META-LEARNING

THE ELSEVIER AND MICCAI SOCIETY BOOK SERIES

Advisory Board

Titles

MICCAI

META-LEARNING
Theory, Algorithms and
Applications

LAN ZOU

ELSEVIER

ACADEMIC PRESS
An imprint of Elsevier

Academic Press is an imprint of Elsevier
125 London Wall, London EC2Y 5AS, United Kingdom
525 B Street, Suite 1650, San Diego, CA 92101, United States
50 Hampshire Street, 5th Floor, Cambridge, MA 02139, United States
The Boulevard, Langford Lane, Kidlington, Oxford OX5 1GB, United Kingdom

Notices
Knowledge and best practice in this field are constantly changing. As new research and experience broaden our
understanding, changes in research methods, professional practices, or medical treatment may become
necessary.

Practitioners and researchers must always rely on their own experience and knowledge in evaluating and using
any information, methods, compounds, or experiments described herein. In using such information or methods
they should be mindful of their own safety and the safety of others, including parties for whom they have a
professional responsibility.

To the fullest extent of the law, neither the Publisher nor the authors, contributors, or editors, assume any liability
for any injury and/or damage to persons or property as a matter of products liability, negligence or otherwise, or
from any use or operation of any methods, products, instructions, or ideas contained in the material herein.

ISBN 978-0-323-89931-4

For information on all Academic Press publications
visit our website at https://www.elsevier.com/books-and-journals

Publisher: Mara E. Conner
Acquisitions Editor: Tim Pitts
Editorial Project Manager: Sara Valentino
Production Project Manager: Kamesh R
Cover Designer: Miles Hitchen

Typeset by STRAIVE, India

To those who explore the world by intelligence.

Contents

Preface

The idea for this book arrived one day when I was walking on the street, taking a break after a long-lasting experiment with my deep learning computer vision model. I saw my neighbor's small public library—an old bookshelf standing in his yard with a sign that said, "Enjoy." This was my "spark moment" to write this book four years ago, and I have appreciated this long journey.

With the support of deep learning technology, many practical solutions reach remarkable performance in various real-world scenarios. In 2016, AlphaGo achieved incredible results in chess-playing with human beings; however, quick learning with few samples remains one of the most complex and common questions in AI research and applications. Meta-learning can solve these issues. Tracing back to 1987, the "Father of modern AI" Jürgen Schmidhuber and 1991 Turing Award recipient Yoshua Bengio began to explore meta-learning. Since 2015, meta-learning has become the most attractive research area in AI communities.

Talking at the BBC about the future of AI, Stephen Hawking, the famous physicist, said "it would take off on its own and re-design itself at an ever-increasing rate" (Cellan-Jones, R. (2014, December 2). Stephen Hawking warns artificial intelligence could end mankind. BBC News. Retrieved from https://www.bbc.com/news/technology-30290540 (Retrieved 7 October 2022).)—this concept has become known as artificial general intelligence (AGI). Meta-learning is an essential technique to achieve the capacity to "re-design itself at an ever-increasing rate." In contrast to AGI, narrow AI means the artificial agent can only tackle one specific task; otherwise, transfer learning or retraining is needed in regimes of varying or dissimilar tasks. AGI, on the other hand, executes the ability of an artificial agent to learn or analyze intelligent tasks as human beings do; even transcending what they can achieve.

Meta-learning used with deep neural networks delivers artificial agents with the ability to solve diverse tasks, even unseen or unknown tasks (or environments), relying on a very small amount of data (such as zero to five samples) within only a couple of gradient steps. Examples of this are covered in Chapter 7, which discusses how meta-reinforcement learning helps artificial agents achieve visual navigation in unseen tasks (or environments), and in Chapter 6, which shows how agents accomplish multilingual neural machine translation tasks with five different target languages in low-source situations.

This book reviews and explores 191 state-of-the-art meta-learning algorithms, involved in more than 450 crucial research. It provides a systematic and detailed investigation of nine essential state-of-the-art meta-learning mechanisms and 11 real-world field applications. This book attempts to solve common problems from deep learning or machine learning and presents the basis for researching meta-learning on a more complex level. It offers answers to the following questions:

What is meta-learning?

Why do we need meta-learning?

In what way are self-improved meta-learning mechanisms heading for AGI?

How can we use meta-learning in our approaches to specific scenarios?

Meta-learning acts as a stepping stone toward AGI, which has become the primary goal of cutting-edge AI research. Optimistically, many professionals believe AGI will be achieved in the coming decades: 45% of scholars think AGI could happen by 2060, according to a survey at EMERJ in 2019 (Faggella, 2019); while Jürgen Schmidhuber estimated it would happen by 2050, and Patrick Winston (former director of MIT AI Lab) suggested 2040, as reported by Futurism (Creighton, 2018). Once AGI is reached, artificial agents will be able to learn, solve problems, think, understand natural language, process, create, perform social and emotional engagement, navigate, and perceive as a human does. Passing the Turing test, the future of AGI heads to artificial superintelligence, where the artificial agents have intelligence far beyond the highest level of human intelligence and human cognitive performance in all domains.

Although this book is a scientific presentation of the theories, algorithms, and applications of meta-learning, I hope it will stimulate readers' curiosity and passion for the role meta-learning can play in artificial intelligence technology.

The Author

References

Creighton, J. (2018). The "father of artificial intelligence" says Singularity is 30 years away. *Futurism*. Retrieved October 7, 2022, from https://futurism.com/father-artificial-intelligence-singularity-decades-away.

Faggella, D. (2019). When will we reach the singularity?—A timeline consensus from AI researchers (AI FutureScape 1 of 6). *Emerj Artificial Intelligence Research*. Retrieved October 7, 2022, from https://emerj.com/ai-future-outlook/when-will-we-reach-the-singularity-a-timeline-consensus-from-ai-researchers/.

Acknowledgments

Many people have made essential contributions during the development of this book through their passion and helpful advice.

I would like to express my sincere thanks to all my team members at Elsevier for their unwavering support throughout the process. My deepest gratitude goes to my editor, Tim Pitts, for his unfailing enthusiasm, valuable experience, and for sharing his beneficial advice during my writing and publishing of this book. I would also like to express my most profound appreciation for my project manager, Sara Valentino, for her thoughtful help as well as her diligent and productive collaboration in supplying me with helpful supporting resources throughout the book's long development. Many thanks also go to my copyright specialist, Swapna Praveen, for her reliable assistance and very professional attitude, and special thanks to my project manager, Kamesh Ramajogi, for his attentive support and effective communication throughout the book's production phase.

The following reviewers contributed constructive suggestions and practical comments in order to improve the accuracy and readability of the book:

- Yu-Xiong Wang, Department of Computer Science, the University of Illinois at Urbana-Champaign
- Pengyu Yuan, Department of Electrical and Computer Engineering, the University of Houston

Finally, I am very grateful to my friends: to Chloe for her uplifting encouragement through the difficult drafting process, and to Zoe for providing instrumental backing despite her hectic schedule.

CHAPTER

1

Meta-learning basics and background

1.1 Introduction

The success of the deep learning strategy has supported a variety of applications (e.g., urban civilization, self-driven vehicles, medicine discovery). It has stimulated machine intelligence into a novel revolution in human technology history. With the benefits of deep learning, voice assistants, automated route planning, and pattern recognition in medical images have become natural parts of human lives and social development. However, the current machine-learning paradigm specifies a single task by training a hand-designed model, where the constraints are obvious (Marcus, 2018); for example:

- Expensive data consumption and requirements of computing resources limit many kinds of research in specific fields, while others are hardly examined.
- Interpretability of the "black box" remains weak. The learning mechanism of hierarchy structure in the deep neural network still contains many unknown processes and a lack of transparency.
- Potential helpful knowledge (e.g., prior knowledge) cannot directly fuse into a deep learning strategy, which thus stays self-isolated from general knowledge.

These factors have led researchers to keep looking for a more reasonable and widely compatible technology to fill these gaps and provide a novel direction—leading to the rise of meta-learning.

The following chapter contains a quick review of the concepts and paradigms involved in the background of meta-learning. Starting from the theoretical formalization of meta-learning, Section 1.2 presents an intro-level picture of this emerging technology. The fundamental knowledge of general machine learning is described in Section 1.3. Section 1.4 examines the development and critical characteristics of deep learning technology. As similar methods that are usually compared with meta-learning, transfer learning and multitask learning are discussed in Section 1.5. Section 1.6 dives into few-shot learning (including zero-shot and one-shot learning) to indicate its relationship with meta-learning. Sections 1.7 and 1.8 recap, separately, the other side of artificial intelligence—probabilistic modeling and Bayesian inference—for better understanding and clarification of the scope of meta-learning.

Meta-Learning
https://doi.org/10.1016/B978-0-323-89931-4.00010-9

1.2 Meta-learning

Meta-learning, also referred to as learning to learn, has been frequently highlighted through its involvement in versatile research and implementations in recent years. As a sub-field of machine learning, it was first heralded by Donald Maudsley (Maudsley, 1979) as "the process by which learners become aware of and increasingly in control of habits of perception, inquiry, learning, and growth that they have internalized." Jürgen Schmidhuber (Schmidhuber, 1987) demonstrated two goals of meta-learning—"solving it, and improving the strategies employed to solve it." He also described its early inspiration from meta-evolution as "prototypical self-referential associating learning mechanisms" (Schmidhuber, 1987). Bengio, Samy, and Gloutier (1991) indicated meta-learning as "mathematically derived and biologically faithful models" based on genetic algorithms and gradient descent.

1.2.1 Definitions

Meta-learning can be formally defined from multiple points of view, as stated by Hospedales, Antoniou, Micaelli, and Storkey (2020); this book mainly focuses on the two most common perspectives: task distribution and bilevel optimization. According to the most regular perspective on meta-learning, **task distribution** emphasizes learning across **a set of** tasks to stimulate better generalization ability for each task. This can be formatted as in Eq. (1.1), where ω is the generic **meta-knowledge** extracted across all tasks, the performance is evaluated over the distribution of tasks $p(T)$, and each task $T = \{D, \mathcal{L}\}$ with a dataset D and a loss function $\mathcal{L}$:

$$\min {}_{\omega} \mathbb{E}_{T \sim p(T)} \ \mathcal{L}(D; \omega) \tag{1.1}$$

Like most machine-learning paradigm, there are two stages in meta-learning: meta-training and meta-testing. Unlike machine-learning methods, each dataset needs an elaborate design. During **meta-training**, a set of S source tasks is presented as $D_{source} = \{(D_{source}^{train}, D_{source}^{val})^{(i)}\}_{i=1}^{S}$, where the D_{source}^{train} is the **support** set and D_{source}^{val} presents the **query** set. In **meta-testing**, a set of G target tasks is denoted as $D_{target} = \{(D_{target}^{train}, D_{target}^{test})^{(i)}\}_{i=1}^{G}$, where D_{target}^{train} is the support set and D_{target}^{test} means the query set. As a term to define the problem settings in some few-shot or meta-learning tasks (e.g., classification), **k-way n-shot** means the k number of classes with n samples per class in *the meta-testing support set*, as demonstrated in Fig. 1.1.

In contrast to the single-level optimization in traditional machine learning and deep learning, meta-learning maintains a **bilevel optimization** with an **inner** loop (i.e., training on a base model like a regular machine-learning or deep-learning paradigm) and an **outer** loop (i.e., training on a meta-learning paradigm). This roughly reflects the idea behind meta-learning: the inner optimization depends on a predefined learning approach ω by the outer optimization (i.e., ω cannot be changed by the inner optimization during the inner loop). The collaboration of this two-level mechanism is presented in Eqs. (1.2), (1.3), where the outer objective function $\mathcal{L}^{meta}$ is shown in Eq. (1.2) and the inner objective function $\mathcal{L}^{task}$ is presented in Eq. (1.3).

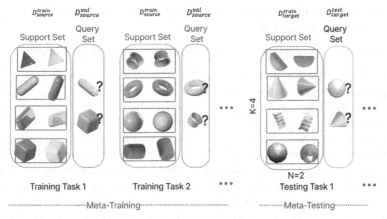

FIG. 1.1 Visualization of task sets in meta-training and meta-testing. Illustration of a four-way two-shot image classification task.

$$\omega^* = arg\,min\,_\omega \sum_{i=1}^{S} \mathcal{L}^{meta}\left(\theta^{*\,(i)}(\omega), \omega, D_{source}^{val\ (i)}\right) \tag{1.2}$$

$$\theta^{*\,(i)}(\omega) = arg\,min\,_\theta \mathcal{L}^{task}\left(\theta, \omega, D_{source}^{train\ (i)}\right) \tag{1.3}$$

ω can be viewed as: (1) a hyper-parameter, (2) a loss function's parameterization for inner optimization, or (3) an "initial condition in non-convex optimization" (Hospedales et al., 2020). For more detail, Saunshi, Zhang, Khodak, and Arora (2020) explored interpretations between convex and nonconvex meta-learning.

1.2.2 Evaluation

Meta-learning is known for many **advantages**, including:

- **Data efficiency** with only minimal training data for each task. Kong, Somani, Song, Kakade, and Oh (2020) examined the reasons and conditions for abundant small-data tasks to compensate for the scarcity of big-data tasks. Kaddour, Sæmundsson, and Deisenroth (2020) suggested a data-sampling method to improve data efficiency. Liu, Davison, and Johns (2019) offered the possibility to increase generalization without further data for supervised tasks.
- **Fast adaptation** usually occurs within a couple of gradient steps, in contrast to the time-consuming training processes needed in machine learning and deep learning. See recent studies as the following. Li, Gu, Zhang, Gool, and Timofte (2020) examined a network-pruning method based on AutoML and neural network search. Park and Oliva (2019) built a framework, Meta-Curvature, to learn the curvature information to accelerate adaptation.
- The practical goal of training a meta-learner usually falls into two categories: creating an optimal initialization and/or learning a meta-policy to guide the further learning

procedures. Good **generalization** and **robustness** with unseen tasks promote meta-learning applicability in research.

However, there remains sufficient space to overcome several **problems**:

- The additional optimization level is powerful but may lead to potential overfitting. **Meta-overfitting** (also known as task-overfitting) is different from regular overfitting in supervised learning. Meta-overfitting occurs when the meta-knowledge learned from source tasks cannot generalize well into target tasks—the meta-learner generalizes well from the meta-training tasks but performs poorly in adapting to unseen tasks. Memorization issues can cause meta-overfitting: instead of learning to adapt to different tasks based on the meta-training tasks, the meta-learner is memorizing a function to process all meta-training data. Careful design of mutually exclusive meta-training tasks can offer one solution to avoid this problem. Furthermore, Yin et al. (2020) offer another solution to learning without memorization, which is introduced in Chapter 5, Section 5.11.6. Additionally, scarce source tasks usually lead to this issue. Rajendran, Irpan, and Jang (2020) generated meta-augmentation to increase randomness in the base model. Tian, Liu, Yuan, and Liu (2020) presented two network-pruning tools to reduce meta-overfitting.
- Another challenging issue is **task heterogeneity**. Some good performances are based on narrow task diversity or modality (e.g., assumption of a unimodal setup), while generalization of various tasks is still difficult (Cho et al., 2014; Rebuffi, Bilen, & Vedaldi, 2017; Yu et al., 2019). Fortunately, recent researches shed light on various directions. Yao, Wei, Huang, and Li (2019) reduced the task uncertainty and heterogeneity through a hierarchically structured meta-learning approach. Liu, Wang, et al. (2020) proposed adaptive task-sampling methods to enhance the model's generalization ability.
- As an **expensive computing process**, bilevel optimization may cause computer memory-hunger and longer training time (since each outer loop demands a couple of inner loops), further limiting research to only few-shot regimes rather than many-shot setups. (For early attempts, see Baydin, Cornish, Martinez-Rubio, Schmidt, & Wood, 2018; Flennerhag et al., 2020; Franceschi, Donini, Frasconi, & Pontil, 2017; Li, Yang, Zhou, & Hospedales, 2019; Liu, Simonyan, & Yang, 2019; Lorraine, Vicol, & Duvenaud, 2020; Micaelli & Storkey, 2020; Pedregosa, 2016; Rajeswaran, Finn, Kakade, & Levine, 2019; Shaban, Cheng, Hatch, & Boots, 2019; Williams & Zipser, 1989).
- A lack of **training task resources** (i.e., task families) persists for specific meta-learning problems or application fields. (For early attempts, see Antoniou & Storkey, 2019; Hsu, Levine, & Finn, 2019; Khodadadeh, Boloni, & Shah, 2019; Li et al., 2019; Meier, Kappler, & Schaal, 2018; Veeriah et al., 2019; Xu, Hasselt, & Silver, 2018; Zheng, Oh, & Singh, 2018).

1.2.3 Datasets and benchmarks

Typical meta-learning datasets and benchmarks for communities of natural language processing, computer vision, and graph neural networks are summarized below.

Natural Language Processing:

- FewRel—a few-shot relation classification benchmark (Han et al., 2018)
- SNIPS—a natural language understanding benchmark (Coucke et al., 2018)

- CLINC150—a dataset for intent classification and out-of-scope prediction (Larson et al., 2019)
- FewGLUE—a dataset for few-shot learning based on GLUE (Schick & Schütze, 2021)

  Graph Neural Network:

- Wiki-One—a dataset with a knowledge graph (Xiong, Yu, Chang, Guo, & Wang, 2018)

  Computer Vision:

- Meta-Dataset—a benchmark for few-shot image classification (Triantafillou et al., 2020)
- Omniglot—a benchmark with handwritten characters at https://omniglot.com.
- *mini*ImageNet—a benchmark with 100 classes randomly selected from ImageNet (Vinyals, Blundell, Lillicrap, & Wierstra, 2016)
- *tiered*ImageNet—a benchmark with 608 classes from ILSVRC-12 (Ren et al., 2018)
- CIFAS-FS—a benchmark for few-shot learning from CIFAR-100 (Bertinetto, Henriques, Valmadre, Torr, & Vedaldi, 2016)
- Fewshot-CIFAS100—a benchmark for few-shot learning as a subset of CIFAS-100 (Oreshkin, Rodriguez, & Lacoste, 2018)
- Caltech-UCSD Birds—a benchmark for fine-grained visual classification (Hilliard et al., 2018)
- Double MNIST and Triple MNIST—datasets for few-shot learning based on MNIST (Sun, 2019)
- PASCAL-5i—a benchmark for object segmentation with sparse data (Shaban, Bansal, Liu, Essa, & Boots, 2017)
- ORBIT—a dataset for real-world, few-shot, object-detection tasks (Massiceti et al., 2021)

A practical implementing toolkit, API Torchmeta, was released by PyTorch to accelerate straightforward applications of meta-learning through existing data loaders and datasets. The official code is available at https://github.com/tristandeleu/pytorch-meta, with the official documentation at https://tristandeleu.github.io/pytorch-meta/. It can be installed from source or using pip via the following code:

```
pip install torchmeta
```

To join a meta-learning community for developers, engineers, scholars, Ph.D. students, researchers, and related professionals, visit the website at https://www.mldcbk.de or https://join.slack.com/t/meta-learning-talk/shared_invite/zt-1gzo81s2o-5QnbVhn0xBmk6BGmOyU90w.

1.3 Machine learning

Machine learning as a field is "concerned with the question of how to construct computer programs that automatically improve with experience." This concise opening appears in the preface of the classical textbook *Machine Learning* by Tom M. Mitchell (Mitchell, 1997). Machine learning is one of the most popular AI tools. Mitchell (1997) presents the formal definition of machine learning as follows:

> A computer program is said to learn from experience E with respect to some class of tasks T and performance measure P, if its performance at tasks in T, as measured by P, improves with experience E.

According to the characteristics of signal and feedback, machine learning approaches are commonly categorized into three groups: supervised learning (Russell & Norvig, 2010), unsupervised learning (Hinton & Sejnowski, 1999), and reinforcement learning (Kaelbling, Littman, & Moore, 1996). Some literature includes semisupervised learning as a fourth approach. Supervised learning primarily relies on labeled training data in input-output pairs. Unsupervised learning draws inferences by extracting features from unlabeled training data. Reinforcement learning, in contrast, depends on rewards, states, and actions to manipulate the optimal policy. Semisupervised learning shares characteristics with supervised learning and unsupervised learning, consuming a mixture of extensive data without ground truth and limited annotated data. Some research associates these described paradigms with meta-learning. For example, Hsu and colleagues (Hsu et al., 2019) employed meta-learning with unsupervised learning based on elementary task construction methods to perform diverse down-sampling tasks. Gemp, Theocharous, and Ghavamzadeh (2017) suggested an automated data-cleaning strategy by learning from the meta-feature representation.

1.3.1 Models

Support vector machine (SVM) is a nonprobabilistic, binary, machine-learning tool for classification and regression. Although regular support-vector machines treat data as a linear classifier, kernel-based SVMs process nonlinear classifications through kernel tricks by projecting training samples into a higher dimension representing space.

Decision tree (DT) is a predictive model used in machine learning, data mining, and statistics with very straightforward algorithms. The training data is recursively partitioned into a smaller subset of the tree by passing from the stem to the leaves. In this tree-structured model, the leaves denote class labels, and the stem contains a conjunction of features leading to the corresponding leaves. Classification trees take discrete data as input, while regression decision trees process continuous data. Pruning techniques are usually considered to reduce overfitting.

Regression analysis uses a wide variety of variations in a statistical model to make predictions by exploring the relationships between different features and input variables. Linear regressions deal with training samples under linearity relationships, while nonlinear regression models—such as logistic regression and kernel regression—handle features with nonlinearity relationships.

K-nearest neighbors (k-NN) method: a nonparametric supervised paradigm that can be used in classification and regression tasks, first proposed in 1951. The inference result of the input data is based on the k nearest training samples as the evidence for output labels in classifications and on the average value of k nearest training data in regression problems. Distance metrics are crucial fundamentals in k-NN; regularly applied distances include the Euclidean distance, Hamming distance, and cosine distance. See Chapter 3, Section 3.1 for an illustration of typical distance in metric learning.

K-means clustering is an unsupervised method with a loose relationship to k-NN. As each observation is assigned to the cluster under the least-squared Euclidean distance, the centroids are constantly updated due to the given observation. The above procedures are repeated over and over again. As long as the assignments are no longer changed, k-means reaches convergence; however, an optimum is not assured.

Ensemble methods contain multiple learning methods to obtain better results than does any constituent learning method alone. Opitz and Maclin (1999) introduced an ensemble method that evolves common algorithm types, including a Bayes Optimal Classifier (Ruck, Rogers, Kabrisky, Oxley, & Suter, 1990), AdaBoost (Freund & Schapire, 1999), Gradient Boosting Decision Tree (GBDT) (Breiman, 1997), Random Forest (Ho, 1995), and others. These techniques can be classified as boosting, stacking, and bagging.

1.3.2 Limitations

A **bias-variance dilemma** refers to a tradeoff between bias and variance when supervised learning algorithms try to minimize these two sources of error simultaneously to generalize patterns beyond training samples. Bias error is the metric to measure the relevance between training features and target outputs, whereas variance error reflects the sensitivity of fluctuations (noise level) in training samples. This dilemma is inevitable in all forms of supervised learning algorithms (Geman, Bienenstock, & Doursat, 1992; Kohavi & Wolpert, 1996; von Luxburg & Schölkopf, 2011).

Inductive bias occurs when a lack of necessary assumptions describes the target outputs given novel inputs (Mitchell, 1980). One goal of the machine learning algorithm is to predict outcomes by learning patterns from given information, even if some of the samples have not been represented during training. This unseen situation may contain arbitrary outputs without such assumptions, failing to approximate outcomes (Gordon & Desjardins, 1995).

Overfitting, which is a common dilemma in machine learning models, occurs when the learning model is too closely aligned with the training data with poor generalization ability in the testing data. The formal definition by Mitchell (Mitchell, 1997) is as follows:

> Given a hypothesis space H, a hypothesis $h \in H$ is said to overfit the training data if there exists some alternative hypothesis $h' \in H$, such that h has a smaller error than h' over the training examples, but h' has a smaller overall error than h over the entire distribution (or data set) of instances.

Although multiple techniques exist to reduce overfitting—such as cross-validation, regularization, drop out, augmentation, and pruning—antioverfitting attracts high-level interest in meta-learning. Shu et al. (2019) constructed a weighting function as a multilayer perceptron with one hidden layer applied in various models to reduce overfitting on biased data, naming their approach Meta-Weight-Net, which is introduced in Chapter 5, Section 5.8.6. Ryu, Shin, Lee, and Hwang (2020) examined a different choice, Meta-Perturb, as regularization and transfer learning are unsuitable for unseen data.

Model selection is the process of choosing a variety of final machine learning models of different complexity and flexibility (Shirangi & Durlofsky, 2016). Probabilistic measures (on training data performance and model complexity) and resampling measures (on validation data performance) are two common ways to propose it. Furthermore, Huang, Huang, Li, and Li (2020) discussed a solution through model averaging over a set of standard models rather than picking an individual model as the final learner by meta-learning the prior knowledge.

Domain adaptation, a field related to machine learning and transfer learning, occurs when learning a model from a source domain and performing an inference in a different but relevant target domain, assuming the source domain and the target domain are under the same feature space. For effective domain adaptation and free of this assumption, Li, Yang, Song, and Hospedales (2017) demonstrated a meta-learning domain generalization method for novel target domains. Li and Hospedales (2020) focused on the initial condition of domain adaptation and improved the performance via a meta-learning semisupervised approach.

1.3.3 Related concepts

Differing from transfer learning (which is explored in Chapter 1, Section 1.5), **knowledge distillation** passes the transferable knowledge from a deeper model with a higher knowledge capacity to a shallow model, widely spread in object detection, natural language processing, etc. However, the technique still suffers from time-consuming methods, expensive computing, and weak compatibility. Liu, Rao, Lu, Zhou, and Hsieh (2020) proposed a meta-learner-optimized label generator to process the feature maps in a top-down order to tackle this problem.

Bilevel optimization, a unique optimization technique, is an interesting topic in machine learning that has obtained both upper-level optimization and lower-level optimization tasks. Franceschi, Frasconi, Salzo, Grazzi, and Pontil (2018) offer a framework for hyper-parameters optimization and meta-learning.

Metric learning mainly falls into supervised learning and weakly supervised learning (Zhou, 2019). It has four axioms to follow: (1) symmetry, (2) nonnegativity, (3) subadditivity, and (4) the identity of the indiscernible. The typical standard metrics include Euclidean distance (Danielsson, 1980), cosine similarity (Singhal, 2001), Manhattan distance (Stigler, 1986), etc. This book follows the definition of metric learning from Torra and Navarro-Arribas (2018):

> In terms of a non-empty set and a distance function or metric, let (S, d) be a metric space, then $d(a, b)$ for a, b measures the distance between the two elements a and b in S.

See Chapter 3, Section 3.1 for a summary of versatile distance metrics and further examination of meta-learning metric-based approaches.

1.3.4 Further Reading

This short section quickly summarizes an outline of concepts and theories in machine learning that are highly related to meta-learning. Some reference sources are provided below for readers who are not already familiar with machine learning. For a comprehensive and systematic understanding of machine learning and related concepts, paradigms, characteristics, and techniques, the following resources may be helpful:

- *Machine Learning*, a classical textbook covering fundamental knowledge of this field, written by Tom Mitchell (Mitchell, 1997), an American computer scientist and the former Chair of the Machine Learning Department at Carnegie Mellon University. Several chapters are available at http://www.cs.cmu.edu/%7Etom/NewChapters.html.

- *Hands-On Machine Learning with Scikit-Learn and TensorFlow: Concepts, Tools, and Techniques to Build Intelligent Systems*, a practical handbook for machine learning coding in Python, was written by Aurélien Géron.

1.4 Deep learning

Tappert's research (Tappert, 2019) points to the book *Principles of Neurodynamics: Perceptrons and the Theory of Brain Mechanisms*, written by American psychologist Frank Rosenblatt, which described the early concepts of today's deep learning system in 1962. Five years later, Alexey Ivakhnenko proposed the first working method—multilayer perceptron. In 1979, Neocognitron, a deep learning technique specific to computer vision problems, was introduced by Kunihiko Fukushima. Backpropagation (i.e., the backward propagation of error) served as the critical logic of supervised learning through neural networks; it was published by Geoffrey Hinton in 1986, although the true inventor remains ambiguous. Rina Dechter introduced the term used today, "deep learning," to the machine learning community. It denotes a subfield of machine learning algorithms for representation learning (i.e., feature learning, which can be categorized into supervised, unsupervised, and semisupervised learning) through neural networks.

Motivated by the biological neural networks in animals' brains, artifical neural networks (ANNs) denotes a computing system that consists of countless artificial neurons to improve the ability (i.e., learning) to tackle a problem (i.e., task) gradually based on given examples, without task-specific programming. A deep neural network (DNN) refers to an ANN of multilayered architectures with five standard components: neurons, synapses (i.e., connections), bias, weights, and activation functions.

Since the deep learning revolution in 2012 and under the support of many essential DNN architectures, groundbreaking computer hardware (e.g., GPUs), global competitions (e.g., ImageNet competition), and practical applications in numerous domains, the entire world has paid close attention to artificial intelligence (AI). Many respected rankings organized by Forbes, MIT Technology Review, and McKinsey note AI technology as one of the top tech trends in the coming decades.

1.4.1 Models

Contemporary deep neural networks typically consist of various architectures of unlimited numbers of layers with limited size. One core concept of these deep neural networks is gradient descent. Gradient descent, a first-order iterative optimization method processed on a differentiable function, aims to find the global minimum in the opposite direction of the approximated gradient or gradient through multiple steps during training for deep neural networks. However, this is not necessarily guaranteed to be a global minimum; it can often be stuck at a local minimum. Gradient descent is the core component of deep learning methods (see Chapter 4 for additional exploration). **Convolutional neural networks** (CNNs), based on a mathematical expression named convolution, are commonly applied in computer vision and natural-language-processing tasks (e.g., intent detection). LeNet-5 is one of the earliest

CNNs and was introduced by LeCun and Bengio (1995). Shift invariant and space invariant are fundamental properties of CNN, which inputs a tensor with the following shape: (number of input) ×(input's height) ×(input's width) ×(input's channels). The main types within the network architecture consist of convolutional layers, pooling layers, and fully connected layers (Stanford-CS231n, 2022). The convolutional layer produces a feature map from the original image in the following shape: (number of input) ×(feature map's height) ×(feature map's width) × (feature map's channels). Each neuron in the convolutional layer processes an input according to the receptive field (i.e., kernel). A dilated convolutional layer inflates the receptive field into a sparser one by adding holes between kernel elements. The receptive field of a fully connected layer is the entire previous layer. The pooling layer reduces data dimensions to save computing complexity through two commonly used pooling methods—average pooling and max pooling.

Sequence model's inputs or outputs are a sequence of data. Unlike other neural networks such as CNN, which assume all inputs are independent of each other, input data is essential to predict the following output in sequence models. Recurrent neural network (RNN), long short-term memory (LSTM) (Gers, Schmidhuber, & Cummins, 1999), and gated recurrent units (GRU) (Cho et al., 2014) are examples of widely used sequence algorithms in natural language processing, speech recognition, sentiment analysis, DNA/gene classification, machine translation, and other areas.

RNN, a class of networks that feeds the output from the previous step as the input of the current step, has versatile variations—see the elaborate workflow of a standard RNN in Fig. 1.2. For each time t, the activation a_t is expressed in Eq. (1.4), while the output y appears in Eq. (1.5), where g_1 and g_2 are activation functions, W and B denotes weight and bias, separately.

$$a_t = g_1 \left(W_{aa} a_{t-1} + W_{ax} x_t + B_a \right) \tag{1.4}$$

$$y_t = g_2 \left(W_{ya} a_t + B_y \right) \tag{1.5}$$

Although RNN offers the advantages of flexible input length and weight sharing between different steps, it is still time-consuming. Longer-period memory is unavailable, which can be

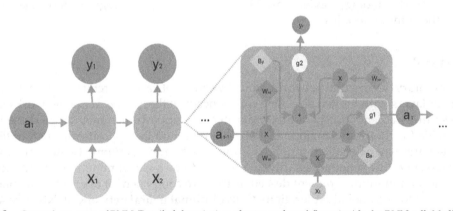

FIG. 1.2   General structure of RNN. Detailed description of gates and workflows inside the RNN cell. *Modified from Amidi, A. & Amidi, S. (2019). Recurrent neural networks cheatsheet.*

easily solved through long short-term memory (LSTM). See precise descriptions of **LSTM** with its structure and methods in Chapter 4, Section 4.2. Other important deep neural network architectures include deep belief network (DBN), autoencoder (AE), variational autoencoder (VAE), and generative adversarial network (GAN).

On the other hand, implicit neural representation offers a different way to parameterize signals, as opposed to only discrete representation. Sitzmann and colleagues (Sitzmann, Chan, Tucker, Snavely, & Wetzstein, 2020) discussed neural implicit shape representations by viewing shape space as a meta-learning problem.

1.4.2 Limitations

Every algorithm has limitations, and deep learning is not a panacea. The **black-box** problem increases the difficulty of comprehending entire computing methods and explaining the learning behavior. The interpretability of deep learning or deep neural networks remains an open discussion. Thus, there is no authoritative guide for selecting the optimal deep learning tools, and "trial-and-error" methods depend on different experiences. **Neural architecture search** through meta-learning provides an automatic design that can outperform handmade neural networks. Elsken, Staffler, Metzen, and Hutter (2020) offered an arbitrary gradient-based meta-learning approach with soft-pruning methods. Chen et al. (2020) proposed a context-based meta-reinforcement learning strategy for vision tasks. Shaw, Wei, Liu, Song, and Dai (2020) accelerated the architecture search through Bayesian formalization of the DARTS (Liu, Simonyan, & Yang, 2019) search space. Liu et al. (2019) proposed an automatic pruning tool to produce weight for pruned structures.

Catastrophic forgetting (also known as catastrophic inference) was first observed by McCloskey and Cohen in 1989. It occurs when an ANN wholly and suddenly forgets the knowledge previously learned as new information arrives. **Continual learning/lifelong learning** usually suffers from catastrophic forgetting. Besides the contemporary solutions—orthogonality, node sharpening, novelty rule, network pretraining, rehearsal mechanism, latent learning, and elastic weight consolidation—several research efforts have attempted to view this problem from a meta-learning perspective. Javed and White (2019) conducted a strategy to accelerate future learning. Luo et al. (2019) concentrated on mining prior knowledge through a Bayesian graph neural network. Gupta, Yadav, and Paull (2020) suggested a look-ahead MAML for online continual learning on visual classification problems. Joseph and Balasubramanian (2020) introduced a VAE backbone for continual learning on meta-distributions over model parameters.

Additionally, the millions or even more parameters are led from the **massive consumption of training** data, as a larger sample size leads to better performance. However, data collection is expensive or sometimes impossible. For example, new data of rare diseases (e.g., porphyria, water allergy, and pica) are challenging to collect because the patients who suffer from these rare diseases are scarce. This is one of the fundamental reasons to introduce meta-learning. It presents various solutions in diverse applications in few-shot, low-source, zero-shot, and one-shot settings. Examples illustrated in Chapters 5–9 include visual recognition, natural language understanding and generation, transportation planning, cold-start problems in recommendation systems, etc. Meta-learning can also tackle rare disease diagnostics, as examined in Chapter 8.

1.4.3 Further readings

Please note this book only provides a shallow overview of deep learning-related concepts, frameworks, models, trends, and applications, while diving more deeply into meta-learning technology. For further understanding and comprehensive interpretations of deep learning—especially if this book is the reader's introduction to deep learning or artificial intelligence—the following resources are strongly recommended to understand systematic theories and practical implementations:

- *Deep Learning*, a brief review of deep learning written by the three Turing Award 2018 winners, Yann LeCun, Yoshua Bengio, and Geoffrey Hinton (LeCun, Bengio, & Hinton, 2015), was published in *Nature* magazine.
- *Deep Learning (Adaptive Computation and Machine Learning series)*, one of the most prestigious textbooks in this field, was written by Ian Goodfellow, Yoshua Bengio, and Aaron Courville (Goodfellow, Bengio, & Courville, 2016).

1.5 Transfer learning

Transfer learning, a popular research area in machine learning, reuses the transferable knowledge learned from one model by applying it to related but different models (see a constrast between transfer learning and knowledge disllation in Chapter 1, Section 1.3.3). Knowledge transfer sheds light on training and testing data from different feature spaces or various distributions and prevents model rebuilding. It allows the domain, distribution, and tasks of training and testing to be different and separately noted as a source and the target domain.

Conventional transfer learning approaches can be divided into three types based on the label set: (1) inductive transfer learning, (2) unsupervised transfer learning, and (3) transductive transfer learning (Xie et al., 2021). On the other hand, transfer learning strategies are categorized into two groups based on space setting: homogeneous and heterogeneous transfer learning.

Transfer learning and meta-learning seem to share a similar idea of referencing previously learned knowledge from one model to another. Nevertheless, they are significantly different. Meta-learning works on unseen samples (or tasks) within only a few gradient descent steps through episode-based training (explained in Chapter 3, Section 3.3). It either learns an initialization that is optimal for both existing samples (or tasks) and new samples (or tasks) or acts as a superlative updating policy to learn unseen samples or tasks quickly and effectively based on only a few samples (usually one to five). Zero-shot, one-shot, and few-shot learning are also achievable through diversified meta-learners. Conversely, transfer learning needs more feeding data based on the pretrained model and must reuse part or all of the source model to reorganize the target model. Furthermore, the relevance between source tasks and target tasks is a vital assumption to note.

Among numerous applications of transfer learning, style transfer (sometimes called neural style transfer) is one of the interesting tasks that interact with computer vision and transfer learning. First introduced by Bozinovski and Fulgosi (1976), neural style transfer offers a straightforward application of transfer learning, which fuses the style of one image and the content of another image. With the development of meta-learning, Zhang, Zhu, and Zhu (2019) attempted to balance the trade-off between speed, various styles (i.e., flexibility), and quality through a MetaStyle in a 2D visual style transfer task.

1.5.1 Multitask learning

Multitask learning is a subcategory of transfer learning, which is to learn a collection of relevant tasks jointly. It enhances the generalization of every single task by leveraging the interconnection across multiple tasks with intertask differences and intertask relevance. Abu-Mostafa (1990) presented an early vision of multitask learning as improving the approach's generalization ability through domain-specific information from the related tasks' training signals. It learns from multiple tasks jointly and shares commonalities simultaneously. Hard parameter sharing and soft parameter sharing are two main techniques in multitask learning. Caruana (1993) applied the hard parameter sharing of hidden layers across all tasks; Baxter (1997) confirmed its effectiveness to decrease overfitting. Soft parameter sharing produces its own model and parameters for each task. The difference between transfer learning and multitask learning is: transfer learning invests more effort into the target tasks than the source tasks, while multitask learning treats each task equally.

Multitask learning has been successfully implemented in computer vision, natural language processing, speech recognition, and drug discovery. Supportive resources for multitask learning/transfer learning and meta-learning are as follows:

- Andrew Ng's presentation involving transfer learning and its current trend in the Conference and Workshop on Neural Information Processing Systems (NeurIPS) 2016 at https://www.youtube.com/watch?v=wjqaz6m42wU
- Nitish Keskar's discussion of multitask learning and meta-learning in computer vision and natural language processing at CVPR 2019

1.6 Few-shot learning

The concept of **few-shot learning** (including one-shot learning and zero-shot learning) was first represented as a solution by Li (2006) in an object categories task. This subfield of machine learning focuses on the minimum amount of training examples, rather than a typical quantity of training data. In support dataset S, k classes have n samples, and each class can be written as *k-way n-shot*: when $k=0$, it is zero-shot learning; when $k=1$, it is one-shot learning. Sun, Liu, Chua, and Schiele (2019) presented a meta-transfer learning strategy with a hard task meta-batch in visual applications. Verma, Brahma, and Rai (2020) produced a meta-learner for challenging a generalized zero-shot learning setup.

Few-shot learning is usually viewed as a task to be solved through the meta-learning paradigm—one of the applications or purposes of meta-learning. While few-shot learning and meta-learning seem similar, the assumptions and definition of meta-learning are much broader than those of few-shot learning.

The basis of few-shot learning is child learning pattern perceptual organization (Biederman, 1987) and rapid cognitive recognition (Li, VanRullen, Koch, & Perona, 2002). When learning new classifications, the method can use prior information in object categories (Li, 2006). Few-shot learning has achieved success in meta-learning, computer vision, natural language processing, and neural architectural searching. (For early attempts, see Bertinetto et al., 2016; Brock, Lim, Ritchie, & Weston, 2018; Finn, Abbeel, & Levine, 2017; Pfister, Charles, & Zisserman, 2014; Ramalho & Garnelo, 2019; Santoro, Bartunov, Botvinick, Wierstra, & Lillicrap, 2016; Triantafillou, Zemel, & Urtasun, 2017; Vinyals et al., 2016; Yan, Yap, & Mori, 2015). Several academic conferences have drawn attention to meta-learning and few-shot learning:

- Finn and Levine (2019) discussed *Meta-Learning: From Few-Shot Learning to Rapid Reinforcement Learning* at the International Conference on Machine Learning (ICML).
- Naik (2019) presented on neural architecture search and meta-learning in CVPR at https://metalearning-cvpr2019.github.io/assets/CVPR_2019_Metalearning_Tutorial_Nikhil_Naik.pdf.

1.7 Probabilistic modeling

Probabilistic modeling, also known as statistical modeling, is a statistical technique that accounts for random events in order to estimate potential outcomes of mathematical expressions across multiple random variables. The probabilistic method was proposed by the prolific Hungarian mathematician Paul Erdős in the late 1940s. This model relied on random variables together with the corresponding cumulative distribution functions to estimate a possible outcome regarding an event or a phenomenon by outputting a probability measure as a solution. Variables can be randomly sampled from standard probability distributions, including normal distribution (i.e., Gaussian distribution), uniform distribution, binomial distribution, Poisson distribution, and Bernoulli distribution. The Central Limited Theorem plays an essential role in formulating large-sized independent random variables into normal distributions.

Probabilistic modeling differs from machine learning and deep learning, as deep learning is an unknown unknown, machine learning is known known, but probabilistic modeling is known unknown. Foong et al. (2020) allowed enhanced dependencies in predictive distributions through a maximum-likelihood meta-learner called Convolutional Neural Process. Wu, Choi, Goodman, and Ermon (2020) presented a meta-amortized variational inference procedure via MetaVAE.

For further information on probabilistic modeling or statistic methods for machine learning, the following textbook is recommended:

- *Probability and Statistical Inference*: this is the classical textbook about fundamental statistics analysis and covers a variety of core probability and statistical theories and methods. It was written by Robert Hogg, Elliot Tanis, and Dale Zimmerman in 2013.

1.8 Bayesian inference

A priori knowledge refers to the knowledge obtained before sampling or observation and is independent of experiments, such as common sense and truth (Sommers, 2003). A priori knowledge is used for constructing an estimation of parameter θ_0, where θ_0 is defined as $(x, f_0 [x, \theta_0])$ from random sampling x, θ_0.

Bayesian inference is an application of Bayes' theorem, which describes the "probability based on prior knowledge of conditions that might be related to the event" (Bayes, 1763; Joyce, 2003). Bayesian inference computes that the posterior probability is expressed in Eq. (1.6) with likelihood $P(E|H)$, prior probability $P(H)$, and marginal likelihood $P(E)$:

$$P(H|E) = \frac{P(E|H)}{P(E)} \, P(H) \tag{1.6}$$

Bayesian inference remains one of the primary applied methods in artificial intelligence. Li, Fergus, and Perona (2003) applied a variational Bayesian framework to the initial few-shot learning unsupervised nonparametric studies. Salakhutdinov, Tenenbaum, and Torralba (2012) proposed a hierarchical Bayesian model on MNIST and MSR Cambridge image datasets. Harrison, Sharma, and Pavone (2018) proposed ALPaCA-modified gradient descent with explicit Gaussian prior. Gordon, Bronskill, Bauer, Nowozin, and Turner (2019) introduced VERSA as a black-box approach for few-shot learning classification and regressions tasks. Garnelo et al. (2018) presented conditional neural processes (CNPs). Gordon et al. (2020) proposed a convolutional conditional neural process (CONVCNP) to model translation equivariance.

Meta-learning also experienced numerous such attempts. Grant, Finn, Levine, Darrell, and Griffiths (2018) improved reformulated model-agnostic meta-learning (MAML, explored in Chapter 4, Section 4.3) as a hierarchical Bayesian inference, with fine-tuning initialization and linked gradient-based meta-learning with hierarchical Bayes. Kim et al. (2018) proposed Bayesian MAML (BMAML) with Bayesian fast adaptation (Williams, 1992) and chaser loss for a meta-update to learn complex uncertainty structures and various reinforcement learning tasks. Finn, Xu, and Levine (2019) introduced a probabilistic MAML. Ravi and Beatson (2019) represented an amortized Bayesian meta-learning approach to generate task-specific posterior approximation. Patacchiola, Turner, Crowley, O'Boyle, and Storkey (2020) applied Bayesian to the inner loop of meta-learning via deep kernels and proposed deep kernel transfer. Hu et al. (2020) presented an empirical Bayesian framework for few-shot visual classification in a multitask setting. Zou and Lu (2020) extended the Bayesian meta-learning framework into a gradient-EM-based algorithm. Wang, Kim, and Kaelbling (2018) estimated the Bayesian prior (which is usually pregiven), and applied it to robotic tasks and motion planning. Jerfel, Grant, Griffiths, and Heller (2019) presented a Dirichlet process mixture of hierarchical Bayesian models for dealing with dissimilar tasks. Xie, Jiang, Liu, Zhao, and Zha (2019) proposed the Hawkes relational meta-learning method for short sequences (HARMLESS) and scaling to more significant problems.

Other beneficial resources on Bayesian inference and meta-learning include:

- Chelsea Finn's 2019 tutorial about meta-learning, memorization, and Bayesian in NeurIPS at https://ai.stanford.edu/~cbfinn/_files/neurips19_memorization.pdf
- Frank Hutter's presentation (Hutter, 2019) at the Conference on Computer Vision and Pattern Recognition (CVPR) at https://metalearning-cvpr2019.github.io/assets/CVPR_2019_Metalearning_Tutorial_Frank_Hutter.pdf

Some solutions and frameworks of meta-learning are briefly introduced in each section from this chapter related to different topics, outlined in Table 1.1. It involves overall 38 advanced pieces of research, which recursively track related bibliographies in papers accepted at premier academic conferences: AAAI, CVPR, ECCV, ICCV, ICLR, ICML, and NeurIPS.

TABLE 1.1   Summary of meta-learning algorithms and frameworks.

Reference	Title	Conference
1.2 Meta-learning		
Kong et al. (2020)	*Meta-Learning for Mixed Linear Regression*	NeurIPS
Yao et al. (2019)	*Hierarchically Structured Meta-Learning*	ICML
Li et al. (2020)	*DHP: Differentiable Meta-Pruning via HyperNetworks*	ECCV
Liu, Wang, et al. (2020)	*Adaptive Task Sampling for Meta-Learning*	ECCV
Ritter et al. (2018)	*Been There, Done That: Meta-Learning with Episodic Recall*	ICML
Saunshi et al. (2020)	*A Sample Complexity Separation between Non-Convex and Convex Meta-Learning*	ICML
Liu, Davison and Johns (2019)	*Self-Supervised Generalization with Meta-Auxiliary Learning*	NeurIPS
Park and Oliva (2019)	*Meta-Curvature*	NeurIPS
Kaddour et al. (2020)	*Probabilistic Active Meta-Learning*	NeurIPS
1.3 Machine Learning		
Hsu et al. (2019)	*Unsupervised Learning via Meta-Learning*	ICLR
Huang et al. (2020)	*Meta-Learning PAC-Bayes Priors in Model Averaging*	AAAI
Shu et al. (2019)	*Meta-Weight-Net: Learning an Explicit Mapping for Sample Weighting*	NeurIPS
Ryu et al. (2020)	*Meta-Perturb: Transferable Regularizer for Heterogeneous Tasks and Architectures*	NeurIPS
Li et al. (2017)	*Learning to Generalize: Meta-Learning for Domain Generalization*	AAAI
Gemp et al. (2017)	*Automated Data Cleansing through Meta-Learning*	AAAI
Li et al. (2020)	*Online Meta-Learning for Multi-Source and Semi-Supervised Domain Adaptation*	ECCV

TABLE 1.1 Summary of meta-learning algorithms and frameworks—cont'd

Reference	Title	Conference
Liu, Rao, et al. (2020)	*Meta-Distiller: Network Self-Boosting via Meta-Learned Top-Down Distillation*	ECCV
Franceschi et al. (2018)	*Bilevel Programming for Hyperparameter Optimization and Meta-Learning*	ICML
Continual Learning		
Javed and White (2019)	*Meta-Learning Representations for Continual Learning*	NeurIPS
Luo et al. (2019)	*Learning from the Past: Continual Meta-Learning with Bayesian Graph Neural Networks*	AAAI
Gupta et al. (2020)	*La-MAML: Look-ahead Meta-Learning for Continual Learning*	NeurIPS
Joseph and Balasubramanian (2020)	*Meta-Consolidation for Continual Learning*	NeurIPS
1.4 Deep Learning		
Elsken et al. (2020)	*Meta-Learning of Neural Architectures for Few-Shot Learning*	CVPR
Chen et al. (2020)	*CATCH: Context-based Meta-Reinforcement Learning for Transferrable Architecture Search*	ECCV
Shaw et al. (2020)	*Meta-Architecture Search*	NeurIPS
Sitzmann et al. (2020)	*Meta-SDF: Meta-learning Signed Distance Functions*	NeurIPS
Liu et al. (2019)	*Meta-Pruning: Meta-Learning for Automatic Neural Network Channel Pruning*	ICCV
1.5 Transfer Learning		
Zhang et al. (2019)	*Meta-Style: Three-Way Trade-Off Among Speed, Flexibility, and Quality in Neural Style Transfer*	AAAI
1.6 Few-Shot Learning		
Sun et al. (2019)	*Meta-Transfer Learning for Few-Shot Learning*	CVPR
Verma et al. (2020)	*Meta-Learning for Generalized Zero-Shot Learning*	AAAI
1.7 Probabilistic Model		
Foong et al. (2020)	*Meta-Learning Stationary Stochastic Process Prediction with Convolutional Neural Processes*	NeurIPS
Wu et al. (2020)	*Meta-Amortized Variational Inference and Learning*	AAAI
1.8 Bayesian Inference		
Patacchiola et al. (2020)	*Bayesian Meta-Learning for the Few-Shot Setting via Deep Kernels*	NeurIPS
Hu et al. (2020)	*Empirical Bayes Transductive Meta-learning with Synthetic Gradients*	ICLR
Zou and Lu (2020)	*Gradient-EM Bayesian Meta-learning*	NeurIPS
Wang et al. (2018)	*Regret Bounds for Meta-Bayesian Optimization with an Unknown Gaussian Process Prior*	NeurIPS
Xie et al. (2019)	*Meta-Learning with Relational Information for Short Sequences*	NeurIPS
Jerfel et al. (2019)	*Reconciling Meta-learning And Continual Learning with Online Mixtures of Tasks*	NeurIPS

Table 1.1 covers the mentioned 38 pieces of research from Sections 1.2–1.8 from premier academic conferences. All this research either achieved state-of-the-art performance or had an influential impact on academia or industry.

In this book, Section 1.2 provides an introduction to meta-learning's historical development, concepts, theories, dataset designs, related terminology, characteristics of techniques, evaluation of benefits, and disadvantages. Meta-learning paradigms can be divided into three types: (1) model-based, (2) metric-based, and (3) optimization-based. Chapters 2–4 discuss the nine most commonly implemented meta-learning algorithms used mainly as backbone models. Chapter 2 offers a detailed exploration of multiple model-based meta-learning methods, including Memory-Augmented Neural Network in Section 2.2 and Meta Network in Section 2.3. Metric-based meta-learning strategies are investigated in Chapter 3: Convolutional Siamese Neural Network in Section 3.2, Matching Network in Section 3.3, Prototypical Network in Section 3.4, and Relation Network in Section 3.5. Chapter 4 reviews the broadly implemented meta-learning algorithms as an excellent companion to deep learning algorithms or optimization-based meta-learning (also called gradient-based meta-learning): LSTM Meta-learner in Section 4.2, Model-Agnostic Meta-learning in Section 4.3, and the variant method Reptile in Section 4.4.

References

Abu-Mostafa, Y. (1990). Learning from hints in neural networks. *Journal of Complexity.* https://doi.org/10.1016/0885-064x(90)90006-y.

Antoniou, A., & Storkey, A. (2019). *Assume, augment and learn: Unsupervised few-shot meta-learning via random labels and data augmentation.*

Baxter, J. (1997). A Bayesian/information theoretic model of learning to learn via multiple task sampling. *Machine Learning, 28,* 7–39.

Baydin, A., Cornish, R., Martinez-Rubio, D., Schmidt, M., & Wood, F. (2018). *Online learning rate adaptation with hypergradient descent.* arXiv.

Bayes, T. (1763). *An essay towards solving a problem in the doctrine of chances.* Royal Society Publishing. https://royalsocietypublishing.org/doi/pdf/10.1098/rstl.1763.0053.

Bengio, Y., Samy, B., & Gloutier, J. (1991). *Learning a synaptic learning rule.* http://bengio.abracadoudou.com/publications/pdf/bengio_1991_ijcnn.pdf.

Bertinetto, L., Henriques, J., Valmadre, J., Torr, P., & Vedaldi, A. (2016). *Learning feed-forward one-shot learners.*

Biederman, I. (1987). Recognition-by-components: A theory of human image understanding. *Psychological Review, 94*(2), 115–147.

Bozinovski, S., & Fulgosi, A. (1976). *The influence of pattern similarity and transfer learning upon the training of a base perceptron B2.*

Breiman, L. (1997). *Arcing the edge.* Berkeley.Edu. https://statistics.berkeley.edu/sites/default/files/tech-reports/486.pdf.

Brock, A., Lim, T., Ritchie, J. M., & Weston, N. (2018). *SMASH: One-shot model architecture search through hypernetworks.* arxiv.org.

Caruana, R. (1993). *Multitask learning: A knowledge-based source of inductive bias.*

Chen, X., Duan, Y., Chen, Z., Xu, H., Chen, Z., Liang, X., et al. (2020). *CATCH: Context-based meta reinforcement learning for transferrable architecture search.*

Cho, K., van Merrienboer, B., Gulcehre, C., Bahdanau, D., Bougares, F., Schwenk, H., et al. (2014). *Learning phrase representations using RNN encoder-decoder for statistical machine translation.* arXiv. http://arXiv:1406.1078.

Coucke, A., Saade, A., Ball, A., Bluche, T., Caulier, A., Leroy, D., et al. (2018). *Snips voice platform: An embedded spoken language understanding system for private-by-design voice interfaces.* arXiv. https://arxiv.org.

Danielsson, P.-E. (1980). Euclidean distance mapping. *Computer Graphics and Image Processing, 14*(3), 227–248.

Elsken, T., Staffler, B., Metzen, J., & Hutter, F. (2020). *Meta-learning of neural architectures for few-shot learning.* Arxiv. Org.

Finn, C., Abbeel, P., & Levine, S. (2017). *Model-agnostic meta-learning for fast adaptation of deep networks.* Arxiv.Org. https://arxiv.org/abs/1703.03400.

Finn, C., & Levine, S. (2019). *Meta-learning: From few-shot learning to rapid reinforcement learning.*

Finn, C., Xu, K., & Levine, S. (2019). *Probabilistic model-Agnostic meta-learning.* Arxiv.Org. https://arxiv.org/pdf/1806.02817.pdf.

Flennerhag, S., Rusu, A., Pascanu, R., Visin, F., Yin, H., & Hadsell, R. (2020). *Meta-learning with warped gradient descent.*

Foong, A., Bruinsma, W., Gordon, J., Dubois, Y., Requeima, J., & Turner, R. (2020). *Meta-learning stationary stochastic process prediction with convolutional neural processes.* arxiv.org.

Franceschi, L., Donini, M., Frasconi, P., & Pontil, M. (2017). *Forward and reverse gradient-based hyperparameter optimization.* arxiv.org.

Franceschi, L., Frasconi, P., Salzo, S., Grazzi, R., & Pontil, M. (2018). *Bilevel programming for hyperparameter optimization and meta-learning.* arxiv.org.

Freund, Y., & Schapire, R. (1999). A short introduction to boosting. *Journal of Japanese Society for Artificial Intelligence, 14*, 771–780. https://cseweb.ucsd.edu/~yfreund/papers/IntroToBoosting.pdf.

Garnelo, M., Rosenbaum, D., Maddison, C., Ramalho, T., Saxton, D., Shanahan, M., et al. (2018). *Conditional neural processes.* Arxiv.Org. https://arxiv.org/pdf/1807.01613.pdf.

Geman, S., Bienenstock, É., & Doursat, R. (1992). Neural networks and the bias/variance dilemma. *Neural Computation.* http://web.mit.edu/6.435/www/Geman92.pdf.

Gemp, I., Theocharous, G., & Ghavamzadeh, M. (2017). *Automated data cleansing through meta-learning.*

Gers, F., Schmidhuber, J., & Cummins, F. (1999). *Learning to forget: Continual prediction with LSTM.*

Goodfellow, I., Bengio, Y., & Courville, A. (2016). *Deep learning.* https://www.deeplearningbook.org/.

Gordon, D., & Desjardins, M. (1995). Evaluation and selection of biases in machine learning. *Machine Learning.* https://doi.org/10.1023/A:1022630017346.

Gordon, J., Bronskill, J., Bauer, M., Nowozin, S., & Turner, R. (2019). *Meta-learning probabilistic inference for prediction.* Arxiv.Org. https://arxiv.org/pdf/1805.09921.pdf.

Gordon, J., Bruinsma, W., Foong, A., Requeima, J., Dubois, Y., & Turner, R. (2020). *Convolutional conditional neural processes.* Arxiv.Org. https://arxiv.org/pdf/1910.13556.pdf.

Grant, E., Finn, C., Levine, S., Darrell, T., & Griffiths, T. (2018). *Recasting gradient-based meta-learning as hierarchical bayes.* Arxiv.Org. https://arxiv.org/pdf/1801.08930.pdf.

Gupta, G., Yadav, K., & Paull, L. (2020). *La-MAML: Look-ahead meta learning for continual learning.*

Han, X., Zhu, H., Yu, P., Wang, Z., Yao, Y., Liu, Z., et al. (2018). *FewRel: A large-scale supervised few-shot relation classification dataset with state-of-the-art evaluation.* arXiv. https://arxiv.org.

Harrison, J., Sharma, A., & Pavone, M. (2018). *Meta-learning priors for efficient online Bayesian regression.* Arxiv.Org. https://arxiv.org/pdf/1807.08912.pdf.

Hilliard, N., Phillips, L., Howland, S., Yankov, A., Corley, C. D., & Hodas, N. O. (2018). *Few-shot learning with metric-agnostic conditional embeddings.* arXiv. https://arxiv.org.

Hinton, G., & Sejnowski, T. (1999). *Unsupervised learning: Foundations of neural computation.* MIT Press.

Ho, T. (1995). *Random decision forests.*

Hospedales, T., Antoniou, A., Micaelli, P., & Storkey, A. (2020). *Meta-learning in neural networks: A survey.*

Hsu, K., Levine, S., & Finn, C. (2019). *Unsupervised learning via meta-learning.*

Hu, S., Moreno, P., Xiao, Y., Shen, X., Obozinski, G., Lawrence, N., et al. (2020). *Empirical bayes transductive meta-learning with synthetic gradients.*

Huang, Y., Huang, W., Li, L., & Li, Z. (2020). *Meta-learning PAC-Bayes priors in model averaging.*

Hutter, F. (2019). *Bayesian optimization and meta-learning.*

Javed, K., & White, M. (2019). *Meta-learning representations for continual learning.*

Jerfel, G., Grant, E., Griffiths, T., & Heller, K. (2019). *Reconciling meta-learning and continual learning with online mixtures of tasks.*

Joseph, K., & Balasubramanian, V. (2020). *Meta-consolidation for continual learning.*

Joyce, J. (2003). Bayes' theorem. In *The Stanford encyclopedia of philosophy* (Spring 2019 Ed.).

Kaddour, J., Sæmundsson, S., & Deisenroth, M. (2020). *Robust meta-learning for mixed linear regression with small batches.*

Kaelbling, L., Littman, M., & Moore, A. (1996). Reinforcement learning: A survey. *Journal of Artificial Intelligence Research, 4*, 237–285. http://arXiv:cs/9605103.

Khodadadeh, S., Boloni, L., & Shah, M. (2019). *Unsupervised meta-learning for few-shot image classification.*

Kim, T., Yoon, J., Dia, O., Kim, S., Bengio, Y., & Ahn, S. (2018). *Bayesian model-agnostic meta-learning.* Arxiv.Org. https://arxiv.org/pdf/1806.03836.pdf.

Kohavi, R., & Wolpert, D. (1996). Bias plus variance decomposition for zero-one loss functions. In *ICML*. https://pdfs. semanticscholar.org/54d4/0c45488e9ecf4da793affb92e08248e3a1a6.pdf.

Kong, W., Somani, R., Song, Z., Kakade, S., & Oh, S. (2020). Meta-learning for mixed linear regression. In *Proceedings of the 37th international conference on machine learning*.

Larson, S., Mahendran, A., Peper, J. J., Clarke, C., Lee, A., Hill, P., et al. (2019). *An evaluation dataset for intent classification and out-of-scope prediction*. arXiv. https://arxiv.org.

LeCun, Y., & Bengio, Y. (1995). *Convolutional networks for images, speech, and time series*.

LeCun, Y., Bengio, Y., & Hinton, G. (2015). Deep learning. *Nature, 521*, 436–444.

Li, D., & Hospedales, T. (2020). *Online meta-learning for multi-source and semi-supervised domain adaptation*. arXiv.

Li, D., Yang, Y., Song, Y.-Z., & Hospedales, T. (2017). *Learning to generalize: Meta-learning for domain generalization*. arXiv.

Li, F., VanRullen, R., Koch, C., & Perona, P. (2002). Rapid natural scene categorization in the near absence of attention. *PNAS, 99*, 9596–9601.

Li, F.-F. (2006). *Knowledge transfer in learning to recognize visual objects classes*. Stanford. http://vision.stanford.edu/documents/Fei-Fei_ICDL2006.pdf.

Li, F.-F., Fergus, R., & Perona, P. (2003). A Bayesian approach to unsupervised one-shot learning of object categories. In *ICCV*. http://vision.stanford.edu/documents/Fei-Fei_ICCV03.pdf.

Li, Y., Gu, S., Zhang, K., Gool, L., & Timofte, R. (2020). *DHP: Differentiable Meta Pruning via HyperNetworks*.

Li, Y., Yang, Y., Zhou, W., & Hospedales, T. (2019). *Feature-critic networks for heterogeneous domain generalization*. arXiv.

Liu, B., Rao, Y., Lu, J., Zhou, J., & Hsieh, C.-J. (2020). MetaDistiller: Network self-boosting via meta-learned top-down distillation. In *Computer vision—ECCV 2020: 16th european conference, Glasgow, UK, August 23–28, 2020, Proceedings, Part XIV* (pp. 694–709). Berlin/Heidelberg: Springer-Verlag. https://doi.org/10.1007/978-3-030-58568-6_41.

Liu, C., Wang, Z., Sahoo, D., Fang, Y., Zhang, K., & Hoi, S. (2020). *Adaptive task sampling for meta-learning*. arXiv.

Liu, H., Simonyan, K., & Yang, Y. (2019). *DARTS: Differentiable architecture search*. arXiv.

Liu, S., Davison, A., & Johns, E. (2019). *Self-supervised generalisation with meta auxiliary learning*.

Liu, Z., Mu, H., Zhang, X., Guo, Z., Yang, X., Cheng, T., et al. (2019). *MetaPruning: Meta learning for automatic neural network channel pruning*. arXiv.

Lorraine, J., Vicol, P., & Duvenaud, D. (2020). *Optimizing millions of hyperparameters by implicit differentiation*. arXiv.

Luo, Y., Huang, Z., Zhang, Z., Wang, Z., Baktashmotlagh, M., & Yang, Y. (2019). *Learning from the past: Continual meta-learning with Bayesian graph neural networks*. arXiv.

Marcus, G. (2018). *Deep learning: A critical appraisal*. arXiv.

Massiceti, D., Zintgraf, L., Bronskill, J., Theodorou, L., Harris, M. T., Cutrell, E., et al. (2021). *ORBIT: A real-world few-shot dataset for teachable object recognition*. arXiv. https://arxiv.org.

Maudsley, D. B. (1979). A theory of meta-learning and principles of facilitation: An organismic perspective. In *A theory of meta-learning and principles of facilitation: An organismic perspective* University of Toronto.

Meier, F., Kappler, D., & Schaal, S. (2018). *Online learning of a memory for learning rates*. arXiv.

Micaelli, P., & Storkey, A. (2020). *Non-greedy gradient-based hyperparameter optimization over long horizons*.

Mitchell, T. (1980). *The need for biases in learning generalizations*. citeseerx. https://citeseerx.ist.psu.edu/viewdoc/summary?doi=10.1.1.19.5466.

Mitchell, T. (1997). *Machine learning*.

Naik, N. (2019). *Neural architecture search a tutorial*.

Opitz, D., & Maclin, R. (1999). *Popular ensemble methods: An empirical study*.

Oreshkin, B. N., Rodriguez, P., & Lacoste, A. (2018). Tadam: Task dependent adaptive metric for improved few-shot learning. In *2018. Advances in neural information processing systems* (pp. 721–731). Neural Information Processing Systems Foundation. https://papers.nips.cc/.

Park, E., & Oliva, J. (2019). *Meta-Curvature*.

Patacchiola, M., Turner, J., Crowley, E., O'Boyle, M., & Storkey, A. (2020). *Bayesian meta-learning for the few-shot setting via deep kernels*.

Pedregosa, F. (2016). *Hyperparameter optimization with approximate gradient*.

Pfister, T., Charles, J., & Zisserman, A. (2014). *Domain-adaptive discriminative one-shot learning of gestures*.

Rajendran, J., Irpan, A., & Jang, E. (2020). *Meta-learning requires meta-augmentation*.

Rajeswaran, A., Finn, C., Kakade, S., & Levine, S. (2019). *Meta-learning with implicit gradients*.

Ramalho, T., & Garnelo, M. (2019). *Adaptive posterior learning: Few-shot learning with a surprise-based memory module*.

Ravi, S., & Beatson, A. (2019). *Amortized Bayesian Meta-learning*. Openreview.Net. https://openreview.net/pdf?id=rkgpy3C5tX.

Rebuffi, S.-A., Bilen, H., & Vedaldi, A. (2017). *Learning multiple visual domains with residual adapters*.

Ren, M., Triantafillou, E., Ravi, S., Snell, J., Swersky, K., Tenenbaum, J. B., et al. (2018). Meta-learning for semi-supervised few-shot classification. In *6th International conference on learning representations, ICLR 2018 – Conference track proceedings. International conference on learning representations, ICLR*. https://dblp.org/db/conf/iclr/iclr2018.html.

Ritter, S., Wang, J., Kurth-Nelson, Z., Jayakumar, S., Blundell, C., Pascanu, R., et al. (2018). Been there, done that: Meta-learning with episodic recall. In *Proceedings of machine learning research: Vol. 80. Proceedings of the 35th international conference on machine mearning* (pp. 4354–4363). Available from: https://proceedings.mlr.press/v80/ritter18a.html.

Ruck, D. W., Rogers, S. K., Kabrisky, M., Oxley, M. E., & Suter, B. W. (1990). The multilayer perceptron as an approximation to a Bayes optimal discriminant function. *IEEE Transactions on Neural Networks, 1*, 296–298. https://ieeexplore.ieee.org/abstract/document/80266.

Russell, S., & Norvig, P. (2010). *Artificial intelligence: A modern approach* (3rd ed.). Prentice Hall.

Ryu, J., Shin, J., Lee, H., & Hwang, S. (2020). *MetaPerturb: Transferable Regularizer for heterogeneous tasks and architectures*.

Salakhutdinov, R., Tenenbaum, J., & Torralba, A. (2012). One-shot learning with a hierarchical nonparametric Bayesian model. *Journal of Machine Learning Research*. http://proceedings.mlr.press/v27/salakhutdinov12a/salakhutdinov12a.pdf.

Santoro, A., Bartunov, S., Botvinick, M., Wierstra, D., & Lillicrap, T. (2016). *Meta-learning with memory-augmented neural networks* (pp. 1842–1850).

Saunshi, N., Zhang, Y., Khodak, M., & Arora, S. (2020). *A sample complexity separation between non-convex and convex meta-learning*.

Schick, T., & Schütze, H. (2021). *It's not just size that matters: Small language models are also few-shot learners*. ArXiv.

Schmidhuber, J. (1987). *Evolutional principles in self-referential learning*. http://people.idsia.ch/~juergen/diploma1987ocr.pdf.

Shaban, A., Bansal, S., Liu, Z., Essa, I., & Boots, B. (2017). One-shot learning for semantic segmentation. In *British machine vision conference 2017, BMVC 2017*BMVA Press. https://doi.org/10.5244/c.31.167.

Shaban, A., Cheng, C.-A., Hatch, N., & Boots, B. (2019). Truncated backpropagation for bilevel optimization. In *AISTATS*.

Shaw, A., Wei, W., Liu, W., Song, L., & Dai, B. (2020). *Meta architecture search*.

Shirangi, M., & Durlofsky, L. (2016). A general method to select representative models for decision making and optimization under uncertainty. *Computers & Geosciences, 96*, 109–123.

Shu, J., Xie, Q., Yi, L., Zhao, Q., Zhou, S., Xu, Z., et al. (2019). *Meta-weight-net: Learning an explicit mapping for sample weighting*.

Singhal, A. (2001). *Modern information retrieval: A brief overview*. Sifaka.Cs.Uiuc.Edu. http://sifaka.cs.uiuc.edu/course/410s12/mir.pdf.

Sitzmann, V., Chan, E., Tucker, R., Snavely, N., & Wetzstein, G. (2020). *MetaSDF: Meta-learning signed distance functions*.

Sommers, T. (2003). *Galen Strawson (interview)*. Believer Magazine.

Stanford-CS231n. (2022). Layers used to build ConvNets. Retrieved from CS231n Convolutional Neural Networks for Visual Recognition: https://cs231n.github.io/convolutional-networks/#add.

Stigler, S. (1986). *The history of statistics: The measurement of uncertainty before 1900*. Harvard University Press.

Sun, Q., Liu, Y., Chua, T.-S., & Schiele, B. (2019). *Meta-transfer learning for few-shot learning*.

Sun, S.-H. (2019). *Multi-digit MNIST for few-shot learning*.

Tappert, C. (2019). *Who is the father of deep learning?* (pp. 343–348). IEEE, ISBN:978-1-7281-5584-5. https://doi.org/10.1109/CSCI49370.2019.00067. S2CID 216043128.

Tian, H., Liu, B., Yuan, X.-T., & Liu, Q. (2020). *Meta-learning with network pruning*.

Torra, V., & Navarro-Arribas, G. (2018). *Probabilistic metric spaces for privacy by design machine learning algorithms: Modeling database changes*. Springer, Lecture Notes in Computer Science.

Triantafillou, E., Zemel, R., & Urtasun, R. (2017). *Few-shot learning through an information retrieval lens*.

Triantafillou, E., Zhu, T. L., Dumoulin, V., Lamblin, P., Xu, K., Goroshin, R., et al. (2020). *Meta-dataset: A dataset of datasets for learning to learn from few examples*. ArXiv.

Veeriah, V., Hessel, M., Xu, Z., Lewis, R., Rajendran, J., Oh, J., et al. (2019). *Discovery of useful questions as auxiliary tasks.*

Verma, V., Brahma, D., & Rai, P. (2020). *Meta-learning for generalized zero-shot learning.*

Vinyals, O., Blundell, C., Lillicrap, T., & Wierstra, D. (2016). Matching networks for one shot learning. *Advances in Neural Information Processing Systems*, 3630–3638.

von Luxburg, U., & Schölkopf, B. (2011). *Statistical learning theory: Models, Concepts, and Results.* https://doi.org/10.1016/B978-0-444-52936-7.50016-1.

Wang, Z., Kim, B., & Kaelbling, L. (2018). *Regret bounds for meta Bayesian optimization with an unknown Gaussian process prior.* arXiv.

Williams, R. (1992). *Simple statistical gradient-following algorithms for connectionist reinforcement learning.* Springer. https://link.springer.com/article/10.1007/BF00992696.

Williams, R., & Zipser, D. (1989). *A learning algorithm for continually running fully recurrent neural networks.* arXiv.

Wu, M., Choi, K., Goodman, N., & Ermon, S. (2020). *Meta-amortized variational inference and learning.* arXiv.

Xie, Y., Jiang, H., Liu, F., Zhao, T., & Zha, H. (2019). *Meta learning with relational information for short sequences.* arXiv.

Xie, K., Wang, C., & Wang, P. (2021). A domain-independent ontology learning method based on transfer learning. *Electronics, 10*(16), 1911. https://doi.org/10.3390/electronics10161911.

Xiong, W., Yu, M., Chang, S., Guo, X., & Wang, W. Y. (2018). *One-shot relational learning for knowledge graphs.* arXiv. https://arxiv.org.

Xu, Z., Hasselt, H., & Silver, D. (2018). *Meta-gradient reinforcement learning.* arXiv.

Yan, W., Yap, J., & Mori, G. (2015). *Multi-task transfer methods to improve one-shot learning for multimedia event detection.* arXiv.

Yao, H., Wei, Y., Huang, J., & Li, Z. (2019). *Hierarchically structured meta-learning.* arXiv.

Yin, M., et al. (2020). *Meta-Learning Without Memorization.* https://arxiv.org/abs/1912.03820.

Yu, T., Quillen, D., He, Z., Julian, R., Hausman, K., Finn, C., et al. (2019). *Meta-world: A benchmark and evaluation for multi- task and meta reinforcement learning.* arXiv.

Zhang, C., Zhu, Y., & Zhu, S.-C. (2019). *MetaStyle: Three-way trade-off among speed, flexibility, and quality in neural style transfer.* arXiv.

Zheng, Z., Oh, J., & Singh, S. (2018). *On learning intrinsic rewards for policy gradient methods.* arXiv.

Zhou, Z.-H. (2019). *A brief introduction to weakly supervised learning.* Semantic Scholar. https://pdfs.semanticscholar.org/3adc/fd254b271bcc2fb7e2a62d750db17e6c2c08.pdf.

Zou, Y., & Lu, X. (2020). *Gradient-EM Bayesian meta-learning.* arXiv.

Theory & mechanisms

2

Model-based meta-learning approaches

2.1 Introduction

Analogous to the concept of "model-based" in the term "model-based design (MBD)" (Reedy & Lunzman, 2010), model-based meta-learning algorithms rely on a controlling model or system designed mainly to guide rapid parameterization for generalization through modeling, analyzing, synthesizing, simulating, and integrating. This controlling model allows users to update parameters efficiently and rapidly within a few training steps through its internal architecture or by another external meta-learner embedded in the pipeline.

Santoro, Bartunov, Botvinick, Wierstra, and Lillicrap (2016) suggested the first model-based meta-learner inspired by the Neural Turing Machine (NTM; Graves, Wayne, & Danihelka, 2014), which built on an external memory buffer with reading heads, writing heads, and creative addressing processes (Hopfield, 1982). This work opened the door for external memory resources that cooperate with a neural network, compared to classical research interests in internal memory like a recurrent neural network (RNN) (Weng, 2018). Following this, the Meta-Networks (Meta-Net) (Munkhdalai & Yu, 2017) meta-learning method presented the integration of fast weights and slow weights via layer augmentation and introduces a different technique rather than standard gradient descent. From that moment, model-based meta-learners attracted more attention in substantial research areas (Le, Tran, & Venkatesh, 2018; Ma et al., 2018).

This chapter sequentially explores the two types of model-based meta-learning strategies, the related essential vanilla models, and various modifications. Section 2.2 introduces the memory-augmented neural network (MANN), explains how the NTM motivated MANN, applies its variations to a visual question answering system (VQA), and offers a write-protected MANN. Section 2.3 discusses Hinton and Plaut's work (1987) on fast weights, and the integration of fast weights and slow weights. This investigation surveys fundamental background knowledge, creative and vital architecture, remarkable techniques, step-by-step algorithms or training methods related to these vanilla models, influential technical contributions or discovery, multiple practical modifications and edge extensions, and the design motivation for such contributions on different model-based meta-learning approaches.

2.2 Memory-augmented neural networks

2.2.1 Background knowledge

As stated by Von Neumann (1945), "external memory can be written to and read from in the course of computation." Many early researchers in psychology and neuroscience (Baddeley, Eysenck, & Anderson, 2009; Hazy, Frank, & O'Reilly, 2006; Wang, 1999) noted the essential connection between memory buffer and attention processes and how biophysical circuits maintain neuronal firing to tackle explicit tasks. Inspired by the Turing Machine (Minsky, 1967), the Neural Turing Machine (NTM; Graves et al., 2014) couples external memory resources with a controller neural network, interacting through attentional processes.

With reference to the Turing Machine, the NTM proposed "read heads" and "write heads" in operating with soft memory to read or write the memory strongly at a specific location and weakly in other spots. The memory acted as a knowledge repository. The attention weights are determined by two mechanisms: content-based addressing (Hopfield, 1982) and location-based addressing. The content-based mechanism focuses on locations by computing the similarity between current values and the value released by the controller. This addressing type offers the advantage of simple retrieval without approximation to parts of the stored information. It generates a normalized weight w_t^c through the cosine similarity $K[\bullet, \bullet]$ between the key vector $\mathbf{k}_t$ and the vector $\mathbf{M}_t(i)$, expressed in Eq. (2.1), where the β_t denotes a positive key strength.

$$w_t^c(i) \leftarrow \frac{\exp\left(\beta_t K[\mathbf{k}_t, \mathbf{M}_t(i)]\right)}{\sum\limits_j \exp\left(\beta_t K[\mathbf{k}_t, \mathbf{M}_t(j)]\right)} \tag{2.1}$$

In contrast, location-based addressing provides recognizable names or an address for an arbitrary variable to which content-based addressing is not well-suited. The location-based addressing controls simple iteration across memory's locations, and random-access jumps through a rotational shift on a weighting (e.g., suppose the weighting fully concentrates on a single location, a rotation of 1 shift to the next location, while a negative shift proceeds the weighting in the reverse direction.) The overall architecture of NTM is displayed in Fig. 2.1.

The **reading** vector r_t in M length is expressed in Eqs. (2.2), (2.3) as a convex combination of i-th row vectors $M_t(i)$ with i-th element weighting $w_t(i)$ in memory:

$$\mathbf{r}_t \leftarrow \sum_i w_t(i) \mathbf{M}_t(i) \tag{2.2}$$

where:

$$\sum_i w_t(i) = 1, 0 \leq w_t(i) \leq 1, \forall i \tag{2.3}$$

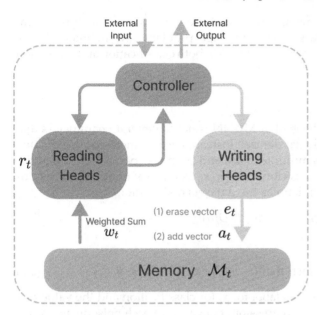

External Input

External Output

FIG. 2.1 General workflow of the neural turing machine. In each updating period, the external input is fed into the controller (*colored green; dark gray in print version*) to read and write the memory through the reading heads (*colored blue; dark gray in print version*) and the writing heads (*colored yellow; light gray in print version*). The Neural Turing Machine is separated from other outside components as denoted by the dashed line.

Modified from Graves, A., Wayne, G., & Danihelka, I. (2014). Neural turing machines. Retrieved from arXiv:1410.5401, 2014.

The **writing** consists of two parts: removing previous content with erase vectors (e_t, presented in Eq. 2.4) followed by inserting the new one through an add vector (a_t, offered in Eq. 2.5), where $\mathbf{M}_{t-1}(i)$ represents the previous step memory vectors:

$$\widetilde{\mathbf{M}}_t(i) \longleftarrow \mathbf{M}_{t-1}(i)[\mathbf{1} - \mathbf{w}_t(i)\mathbf{e}_t] \tag{2.4}$$

$$\mathbf{M}_t(i) \longleftarrow \widetilde{\mathbf{M}}_t(i) + \mathbf{w}_t(i)\mathbf{a}_t \tag{2.5}$$

To encode new information rapidly, scalable and valid strategies have two basic requirements: (1) the data stored in memory capacity needs to be stable (for accessing reliably) and element-wise addressable (for accessing selectively) and (2) the number of parameters is not dependent on memory size. Thus, existing neural networks like long short-term memory (LSTM) and RNN cannot be used, but NTM and MANN are satisfactory. The NTM, memory network (Weston, Chopra, & Bordes, 2015), and memory-augmented neural network all belong to the category of **external**-memory sources. In contrast, LSTM (Hochreiter & Schmidhuber, 1997), vanilla RNN (Schmidhuber, 1993b), and gated recurrent unit (GRU) (Cho et al., 2014) are considered as internal memory capacity-equipped structures.

2.2.2 Methodology

Motivated by NTM, Santoro et al. (2016) introduced an evolutional model-based meta-learning approach—the **memory-augmented neural network** (MANN)—an external-memory resources-equipped architecture that can rapidly and effectively encode and retrieve information, as well as make accurate predictions and adapt to new tasks based on few-shot samples. Like NTM, this external memory is independent of the process-controlling mechanisms, where such controlling mechanisms can be fed forward networks, LSTM, or other neural networks. MANN achieved promising results in various tasks from small programming topics (Graves et al., 2014) to large-scale language problems (Munkhdalai & Yu, 2017; Weston et al., 2015). It has shown good performance in both classification and regression tasks using sparse training samples.

Task setup

Unlike most deep learning models, the goal of MANN is not to generate parameters that minimize the cost function across a particular dataset. Instead, it learns meta-parameters that could minimize the cost function across multiple tasks, and produces parameters θ that decrease the expected cost function across a distribution $p(y_t | x_t, D_{1:t-1}; \theta)$ of multiple datasets, as expressed in Eqs. (2.6), (2.7), where $p(D)$ denotes the datasets distribution.

$$\theta^* = argmin_\theta E_{D \sim p(D)}[\mathcal{L}(D; \theta)] \tag{2.6}$$

where:

$$D = \{d_t\}_{t=1}^T = \left\{ (x_t\, y_t) \right\}_{t=1}^T \text{ such that } (x_1\ null), (x_2\ y_1), ..., (x_T\ y_{T-1}) \tag{2.7}$$

As demonstrated in Eq. (2.7), y_t is the class label for x_t for classification and the value of a hidden function associated with factor x_t in regression. However, in each episode, y_{t-1} is offered with a **one-step offset** as (x_t, y_{t-1}), so that y_{t-1} is the correct label at time $t-1$ as well as part of the input at time t.

Memory retrieval

Based on shuffled labels, the system is stimulated to hold the current input in memory until the correct label is presented at a later time-step and then to retrieve the corresponding old sample-label bound information to make a prediction appropriately. To retrieve the old bound memory, similar to NTM, the cosine similarity is computed using Eq. (2.8), where M_t denotes the memory matrix, and k_t presents the key generated by the controller:

$$K(k_t, M_t(i)) = \frac{k_t \cdot M_t(i)}{\| k_t \| \ \| M_t(i) \|} \tag{2.8}$$

The **reading vector**, which is denoted as r_t, with reading weight is expressed in Eq. (2.9):

$$r_t \leftarrow \sum_i w_t^r(i) M_t(i) \tag{2.9}$$

The **reading weight**, which is denoted as w_t^r, is presented in Eq. (2.10):

$$w_t^r(i) \leftarrow \frac{\exp\left(K(k_t, M_t(i))\right)}{\sum_j \exp\left(K(k_t, M_t(j))\right)} \tag{2.10}$$

Least recently used access

Unlike the two original addressing methods (location-based addressing and content-based) in NTM, MANN creates a novel structure with a purely content-based memory writer, which is named the least recently used access module (LRUA). Cache replacement (Smith, 1987), a techinque that motivated how LRUA is conducted; it addresses either the least-used memory (Lee et al., 2001) or the most recently used memory (Chou & Dewitt, 2006). Location-based addressing offers the advantages of long-distance jumping and iterative steps in sequence-based tasks but not for tasks with conjunctive coding of memory independent of sequence. Depending on the writing vector, LRUA addresses memory in two locations: either the least-used memory spots for frequently used information or the most recently used memory spots that would not be called on for a while.

The **writing vector,** which is denoted as w_t^w, reflects an interpolation between previous reading weights (so that the system will address to the most recently used location) and the previous least-used weights (so that the system will address to the lease-used location). This interpolation is denoted as a sigmoid function of hyperparametric α in Eq. (2.11), representing a learnable sigmoid gate to compute convex combinations of both read weight and least-used weight in the previous time step:

$$w_t^w \leftarrow \sigma(\alpha)w_{t-1}^r + (1 - \sigma(\alpha))w_{t-1}^{lu} \qquad (2.11)$$

The **usage weight,** which is denoted as w_t^u, is updated at each time step through the decay parameter γ on its previous usage weight. It is the sum of write weight w_t^w, read weight w_t^r, and the decayed usage weight w_{t-1}^u at the previous time step. See Eq. (2.12) for this expression:

$$w_t^u \leftarrow \gamma w_{t-1}^u + w_t^r + w_t^w \qquad (2.12)$$

The **least-used weight,** which is denoted as w_t^{lu}, is determined by the usage weight w_t^u at time t, where $m(v, n)$ is the nth smallest element in vector **v**. See Eq. (2.13) for this expression:

$$w_t^{lu}(i) = \begin{cases} 0 \; if \; w_t^u(i) > m(w_t^u, n) \\ 1 \; if \; w_t^u(i) \leq m(w_t^u, n) \end{cases} \qquad (2.13)$$

After the least-used memory is set to zero, the memory is updated by row, as expressed in Eq. (2.14):

$$M_t(i) \leftarrow M_{t-1}(i) + w_t^w(i)k_t, \forall i \qquad (2.14)$$

2.2.3 Extended algorithm 1

Le et al. (2018) proposed a dual controller write-protected MANN (DCw-MANN), with one LSTM$_E$ controller as an encoder and another LSTM$_D$ controller as a decoder to generate treatment options. This tackled two healthcare treatment tasks based on the MIMIC-III (Johnson et al., 2016) dataset—procedure prediction and medication prescription. This approach is based on differentiable neural computer (DNC) (Graves et al., 2016), a special version of MANN as a completely differentiable MANN. During encoding, the memory keeps updating as feeding the new inputs through the embedding layer W_E to the controller LSTM$_E$. Hence, LSTME interprets from and edits the memory of essential data for the underlying decoding phase (Le, 2021). In the end, LSTM$_E$ maintains the medical history and knowledge of current diseases. In the decoding process, after receiving the states from LSTM$_E$, the memory is write-protected, meaning the decoder cannot write to the memory in the decoding

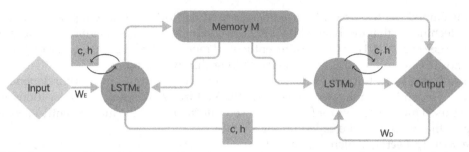

FIG. 2.2   General workflow of dual controller write-protected memory augmented neural network. Input is fed through the embedding layer W_E into the controller $LSTM_E$, which can write and read into the memory M. Hence, the cell memory c and hidden state h is passing to the controller $LSTM_D$ to produce outputs.
Adapted from Springer, ACL, Dual Control Memory Augmented Neural Networks for Treatment Recommendations, Le, H., Tran, T., & Venkatesh, S. (2018).

phase. It is difficult for a sole controller to learn enormous approaches simultaneously (Le, 2021). In contrast, two controllers make processing the learning easier to handle. This is the reason for DCw-MANN with two controllers rather than one. The overall workflow is indicated in Fig. 2.2. With the benefits of DNC, this strategy supports dynamic memory allocation and temporal memory linkage. DNC also produces a key to determine read and write memory locations on the memory matrix.

The cell memory and the hidden state related to these two controllers are expressed in Eq. (2.15), where v_{d_t} is the one-hot vector for input sequence representation, and v_{p_t} is the predicted one-hot vector describing decoder output, as shown in Eq. 2.16. r_t means the read value. v_{d_t} presents a one-hot embedding representation of the input at time $t \leq L_{in}$, whereas v_{p_t} is the predicted one-hot embedding representation of output from decodes at time $t > L_{in}$. o_t denotes the control's output.

$$h_{t+1}, c_{t+1} = \begin{cases} LSTM\ M_E([W_E v_{d_t}, r_t], h_t, c_t); & t \leq L_{in} \\ LST\ M_D([W_D v_{p_t}, r_t], h_t, c_t); & t > L_{in} \end{cases} \tag{2.15}$$

$$v_{p_t}[i] = \begin{cases} 1 & ; i = \underset{1 \leq j \leq |C_p|}{\mathrm{argmax}}(o_t[j]) \\ 0 & ; \text{otherwise} \end{cases} \tag{2.16}$$

The write-protected update rule is presented in Eq. (2.17), where w_t^w denotes the write-weights. E presents a matrix of ones, and e_t and v_t mean an erase vector and write vector, respectively. L_{in} denotes the input's length, and $\circ$ indicates the point-wise multiplication:

$$M_t = \begin{cases} M_{t-1} \circ (E - w_t^w e_t^T) + w_t^w v_t^T; & t \leq L_{in} \\ M_{t-1}; & t > L_{in} \end{cases} \tag{2.17}$$

2.2.4   Extended algorithm 2

Ma et al. (2018) proposed a modified MANN approach to predict correct answers in a visual question answering system with high-tailed distribution data. MANN is conducted to process long-tailed pair-wise question and answer samples, which can maintain optimal generalization in low-data situations. Unlike MANN, this approach implements a coattention mechanism to input visual and question feature vectors, denoted as v_0 and q_0, as expressed in Eqs. (2.18)–(2.20). $\mathbf{v}_n$ denotes the visual feature vector, whereas $\mathbf{q}_t$ presents the question feature vector. $\odot$ means element-wise production.

$$\mathbf{m}_0 = \mathbf{v}_0 \odot \mathbf{q}_0 \tag{2.18}$$

where:

$$\mathbf{v}_0 = \tanh\left(\frac{1}{N}\sum_n \mathbf{v}_n\right) \tag{2.19}$$

$$\mathbf{q}_0 = \frac{1}{T}\sum_t \mathbf{q}_t \tag{2.20}$$

A memory-augmented neural network is employed through an LSTM as the controller for taking input $\mathbf{x}_t$ and communicating with external memory $\mathbf{M}_t$ with multiple read and write heads. In Eq. (2.21), the LSTM is fed with input and the hidden state $\mathbf{h}_{t-1}$ at the previous $t-1$:

$$\mathbf{h}_t = \text{LSTM}(\mathbf{x}_t, \mathbf{h}_{t-1}) \tag{2.21}$$

The read weight vector w_t^r obtains the class probability based on the cosine distance between the external memory $\mathbf{M}_t$ and the hidden state $\mathbf{h}_t$, as expressed in Eq. (2.22):

$$w_t^r(i) = \text{softmax}(D(\mathbf{h}_t, \mathbf{M}_t(i)) \tag{2.22}$$

Thus, a retrieval memory $\mathbf{r}_t$ is expressed in Eq. (2.23):

$$\mathbf{r}_t = \sum_i w_t^r(i)\mathbf{M}_i \tag{2.23}$$

Like MANN, the usage weight controls the memory writing. The current usage weight is updated by decaying the pervious usage weight through Eq. (2.24), where γ denotes the decay parameter, and $\mathbf{w}_t^w$ and $\mathbf{w}_t^r$ represent the current write and read weights, respectively:

$$\mathbf{w}_t^u = \gamma\mathbf{w}_{t-1}^u + \mathbf{w}_t^r + \mathbf{w}_t^w \tag{2.24}$$

Where, the write weights are expressed in Eq. (2.25), $m(\mathbf{w}_{t-1}^u, n)$ denotes the n-th smallest component of $\mathbf{w}_{t-1}^u$, σ means the sigmoid activation, and α represents a scalar gate parameter; both α and γ are utlized to adjust the writing rate of the external memory, which results in a more flexible regularization on memory update, and $\mathbb{1}(x)$ denotes an indicator, which equals 1 as (x) is true and 0 for other situations:

$$\mathbf{w}_t^w = \sigma(\alpha)\mathbf{w}_{t-1}^r + (1 - \sigma(\alpha))\mathbb{1}\left(\mathbf{w}_{t-1}^u \leq m\left(\mathbf{w}_{t-1}^u, n\right)\right) \tag{2.25}$$

Finally, the memory is written with the hidden state and write weight as Eq. (2.26):

$$\mathbf{M}_t^i = \mathbf{M}_{t-1}(i) + w_t^w(i)\mathbf{h}_t \tag{2.26}$$

A one-layer perceptron equips a linear hidden layer to generate a categorical distribution to output answers through the sigmoid or softmax function, as expressed in Eqs. (2.27), (2.28).

$\mathbf{h}_t$ means the hidden state, and $\mathbf{r}_t$ presents the reading memory, such as the final embedding representation $\mathbf{o}_t = [\mathbf{h}_t, \mathbf{r}_t]$. $\mathbf{W}_o$, $\mathbf{W}_h$ denotes the linear layer parameters, and $\mathbf{p}_t$ the output probability of each class:

$$\mathbf{h}_t = \tanh\left(\mathbf{W}_o\mathbf{o}_t\right) \tag{2.27}$$

$$\mathbf{p}_t = \text{softmax}(\mathbf{W}_h\mathbf{h}_t) \tag{2.28}$$

2.3 Meta-networks[a]

2.3.1 Background knowledge

Hinton and Plaut (1987) first suggested applying two weights to deblur old memory—slow weights for maintaining long-term memory and fast weights for storing temporary memory and spontaneously declining toward zero. In this work, Hinton and Plaut (1987) stated that: (1) fast weights could change quickly and regularly revert towards zero, which guarantees that their magnitude exclusively depends on their immediate past; and (2) slow weights, on the other hand, change steadily and maintain the comprehensive long-term information in the architecture. The normal weights generated from stochastic gradient descent are categorized as slow weights. Fast weights support the temporary deblurring of old memories without leading essential interference to new memories. After the fast weight declines to zero, the new memories are reinstated. Hinton and Plaut's work provides a detailed geometrical explanation and mathematical analysis of how this occurs if any interested.

This temporary memory performs several functions:

- Fast temporary learning
- Constructing temporary bindings of a range of features
- Powerful recursive processing (Schmidhuber, 1992, 1993a later implemented fast weights in recursive nets)
- Offering the shortest descent to minimize interference effects by new learning

2.3.2 Methodology

Munkhdalai and Yu (2017) proposed a two-level (meta-space and task space) strategy—the Meta-Networks (Meta-Net)—in which the meta-learner is extracting meta-knowledge across multiple tasks while the base learner supports learning within each task. The base learner provides the meta-knowledge as higher-order feedback about "its own status in the current task space" (Munkhdalai & Yu, 2017). Meta-Net is designed for shifting inductive biases and rapidly generating parameters based on just a few samples. This strategy has been evaluated on

---

[a]These meta networks are not to be confused with the style transfer framework with the same name in computer vision 2D imagery.

two public datasets—Omniglot (Ager, 2021) and Mini-ImageNet (Ravi & Larochell, 2017)—
with reported state-of-the-art (SOTA) performance on both. This framework is highly generic.
It can be applied to reinforcement learning and imitation learning, as well as to language understanding and sequence modeling tasks with the help of recurrent networks. However, it
may seem vague to some newcomers in AI or deep learning areas.

Slow weights and fast weights

Adopting the consideration of slow weights and fast weights from Hinton and Plaut (1987),
Meta-Net implements these two weight types on one-shot meta-learning: the fast weight is
read by soft attention (Ba, Hinton, Mnih, Leibo, & Ionescu, 2016; Bahdanau, Cho, & Bengio,
2015), and the slow weight is the ordinary weight generated from gradient descent. The overall step-by-step algorithm is displayed in Table 2.1, followed by three main procedures: (1)
acquisition of meta-information, (2) generation of fast weights, and (3) optimization of slow
weights.

TABLE 2.1 Training methods of Meta-Net in one-shot supervised
learning.

Input: $\{x_i', y_i'\}_{i=1}^N$, support set
$\{x_i, y_i\}_{i=1}^L$, training set
Fast weight generation functions m and d
$\theta = \{W, Q, Z, G\}$, slow weight
b, base learner
u, dynamic representation learning function
Output: $\theta = \{W, Q, Z, G\}$, updated slow weight

---

1 **for** $i = 1, ..., T$ **do**
    # compute embedding loss function
2   Obtain $\mathcal{L}_i \leftarrow loss_{emb}\big(u(Q, x_i'), y_i'\big)$
3   Obtain $\nabla_i \leftarrow \nabla_Q \mathcal{L}_i$
4 **end for**

    # compute task-level fast weights
5 $Q^* = d\big(G, \{\nabla\}_{i=1}^T\big)$

    # compute example-level fast weights while updating memories
6 **for** $i = 1, ..., N$ **do**
7      $\mathcal{L}_i \leftarrow loss_{task}\big(b(W, x_i'), y_i'\big)$
8      $\nabla_i \leftarrow \nabla_W \mathcal{L}_i$
9      $W_i^* \leftarrow m(Z, \nabla_i)$
10   Keep W_i^* in i^{th} position of memory M
11     $r_i' = u(Q, Q^*, x_i')$
12   Keep r_i' in i^{th} position of index memory R
13 **end for**

14 Initialize $\mathcal{L}_{train} = 0$
    # compute training loss on test set
15 **for** $i = 1, ..., L$ **do**
    # encode the samples to task-specific input representations
16     $r_i' = u(Q, Q^*, x_i')$

Continued

I. Theory & mechanisms

TABLE 2.1   Training methods of Meta-Net in one-shot supervised learning—cont'd

	# generic attention mechanism
17	Let $a_i = attention(R, r_i)$
18	Obtain $W_i^* = softmax(a_i)^\mathsf{T} M$
	# update training loss
19	Evaluate $\mathcal{L}_{train} \leftarrow \mathcal{L}_{train} + loss_{task}\big(b\big(W, W_i^*, x_i\big), y_i\big)$
20	**end for**
	# update all parameters
21	Update θ using $\nabla_\theta \mathcal{L}_{train}$

Modified from Munkhdalai, T., & Yu, H. (2017). Meta networks. Retrieved from arxiv https://arxiv.org/abs/1703.00837.

During this training, three levels of weights are updated at **different time scales**:

- Regular slow-weight updating through a learning algorithm denoted as Q and W
- Task-level fast-weight updating within each task, denoted as Q^*
- Example-level fast-weight updating for a particular input example, denoted as W^* through line 6 to 13 in Table 2.1

Memory M aims to store the example-level fast weight W^* as $M = \{W_i^*\}_{i=1}^N$, while memory M is indexed with task-specific input representation $R = \{r_i'\}_{i=1}^N$. Hence, the meta-learner is parametrized with the base learner through the example-level fast weights W^*. A soft attention mechanism is employed to read the memory.

The way to generate fast weight is expressed below, and the task-level fast weights Q^* and slow weights Q are explored in Eqs. (2.29)–(2.31).

$$\mathcal{L}_i = loss_{emb}\big(u\big(Q, x_i'\big), y_i'\big) \tag{2.29}$$

$$\nabla_i = \nabla_Q \mathcal{L}_i \tag{2.30}$$

$$Q^* = d\Big(G, \{\nabla\}_{i=1}^T\Big) \tag{2.31}$$

Layer augmentation

This layer of fast-weight and slow-weight augmented neural nets is a feature detector that processes in two different numeric spaces. The slow weights on the base learner are equipped with their corresponding fast weights to generalize parameters rapidly. Combining fast weights and slow weights with layer augmentation leads Meta-Net to converge successfully; whereas, experiments indicated that Meta-Net would fail to converge without layer augmentation.

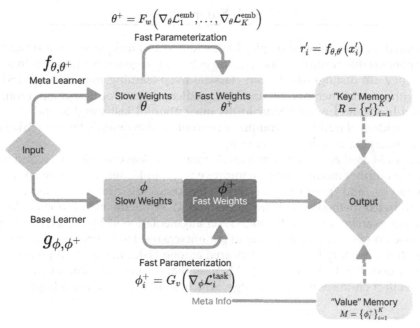

FIG. 2.3 General Workflow of Meta-Net.
Modified from Jadon, S. (2020). An overview of deep learning architectures in few-shot learning domain. arXiv preprint arXiv:2008.06365.

2.3.3 Main loss functions and representation loss functions

Meta-Net consists of three main modules, as displayed in Fig. 2.3: a base learner, a meta-learner, and an external memory for fast learning and powerful generalization. The base learner aims to perform the primary learning tasks, usually through a deep neural network, while the meta-learner accelerates the parameterization and parametizes the base learner through the example-level fast weights.

Two distinguished loss functions are utilized in this method:

(1) An embedding loss function in meta-learner verifies two input vectors from the same class through the contrastive loss (Hadsell, Chopra, & LeCun, 2006; see Chapter 3, Section 3.2) to reflect positive or negative value, as expressed in Eq. 2.32:

$$\mathcal{L}_i = \text{loss}_{emb}\left(u(Q, x'_{1,i}), u(Q, x'_{2,i}), l_i\right) \qquad (2.32)$$

(2) The main loss function in the base learner is learning a task, as indicated in Eqs. (2.33) and (2.34). Cross-entropy is used in one-shot classification, but overall, this loss function is generic to various forms, such as MSE or reward function:

$$\mathcal{L}_i = \text{loss}_{task}\left(b(W, x'_i), y'_i\right) \qquad (2.33)$$

$$\nabla_i = \nabla_W \mathcal{L}_i \qquad (2.34)$$

2.4 Summary

Model-based meta-learning strategies have exciting and unique internal structures or external components that control the system and achieve fast generalization within a few training steps. They are distinguished from classical deep-learning methods like LSTM, other networks with internal memory, or standard gradient descent optimization. From memory buffers, read heads, and write heads, to the integration of fast weights and slow weights, the interesting ideas of traditional computer concepts and geometric theories drive contributions in this emerging area of meta-learning.

In fact, model-based approaches remain heuristic and leave ample space, and most strategies may need further modifications to improve their applicability. Current approaches still have drawbacks, and performances drop for out-of-distribution tasks compared to optimization-based methods (explored in Chapter 4). While the integration of slow weights and fast weights can be achieved through layer augmentation in Meta-Net, the current solution will cause trouble if additional types of parameters need to be processed at many distinct time scales. If the memory buffer is not cleared among tasks, unexpected proactive interference (Underwood, 1957) will occur in MANN, so that the previous knowledge produces an interference effect on the newer knowledge, which is an effect that often happens in human memory.

References

Ager, S. (2021). *Omniglot – writing systems and languages of the world.* Retrieved from: https://omniglot.com.

Ba, J., Hinton, G., Mnih, V., Leibo, J. Z., & Ionescu, C. (2016). *Using fast weights to attend to the recent past.* Retrieved from arXiv https://arxiv.org/abs/1610.06258.

Baddeley, A., Eysenck, M., & Anderson, M. (2009). *Memory.* Psychology Press.

Bahdanau, D., Cho, K., & Bengio, Y. (2015). Neural machine translation by jointly learning to align and translate. In *International conference on learning representations.*

Cho, K., van Merrienboer, B., Gulcehre, C., Bahdanau, D., Bougares, F., Schwenk, H., & Bengio, Y. (2014). *Learning phrase representations using RNN encoder-decoder for statistical machine translation.* Retrieved from arXiv:1406.1078.

Chou, H.-T., & Dewitt, D. J. (2006). *An evaluation of buffer management strategies for relational database systems.* Retrieved from http://www.vldb.org/conf/1985/P127.PDF.

Graves, A., Wayne, G., & Danihelka, I. (2014). *Neural turing machines.* Retrieved from arXiv:1410.5401, 2014.

Graves, A., Wayne, G., Reynolds, M., Harley, T., Danihelka, I., Grabska-Barwińska, A., … Agapiou, J. (2016). Hybrid computing using a neural network with dynamic external memory. *Nature, 538*(7626), 471–476.

Hadsell, R., Chopra, S., & LeCun, Y. (2006). Dimensionality reduction by learning an invariant mapping. In *CVPR.*

Hazy, T. E., Frank, M. J., & O'Reilly, R. C. (2006). Banishing the homunculus: Making working memory work. *Neuroscience, 139*, 105–118.

Hinton, G. E., & Plaut, D. C. (1987). Using fast weights to deblur old memories. In *Proceedings of the ninth annual conference of the Cognitive Science Society.*

Hochreiter, S., & Schmidhuber, J. (1997). Long short-term memory. *Neural Computation.* https://doi.org/10.1162/neco.1997.9.8.1735. 9377276. Retrieved from S2CID 1915014.

Hopfield, J. J. (1982). Neural networks and physical systems with emergent collective computational abilities. *PNAS.* https://doi.org/10.1073/pnas.79.8.2554. Retrieved from.

Johnson, A. E., Pollard, T. J., Shen, L., Lehman, L.-W. H., Feng, M., Ghassemi, M., … Mark, R. G. (2016). MIMIC-III, a freely accessible critical care database. *Scientific Data, 3,* 160035.

Le, H. (2021). *Memory and attention in deep learning.* arXiv preprint arXiv:2107.01390.

Le, H., Tran, T., & Venkatesh, S. (2018). Dual control memory augmented neural networks for treatment recommendations. In *ACL.*

Lee, D., Choi, J., Kim, J.-H., Noh, S. H., Min, S. L., Cho, Y., & Kim, C. S. (2001). *LRFU: A spectrum of policies that subsumes the least recently used and least frequently used policies.* Retrieved from IEEE https://ieeexplore.ieee.org/document/970573.

Ma, C., Shen, C., Dick, A., Wu, Q., Wang, P., Hengel, A. V., & Reid, I. (2018). Visual question answering with memory-augmented networks. In *CVPR*.

Minsky, M. L. (1967). *Computation: Finite and infinite machines.*

Munkhdalai, T., & Yu, H. (2017). *Meta networks.* Retrieved from arxiv https://arxiv.org/abs/1703.00837.

Ravi, S., & Larochell, H. (2017). Optimization as a model for few-shot learning. In *ICLR*.

Reedy, J., & Lunzman, S. (2010). *Model based design accelerates the development of mechanical locomotive controls.* https://doi.org/10.4271/2010-01-1999.

Santoro, A., Bartunov, S., Botvinick, M., Wierstra, D., & Lillicrap, T. (2016). *Meta-learning with memory-augmented neural networks.* Retrieved from http://proceedings.mlr.press/v48/santoro16.pdf.

Schmidhuber, J. (1992). Learning to control fast-weight memories: An alternative to dynamic recurrent networks. *Neural Computation, 4*, 131–139.

Schmidhuber, J. (1993a). *Habilitation thesis: System modeling and optimization.* Retrieved from ftp://ftp.idsia.ch/pub/juergen/habilitation.pdf.

Schmidhuber, J. (1993b). *Reducing the ratio between learning complexity and number of time varying variables in fully recurrent nets.* Springer. https://doi.org/10.1007/978-1-4471-2063-6 110. Retrieved from.

Smith, A. J. (1987). *Design of CPU cache memories.* Retrieved from IEEE TENCON https://www2.eecs.berkeley.edu/Pubs/TechRpts/1987/CSD-87-357.pdf.

Underwood, B. J. (1957). Interference and forgetting. *Psychological Review, 64*, 49–60.

von Neumann, J. (1945). *First draft of a report on the EDVAC.*

Wang, X.-J. (1999). Synaptic basis of cortical persistent activity: The importance of nmda receptors to working memory. *The Journal of Neuroscience, 19*, 9587–9603.

Weng, L. (2018). *Meta-learning: Learning to learn fast November.* Retrieved from OpenAI Blog. https://lilianweng.github.io/lil-log/2018/11/30/meta-learning.html#model-based.

Weston, J., Chopra, S., & Bordes, A. (2015). Memory networks. In *The International conference on representation learning. ICLR*.

Metric-based meta-learning approaches

3.1 Introduction

Like the k-nearest neighbors algorithm (k-NN) (Altman, 1992) and k-means clustering (MacQueen, 1967), metric-based meta-learning generates weights via kernel function (Aizerman, Braverman, & Rozonoer, 1964; Theodoridis, 2008) by measuring the distance between two samples. See Chapter 1, Section 1.2 for a brief review of metric learning. A proper distance metric is essential to the performance of the learned model; it should represent the relationship between inputs in metric space and aid in problem-solving.

Six types of common distance metrics can be specified:

- **Euclidean distance** of a and b is expressed by Eq. (3.1) for n-dimensional space (Liberti, Lavor, Maculan, & Mucherino, 2014):

$$D(\boldsymbol{a},\boldsymbol{b}) = \sqrt{(a_1 - b)^2 + (a_2 - b_2)^2 + \ldots + (a_n - b_n)^2} = \sqrt{\sum_{i=1}^{n}(a_i - b_i)^2} \qquad (3.1)$$

- **Manhattan distance** (Black, 2019):

$$D_1(\boldsymbol{a},\boldsymbol{b}) = ||\boldsymbol{a} - \boldsymbol{b}||_1 = \sum_{i=1}^{n}|a_i - b_i| \qquad (3.2)$$

- **Hamming distance** (Yamada, 1990):

$$D(\boldsymbol{a},\boldsymbol{b}) = \sum_{i=1}^{n}\delta(a_i, b_i), where\ \delta(a_i, b_i) = \begin{cases} 0\ if\ a_i = b_i \\ 1\ if\ a_i \neq b_i \end{cases} \qquad (3.3)$$

Meta-Learning
https://doi.org/10.1016/B978-0-323-89931-4.00003-1

- **Cosine distance** or cosine similarity (Korenius, Laurikkala, & Juhola, 2007):

$$\text{Cosine distance} = 1 - \text{consine similarity} \tag{3.4}$$

$$\text{Cosine similarity} = \frac{\sum_{i=1}^{n} a_i b_i}{\sqrt{\sum_{i=1}^{n} a_i^2} \sqrt{\sum_{i=1}^{n} b_i^2}} \tag{3.5}$$

- **Minkowski distance** (NIST, 2017):

$$D(\boldsymbol{a}, \boldsymbol{b}) = \left(\sum_{i=1}^{n} |a_i - b_i|^p \right)^{1/p}, \text{where}$$

Manhattan distance if $p = 1$,

Euclidean distance if $p = 2$,

Chebyshev distance if $p = \infty$
$$\tag{3.6}$$

- **Mahalanobis distance** (De Maesschalck, Jouan-Rimbaud, & Massart, 2000) regarding the probability distribution P on $\mathbb{R}^N$, where $\boldsymbol{a}$ and $\boldsymbol{b}$ are two points in $\mathbb{R}^N$ and S denotes a nonsingular covariance matrix:

$$D_M(\boldsymbol{a}; \boldsymbol{b}; P) = \sqrt{(\boldsymbol{a} - \boldsymbol{b})^T S^{-1} (\boldsymbol{a} - \boldsymbol{b})} \tag{3.7}$$

Koch, Zemel, and Salakhutdinov (2015) proposed the first meta-learning metrics-based algorithms via the Siamese neural network (SNN) (Chopra, Hadsell, & LeCun, 2005). The SNN could also be trained in triplet loss (Schroff, Kalenichenko, & Philbin, 2015) to compare the similarity of queries and samples in the embedding space. In both a Matching Network (Vinyals, Blundell, Lillicrap, Kavukcuoglu, & Wierstra, 2016) and a Prototypical Network (Snell, Swersky, & Zemel, 2017), a neural network was embedded in the sample set and query set, using the nearest neighbor classifier with a given metric. Since that time, the interest in devising the proper metrics has produced extensive research (Mishra, Rohaninejad, Chen, & Abbeel, 2018; Munkhdalai, Yuan, Mehri, & Trischler, 2018).

Many meta-learning metric-based variations have extended Prototypical Networks in various ways. Oreshkin, Rodriguez, and Lacoste (2019) developed an end-to-end optimizer to learn task-conditioning metric spaces and proposed metric scaling based on auxiliary task cotraining. Fort (2017) introduced a Gaussian prototypical network that was specific to image classification. It contained an encoder to produce confidence region estimation via the Gaussian covariance matrix, using a variance-weighted linear combination of embedding vectors of individual samples to define classes. Sung et al. (2018) proposed the Relation Network to compute the relation score between query data and a few samples from each new class without updating the network parameters. This network relied on end-to-end episode-based training and showed promising results in both few-shot learning and zero-shot learning. Li, Eigen, Dodge, Zeiler, and Wang (2019) offered a category traversal module (CTM) as a plug-and-play component to insert into a common meta-learning-based few-shot learner. This CTM consisted of: (1) a concentrator to find global features of all samples in each class, (2) a projector to map the relevant features of query and support sets, and (3) a reshaper to scale the shapes between each module.

Debating the outperformance among different metrics, Snell et al. (2017) and Oreshkin et al. (2019) presented opposite opinions on Euclidean distance and cosine similarity. The former argued Euclidean distance improved outcomes over cosine similarity on miniImageNet (Liu, 2018) and Omniglot (Ager & Kualo, 1998) datasets with both the Matching Network and Prototypical Network. However, the latter suggested scaled cosine similarity surpassed Euclidean distance in miniImageNet and CIFAR100 (Krizhevsky, 2009), as cross-validation determined the scaling parameter.

The remainder of this chapter chronologically discusses the four types of metric-based meta-learning and major baseline models, including convolutional Siamese neural network in Section 3.2, Matching Network in Section 3.3, Prototypical Network in Section 3.4, and Relation Network in Section 3.5. These explorations cover background knowledge and describe the remarkable developments of the essential techniques used, the methodology of the baseline models, innovative and influential technical contributions, and multiple state-of-the-art extended variations and design motivations within each type of metric-based meta-learning algorithm. The research recursively tracks related bibliographies in papers accepted at premier academic conferences, including ICML, ICLR, ICCV, CVPR, and NeurIPS.

3.2 Convolutional Siamese neural networks

3.2.1 Background knowledge

Bromley, Guyon, LeCun, Säckinger, and Shah (1994) introduced twin neural networks, named the Siamese neural network (SNN), as a novel structure with shared weights between two identical and symmetric neural networks. It compared the similarity of two inputs via **contrastive loss** (Hadsell, Chopra, & LeCun, 2006) in a signature recognition task. This loss was a pairwise distance-based loss, expressed as Eq. (3.8), where D_w denotes the eculidean distance of X_1 and X_2. $Y = 1$ if X_1 is dissimilar to X_2; otherwise, $Y = 0$ if X_1 and X_2 are similar to each other:

$$L(W, Y, X_1, X_2) = (1 - Y)\frac{1}{2}(D_w)^2 + (Y)\frac{1}{2}\{max\,(0, m - D_w)\}^2 \qquad (3.8)$$

It decreased if the positive samples encoded were more closely represented; otherwise, it increased if negative samples encoded were further described. Contrastive loss recently showed state-of-the-art results in numerous unsupervised and self-supervised research efforts, including momentum contrast (MoCo) (He, Fan, Wu, Xie, & Girshick, 2019), pretext-invariant representation learning (PIRL) (Misra & Maaten, 2019), and SimCLR (Chen, Kornblith, Norouzi, & Hinton, 2020).

The Siamese neural network is commonly used when two inputs are highly similar, such as a comparison between two sentences, two vocabulary items, and objects tracking (Bertinetto, Valmadre, Henriques, Vedaldi, & Torr, 2016). For the observation between two distinguished inputs like title and context, a pseudo-Siamese network (Hughes, Schmitt, Mou, Wang, &

Zhu, 2018) is more suitable. Aguilera, Aguilera, Sappa, Aguilera, and Toledo (2016) compared the neural network structure and performance with regard to the similarity of cross-spectral image patches among Siamese with shared Fweights (frequency weights), pseudo-Siamese with independent weights, and 2-channel networks.

3.2.2 Methodology

Koch et al. (2015), proposed a **convolutional Siamese neural network** for one-shot image classification on character recognition without prior knowledge. This is known as the first metric-based meta-learning algorithm. It assumes that new tasks should be highly similar to original ones so that the learned embedding knowledge can be beneficial in measuring the distance between the image and unknown classes. The approach proposes: (1) a trained binary classifier to distinguish the same or different pairs of given classes and (2) a learner to evaluate new categories based on learned mapping features. The network selection considers the following factors: (1) being capable of few-shot learning, (2) dealing with pairwise data with the standard optimizer, and (3) learning beyond domain-specific knowledge.

A convolutional Siamese network was proposed as a standard model to encode two images to the outputs feature vectors from twin branches in Eqs. (3.9), (3.10), displayed in Fig. 3.1, where a hidden vector $h_{1,l}$ is in l layer for the first twin network. The valid convolutional operation $\ast$ only proposes to the output units, which have a complete overlap between each convolutional filter and input feature map. As a 3D tensor, $W_{l-1, l}^{(k)}$ presents to the feature embedding for layer l at epoch k, and b_l means bias for layer l. $h_{1,(l-1)}$ and $h_{2,(l-1)}$ mean hidden vector for layer l in the first twin and in the second twin, separately.

$$a_{1,m}^{(k)} = max\,pool\left(\max\left(0, W_{l-1,l}^{(k)}\ast h_{1,(l-1)} + b_l\right), 2\right) \tag{3.9}$$

$$a_{2,m}^{(k)} = max\,pool\left(\max\left(0, W_{l-1,l}^{(k)}\ast h_{2,(l-1)} + b_l\right), 2\right) \tag{3.10}$$

Combination of the twin Siamese networks

The prediction vector p of the final distance between the Siamese twins is computed by a single sigmoid unit, as noted in Eq. (3.11). A weighted L_1 distance (Manhattan distance) computes the similarity scores between twin feature vectors h_1 and h_2, and the weighting parameter reflects the importance of component-wise distance. The L_1 distance can be replaced with other distance metrics, such as cosine similarity, as long as it is differentiable.

$$p = \sigma\left(\sum_j \alpha_j |h_{1,L-1}^{(j)} - h_{2,L-1}^{(j)}|\right) \tag{3.11}$$

Objective function

The binary classifier of same/distinguish classes is proposed by a cross-entropy loss, expressed in Eqs. (3.12), (3.13). For i-th mini-batch among overall M mini-batch, y presents an M-length vector with labels of this mini-batch, p is the prediction vector, and λ is the regularization penalty from 0 to 0.1.

FIG. 3.1 Architecture of convolutional Siamese neural network. Siamese twin architecture is applied in convolutional Siamese neural network. Two hand-written characters are fed into this pipeline and ended up with a join after 4096 units with L1 component-wise distance.

Modified from Koch, G., Zemel, R., & Salakhutdinov, R. (2015). Siamese neural networks for one-shot image recognition. cs. toronto.edu. Retrieved from: http://www.cs.toronto.edu/~rsalakhu/papers/oneshot1.pdf.

$$\mathcal{L}\left(x_1^{(i)}, x_2^{(i)}\right) = y\left(x_1^{(i)}, x_2^{(i)}\right) log\; p\left(x_1^{(i)}, x_2^{(i)}\right) + \left(1 - y\left(x_1^{(i)}, x_2^{(i)}\right)\right) log\left(1 - p\left(x_1^{(i)}, x_2^{(i)}\right)\right) + \lambda^T |W|^2$$
(3.12)

where:

$$y\left(x_1^{(i)}, x_2^{(i)}\right) = \begin{cases} 0, if\; x_1\; and\; x_2\; from\; same\; class \\ 1, otherwise \end{cases}$$
(3.13)

Optimization

The goal is to conduct optimization through standard backpropagation. Due to the "tied weights," the gradient is addictive across the twin networks. Eqs. (3.14), (3.15) express layer-wise updates with momentum μ_j and L_2 regulation weights λ_j, where $\nabla\omega_{kj}$ is the weight between j^{th} neuron in some layer and k^{th} neuron in the next layer.

$$w_{kj}^{(T)}\left(x_1^{(i)}, x_2^{(i)}\right) = w_{kj}^{(T)} + \Delta w_{kj}^{(T)}\left(x_1^{(i)}, x_2^{(i)}\right) + 2\lambda_j |w_{kj}|$$
(3.14)

$$\Delta w_{kj}^{(T)}\left(x_1^{(i)}, x_2^{(i)}\right) = -\eta_j \nabla\omega_{kj}^{(T)} + \mu_j \Delta w_{kj}^{(T-1)}$$
(3.15)

3.2.3 Extended algorithm 1

Garcia and Bruna (2018) proposed a **graph neural network** (GNN) learner focused on Euclidean space as a few-shot learner. It can be extended to become a semisupervised and active-learning system. This approach tries to interpret Siamese neural network as a single layer "message-passing" iteration in this GNN-based work via a nontrainable edge feature demonstrated, shown in Eq. (3.16), where φ represents a parametrized symmetric function of a neural network, ϕ denotes the embedding function, and A is the edge feature kernel:

$$\varphi(x_i, x_j) = || \phi(x_i) - \phi(x_j)||, \tilde{A}^{(0)} = softmax(-\varphi)$$
(3.16)

The resulting label estimation is shown in Eq. (3.17), where u chooses the label field based on x. By implementing Siamese neural network, this method focused on learning the image embedding is consistent with the label similarity based on Euclidean distance.

$$\hat{Y}_* = \sum_j \tilde{A}_{*j}^{(0)}\left\langle x_j^{(0)}, u \right\rangle$$
(3.17)

3.3 Matching networks

3.3.1 Background knowledge

This work is a re-discussion of the neural network with external memory. Long short-term memory (LSTM) achieves a memory-augmented system and makes a significant contribution to many AI application fields such as speech recognition (Hochreiter & Schmidhuber, 1997) and natural language processing. After the adoption of LSTMs, Hyun and Bengio (2016) introduced content-based attention in machine translation by a bidirectional recurrent neural network (BRNN) encoding a fixed-length vector from source sentences in English and decoding the translation to French. This research also discovered a linguistically plausible (soft) alignment between target and source sentences.

Graves, Wayne, and Danihelka (2014) developed the end-to-end neural turing machine (NTM), which was trained by gradient descent for copying and recalling from inputs or outputs, as well as priority sorting tasks via a reading head and writing head imported and exported from the memory matrix. This machine consisted of two primary modules: a neural network controller and a memory bank. See Chapter 2, Section 2.2.1 for details or NTM. Santoro, Bartunov, Botvinick, Wierstra, and Lillicrap (2016) proposed a promising paradigm to combine meta-learning and memory-augmented neural networks inspired by NTM. The machine is capable of efficiently understanding new data without relearning, and it can predict accurately based on just a few samples.

3.3.2 Methodology

Vinyals et al. (2016) proposed the nonparametric Matching Network (also named Matching Net), utilizing an attention mechanism and external memory structure for image and language classification tasks. It can: (1) produce labels for unobserved classes without changing the network and (2) perform few-shot learning within a set-to-set framework in Omniglot, ImageNet, and Penn Treebank (Marcus et al., 1992) datasets. Set-to-set framework, which is an extension of seq2seq framework, inputs or outputs sets of data (e.g., set{(I,1), (eat,2), (ice,3), (cream,4)} transfer from sequence "I eat ice cream").

Given a test sample $\hat{x}$, the model aims to determine the probability distribution over output $\hat{y}$ by learning from the mapping of the new support set S' sampled from support set $S = \{(x_i, y_i)\}_{i=1}^{k}$ to the classifier $c_S(\hat{x})$. The mapping of $S \rightarrow c_S(\hat{x})$ with the input pair (x_i, y_i) is expressed in Eqs. (3.18), (3.19). It approximates a kernel density estimator, considering neural attention mechanism a is a kernel on $X \times X$.

$$\hat{y} = \sum_{i=1}^{k} a(\hat{x}, x_i) y_i \qquad (3.18)$$

where:

$$a(\hat{x}, x_i) = \begin{cases} 0, & \textit{for } b \text{ furthest } x_i \text{ from } \hat{x} \\ \text{appropriate constant}, \text{otherwise} \end{cases} \qquad (3.19)$$

This nonparametric strategy consists of two components: (1) a kernel attention mechanism and (2) full context embedding.

The attention kernel

The attention kernel relies on softmax normalization over cosine distance, expressed in Eq. (3.20), with embedding functions f and g to embed $\hat{x}$ and x_i separately, as shown in Fig. 3.2. In a computer vision problem, f and g are parameterized as an artificial neural

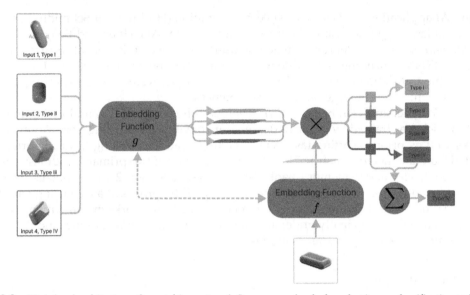

FIG. 3.2   High-level architecture of a matching network. In an example of a few-shot image classification task, various inputs under different categories are fed into the network after embedding function g. The query image is represented through embedding function f to generate the output label.
Modified from Vinyals, O., Blundell, C., Lillicrap, T., Kavukcuoglu, K., & Wierstra, D. (2016). Matching networks for one shot learning. NIPS Retrieved from: http://papers.nips.cc/paper/6385-matching-networks-for-one-shot-learning.pdf.

network and as word embedding in natural language processing tasks. This attention kernel classifier is discriminative. Given the support set S and sample, as long as $\widehat{x}$ is aligned with pair $(x',y') \in S$ such that $y' = y$ and misaligned with the rest, the classifier can classify test sample $\widehat{x}$. The objective becomes to transfer to a multimethod, one-shot classification.

$$a(\widehat{x},\ x_i) = \frac{e^{cosine\ distance\left(f\left(\widehat{x}\right)g(x_i)\right)}}{\sum_{j=1}^{k} e^{cosine\ distance\left(f\left(\widehat{x}\right)g(x_j)\right)}} \tag{3.20}$$

Full context embedding

The function g changes to $g(S,x_i)$ by encoding both x_i and the complete support set S. $g(S,x_i)$, a function of the entire support set, can decide how to encode x_i. This is particularly helpful when x_j and x_i are closed. In the context of the support set, Matching Network uses bidirectional LSTM (Graves, Fernández, & Schmidhuber., J., 2005) to encode x_i. An embedding function $f'(\widehat{x})$ involves the input of an LSTM with read-attention over the entire support set S. Eqs. (3.21)–(3.24) describe the recurrence over k processing steps, where a is the content-based attention mechanism (Bahdanau, Cho, & Bengio, 2014). x, h, and c represent input, output, and the cell, respectively.

$$\widehat{h}_k, c_k = LSTM\left(f'(\widehat{x}), [h_{k-1}, r_{k-1}], c_{k-1}\right) \tag{3.21}$$

$$h_k = \widehat{h}_k + f'(\widehat{x}) \tag{3.22}$$

After proposing K steps of "read," h_K is expressed in Eq. (3.22), and then $f(S,\widehat{x}) = h_K$.

$$r_{k-1} = \sum_{i=1}^{|S|} a(h_{k-1}, g(x_i)) g(x_i) \tag{3.23}$$

$$a(h_{k-1}, g(x_i)) = \frac{e^{h_{k-1}^T g(x_i)}}{\sum_{j=1}^{|S|} e^{h_{k-1}^T g(x_j)}} = softmax\left(e^{h_{k-1}^T g(x_i)}\right) \tag{3.24}$$

Episode-based training

Matching Network adopted an episode-based training method, which is a training strategy widely used in meta-learning algorithms, such as Prototypical Network and Relation Network. First, this method samples L from T, where task T is defined as a distribution over possible label set L. Then, batch B and support set S are sampled from L. The purpose of training θ is to minimize error when predicting labels based on S over batch B, expressed in Eq. (3.25). The nonparametric model performs well in predicting new classes that the model never sees during training, and no fine-tuning is required. As long as a new task T' is similar to T, the learner works well.

$$\theta = arg \max_{\theta} E_{L \sim T}\left[E_{S \sim L, B \sim L}\left[\sum_{(x,y) \in B} log\, P_\theta(y|x,S) \right] \right] \tag{3.25}$$

3.3.3 Extended algorithm 1

Wang and colleagues (Wang, Girshick, Hebert, & Hariharan, 2018) introduced a "**hallucinator**" as another solution for meta-learning-based few-shot learning with Euclidean distance. It can generate additional training samples from existing datasets in order to build an accurate classifier and optimize both the hallucinator and Matching Network meta-learner jointly. This learner maps existing samples to hallucinated examples; it is also a universal model combined with different meta-learners. h is a learning classification algorithm, S_{train} means a training set, $\widehat{p}$ denotes the estimated probability distribution of multiple labels, and d represents the distance metrics.

$$h(x, S_{train},; w) = \widehat{p}(x) \tag{3.26}$$

$$\widehat{p}_k(x) = \frac{\sum_{(x_i,y_i) \in S_{train}} e^{-d(f(x),g(x_i))} I[y_i = k]}{\sum_{(x_i,y_i) \in S_{train}} e^{-d(f(x),g(x_i))}} \tag{3.27}$$

In the case of Matching Network, it generates a contextual embedding $\{g(x_i)\}_{i=1}^N$ of the training via bidirectional long-short term memory (BiLSTM) in Eq. (3.28), along with another embedding function $f(x)$ of the testing dataset via a long-short term memory attention mechanism (AttLSTM) in Eq. (3.29). d is the distance metric, and w_f, w_g, and w_ϕ are learnable parameters.

$$f(x) = AttLSTM\left(\phi(x; w_\phi), \{g(x_i)\}_{i=1}^{N}; w_f\right) \qquad (3.28)$$

$$\{g(x_i)\}_{i=1}^{N} = BiLSTM\left(\{\phi(x_i; w_\phi)\}_{i=1}^{N}; w_g\right) \qquad (3.29)$$

To one's further interest, the combination of the prototypical network and prototypical matching network can be found in Section 3 from Wang et al. (2018).

3.4 Prototypical networks

3.4.1 Background knowledge

A prototypical network is inspirited from nonlinear neighborhood component analysis (NCA) and the nearest class mean (NCM) approaches. Goldberger, Hinton, Roweis, and Salakhutdinov (2004) proposed nonparametric NCA measuring the Mahalanobis distance used in k-NN to optimize a leave-one-out classification by maximizing stochastic (soft) neighbor assignments on the training dataset. Mensink, Verbeek, Perronnin, and Csurka (2013) introduced an improvement of an NCM classifier based on: (1) multiclass logistic discrimination to maximize log-likelihood and (2) the implementation of multiple centroids per class to transfer the NCM as a nonlinear classifier.

$$c^* = arg \min_{c\in\{1,...,C\}} d(x,\mu_c) \qquad (3.30)$$

NCM classifier assigns the query point x to a target class $c^* \in \{1, ..., C\}$ through the class mean μ_c measured by Euclidean distance, as expressed in Eqs. (3.30), (3.31), where y_i denotes image i's ground truth.

$$\mu_c = \frac{1}{N_c} \sum_{i:y_i=c} x_i \qquad (3.31)$$

The Prototypical Network shares the basic idea of the NCM but applies a deep neural network to represent nonlinear metrics. Compared to the Matching Network mentioned in Section 3.3 above, both the Prototypical Network and Matching Network solve few-shot learning problems; the former reduces learnable parameters from the latter.

3.4.2 Methodology

Snell et al. (2017) introduced the supervised **Prototypical Network** (Proto Net) extended from the k-means to solve few-shot and zero-shot classification tasks by learning a distance to the prototype representations of each class. It assumed an embedding space existed that represented a cluster around a single prototype description of this class, using Bregman divergence (Banerjee,

Merugu, Dhillon, & Ghosh, 2005) to compute this distance (e.g., squared Euclidean distance and Mahalanobis distance). The prototypical network uses a deep neural network to map "the nonlinear relationship of input points into an embedding space" (Snell et al., 2017).

c_k represents the mean of the support set via the prototype of a class displayed in Fig. 3.3 (left). The classification of the embedded query points relies on the nearest prototype, particularly in zero-shot learning in Fig. 3.3 (right), where c_k is described by embedding class meta-data v_k. The meta-data embedding vector is defined as $c_k = g_v(v_k)$ in zero-shot learning. It is helpful to set up prototype embedding function g in unit length, as query data and meta-data vectors are gathered from different domains. The prototypical network reports promising results in the Caltech UCSD bird dataset (CUB-2002011) (Welinder et al., 2010).

As the prototype in the M dimension of each class, $c_k \in \mathbb{R}^M$ calculated from the embedding function represents vectors $f_\phi: \mathbb{R}^D \to \mathbb{R}^M$, where ϕ is a learnable parameter. The mean vector of support for embedded points of each class is the prototype c_k expressed as Eq. (3.32), where the support set S of N sample-label pair (x_i, y_i) s. t. $S = \{(x_1, y_1), (x_2, y_2), \ldots, (x_N, y_N)\}$. Each sample x_i is represented as a D-dimensional feature vector s. t. $x_i \in \mathbb{R}^D$, and y_i denotes the corresponding label s. t. $y_i \in \{1, 2, \ldots, K\}$.

$$c_k = \frac{1}{|S_k|} \sum_{(x_i, y_i) \in S_k} f_\phi(x_i) \tag{3.32}$$

where S_k indicates the set of samples in class k.

Proto Net computes the distribution via a softmax function over the distance between query point x to its prototype c_k, expressed in Eq. (3.33), where the nonnegative distance function d s.t. $d: \mathbb{R}^M \times \mathbb{R}^M \to [0, +\infty)$.

$$p_\phi(y = k | x) = \frac{exp\left(-d\left(f_\phi(x), c_k\right)\right)}{\sum_{k'} exp\left(-d\left(f_\phi(x), c_{k'}\right)\right)} \tag{3.33}$$

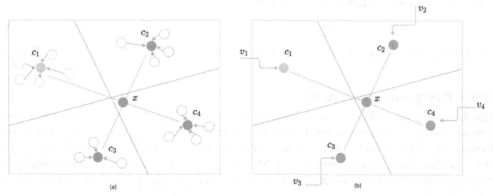

(a)   (b)

FIG. 3.3 Prototypical networks in few-shot and zero-shot regimes. (A) The mean of embedding support samples determines the few-shot prototypes c_k of k class. (B) The meta-data v_k supports the zero-shot prototypes c_k. *Modified from Snell, J., Swersky, K., & Zemel, R. (2017). Prototypical networks for few-shot learning. NIPS Retrieved from: http://papers.nips.cc/paper/6996-prototypical-networks-for-few-shot-learning.pdf.*

TABLE 3.1 Training methods of Prototypical Network.

Input: D, training dataset s. t. $D = \{(x_1, y_1), \ldots, (x_N, y_N)\}$, for each $y_i \in \{1, \ldots, K\}$
D_k, subset of D with all elements (x_i, y_i) s.t. $y_i = k$
N, sample size of D
K, number of classes in D
N_C, number of classes for each episode
N_S, sample size of support set for each class
N_Q, sample size of query set for each class
Random Sample(S, N), a shuffle set with N elements that are uniformly chosen from set S
without replacement

1 Randomly select class indices using $V \leftarrow RANDOMSAMPLE(\{1, \ldots, K\}, N_C)$
2 **for** k in $\{1, \ldots, N_C\}$ **do**
3   Construct support samples using $S_k \leftarrow RANDOMSAMPLE(D_{V_k}, N_S)$
4   Construct query samples using $Q_k \leftarrow RANDOMSAMPLE(D_{V_k} \setminus S_k, N_Q)$
5   Obtain prototype by embedding support samples using $c_k \leftarrow \dfrac{1}{N_C} \sum_{(x_i, y_i) \in S_k} f_\phi(x_i)$
6 **end for**

    # loss initialization
7 $J \leftarrow 0$

8 **for** k in $\{1, \ldots, N_C\}$ **do**
9   **for** (x, y) in Q_k **do**
10   Update loss using $J \leftarrow J + \frac{1}{N_C N_Q}\left[d\left(f_\phi(x), c_k\right) + log \sum_{k'} \exp\left(-d\left(f_\phi(x), c_{k'}\right)\right)\right]$
11   **end for**
12 **end for**

Modified from Snell, J., Swersky, K., & Zemel, R. (2017). Prototypical networks for few-shot learning. NIPS Retrieved from: http://papers.nips.cc/paper/6996-prototypical-networks-for-few-shot-learning.pdf.

This work aims to minimize the negative log-probability loss function $J(\phi)$ via stochastic gradient descent (SGD), denoted in Eq. (3.34):

$$J(\phi) = -\log p_\phi(y = k|x) \tag{3.34}$$

The pseudocode of training the loss function $J(\phi)$ in each episode is outlined in Table 3.1.

Bregman divergence requirement

The distance used in Prototypical Network needs to satisfy regular Bregman divergence; otherwise, the equivalence to mixture density estimation on the support set will not be held. Although any distance metric in Proto Net is permissible, squared Euclidean distance (rather than the widely used cosine similarity in Matching Network) generated promising results during experiments. Examples of Bregman divergence include squared Euclidean distance $D = ||z - z'||^2$ and Mahalanobis distance $D_M(x) = \sqrt{(x - \mu)^T S^{-1}(x - \mu)}$. By applying squared Euclidean distance, Proto Net produces a linear classifier, compared to the weighted nearest neighbor used in classifier Matching Net. Bregman divergence (Banerjee et al., 2005) is defined in Eq. (3.35):

$$d_\varphi(z, z') = \varphi(z) - \varphi(z') - (z - z')^T \nabla\varphi(z') \tag{3.35}$$

Regular exponential distribution $p_\psi(z|\boldsymbol{\theta})$ can be written as Bregman divergence with parameter $\boldsymbol{\theta}$ and cumulant function φ, as described in Eq. (3.36).

$$p_\psi(z|\boldsymbol{\theta}) = \exp\left\{z^T\boldsymbol{\theta} - \psi(\boldsymbol{\theta}) - g_\psi(z)\right\} = \exp\left\{-d_\varphi(z,\boldsymbol{\mu}(\boldsymbol{\theta})) - g_\psi(z)\right\} \quad (3.36)$$

Given the parameter $\boldsymbol{\Gamma} = \{\boldsymbol{\theta}_k, \pi_k\}_{k=1}^K$, the semiparametric learner is demonstrated in Eq. (3.37):

$$p(z|\boldsymbol{\Gamma}) = \sum_{k=1}^K \pi_k p_\psi(z|\boldsymbol{\theta}_k) = \sum_{k=1}^K \pi_k \exp\left\{-d_\varphi(z,\boldsymbol{\mu}(\boldsymbol{\theta}_k)) - g_\psi(z)\right\} \quad (3.37)$$

The estimation of the cluster assignment y with respect to the unlabeled point z is expressed in Eq. (3.38):

$$p(y=k|z) = \frac{\pi_k \exp\left(-d_\varphi(z,\boldsymbol{\mu}(\boldsymbol{\theta}_k))\right)}{\sum_{k'} \pi_{k'} \exp\left(-d_\varphi(z,\boldsymbol{\mu}(\boldsymbol{\theta}_k))\right)} \quad (3.38)$$

A detailed exploration of exponential family distribution in terms of Bregman divergence is provided in Section 2.3 "Prototypical Networks as Mixture Density Estimation" from Snell et al. (2017).

3.4.3 Extended algorithm 1

Liu and colleagues (Liu, Zhou, Long, Jiang, & Zhang, 2019) introduced the **gated propagation network** (GPN). A meta-learner transfers information between prototypes of different classes on the graph, followed by the few-shot classification benefits from the data of related neighboring classes. This work serves as an extension of the Prototypical Network by improving a single prototype of each class to several adaptive prototypes per class. Thus, the feature space can be extended and improved by scaling features with respect to various tasks. The aggregated knowledge $P_{\mathcal{N}_y \to y}^{t+1}$ from the neighbors $\mathcal{N}_y$ for class y at step $t+1$ is obtained by the dot product of attention $a(p,q)$, where h is learnable transformations, P_z^t presents prototype of class z at step t, and P_y^t means prototype of class y at step t.

$$P_{\mathcal{N}_y \to y}^{t+1} \triangleq \sum_{z \in \mathcal{N}_y} a\left(P_{y'}^t, P_z^t\right) \times P_z^t, a(p,q) = \frac{\langle h_1(p), h_2(q) \rangle}{|h_1(p)| \times |h_2(q)|} \quad (3.39)$$

The attention mechanism combines information from multiple neighboring classes of each class, as expressed in Eq. (3.39), where a gate g can select information from related classes in Eq. (3.40). $P_{y \to y}^{t+1}$ presents a message from class y to itself at step $t+1$, γ denotes a temperature hyperparameter for determining how the softmax function smooths, and P_y^0 is the prototype of class y at step 0.

$$P_y^{t+1} \triangleq g P_{y \to y}^{t+1} + (1-g) P_{\mathcal{N}_y \to y'}^{t+1} \quad (3.40)$$

$$g = \frac{\exp\left[\gamma \cos\left(P_y^0, P_{y\to y}^{t+1}\right)\right]}{\exp\left[\gamma \cos\left(P_y^0, P_{y\to y}^{t+1}\right)\right] + \exp\left[\gamma \cos\left(P_y^0, P_{N_y\to y}^{t+1}\right)\right]}$$

The PyTorch code of GPN and the proposed dataset were released at https://github.com/liulu112601/Gated-Propagation-Net.

3.4.4 Extended algorithm 2

Ren et al. (2018) provided an interesting extension of the prototypical network for an unlabeled sample and used it in two scenarios: (1) the new class contains all unlabeled samples, and (2) the images of a new class to be learned are distracted among a pool of unlabeled samples named the "distractors" class. In contrast to the typical situation described above in regular prototypical network, this approach employs a prototypical network when each episode has an unlabeled sample set. This model creates a partial assignment $\tilde{z}_{j,c}$ for the unlabeled sample based on a distance metric to each cluster, generating the refined prototype $\tilde{p}_c$, as expressed in Eq. (3.41):

$$\tilde{p}_c = \frac{\sum_i h(x_i)z_{i,c} + \sum_j h(\tilde{x}_j)\tilde{z}_{j,c}}{\sum_i z_{i,c} + \sum_j \tilde{z}_{j,c}}, \tilde{z}_{j,c} = \frac{\exp\left(-\left|h(\tilde{x}_j) - p_c\right|_2^2\right)}{\sum_{c'} \exp\left(-\left|h(\tilde{x}_j) - p_{c'}\right|_2^2\right)} \tag{3.41}$$

It uses soft-masking $m_{j,c}$ with sigmoid function to model the unlabeled sample by the normalizing distance between unlabeled samples $\tilde{x}_j$ and prototype p_c in Eq. (3.42):

$$\tilde{d}_{j,c} = \frac{d_{j,c}}{\frac{1}{M}\sum_j d_{j,c}}, d_{j,c} = \left|h(\tilde{x}_j) - p_c\right|_2^2 \tag{3.42}$$

A neural network predicted each prototype's slope γ_c and soft threshold β_c from the normalized distance $\tilde{d}_{j,c}$ in Eqs. (3.43), (3.44):

$$[\beta_c, \gamma_c] = MLP\left(\left[\min_j\left(\tilde{d}_{j,c}\right), \max_j\left(\tilde{d}_{j,c}\right), var_j\left(\tilde{d}_{j,c}\right), \text{skew}_j\left(\tilde{d}_{j,c}\right), \text{kurt}_j\left(\tilde{d}_{j,c}\right)\right]\right) \tag{3.43}$$

$$\tilde{p}_c = \frac{\sum_i h(x_i)z_{i,c} + \sum_j h(\tilde{x}_j)\tilde{z}_{j,c}m_{j,c}}{\sum_i z_{i,c} + \sum_j \tilde{z}_{j,c}m_{j,c}}, m_{j,c} = \sigma\left(-\gamma_c\left(\tilde{d}_{j,c} - \beta_c\right)\right) \tag{3.44}$$

3.4.5 Extended algorithm 3

Zhang and colleagues (Zhang, Wang, & Qiao, 2019) introduced **Meta-Cleaner**; a shot-free meta-learner that can represent hallucinated clean description v_c of samples V with noisy-labels in object recognition tasks. This hallucination is expressed in Eq. (3.45). The module can be directly inserted into the regular training of deep neural networks to improve the robustness of noisy-label and generalization capability and to reduce overfitting.

$$v_c = MetaCleaner(V)$$

$$= E[v \cdot p_{clean}(v|V)] \approx \frac{1}{\sum_{i=1}^{N} p_{clean}(v_i|V)} \sum_{i=1}^{N} v_i \cdot p_{clean}(v_i|V) \qquad (3.45)$$

To estimate the value of $p_{clean}(v_i | V)$, this Meta-Cleaner contains two main components: (1) noisy weighting to generate confidence scores of all noisy-labeled images through deep feature joint analysis, and (2) clean hallucination to produce a clean representation of such images by integrating these noisy-label images and their confidence scores. Noisy weighting is demonstrated in Eq. (3.46), where $f_{Noisy\ Weighting}$ involves nonlinear mapping via a two-layer multilayer perceptron:

$$[\alpha_1, ..., \alpha_N] = f_{Noisy\ Weighting}([v_1, ..., v_N]) \qquad (3.46)$$

Clean hallucination is built as a training sample classifier expressed in Eq. (3.47). The weights of different images generate a softmax classifier in the end-to-end training method, which will be fed with the image feature vector in the testing method.

$$v_c = \frac{\sum_i \alpha_i v_i}{\sum_i \alpha_i} \qquad (3.47)$$

3.5 Relation network

3.5.1 Background knowledge

This work is related to Matching Network (Vinyals et al., 2016) and Prototypical Network (Snell et al., 2017), not the one with same name innovated by DeepMind or in object detection by MSRA. In contrast to Matching Network and Prototypical Network, the Relation Network differs from most metric strategies' attempts to learn the transferrable deep metric, while the prior works focus on learning a transferrable embedding and carries predefined fixed metrics. The Relation Network tries to align the image with category embedding and attempts to predict the matching relationship between the query image and candidate category embeddings. The classical embedding method relies on research from, but not limited to, Frome et al. (2013), Akata, Reed, Walter, Lee, and Schiele (2015), Yang and Hospedales (2015), and Zhang and Saligrama (2015).

Frome et al. (2013) proposed a deep visual-semantic embedding model (DeViSE) for object recognition based not only on labeled visual images via traditional visual models but also on semantic information from unannotated natural language text by a skip-gram (Mikolov, Chen, Corrado, & Dean, 2013) language model. To emphasize the dot product similarity between visual model output and correct text-embedding vectors, this model uses the hinge rank loss described in Eq. (3.48):

$$L(image, label) = \sum_{j \neq label} \max \left[0, margin - t_{label} M v(image) + t_j M v(image)\right] \qquad (3.48)$$

This work reports that the mapping of images to semantic embedding space demonstrated promising improvements in zero-show learning on the ImageNet 2011 21 K (Russakovsky et al., 2015) dataset that excluded the Large Scale Visual Recognition Challenge 2012 1 K (ILSVRC 2012) (Russakovsky et al., 2015), which was a DeViSE training dataset.

Akata et al. (2015) introduced a fine-grained classification unsupervised model based on an attribute (Farhadi, Endres, Hoiem, & Forsyth, 2009; Ferrari & Zisserman, 2007; Lampert, Nickisch, & Harmeling, 2013) and class embedding from unlabeled text terms through a structured joint embedding (SJE) framework (Akata, Lee, & Schiele, 2014). This model considered three types of embedding to generate compatibility scores:

1. Embedding from the attribute, $F_1(x_i, y_i; W_1)$
2. Label embedding from the text, $F_2(x_i, y_i; W_2)$ from Word2Vec (Mikolov, Sutskever, Chen, Corrado, & Dean, 2013), GloVe (Pennington, Socher, & Manning, 2014), weakly supervised Word2Vec, and bag-of-word (Harris, 1954)
3. Hierarchical embedding, $F_3(x_i, y_i; W_3)$

This approach was trained on Caltech UCSD, the fine-grained dataset Stanford Dogs, and the standard zero-shot classification dataset Animals with Attributes (AWA). The combined compatibility score is evaluated in Eq. (3.49):

$$F(x, y; \{W\}_{1,\ldots,K}) = \sum_k \alpha_k \theta(x)^T W_k \varphi_k(y)$$
$$\text{such that} \sum_k \alpha_k = 1 \tag{3.49}$$

3.5.2 Methodology

Sung et al. (2018) proposed an end-to-end two-branch model Relation Network (RN) based on few-shot learning and zero-shot learning. The RN learns the deep metric to discover the connections between different images for few-shot learning and between pictures and class description for zero-shot learning, rather than simply referring to fixed embedding vectors. The Relation Network implements a convolutional neural network (CNN) classifier to learn deep, nonlinear, and learnable metrics, rather than nonlearnable, simple, and linear distance metrics. Fig. 3.4 illustrates a five-way one-shot task with one query image, as an example architecture of Relation Network. The embedding function f_φ first represents query and training images. Based on these embedding vectors, the relation function g_ϕ decides whether they are from matching categories. Similar to the Matching Network, the Relation Network can predict novel labels that the learner never observed during training without further updating the network or fine-tuning.

The detailed architecture of the Relation Network is motivated from the Prototypical Network (Snell et al., 2017) and Matching Net (Vinyals et al., 2016). The architecture of the Relation Network for few-shot learning is as follows: convolutional block—max pooling 2 × 2—convolutional block—max pooling 2 × 2—two convolutional blocks—feature concentration—convolutional block—max pooling 2 × 2—convolutional block—max pooling 2 × 2—Fully Connected (FC) ReLU H × 8—FC sigmoid 8 × 1—relation score output. The convolutional block consists of ReLU activation and batch normalization in 3 × 3 Conv with 64 kernels. On the other hand, the zero-shot Relation Network structure can be explored as

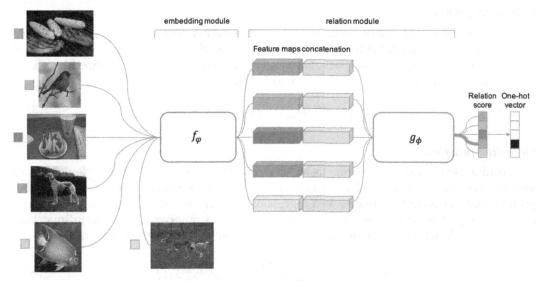

FIG. 3.4 Architecture of the relation network. This example is a five-way one-shot image classification task with one query image. After the inputs pass through the embedding module f, the feature maps are concatenated and sent to the relation net g. The output label is produced based on the relation scores.

feature concentration from two FC ReLU Weight Decay from one side and deep neural network for another side, then FC with ReLU activation and FC with sigmoid activation, finally output relation score.

C-Way one-shot

Suppose there is a sample-label pair in the query set $Q = \{(x_j, y_j)\}_{j=1}^{n}$ and sample set $S = \{(x_i, y_i)\}_{i=1}^{m}$ such that $m = K \times C$, where $K = 1$. The Relation Network contains an embedding module f_φ that is fed with a sample from the query set x_j and from the sample set x_i, generating feature maps $f_\varphi(x_i)$ and $f_\varphi(x_j)$. $C\left(f_\varphi(x_i), f_\varphi(x_j)\right)$ is the concatenation of these feature maps. The relation module g_φ computes the relation score $r_{i,\,j} \in \{0, 1\}$ between the query input and the sample input from this feature map combination.

C-Way K-shot

Each class has more than one sample (i.e., $K > 1$). Summing all the samples' comprehensive embedding component outputs from every training class constructs the feature map of the pooled class (Sung et al., 2018) builds the feature map of the pooled class. This allows for the number of relation scores to C and maintains the relationship demonstrated as Eq. (3.50):

$$r_{ij} = g_\varphi\left(C\left(f_\varphi(x_i), f_\varphi(x_j)\right)\right), \text{where } i = 1, 2, ..., C \qquad (3.50)$$

C-Way zero-shot

Given a semantic vector v_c for each class, an additional heterogeneous embedding component $f_{\varphi 2}$ replaces the normal embedding vector of the sample from the support set $f_\varphi(x_i)$ used in a one-shot or k-shot scenario. The relation score between $f_{\varphi 2}(x_j)$ and the embedding function of the semantic vector $f_{\varphi 1}(v_c)$ is indicated in Eq. (3.51):

$$r_{i,j} = g_\varphi\left(\mathcal{C}\left(f_{\varphi 1}(v_c), f_{\varphi 2}(x_j)\right)\right), where\ i = 1, 2, ..., C \tag{3.51}$$

Objective function

In contrast to typical classification tasks via cross-entropy loss, the Relation Network aims to minimize the mean squared error (MSE) between the predicted relation score $r_{i,j}$ and ground truth, viewing this process as a regression problem in Eq. (3.52). Relation similarity consists of $r_{i,j} = 1$ as a query-and-sample-matched pair and, otherwise, $r_{i,j} = 0$ as mismatched. This objective function stays workable for one-shot, few-shot, or zero-shot learning.

$$\varphi, \phi \leftarrow \arg\min_{\varphi, \phi} \sum_{i=1}^{m} \sum_{j=1}^{n} \left(r_{i,j} - \mathbf{1}\left(y_i == y_j\right)\right)^2 \tag{3.52}$$

3.6 Summary

The metric-based approach is a crucial component of meta-learning algorithms. The choice of a specific metric-based algorithm usually depends on various factors, such as sample size, focused domains, types of tasks, and method of computation. It significantly affects the performance of the underlying system in terms of accuracy, complexity, and training strategies. Convolutional Siamese neural network, as the first metric-based meta-learner, equips a twin Siamese network and cross-entropy loss for image classification tasks without prior knowledge. As a nonparametric model, Matching Network conducts an attention kernel over cosine distance and external memory module for image and language tasks. Prototypical networks tackle classification tasks through a distance to the prototype representation of each class and employ a nonlinear model for embedding. However, each approach has its own merits and drawbacks. Matching Network with nonparametric structure is highly adaptive to new training sets, but its gradient updates become expensive as sample size increases. Relation Network with learnable distance metric provides a nonlinear comparator between queries and samples, whereas Prototypical Network constructs nonlinear mapping between inputs and embedding space but with a linear comparator. Besides the few-shot classification, this technique has been proposed for multiple applications, such as image cleaning, data generation, visual tracking, word embedding, adversarial attacks, etc.

References

Ager, S., & Kualo, H. B. (1998). *Omniglot*. Retrieved from Omniglot www.omniglot.com.
Aguilera, C. A., Aguilera, F. J., Sappa, A. D., Aguilera, C., & Toledo, R. (2016). *Learning cross-spectral similarity measures with deep convolutional neural networks*. Retrieved from CVPR https://www.cv-foundation.org//openaccess/content_cvpr_2016_workshops/w9/papers/Aguilera_Learning_Cross-Spectral_Similarity_CVPR_2016_paper.pdf.

Aizerman, M. A., Braverman, E. M., & Rozonoer, L. I. (1964). Theoretical foundations of the potential function method in pattern recognition learning. *Automation and Remote Control, 25,* 821–837. Retrieved from https://citeseerx.ist.psu.edu/viewdoc/summary?doi=10.1.1.17.7215.

Akata, Z., Lee, H., & Schiele, B. (2014). *Zero-shot learning with structured embeddings.* arxiv.org. Retrieved from https://arxiv.org/pdf/1409.8403v1.pdf.

Akata, Z., Reed, S., Walter, D., Lee, H., & Schiele, B. (2015). *Evaluation of output embeddings for fine-grained image classification.* Retrieved from CVPR https://www.cv-foundation.org/openaccess/content_cvpr_2015/papers/Akata_Evaluation_of_Output_2015_CVPR_paper.pdf.

Altman, N. S. (1992). An introduction to kernel and nearest-neighbor nonparametric regression. *The American Statistician, 46*(3), 175–185. Retrieved from The American Statistician https://doi.org/10.1080/00031305.1992.10475879.

Bahdanau, D., Cho, K., & Bengio, Y. (2014). Neural machine translation by jointly learning to align and translate. In *ICLR.* Retrieved from.

Banerjee, A., Merugu, S., Dhillon, I. S., & Ghosh, J. (2005). Clustering with Bregman divergences. *Journal of Machine Learning Research.* Retrieved from http://www.jmlr.org/papers/volume6/banerjee05b/banerjee05b.pdf.

Bertinetto, L., Valmadre, J., Henriques, J. F., Vedaldi, A., & Torr, P. H. (2016). *Fully-convolutional Siamese networks for object tracking.* Spinger. Retrieved from https://link.springer.com/chapter/10.1007/978-3-319-48881-3_56.

Black, P. E. (2019). *"Manhattan distance". Dictionary of algorithms and data structures.* Dictionary of Algorithms and Data Structures. Retrieved from.

Bromley, J., Guyon, I., LeCun, Y., Säckinger, E., & Shah, R. (1994). Signature verification using a "Siamese" time delay neural network. *Advances in Neural Information Processing Systems, 6,* 737–744.

Chen, T., Kornblith, S., Norouzi, M., & Hinton, G. (2020). *A simple framework for contrastive learning of visual representations.* arxiv.org. Retrieved from https://arxiv.org/abs/2002.05709.

Chopra, S., Hadsell, R., & LeCun, Y. (2005). Learning a similarity metric discriminatively, with application to face verification. In *Vol. 1. Computer vision and pattern recognition, 2005 (CVPR)* (pp. 539–546).

De Maesschalck, R., Jouan-Rimbaud, D., & Massart, D. L. (2000). The Mahalanobis distance. *Chemometrics and Intelligent Laboratory Systems, 50*(1), 1–18. https://doi.org/10.1016/s0169-7439(99)00047-7.

Farhadi, A., Endres, I., Hoiem, D., & Forsyth, D. (2009). Describing objects by their attributes. In *CVPR.*

Ferrari, V., & Zisserman, A. (2007). Learning visual attributes. In *NIPS.*

Fort, S. (2017). *Gaussian prototypical networks for few-shot learning on Omniglot.* arxiv.org. Retrieved from https://arxiv.org/pdf/1708.02735.pdf.

Frome, A., Corrado, G. S., Shlens, J., Dean, S. B., Ranzato, M., & Mikolov, T. (2013). DeViSE: A deep visual-semantic embedding model. In *NIPS.*

Garcia, V., & Bruna, J. (2018). Few-shot learning with graph neural networks. In *ICLR.*

Goldberger, J., Hinton, G. E., Roweis, S. T., & Salakhutdinov, R. (2004). Neighbourhood components analysis. In *Advances in neural information processing systems* (pp. 513–520). MIT Press.

Graves, A., Fernández, S., & Schmidhuber., J. (2005). *Bidirectional LSTM networks for improved phoneme classification and recognition.* ICANN. Retrieved from: https://mediatum.ub.tum.de/doc/1290195/file.pdf.

Graves, A., Wayne, G., & Danihelka, I. (2014). *Neural turing machines.* arxiv.org. Retrieved from https://arxiv.org/abs/1410.5401.

Hadsell, R., Chopra, S., & LeCun, Y. (2006). Dimensionality reduction by learning an invariant mapping. In *CVPR.* Retrieved from http://yann.lecun.com/exdb/publis/pdf/hadsell-chopra-lecun-06.pdf.

Harris, Z. (1954). *Distributional structure.*

He, K., Fan, H., Wu, Y., Xie, S., & Girshick, R. (2019). *Momentum contrast for unsupervised visual representation learning.* arxiv.org. Retrieved from https://arxiv.org/abs/1911.05722.

Hochreiter, S., & Schmidhuber, J. (1997). Long short-term memory. *Neural Computation, 9,* 1735–1780. Retrieved from https://doi.org/10.1162/neco.1997.9.8.1735.

Hughes, L. H., Schmitt, M., Mou, L., Wang, Y., & Zhu, X. X. (2018). *Identifying corresponding patches in SAR and optical images with a pseudo-siamese CNN.* arxiv.org. Retrieved from https://arxiv.org/abs/1801.08467.

Hyun, K., & Bengio, C. Y. (2016). *Neural machine translation by jointly learning to align and translate.* arxiv.org. Retrieved from https://arxiv.org/pdf/1409.0473.pdf.

Koch, G., Zemel, R., & Salakhutdinov, R. (2015). *Siamese neural networks for one-shot image recognition.* cs.toronto.edu. Retrieved from http://www.cs.toronto.edu/~rsalakhu/papers/oneshot1.pdf.

Korenius, T., Laurikkala, J., & Juhola, M. (2007). *On principal component analysis, cosine and Euclidean measures in information retrieval.*

I. Theory & mechanisms

Krizhevsky, A. (2009). *Learning multiple layers of features from tiny images.* University of Toronto.

Lampert, C., Nickisch, H., & Harmeling, S. (2013). Attribute-based classification for zero-shot visual object categorization. In *TPAMI*.

Li, H., Eigen, D., Dodge, S., Zeiler, M., & Wang, X. (2019). *Finding task-relevant features for few-shot learning by category traversal.* CVPR. Retrieved from http://openaccess.thecvf.com/content_CVPR_2019/papers/Li_Finding_Task-Relevant_Features_for_Few-Shot_Learning_by_Category_Traversal_CVPR_2019_paper.pdf.

Liberti, L., Lavor, C., Maculan, N., & Mucherino, A. (2014). Euclidean distance geometry and applications. *SIAM Review, 56.* https://doi.org/10.1137/120875909.

Liu, L., Zhou, T., Long, G., Jiang, J., & Zhang, C. (2019). *Learning to propagate for graph meta-learning.* arxiv.org. Retrieved from https://arxiv.org/pdf/1909.05024.pdf.

Liu, Y.-Y. (2018). Yaoyao-liu/mini-imagenet-tools. In *Meta-transfer leaning CVPR 2019.* Retrieved from https://github.com/yaoyao-liu/mini-imagenet-tools.

MacQueen, J. B. (1967). Some methods for classification and analysis of multivariate observations. In *5th Berkeley symposium on mathematical statistics and probability* (pp. 281–297).

Marcus, M., Taylor, A., MacIntyre, R., Bies, A., Cooper, C., Ferguson, M., et al. (1992). *The Penn treebank project.* Retrieved from https://web.archive.org/web/19970614160127/http://www.cis.upenn.edu/~treebank/.

Mensink, T., Verbeek, J., Perronnin, F., & Csurka, G. (2013). Distance-based image classification: Generalizing to new classes at near-zero cost. *IEEE Transactions on Pattern Analysis and Machine Intelligence, 35*(11), 2624–2637.

Mikolov, T., Chen, K., Corrado, G. S., & Dean, J. (2013). In *Efficient estimation of word representations in vector space International conference on learning representations (ICLR), Scottsdale, Arizona, USA.*

Mikolov, T., Sutskever, I., Chen, K., Corrado, G. S., & Dean, J. (2013). Distributed representations of words and phrases and their compositionality. In *NIPS*.

Mishra, N., Rohaninejad, M., Chen, X., & Abbeel, P. (2018). A simple neural attentive meta-learner. In *ICLR*.

Misra, I., & Maaten, L. V. (2019). *Self-supervised learning of pretext-invariant representations.* arxiv. Retrieved from https://arxiv.org/abs/1912.01991.

Munkhdalai, T., Yuan, X., Mehri, S., & Trischler, A. (2018). Rapid adaptation with conditionally shifted neurons. In *ICML*.

National Institute of Standards and Technology. (2017). *Minkowski distance.* https://www.itl.nist.gov/div898/software/dataplot/refman2/auxillar/minkdist.htm.

Oreshkin, B. N., Rodriguez, P., & Lacoste, A. (2019). *TADAM: Task dependent adaptive metric for improved few-shot learning.* arxiv.org. Retrieved from: https://arxiv.org/abs/1805.10123.

Pennington, J., Socher, R., & Manning, C. D. (2014). Glove: Global vectors for word representation. In *EMNLP*.

Ren, M., Triantafillou, E., Ravi, S., Snell, J., Swersky, K., Tenenbaum, J. B., et al. (2018). Meta-learning for semi-supervised few-shot classification. In *ICLR*. Retrieved from https://openreview.net/pdf?id=HJcSzz-CZ.

Russakovsky, O., Deng, J., Su, H., Krause, J., Satheesh, S., Ma, S., et al. (2015). *ImageNet large scale visual recognition challenge 2012 (ILSVRC2012).* Retrieved from IJCV http://www.image-net.org/challenges/LSVRC/2012/.

Santoro, A., Bartunov, S., Botvinick, M., Wierstra, D., & Lillicrap, T. (2016). *Meta-learning with memory-augmented neural networks.* Retrieved from http://proceedings.mlr.press/v48/santoro16.pdf.

Schroff, F., Kalenichenko, D., & Philbin, J. (2015). *FaceNet: A unified embedding for face recognition and clustering.* arxiv.org. Retrieved from https://arxiv.org/pdf/1503.03832.pdf.

Snell, J., Swersky, K., & Zemel, R. (2017). *Prototypical networks for few-shot learning.* NIPS. Retrieved from http://papers.nips.cc/paper/6996-prototypical-networks-for-few-shot-learning.pdf.

Sung, F., Yang, Y., Zhang, L., Xiang, T., Torr, P. H., & Hospedales, T. M. (2018). *Learning to compare: Relation network for few-shot learning.* CVPR. Retrieved from http://openaccess.thecvf.com/content_cvpr_2018/papers_backup/Sung_Learning_to_Compare_CVPR_2018_paper.pdf.

Theodoridis, S. (2008). *Pattern recognition.* Elsevier.

Vinyals, O., Blundell, C., Lillicrap, T., Kavukcuoglu, K., & Wierstra, D. (2016). *Matching networks for one shot learning.* NIPS. Retrieved from http://papers.nips.cc/paper/6385-matching-networks-for-one-shot-learning.pdf.

Wang, Y.-X., Girshick, R., Hebert, M., & Hariharan, B. (2018). *Low-shot learning from imaginary data.* arxiv.org. Retrieved from https://arxiv.org/pdf/1801.05401.pdf.

Welinder, P., Branson, S., Mita, T., Wah, C., Belongie, S., & Perona, P. (2010). *Caltech-UCSD birds 200, technical report CNS-TR-2010-001.* California Institute of Technology.

Yamada, T. (1990). *Essentials of error-control coding techniques*. Science Direct. Retrieved from https://www.sciencedirect.com/topics/engineering/hamming-distance.

Yang, Y., & Hospedales, T. M. (2015). A unified perspective on multi-domain and multi-task learning. In *ICLR*. Retrieved from https://arxiv.org/pdf/1412.7489.pdf.

Zhang, W., Wang, Y., & Qiao, Y. (2019). MetaCleaner: Learning to hallucinate clean representations for noisy-labeled visual recognition. In *CVPR*.

Zhang, Z., & Saligrama, V. (2015). *Zero-shot learning via semantic similarity embedding*. Retrieved from arxiv.org. https://arxiv.org/pdf/1509.04767.pdf.

I. Theory & mechanisms

Optimization-based meta-learning approaches

4.1 Introduction

The gradient represents the core concept of neural networks in processing large-scale datasets through backpropagation. However, a gradient-based optimization algorithm consumes giant iterative steps over extensive samples to achieve adequate performance. To address these shortcomings, optimization-based meta-learning strategies are designed for quick convergence of training based on a few samples of each class while maintaining solid generalization ability.

Ravi and Larochelle (2017) contributed one of the most fundamental optimization-based meta-learners, motivated by the long short-term memory (LSTM) cell (Chevalier, 2018), which presents a different view of gradient-based optimizers. Then, encouraged by the insight of fine-tuning, Finn, Abbeel, and Levine (2017) proposed a model-agnostic meta-learning (MAML) approach that is broadly appropriate for many scenarios. This led to a large family of variations, of which Reptile (Nichol, Achiam, & Schulman, 2018) is the most widely used and easy to implement. Reptile provides cheap computation and better performance than MAML through removing the second derivative.

The rest of this chapter will explore three types of optimization-based meta-learning methods with their models, motivations, character of techniques, and extended modifications. Section 4.2 presents the development of LSTM, a brief introduction of several gradient-based optimizers (Momentum, AdaGrad, AdaDelta, and ADAM), a historical study of batch normalization, and an overview of the first gradient-based meta-learner, the LSTM meta-learner. Meta-SGD is described concisely as a contrasting but related algorithm to the LSTM meta-learner. Section 4.3 explains one of the most widely adopted frameworks, MAML, and many modifications from this design—regarding reinforcement learning, intimation learning, and few-learning classification and regression. Section 4.4 presents the first-order model-agnostic meta-learning (FOMAML) as background knowledge and focuses on Reptile. It offers a complete comparison between MAML, FOMAML, and Reptile, and their expectations. Finally, this chapter presents three extended frameworks of Reptile regarding pruning, regularization, and application in reinforcement learning.

This exploration will cover background knowledge, the motivation behind the design, critical technical distributions, detailed structures and architectures, and numerous modified algorithms on each method of optimization-based meta-learning. This research recursively tracks related bibliographies in papers accepted at premier academic conferences, including ICLR, ICML, CVPR, and ECCV.

4.2 LSTM meta-learner

4.2.1 Background knowledge

Covariate shift

Shimodaira (2000) described the **covariate shift** in distribution when the covariate (Glen, 2021) in observed samples follows a distinct distribution from the whole population data. For instance, in the Kullback-Leibler loss function expressed Eq. (4.1), $q_0(x)$ is denoted as the density of x in observed samples (i.e., density determined by samples), and $q_1(x)$ is the density of x for the evaluation of estimated performance (i.e., density determined by population). $q(y|x)$ is the conditional density over x and y, where x is the undependable or explanatory variable while y is the dependable or response variable. $p(y|x,\theta)$ represents the model of the conditional density parameterized by θ.

$$\text{loss}_i(\theta) := -\int q_i(x) \int q(y|x) \log p(y|x,\theta) dy dx \qquad (4.1)$$

A covariate shift in distribution occurs when $q_0(x) \neq q_1(x)$, which is usually observed in the following situations:

(1) In regression analysis, experiment design or resource constraints may lead to its appearance.
(2) Under active learning (also named optimal experimental design in some statistics literature; Settles, 2010) in neural network processing, the distribution of x in future samples may differ from that of past samples. Instead, an imaginary $q_1(x)$ is identified to a particular region of x where the estimation accuracy needs to be controlled.

Batch normalization

Seeking to reduce the covariate shift phenomenon (Shimodaira, 2000), Ioffe and Szegedy (2015) presented one of the most classical and broadly implemented deep neural network techniques, **batch normalization** (BN). Ioffe and Szegedy (2015) defined internal covariate shift (ICS) as "the change in the distribution of network activations due to the change in network parameters during training." Referred to as the benefit of whitening (LeCun, Bottou, Orr, & Muller, 1998; Wiesler & Ney, 2011) but lacking thorough step-to-step mathematical proof, this design is supposed to reduce ICS through the transformation expressed in Table 4.1. Its effectiveness is explained by reducing each layer's input distribution changes via controlling the mean and standard deviation of layer inputs.

TABLE 4.1 Batch normalization of a mini-batch.

Input: $\mathcal{B} = \{x_{1...m}\}$ as mini-batch of x
        γ and β, learnable parameters
Output: $\{y_i = BN_{\gamma,\beta}(x_i)\}$

1 Evaluate the mini-batch mean using $\mu_\mathcal{B} \leftarrow \frac{1}{m} \sum\limits_{i=1}^{m} x_i$

2 Evaluate the mini-batch variance using $\sigma_\mathcal{B}^2 \leftarrow \frac{1}{m} \sum\limits_{i=1}^{m} (x_i - \mu_\mathcal{B})^2$

3 Perform the normalization using $\widehat{x}_i \leftarrow \frac{x_i - \mu_\mathcal{B}}{\sqrt{\sigma_\mathcal{B}^2 + \epsilon}}$

4 Obtain $y_i \leftarrow \gamma \widehat{x}_i + \beta \equiv BN_{\gamma,\beta}(x_i)$ by adding scale and shift terms

Modified from Ioffe, S., & Szegedy, C. (2015). Batch normalization: Accelerating deep network training by reducing internal covariate shift. Retrieved from CoRR: http://arxiv.org/abs/1502.03167.

Batch normalization achieved essential success and offered many significant contributions in practical faster learning, including:

- Accelerating the gradient descent with stable training
- Enabling deep neural network training with a more considerable learning rate
- Substituting drop-out at some level
- Regulating the model

However, Santurkar, Tsipras, Ilyas, and Madry (2018) questioned the theoretical and rigorous reasons behind BN's success and brought BN's ability to eliminate ICS into **doubt**. They argued that BN makes the ICS effects even worse. After experiments with noise samples (nonzero mean and nonunit variance distribution) on CIFAR-10 (Krizhevsky, 2009) through standard VGG (Simonyan & Zisserman, 2015) with and without BN, Santurkar addressed the gaps in understanding why batch normalization works with the following conclusions and published these findings at the NeurIPS conference:

1. The effectiveness of batch normalization is unrelated to the internal covariate shift.
2. The root of batch normalization's success is the smoothness of the optimization landscape, which generates more predictive, stable, faster, and more effective gradient behavior.

Long short-term memory

Hochreier and Schmidhuber proposed one of the most essential and highly cited neural networks, **long short-term memory** (LSTM; Chevalier, 2018; Gers, Schmidhuber, & Cummins, 2000; Hochreiter, 1991). LSTM presents feedback connections and can process both single-point data (e.g., image) and sequences of data (e.g., sentence understanding, speech recognition, video analysis). It tackles various tasks ranged from prediction classification to processing sequential data. Under the long-term evolution of LSTM, a standard LSTM unit often refers to an input gate, an output gate, a memory cell, and a forget gate. The workflow and component structure is represented in Fig. 4.1, where the inputs are shown in *blue* (*dark gray* in print version) and the outputs in *green* (*light gray* in print version).

From Eqs. (4.2) to (4.7), the element-wise product is presented as an operator ∘, and the element-wise addition as operator +; $x_t \in \mathbb{R}^d$ is the input vector to an LSTM unit. The weight and bias metrics $W \in \mathbb{R}^{h \times d}$, $U \in \mathbb{R}^{h \times h}$, and $b \in \mathbb{R}^h$ are learnable during training.

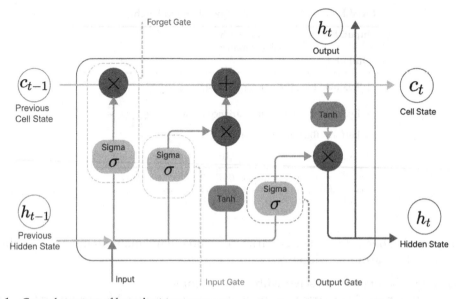

FIG. 4.1 General structure of long short-term memory.
Modified from Chevalier, G. (2018). *LARNN: Linear attention recurrent neural network.* arXiv.org. Retrieved June 27, 2022, from *https://arxiv.org/abs/1808.05578.*

The forget gate's activation vector through a sigmoid layer and corresponded bias b_f, denoted as f_t, is expressed in Eq. (4.2).

$$f_t = \sigma_g(W_f x_t + U_f h_{t-1} + b_f) \tag{4.2}$$

The input or update gate's activation vector through a sigmoid layer, which is denoted as i_t, is expressed in Eq. (4.3). The c_{t-1} denotes the previous cell state, h_{t-1} is the previous hidden state, and σ_g is sigmoid function and corresponded to bias b_i:

$$i_t = \sigma_g(W_i x_t + U_i h_{t-1} + b_i) \tag{4.3}$$

The output gate's activation vector through a sigmoid layer, which is denoted as o_t, is expressed in Eq. (4.4) and corresponded to bias b_o:

$$o_t = \sigma_g(W_o x_t + U_o h_{t-1} + b_o) \tag{4.4}$$

The cell input activation vector, denoted as $\tilde{c}_t$, is expressed in Eq. (4.5) and corresponded to bias b_c:

$$\tilde{c}_t = \tanh(W_c x_t + U_c h_{t-1} + b_c) \tag{4.5}$$

The cell state vector, which is denoted as c_t, is expressed in Eq. (4.6):

$$c_t = f_t \circ c_{t-1} + i_t \circ \tilde{c}_t \tag{4.6}$$

The output vector of an LSTM unit or the hidden state vector, which is denoted as h_t, is expressed in Eq. (4.7):

$$h_t = o_t \circ \tanh(c_t) \tag{4.7}$$

Additionally, a significant number of variations of LSTM with superior structures are proposed chronologically: the earliest vanilla LSTM without a forget gate (Chevalier, 2018), and the standard LSTM with a forget gate (Gers et al., 2000), which is discussed above. The peephole LSTM (Gers & Schmidhuber, 2001) presented a peephole connection with every gate or partial gate. Another widely used RNN encoder-decoder memory unit—the gated recurrent unit (GRU; Cho, Bahdanau, Bougares, Schwenk, & Bengio, 2014)—simplifies LSTM by redefining the update gate and reset gate. Greff and colleagues introduced the coupled input and forget gate LSTM (CIFG-LSTM; Greff, Srivastava, Koutník, Steunebrink, & Schmidhuber, 2015), which effectively reduces the computational cost.

LSTM has become one of the most distinguished methods in a variety of areas. Researchers have conducted in-depth investigations into its structure, performance, and modifications, and hold distinct opinions. Greff argued that the forget gate and output gate are the most essential components of this method among more than 10,000 LSTM modifications. Thus, removing any of them will considerably reduce its performance (Greff et al., 2015). Jozefowicz, Zaremba, and Sutskever (2015) noted that "GRU outperforms LSTM in all tasks except for language modeling," and "LSTM with the large forget gate bias outperforms both the LSTM and GRU on almost all tasks." Conversely, Greff et al. (2015) stated that the standard LSTM with a forget gate performs well on multiple datasets after comparing many LSTM variations.

Gradient-based optimization

Gradient descent is deep learning's critical core concept and technology. For stochastic gradient descent (SGD), one of the classic techniques, Momentum (Nesterov, 1983), uses the current step's gradient to navigate the direction and the past steps to guide the search. Duchi, Hazan, and Singer (2011) proposed AdaGrad, which assigns different behaviors to different parameters. It navigates a higher learning rate to parameters with infrequently accruing features and a lower rate to those with frequently occurring features. Zeiler (2012) offered a more powerful AdaGrad extension, AdaDelta, which narrows the window of the cumulative past steps and adjusts the learning rate based on the moving window of gradient update. No global learning rate must be determined under AdaDelta, and it prevents the aggressive learning rate decay that occurred under AdaGrad. Kingma and Ba (2014) provided the Adaptive Moment Estimation (ADAM), an adaptive learning rate technique through both the gradient and the second momentum of gradients. It can be viewed as integrating benefits from AdaGrad and RMSProp (Hinton, 2013) to handle the sparse gradient and noise issue.

Despite the general acceptance of these gradient-based optimizers, two primary defects remain:

- These optimizations cannot guarantee a fast convergence in nonconvex optimization situations.
- The algorithm must restart from random initialization in each dataset, damaging its capability of converging to optimal parameters within a couple of updates.

4.2.2 Methodology

Differing from traditional gradient-based optimizations like Momentum, ADAM, and the others introduced above (Duchi et al., 2011; Kingma & Ba, 2014; Nesterov, 1983; Zeiler, 2012), a novel gradient-based optimizer—the LSTM meta-learner (also called meta-LSTM)—was proposed by Ravi and Larochelle (2017). Meta-LSTM aims to converge rapidly within few-shot learning using a large set of different datasets, each with few labeled examples per class. It also avoids the error in transfer learning when networks are trained on divergences from target tasks (Yosinski, Clune, Bengio, & Lipson, 2014). Meta-LSTM analyzes the samples at two levels to capture short-term knowledge within a task and fundamental long-term knowledge shared across multiple tasks.

In a K-shot N-class image classification task, the update rule coordinates with the cell state in LSTM, as described in Eq. (4.8).

$$c_t = f_t \odot c_{t-1} + i_t \odot \tilde{c}_t \tag{4.8}$$

$$as\ f_t = 1, c_{t-1} = \theta_{t-1}, i_t = \alpha_t, \tilde{c}_t = -\nabla_{\theta_{t-1}} \mathcal{L}_t$$

In the case of the forget gate $f_t \neq 1$, this framework applied the forget gate as a function of the previous value of the forget gate f_{t-1}, the current loss $\mathcal{L}_t$, the loss gradient concerning parameters $\nabla_{\theta_{t-1}} \mathcal{L}_t$, and the previously updated parameters of the learner θ_{t-1}, as expressed in Eq. (4.9):

$$f_t = \sigma\big(W_F \cdot \big[\nabla_{\theta_{t-1}}\mathcal{L}_t, \mathcal{L}_t, \theta_{t-1}, f_{t-1}\big] + b_F\big) \tag{4.9}$$

To diminish divergence and achieve rapid training, Ravi and Larochelle (2017) formulated the learning rate in terms of a function concerning the parameter value θ_{t-1} after $t-1$ updating, the current loss $\mathcal{L}_t$, the gradient $\nabla_{\theta_{t-1}} \mathcal{L}_t$ on parameter θ_{t-1}, and the learning rate i_{t-1} in the previous time step, as expressed in Eq. (4.10):

$$i_t = \sigma\big(W_I \cdot [\nabla_{\theta_{t-1}}\mathcal{L}_t, \mathcal{L}_t, \theta_{t-1}, i_{t-1}] + b_I\big) \tag{4.10}$$

See Fig. 4.2 for the computational visualization and Table 4.2 for the corresponding training of Meta-LSTM.

During training, some implementations need more attention, as outlined below.

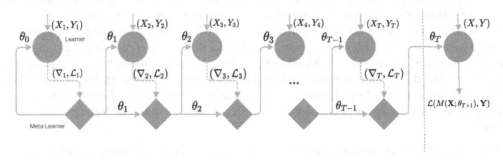

FIG. 4.2 High-level structure of LSTM meta-learner.
Modified from Ravi, S., & Larochelle, H. (2017). Optimization as a model for few-shot learning. Retrieved from ICRL: https://openreview.net/pdf?id=rJY0-Kcll.

TABLE 4.2 General training methods of LSTM meta-learner.

Input: $\mathcal{D}_{meta-train}$, meta-training set
$\quad\quad\quad$ R, LSTM meta-learner parameterized by Θ
$\quad\quad\quad$ M, based learner parameterized by θ
Output: Θ_d, updated parameters

1 $\quad \Theta_0 \leftarrow random\ initialization$

2 $\quad$ **for** $d = 1,...,n$ **do**
3 $\quad\quad$ Construct $\mathcal{D}_{train}, \mathcal{D}_{test} \leftarrow random\ dataset\ from\ \mathcal{D}_{meta-train}$
4 $\quad\quad$ Initialize learner parameters as $\theta_0 \leftarrow c_0$

5 $\quad\quad$ **for** $t = 1,...,T$ **do**
6 $\quad\quad\quad$ Construct $X_t, Y_t \leftarrow randombatchfrom\ \mathcal{D}_{train}$
7 $\quad\quad\quad$ Obtain the loss of learner on train batch using $\mathcal{L}_t \leftarrow \mathcal{L}(M(X_t;\theta_{t-1}),Y_t)$
8 $\quad\quad\quad$ Obtain update of meta-learner using $c_t \leftarrow R((\nabla_{\theta_{t-1}}\mathcal{L}_t, \mathcal{L}_t); \Theta_{d-1})$
9 $\quad\quad\quad$ Update learner parameters using $\theta_t \leftarrow c_t$
10 $\quad\quad$ **end for**

11 $\quad\quad$ Let $X, Y \leftarrow \mathcal{D}_{test}$
12 $\quad\quad$ Obtain the loss of learner on test batch using $\mathcal{L}_{test} \leftarrow \mathcal{L}(M(X;\theta_T),Y)$
13 $\quad\quad$ Update meta-learner parameters Θ_d using $\nabla_{\Theta_{d-1}}\mathcal{L}_{test}$

14 $\quad$ **end for**

Modified from Ravi, S., & Larochelle, H. (2017). Optimization as a model for few-shot learning. Retrieved from ICRL: https://openreview.net/pdf?id=rJY0-Kcll.

Gradient independent assumption and initialization

According to previous work by Andrychowicz et al. (2016), this framework ignores the dependency of loss $\mathcal{L}_t$ and gradients $\nabla_{\theta_{t-1}}\mathcal{L}_t$ of the learner M on the meta-learner's parameter Θ to prevent expensive computation costs from second derivatives.

This framework follows Jozefowicz et al. (2015) suggestion of a small random-weight initialization with a big value on the forget gate bias to enable gradient flow. A small value on the input gate bias is advised in this model to achieve a slow learning rate and steady training stability.

Meta-training and meta-testing batch normalization

This method utilizes a hybrid approach to collect mean and variance to eliminate information leaks between different datasets or episodes. During meta-training, it uses batch normalization for both the training set and testing set. However, during meta-testing, it relies on batch statistics solely for the training set and calculates the running averages; then, it implements the running average in testing. Greater preference is given to the later values in running averages since this method only runs a few training steps.

Parameter sharing

To block the explosion of parameters, this framework built on Andrychowicz et al. (2016), sharing parameters across all coordinates of the learner gradient to implement identical update rules for each coordinate. To normalize the multiple scales of gradient and loss while maintaining the sign and magnitude of inputs, Andrychowicz proposed the preprocessing procedure presented in Eq. (4.11) as the recommended value $p=10$:

$$x \rightarrow \begin{cases} \left(\dfrac{\log(|x|)}{p}, sgn(x)\right), & \text{if } |x| \geq e^{-p} \\ (-1, e^{p}x), & \text{otherwise} \end{cases} \qquad (4.11)$$

4.3 Model-agnostic meta-learning

4.3.1 Background knowledge

Transfer learning

Transfer learning is a fascinating research area in machine learning that involves keeping knowledge gained by tackling a task and reusing it for a different but relevant task (West, Ventura, & Warnick, 2007). Goodfellow, Bengio, and Courville (2016) defined this entity as follows: "transfer learning and domain adaptation refer to the situation where what has been learned in one setting is exploited to improve generalization in another setting."

Fine-tuning

Yosinski and colleagues (Yosinski et al., 2014) discussed fine-tuning, a common technique for transfer learning (Bengio, 2011; Bengio et al., 2011; Caruana, 1995). Fine-tuning is implemented when target datasets share a high degree of relevance and similarity with the source dataset. If two datasets significantly differ, the transferable knowledge could be limited. One common transfer learning approach with fine-tuning is to copy the first couple of layers from the pretrained (i.e., source) model to the target model while training the other layers in the target network with random initialization toward the target model. The layers can be left unchanged (frozen) or adopted (fine-tuning) by the source model during training.

Fine-tuning uses gradient-based learning tools to learn transferable knowledge in training. This idea motivated Finn and colleagues (Finn et al., 2017) to design a meta-learning model accordingly; their resulting MAML algorithm offered a gradient-based learning rule that could rapidly generate new tasks with no overfitting.

For a deeper look at transfer learning, see Chapter 1.

4.3.2 Methodology

Finn and colleagues (Finn et al., 2017) introduced the MAML, which attracted academic interest and led to the production of various extensions (e.g., Dou, Yu, & Anastasopoulos, 2019; Guo, Tang, Duan, Zhou, & Yin, 2019; Huang, Wang, Singh, Yih, & He, 2018; Jung, You, Noh, Cho, & Han, 2020; Nichol, Achiam and Schulman, 2018; Obamuyide & Vlachos, 2019; Soh, Cho, & Cho, 2020; Wang, Luo, Sun, Xiong, & Zeng, 2020; Wu et al., 2020). MAML achieved state-of-the-art performance in versatile, classical learning problems from different domains, including few-shot learning in supervised classification and regression and reinforcement learning.

This universally task-agnostic meta-learner is not only applicable to deep learning techniques but also to any architecture that allows gradient descent (Lemaréchal, 2012) to be applied to the differentiable (smooth) loss function (Banach, 1931). It maintains the advantage of rapid adaptation through only one or five examples per class—which leads a comparatively small number of parameters—and requires just a few gradient descent steps to achieve excellent performance.

Task adaptation

MAML aims to maximize the sensitivity of loss functions of new tasks regrading the parameters. It distinguishes the model parameters according to their sensitivity in different numbers of tasks and trains the ones that are sensitive to changes in the task. As a result, small changes in the tasks will lead to a considerable improvement in loss function among distinct tasks and signal to change the gradient descent direction. Fig. 4.3 displays how MAML achieves rapid adaptation to new tasks through a representation θ.

If a model f_θ with parameter θ seeks to adapt a new task $\mathcal{T}_i$ with the corresponding dataset $(D_{train}^{(i)}, D_{test}^{(i)})$, the adjusted parameter θ_i' is updated through one or more gradient steps. The step size is a fixed hyperparameter or meta-learned, denoted as α. Eq. (4.12) illustrates one gradient descent step; multiple gradient steps are a straightforward extension.

$$\theta_i' = \theta - \alpha \nabla_\theta \mathcal{L}_{\mathcal{T}_i}(f_\theta) \tag{4.12}$$

Every task $\mathcal{T}_i = \{\mathcal{L}_{\mathcal{T}_i}(x_1, a_1, ..., x_H, a_H), q(x_1), q(x_{t+1}|x_t, a_t), H\}$ is defined with the observation and action pair (x_i, a_i) in a transition distribution $q(x_{t+1}|x_t, a_t)$ with an episode length H among all tasks $p(\mathcal{T})$. The initial observation is denoted as $q(x_1)$, and a task-specific loss function is $\mathcal{L}_{\mathcal{T}_i}$. Eq. (4.13) constructs an optimization for only one task. For learning productive generalization across multiple tasks, the meta-objective function aims to find optimal θ^* so that the task-specific fine-tuning is more constructive.

$$\theta^* = \min_\theta \sum_{\mathcal{T}_i \sim p(\mathcal{T})} \mathcal{L}_{\mathcal{T}_i}\left(f_{\theta_i'}\right) = \min_\theta \sum_{\mathcal{T}_i \sim p(\mathcal{T})} \mathcal{L}_{\mathcal{T}_i}\left(f_{\theta - \alpha \nabla_\theta \mathcal{L}_{\mathcal{T}_i}(f_\theta)}\right) \tag{4.13}$$

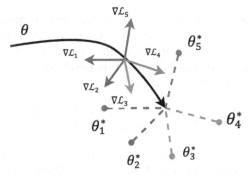

FIG. 4.3 MAML optimizes for a representation, θ, which supports rapid adaptation to new tasks.
Modified from Finn, C., Abbeel, P., & Levine, S. (2017). Model-agnostic meta-learning for fast adaptation of deep networks. Retrieved from arxiv.org: https://arxiv.org/pdf/1703.03400.pdf.

TABLE 4.3   General training methods of model-agnostic meta-learning.

Input: $p(\mathcal{T})$, tasks distribution
      α, β, hyper-parameters of step size
      D, training dataset
      D', a different dataset than D

Output: θ, updated parameters

---

1   $\theta \rightarrow$ random initialization

2   **while** not meeting stopping criteria **do**
3   Randomly select a batch of tasks $\mathcal{T}_i$ from $p(\mathcal{T})$

4   **for** each $\mathcal{T}_i$ **do**
5   Compute $\nabla_\theta \mathcal{L}_{\mathcal{T}_i}(f_\theta)$ corresponding to K examples
6   Obtain adjusted parameters through gradient descent using $\theta_i^* = \theta - \alpha \nabla_\theta \mathcal{L}_{\mathcal{T}_i}(f_\theta)$
7   **end for**

8   Update gradient descent based on the new dataset D' using $\theta \leftarrow \theta - \beta \nabla_\theta \mathcal{L}_{\mathcal{T}_i \sim p(\mathcal{T})}\left(f_{\theta_i'}\right)$
9   **end while**

Modified from Finn, C., Abbeel, P., & Levine, S. (2017). Model-agnostic meta-learning for fast adaptation of deep networks. *Retrieved from arxiv.org: https://arxiv.org/pdf/1703.03400.pdf.*

To update gradient descent, this framework selects the stochastic gradient descent (SGD) as Eq. (4.14), where β is the meta-step size:

$$\theta \leftarrow \theta - \beta \nabla_\theta \sum_{\mathcal{T}_i \sim p(\mathcal{T})} \mathcal{L}_{\mathcal{T}_i}\left(f_{\theta_i'}\right) \tag{4.14}$$

After training on K samples with a loss function $\mathcal{L}_{\mathcal{T}_i}$, the performance is measured by the test error on a task $\mathcal{T}_i$ based on unseen samples. The step-by-step training pseudocode is shown in Table 4.3.

4.3.3 Illustration 1: Few-shot regression and few-shot classification

In addition to the original, MAML developed many extensions, including classification and regression based on only a few samples. Cross entropy and mean-squared error (MSE) are two standard loss functions in regression tasks, whereas other supervised regression loss functions are also open. The MSE loss function is shown in Eq. (4.15), where ϕ presents the task-specific parameters:

$$\mathcal{L}_{\mathcal{T}_i}\left(f_\phi\right) = \sum_{x^{(j)}, y^{(j)} \sim \mathcal{T}_i} \left| f_\phi\left(x^{(j)}\right) - y^{(j)} \right|_2^2 \tag{4.15}$$

Here, $j \in \{1, 2, \dots, N\}$ for an N-shot regression problem, and $x^{(j)}$ and $y^{(j)}$ are an input-output pair from task $\mathcal{T}_i$. Conversely, the loss function of a discrete classification is displayed in Eq. (4.16):

$$\mathcal{L}_{\mathcal{T}_i}\left(f_\phi\right) = \sum_{x^{(j)}, y^{(j)} \sim \mathcal{T}_i} y^{(j)} \log f_\phi\left(x^{(j)}\right) + \left(1 - y^{(j)}\right) \log \left(1 - f_\phi\left(x^{(j)}\right)\right) \tag{4.16}$$

TABLE 4.4 General training methods of MAML for supervised few-shot learning.

Input: $p(\mathcal{T})$, tasks distribution
       α, β, hyper-parameters of step size
       D, training dataset
       D', a different dataset than D

Output: θ, updated parameters

1 $\theta \rightarrow$ random initialization

2 **while** not meeting stopping criteria **do**
3   Randomly select a batch of tasks $\mathcal{T}_i$ from $p(\mathcal{T})$
4   **for** each $\mathcal{T}_i$ **do**
5   Randomly sample K data points $D = \{x^{(j)}, y^{(j)}\}$ from $\mathcal{T}_i$
6   Compute $\nabla_\theta \mathcal{L}_{\mathcal{T}_i}(f_\theta)$ using D and $\mathcal{L}_{\mathcal{T}_i}$ in Eq. (4.15) or (4.16) stated above
7   Obtain adapted parameters with gradient descent using $\theta'_i = \theta - \alpha \nabla_\theta \mathcal{L}_{\mathcal{T}_i}(f_\theta)$
8   Sample data points $D_i' = \{x^{(j)}, y^{(j)}\}$ from $\mathcal{T}_i$ for meta-update
9   **end for**
10   Update gradient descent based on the new dataset D' using $\theta \leftarrow \theta - \beta \nabla_\theta \mathcal{L}_{\mathcal{T}_i \sim p(\mathcal{T})}\left(f_{\theta'_i}\right)$ using D' and $\mathcal{L}_{\mathcal{T}_i}$ in Eq. (4.15) or (4.16) stated above

11 **end while**
12 return θ

Modified from Finn, C., Abbeel, P., & Levine, S. (2017). Model-agnostic meta-learning for fast adaptation of deep networks. Retrieved from arxiv.org: https://arxiv.org/pdf/1703.03400.pdf.

The detailed pseudocode is outlined in Table 4.4. One can insert either Eq. (4.15) for regression or Eq. (4.16) for classification in the corresponding steps.

4.3.4 Illustration 2: Policy gradient reinforcement learning

As in Chapter 7, Section 7.1, which introduces the fundamental concept of reinforcement learning (RL), gradient-based methods (policy gradient; Sutton, McAllester, Singh, & Mansour, 1999) are essential reinforcement learning components. The gradient in policy gradient is used to estimate both the learner gradient updates and the meta-optimization.

The objective function of MAML for reinforcement learning is demonstrated in Eq. (4.17), where $R_i(x_t, a_t)$ is the reward function of each task $\mathcal{T}_i$, where ϕ presents the task-specific parameters:

$$\mathcal{L}_{\mathcal{T}_i}\left(f_\phi\right) = -\mathbb{E}_{x_t, a_t \sim f_\phi, q\mathcal{T}_i}\left[\sum_{t=1}^{H} R_i(x_t, a_t)\right] \tag{4.17}$$

The specific pseudocode RL gradient policy MAML is described in Table 4.5.

4.3.5 Illustration 3: Meta-imitation learning

The modified MAML with imitation learning (Finn, 2018; Hussein, Gaber, Elyan, & Jayne, 2016) aims to learn a policy for adapting new tasks through a single demonstration applied in a real robotic system. The range of corresponding tasks involves simulated reaching, simulated pushing, and real-world placing. The mean square-error loss function of policy

TABLE 4.5   General training methods of MAML for reinforcement learning.

Input: $p(\mathcal{T})$, tasks distribution
   α, β, hyper-parameters of step size
   D, training dataset
   D', a different dataset than D

Output: θ, updated gradient descent

1 $\theta \rightarrow$ random initialization

2 **while** not meeting stopping criteria **do**
3   Randomly select a batch of tasks $\mathcal{T}_i$ from $p(\mathcal{T})$

4   **for** each $\mathcal{T}_i$ **do**
5   Randomly sampling trajectories from the environment related to task $\mathcal{T}_i$
6   Randomly sample K trajectories $D = \{(x_1, a_1, \ldots x_H)\}$ with f_θ in $\mathcal{T}_i$
7   Compute $\nabla_\theta \mathcal{L}_{\mathcal{T}_i}(f_\theta)$ using D and $\mathcal{L}_{\mathcal{T}_i}$ in Eq. (4.18)
8   Obtain adapted parameters with gradient descent using $\theta'_i = \theta - \alpha \nabla_\theta \mathcal{L}_{\mathcal{T}_i}(f_\theta)$
9   Sample trajectories $D_i' = \{(x_1, a_1, \ldots x_H)\}$ using $f_{\theta'_i}$ in $\mathcal{T}_i$
10   **end for**

11   # Update gradient descent using new dataset D' using $\theta \leftarrow \theta - \beta \nabla_\theta \mathcal{L}_{\mathcal{T}_i \sim p(\mathcal{T})}\left(f_{\theta'_i}\right)$ with each D_i' and
       $\mathcal{L}_{\mathcal{T}_i}$ in Eq. (4.18)
12 **end while**
13 return θ

Modified from Finn, C., Abbeel, P., & Levine, S. (2017). Model-agnostic meta-learning for fast adaptation of deep networks. Retrieved from arxiv.org: https://arxiv.org/pdf/1703.03400.pdf.

parameters ψ is expressed in Eq. (4.18), where the demonstration trajectory is denoted as $\tau := \{ O_1, a_1, \ldots, O_T, a_T\}$:

$$\mathcal{L}(\psi, D_{T_i}) = \sum_{\tau^{(j)} \sim D_{T_i}} \sum_t \left\| f_\psi\left(o_t^{(j)}\right) - a_t^{(j)} \right\|_2^2 \tag{4.18}$$

See Table 4.6 for a summary of pseudocode described meta-imitation learning with MAML.

4.3.6 Related Algorithm 1: Meta-SGD

An SGD-like meta-learner was developed based on few-shot samples in reinforcement learning and supervised learning on classification and regression tasks—meta-SGD (Li, Zhou, Chen, & Li, 2017). It learns faster and is easier to train than the LSTM meta-learner, and it has a higher capacity than the MAML for 2D navigation. This framework is not an extension of the LSTM meta-learner, but rather another gradient-based algorithm to select all optimizer components (initialization, learning rate, and direction update) automatically, as shown in Eq. (4.19).

$$\theta' = \theta - \alpha \circ \nabla \mathcal{L}_T(\theta) \tag{4.19}$$

where θ denotes the learnable meta-parameter as the state of a learner and the initialization term in new tasks, and the adaption term $\alpha \circ \nabla \mathcal{L}_T(\theta)$ represents the meta-SGD updating direction through its direction and learning rate by its length.

TABLE 4.6 General training methods for meta-imitation with MAML.

Input: $p(T)$, distribution of tasks
α, β, hyperparameters of step size

1   $\theta\leftarrow$random initialization

2   **while** not meeting stopping criteria **do**
3   Randomly select a batch of tasks $\mathcal{T}_i \sim p(\mathcal{T})$

4   **for** each T_i **do**
5   Randomly sample demonstration $\tau_i = \{o_1, a_1, ..., o_T, a_T\}$ from D_{T_i}

6   Compute $\nabla_\theta \mathcal{L}(\theta, \{\tau_i\})$ through $\mathcal{L}$ using $\mathcal{L}(\psi, D_{T_i}) = \sum_{\tau^{(j)} \sim D_{T_i}} \sum_t \left\| f_\psi \left(o_t^{(j)} \right) - a_t^{(j)} \right\|_2^2$

7   Obtain adapted parameters with gradient descent using $\phi_i = \theta - \alpha \nabla_\theta \mathcal{L}(\theta, \tau_i)$
8   Randomly sample demonstration $\tau_i' = \{o_1', a_1', ..., o_T', a_T'\}$ from $D_{T_i} \backslash \{\tau_i\}$ for the meta-update

9   Update $\theta \leftarrow \theta - \beta \nabla_\theta \sum_{T_i \sim p(T)} \mathcal{L}(\phi_i, \{\tau_i\})$ through each $\mathcal{L}$ using $\mathcal{L}(\psi, D_{T_i})$

$$= \sum_{\tau^{(j)} \sim D_{T_i}} \sum_t \left\| f_\psi \left(o_t^{(j)} \right) - a_t^{(j)} \right\|_2^2$$

10   **Return** parameters θ for rapid adaptation of new tasks through imitation

Modified from Finn, C., Abbeel, P., & Levine, S. (2017). Model-agnostic meta-learning for fast adaptation of deep networks. Retrieved from arxiv.org: https://arxiv.org/pdf/1703.03400.pdf.

The loss function in supervised learning is expressed in Eq. (4.20), while the loss function in reinforcement learning is expressed in Eq. (4.21).

$$\min_{\theta, \alpha} E_{T \sim p(T)} \left[\mathcal{L}_{test(T)}(\theta') \right] = E_{T \sim p(T)} \left[\mathcal{L}_{test(T)} \left(\theta - \alpha \circ \nabla \mathcal{L}_{train(T)}(\theta) \right) \right] \tag{4.20}$$

$$\min_{\theta, \alpha} E_{T \sim p(T)} [\mathcal{L}_T(\theta')] = E_{T \sim p(T)} [\mathcal{L}_T(\theta - \alpha \circ \nabla \mathcal{L}_T(\theta))] \tag{4.21}$$

The summary for supervised learning is outlined in Table 4.7, and Table 4.8 develops the meta-SGD reinforcement learning methods.

4.3.7 Related Algorithm 2: Feature reuse—The effectiveness of MAML

As one of the most promising meta-learning frameworks, MAML employs a bi-level optimization structure. The inner optimization (i.e., the inner loop) performs the powerful adaptation by taking the initialization from the outer optimization and producing a task-specific gradient update based on only minimal samples. The outer optimization (i.e., the outer loop or meta-update) updates the impressive meta-initialization.

Raghu, Raghu, Bengio, and Vinyals (2019) furthered the discussion of MAML, and attempted to determine the reason behind its effectiveness, investigating whether the feature reuse or the rapid learning promotes its generalization on novel tasks. They argued that feature reuse is the primary controlling component of MAML's generalization capability based on their layer-freezing experiences and latent representational analysis.

TABLE 4.7   General training methods of meta-SGD for supervised learning.

Input: $p(T)$, task distribution
       β, hyperparameter of learning rate
Output: θ, α, learnable parameter

---

1   θ, $\alpha \leftarrow$ initialization

2   **while** not meeting stopping criteria **do**
3   Randomly select a batch of tasks T_i from $p(T)$
4   **for** each T_i **do**
5   Compute $\mathcal{L}_{train(T_i)}(\boldsymbol{\theta}) \leftarrow \frac{1}{|train(T_i)|} \sum_{(x,y) \in train(T_i)} \ell(f_{\boldsymbol{\theta}}(\boldsymbol{x}), \boldsymbol{y})$

6   Obtain $\boldsymbol{\theta}_i' \leftarrow \boldsymbol{\theta} - \boldsymbol{\alpha} \circ \nabla \mathcal{L}_{train(T_i)}(\boldsymbol{\theta})$

7   Evaluate $\mathcal{L}_{test(T_i)}(\boldsymbol{\theta}_i') \leftarrow \frac{1}{|test(T_i)|} \sum_{(x,y) \in test(T_i)} \ell(f_{\theta_i'}(\boldsymbol{x}), \boldsymbol{y})$

8   **end for**
9   Obtain $(\theta, \alpha) \leftarrow (\theta, \alpha) - \beta \nabla_{(\theta, \alpha)} \sum_{T_i} \mathcal{L}_{test(T_i)}(\boldsymbol{\theta}_i')$
10   **end**

Modified from Li, Z., Zhou, F., Chen, F., & Li, H. (2017). Meta-SGD: Learning to learn quickly for few-shot learning. Retrieved from https://arxiv.org/pdf/1707.09835.pdf.

TABLE 4.8   General training methods of meta-SGD for reinforcement learning.

Input: $p(T)$, task distribution
       β, hyperparameter of learning rate
Output: θ, α, learnable parameter

---

1   θ, $\alpha \leftarrow$ initialization
2   **while** not meeting stopping criteria **do**
3   Randomly select a batch of tasks T_i from $p(T)$
4   **for** each T_i **do**
5   Randomly sample N_1 trajectories concerning f_θ
6   Evaluate policy gradient $\nabla \mathcal{L}_{T_i}(\boldsymbol{\theta})$
7   Obtain $\boldsymbol{\theta}_i' \leftarrow \boldsymbol{\theta} - \boldsymbol{\alpha} \circ \nabla \mathcal{L}_{T_i}(\boldsymbol{\theta})$
8   Randomly sample N_2 trajectories concerning $f_{\theta_i'}$
9   Evaluate policy gradient $\nabla_{(\theta, \alpha)} \mathcal{L}_{T_i}(\boldsymbol{\theta}_i')$
10   **end for**

11   Obtain $(\theta, \alpha) \leftarrow (\theta, \alpha) - \beta \nabla_{(\theta, \alpha)} \sum_{T_i} \mathcal{L}_{T_i}(\boldsymbol{\theta}_i')$
12   **End while**

Modified from Li, Z., Zhou, F., Chen, F., & Li, H. (2017). Meta-SGD: Learning to learn quickly for few-shot learning. Retrieved from https://arxiv.org/pdf/1707.09835.pdf.

In this way, a simplified version of MAML was introduced by Raghu and colleagues (2020) entitled Almost No Inner Loop (ANIL). It only preserves the inner optimization for the task-specific head of the corresponding neural networks during training and testing; this means only the final layer obtains inner loop updating, and ANIL withdraws the inner loop for all other procedures. This can be expressed as $\theta_m^{(b)} = \left(\theta_1, \dots, (\theta_l)_{m-1}^{(b)} - \alpha\nabla_{(\theta_l)_{m-1}^{(b)}} \mathcal{L}_{S_b}\left(f_{\theta_{m-1}^{(b)}}\right)\right)$. The unofficial but popular code for ANIL is available at https://github.com/learnables/learn2learn.

The ANIL is updated according to Eqs. (4.22) and (4.23), as compared to MAML updating in Eqs. (4.24) and (4.25).

$$\theta_1 \leftarrow \theta_1 - \sum_{t=1}^{N} \frac{\partial L\left(\widehat{y}\left(x_2^{(t)};\boldsymbol{\theta}_{\text{ANIL}}^{(t)}\right), y_2^{(t)}\right)}{\partial \theta_1} \tag{4.22}$$

$$\widehat{y}\left(x_2^{(t)};\boldsymbol{\theta}_{\text{ANIL}}^{(t)}\right) = \left(\left[\theta_2 - \frac{\partial L\left(\widehat{y}\left(x_1^{(t)};\boldsymbol{\theta}\right), y_1^{(t)}\right)}{\partial \theta_2}\right] \cdot \theta_1 \cdot x_2\right) \tag{4.23}$$

$$\theta_1 \leftarrow \theta_1 - \sum_{t=1}^{N} \frac{\partial L\left(\widehat{y}\left(x_2^{(t)};\boldsymbol{\theta}_{\text{MAML}}^{(t)}\right), y_2^{(t)}\right)}{\partial \theta_1} \tag{4.24}$$

$$\widehat{y}\left(x_2^{(t)};\boldsymbol{\theta}_{\text{MAML}}^{(t)}\right) = \left(\left[\theta_2 - \frac{\partial L\left(\widehat{y}\left(x_1^{(t)};\boldsymbol{\theta}\right), y_1^{(t)}\right)}{\partial \theta_2}\right] \cdot \left[\theta_1 - \frac{\partial L\left(\widehat{y}\left(x_1^{(t)};\boldsymbol{\theta}\right), y_1^{(t)}\right)}{\partial \theta_1}\right] \cdot x_2\right) \tag{4.25}$$

This approach is assessed on various tasks, including few-shot multiclass classification, multitask learning, and others, on datasets Omniglot and MiniImageNet. The performances show similar results between MAML and ANIL, and removing the inner optimization does not hurt the performance.

4.3.8 Related Algorithm 3: Adaptive hyperparameter generation for fast adaptation

Although MAML has become popular as one of the most successful learning approaches, its efficiency is questionable, as the training and testing tasks vary. Related Algorithm 3 offers adaptive learning of the hyperparameters for fast adaptation to tackle this issue.

MAML is a widely used optimization-based framework with remarkable benefits in both impressed compatibility on top of gradient-based paradigms and rapid adaptation (i.e., inner-optimization or inner loop) with optimal initialization for new tasks. It aims to leverage the prior knowledge of sample tasks as the shared initial weight θ across multiple tasks in the neural network f_θ to lead to an optimal initialization for fast adaptation. The weights update during inner-optimization as $\theta_{i,j+1} = \theta_{i,j} - \alpha\nabla_\theta\mathcal{L}_{T_i}^{D_i}\left(f_{\theta_{i,j}}\right)$ for sample task T_i with examples D_i, where $\mathcal{L}_{T_i}^{D_i}$ denotes the loss function. The outer-optimization updating rule is expressed as $\theta \leftarrow \theta - \eta\nabla_\theta\sum_{T_i}\mathcal{L}_{T_i}^{D_i'}\left(f_{\theta_{i,j}}\right)$.

However, current research has cast doubt on the effectiveness of MAML's initialization, particularly for tasks that are dissimilar between training and testing tasks. Many developments offer improvements on the fast adaptation in MAML. Baik, Choi, Choi, Kim, and Lee (2020) proposed an adaptive hyperparameters paradigm to improve inner-loop optimization. This proposed method regulates the adaptation procedure via a learned updating rule. It generates two hyperparameters—weight decay coefficients and learning rates—based on the gradient values and weights of the base learners, specifically to every updating step and task. This proposed method is called Adaptive Learning of Hyperparameters for Fast Adaptation (ALFA), which was mainly designed for meta-learning practices, allowing fast adaptation based on random initialization. The official code is available at https://github.com/baiksung/ALFA.

The ℓ_2 regularization is added to the loss function $\mathcal{L}_{T_i}$ in adaptive learning of hyperparameters for fast adaptation. The inner-loop updating rule is expressed in Eq. (4.26):

$$
\begin{aligned}
\theta_{i,j+1} &= \theta_{i,j} - \alpha \left(\nabla_\theta \mathcal{L}_{T_i}^{D_i} \left(f_{\theta_{i,j}} \right) + \lambda \theta_{i,j} \right) \\
&= \beta \theta_{i,j} - \alpha \nabla_\theta \mathcal{L}_{T_i}^{D_i} \left(f_{\theta_{i,j}} \right)
\end{aligned}
\tag{4.26}
$$

Learnable parameters $\alpha_{i,j}$ and $\beta_{i,j}$ replace the predefined hyperparameters as learning rate and weight decay coefficients. The final inner-loop equation is indicated in Eq. (4.27):

$$
\theta_{i,j+1} = \beta_{i,j} \odot \theta_{i,j} - \alpha_{i,j} \odot \nabla_\theta \mathcal{L}_{T_i}^{D_i} \left(f_{\theta_{i,j}} \right)
\tag{4.27}
$$

The outer-loop optimization with new examples D_i' and task-adapted weights θ_i' is shown in Eq. (4.28):

$$
\phi \leftarrow \phi - \eta \nabla_\phi \sum_{T_i} \mathcal{L}_{T_i}^{D_i'} \left(f_{\theta_i'} \right)
\tag{4.28}
$$

Table 4.9 summarizes the methods of ALFA.

This proposed paradigm is evaluated in cases of (1) 5-way and 20-way classification; (2) 5-way 5-shot cross-domain classification; and (3) 5-shot, 10-shot, and 20-shot regression in multiple public datasets, including miniImageNet and tieredImageNet from ILSVRC-12 and CUB (Wah, Branson, Perona, & Belongie, 2011).

4.4 Reptile

4.4.1 Background knowledge

First-order model-agnostic meta-learning

The MAML, discussed in Section 4.3, heavily depends on second-order derivatives, which cause colossal computing complexity. FOMAML, an approximation of MAML that ignores the second-order derivatives, is introduced as a simplified modification to reduce expensive computation.

It starts by rewriting the update rule indicated in Eqs. (4.29)–(4.31).

TABLE 4.9 General training methods of adaptive learning of hyperparameters for fast adaptation.

Require: $p(\mathcal{T})$, task distribution
$\quad\quad$ η, hyperparameter of learning rate
$\quad\quad$ θ, arbitrary given initialization

1: $\quad$ ϕ random initialization

2: $\quad$ **while** not meeting stopping criteria **do**
3: $\quad\quad$ Randomly select a batch of tasks $\mathcal{T}_i$ from $p(\mathcal{T})$

4: $\quad\quad$ **for** each $\mathcal{T}_i$ **do**
5: $\quad\quad\quad$ $\theta_{i,0} = \theta$
6: $\quad\quad\quad$ Randomly sample disjoint examples $(\mathcal{D}_i, \mathcal{D}_i')$ from $\mathcal{T}_i$
7: $\quad\quad\quad$ **for** inner-loop step $j:0, \ldots, S-1$ **do**
8: $\quad\quad\quad\quad$ Obtain loss $\mathcal{L}_{\mathcal{T}_i}^{\mathcal{D}_i}\left(f_{\theta_{i,j}}\right)$ using $\mathcal{L}_{\mathcal{T}_i}$ w.r.t. $\mathcal{D}_i$
9: $\quad\quad\quad\quad$ Evaluate task-specific learning state $\tau_{i,j} = \left[\nabla_\theta \mathcal{L}_{\mathcal{T}_i}^{\mathcal{D}_i}\left(f_{\theta_{i,j}}\right), \theta_{i,j}\right]$
10: $\quad\quad\quad\quad$ Obtain hyperparameters $(\boldsymbol{\alpha}_{i,j}, \boldsymbol{\beta}_{i,j}) = g_\phi(\tau_{i,j})$
11: $\quad\quad\quad\quad$ Conduct gradient descent for adapted weights:

$$\theta_{i,j+1} = \beta_{i,j} \odot \theta_{i,j} - \alpha_{i,j} \odot \nabla_\theta \mathcal{L}_{\mathcal{T}_i}^{\mathcal{D}_i}\left(f_{\theta_{i,j}}\right)$$

12: $\quad\quad\quad$ **end for**
13: $\quad\quad\quad$ Evaluate $\mathcal{L}_{\mathcal{T}_i'}'\left(f_{\theta_i'}\right)$ through $\mathcal{L}_{\mathcal{T}_i}$ w.r.t. $\mathcal{D}_i'$ and task-adapted weights $\theta_i' = \theta_{i,S}$
14: $\quad\quad$ **end for**
15: $\quad\quad$ Conduct gradient descent for weights updating: $\phi \leftarrow \phi - \eta \nabla_\phi \sum_{\mathcal{T}_i} \mathcal{L}_{\mathcal{T}_i}'\left(f_{\theta_i'}\right)$
16: **end while**

Modified from Baik, S., Choi, M., Choi, J., Kim, H., & Lee, K. M. (2020). Meta-learning with adaptive hyperparameters. Advances in Neural Information Processing Systems, 33, 20755–20765.

$$\theta \leftarrow \theta - \beta \nabla_\theta \sum_{\mathcal{T}_i \sim p(\mathcal{T})} \mathcal{L}_{\mathcal{T}_i}\left(f_{\theta_i'}\right) \tag{4.29}$$

to:

$$\theta \leftarrow \theta - \beta g_{MAML} \tag{4.30}$$

where:

$$
\begin{aligned}
g_{MAML} &= \nabla_\theta \mathcal{L}'(\theta_k) \\
&= \nabla_{\theta_k} \mathcal{L}'(\theta_k) \cdot \left(\prod_{i=1}^{k} \nabla_{\theta_{i-1}} \theta_i\right) \cdot I \\
&= \nabla_{\theta_k} \mathcal{L}'(\theta_k) \cdot \prod_{i=1}^{k} \nabla_{\theta_{i-1}}(\theta_{i-1} - \alpha \nabla_\theta \mathcal{L}(\theta_{i-1})) \\
&= \nabla_{\theta_k} \mathcal{L}'(\theta_k) \cdot \prod_{i=1}^{k} (I - \alpha \nabla_{\theta_{i-1}}(\nabla_\theta \mathcal{L}(\theta_{i-1})))
\end{aligned}
\tag{4.31}
$$

It disregards the second-order derivative and only focuses on the first-order derivative, expressed in Eq. (4.32). It is finally equivalent to Eq. (4.33).

I. Theory & mechanisms

$$gMAML = \nabla_{\theta_k} \mathcal{L}'(\theta_k) \prod_{i=1}^{k} (I - \alpha) \tag{4.32}$$

$$gFOMAML = \nabla_{\theta_k} \mathcal{L}'(\theta_k) \tag{4.33}$$

4.4.2 Methodology

Nichol et al. (2018)[a], inspired by joint training (Bourlard, Konig, & Morgan, 1995; Morin & Bengio, 2005; Ning et al., 2005) and FOMAML, proposed Reptile, a first-order gradient-based MAML method. Reptile focuses on minimizing expectation loss function and maximizing generalization ability within each task. Like MAML, Reptile works quickly by fine-tuning through gradient descent. Differing from standard MAML, Reptile does not need training via testing data cross-validation (Allen, 1974) for each task.

Reptile depends on a second-order derivative rather than the first-order derivative. It performed an excellent benchmark in MiniImageNet (Vinyals, Blundell, Lillicrap, Kavukcuoglu, & Wierstra, 2016) and Omniglot (Lake, Salakhutdinov, & Tenenbaum, 2015) dataset. The official code is available at https://github.com/openai/supervised-reptile.

Reptile defined $\left(\widetilde{\phi}_i - \phi\right)/\alpha$ as its gradient for ith task $\mathcal{T}_i$, where α is the step size in SGD. An optimizer other than SGD is also workable.

In short, Reptile repeatedly iterates by the following (in both serial version and batch version):

- Randomly sampling a task from tasks pool
- Training on the selected task by multiple-step gradient descent through an optimizer
- Adjusting the weights toward the new parameters

4.4.2.1 Serial version

The exhaustive serial version of Reptile with SGD or Adam as the optimizer is introduced in Table 4.10; another optimization could substitute as well. The parameter vector of a model is shown as ϕ with a task τ, and $SGD(\mathcal{L}, \phi, k)$ denotes the function that executed k steps of gradient descent on loss function $\mathcal{L}$ starting with vector ϕ. The direction of $W - \phi$ is the direction of gradient descent.

4.4.2.2 Parallel or batch version

The latest optimal batch version of Reptile is similar to the SimuParallelSGD (Nichol et al., 2018; Zinkevich, Weimer, Li, & Smola, 2010), a communication-efficient distributional

---

[a] Two versions of this paper are both trackable in arXiv.org: the previous version (Reptile: a Scalable Meta-Learning Algorithm published in March 2018) and the latest one (On First-Order Meta-Learning Algorithms in October 2018). The material is slightly different. The earlier one has more precise algorithm explanations, whereas the latter focuses on more comprehensive analyses and experiments.

TABLE 4.10 General training methods of Reptile algorithm (serial version).

Input: $\mathcal{T}$, sample task
$\quad\quad\epsilon$, hyperparameter of step size
Output: ϕ, updated gradient descent

1 $\phi\rightarrow$ initialization
2 **for** each iteration **do**
3 $\quad$ Randomly select a task $\mathcal{T}$, concerning loss $\mathcal{L}_\mathcal{T}$ on weight vectors W
4 $\quad$ Perform multiple gradient descent step k using $W = SGD(\mathcal{L}_\mathcal{T},\phi,k)$
5 $\quad$ Update gradient descent using $\phi\leftarrow\phi+\epsilon(W-\phi)$
6 **end for**
7 return ϕ

Modified from Nichol, A., Achiam, J., & Schulman, J. (2018). On first-order meta-learning algorithms. Retrieved from arxiv.org: https://arxiv.org/pdf/1803.02999.pdf.

approach to updating gradient locally. It maintains high latency tolerance, a MapReduce framework (Dean & Ghemawat, 2004), and linearity scalability in a large-scale learning paradigm.

The update rule on the ith task of parallel or batch version is expressed in Eq. (4.34), which accesses n tasks each iteration and adjusts the initialization as follows:

$$\phi \leftarrow \phi + \epsilon\frac{1}{n}\sum_{i=1}^{n}\left(\widetilde{\phi}_i - \phi\right), \text{ where } \widetilde{\phi}_i = U_{\mathcal{T}_i}^k(\phi) \tag{4.34}$$

In contrast, an early-stage batch version was published on the first version of the Reptile paper (Nichol & Schulman, 2018), as outlined in Table 4.11.

TABLE 4.11 General training methods of Reptile algorithm (batch version).

Input: n, number of sample tasks
$\quad\quad\epsilon$, hyperparameter of step size
Output: ϕ, updated gradient descent

1 $\phi\rightarrow$ initialization
2 **for** iteration $= 1, 2, \ldots$ **do**
3 $\quad$ Randomly sample a task $\mathcal{T}_1, \mathcal{T}_2, \ldots, \mathcal{T}_n$
4 $\quad$ **for** $i = 1, 2, \ldots, n$ **do**
5 $\quad\quad$ Evaluate loss function $\mathcal{L}_{\mathcal{T}_i}$ of multiple k steps using $W_i = SGD(\mathcal{L}_{\mathcal{T}_i}, k, \phi)$
6 $\quad$ **end for**
7 $\quad$ Update gradient descent using $\phi \leftarrow \phi + \epsilon\frac{1}{k}\sum_{i=1}^{n}(W_i - \phi)$
8 $\quad$ **end for**
9 return ϕ

Modified from Nichol, A., & Schulman, J. (2018a). Reptile: A scalable metalearning algorithm. Retrieved from Arxiv: https://arxiv.org/pdf/1803.02999v1.pdf, version 1.

The optimization assumption

This assumes that the single point Reptile converges to is close enough to each task T_i's optimal solution, measured in Euclidean distance.

The goal is to minimize the Euclidean distance $D(\phi, W_T^*)$ between W_T^* and ϕ, where W_T^* presents the set of optimal weights of task T computed by neural networks, and ϕ is the network initialization, as expressed in Eqs. (4.35) to (4.37):

$$\min_{\phi} \mathbb{E}_T \left[\frac{1}{2} D(\phi, W_T^*)^2 \right] \tag{4.35}$$

$$\nabla_{\phi} \mathbb{E}_T \left[\frac{1}{2} D(\phi, W_T^*)^2 \right] = \mathbb{E}_T \left[\frac{1}{2} \nabla_{\phi} D(\phi, W_T^*)^2 \right]$$
$$= \mathbb{E}_T \left[\phi - W_T^* \right] \tag{4.36}$$

$$\text{where } W_T^*(\phi) = \underset{W \in W_T^*}{\text{argmin}} D(W, \phi) \tag{4.37}$$

Each iteration of Reptile will sample a task T and execute SGD, as expressed in Eq. (4.38). In the last step, SGD replaces W_T^* due to the approximation of W_T^* in Reptile, where ϵ is the hyperparameter of step size.

$$\phi \leftarrow \phi - \epsilon \nabla_{\phi} \frac{1}{2} D(\phi, W^*)^2$$
$$= \phi - \epsilon(\phi - W_T^*(\phi))$$
$$= (1 - \epsilon)\phi + \epsilon W_T^*(\phi) \tag{4.38}$$
$$\sim (1 - \epsilon)\phi + \epsilon SGD(\mathcal{L}_{T_i}, k, \phi) \text{ (for Reptile)}$$

Analysis

When the gradient from a different mini-batch produces a positive inner product, taking a gradient step on one mini-batch also improves the performance of another mini-batch. Taylor series expansion (Taylor, 1715) is used to approximate the update executed by MAML and Reptile, as expressed in Eq. (4.39), where Taylor approximation is only appropriate for a small αk (α is denoted as step size and k as the number of iterations). The operator U_i corresponds to updating parameters on minibatch i, which is denoted as $U_i(\phi) = \phi - \alpha \mathcal{L}_i'(\phi)$ and $U_i'(\phi) = I - \alpha \mathcal{L}_i''(\phi)$.

$$gMAML = \frac{\partial}{\partial \phi_1} \mathcal{L}_k(\phi_k)$$
$$= U_1'(\phi_1)...U_{k-1}'(\phi_{k-1})\mathcal{L}_k(\phi_k) \tag{4.39}$$
$$= \left(\prod_{j=1}^{k-1} \left(I - \alpha \mathcal{L}_j''(\phi_j)\right) \right) g_k$$

The more general cases ($k \geq 2$) of multiple-step gradient descent through the Taylor series expansion of MAML, FOMAML, and Reptile, and the relationships among them are expressed in Eqs. (4.40)–(4.42). $g_i = \mathcal{L}_i'(\phi_i)$ as gradient obtained during SGD, $\phi_{i+1} = \phi_i - \alpha g_i$

as the sequence of parameter vectors, $\bar{g}_i = \mathcal{L}'_i(\phi_1)$ as gradient at the initial point, and $\overline{H}_i = \mathcal{L}''_i(\phi_1)$ as Hessian at the initial point.

$$gFOMAML = \bar{g}_k - \alpha \overline{H}_k \sum_{j=1}^{k-1} \bar{g}_j + O(\alpha^2) \tag{4.40}$$

$$gMAML = \bar{g}_k - \alpha \overline{H}_k \sum_{j=1}^{k-1} \bar{g}_j + O(\alpha^2) - \alpha \sum_{j=1}^{k-1} \overline{H}_j \bar{g}_k = gFOMAML - \alpha \sum_{j=1}^{k-1} \overline{H}_j \bar{g}_k \tag{4.41}$$

$$gReptile = \sum_{i=1}^{k} \bar{g}_i - \alpha \sum_{i=1}^{k} \sum_{j=1}^{i-1} \overline{H}_i \bar{g}_j + O(\alpha^2) = \sum_{i=1}^{k-1} \bar{g}_i - \alpha \sum_{i=1}^{k-1} \sum_{j=1}^{i-1} \overline{H}_i \bar{g}_j + gFOMAML \tag{4.42}$$

There are only two terms in the expectation of *gMAML*, *gFOMAML*, and *gReptile*: AvgGradInner and AvgGrad. AvgGrad is defined as the gradient of expected loss, as expressed in Eq. (4.43):

$$AvgGrad = \mathbb{E}_{T,1}\left[\bar{g}_1\right] \tag{4.43}$$

AvgGradInner is demonstrated in Eq. (4.44), where the direction of negative AvgGradInner (i.e., – AvgGradInner) indicates the direction to minimize the "joint training" problem—the direction to expand the inner product between two gradients of different minibatches and boost generalization.

$$\begin{aligned} AvgGradInner &= \mathbb{E}_{T,1,2}\left[\overline{H}_2 \bar{g}_1\right] \\ &= \mathbb{E}_{T,1,2}\left[\overline{H}_1 \bar{g}_2\right] \\ &= \frac{1}{2}\mathbb{E}_{T,1,2}\left[\overline{H}_2 \bar{g}_1 + \overline{H}_1 \bar{g}_2\right] \\ &= \frac{1}{2}\mathbb{E}_{T,1,2}\left[\frac{\partial}{\partial \phi_1}\left(\bar{g}_1 \cdot \bar{g}_2\right)\right] \end{aligned} \tag{4.44}$$

Overall, in the multistep gradient cases ($k \geq 2$), the meta-gradients of MAML, FOMAML, and Reptile are described in Eqs. (4.45)–(4.47). Among these three algorithms, the gradient operations determine the minimum of expected loss for tasks through the term *AvgGrad*; hence, fast adaptation is executed through the high-order of *AvgGradInner*.

$$\mathbb{E}[gMAML] = (1)AvgGrad - (2(k-1)\alpha)AvgGradInner \tag{4.45}$$

$$\mathbb{E}[gFOMAML] = (1)AvgGrad - ((k-1)\alpha)AvgGradInner \tag{4.46}$$

$$\mathbb{E}[gReptile] = (k)AvgGrad - \left(\frac{1}{2}k(k-1)\alpha\right)AvgGradInner \tag{4.47}$$

4.4.3 Related Algorithm 1

Li et al. (2020) proposed a framework in visual navigation for tackling interchangeable meta-skills that relied on unannotated environments without support from supervisory

TABLE 4.12   General training methods for unsupervised reinforcement learning of transferable meta-skills.

1   $\theta, \phi, \mu \leftarrow$ random initialization
2   Let $\Pi \leftarrow [\,]$
3   **while** not converged **do**
4   Let $s_o \leftarrow e_i.\ start\_state$
5   Gather rollout $\tau_i^G(s_o, s_1, ..., s_T)$ through π_μ^G
6   Let $s^* \leftarrow s_T$
7   Let $o^* \leftarrow o_T$
8   Set task $\tau_i = SetTask\ (s_o, s^*, o^*)$
9   # **warmup period**
10   **for** $w = 0, 1, ..., W$ **do**
11   Gather rollout τ_i^w through $\tau_{\phi_i,\theta}^M$
12   Update $\phi_i \leftarrow \phi_i + \alpha \nabla_\phi J(\tau_i^w, \tau_{\phi_i,\theta}^M)$
13   **end for**
14   Let $\tilde{\theta} = \theta$
15   # **joint update period**
16   **for** j $= 0,1,..., J$ **do**
17   Gather rollout τ_i^j through $\tau_{\phi_i,\tilde{\theta}}^M$
18   Update $\phi_i \leftarrow \phi_i + \alpha \nabla_\phi J\left(\tau_i^j, \tau_{\phi_i,\tilde{\theta}}^M\right)$
19   Update $\tilde{\theta} \leftarrow \tilde{\theta} + \alpha \nabla_\phi J\left(\tau_i^j, \tau_{\phi_i,\tilde{\theta}}^M\right)$
20   **end for**
21   $\theta \leftarrow \theta + \beta\left(\tilde{\theta} - \theta\right)$
22   Compute R_G using $R_G = k*(1-r) - \lambda*n + \eta*\sum_{s_t \in \tau}\sum_{\pi' \in \Pi} D_{KL}\left(\pi'(\bullet|s_t)\,\big\|\,\pi(\bullet|s_t)\right)$ and update π_μ^G
23   If $len(\Pi) == 4$ **then**
24           $\Pi.\ pop(0)$
25   **end if**
26       $\Pi.\ append(\mu)$
27   **end while**

Modified from Li, J., Wang, X., Tang, S., Shi, H., Wu, F., Zhuang, Y., et al. (2020). Unsupervised reinforcement learning of transferable meta-skills for embodied navigation. In CVPR.

guidance. It is named unsupervised reinforcement learning of transferable meta-skills (ULTRA). Rather than updating all parameters in Reptile, ULTRA adjusts only the subpolicy parameters and fixes them in testing. It applies Reptile by updating hierarchical policy in the meta-learner in the warm-up phase for fine-tuning the main policy. Table 4.12 summarizes the pseudocode.

4.4.4 Related Algorithm 2

Goldblum et al. (2020) proposed a weight-clustering regularized Reptile format to improve the regular training procedure of few-shot classification by helping find local minima. This optimizer penalizes the squared ℓ_2 distance from current task parameters to the average of the parameters across all the tasks in the current batch. It is formulated as Eq. (4.48):

$$R_i\left(\left\{\widetilde{\theta}_p\right\}_{p=1}^{m}\right) = d\left(\widetilde{\theta}_i, \frac{1}{m}\sum_{p=1}^{m}\widetilde{\theta}_p\right)^2 \tag{4.48}$$

where the network parameter is $\widetilde{\theta}_p$ on task p and the filter-normalized ℓ_2 is d. See the comprehensive algorithm in Table 4.13.

4.4.5 Related Algorithm 3

Tian, Liu, Yuan, and Liu (2020) introduced a cardinality-constrained meta-learning strategy based on Reptile with network pruning through Dense-Sparse-Dense (DSD; Han et al., 2016) and Iterative Hard Thresholding (IHT; Jin, Yuan, Feng, & Yan, 2016). This research demonstrated that the sparse meta-learner's generalization gap bounds hold polynomial reliance on the sparsity level instead of the number of parameters. It aims to control the overparameterized neural network. See detailed methods in Table 4.14.

TABLE 4.13 General training methods of Retile with weight-clustering regularization.

Input: θ, initial parameter
  γ, learning rate in the outer loop
  η, learning rate in the inner loop
  α, regularization coefficient
  $p(T)$, distribution over tasks

1 **for** meta-step $= 1, ..., $n **do**
2   Randomly sample batch of tasks, $\{T_i\}_{i=1}^{m} \sim p(T)$
3   Initialize $\widetilde{\theta}_i^0 = \theta$ for each task

4   **for** j $= 1, ...,$k **do**
5   **for** I $= 1, ..., $m **do**
6   Compute $\mathcal{L} = \mathcal{L}_{T_i}^{j} + \alpha R_i\left(\left\{\widetilde{\theta}_p^{j-1}\right\}_{p=1}^{m}\right)$

7   Update $\widetilde{\theta}_p^{j} = \widetilde{\theta}_p^{j-1} - \eta\nabla_{\widetilde{\theta}_i}\mathcal{L}$
8   **end for**

9   **end for**
10   Evaluate difference vectors $\left\{g_i = \widetilde{\theta}_i^k - \widetilde{\theta}_i^0\right\}_{i=1}^{m}$
11   Update $\theta \leftarrow \theta - \frac{\gamma}{m}\sum_i g_i$
12 **end for**

Modified from Goldblum, M., Reich, S., Fowl, L., Ni, R., Cherepanova, V., & Goldstein, T. (2020). Unraveling meta-learning: Understanding feature representations for few-shot tasks. In ICML.

TABLE 4.14   General training methods of Reptile with iterative network pruning.

Input: η, hyperparameter of learning rate in the inner loop
β, hyperparameter of learning rate in the outer loop
$\{k_l\}_{l=1}^L$, layer-wise sparsity level
s, size of a mini-batch
Output: $\theta^{(t)}$, learnable parameter

1 $\theta^{(0)} \leftarrow$ random initialization
   # pre-training using Reptile
2 **while** not done **do**
3   Let $\theta^{(0)} = Reptile\,(\theta^{(0)}, \eta, \beta, s)$
4 **end while**

5 **for** each t **do**

       # prune conducting phase
6   Produce a network mask $\mathcal{M}^{(t)}$ (zero-one) where each layer l
       has nonzero entries (i.e., top k_l entries of $\theta_l^{(t)}$)
7   Evaluate $\theta_{\mathcal{M}}^{(t)} = \theta^{(t)} \odot \mathcal{M}^{(t)}$

       # subnetwork fine-tune using Reptile
8   **while** not done **do**
9   Let $\theta^{(t)} = Reptile\left(\theta_{\mathcal{M}}^{(t)}, \eta, \beta, s\right)$
10   **end while**

       # retraining phase
11   **while** not done **do**
12   Let $\theta^{(t)} = Reptile\,(\theta^{(t)}, \eta, \beta, s)$
13   **end while**
14 **end for**

Modified from Tian, H., Liu, B., Yuan, X.-T., & Liu, Q. (2020). Meta-learning with network pruning. In ECCV.

4.4.6 Related Algorithm 4

Zügner and Günnemann (2019) used meta-learning in a learning efficiency study. This work investigated training-time attacks on GNN and attempted to solve the bilevel optimization problem of poisoning attacks via meta-gradients by setting the graph structure matrix as a hyperparameter. This approach trains meta-gradients in an opposite way: to worsen the generalization after training. Reptile as a heuristic intuition of meta-gradient is employed in this adversarial attack approach.

The posttraining gradient of the attacker's loss is expressed in Eq. (4.49), where $\mathcal{L}_{atk}$ presents the attacker loss, $\mathcal{L}_{train}$ is the training loss, *opt* means the differentiable optimization, and G stands for GNN:

$$\nabla_G^{meta} := \nabla_G \mathcal{L}_{atk}\left(f_{\theta^*}(G)\right),\ s.t.\theta^* = opt_\theta\left(\mathcal{L}_{train}\left(f_\theta(G)\right)\right) \tag{4.49}$$

The combined approximation of the meta-gradient in Eq. (4.50), where A denotes the adjacency matrix, and θ_T presents parameters at local optimum:

$$\nabla_A^{meta} := \nabla_A \mathcal{L}_{atk}\left(f_{\theta_T}(A)\right) \approx \nabla_A \mathcal{L}_{atk}\left(f_{\tilde{\theta}_T}(A)\right) = \nabla_f \mathcal{L}_{atk}\left(f_{\tilde{\theta}_T}(A)\right) \times \nabla_A f_{\tilde{\theta}_T}(A) \tag{4.50}$$

4.5 Summary

Compared to other categories of meta-learning approaches, optimization-based meta-learners are more generic and scalable to implement at a practical level, and the gradient-based algorithms are model-agnostic to any differentiable neural network. MAML uses backpropagation to compute meta-loss through the inner loop. In contrast, Reptile reduces computing complexity through Hessian to adjust the meta-parameters as multistep stochastic gradient descent updates. The LSTM meta-learner constructs an exact optimization algorithm for learning another neural network in a few-shot classification. MAML, FOMAML, Reptile, and their variations characterize gradient-based meta-learning and are essential in diverse areas, particularly computer vision and reinforcement learning.

References

Allen, D. M. (1974). The relationship between variable selection and data agumentation and a method for prediction. *Technometrics, 16*(1), 125–127.

Andrychowicz, M., Denil, M., Gomez, S., Hoffman, M. W., Pfau, D., Schaul, T., & Freitas, N. (2016). *Learning to learn by gradient descent by gradient descent*. Retrieved from CoRR http://arxiv.org/abs/1606.04474.

Baik, S., Choi, M., Choi, J., Kim, H., & Lee, K. M. (2020). Meta-learning with adaptive hyperparameters. *Advances in Neural Information Processing Systems, 33*, 20755–20765.

Banach, S. (1931). Über die Baire'sche Kategorie gewisser Funktionenmengen. *Studia Mathematica, 1*(3), 174–179.

Bengio, Y. (2011). Deep learning of representations for unsupervised and transfer learning. In *JMLR W&CP: Proc. unsupervised and transfer learning*.

Bengio, Y., Bastien, F., Bergeron, A., Boulanger-Lewandowski, N., Breuel, T., Chherawala, Y., ... Sicard, G. (2011). Deep learners benefit more from out-of-distribution examples. In *JMLR W&CP: Proc. AISTATS'2011*.

Bourlard, H., Konig, Y., & Morgan, N. (1995). Remap: Recursive estimation and maximization of a posteriori probabilities in connectionist speech recognition. In *EUROSPEECH*.

Caruana, R. (1995). *Learning many related tasks at the same time with backpropagation* (pp. 657–664). MIT Press.

Chevalier, G. (2018). *LARNN: Linear attention recurrent neural network. arXiv.org*. Retrieved June 27, 2022, from https://arxiv.org/abs/1808.05578.

Cho, K., Bahdanau, D., Bougares, F., Schwenk, H., & Bengio, Y. (2014). *Learning phrase representations using RNN encoder–decoder for statistical machine translation*. Retrieved from https://arxiv.org/pdf/1406.1078v3.pdf.

Dean, J., & Ghemawat, S. (2004). *MapReduce: Simplified data processing on large clusters*. Retrieved from research.google http://static.googleusercontent.com/media/research.google.com/es/us/archive/mapreduce-osdi04.pdf.

Dou, Z.-Y., Yu, K., & Anastasopoulos, A. (2019). Investigating meta-learning algorithms for low-resource natural language understanding tasks. In *ACL*.

Duchi, J., Hazan, E., & Singer, Y. (2011). Adaptive subgradient methods for online learning and stochastic optimization. *Journal of Machine Learning Research, 12*, 2121–2159. ISSN 1532-4435. Retrieved from http://dl.acm.org/citation.cfm?id=1953048.2021068.

Finn, C. B. (2018). *Learning to learn with gradients*. Retrieved from https://ai.stanford.edu/~cbfinn/_files/dissertation.pdf.

Finn, C., Abbeel, P., & Levine, S. (2017). *Model-agnostic meta-learning for fast adaptation of deep networks*. Retrieved from arxiv.org https://arxiv.org/pdf/1703.03400.pdf.

Gers, F. A., & Schmidhuber, E. (2001). LSTM recurrent networks learn simple context-free and context-sensitive languages. *IEEE Transactions on Neural Networks, 12*(6), 1333–1340.

Gers, F. A., Schmidhuber, J., & Cummins, F. (2000). Learning to forget: Continual prediction with LSTM. *Neural Computation, 12*(10), 2451–2471.

Glen, S. (2021). *Covariate definition in statistics*. Retrieved from StatisticsHowTo.com: Elementary Statistics for the rest of us! https://www.statisticshowto.com/covariate/.

Goldblum, M., Reich, S., Fowl, L., Ni, R., Cherepanova, V., & Goldstein, T. (2020). Unraveling meta-learning: Understanding feature representations for few-shot tasks. In *ICML*.

Goodfellow, I., Bengio, Y., & Courville, A. (2016). *Deep learning*. MIT Press.

Greff, K., Srivastava, R. K., Koutník, J., Steunebrink, B. R., & Schmidhuber, J. (2015). *LSTM: A search space odyssey*. Retrieved from arXiv.org.

Guo, D., Tang, D., Duan, N., Zhou, M., & Yin, J. (2019). Coupling retrieval and meta-learning for context-dependent semantic parsing. In *ACL*.

Han, S., Pool, J., Narang, S., Mao, H., Gong, E., Tang, S., … Tran, J. (2016). Dense-sparse-dense training for deep neural networks. In *International conference on learning representations*.

Hinton, G. (2013). *Lecture 6e rmsprop: Divide the gradient by a running average of its recent magnitude*. Retrieved from https://www.cs.toronto.edu/~hinton/coursera/lecture6/lec6.pdf.

Hochreiter, S. (1991). *Untersuchungen zu dynamischen neuronalen Netzen (diploma thesis)*. Technical University Munich, Institute of Computer Science.

Huang, P.-S., Wang, C., Singh, R., Yih, W.-T., & He, X. (2018). Natural language to structured query generation via meta-learning. In *ACL*.

Hussein, A., Gaber, M. M., Elyan, E., & Jayne, C. (2016). Imitation learning: A survey of learning methods. *ACM Computing Surveys (CSUR)*, *50*(2), 1–35.

Ioffe, S., & Szegedy, C. (2015). *Batch normalization: Accelerating deep network training by reducing internal covariate shift*. Retrieved from CoRR http://arxiv.org/ abs/1502.03167.

Jin, X., Yuan, X., Feng, J., & Yan, S. (2016). *Training skinny deep neural networks with iterative hard thresholding methods*. Retrieved from arXiv: arXiv:1607.05423.

Jozefowicz, R., Zaremba, W., & Sutskever, I. (2015). An empirical exploration of recurrent network architectures. In *International conference on machine learning* (pp. 2342–2350). PMLR. http://proceedings.mlr.press/v37/jozefowicz15.pdf.

Jung, I., You, K., Noh, H., Cho, M., & Han, B. (2020). Real-time object tracking via meta-learning: Efficient model adaptation and one-shot channel pruning. In *AAAI*.

Kingma, D. P., & Ba, J. (2014). *Adam: A method for stochastic optimization*. Retrieved from CoRR, abs/1412.6980 http://arxiv.org/abs/1412.6980.

Krizhevsky, A. (2009). *Learning multiple layers of features from tiny images*. Technical report.

Lake, B. M., Salakhutdinov, R., & Tenenbaum, J. B. (2015). Human-level concept learning through probabilistic program induction. *Science*, *350*(6266), 1332–1338. Retrieved from https://github.com/brendenlake/omniglot/.

LeCun, Y., Bottou, L., Orr, G., & Muller, K. (1998). Efficient backprop. In G. Orr, & K.-R. Müller (Eds.), *Neural networks: Tricks of the trade* Springer.

Lemaréchal, C. (2012). Cauchy and the gradient method. *Doc Math Extra*, 251–254.

Li, J., Wang, X., Tang, S., Shi, H., Wu, F., Zhuang, Y., & Wang, W. Y. (2020). Unsupervised reinforcement learning of transferable meta-skills for embodied navigation. In *CVPR*.

Li, Z., Zhou, F., Chen, F., & Li, H. (2017). *Meta-SGD: Learning to learn quickly for few-shot learning*. Retrieved from https://arxiv.org/pdf/1707.09835.pdf.

Morin, F., & Bengio, Y. (2005). Hierarchical probabilistic neuralnet work language model. In *Proceedingsofthe tenth international workshop on artificial intelligence and statistics*.

Nesterov, Y. E. (1983). A method for solving the convex programming problem with convergence rate O $(1/k^2)$. *Dokl. Akad. Nauk SSSR*, *269*, 543–547.

Nichol, A., Achiam, J., & Schulman, J. (2018). *On first-order meta-learning algorithms*. Retrieved from arxiv.org https://arxiv.org/pdf/1803.02999.pdf.

Nichol, A., & Schulman, J. (2018). *Reptile: A scalable metalearning algorithm*. Retrieved from Arxiv https://arxiv.org/pdf/1803.02999v1.pdf.

Ning, F., Delhomme, D., LeCun, Y., Piano, F., Bottou, L., & Barbano, P. E. (2005). *Toward automatic phenotyping of developing embryos from videos*. Retrieved from IEEE https://ieeexplore.ieee.org/abstract/document/1495508.

Obamuyide, A., & Vlachos, A. (2019). Model-agnostic meta-learning for relation classification with limited supervision. In *ACL*.

Raghu, A., Raghu, M., Bengio, S., & Vinyals, O. (2019). Rapid learning or feature reuse? Towards understanding the effectiveness of MAML. *arXiv preprint*, arXiv:1909.09157.

Ravi, S., & Larochelle, H. (2017). *Optimization as a model for few-shot learning.* Retrieved from ICRL https://openreview.net/pdf?id=rJY0-Kcll.

Santurkar, S., Tsipras, D., Ilyas, A., & Madry, A. (2018). How does batch normalization help optimization? In *NeurIPS*.

Settles, B. (2010). *Active learning literature survey.* Computer sciences technical report 1648. University of Wisconsin–Madison.

Shimodaira, H. (2000). Improving predictive inference under covariate shift by weighting the log-likelihood function. *Journal of Statistical Planning and Inference, 90*(2), 227–244.

Simonyan, K., & Zisserman, A. (2015). Very deep convolutional networks for large-scale image recognition. In *ICLR*.

Soh, J. W., Cho, S., & Cho, N. I. (2020). Meta-transfer learning for zero-shot super-resolution. In *CVPR*.

Sutton, R. S., McAllester, D., Singh, S., & Mansour, Y. (1999). Policy gradient methods for reinforcement learning with function approximation. In *NIPS*.

Taylor, B. (1715). *Methodus incrementorum directa & inversa. Auctore Brook Taylor, LL. D. & Regiae Societatis Secretario.* typis Pearsonianis: prostant apud Gul. Innys ad Insignia Principis in Coemeterio Paulino.

Tian, H., Liu, B., Yuan, X.-T., & Liu, Q. (2020). Meta-learning with network pruning. In *ECCV*.

Vinyals, O., Blundell, C., Lillicrap, T., Kavukcuoglu, K., & Wierstra, D. (2016). *Matching networks for one shot learning.* Retrieved from http://papers.nips.cc/paper/6385-matching-networks-for-one-shot-learning.pdf.

Wah, C., Branson, S., Perona, P., & Belongie, S. (2011). Multiclass recognition and part localization with humans in the loop. In *2011 International conference on computer vision* (pp. 2524–2531). IEEE. https://doi.org/10.1109/ICCV.2011.6126539.

Wang, G., Luo, C., Sun, X., Xiong, Z., & Zeng, W. (2020). Tracking by instance detection: A meta-learning approach. In *CVPR*.

West, J., Ventura, D., & Warnick, S. (2007). *Spring research presentation: A theoretical foundation for inductive transfer.* Brigham Young University, College of Physical and Mathematical Sciences.

Wiesler, S., & Ney, H. (2011). A convergence analysis of log-linear training. *Advances in Neural Information Processing Systems, 24,* 657–665.

Wu, Q., Lin, Z., Wang, G., Chen, H., Karlsson, B. F., Huang, B., & Lin, C.-Y. (2020). Enhanced meta-learning for cross-lingual named entity recognition with minimal resources. In *AAAI*.

Yosinski, J., Clune, J., Bengio, Y., & Lipson, H. (2014). How transferable are features in deep neural networks? In *NeurIPS*.

Zeiler, M. D. (2012). *ADADELTA: An adaptive learning rate method.* Retrieved from CoRR http://arxiv.org/abs/1212.5701.

Zinkevich, M., Weimer, M., Li, L., & Smola, A. (2010). Parallelized stochastic gradient descent. *Advances in Neural Information Processing Systems, 23,* 2595–2603.

Zügner, D., & Günnemann, S. (2019). Adversarial attacks on graph neural networks via meta learning. *arXiv preprint,* arXiv:1902.08412.

I. Theory & mechanisms

## PART II

Applications

5

Meta-learning for computer vision

5.1 Introduction

Computer vision is an interdisciplinary field involving engineering, physics, mathematics, biology, and psychology. It focuses on addressing how computers obtain a high-level interpretation of digital images and videos. Computer vision includes extensive subfields, such as object tracking, motion estimation, scene reconstruction, virtual reality, face recognition, three-dimensional pose estimation, and event detection.

Regular computer vision tasks aim to improve a machine's ability to obtain, process, analyze, and interpret digital images and video, thereby capturing high-level information to generate or execute corresponding decisions (e.g., prediction, estimation, detection, and localization). The visual data format may rely on a range of visual signals sourced from, e.g., medical scanning machines, video frames, images taken by a single camera, a scene sourced from multiple cameras, and multimodal data related to natural language.

As the most developed and mature subfield in artificial intelligence (AI), to some degree, the history of computer vision is also the history of AI. Many classical experiments, fundamental theories, and observations on visual perceptron and neurophysiology can be traced to research conducted from the 1950s to 1960s. In 1956, the term "artificial intelligence" was proposed at the Dartmouth conference. Computer vision emerged in the 1960s as a steppingstone toward achieving true AI in many pioneering universities, where it aimed to simulate the human visual system for visual analysis and implement it within robotic systems to enable intelligent capabilities and behavior. Early researchers in the field were very optimistic about this technology and its capability to transform the world. In the 1970s, the fundamentals of early computer vision began to be formulated. Today, some concepts and theories are still influenced by these early principles, such as motion estimation and optical flow.

Two decades later, mathematical tools and quantitative analysis began shaping the development of computer vision. Researchers discovered that mathematical concepts could be applied to computer vision algorithms in the form of regularization and Markov random fields. Conversely, photogrammetry also provided the means for an in-depth investigation of several vital computer vision theories. In the late 1990s, statistical analysis was for the first time implemented in the field of facial recognition (FR), while graph-cut variations addressed the task of image segmentation. Various additional achievements followed as a result of the interaction between computer graphics and computer vision, such as image morphing.

Modern studies in computer vision heavily rely on feature representation through machine learning frameworks or optimization algorithms. With the support of a dramatically increasing amount of data, the 2012 ImageNet Large Scale Visual Recognition Challenge served as a milestone for clearing the existing bottleneck within the field of computer vision. The error rate of the 2010 benchmark was approximately 26%; however, with the emergence of AlexNet in 2012, this rate reduced to 16%. After that, deep learning technology, particularly deep convolutional neural networks (DCNNs), began dominating a range of computer vision tasks in a variety of fields, including medicine, the military, machine vision, and automatic vehicles.

5.1.1 Limitations

However, deep learning is not universal to the field of computer vision, and several limitations reduce its scope, as follows:

- Deep learning is a **data-hungry** technology. Although some classic computer vision tasks include extensive datasets, the quality of these datasets suffer from: (1) noisy labels; (2) long-tailed and imbalanced data distribution; and (3) the dataset scales are constrained due to monetary costs or rare categories where data collection is impossible (e.g., rare diseases or endangered animals). For example, instance-level visual tasks require hand-crafted annotation that encompasses more details, such as segmentation tasks or bounding boxes, which are more expensive.
- **Poor generalization in real-world scenarios** but excellent performance involving benchmarked datasets. This may occur frequently as the data distribution of the training dataset is significantly different from real-world samples, causing bias to occur. Additionally, due to the need to rapidly adapt to unseen situations (e.g., novel tasks or novel classes), deep neural networks perform weakly in terms of generalization.
- Nonoptimal performance in situations where **active updating or** continuous learning is required. As an increase in lifelong leaning or continuous learning is applied to visual tasks, the capability of continuously updating target information (e.g., the target object's appearance) is a key component of desired models.
- Due to the **self-awareness** of a DCNN, an open-set visual task is not preferred. A DCNN maintains intelligent self-awareness to determine if a task is favorable; the network will accept and execute what it is good at and reject what it cannot do; as such, an open-set visual task will be denied.
- Although domain adaptation issues can to some degree be solved by transfer learning within cross-domain visual tasks, **overfitting** caused by fine-tuning and the assumption of **relevance** between the source and the target domain of tasks will give rise to further uncertainty. Additionally, transfer learning is no longer an optimal method when target domains or tasks remain unknown or inaccessible. Conversely, even immense datasets, such as ImageNet, can provide helpful solutions for pretrained models; however, ImageNet data distribution could potentially be differentiated from that of target samples.
- The **time-consuming** aspect of deep learning can result from multiple factors, such as complicated neural network architecture or a thousand steps of gradient descent.

Fortunately, meta-learning can help to shed light on these issues. In the past few years, there has been significant growth in the possibilities of versatile computer vision tasks through the implementation of the meta-learning paradigm, including optimizing and improving performances, re-discussing the relationships among different tasks, and enhancing learning abilities and the rapid generalization of unseen tasks. This has signaled major progress in the field of AI, moving from immediate representation learning and objective function learning to "learning to learn" representation.

This chapter investigates 49 recent state-of-the-art works of research, all of which can be divided into 10 taxonomies according to the tasks that require solving, as follows: image classification, face recognition and face representation attacks, object detection, fine-grained image recognition, image segmentation, object tracking, label noise, super-resolution, multimodal learning, and other emerging applications related to computer vision. For each subfield, this chapter outlines its terminology and definition, historical background, developments before and after deep neural networks, influential characteristics of specific techniques, the taxonomy of typical learning methods, evaluation metrics, public benchmarks, corresponding framework-conducted meta-learning, algorithms with pseudocode, and the repository of the official code.

In the following chapters, these approaches have been selected due to their fundamental influence on current methods or theories, with a particular focus on: (a) their significant and broadly practical contributions in diverse applications; (b) their remarkable influence in academia according to their advanced performance and significant potential for further investigation; and (c) the impressive solutions they present as integral components, which are rarely discussed but important to meta-learning in computer vision. This research recursively tracked the related bibliographies in papers accepted at premier academic conferences, including AAAI, CVPR, ECCV, ECML, ICCV, ICLR, ICML, IJCAI, and NeurIPS, as summarized in Table 5.1.

TABLE 5.1 Summary of meta-learning techniques for computer vision.

Reference	Tasks	Method	Conference
5.2 Image classification			
Zhang, Che, Ghahramani, Bengio, and Song (2018)	Decision boundary sharpness and few-shot image classification	MetaGAN	NeurIPS
Ren et al. (2018)	Semisupervised few-shot image classification with refined prototypical network	Prototypical network-based	ICLR
Khodadadeh, Bölöni, and Shah (2019)	Few-shot unsupervised image classification	Unsupervised meta-learning with tasks constructed by random sampling and augmentation (UMTRA)	CVPR
Chen et al. (2019)	One-shot image deformation	Image deformation meta-network (IDeMe-Net)	CVPR
Requeima, Gordon, Bronskill, Nowozin, and Turner (2020)	Heterogeneous multitask learning in image classification	Conditional neural adaptive processes (CNAPs)	NeurIPS

Continued

TABLE 5.1 Summary of meta-learning techniques for computer vision—cont'd

Reference	Tasks	Method	Conference
Liu et al. (2018)	Few-shot classification with transductive inference	Transductive propagation network (TPN)	ICLR
Bertinetto, Henriques, Torr, and Vedaldi (2018)	Closed-form base learners	Ridge regression differentiable discriminator (R2-D2), logistic regression differentiable discriminator (LR-D2)	ICLR
Ren et al. (2020)	Long-tailed image classification	Balanced meta-softmax (BALMS)	NeurIPS
Rajasegaran, Khan, Hayat, Khan, and Shah (2020)	Image classification via incremental learning without forgetting	Incremental task-agnostic meta-learning (iTAML)	CVPR
Liu, Kang, Li, Hua and Vasconcelos (2020)	Few-shot open set recognition	Open set meta-learning (PEELER)	CVPR
Yue, Zhang, Sun, and Hua (2020)	Deficiency of pretrained knowledge in few-shot learning	Interventional few-shot learning (IFSL)	NeurIPS
Patacchiola, Turner, Crowley, O'Boyle, and Storkey (2020)	Bayesian strategy with deep kernel for regression and cross-domain image classification in a few-shot setting	Deep kernel transfer (DKT)	NeurIPS
Dinh, Tran, and Nguyen (2020)	Statistical diversity in personalized models of federated learning	Personalized FL (pFedMe)	NeurIPS
Chen, Liu, Xu, Darrell, and Wang (2021)	Meta-learning deficiency in few-shot learning	Meta-baseline, classifier-baseline	ICCV
5.3 Face recognition and face presentation attack			
Zakharov, Shysheya, Burkov, and Lempitsky (2019)	Person-specific talking head generation for unseen people and portrait painting in few-shot regimes	Realistic neural talking head models	ICCV
Shao, Lan, and Yuen (2020)	Face presentation attack and domain generalization	Regularized fine-grained meta-learning face antispoofing	AAAI
Qin et al. (2020)	Anti-face-spoofing in few-shot and zero-shot scenarios	Adaptive inner-update meta-face antispoofing (AIM-FAS)	AAAI
Guo, Zhu, et al. (2020)	Generalized face recognition in unseen domain	Meta-face recognition (MFR)	CVPR
5.4 Object detection			
Wang, Ramanan and Hebert (2019)	Long-tailed data object detection in few-shot scenarios	MetaDet	ICCV
Kang et al. (2019)	Object detection in few-shot scenarios	CNN-based	ICCV
Xiao and Marlet (2020)	Unseen object detection and viewpoint estimation in low-data setting	Few-shot object detection, few-shot viewpoint estimation	ECCV

TABLE 5.1 Summary of meta-learning techniques for computer vision—cont'd

Reference	Tasks	Method	Conference
5.5 Fine-grained image recognition			
Zhang et al. (2018)	Fine-grained visual categorization	MetaFGNet	ECCV
Tsutsui, Fu, and Crandall (2019)	One-shot fine-grained visual recognition	Meta-image reinforcing network (MetaIRNet)	NeurIPS
Zhu, Liu, and Jiang (2020)	Few-shot fine-grained image recognition	Multiattention meta-learning (MattML)	IJCAI
5.6 Image segmentation			
Tian et al. (2020)	Multiobject few-shot semantic segmentation	MetaSegNet	AAAI
Yan et al. (2020)	Few-shot static object instance-level detection	Meta R-CNN	ICCV
5.7 Object tracking			
Park and Berg (2018)	Offline object tracking	Meta-tracker	ECCV
Choi, Kwon, and Lee (2019)	Real-time online object tracking	Siamese matching network-based	ICCV
Jung, You, Noh, Cho, and Han (2020)	Real-time object tracking with channel pruning	MAML-based	AAAI
Wang, Hu, and Hu (2020)	Object tracking via instance detection	Retina-MAML, FCOS-MAML	CVPR
5.8 Label noise			
Ren et al. (2018)	Reweighting examples through online approximation	Meta-learning reweighting	ICML
Zhang, Wang, and Qiao (2019)	Hallucinated clean representation for noisy-labeled visual recognition	MetaCleaner	CVPR
Yoon, Arik, and Pfister (2020)	Data valuation	Data valuation using reinforcement learning (DVRL)	ICML
Li, Chen, and Liu (2019)	Teacher-student networks for image classification on noisy labels	Meta-learning based noise-tolerant (MLNT)	CVPR
Shu et al. (2019)	Sample reweighting function construction	Meta-weight-Net (MW-Net)	NeurIPS
Wang, Hu and Hu (2020)	Loss correction approach	Meta-loss correction (MLC)	CVPR
Zhang, Zhang, Arik, Lee, and Pfister (2020)	Meta-re-labelling through data coefficients	Data coefficients, L2R	CVPR
Zheng, Awadallah, and Dumais (2021)	Meta-label correction	Meta-label correction (MLC)	AAAI

Continued

II. Applications

TABLE 5.1   Summary of meta-learning techniques for computer vision—cont'd

Reference	Tasks	Method	Conference
5.9 Super resolution			
Soh, Cho, and Cho (2020)	Meta-transfer zero-shot super-resolution	MAML-based	CVPR
Park, Yoo, Cho, Kim, and Kim (2020)	LR-HR image pair super-resolution	MLSR	CVPR
Zhu et al. (2020)	No-reference image quality assessment	MetaIQA	CVPR
5.10 Multimodal			
Teney and van den Hengel (2018)	Visual question answering system	Nonlinear transformation and classifier	ECCV
5.11 Other emerging applications related to computer vision			
Balaji et al. (2018)	Domain generalization	MetaReg	NeurIPS
Park et al. (2019)	High-accuracy 3D appearance-based gaze estimation in few-shot regimes	Few-shot adaptive gaze estimation (FAZE)	ICCV
Guo, Codella, et al. (2020)	Benchmark of cross-domain few-shot learning in vision tasks	Broader study of cross-domain few-shot learning (BSCD-FSL)	ECCV
Rusu et al. (2018)	Latent embedding optimization in low-dimensional space	Latent embedding optimization (LEO)	ICLR
Li, Wong, Zhao, and Kankanhalli (2019)	Image captioning	MAML-based	AAAI
Yin, Tucker, Zhou, Levine, and Finn (2019)	Memorization issue	Meta-regularization	ICLR
Pham, Dai, Xie, Luong, and Le (2021)	Meta-pseudo label	Meta-pseudo label	CVPR

5.2 Image classification

5.2.1 Introduction

The term "object recognition" broadly describes a set of relevant computer vision tasks involving object identification. The interchangeable use of "object recognition" and "object detection" can cause confusion. There are explanations regarding the three typical object-related tasks as follows:

- Image classification: a task to determine the class or type of a given object in an image, usually for a single object, with an output of the class label.

- Object localization: a task to locate and demonstrate the spatial location of objects in a given image, with an output of one or more spatial locations.
- Object detection: a task to demonstrate the location of objects in a given image and identify the types or class of the located object, with an output of one or more spatial locations and a class label of each related object.

Section 5.1 explores image classification, face recognition is examined in Section 5.2, Section 5.3 suggests meta-learning in object detection, whereas section 5.4 outlines fine-grained image classification.

Image classification is a fundamental problem that aims to assign an image into a particular label by processing and understanding the entire image as a whole. Image classification commonly deals with a single object, whereas object detection and instance segmentation focus on multiple objects in one image. This idea has attracted much attention from remote-sensing research since its early study, and the result of classification has played a significant role in environmental and socioeconomic implementations, historically.

Humans can identify "3000 entry-level categories and 30,000 visual categories overall" (Liu et al., 2020). Biederman (1987) reported that an effective and robust system could achieve human-level performance in the detection and recognition of 10,000–100,000 categories.

Development

Concerning development and maturity, object recognition has two main eras: scale-invariant feature transform (SIFT) and DCNN. The global representations of appearance features (Murase & Nayar, 1995; Swain & Ballard, 1991; Turk & Pentland, 1991) change to local representations—which is invariant to resize, rotation, cropping, flipping, viewpoint, occlusion, translation, padding, affine transformation, and occlusion. The implementation of local descriptors became widely used, such as Haar-Like Features (Viola & Jones, 2001), Shape Context (Belongie, Malik, & Puzicha, 2002), and Histogram of Oriented Gradients (HOG; Dalal & Triggs, 2005).

Since 2012, when the ImageNet achieved a significant breakthrough in image classification, deep neural networks have attracted increasing attention from researchers in visual recognition. Large-scale datasets, billions of parameters, and the computing capacity of GPU supported the early success of deep-learning recognizers. Several classic DCNN frameworks dominate the object-recognition domains: GoogleNet (Szegedy et al., 2014), VGG series (Simonyan & Zisserman, 2014), and ResNet series (He, Zhang, Ren, & Sun, 2016).

Approaches

The essential methods of image classification can be divided into multiple categories depending on distinctive criteria: supervised classification (e.g., decision tree) and unsupervised classification (e.g., K-means), or parametric classifiers (e.g., logistic regression), and nonparametric classifiers (e.g., K-nearest neighbors), per-pixel classifiers (most of the classifiers) and subpixel classifiers (e.g., fuzzy-set classifiers), object-oriented classifiers (e.g., eCognition) and per-field classifiers (e.g., geographical system-based), hard classifiers and soft (fuzzy) classifiers, and spatial/contextual/spectral-contextual classifiers (Lu & Weng, 2007).

Along with the development of deep learning, the convolutional neural network (CNN) illuminates many complex problems. The general steps of image classification through CNN are:

1. Selecting a dataset
2. Preprocessing (e.g., image denoise, augmentation, shuffle, splitting data set)
3. Defining, compiling, and training a CNN-based model
4. Evaluation/inference

Although multiple neural network architectures—like LSTM—can be used in image classification, CNN is still the most effective and widely used one. Some popular CNN backbone approaches include Xception (Chollet, 2016), VGG-16/VGG-19 (Simonyan & Zisserman, 2014), ResNet50 (He et al., 2016), Inception3 (Szegedy, Vanhoucke, Ioffe, Shlens, & Wojna, 2015), DenseNet, MobileNet (Howard et al., 2017), NASNet (Zoph, Vasudevan, Shlens, & Le, 2018), and EfficientNet (Tan & Le, 2020).

Benchmarks

Besides the well-known benchmarks of general image classification—Open Image dataset, CIFAR-10, Omniglot, ImageNet (Russakovsky et al., 2015), Places (Zhou, Lapedriza, Khosla, Oliva, & Torralba, 2017)—there are many public datasets of image classification for specific fields. Benchmarks for medicine include TensorFlow patch_camelyon Medical Image (TensorFlow, 2021a, 2021b), Recursion Cellular Image Classification (xhlulu, 2019), Blood Cell Images (Mooney, 2018), and ChestX-ray8 (Wang et al., 2017). Datasets for agriculture and science include Indoor Scenes Images (Ahmad, 2019), Images for Weather Recognition (Ajayi, 2018), Intel Image Classification (Bansal, 2019), TensorFlow Sun397 Image Classification Dataset (TensorFlow, 2021a, 2021b), and CoastSat Image Classification Dataset (Vos, 2019). Other datasets for specific objects include Image Classification: People and Food (CrowdFlower, 2016), Images of Cracks in Concrete for Classification (Özgenel, 2019), Architectural Heritage Elements (Llamas, 2021), and Fruits 360 (Oltean, 2021).

One-stage semisupervised learning

In real-world scenarios, large-scale datasets are expensive and impractical; thus, unsupervised and semisupervised options have gained increasing attention (Schmarje, Santarossa, Schroder, & Koch, 2021). One-stage semisupervised learning is set up during training with a combination of labeled and unlabeled data by integrating a few unsupervised losses to the supervised loss. Common approaches include Pseudo-Labels (Lee, 2013), π-Model and Temporal Ensembling (Laine & Aila, 2017), Mean Teacher (Tarvainen & Valpola, 2017), Fast-Stochastic Weight Averaging (fast-SWA; Izmailov, Podoprikhin, Garipov, Vetrov, & Wilson, 2018), Virtual Adversarial Training (VAT; Miyato, Maeda, Koyama, Ishii, & Koyama, 2018), Interpolation Consistency Training (ICT; Verma et al., 2019), MixMatch (Berthelot et al., 2019), Ensemble AutoEndocing Transformation (EnAET; Wang et al., 2019), Unsupervised Data Augmentation (UDA; Cubuk, Zoph, Mane, Vasudevan, & Le, 2019), Self-Paced Multi-View Co-Training (SpamCo; Ma et al., 2020; Ma, Meng, Dong, & Yang, 2020), ReMixMax (Berthelot et al., 2020), and FixMatch (Sohn et al., 2020).

One-stage unsupervised learning

One-stage unsupervised learning is conducted through a range of unsupervised loss functions (Chang, Wang, Meng, Xiang, & Pan, 2017; Vedaldi, Ji, Henriques, & Vedaldi, 2019; Xie, Girshick, Farhadi, Cs, & Edu, 2016). Regular strategies include Deep Adaptive Image Clustering (DAC; Chang et al., 2017), Information Maximizing Self-Augmented Training (IMSAT; Hu, Miyato, Tokui, Matsumoto, & Sugiyama, 2017), Invariant Information Clustering (IIC; Vedaldi et al., 2019), and Semantic Clustering by Adopting Nearest Neighbors (SCAN; (Gansbeke, Vandenhende, Georgoulis, Proesmans, & Gool, 2020).

Multistage semisupervised learning

Multistage semisupervised learning usually involves training in two stages with fine-tuning in the second stage. Common methods include Exemplar (Dosovitskiy, Fischer, Springenberg, Riedmiller, & Brox, 2018), Context (Doersch, Gupta, & Efros, 2015), Jigsaw (Noroozi & Favaro, 2016), DeepCluster (Caron, Bojanowski, Joulin, & Douze, 2018), Rotation (Gidaris, Singh, & Komodakis, 2018), Contrastive Predictive Coding (CPC; Henaff et al., 2020; Oord, Li, & Vinyals, 2018), Contrastive Multiview Coding (CMC), Deep InfoMax (DIM; Hjelm et al., 2019), Augmented Multiscale Deep InfoMax (AMDIM; Bachman, Hjelm, & Buchwalter, 2019), Deep Metric Transfer (DMT), Self-Supervised Semi-Supervised Learning (S^{4}L; Zhai, Oliver, Kolesnikov, & Beyer, 2019), SimCLR, Fuzzy Overclustering (FOC; Schmarje et al., 2020), Momentum Contrast (MoCo; He, Fan, Wu, Xie, & Girshick, 2020), BYOL (Grill et al., 2020), and SimCLRv2.

Image classification is the most classical vision task and possesses countless solutions, but some drawbacks remain. Current studies rely heavily on an extensive dataset for training, even with weak adaptation capability on previously unseen novel classes, and overfitting frequently occurs in long-tailed or imbalanced datasets. In addition, catastrophic forgetting occurs in image classification as more new tasks are fed into the system. Unlike supervised learning, pretrained knowledge can confuse the model in few-shot regimes. Many visual tasks treat images like a black box without understanding their internal structure or deformation analysis, in contrast with the human visual system. Classification models have to learn from heterogeneous datasets to acquire a global model in federated learning. Failure to handle these heterogeneous distributions may lead to unsatisfactory performance.

On the other hand, meta-learning specifies some new solutions. It is equipped with the generative adversarial network (GAN) to generate synthesized samples and sharpen the decision boundary for classifying few-shot images. This semisupervised solution is incorporated with a refined prototypical network to tackle few-shot classification. Furthermore, unsupervised learning with statistical diversity properties and domain-specific augmentation achieves remarkable success in classifying without any clustering algorithm. The meta-learning framework also analyzes semantic image information and determines sharp classification decision boundaries.

This section investigates multiple potential issues in image classification and addresses a variety of solutions incorporated with meta-learning. Section 5.2.2 provides a semisupervised method to sharpen decision boundary in few-shot image classification. Semisupervised K-shot N-way image classification relies on unlabeled and labeled low-data regimes. Section 5.2.3 suggests the modified prototypical network with refinements. Section 5.2.4

introduces an upgrade of supervised MAML so that an utterly unlabeled dataset can be learned directly under a few labeled data elements in target tasks. Section 5.2.5 discusses an improvement toward an image structure and deformation analysis. The following sections provide detailed reviews of a couple of meta-learners to deal with heterogeneous distributions that occur in various situations: federated learning regimes, multitask learning, and initialization in MAML with dissimilar testing and training tasks. Section 5.2.6 looks into diverse data distribution in high-data and low-data setups without retraining for multitask image classification and the corresponding solution—Conditional Neural Adaptive Processes (CNAPs). Section 5.2.7 concentrates on using transductive inference for few-shot image classification in the meta-learning framework Transductive Propagation Network (TPN).

Rather than a typical neural network-based image classifier, Section 5.2.8 explores two base learners with closed-form methods—Ridge Regression Differentiable Discriminator and Logistic Regression Differentiable Discriminator in image classification problem. Section 5.2.9 tackles the problem of long-tailed data in image processing through Balanced Softmax and a bi-level meta-learner. Section 5.2.10 examines a task-agnostic meta-solver to avoid catastrophic forgetting in incremental learning and balance old and new examples. Section 5.2.11 provides an open-set visual recognition solution based on few-shot regimes to replace the traditional approached trained on large-scale dataset.

As (Yue et al., 2020) reported, the golden rule in supervised learning—that more robust pretrained knowledge always leads to better downstream performance—actually confused the few-shot model; Section 5.2.12 traces back to a meta-learner to deal with this hitch. Section 5.2.13 offers a kernel-based solution with Bayesian meta-learning for two tasks: regression and cross-domain image classification. Unlike most machine learning tasks with independent and identically distributed data (IID data or i.i.d. data), federated learning processes non-IID samples, while Section 5.2.14 suggests a solution for heterogeneity. Even though meta-learning techniques have been broadly implemented in various fields, Section 5.2.15 cautions skepticism of the efficiency of meta-learning procedures in few-shot regimes by comparing the whole-classifier and meta-learning-based classifier.

5.2.2 Decision boundary sharpness and few-shot image classification

Despite the broad success achieved by deep learning in computer vision, it is still unable to learn as fast as human adaptability in unseen situations. The current deep learning-based visual tasks face several challenges: (1) being data-hungry, with a large amount of data consumption, and (2) fast adaptation of novel tasks within a few gradient descents. In few-shot visual tasks, the optimal decision boundary among multiple classes is a highly demanded generalization. Fortunately, meta-learning overcomes these issues.

Inspired by similar research by Salimans et al. (2016), Zhang and coresearchers (2018) developed a GAN-based (Goodfellow et al., 2014) meta-learning strategy named MetaGAN to sharpen the decision boundary for classifying few-shot images. MetaGAN integrates MAML and the Relation Network (Sung et al., 2018). It can convert supervised models by incorporating unlabeled data and processes as semisupervision methods on sample-level and task-level elements (Ren et al., 2018). The fundamental idea of this model argued that the generators from GAN models could produce a great deal of fake data among the manifolds from various real data classes, which offers supplementary guidance for the classifier and leads to the decision boundaries being much more accurate.

The objective functions $\mathcal{L}_D^{\mathcal{T}}$ for task $\mathcal{T}$ of the few-shot N-way fake/real sample classification in a discriminator are outlined in Eqs. (5.1)–(5.3), where $Q_{\mathcal{T}}^s = \{(x_1, y_1), ..., (x_T, y_T)\}$ is the supervised query dataset, and $Q_{\mathcal{T}}^u$ denotes the optional unlabeled query dataset:

$$\mathcal{L}_D^{\mathcal{T}} = \mathcal{L}_{supervision} + \mathcal{L}_{unsupervision} \tag{5.1}$$

$$\mathcal{L}_{supervision} = \mathbb{E}_{x,y \sim Q_{\mathcal{T}}^s} \log p_D(y|x, y \leq N) \tag{5.2}$$

$$\mathcal{L}_{unsupervision} = \mathbb{E}_{x \sim Q_{\mathcal{T}}^u} \log p_D(y \leq N|x) + \mathbb{E}_{x \sim P_G^{\mathcal{T}}} \log p_D(1 + N|x) \tag{5.3}$$

The nonsaturating loss function for a generator is summarized in Eq. (5.4):

$$\mathcal{L}_D^{\mathcal{T}}(D) = -\mathbb{E}_{x \sim P_G^{\mathcal{T}}} \left[\log \left(p_D(y \leq N|x) \right) \right] \tag{5.4}$$

Employed with MAML, according to the loss function in Eq. (5.5), the discriminator of MetaGAN $D(\theta_d)$ is expressed by parameter θ_d and updating parameter $\theta_d' = \theta_d - \alpha \nabla_{\theta_d} \ell_D^{\mathcal{T}}$, where $T \sim P(T)$ denotes a specific task:

$$\ell_D^{\mathcal{T}} = -\mathbb{E}_{x,y \sim S_{\mathcal{T}}^s} \log p_D(y|x, y \leq N) - \mathbb{E}_{x \sim S_{\mathcal{T}}^u} \log p_D(y \leq N|x) - \mathbb{E}_{x \sim P_G^{\mathcal{T}}} \log p_D(N + 1|x) \tag{5.5}$$

The overall objective functions that combined MetaGAN with MAML are expressed in Eqs. (5.6), (5.7) for the discriminator and the generator, respectively:

$$\mathcal{L}_D = \max_D \mathbb{E}_{T \sim P(T)} \mathcal{L}_D^{\mathcal{T}} \tag{5.6}$$

$$\mathcal{L}_G = \min_G \mathbb{E}_{T \sim P(T)} \mathcal{L}_G^{\mathcal{T}} \tag{5.7}$$

The softmax function for the multiclass classification of MetaGAN equipped with a Relation Network is expressed in Eq. (5.8). Unlike a standard Relation Network, there is no restriction of $r_{i,j} \in [0,1]$ and $r_{i,j} = g_\psi(C(f_\phi(x_i), f_\phi(x_j)))$, where g_ψ denotes the relation module, C is concatenation operation, and f_ϕ presents the feature embedding network.

$$p_D(y = k|x_j) = \frac{\exp(r_{k,j})}{1 + \sum_{i=1}^N \exp(r_{i,j})} \tag{5.8}$$

MetaGAN consists of two modules in the generator: an instance-encoder module and a feature-aggregation module, encouraged by Edwards and Storkey (2017).

MetaGAN mainly focused on the following three scenarios and has been evaluated on Omniglot (Ager, 2020) and *mini*ImageNet (Dhillon, Chaudhari, Ravichandran, & Soatto, 2020) datasets:

- Supervised few-shot learning
- Sample-level semisupervised few-shot learning (similar to the research of Ren et al., 2018)
- Task-level semisupervised few-shot learning

5.2.3 Semisupervised few-shot image classification with refined prototypical network

Deep learning technologies perform well with large volumes of training data, but quality labeled data is often limited in real-world scenarios. Moreover, although the overall number of samples is high for long-tailed or imbalanced datasets, certain specific classes tend to contain only a few annotated examples.

Ren et al. (2018) introduced a semisupervised few-shot learning approach to tackle K-shot N-way classification. The goal is to create a classifier for category testing samples belonging to novel classes that have never been seen during episodic training, based on a small number of labeled and unlabeled samples in each episode. According to the distribution of unlabeled data, there are two different situations:

1. A basic situation where all unannotated data are from the same classes as the annotated samples in each episode
2. A challenging situation where some examples belong to other classes (i.e., distractor classes)

This approach extends the meta-learning algorithm Prototypical Network (see Section 3.4 for a detailed overview) to a semisupervised image classification problem. See the overall architecture in Fig. 5.1. In contrast with the regular prototypes p_c of the standard prototypical network (at the left), this method focusses on the refined prototypes $\widetilde{p}_c$ with an additional unannotated dataset R in each episode (at the right). The official code is available at https://github.com/renmengye/few-shot-ssl-public.

There are three ways to leverage unannotated data to obtain refined prototypes in this semisupervised prototypical network, where the training set is a hybrid collection of annotated samples and unannotated samples (S, R):

1. The soft k-means are employed with the prototypical network. Each prototype can be treated as the center of a cluster; the refinement process aims to modulate the location of a cluster to a better place, considering both the support sets and unannotated sets. The assumption in this situation is each item of unannotated data can be classified to one of the

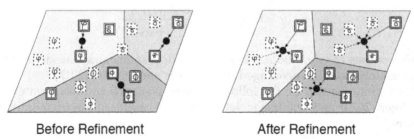

Before Refinement   After Refinement

FIG. 5.1 regular prototypical network vs. regined prototypical network.
From Ren, M., Triantafillou, E., Ravi, S., Snell, J., Swersky, K., Tenenbaum, J. B., ... & Zemel, R. S. (2018). Meta-learning for semi-supervised few-shot classification. arXiv preprint arXiv:1803.00676.

N classes in an episode. Based on the cluster location from the regular Prototypical Network's prototypes p_c, the unannotated samples obtain a partial assignment $\widetilde{z}_{j,c}$ on each cluster through Euclidean distance. The prototype $\widetilde{p}_c$ per class c with refinement is expressed in Eqs (5.9), (5.10), where $h(x)$ denotes the embedding function.

$$\widetilde{p}_c = \frac{\sum_i h(x_i)z_{i,c} + \sum_j h(\widetilde{x}_j)\widetilde{z}_{j,c}}{\sum_i z_{i,c} + \sum_j \widetilde{z}_{j,c}} \tag{5.9}$$

where

$$\widetilde{z}_{j,c} = \frac{\exp\left(-\| h(\widetilde{x}_j) - p_c \|_2^2\right)}{\sum_{c'} \exp\left(-\| h(\widetilde{x}_j) - p_{c'} \|_2^2\right)} \tag{5.10}$$

2. The soft k-means with a distractor cluster is employed in the prototypical network. This case frees the assumption in the first situation noted above and applies to a more realistic assumption: the unannotated data can belong to a class other than the existing classes, which are termed distractor classes. To address the confusion between the existing and distractor classes, an additional catch-all cluster is presented to split the distractors and avoid fooling the clusters of the classes of interest. This is expressed in Eq. (5.11):

$$p_c = \begin{cases} \dfrac{\sum_i h(x_i)z_{i,c}}{\sum_i z_{i,c}} & \text{for } c = 1...N \\ 0 & \text{for } c = N + 1 \end{cases} \tag{5.11}$$

where r_c denotes the length scales to indicate the variations from within-cluster distances for a distractor cluster.

$$\widetilde{z}_{j,c} = \frac{\exp\left(-\frac{1}{r_c^2}\|\widetilde{x}_j - p_c\|_2^2 - A(r_c)\right)}{\sum_{c'} \exp\left(-\frac{1}{r_{c'}^2}\|\widetilde{x}_j - p_{c'}\|_2^2 - A(r_{c'})\right)}, \text{where } A(r) = \tfrac{1}{2}\log(2\pi) + \log(r)$$

3. The soft k-means and soft-masking mechanism are employed in the prototypical network. This case generalizes the assumption, as each distractor's unannotated data may belong to more than one cluster. Rather than the simple high-variance cluster conducted in the second approach, a distractor is viewed as an instance that does not belong to any legitimate class prototypes. The goal is to make the unannotated sample less masked as it gets closer to a prototype, and more as it moves further away, by applying a soft-mask mechanism. This procedure is summarized in Eqs. (5.12)–(5.16). The normalized distance $\widetilde{d}_{j,c}$ between prototypes p_c and samples $\widetilde{x}_j$ is computed in Eqs. (5.12), (5.13):

$$\widetilde{d}_{j,c} = \frac{d_{j,c}}{\frac{1}{M}\sum_j d_{j,c}} \tag{5.12}$$

where:

$$d_{j,c} = \| h(\widetilde{x}_j) - p_c \|_2^2 \tag{5.13}$$

The soft threshold β_c and slope γ_c are expressed in Eq. (5.14):

$$[\beta_c, \gamma_c] = \text{MLP}\left(\left[\min_j\left(\tilde{d}_{j,c}\right), \max_j\left(\tilde{d}_{j,c}\right), \text{var}_j\left(\tilde{d}_{j,c}\right), \text{skew}_j\left(\tilde{d}_{j,c}\right), \text{kurt}_j\left(\tilde{d}_{j,c}\right)\right]\right) \qquad (5.14)$$

The final prototype $\tilde{p}_c$, after refinement with soft mask $m_{j,c}$, is expressed in Eqs. (5.15), (5.16):

$$\tilde{p}_c = \frac{\sum_i h(x_i)z_{i,c} + \sum_j h(\tilde{x}_j)\tilde{z}_{j,c}m_{j,c}}{\sum_i z_{i,c} + \sum_j \tilde{z}_{j,c}m_{j,c}} \qquad (5.15)$$

where:

$$m_{j,c} = \sigma\left(-\gamma_c\left(\tilde{d}_{j,c} - \beta_c\right)\right) \qquad (5.16)$$

This paradigm is evaluated on three public benchmarks, including two existing datasets (Omniglot and *mini*ImageNet) and a widely used dataset *tiered*ImageNet initially proposed by this research. *Tiered*ImageNet is a large-scale dataset for few-shot classification with unlabeled and labeled sample splitting. It also contains hierarchical labels with diverse categories for training and testing. The assessment discusses one-shot and five-shot accuracy with distractors (the primary situation) and without distractor classes (the challenging situation).

5.2.4 Few-shot unsupervised image classification

An extensive request of large-scale labeled data for a range of various tasks demands significant monetary outlay as well as being time-consuming for expert labeling and data collection. Additionally, even after all these have been done successfully, labeled training samples must be carried out for each task, $T_1, T_2, ..., T_{n-1}$, to learn the target T_n. This strategy will constrain the variety of task types to investigate.

Khodadadeh et al. (2019) aim to solve this problem through an unsupervised model-agnostic few-shot classification, namely Unsupervised Meta-learning with Tasks constructed by Random Sampling and Augmentation (UMTRA).

Traditional supervised MAML needs more than a thousand labeled data and implements CACTUs algorithms involving robust clustering algorithms; for example, DeepCluster (Caron et al., 2018) or ACAI (Berthelot, Raffel, Roy, & Goodfellow, 2018). In contrast, UMTRA starts with training on an unlabeled dataset; it only requires a few labeled data in the final target tasks—this is even possible with just one sample per class—with no clustering method. UMTRA is built on a MAML-based procedure equipped with statistical diversity properties and domain-specific augmentation (Antoniou & Storkey, 2019). The official code is available at https://github.com/siavash-khodadadeh/UMTRA-Release.

Unlike supervised MAML, this method randomly selects N samples x_i from the dataset as training data, whereas validation data is generated through each training sample's augmentation function $\mathcal{A}$. See Fig. 5.2 for visualization.

The complete detailed algorithm is shown in Table 5.2.

UMTRA offers a significant improvement over the Omniglot (Ager, 2020) and *mini*ImageNet (Dhillon et al., 2020) benchmarks as a substitute for supervised MAML performance in and of unsupervised CACTUs algorithm (Hsu, Levine, & Finn, 2018). For instance, supervised MAML reached 98.83% accuracy with 24,025 labels, while UMTRA achieved 95.43% accuracy with only 25 labels in five-way five-shot Omniglot classification.

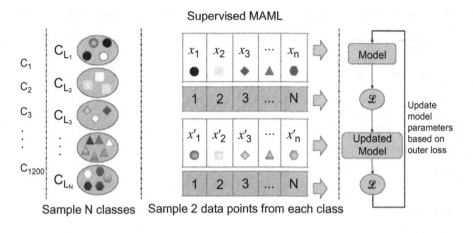

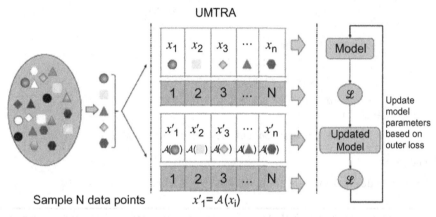

FIG. 5.2 General workflow of unsupervised meta-learning with tasks constructed by random sampling and augmentation.

From Khodadadeh, S., Bölöni, L., & Shah, M. (2019). Unsupervised meta-learning for few-shot image classification. In: CVPR.

5.2.5 One-shot image deformation

In spite of the promising results, the current meta-learning methods on visual tasks still view images as a black box without understanding their structure. In this way, an improvement in the direction of an image structure and deformation analysis like that of the human eyes and brain is required.

Inspirited by Wang, Girshick, Hebert, and Ran (2018) and Zhang et al. (2018), Chen et al. (2019) provided a simple but robust end-to-end meta-learning image deformation network (Boccolini, Fedrizzi, & Faccio, 2019; Vermaak, Maskell, & Briers, 2005) named Image Deformation Meta-Network (IDeMe-Net), for image semantic information analysis and formulating classification decision boundaries. Common examples of image deformations include ghosting, stitching, montaging, and partially occluding. To address a one-shot learning problem, IDeMe-Net can generate extra examples for more accurate and robust classification. The official code is available at https://github.com/tankche1/IDeMe-Net.

TABLE 5.2   General methods of unsupervised meta-learning with tasks constructed by random sampling and augmentation.

Input: *N*: class-count.
        N_{MB}: size of meta-batch
        N_U: number of updates
        $\mathcal{U} = \{...x_j...\}$: unlabeled dataset
        α, β: hyperparameters of step size
        $\mathcal{A}$: augmentation function

```
1  θ random initialization
2  while not meeting stopping criteria do

3       for i = 1...N_MB do
4             Select N instance x_1...x_N from dataset U
5             T_i ← {x_1,...x_N}
6       end for

7       for each T_i do
8             Produce training set D_i = {(x_1,1),...,(x_N,N)}
9             θ_i'=θ;

10            for j = 1...N_U do
11                  Compute ∇_θ_i L_T_i(f_θ_i)
                    # Obtain adapted parameters
12                  θ'_i = θ'_i - α∇_θ_i L_T_i(f_θ_i)
13            end for

                # Produce validation set used for meta-updating
14            D'_i = {(A(x_1),1),...,(A(x_N),N)}
15      end for

16      Update model parameters by θ ← θ - β∇_θ∑_T_i L_T_i(f_θ_i) with each D'_i
17 end while
```

Modified from Khodadadeh, S., Bölöni, L., & Shah, M. (2019). Unsupervised meta-learning for few-shot image classification. In: CVPR.

This framework consists of two submodules (and see the overall workflow):

1. The deformation subnetwork produces additional deformed images via the linear fusion on the patches of probe images and gallery images. After splitting the gallery images and probe images into nine patches, this deformation subnetwork starts to evaluate the fusing weight of each patch.
2. The embedding subnetwork employs a convolutional neural network (e.g., ResNet) for feature extraction and equips a nonparametric classification model based on prototype vectors in one-shot scenarios.

The prototype loss function is employed in the deformation subnetwork as expressed in Eq. (5.17), where *S* is support set, *Q* present query set, and *G* consists of a random sample from per base class from the base dataset D_{base}:

$$\min_\theta \mathbb{E}_{L \sim D_{base}} \mathbb{E}_{S,G,Q \sim L} \left[\sum_{(I_i,t_i) \in Q} - \log P_\theta(y_i | \mathbf{I}_i) \right] \tag{5.17}$$

TABLE 5.3   General training methods of image deformation meta-network.

Input: G, the fixed gallery collected from $\mathcal{C}_{\text{base}}$

\# The procedure of one single episode of meta-train

1: $L \sim \mathcal{C}_{\text{base}} \leftarrow$ randomly samples N classes

2: \# construct the support set
3: $S \sim L \leftarrow$ randomly sample instances
4: \# construct the query set
5: $Q \sim L \leftarrow$ randomly sample instances

6: train the prototype classifier $P \sim f_{\theta_{\text{emb}}}(S)$
7: \# initialize the augment support set
8: $\widetilde{S} \leftarrow S$
9: \# enumerate the chosen classes
10: for c in L do
11:      $pool \leftarrow$ Utilized P to choose $\epsilon\%$ images of G, which rank the greatest probability of c
12:      for (I_{probe}, c) in S_c do
13:          for $j=1$ to n_{aug} do
14:              $I_{\text{gallery}} \sim pool \leftarrow$ randomly sample instances
15:              $I_{\text{syn}} \leftarrow f_{\theta_{\text{def}}}(I_{\text{probe}}, I_{\text{gallery}})$
16:              $\widetilde{S} \leftarrow \widetilde{S} \cup (\mathbf{I}_{syn}, c)$
17:          end for
18:      end for
19: end for

20: Train the prototype classifier $\widetilde{P} \sim f_{\theta_{\text{emb}}}(\widetilde{S})$
21: Use $\widetilde{P}$ to classify $f_{\theta_{\text{emb}}}(Q)$ and evaluate the prototype loss
22: Classify $f_{\theta_{\text{emb}}}(\widetilde{S})$ using the softmax classifie and evaluate the cross entropy loss
23: Update θ_{emb} through the cross entropy loss
24: Update θ_{def} through the prototype loss
25: end procedure

Modified from Chen, Z., Fu, Y., Wang, Y. X., Ma, L., Liu, W., & Hebert, M. (2019). Image deformation meta-networks for one-shot learning. In: Proceedings of the IEEE/CVF conference on computer vision and pattern recognition (pp. 8680–8689).

Table 5.3 shows the step-by-step pseudocode of meta-training in IDeMe-Net.

This model is assessed on *mini*ImageNet and ImageNet 1K Challenge datasets (Hariharan & Girshick, 2017), as the number of images in each class ranges from 1 to 20.

5.2.6 Heterogeneous multitask learning in image classification

Requeima et al. (2020) aimed to solve the image classification multitask from many data distributions under both high- and low-data setups without retraining, as the current solutions involving few-shot learning and meta-learning have two issues under multitask learning settings: (1) the number of parameters adapted in each task and (2) the adaptation approaches. Requeima and team proposed a model class named CNAPs to handle these two drawbacks efficiently. CNAPs extended the conditional neural processes (CNP) framework in a multitask classification setting to maintain fast adaptation for new tasks during inference time and to prevent overfitting under low-data environments and underfitting in a high-shot situation. The official code is available at https://github.com/cambridge-mlg/cnaps.

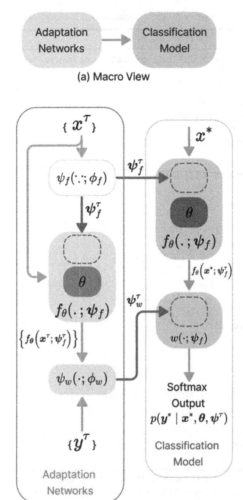

(a) Macro View

(b) Detail of the Proposed Pipeline

FIG. 5.3 General pipeline of conditional neural adaptive processes.
Modified from Requeima, J., Gordon, J., Bronskill, J., Nowozin, S., & Turner, R. E. (2020, January 7). Fast and flexible multi-task classification using conditional neural adaptive processes. arXiv.org. Retrieved June 4, 2022, from https://arxiv.org/abs/1906.07697.

This proposed method has two main modules: the classification model serves as the main model with adaptation networks as a supplementary model. CNAPs consist of both global and local parameters to improve flexibility and robustness. The overall high-level architecture is shown in Fig. 5.3, where $D^{\mathcal{T}}$ is the context set and $\psi^{\mathcal{T}}$ denotes the local task-specific parameters. ϕ presents the adaptation network parameters worked as a collection of global parameters θ. For reducing extra parameters and overfitting in a few-shot setting, CNAPs feed the context set into a function (e.g., neural network) and yield an output of the task-specific parameters, such that $\psi^{\mathcal{T}} = \psi_{\phi}(D^{\mathcal{T}})$. These adaptation network parameters are trained on multiple tasks to pursue an optimal learning policy to generate local parameters for solid generalization—a scheme of meta-learning.

CNAPs also employ a feature-wise linear modulation layer (FiLM) to maintain expressiveness while saving parameters during feature adaptation. This proposed method is evaluated on several public benchmarks, including Meta-Dataset, CIFAR-10, CIFAR-100, and MNIST.

5.2.7 Few-shot classification with transductive inference

One of the traditional approaches to the few-shot learning classification problem is relying on a generic meta-learning classifier by episodic learning from a large labeled dataset of multiclass tasks and implementing this classifier using a novel class with low-data regimes. This powerful generalization and adaptation on unseen tasks is effective, robust, and avoids overfitting, but the problem of leveraging limited samples in unseen classification remains. In this way, transductive inference—focusing on the relationship between testing samples and predicting outcomes for the entire testing set—highlights a new research direction. A framework named the TPN, proposed by Liu et al. (2018), tackles this problem by exploiting the whole query set for transductive inference and label propagation (i.e., offering a semisupervised machine learning method to assign labels to unannotated samples). The official code with PyTorch implementation is available at https://github.com/csyanbin/TPN.

TPN mainly consists of four main procedures:

1. In the feature-embedding module, a deep neural network f_φ with parameters φ is applied to project the inputs x_i into an embedding space through a feature map $f_\varphi(x_i; \varphi)$. Both the query set Q and support set S are represented by the same embedding function.
2. The graph construction module is the most important and complex procedure. It leverages the manifold structure from the novel class space of all examples (i.e., $x_i \in S \cup Q$) from the support set or query set. The example-wise length-scale parameter $\sigma_i = g_\phi(f_\varphi(x_i))$ is generated through a CNN g_ϕ.
3. Per the graph structure, label propagation, passing labels from support set S to query set Q, is conducted through iterative label propagation; hence, the closed-form solution about prediction score $F^* = (I - \alpha S)^{-1} Y$ is produced. I denotes an identity matrix, S is the normalized weight, $\alpha \in (0, 1)$ determines the load of propagated information, and Y presents the label matrix.
4. Based on the ground-truth label y from the union of the support set and query set and the propagated score F^*, a cross-entropy classification loss jointly trains the parameters in this framework. Eq. (5.18) presents the N-way K-shot classification loss function, where $\tilde{y}$ denotes the final prediction label and T is a dimension size:

$$J(\varphi, \phi) = \sum_{i=1}^{N \times K + T} \sum_{j=1}^{N} -\mathbb{I}(y_i == j) \log\left(P(\tilde{y}_i = j | x_i)\right) \tag{5.18}$$

This framework is assessed in two public benchmarks: *mini*ImageNet and *tiered*ImageNet (i.e., a subset of ILSVRC-12), in one-shot, five-shot, five-way, and ten-way settings.

5.2.8 Closed-form base learners

Among most of the current research previously introduced in this book, meta-learning technology is embedded into a variety of deep learning methods as an executing paradigm to adopt new tasks rapidly within a few steps of gradients. Briefly, it seeks to implement different deep-learning or machine-learning methods to tackle challenging or unsolved problems by yielding feature representations for the base learners. At the same time, meta-learning algorithms operate as meta-learners to learn across different tasks. In this way, shaping an optimal initialization and retaining a meta-policy for "learning to learn" become the two primary goals.

Alternatively, can meta-learning lead deep neural networks to manipulate regular machine learning tools? Bertinetto et al. (2018) proposed an interesting meta-learning method to guide deep neural networks to operate machine learning tools in a few-shot image classification task. This rapid convergence allows fast adaptation on novel tasks by implementing the base learner Λ as two closed-form strategies (see its overall architecture in Fig. 5.4): Ridge Regression Differentiable Discriminator (R2-D2) and Logistic Regression Differentiable Discriminator (LR-D2). In the base learner, a regular CNN is equipped as a feature extractor ϕ, and a linear predictor f is the last layer for classifying with parameters ω_e. These strategies handle limited training data in high dimensionality with support from back-propagation errors and Woodbury identity. The official code is available at https://github.com/bertinetto/r2d2.

The Ridge Regression Differentiable Discriminator conducts a least-squared-based ridge regression strategy. The ℓ_2 regularization is employed to reduce overfitting, as expressed in Eq. (5.19), where Z denotes samples with weights such that $W = \Lambda(Z)$. This strategy balances the adaptation on new episodes and the expensive computing cost in iterative methods, where X and Y have n pair-wise samples from input embedding and output of Z, λ is a positive hyper-parameter of the base learner, and I denotes identity matrix.

$$\Lambda(Z) = \arg\min_{W} \| XW - Y\|^2 + \lambda \| W\|^2$$

$$= \left(X^T X + \lambda I\right)^{-1} X^T Y \tag{5.19}$$

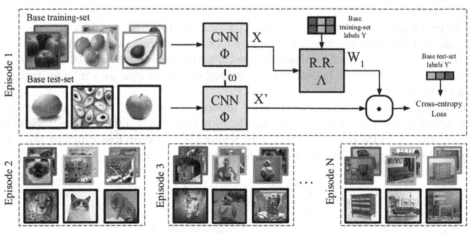

FIG. 5.4 Overall pipeline of the proposed meta-learning solution.
From Bertinetto, L., Henriques, J.F., Torr, P.H., & Vedaldi, A. (2018). Meta-learning with differentiable closed-form solvers. arXiv preprint arXiv:1805.08136.

To avoid the quadratic growth of matrix $X^T X \in \mathbb{R}^{e \times e}$, the Woodbury identity is applied in the R2-D2 strategy, as expressed in Eq. (5.20):

$$W = \Lambda(Z) = X^T \left(XX^T + \lambda I \right)^{-1} Y \tag{5.20}$$

Hence, the classification prediction can be expressed as Eq. (5.21), where α and β are hyperparameters of the base learner:

$$\widehat{Y} = \alpha X'W + \beta \tag{5.21}$$

In LR-D2, Newton's method is applied to obtain parameter ω_i, as expressed in Eq. (5.22), where $\mu_i = \sigma\left(\omega_{i-1}^T X\right)$, $z_i = \omega_{i-1}^T X + \frac{(y-\mu_i)}{s_i}$, and $s_i = \mu_i(1 - \mu_i)$:

$$w_i = \left(X^T \operatorname{diag}(s_i) X + \lambda I \right)^{-1} X^T \operatorname{diag}(s_i) z_i \tag{5.22}$$

Similarly, the Woodbury identity is applied in the LR-D2 strategy to obtain Eq. (5.23):

$$w_i = X^T \left(XX^T + \lambda \operatorname{diag}(s_i)^{-1} \right)^{-1} z_i \tag{5.23}$$

These two strategies (i.e., R2-D2 and LR-D2) are evaluated in multiple public few-shot classification benchmarks, including Omniglot, *mini*ImageNet, and CIFAR-FS.

5.2.9 Long-tailed image classification

Regular public datasets or benchmarks aim to be balanced among different classes, meaning the sample size of each class is about the same or similar to every other. For example, samples related to the label "cat," "ant," "fish," and "dog" are all-around 100,000, individually. However, real-world datasets frequently experience long-tailed or skewed distributions—an extensive amount of training data concentrated on a few classes and a small number of training data spread to multiple classes. In a long-tailed dataset, the number of classes decreases from the head classes (i.e., high-frequency classes) to tail classes (i.e., low-frequency classes). For instance, 100,000 samples have a "cat" label, while "ant," "dog," and "fish" labels overall have 1000 samples in total. This long-tailed dataset increases difficulty on biases handling and inference on balanced testing dataset.

Ren et al. (2020) introduced Balanced Meta-Softmax (BALMS) to overcome the common issue in long-tailed visual recognition (Jamal, Brown, Yang, Wang, & Gong, 2020; Ren, Zeng, Yang, & Urtasun, 2018; Shu et al., 2019)—distribution shifts between training and test data. This strategy integrates generalization error-bound theory into meta-learning.

BALMS consists of two components: (1) Balanced Softmax and (2) Meta Sampler. This framework equipped a Balanced Softmax function to narrow the generalization error bound to construct an optimal Meta-Sampler, and benefit the performance based on large-size skewed datasets (Ren et al., 2020). The official code is available at https://github.com/jiawei-ren/BalancedMetaSoftmax.

Balanced Softmax (BS) is an unbiased modification of the standard Softmax function to address the common biased gradient assessment due to long-tailed composition. BS reduces the variations between the posterior distribution over training and testing samples, which is defined in Eq. (5.24), where η denotes the model output, and $\widehat{\phi_y}$ is the conditional probability of the imbalanced training set:

$$\hat{\ell}(\theta) = -\log\left(\widehat{\phi_y}\right) = \log\left(\frac{n_y e^{\eta_y}}{\sum_{i=1}^{k} n_i e^{\eta_i}}\right) \tag{5.24}$$

Generalization Error Bound offers the upper bound of the related testing error based on its training error. The margin bound is built on negative log-likelihood (NLL) as expressed in Eq. (5.25), where $l_j(\theta)$ is the NLL with Softmax and t is always nonnegative for any threshold:

$$err(t) = Pr\left[t < \log\left(1 + \sum_{i \neq y} e^{\theta_i^T f(x) - \theta_y^T f(x)}\right)\right] = Pr[\ell(\theta) > t] \tag{5.25}$$

The desired training loss $\hat{l}_j^*(\theta)$ for every class j is presented in Eqs. (5.26), (5.27), where optimal γ_j^* is offered by the Cauchy-Schwarz inequality, and ϕ_j is the conditional probability from Bayesian inference:

$$\hat{\ell}_j^*(\theta) = \ell_j(\theta) + \gamma_j^* \tag{5.26}$$

where

$$\ell_j(\theta) = -\log\left(\phi_j\right) \tag{5.27}$$

$\hat{\ell}_j(\theta)$ can approximate $\hat{\ell}_j^*(\theta) = \ell_j(\theta) + \gamma_j^* = \ell_j(\theta) + \frac{\beta n_j^{-1/4}}{\sum_{i=1}^{k} n_i^{-1/4}}$, where $\beta = \sum_{j=1}^{k} \gamma_j$, as shown in Eqs. (5.28), (5.29):

$$\hat{\ell}_j(\theta) = -\log\left(\phi_j\right) \tag{5.28}$$

$$\widehat{\phi}_j = \frac{e^{\eta_y - \log \gamma_j^*}}{\sum_{i=1}^{k} e^{\eta_i - \log \gamma_i^*}} = \frac{n_j^{1/4} e^{\eta_j}}{\sum_{i=1}^{k} n_i^{1/4} e^{\eta_i}} \tag{5.29}$$

Meta Sampler is a resampling approach of the long-tailed data with a bi-level meta-learning strategy (Kang et al., 2020; Zhou, Cui, Wei, & Chen, 2019):

1. For the inner loop, it updates the sample distribution π_ψ's parameters ψ;
2. For the outer loop, it updates the classifier parameters θ. See Eqs. (5.30), (5.31):

$$\pi_\psi^* = \arg\min_\psi L_{D_{meta}}\left(\theta^*\left(\pi_\psi\right)\right) \tag{5.30}$$

where

$$\theta^*\left(\pi_\psi\right) = \arg\min_\theta \widehat{L}_{D_{q(x,y;\pi_\psi)}}(\theta) \tag{5.31}$$

This approach is evaluated in five public datasets: LVIS (Gupta, Dollar, & Girshick, 2019) for instance segmentation, CIFAR-10/100-LT (Krizhevsky, 2009), ImageNet-LT (Liu et al., 2018), and Places-LT (Zhou et al., 2017) for image classification.

5.2.10 Image classification via incremental learning without forgetting

To avoid catastrophic forgetting (Li & Hoiem, 2018; Pfulb & Gepperth, 2019; see the limitations of deep learning in Chapter 1, Section 1.3 for exploration) in order to balance old and new tasks, Rajasegaran et al. (2020) introduced a momentum-based framework to prevent forgetting, named Incremental Task-Agnostic Meta-learning (iTAML)—a task-agnostic meta-learning algorithm for an incremental learning setup. This method can automatically recognize a new task and quickly adapt it within a single update in an image classification task. Instead of typical one-fits-all solutions (Riemer et al., 2019), iTAML provides a generic framework that can quickly adapt to the target task and apply meta-learning through task prediction and class prediction. iTAML has demonstrated the lower bound of sample numbers in the data continuum to feed into the framework during inference for meta-updating. The official code is available at https://github.com/brjathu/iTAML.

The two-stage inference consists of the following steps:

1. The desired task is predicted through the generalized parameters. In Table 5.4, Φ^t presents the trained model for the unknown task t under U classes in each task, and $\mathcal{C}(p) = \{x_j : \ell_j = m\}_{j=1}^{p}$ denotes the data continuum.
2. The generalized parameters from Stage 1 are updated to task-specific parameters in order to assign the correct label to a specific task. See Table 5.5.

Comparison and contrast of iTAML and reptile

iTAML maintains two properties differing from Reptile (Nichol & Schulman, 2018):

1. Supporting with a balancing factor for new and old tasks
2. iTAML can perform single inner-loop updating ($r \geq 1$), whereas Reptile requires numerous inner-loop updates ($r > 1$)

The inner loop is responsible for producing task-specific models for each task via a binary cross-entropy loss where the classification parameters ϕ_i can update in the inner loop independently on each task I; in contrast, the outer loop integrates all task-specific models into an overall generic model.

The meta-training methods are summarized in Table 5.6.

TABLE 5.4 Methods of Stage 1.

```
Input:  Φᵗ,
        C(p) = {xⱼ}ᵖⱼ₌₁
        U, T

1: # initialize scores with zero vector
2:     Q ← [0, 0, 0, ..., 0]
3:     for j = [1, 2, ...., p] do
4:         ŷʲ ← Φᵗ(xⱼ)
5:         for i = [1, 2, ..., r] do
6:             Q[i] ← Q[i] + max(ŷʲ[i · U : (i + 1) · U])
7:     return t_pred ← argmax(Q)
```

Modified from Rajasegaran, J., Khan, S., Hayat, M., Khan, F. S., & Shah, M. (2020). iTAML: An incremental task-agnostic meta-learning approach. In: CVPR.

TABLE 5.5 Methods of Stage 2.

Input: Φ^t
$C(p)$
t_{pred}
memory $\mathcal{M}(t)$

1:   $\widehat{\mathcal{M}}_{t_{\text{pred}}} \leftarrow$ filter $(\mathcal{M}(t), t_{\text{pred}})$
2:   $\Phi_{new} \leftarrow \{\theta, \phi_{t_{\text{pred}}}\}$
3:   for i iterations do
4:       # mini batch with Q samples
5:           $\mathcal{B}'_m \sim \widehat{\mathcal{M}}_{t_{\text{pred}}}$
6:           $\{\hat{y}_q\}_{j=1}^{Q} \leftarrow \Phi_{new}(\mathcal{B}'_m)$
7:           loss $\leftarrow \sum_j \text{BCE}(y_j, \hat{y}_j)$
8:           $\Phi_{new} \leftarrow$ Optimization $(\Phi_{new}, \text{loss})$
9:   end for
10: for $j \in [1, p]$ do
11:      $\hat{y}_j \leftarrow \Phi_{new}(x_j)$
12:      subclass $\leftarrow$ argmax$\left(\hat{y}_j[U \cdot t_{\text{pred}} : U(t_{\text{pred}}+1)]\right)$
13:      $C^j_{\text{pred}} \leftarrow t_{\text{pred}} \cdot U +$ subclass
14: end for
15: return $C_{\text{pred}} = \{C^j_{\text{pred}}\}_{j=1}^{p}$

Modified from Rajasegaran, J., Khan, S., Hayat, M., Khan, F. S., & Shah, M. (2020). iTAML: An incremental task-agnostic meta-learning approach. In: CVPR.

TABLE 5.6 Training methods of iTAML.

Input: Φ^{t-1},
$\mathcal{D}(t)$,
$\mathcal{M}(t-1)$,
t, T and U

1:   $\Phi \leftarrow \Phi^{t-1}$
2:   for e iterations do
3:       $\Phi_{base} \leftarrow \Phi$
4:       $\mathcal{B}_m \sim \{\mathcal{D}(t) \cup \mathcal{M}(t-1)\}$
5:       for $i \in [1, t]$ do
6:           $\Phi_i \leftarrow \{\theta, \phi_i\}$
7:           $\mathcal{B}^i_\mu \leftarrow$ filter $(\mathcal{B}_m, i)$
8:           for r iterations do
9:               $\{\hat{y}_j\}_{j=1}^{J} \leftarrow \Phi_i\left(\{x_j\}_{j=1}^{J}\right)$
10:              loss $\leftarrow \sum_j \text{BCE}(y_j, \hat{y}_j)$
11:              $\Phi_i \leftarrow$ Optimization (Φ_i, loss)
12:      $\eta \leftarrow \exp\left(-\beta \cdot \frac{i}{t}\right)$
     # update model parameters by
13:      $\Phi \leftarrow \eta \cdot \frac{1}{t}\Sigma_i \Phi_i + (1-\eta) \cdot \Phi_{base}$
14: return $\Phi^t \leftarrow \Phi$

Modified from Rajasegaran, J., Khan, S., Hayat, M., Khan, F. S., & Shah, M. (2020). iTAML: An incremental task-agnostic meta-learning approach. In: CVPR.

TABLE 5.7 Methods of lower bound (minimum number) of sample.

Input:	P_0, minimum class prediction accuracy required task accuracy γ, U and t

1:	$N \leftarrow t \cdot U$
2:	$\hat{P}_0 \leftarrow \frac{U-1}{N-1} \cdot (1 - P_0)$
3:	$\min(n)$ with constraint such that
4:	$\sum_{k=\text{round}(\frac{n}{t})+1}^{n} \binom{n}{k} \left(\hat{P}_0\right)^k \left(1 - \hat{P}_0\right)^{n-k} > \gamma$
5:	return n

Modified from Rajasegaran, J., Khan, S., Hayat, M., Khan, F. S., & Shah, M. (2020). iTAML: An incremental task-agnostic meta-learning approach. In: CVPR.

Lower bound of sample

Considering the limited number of samples in a practical case, the lower bound (minimum number) of samples in a data continuum needed to maintain task prediction accuracy is determined according to the methods shown in Table 5.7. Otherwise, a larger sample size leads to a more accurate prediction.

This model was evaluated in diverse public datasets, including CIFAR100, MS-Celeb (Wu et al., 2019), ImageNet, MNIST, and SVHN (Netzer et al., 2011).

5.2.11 Few-shot open set recognition

Typical open-set visual recognition (i.e., the testing classes are unseen during training) is discussed based on large-scale datasets through a CNN-based classification. However, the practical approaches of open-set recognition with a small number of training samples (few-shot open-set recognition) are limited. As CNN self-awareness has increasingly been encouraged in recent research, CNN has the ability to identify and accept what it is good at and reject what it cannot do—open-set recognition is denied. Additionally, few-shot classification and domain adaptation also release pressures on the generalization capability of the potential strategies.

Liu et al. (2020) introduced a prototypical network (Snell, Swersky, & Zemel, 2017) backbone meta-learner, namely, oPen sEt mEta LEaRning (PEELER). They viewed open-set image recognition (Bendale & Boult, 2016; Ge, Demyanov, & Garnavi, 2019; Neal, Olson, Fern, Wong, & Li, 2018; Schlachter, Liao, & Yang, 2019) as a few-shot problem inspired by randomization and posterior knowledge postprocessing.

This model provided three interesting components that combined the open-set into traditional meta-learning: (1) a loss function OpLoss, (2) Open-set episode training, and (3) Gaussian embedding GaussianE. The official code is available at https://github.com/BoLiu-SVCL/meta-open.

OpLoss is introduced as a novel open-set loss that tackles assigning a sample to the unseen classes $\mathbb{C}_i^u$ by maximizing the entropy of seen class $\mathbb{C}_i^s$ probabilities via a negative entropy, as expressed in Eq. (5.32), where:

$$L_o[\boldsymbol{x}] = \sum_{k \in \mathbb{C}_i^s} p(y = k|\boldsymbol{x}) \, \log p(y = k|\boldsymbol{x}) \tag{5.32}$$

PEELER is based on open-set episode training, unlike the regular episode strategy used by Vinyals, Blundell, Lillicrap, Kavukcuoglu, and Wierstra (2016): the training set remains the same, whereas the test set is "augmented with unseen classes." The optimization steps are presented in Eq. (5.33), where L_c denotes a classification loss, L_o is an open-set loss, h represents the meta-model, h' is an estimated optimal model for the training set, and λ is a hyper-parameter:

$$h^* = \underset{h}{\arg\min} \left\{ \sum_{(x_k,y_k) \in \mathbb{T}_i^s | y_k \in \mathbb{C}_i^s} L_c \left[y_k, h'(x_k) \right] + \lambda \sum_{(x_k,y_k) \in \mathbb{T}_i^s | y_k \in \mathbb{C}_i^u} L_o \left[y_k, h'(x_k) \right] \right\} \qquad (5.33)$$

GaussianE was constructed to avoid the unstable optimal boundary shape between seen and unseen classes. The Euclidean distance in Prototypical Network is also replaced by Mahalanobis distance, summarized in Eq. (5.34), where μ_k is the mean of Gaussian distribution of class k, and f_ϕ is the embedding function. Based on the assumption of diagonal covariance matrices, this new embedding function g_φ is involved in Eq. (5.35), where A_k is the parameters directly obtained from back-propagation.

$$d\left(f_\phi(x), \mu_k \right) = \left[f_\phi(x) - \mu_k \right]^T \sum_k^{-1} \left[f_\phi(x) - \mu_k \right] \qquad (5.34)$$

$$A_k = \frac{1}{|S_k|} \sum_{(x_i,y_i) \in S_k} g_\varphi(x_i) \qquad (5.35)$$

PEELER is assessed as offering state-of-the-art performance in metrics of the area under the ROC curve (AUROC) on CIFAR-10 (He et al., 2016) and miniImageNet (Dhillon et al., 2020) datasets. Besides classical image recognition, the weakly supervised video object recognition tasks may also involve this model, as its effectiveness has been reported on the XJTU-Stevens dataset.

5.2.12 Deficiency of pretrained knowledge in few-shot learning

Few-shot learning can drive prediction while relying on only a few samples. It is motivated by the human learning ability to refer to and transfer previous related experience or knowledge to the new situation. Researchers have pursued a surge of interest in how to exploit transferable knowledge. One of the common approaches is to obtain a robust deep neural network by leveraging a dataset with sufficient, perfect annotated data and implementing this pretrained knowledge into fine-tuning or meta-learning methods.

However, this common approach is not always flawless. In supervised learning, more robust pretrained knowledge always leads to better downstream performance. However, the solid pretrained knowledge may be a confounder, confusing the model when samples from a query set are dissimilar to those of the support set in few-shot regimes

(Yue et al., 2020). This is rarely noticed but systematically influences few-shot learning. To overcome a pretrained knowledge deficiency, (Yue et al., 2020) proposed a widely implemented paradigm through backdoor adjustment in low-data regimes, namely Interventional Few-Shot Learning (IFSL). The official code is available at https://github.com/yue-zhongqi/ifsl.

This adjustment approach can be divided into three implementations:

- In feature-wise adjustment, the **x**-dimensioned feature vector is divided into n disjointed subsets with the same size to obtain one classifier per subset. The feature-wise adjustment is expressed in Eq. (5.36). $\mathcal{F}$ denotes the index set of x's feature dimension, $\mathcal{I}_t$ is the index set with x's absolute values which exceed the threshold t, and $[x]_c$ denotes a feature selector that selected the dimension of x w.r.t. the index set c.

$$P(Y|do(X = x)) = \frac{1}{n} \sum_{i=1}^{n} P(Y|[x]_c), \text{where } c = \{k|k \in \mathcal{F}_i \cap \mathcal{I}_t\} \quad (5.36)$$

- In a class-wise adjustment, as expressed in Eq. (5.37), m pretraining classes $a_1, \ldots, a_m$ denote m stratum of pretrained knowledge, where $\oplus$ represents vector concatenation:

$$P(Y|do(X = x)) = \frac{1}{m} \sum_{i=1}^{m} P(Y|x \oplus P(a_i|x)\overline{x_i}) \approx P\left(Y|x \oplus \frac{1}{m} \sum_{i=1}^{m} P(a_i|x)\overline{x_i}\right) \quad (5.37)$$

- The combined adjustment integrates the two adjustments mentioned above, as expressed in Eqs. (5.38), (5.39):

$$P(Y|do(X = x)) \approx \frac{1}{n} \sum_{i=1}^{n} P(Y|[x]_c \oplus \frac{1}{m} \sum_{j=1}^{m} \left[P(a_j|x)\overline{x_j}\right]_c) \quad (5.38)$$

where

$$c = \{k|k \in \mathcal{F}_i \cap \mathcal{I}_t\} \quad (5.39)$$

This paradigm can be widely applied to a variety of meta-learning approaches:

- Matching network (see Chapter 3, Section 3.3)
- Synthetic information bottleneck (SIB)
- Latent embedding optimization (LEO; see Section 5.11.4)
- Meta-transfer learning (MTL)
- Model-agnostic meta-learning (MAML; see Chapter 4, Section 4.3)

The summarized methods of using IFSL in diverse approaches are outlined in Tables 5.8 and 5.9.

This paradigm is assessed on public benchmarks—*mini*ImageNet and *tiered*ImageNet—for one-shot and five-shot regimes in terms of Conventional Acc, Hardness-Specific Acc, CAM-Acc, and cross-domain evaluation.

TABLE 5.8 Methods of Interventional Few-Shot Learning incorporated with meta-learning.

```
Input: D, training dataset
Output: φ, the meta-parameters after optimization
```

```
# Procedure of Meta-learning + IFSL

1. φ initialization

2. while not converged do
3.        Randomly sample (Sᵢ,Qᵢ) ∼ D;
4.        θ classifier initialization through φ,Sᵢ;
5.        Perform fine-tuning θ via procedure of fine-tuning + IFSL based on φ;
6.        Estimate query through Pφ(y|do(x);θ);
7.        Update φ via Lφ(Sᵢ,Qᵢ;θ)
8. return φ
```

Modified from Yue, Z., Zhang, H., Sun, Q., & Hua, X.S. (2020). Interventional few-shot learning. Advances in Neural Information Processing, 33, 2734–2746.

TABLE 5.9 Methods of Interventional Few-Shot Learning incorporated with fine tuning.

```
Input: S = {(xᵢ,yᵢ)}ⁱ₌₁ⁿˢ, the support set
Output: θ, the classifier parameters after fine-tuning
```

```
# Procedure of fine-tuning + IFSL

1. θ initialization
2. while not converged do

3.        for i=1, ..., nₛ do

4.            for d∈D do
5.                Evaluate c=g(x,d);
6.                Obtain P(Y|xᵢ,c,d;θ), P(d)

7.            Estimate ŷᵢ = P(y|do(x);θ);
8.            Update θ via L(ŷᵢ,yᵢ)
9. return θ
```

Modified from Yue, Z., Zhang, H., Sun, Q., & Hua, X.S. (2020). Interventional few-shot learning. Advances in Neural Information Processing, 33, 2734–2746.

5.2.13 Bayesian strategy with deep kernel for regression and cross-domain image classification in a few-shot setting

Patacchiola et al. (2020) proposed a Bayesian meta-learning strategy with the deep kernel, Deep Kernel Transfer (DKT). This method targets two different tasks under low-data regimes: regression (i.e., head pose regression and unknown periodic function estimation) and cross-domain image classification. One hitch of the common differentiable gradient-based meta-learners is the instability caused by the joint training of parameters from two-level optimizations and the demand of higher-order derivatives during weight adjusting. DKT aims to solve few-shot problems through deep kernel learning, where the task-specific parameters' posterior distribution is omitted. An analytical marginal likelihood alternates the inner loop optimization to reduce model complexity, which attempts to estimate data expectedness

TABLE 5.10   Training and testing methods of deep kernel transfer.

Input: $\mathcal{D} = \{\mathcal{T}_n\}_{n=1}^{N}$ training dataset
$\quad\quad \mathcal{T}_* = \{\mathcal{S}_*, \mathcal{Q}_*\}$ testing task
$\quad \hat{\theta}$ kernel hyperparameters through random initialization
$\quad\quad \hat{\phi}$ neural network weights through random initialization
$\quad \alpha, \beta$: step size

\# Procedure of Training
1: function TRAIN $\left(\mathcal{D}, \alpha, \beta, \hat{\theta}, \hat{\phi}\right)$

2: $\quad\quad\quad$ while not done do
3: $\quad\quad\quad\quad\quad$ Randomly sample task $\mathcal{T} = \{\mathcal{S}, \mathcal{Q}\}$ from $\mathcal{D}$
4: $\quad\quad\quad\quad\quad$ Set $\mathcal{T}^x \leftarrow \forall x \in \mathcal{S} \cup \mathcal{Q}$ as well as $\mathcal{T}^y \leftarrow \forall y \in \mathcal{S} \cup \mathcal{Q}$
5: $\quad\quad\quad\quad\quad$ Obtain $\mathcal{L} = -\log p\left(\mathcal{T}^y | \mathcal{T}^x, \hat{\theta}, \hat{\phi}\right)$, where $p\left(\mathcal{D}^y | \mathcal{D}^x, \hat{\theta}, \hat{\phi}\right) = \prod_t P\left(\mathcal{T}_t^y | \mathcal{T}_t^x, \hat{\theta}, \hat{\phi}\right)$
6: $\quad\quad\quad\quad\quad$ Evaluate $\hat{\theta} \leftarrow \hat{\theta} - \alpha \nabla_{\hat{\theta}} \mathcal{L}$ and $\hat{\phi} \leftarrow \hat{\phi} - \beta \nabla_{\hat{\phi}} \mathcal{L}$
7: $\quad\quad\quad$ end while
8: return $\hat{\theta}, \hat{\phi}$
9: end function

\# Procedure of Testing
10: function TEST $\left(\mathcal{T}_*, \hat{\theta}, \hat{\phi}\right)$

11: $\quad$ Set $\mathcal{T}_*^x \leftarrow \forall x \in \mathcal{S}_*, \mathcal{T}_*^y \leftarrow \forall y \in \mathcal{S}_*$, and $x_* \leftarrow x \in \mathcal{Q}_*$

12: $\quad$ return $p\left(y_* | x_*, \mathcal{T}_*^x, \mathcal{T}_*^y, \hat{\theta}, \hat{\phi}\right)$, where $p\left(y_* | x_*, \mathcal{T}_{t_*}^x, \mathcal{T}_{t_*}^y\right) \approx p\left(y_* | x_*, \mathcal{T}_{t_*}^x, \mathcal{T}_{t_*}^y, \hat{\theta}, \hat{\phi}\right)$

13: end function

Modified from Patacchiola, M., Turner, J., Crowley, E.J., O'Boyle, M., & Storkey, A.J. (2020). Bayesian meta-learning for the few-shot setting via deep kernels. Advances in Neural Information Processing Systems, 33, 16108–16118.

with the parameters provided. Unlike traditional bi-level optimization-based approaches, this single-optimization meta-learner offers benefits over few-shot regimes in simplicity, flexibility, efficiency, and robustness without task-specific parameters. The official code is available at https://github.com/BayesWatch/deep-kernel-transfer.

The summarized methods of DKT are outlined in Table 5.10.

For regression, the original log marginal likelihood (line 5 in Table 5.10) is replaced by Eq. (5.40), where D^y and D^x denote input dataset (query and support) and target dataset, $\hat{\theta}$ is task-common hyper-parameter, $\hat{\phi}$ represents other task-common parameters, K_t means the kernel function, and c denotes a constant:

$$\log P\left(D^y | D^x, \hat{\theta}, \hat{\phi}\right) = \sum_t \overbrace{-\frac{1}{2} y_t^\top \left[K_t\left(\hat{\theta}, \hat{\phi}\right)\right]^{-1} y_t}^{data-fit} \overbrace{-\frac{1}{2}\log|K_t\left(\hat{\theta}, \hat{\phi}\right)|}^{penalty} + c \tag{5.40}$$

In image classification, the initial log marginal likelihood (line 5 in Table 5.10) is expressed in Eq. (5.41), where y_c is an output of class c:

$$\log p\left(y | x, \hat{\theta}, \hat{\phi}\right) = \sum_{c=1}^{C} \log p\left(y_c | x, \hat{\theta}, \hat{\phi}\right) \tag{5.41}$$

This method is assessed in several public datasets regarding different tasks:

- Queen Mary University of London (QMUL) multiview face dataset for head pose trajectory estimation
- *mini*ImageNet and Caltech-UCSD Birds (CUB-200) for classification

5.2.14 Statistical diversity in personalized models of federated learning

Federated Learning (also called collaborated learning) aims to obtain an algorithm based on multiple clients connected to a global server. The clients store and keep samples locally, without data interchanging, for privacy protection (e.g., personal bank account information, see a brief description in Section 9.2) and data efficiency. This decentralized concept fundamentally focuses on learning from heterogeneous datasets to acquire a global model shared by all clients. Instead of exchanging data, federated learning passes model parameters between global and local models. The typical approach of standard federated learning follows four steps:

1. After initialization, the global model parameters are transferred to local clients in each iteration
2. Local clients update their local model parameters
3. The global server gathers local model parameters to update global parameters
4. These steps are repeated until local and global parameters converge

The federated learning approach requires high local memory capability, computing power, and bandwidth connections. Additionally, this global model learns from non-IID data; the generalization performances vary due to local data distribution. Imbalance, covariate shifts, prior probability shift, concept drift, and concept shift are the primary deficiencies in these distributions. Statistical diversity issues occur when a variety of N clients incorporate with a shared server to process a global machine-learning model w. Other significant challenges include the heterogeneous distributions among local datasets and the local dataset that generates various distributions in different timestamps (i.e., the temporal heterogeneity).

To tackle these statistical distribution issues, Dinh et al. (2020) proposed a personalized federate learning solution through a meta-learning paradigm named personalized FL (pFedMe). Moreau envelopes are equipped in pFedMe for a "regularized loss function" with the l_2-norm in the local models from the client side; this provides a novel direction to solve personalized federated learning by separating "personalized model optimization from global model learning methods," and then conducting a "bi-level" optimization (Dinh et al., 2020). The official code is available at https://github.com/CharlieDinh/pFedMe.

pFedMe allows each client to train their local model with diverse directions based on reference point w, which is contributed by every client. The bi-level problem can be formulated into Eqs. (5.42), (5.43), where w denotes the reference point for each client as they develop a model in various directions, θ_i is the personalization model for client i, $F_i(w)$ denotes the Moreau envelope, λ represents a regularization parameter, and f_i means the expected loss of data distribution of client i:

$$\min_{w \in \mathbb{R}^d} \left\{ F(w) := \frac{1}{N} \sum_{i=1}^{N} F_i(w) \right\} \qquad (5.42)$$

where

$$F_i(w) = \min_{\theta_i \in \mathbb{R}^d} \left\{ f_i(\theta_i) + \frac{\lambda}{2} \| \theta_i - w \|^2 \right\} \tag{5.43}$$

Hence, the optimal personalized model can be expressed in Eq. (5.44), where "prox" stands for proximal operation:

$$\hat{\theta}_i(w) := \text{prox}_{f_i/\lambda}(w) = \arg\min_{\theta_i \in \mathbb{R}^d} \left\{ f_i(\theta_i) + \frac{\lambda}{2} \| \theta_i - w \|^2 \right\} \tag{5.44}$$

Since the closed-form cannot be directly accessible, the first-order approximation over the mini-batch of data $\mathcal{D}_i$ is conducted instead, as shown in Eq. (5.45), where $w_{i,r}^t$ denotes a local model at global round t and local round r for client i:

$$\tilde{h}_i\left(\theta_i; w_{i,r}^t, \mathcal{D}_i\right) := \tilde{f}_i(\theta_i; \mathcal{D}_i) + \frac{\lambda}{2} \| \theta_i - w_{i,r}^t \|^2 \tag{5.45}$$

The gradient descent of this first-order approximation $\tilde{h}_i\left(\theta_i; w_{i,r}^t, \mathcal{D}_i\right)$ is conducted as Eq. (5.46), in which ν denotes the accuracy level:

$$\| \nabla \tilde{h}_i\left(\tilde{\theta}_i; w_{i,r}^t, \mathcal{D}_i\right) \|^2 \leq \nu \tag{5.46}$$

The summarized methods of pFedMe are outlined in Table 5.11.

This method is evaluated on public benchmark MNIST and synthesis datasets; it outperforms FedAvg and the meta-learning approach Per-FedAvg with an efficient convergence rate.

TABLE 5.11 Training methods of pFedMe.

```
1:  # Global communication
2:  for t=0, ..., T-1 do

3:       Global server pass w_t to all local clients

4:       for i=1,..., N do
5:            w_{i,0}^t = w_t

6:       # Local update rounds
7:            for r=0 to R-1 do
8:                 Randomly sample a new mini-batch D_i in size |D| and minimize
     h_i(θ_i; w_{i,r}^t, D_i) toward an accuracy level to obtain a δ-approximate θ_i(w_{i,r}^t)
9:                 Compute w_{i,r+1}^t = w_{i,r}^t - ηλ(w_{i,r}^t - θ̃_i(w_{i,r}^t))

10:      Global server uniformly samples a subcollection of clients S^t in size S in a
         uniform way, then, every selected client passes the local model w_{i,R}^t, where ∀i∈S^t, to
         the global server

11:      Global server updates the global model through w_{t+1} = (1-β)w_t + β∑_{i∈S^t} (w_{i,R}^t)/S
```

Modified from Dinh, C., Tran, N., & Nguyen, J. (2020). Personalized federated learning with moreau envelopes. Advances in Neural Information Processing Systems, 33, 21394–21405.

5.2.15 Meta-learning deficiency in few-shot learning

Although meta-learning has attracted interest within discussions of few-shot learning in recent years, some contemporary researchers proposed questions and limitations about meta-learning. They argued that the performance of whole-classification may approximate or exceed that of numerous meta-learning approaches (Chen, Liu, Kira, Wang, & Huang, 2019; Gidaris et al., 2018). The whole-classification comprises the entire label set from the base classes.

Targeting the under-explored space regarding the effectiveness and limitations of meta-learning in few-shot regimes, (Chen et al., 2021) examined the generalization capability of meta-learning and the trade-offs of the objectives of whole-classification and meta-learning. The conclusion confirmed the meta-learning objective discrepancy in few-shot learning. Meta-learning paradigms perform better on novel tasks belonging to base classes (i.e., base class generalization). Still, they remain deficient on tasks associated with novel classes (i.e., novel class generalization) compared to whole-classification. The issues of class transferability in meta-learning are the critical factor that limits its performance.

To compare the capability of the meta-learning paradigm under few-shot regimes, two approaches are studied and compared: Classifier-Baseline and Meta-Baseline in N-way K-shot classification tasks. The official code is available at https://github.com/yinboc/few-shot-meta-baseline.

1. Classifier-Baseline conducts a whole-classification procedure trained on base classes with a removal at the last fully connected layer. The average embedding w_c involved the centroids in class c, such that $w_c = \frac{1}{|S_c|} \sum_{x \in S_c} f_\theta(x)$, where f_θ denotes encoder and S_c presents samples in class c. The query data are categorized into the nearest centroid through cosine distance as $p(y = c \,|x) = \frac{exp\left(\langle f_\theta(x), w_c \rangle\right)}{\sum_{c'} exp\left(\langle f_\theta(x), w_{c'} \rangle\right)}$.

2. Meta-Baseline has an analogous structure to Matching Network or Prototypical Network equipped with a pretraining classification. The overall pipeline consists of two stages: classification training followed by the Classifier-Baseline and meta-learning. The primary goal of Meta-Baseline is to verify the effectiveness of the meta-learning objective from the Classifier-Baseline. The query sample is computed through the nearest centroid through the cosine distance with a learnable scalar τ as $p(y = c \,|x) = \frac{exp\left(\tau \cdot \langle f_\theta(x), w_c \rangle\right)}{\sum_{c'} exp\left(\tau \cdot \langle f_\theta(x), w_{c'} \rangle\right)}$.

This method is evaluated in public benchmarks in *mini*ImageNet, *tiered*ImageNet, and ImageNet-800 (which is a subset randomly sampled from ILSVRC-2012 1K; Russakovsky et al., 2015) under one-shot and five-shot regimes. The Meta-Baseline outperforms multiple frameworks over the given datasets to be viewed as the representative of meta-learning methods. These frameworks include:

- Matching Networks (see Chapter 3, Section 3.3)
- Prototypical Networks (see Chapter 3, Section 3.4)
- Activation to Parameters (Qiao, Liu, Shen, & Yuille, 2018)
- LEO (see section 5.11.4)
- Baselines ++ (Chen, Liu, et al., 2019)

- SNAIL (Mishra, Rohaninejad, Chen, & Abbeel, 2018)
- AdaResNet (Munkhdalai, Yuan, Mehri, Wang, & Trischler, 2017)
- TADAM (Oreshkin, López, & Lacoste, 2018)
- MTL (Sun, Liu, Chua, & Schiele, 2019)
- MetaOptNet (Lee, Maji, Ravichandran, & Soatto, 2019)
- SLA-AG (Lee, Hwang, & Shin, 2020)
- ConstellationNet (Xu, Xu, Wang, & Tu, 2021)

5.3 Face recognition and face presentation attack

5.3.1 Introduction

Facial recognition

Facial recognization (FR), which has become a well-studied biometric technology since the 1990s, attempts to retrieve a face query image from a face image dataset. In this way, a classical or deep learning-based paradigm can achieve feature representation of the face image. The deep learning approach relies heavily on extensive samples during a training phase. However, it is not practical to maintain a large volume of training samples from candidates' faces in real scenarios; as a result, FR was developed as a zero-shot learning task. Due to the similarity of human facial shapes and textures, "the representation learned from a small proportion of faces can generalize well to the rest" (Wang & Deng, 2020). With the emerging development of deep-learning techniques, many significant signs of progress have been achieved in multiple pieces of research, including DeepFace (Taigman & Yang, 2014), Deep IDs (Sun, Wang, & Tang, 2015), VGG Face (Parkhi, Vedaldi, & Zisserman, 2015), Face Net (Schroff, Kalenichenko, & Philbin, 2015), ArcFace (Deng, Guo, Xue, & Zafeiriou, 2019), and SphereFace. Common loss functions can be categorized into different groups: loss function with Euclidean distance, loss function with angular-margin or cosine-margin, and SoftMax loss and its modifications (Wang & Deng, 2020).

Face antispoofing

Amidst the evolution of face recognition, face presentation attack detection (PAD)—or face antispoofing—has played an important role in the cybersecurity of face authentication systems to defend against presentation attacks (PAs). Presentation attacks can be divided into two types (Ming, Visani, Luoman, & Burie, 2020): impersonation (spoofing) attacks and obfuscation attacks. In impersonation attacks, impostors use photos or videos to fool the authentication system, whereas obfuscation attacks occur when someone avoids being identified by the face authentication system. Common impersonation attacks consist of print attacks, email account attacks, video replay attacks, cousin domain attacks, and unknown-type attacks (e.g., complex attacks that do not belong to any existing category). For example, DeepFake technology generates falsified videos with synthesizing faces. Extreme makeup, partial occlusion, and plastic surgery are three main subtypes of obfuscation attacks.

There are several PAD methods, including:

- texture cues ("the texture properties of the object presented to the system," per Ming et al., 2020)
- 3D geometric cues
- Liveness cues (any dynamic physiological signals of life)
- Multiple cues (combination of liveness cues, 3D geometric cues, and texture cues)
- Voluntary reactions (user completing predefined tasks)
- New trends in neural architecture search, zero/few-shot learning, and domain adaption

Developing face recognition techniques that are robust against PAs is the most effective strategy. Supervised learning methods of face antispoofing require massive training data; on the other hand, techniques that allow generalization for unseen spoofing types through the discriminative features could be more appropriate for this issue. Thus, zero-shot learning, which leverages general discriminative features and performs fast adaptation, is favorable in this scenario. For zero/few-shot face antispoofing approaches, Arashloo, Kittler, and Christmas (2017) proposed the first solution of unseen attack detection through a one-class SVM. This motivated Nikisins, Mohammadi, Anjos, and Marcel (2018) to develop a one-class Gaussian mixed model (GMM) for unseen attack detection. Liu et al. (2018) introduced a CNN-backbone deep tree network (DTN) addressing impersonation and obfuscation attacks. Shao et al. (2020) proposed the first domain adaption strategies based on adversarial learning to improve the generalization ability to existing approaches, while Pereira, Anjos, Martino, and Marcel (2013) presented the first combination dataset for domain adaption.

Even though current studies include a range of practical strategies for face recognition and antifacespoofing, some deficiencies remain. The current error rate of the human talking head is low, however, it is still inferior to the sensitive human visual system due to the complexity of the human head and the uncanny valley effect. Furthermore, when the testing domain is unknown or inaccessible, the performance fluctuates. In addition, during training in antifacespoofing tasks, the generalization ability remains questionable against unseen attacks. The model struggles with domain adaptation from a source dataset and testing in another shifted dataset.

Meta-learning sheds light on these issues. The meta-learning frameworks leverage pose-independent information and face landmarks to generate a synthesized image, passed to the discriminator with ground truth based on a small number of video streams. A meta-learning method can also quickly adapt to unseen situations or novel domains.

The following three sections will investigate face recognition and presentation attacks. Personalized virtual talking head generation is examined in Section 5.3.2. This is achievable in a few-shot regime of novel people's faces and shows promising outcomes for portrait paintings of human faces.

Section 5.3.3 primarily introduces meta-learning face recognition, Section 5.3.4 presents an antispoofing meta-learner from a domain-generalization perspective, and Section 5.3.5 studies a zero-shot/few-shot antispoofing strategy.

5.3.2 Person-specific talking head generation for unseen people and portrait painting in few-shot regimes

A talking head synthesis system faces two major difficulties: human head complexity and the uncanny valley effect. Due to the challenging complexity of the human head's photometric, kinematics, and geometrics, every small detail (e.g., hair, beard, garments, wrinkles, and mouth cavity) are complicated to model. The uncanny valley effect describes the relationship between the human-like appearance of a computer-generated object and the emotional reaction it evokes. The extremely high sensitivity of the human visual system leads to an incredibly low error tolerance for human head-appearance modeling.

Zakharov et al. (2019) presented a meta-learning framework of adversarial generative models to create person-specific virtual talking heads with a variety of facial expressions and facial appearances. In contrast with the traditional data-hungry deep learning strategy, the proposed framework processes a dataset of numerous videos. Then, it generates photorealistic person-specific talking head images with a collection of facial landmarks. It synthesizes highly realistic personalized head models for new people or portrait paintings with only a few photographs or videos as inputs. An unofficial but widely applied code is available at https://github.com/vincent-thevenin/Realistic-Neural-Talking-Head-Models.

This framework consists of three main modules:

- An embedder $E(x_i(s), y_i(s); \phi)$, where $x_i(\cdot)$ denotes the video frame and $y_i(\cdot)$ means the landmark image. Both $x_i(\cdot)$ and $y_i(\cdot)$ are projecting to N-dimensional space $\widehat{e}_i(\cdot)$. Parameters ϕ are obtained during meta-training, so $\widehat{e}_i(\cdot)$ carries video-specific postinvariant knowledge.
- A generator $G(y_i(t), \widehat{e}_i; \psi, P)$, where ψ presents person-generic parameters that are learned in meta-training, while ψ_i indicates person-specific parameters that are estimated by $\widehat{e}_i$ with projection matrix P: $\widehat{\psi}_i = P\widehat{e}_i$.
- A discriminator $D(x_i(t), y_i(t), i; \theta, W, w_0, b)$, where θ, W, w_0, b are all learnable parameters.

See the general workflow of this strategy in Fig. 5.5.

During the meta-learning stage, the parameters of embedder and generator are learned through the loss function shown in Eq. (5.47), where $\mathcal{L}_{CNT}$ is the content loss and $\mathcal{L}_{MCH}$ denotes the embedding matching loss:

$$\mathcal{L}(\phi, \psi, \mathbf{P}, \theta, \mathbf{W}, \mathbf{w}_0, b) = \mathcal{L}_{CNT}(\phi, \psi, \mathbf{P}) + \mathcal{L}_{ADV}(\phi, \psi, \mathbf{P}, \theta, \mathbf{W}, \mathbf{w}_0, b) + \mathcal{L}_{MCH}(\phi, \mathbf{W}) \qquad (5.47)$$

The adversarial $\mathcal{L}_{ADV}$ is computed in Eq. (5.48), which is involved in the realism score by a discriminator and a feature-matching $\mathcal{L}_{FM}$:

$$\mathcal{L}_{ADV}(\phi, \psi, \mathbf{P}, \theta, \mathbf{W}, \mathbf{w}_0, b) = -D(\hat{\mathbf{x}}_i(t), \mathbf{y}_i(t), i; \theta, \mathbf{W}, \mathbf{w}_0, b) + \mathcal{L}_{FM} \qquad (5.48)$$

The hinge loss function aims to simulate a higher realism score from a real image $x_i(t)$ and reduce the score of synthesized images $\widehat{x}_i(t)$, as expressed in Eq. (5.49):

$$\mathcal{L}_{DSC}(\phi, \psi, \mathbf{P}, \theta, \mathbf{W}, \mathbf{w}_0, b) = \max\left(0, 1 + D(\hat{\mathbf{x}}_i(t), \mathbf{y}_i(t), i; \phi, \psi, \theta, \mathbf{W}, \mathbf{w}_0, b)\right)$$
$$+ \max\left(0, 1 - D(\mathbf{x}_i(t), \mathbf{y}_i(t), i; \theta, \mathbf{W}, \mathbf{w}_0, b)\right) \qquad (5.49)$$

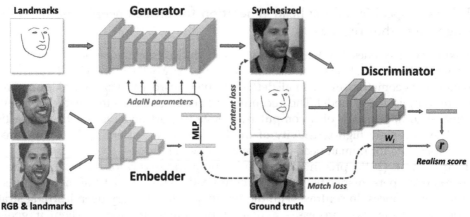

FIG. 5.5 General pipeline of the proposed method.
© *2022 IEEE. Reprinted, with permission, from Zakharov, E., Shysheya, A., Burkov, E., & Lempitsky, V. (2019, September 25). Few-shot adversarial learning of realistic neural talking head models. arXiv.org. Retrieved June 4, 2022, from https://arxiv.org/abs/1905.08233.*

This method is evaluated in dataset X2Face (Wiles, Koepke, & Zisserman, 2018) and Pix2pixHD (Wang et al., 2018).

5.3.3 Face presentation attack and domain generalization

Progress in face antispoofing has experienced impressive advancements, but its ability to generalize remains questionable when faced with previously unseen attacks. As a result, domain adaptation is required. Because the model is trained and tested on the same dataset, the outcome of intra-class experiments tends to be favorable. However, cross-dataset performance becomes less efficacious, since the model is trained on a source dataset and tested on another shifted dataset. In this case, the model relies heavily on specific dataset-biased cues and loses its ability to accurately detect different distributions from a related but distinct dataset.

Shao et al. (2020) offered an antispoofing meta-learner with a distinguishing generalization ability to unseen federal credit face presentation attacks by viewing it as a domain generalization (DG) problem (Balaji et al., 2018; Nichol, Achiam, & Schulman, 2018; Shao, Lan, Li, & Yuen, 2019). This model maintains good performance in simultaneously simulated domain shifts on diverse scenarios via regularized fine-grained meta-learning to find an optimal direction during the meta-optimizing. The official code is available at https://github.com/rshaojimmy/AAAI2020-RFMetaFAS.

This method consists of three parts: meta-train, meta-test, and meta-optimization. Table 5.12 summarizes this step-by-step pseudocode.

This strategy is focused on photo attacks and video replay attacks based on four public datasets, consisting of:

- Oulu-NPU (Boulkenafet, 2017)
- CASIA-MFSD (He et al., 2016)
- Idiap Replay-Attack (Chingovska, Anjos, & Marcel, 2012)
- MSU-MFSD (Wen, Han, & Jain, 2015)

TABLE 5.12 General methods of the proposed method.

Input: $D=[D_1,D_2,\ldots,D_N]$, N source domains
      α, β, hyperparameters
Output: updated parameters θ_F, θ_D, θ_M

Initialize θ_F, θ_D, θ_M

1: **while** not meeting stopping criteria **do**

2:     Randomly choose (N-1) source domains from D as training domains D_{trn}, and the rest of the validation domains as D_{val}

    # Meta-training

3:     Selecting batch from each domain in D_{trn} as T_i (i=1,...,N-1)

4:     **for** each T_i **do**

5:         $\mathcal{L}_{Cls\left(\widehat{T_i}\right)}(\theta_F,\theta_M) = \sum_{(x,\widehat{T})} y\log M(F(x)) + (1-y)\ \log(1-M(F(x)))$

6:         $\theta_{M_i}' = \theta_M - \alpha\nabla_{\theta_M}\mathcal{L}_{Cls\left(\widehat{T_i}\right)}(\theta_F,\theta_M)$

7:         $\mathcal{L}_{Dep\left(\widetilde{T}\right)}(\theta_F,\theta_D) = \sum_{(x,I)\sim\widetilde{T}} \|D(F(x)) - I\|^2$

8:     **end for**

    # Meta-testing

9:     Selecting batch from D_{val} as $\widetilde{T}$

10:     $\sum_{i=1}^{N-1}\mathcal{L}_{Cls\left(\widetilde{T}\right)}\left(\theta_F,\theta_{M_i}'\right) = \sum_{i=1}^{N-1}\sum_{\widetilde{T}} y\log M_i'(F(x)) + (1-y)\log(1-M_i'(F(x)))$

11:     $\mathcal{L}_{Dep\left(\widetilde{T}\right)}(\theta_F,\theta_D) = \sum_{(x,I)\sim\widetilde{T}} \|D(F(x)) - I\|^2$

    # Meta-optimizing, model parameters updating by:

12:     $\theta_M \leftarrow \theta_M - \beta\nabla_{\theta_M}\left(\sum_{i=1}^{N-1}\left(\mathcal{L}_{Cls\left(\widehat{T_i}\right)}(\theta_F,\theta_M) + \mathcal{L}_{Cls\left(\widetilde{T}\right)}\left(\theta_F,\theta_{M_i}'\right)\right)\right)$

13:     $\theta_F \leftarrow \theta_F - \beta\nabla_{\theta_F}\left(\mathcal{L}_{Dep\left(\widetilde{T}\right)}(\theta_F,\theta_D) + \sum_{i=1}^{N-1}\left(\mathcal{L}_{Cls\left(\widehat{T_i}\right)}(\theta_F,\theta_M) + \mathcal{L}_{Dep\left(\widehat{T_i}\right)}(\theta_F,\theta_D) + \mathcal{L}_{Cls\left(\widetilde{T}\right)}\left(\theta_F,\theta_{M_i}'\right)\right)\right)$

14:     $\theta_D \leftarrow \theta_D - \beta\nabla_{\theta_D}\left(\mathcal{L}_{Dep\left(\widetilde{T}\right)}(\theta_F,\theta_D) + \sum_{i=1}^{N-1}\left(\mathcal{L}_{Dep\left(\widehat{T_i}\right)}(\theta_F,\theta_D)\right)\right)$

15: **end while**

16: **return** updated parameters θ_F, θ_D, θ_M

Modified from Shao, R., Lan, X., & Yuen, P. C. (2020). Regularized fine-grained meta face anti-spoofing. In: AAAI.

5.3.4 Anti-face-spoofing in few-shot and zero-shot scenarios

Large-scale data consumption and adaptation to novel presentation attacks and unseen application scenarios present challenges to traditional deep learning models. Qin et al. (2020) viewed the face antispoofing task as a few-shot and zero-shot meta-learning problem rather than a supervised learning one. Traditional supervised FAS needs large training samples and easy overfitting on existing attacks plus providing inadequate generalization ability on unseen tasks. Qin and colleagues proposed Adaptive Inner-Update Meta Face Antispoofing (AIM-FAS) under the fusion training (FT) method through predetermined living and fake human faces, as well as examples of novel attacks that have never been processed before. The official code is available at https://github.com/qyxqyx/AIM_FAS.

AIM-FAS attempts to:

- leverage discriminative features from predetermined presentation attacks by reusing them in case of unknown spoofing types
- Offer quick adaption of few-shot predefined attacks from new spoofing types

In general workflow of Adaptive Inner-Update Meta Face Anti-Spoofing, the zero- or few-shot FAS tasks are produced through task generation based on a fine-grained FAS dataset that consists of living ($L_1, L_2,..., L_p$) and spoofing ($S_1, S_2,..., S_p$) types. The support set in AIM-FAS for zero-shot tasks contains only predefined living and spoofing data samples, whereas the few-shot element has predefined data and adds unseen living and spoofing data. This dataset setting distinguishes AIM-FAS under meta-learning from traditional FAS solutions. During meta-training, the meta learner inner updates based on the support set from zero-or few-shot FAS tasks modulates θ to $\theta^{(u)}$ after u steps. By testing on the query set, meta-loss and zero- or few-shot learning performance are generated via the updated meta-learner.

The meta-learner's loss on support set $\mathcal{L}_s$ and update rules in the inner-update stage are expressed in Eqs. (5.50), (5.51), where for each task τ_i, $\theta_i^{(j)}$ denotes the weight of meta-learner after j inner updating, $\|s(\tau_i)\|$ means the number of instance in support set, and α and γ are scalar parameters:

$$\mathcal{L}_{s(\tau_i)}\left(\theta_i^{(j)}\right) \leftarrow \frac{1}{\|s(\tau_i)\|}\sum_{x,y \in s(\tau_i)} \ell\left(f_{\theta_i^{(j)}}(x), y\right) \tag{5.50}$$

$$\theta_i^{(j+1)} \leftarrow \theta_i^{(j)} - \alpha \cdot \gamma^j \cdot \nabla_{\theta_i^{(j)}} \mathcal{L}_{s(\tau_i)}\left(\theta_i^{(j)}\right) \tag{5.51}$$

The meta-learner's loss on query set $\mathcal{L}_q$ and update rules of the optimization stage on the query set with new unseen samples are shown in Eqs. (5.52), (5.53), where $\|q(\tau_i)\|$ means the number of instances in the query set, and $\theta_i^{(u)}$ denotes the weight of meta-learner after u inner updating:

$$\mathcal{L}_{q(\tau_i)}\left(\theta_i^{(u)}\right) \leftarrow \frac{1}{\|q(\tau_i)\|}\sum_{x,y \in q(\tau_i)} \ell\left(f_{\theta_i^{(u)}}(x), y\right) \tag{5.52}$$

$$(\theta, \gamma, \alpha) \leftarrow (\theta, \gamma, \alpha) - \beta \cdot \nabla_{(\theta,\alpha,\gamma)} \mathcal{L}_{q(\tau_i)}\left(\theta_i^{(u)}\right) \tag{5.53}$$

Fusion training—training simultaneously on zero-shot tasks and few-shot tasks—is utilized in AIM-FAS and reported as an improvement on the generalization ability of both zero- and few-shot FAS outcomes. The step-by-step training and testing stages are provided in Tables 5.13 and 5.14, respectively.

This solution is valid across benchmarks of CASIA (Zhang et al., 2012) and MSU-MFSD (Wen et al., 2015). The evaluating metrics involved attack presentation classification error rate (APCER), bona fide presentation classification error rate (BPCER), average classification error rate (ACER), and area under the curve (AUC).

TABLE 5.13 Summarized meta-training methods of adaptive inner-update meta-face antispoofing.

Input: Ψ_t, K-shot ($K >= 0$) FAS training tasks
  β, hyperparameter of learning rate
  u, number of inner-update steps
  α, γ, AIU parameters
Output: updated θ, α, γ.

1: Initialize θ, α, and γ
2: Obtain a pretrained meta-learner based on the training dataset
3: while not meeting requirements do
4:    sample a batch of tasks $\tau_i \in \Psi_t$
  # meta-training procedure
5:    for each task τ_i do
6:    $\theta_i^{(0)} = \theta$
7:      for $j < u$ do
8:        $\mathcal{L}_{s(\tau_i)}\left(\theta_i^{(j)}\right) \leftarrow \frac{1}{\|s(\tau_i)\|} \sum_{x,y \in s(\tau_i)} l\left(f_{\theta_i^{(j)}}(x), y\right)$
        # update model parameters by
9:        $\theta_i^{(j+1)} \leftarrow \theta_i^{(j)} - \alpha \cdot \gamma^j \cdot \nabla_{\theta_i^{(j)}} \mathcal{L}_{s(\tau_i)}\left(\theta_i^{(j)}\right)$
10:       $\mathcal{L}_{q(\tau_i)}\left(\theta_i^{(j+1)}\right) \leftarrow \frac{1}{\|q(\tau_i)\|} \sum_{x,y \in q(\tau_i)} l\left(f_{\theta_i^{(j+1)}}(x), y\right)$
11:       $j = j + 1$
12:     end for

13:   end for
    # update model parameters by
14:   $(\theta, \alpha, \gamma) \leftarrow (\theta, \alpha, \gamma) - \beta \cdot \nabla_{(\theta, \alpha, \gamma)} \sum_{\tau_i} \mathcal{L}_{q(\tau_i)}\left(\theta_i^{(u)}\right)$

15: end while

Modified from Qin, Y., Zhao, C., Zhu, X., Wang, Z., Yu, Z., Fu, T., ... Lei, Z. (2020). Learning meta model for zero- and few-shot face antispoofing. In: AAAI.

TABLE 5.14 Summarized meta-testing methods of adaptive inner-update meta-face antispoofing.

Input: Ψ_v, K-shot FAS testing tasks
  u, number of inner-update steps
  θ, parameter of meta-learner
  α, γ, AIU parameters
Output: Meta-learner's performance P

1: for each task $\tau_i \in \Psi_v$ do
2:    $\theta_i^{(0)} = \theta$
  # meta-test procedure
3:    for $j < u$ do
4:      $\mathcal{L}_{s(\tau_i)}\left(\theta_i^{(j)}\right) \leftarrow \frac{1}{\|s(\tau_i)\|} \sum_{x,y \in s(\tau_i)} l\left(f_{\theta_i^{(j)}}(x), y\right)$
      # update model parameters by
5:      $\theta_i^{(j+1)} \leftarrow \theta_i^{(j)} - \alpha \cdot \gamma^j \cdot \nabla_{\theta_i^{(j)}} \mathcal{L}_{s(\tau_i)}\left(\theta_i^{(j)}\right)$
6:      $j = j + 1$
7:    end for

8:    $P_{q(\tau_i)} \leftarrow p(f_{\theta\{u\}}(X_{q(\tau_i)}), Y_{q(\tau_i)})$
9: end for

10: $P \leftarrow \frac{1}{\|\Psi_v\|} \sum_{\tau_i \in \Psi_v} P_{q(\tau_i)}$

Modified from Qin, Y., Zhao, C., Zhu, X., Wang, Z., Yu, Z., Fu, T., ... Lei, Z. (2020). Learning meta model for zero- and few-shot face antispoofing. In: AAAI.

5.3.5 Generalized face recognition in the unseen domain

There are two types of difficulties related to domains in face recognition. In type 1, the target domain D_T is predetermined and accessible. The domain adaptation solutions concentrate on a source domain D_S with labeled data, and the target domain D_T may contain or not contain labels. The strategy tries to leverage knowledge extracted from the source domain to generalize and reuse in the target domain. For type 2, the target domain is unknown, or the data is unseen—known as generalized face recognition. In this situation, the domain generalization strategies are conducted.

Inspired by meta-learning domain-generalization methods by Li's team (2018) and domain generalizable person re-identification strategy by Song, Kim, and Lee (2019), Guo, Zhu, et al. (2020) introduced a novel meta-learner on unseen target-domain face recognition without any updating, named meta-face recognition (MFR).

MFR purely focuses on the generalized face recognition scenario where the target domain is unseen. It is built on a MAML-modified backbone. The official code is available at https://github.com/cleardusk/MFR.

MFR can be divided into three main modules:

- Domain-level sampling from source domains to imitate domain shifts
- Distributions optimization over multiple domains to leverage face embedding
- Meta-optimization to enhance generalization ability

In the optimization of the multiple-domain distribution stages, this model consists of three specific loss functions to "domain-invariant and discriminative face" (Guo, Zhu, et al., 2020) representation extracted from different domain distributions:

1. Hard-pair attention loss $\mathcal{L}_{hp}$ to optimize hard positive and hard negative pairs, expressed in Eq. (5.54), where $\mathcal{P}$ is the indices of hard positive pairs, $\mathcal{N}$ denotes the indices of hard negative pairs, F_g denotes the gallery embedding, and F_p is probe embedding:

$$\mathcal{L}_{hp} = \frac{1}{2|\mathcal{P}|} \sum_{i \in \mathcal{P}} \left\| F_{g_i} - F_{p_i} \right\|_2^2 - \frac{1}{2|\mathcal{N}|} \sum_{(i,j) \in \mathcal{P}} \left\| F_{g_i} - F_{p_j} \right\|_2^2 \qquad (5.54)$$

2. Soft-classification loss $\mathcal{L}_{cls}$ to classify within a single batch, as in Eq. (5.55), where B represents identities, CE denotes cross-entropy loss, $F_{g_i} W^\top$ or $F_{p_i} W^\top$ represents the logit of identity i, and s is a fixed scaling parameter:

$$\mathcal{L}_{cls} = \frac{1}{2B} \sum_{i=1}^{B} \left(CE\left(y_i, s \cdot F_{g_i} W^\top\right) + CE\left(y_i, s \cdot F_{p_i} W^\top\right) \right) \qquad (5.55)$$

3. Domain alignment loss $\mathcal{L}_{da}$ to narrow gaps between meta-train domains, as in Eqs. (5.56), (5.57), where c_j indicates the mean embedding of a sampled batch of domain $\mathcal{D}_j$, c_{mtr} denotes the embedding center of all mean embedding in the n meta-train domains, and F_g and F_p become normalized embedding:

$$c_j = \frac{1}{B} \sum_{i=1}^{B} \left(\frac{F_{g_i}^{\mathcal{D}_j} + F_{p_i}^{\mathcal{D}_j}}{2} \right) \qquad (5.56)$$

TABLE 5.15   General meta-optimization methods of meta-face recognition.

```
Input: Source (training) domains 𝒟_S = {𝒟_1, 𝒟_2, ..., 𝒟_N}
       f(θ) pretrained model of θ
       α, β, γ, hyperparameters
       B, batch size
```

```
1  for iteration = max_iterations do
2      Zero initialization for gradient g_θ
       # For each meta-batch, where 𝒟_mte denotes meta-test domain
3      for each 𝒟_mte from 𝒟_S do

           # For each batch
4          Sample the rest of the domains as meta-train domains 𝒟_mtr

5          # Meta-training
6          Sample 𝒳_S : B paired images with B identities in 𝒟_mtr
7          ℒ_S = ℒ_hp(𝒳_S;θ) + ℒ_cls(𝒳_S;θ) + ℒ_da(𝒳_S;θ)
8          θ' = θ − α∇_θℒ_S(θ);

9          # Meta-testing
10         Sample 𝒳_T : B paired images with B identities in 𝒟_mte
11         ℒ_T = ℒ_hp(𝒳_T;θ') + ℒ_cls(𝒳_T;θ')

13         g_θ ← g_θ + γ∇_θℒ_S + (1−γ)∇_θℒ_T

14     end for

15     # Meta-optimization with SGD, update model parameters by
16     θ ← θ − ℓ/n g_θ

17 end for
```

Modified from Guo, J., Zhu, X., Zhao, C., Cao, D., Lei, Z., & Li, S. Z. (2020). Learning meta face recognition in unseen domains. In: CVPR.

$$c_{mtr} = \frac{1}{n}\sum_{j=1}^{n} c_j$$

$$\mathcal{L}_{da} = \frac{1}{n}\sum_{i=1}^{B} \left\| s \cdot (c_j - c_{mtr}) \right\|_2^2 \tag{5.57}$$

The overview of meta-optimization is summarized in Table 5.15.

The benchmarks are evaluated via a receiver-operating characteristic curve (ROC) and rank-1 accuracy in five public target datasets: CACD-VS (Chen, Chen, & Hsu, 2014), CASIA NIR-VIS 2.0 (Li, Yi, Lei, & Liao, 2013), MultiPIE (Gross, Matthews, Cohn, Kanade, & Baker, 2010), MeGlass (Guo, Zhu, Lei, & Li, 2018), and Public-IvS (Zhu et al., 2019).

5.4 Object detection

5.4.1 Introduction

Object detection is an elemental task in computer vision and remarkably important for a variety of complex vision tasks, for instance, image retrieval, segmentation, people detection, object tracking, medical feature detection, and image captioning. Other applications—for example, self-driven vehicles, augmented reality, and human-machine interactions—also rely heavily on object detection.

Object detection is a task that seeks (a) to determine in an image if there are any instances of specific objects belonging to a given category and, if any do exist, (b) to output the extent and spatial location of each object instance. In other words, if the object exists, both the spatial location information and classification labels need to return. The spatial location can be expressed through a bounding box, a segmentation mask, or a closed boundary.

Approaches

Current detection tasks mainly focus on structured objects (e.g., pedestrians, birds, flowers, and human faces) rather than unstructured scenes (e.g., clouds). Object detection can be categorized into two types: generic object detection (for broad categories like cat, taxi, or boat) and specific object detection (for specific instances like the Empire State Building or the face of a certain person).

In the broad usage of deep neural networks, the CNN is a dominating model in this task. Early deep neural network-based approaches include:

- Region Proposal, including Region CNN (R-CNN; Girshick, Donahue, Darrell, & Malik, 2013), Fast RCNN (Girshick, 2015), and Mask RCNN (He, Gkioxari, Dollár, & Girshick, 2017; He, Zhang, & Sun, 2017)
- You Only Look Once (YOLO; Redmon, Divvala, Girshick, & Farhadi, 2016) and its variations
- Single Shot Multibox Detector (SSD; Liu et al., 2016)
- RefineNet (Lin, Shen, Hengel, & Reid, 2016)
- RetinaNet (Lin, Goyal, Girshick, He, & Dollar, 2017)
- Deformable ConvNets (Dai, 2017) and its variations

  There are multiple criteria for an optimal generic object detector to address, including:

- High accuracy (e.g., location accuracy and recognition accuracy)
- High efficiency
- High robustness regarding intra-class variations (e.g., image noise, object instance diversities)
- High distinctiveness (e.g., interclass ambiguities)

Benchmarks

The common benchmarks for assessments include:

- PASCAL VOC (Everingham et al., 2015)
- MS COCO (Lin et al., 2014)
- Open Images (Kuznetsova et al., 2018)
- LVIS (Gupta et al., 2019)

During experiments, the typical evaluation metrics include detection speed in frames per second (FPS), precision (e.g., average precision), mean average precision, recall, true positive (TP), false positive (FP), and overlap ratio intersection over union (IOU).

Although with benefits among the diverse deep learning frameworks described above, some challenging situations remain in few-shot regimes as extensive datasets are inaccessible. Accurate localization based on a minimal number of samples is under-explored in a few-shot object detection model and leaves vast potential for further examination. Additionally, deep neural networks cannot handle the overfitting and poor generalization capability of a low-data setting, and so novel classes that are unseen during training are still full of uncertainty.

Meta-learning offers multiple end-to-end solutions to handle object detection in a few-show setting and unseen situations. It also offers variations of existing object detection models to tailor to the low-data setup, by modifying and incorporating the widely-used DCNN object detection (e.g., decoupling the category-agnostic and category-specific elements or leveraging task-specific and task-agnostic knowledge). In addition, meta-learners capture the meta-feature, which contains meta-knowledge to be generalized to unseen situations. The global feature, which contains information of the novel classes, is employed to adjust the meta-feature for an appropriate and accurate generalization.

This section investigates multiple potential issues in object detection and addresses a variety of solutions incorporated with meta-learning. A practical meta-solution in object detection for long-tailed data is presented in Section 5.4.2. Section 5.4.3 investigates few-shot novel object and viewpoint detection with approaches motivated by Meta R-CNN and PostFromShape. In Section 5.4.4, base classes are leveraged with abundant perfectly annotated training samples through a one-staged meta-feature learner to adapt low-data unseen classes quickly.

5.4.2 Long-tailed data object detection in few-shot scenarios

Few-shot learning has continuously attracted a high level of interest. Few-shot object detection consists of a localizer for multiple object positions and a classifier to recognize the categories of certain objects. However, localizing based on few-shot samples is under-explored in few-shot object detection models and remains an important avenue for further investigation.

Wang, Ramanan, and Hebert (2019) constructed a Faster R-CNN-modified (Ren, He, Girshick, & Sun, 2015) few-shot object detection framework named MetaDet. It can simultaneously address the problems of few-shot object classification (Vinyals et al., 2016) and multiobjects localization. MetaDet is a parameterized weight prediction framework trained on an end-to-end meta-learning procedure. Inspired by early research (Andrychowicz et al., 2016; Hu, Dollar, He, Darrell, & Girshick, 2018; Hu, Shen, & Sun, 2018; Li & Malik, 2017; Sinha, Sarkar, Mukherjee, & Krishnamurthy, 2017; Wang & Hebert, 2016a, 2016b), this model focuses on leveraging category-specific and category-agnostic components from a detection model with a convolutional neural network backbone.

MetaDet learns both knowledges from large-scale datasets efficiently and transferable meta-knowledge from base classes with numerical annotated bounding boxes to guide few-shot detection tasks for unseen classes (Chen, Wang, Wang, & Qiao, 2018; Kang et al., 2019; Schwartz et al., 2019).

The meta-objective function for each class c is expressed in Eq. (5.58). MetaDet is flexible to any other CNN backbone object detectors as its base detector for equivalent functionality of the current Fast R-CNN module in the inner loop.

$$\left\| \mathcal{T}\left(w_{det}^c; \phi\right) - w_{det}^{c,*}\right\|^2 + \lambda \sum_{(x,y) \in RoI^c} loss\left(\mathcal{D}\left(x; \mathcal{T}\left(w_{det}^c; \phi\right)\right), y\right) \qquad (5.58)$$

This evaluation explores different "novel" classes:

1. The unseen classes
2. The classes that have solely seen global image-level labels
3. The classes that have been seen as background but with no labels

Multiple scenarios have been experimented during evaluation on public datasets of PASCAL VOC (Everingham et al., 2015), MS-COCO (Lin et al., 2014), ImageNet, and iNaturalist:

1. The within-domain
2. The cross-domain
3. The long-tailed setup

5.4.3 Object detection in few-shot scenarios

DCNNs have experienced remarkable progress in object detection. However, several drawbacks are also worthy of attention. Due to the nature of object detection, annotated training data requires both classification labels and accurate bounding boxes. When considering DCNN-based solutions, large volumes of annotated data with bounding boxes and ground-truth labels are required, yet this is expensive and samples are often scarce. Training deep neural networks on a small-scale dataset frequently leads to overfitting and weak generalization capabilities.

To detect objects in low-data regimes, Kang et al. (2019) suggested a few-shot object detector for 2D visual recognition. This has an end-to-end architecture with a straightforward learning strategy—exploiting meta-knowledge learned from base classes (i.e., plentiful training samples with perfect annotation) through a one-stage detector structured meta-feature learner and then rapidly adapting to unseen classes (i.e., limited annotated data). The official code is available at https://github.com/bingykang/Fewshot_Detection.

This model has three main modules (see Fig. 5.6 for the overall pipeline):

- A meta-feature learner D captures meta-features—which can be generalized to N novel object classes—by leveraging the perfectly annotated base classes with a large amount of data through the DarkNet-19 backbone.
- Within a lightweight reweighting module M, the support samples from N unseen classes are converted to N global feature representations (i.e., the reweighting vectors, which indicate the relevance between support samples and meta-features). These N global feature vectors are embedded into N reweighting vectors to adjust the meta-features.
- A detection prediction module P inputs N adapted meta-features to generate bounding box location (x, y, h, w), a classification score (c), and an objectness score (o) for unseen objects. The overall loss function is expressed in Eqs. (5.59), (5.60), where $\hat{c}_i$ denotes

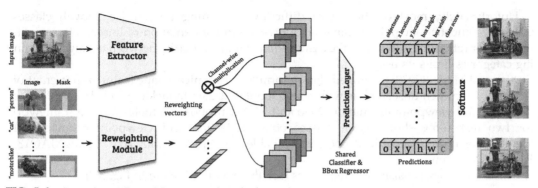

FIG. 5.6 General workflow of the proposed method.
© 2022 IEEE. Reprinted, with permission, from Kang, B., Liu, Z., Wang, X., Yu, F., Feng, J., & Darrell, T. (2019). Few-shot object detection via feature reweighting. In: ICCV.

calibrated scores for class i, and $\mathcal{L}_c$, $\mathcal{L}_{bbx}$, $\mathcal{L}_{obj}$ represents the loss of classification score, loss of bounding box location, and loss of objectness score, respectively:

$$\mathcal{L}_{\text{det}} = \mathcal{L}_c + \mathcal{L}_{bbx} + \mathcal{L}_{obj} \tag{5.59}$$

where

$$\mathcal{L}_c = -\sum_{i=1}^{N} \mathbb{1}(\cdot, i) \log(\hat{c}_i) \tag{5.60}$$

This strategy consists of a two-step learning procedure:

1. The base training procedure extracts the meta-features and creates optimal reweighting modules based on base classes.
2. The detection prediction model is fine-tuned to modulate novel classes in the few-shot fine-tuning procedure.

The method is evaluated on datasets MS-COCO, VOC 2012, VOC 2007, and PASCAL VOC.

5.4.4 Unseen object detection and viewpoint estimation in low-data settings

Viewpoint estimation involves determining the viewpoint of an object that belongs to a known category in a given image. It is widely used in virtual reality, scientific understanding and reconstruction, object detection, and robotics. The traditional primary research focused on large datasets under deep learning techniques; however, the approach's generalization in novel classes is still problematic. Peering approaches under few-shot learning shed light on this field but remain under-explored.

Viewpoint estimation using deep learning approaches can be divided into three groups:

- Euler angles computing
- Key point detection supported by 3D bounding box corners or semantic key points
- Template-based matching

Unfortunately, most of them face difficulty examining unseen (i.e., novel) classes. Category-agnostic viewpoint estimation allows the implementation of unseen classes with no need for retraining. However, the assumption of high similarity between testing and training categories limits its usage.

Xiao and Marlet (2020) leveraged class-informative canonical shape feature representation captured from each unseen class with a few annotated data to tackle novel classes of object detection and viewpoint estimation. Xiao and Marlet proposed a meta-learning framework for two tasks—few-shot unseen classes object detection and viewpoint estimation in low-data regimes. The official code is available at https://github.com/YoungXIAO13/FewShotDetection.

This framework consists of three stages (see the overall pipeline in Fig. 5.7):

1. The query sample x is fed into the query encode $\mathcal{F}^{qry}$; in the meantime, the class encoder $\mathcal{F}^{cls}$ takes class-informative data z_c as input. The goal of this step is to produce feature representations.
2. The feature aggregator $\mathcal{A}$ integrates query feature vectors and class feature vectors.
3. The task-specific predictor $\mathcal{P}$ inputs the integrated feature vectors in both object detection and viewpoint estimation. However, the outputs differ by task during the final stage.

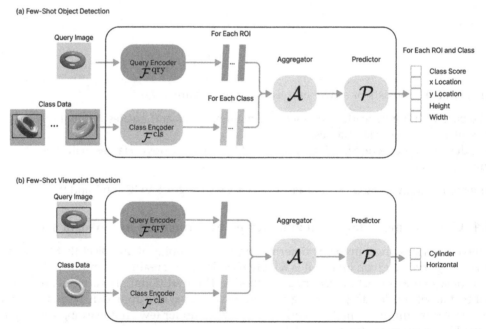

FIG. 5.7　(A) General workflow of few-shot object detection. (B) General workflow of few-shot viewpoint estimation.
Adapted from Springer, ECCV, Few-Shot Object Detection and Viewpoint Estimation for Objects in the Wild, Yang Xiao, Renaud Marlet (2020).

○ The output for few-shot object detection includes the class score and object location per region of interest and class.

The object detection loss function is motivated by Meta R-CNN (see Section 5.6.3), as expressed in Eq. (5.61). The original meta-loss term is removed to focus on interclass similarities without interclass knowledge. $\mathcal{L}_{rpn}$ is employed on RPN's output to separate the foreground and background, and $\mathcal{L}_{meta}$ presents the cross-entropy loss to increase the variety of class features among different classes. $\mathcal{L}_{cls}$ and $\mathcal{L}_{loc}$ denote the cross-entropy loss and smoothed-L1 loss, respectively, for box classification.

$$\mathcal{L} = \mathcal{L}_{\text{rpn}} + \mathcal{L}_{\text{cls}} + \mathcal{L}_{\text{loc}} + \mathcal{L}_{\text{meta}} \tag{5.61}$$

○ In the few-shot viewpoint estimation, the output is the quantized angle purified by regressed angular offsets.

Analogous to PostFromShape, the viewpoint estimation loss function is expressed in Eq. (5.62), where θ represents the Euler angle. $\mathcal{L}_{cls}^{\theta}$ denotes the cross-entropy loss to the classification of Euler angles, and $\mathcal{L}_{reg}^{\theta}$ offers a smoothed-L1 loss to regression of angular offsets, where $(azi, ele, inp) = \mathcal{P}\left(\mathcal{A}\left(f^{qry}, f^{cls}\right)\right)$, and $\mathcal{A}$ is the mean aggregator.

$$\mathcal{L} = \sum_{\theta \in \{azi, ele, inp\}} \mathcal{L}_{\text{cls}}^{\theta} + \mathcal{L}_{\text{reg}}^{\theta} \tag{5.62}$$

This framework is evaluated on four public benchmarks for two tasks:

- PASCAL VOC and MS COCO (Lin et al., 2014) for novel object detection in low-data regimes
- Inter-dataset between Pasacal3D+ and ObjectNet3D and intra-dataset ObjectNet3D for viewpoint estimation in a few-shot setup

5.5 Fine-grained image recognition

5.5.1 Introduction

In contrast to generic image recognition, fine-grained image recognition focuses on visually processing and analyzing objects from a secondary level of categories related to a specific domain. For example, generic image recognition discusses the classification of a super-category (e.g., flowers, trees, and buildings), whereas fine-grained image recognition explores various subcategories (e.g., different types of roses: climbing roses, hybrid tea roses, grandiflora roses, floribunda roses, polyantha roses, and miniature roses). This task seeks to identify visual objects against multiple species of a super-category. The significant intra-class variations caused by pose and rotation, and the minor interclass variations shared by largely similar species make it a tricky and complex task in machine learning (Wei, Cui, Yang, Wang, & Liu, 2019; Wei, Wu, & Cui, 2019).

Approaches

There are three paradigm types of fine-grained image recognition:

1. Part-based recognition aims to learn the discriminative semantic part of fine-grained visual recognition through bounding box, segmentation mask, etc. The mid-level/part-level knowledge can improve classification accuracy. This method is also called localization classification subnetworks.
2. End-to-end feature encoding aims to employ a deep neural network to learn distinctive knowledge through deep neural networks, such as Bilinear CNN (Lin, RoyChowdhury, & Maji, 2015). The frameworks stated below belong to this category (see Charikar, Chen, & Farach-Colton, 2002; Cui et al., 2017; Dubey, Gupta, Raskar, & Naik, 2018; Gao, Beijbom, Zhang, & Darrell, 2016; Kong & Fowlkes, 2017; Pham & Pagh, 2013).
3. External information aims to capture information from the web, text explanations, human-computer interactions, and multimodal data.

Benchmarks

Some public benchmark datasets of fine-grained image analysis include:

- Oxford Flower (Nilsback & Zisserman, 2008)
- CUB200-2011 (Wah, Branson, Welinder, Perona, & Belongie, 2011), focused on bird subcategories
- Stanford Dog (Khosla, Jayadevaprakash, Yao, & Li, 2011)
- Stanford Car (Krause, Stark, Deng, & Fei-Fei, 2013)
- FGVC Aircraft (Maji, Kannala, Rahtu, Blaschko, & Vedaldi, 2013; Maji, Rahtu, Kannala, Blaschko, & Vedaldi, 2013), focused on aircraft subcategories
- Birdsnap (Berg et al., 2014)
- Fru92 (Hou, Feng, & Wang, 2017), focused on fruit subcategories
- Veg200 (Hou et al., 2017), focused on vegetable subcategories
- iNat2017 (Horn et al., 2017), focused on plant and animal subcategories
- RPC (Wei, Cui, et al., 2019; Wei, Wu, & Cui, 2019), focused on retail items subcategories

Many difficulties need to be solved at the practical level of the above approaches. First, due to the lack of large-scale datasets, and because certain rare categories are extremely challenging to collect (such as endangered animals or rare diseases), increasing attention focuses on few-shot learning strategies. The traditional method of mining distinctive knowledge from different categories reaches its limits when handling few-shot regimes. Additionally, transfer learning may solve the domain adaptation issues to some degree but lead to overfitting in rare categories. This is because the number of samples in rare categories is extremely minimal compared to other common categories with massive data.

Current studies of meta-learning shed light on these dilemmas. Meta-learning offers a novel regularizer to manage the overfitting in a low-quality setup by encoding generic knowledge or semantically relevant information from auxiliary data. Moreover, to generate more synthesis samples, meta-learning supports an off-the-shelf generator mainly designed for a few-shot setting, which can be conducted in one-shot regimes as well. It can successfully handle the biases in the synthesis images caused by the original image distribution. Meta-learning also enhances the part-based recognizer by thoroughly investigating the distinctive knowledge using only a small number of samples.

The following sections concentrate on various solutions equipped with a meta-learning framework to tackle the fine-grained issue. Section 5.5.2 addresses a common problem in transfer learning by providing a regularized objective function. Section 5.5.3 presents a GAN-based one-shot object classifier to enhance generated images. Section 5.5.4 discusses a two-stage learner for few-shot fine-grained visual recognition.

5.5.2 Fine-grained visual categorization

Collecting data for subordinate object classification remains challenging. In some cases, only a small number of samples can be gathered for each category. Many attempts focus on using global or regional discriminative knowledge to distinguish between the subtle subordinate object categories. However, such data mining has already reached its limit in terms of improved generalization, as only a few samples can be supplied for each category. Transfer learning or domain adaptation with fine-tuning is a common strategy to counter this; however, overfitting occurs frequently. Meta-learning thus becomes an ideal strategy for reducing the negative effects of overfitting and domain adaptation based on only a few samples.

Zhang et al. (2018) suggested a fine-grained visual categorization (FGVC) meta-solver based on a novel regularized meta-learning objective named MetaFGNet, motivated by fundamental few-shot meta-learning frameworks (e.g., Ravi & Larochelle, 2017; Vinyals et al., 2016). This framework addresses the common issue in traditional transfer learning-based approaches due to an implicit regularization: pretraining without considering the target task is not the best optimal strategy for fine-tuning to avoid overfitting. The official code is available at https://github.com/Gorilla-Lab-SCUT/MetaFGNet.

This strategy proposed a novel regularized objective function—an explicit regularization. It learns the parameters of base neural networks for encoding mutual or semantically relevant knowledge extracted from auxiliary data—this is the objective of regularized meta-learning in the fine-grained classification tasks, as expressed in Eq. (5.63), which represents the step size. $\mathcal{T}$ is the training set, η presents the step size, $R(S;\theta^s)$ mean the regularizer of auxiliary data S and source model θ^s, θ^t denotes the target model, and θ_b is the base model.

$$\min_{\theta_b, \theta_{c'}^t, \theta_c^s} \frac{1}{|\mathcal{T}|} L\left(\mathcal{T};\theta^t - \eta \frac{1}{|\mathcal{T}|} \nabla_{\theta^t} L(\mathcal{T};\theta^t)\right) + \frac{1}{|S|} R(S;\theta^s) \tag{5.63}$$

The overall architecture is displayed in Fig. 5.8.

Comprehensive training is summarized in Table 5.16.

This method has been trained and evaluated on public datasets CUB-200-2011 (Wah et al., 2011) and Stanford Dogs (Khosla et al., 2011), as well as ImageNet Subset and L-Bird Subset (Krause, Johnson, Krishna, & Li, 2016; Krause et al., 2016) separately.

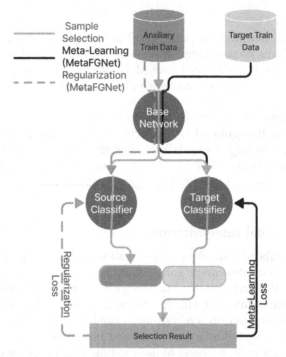

FIG. 5.8 High-level pipeline of MetaFGNet.
Adapted from Springer, ECCV, Fine-Grained Visual Categorization using Meta-Learning Optimization with Sample Selection of Auxiliary, Yabin Zhang, Hui Tang, Kui Jia (2018).

TABLE 5.16 General training methods of MetaFGNet.

Input: $\mathcal{T}$: target train data
$\mathcal{S}$: auxiliary train data
η, α: hyperparameters of step size

1: Initialize θ_b, θ_c^t, θ_c^s

2: **while** not meeting requirement **do**
3:     Select mini-batches $\mathcal{T}_i$, $\mathcal{S}_i$ from $\mathcal{T}$, $\mathcal{S}$
4:     Compute:
$$\left[\Delta(\theta_b;\mathcal{S}_i),\Delta(\theta_c^s;\mathcal{S}_i)\right] = \tfrac{1}{|\mathcal{S}_i|}\nabla_{\theta^s}R(\mathcal{S}_i;\theta^s)$$
$$\left[\Delta(\theta_b;\mathcal{T}_i),\Delta(\theta_c^t;\mathcal{T}_i)\right] = \tfrac{1}{|\mathcal{T}_i|}\nabla_{\theta^t}L(\mathcal{T}_i;\theta^t)$$
5:     Evaluate adapted parameters with SGD:
$$\sum_{k=\text{round}\left(\frac{n}{2}\right)+1}^{n}\binom{n}{k}\left(\hat{P}_0\right)^k\left(1-\hat{P}_0\right)^{n-k} > \gamma$$
6:     Sample a different mini-batch $\mathcal{T}_j$ from $\mathcal{T}$
7:     Compute:
$$\left[\Delta(\theta_b;\mathcal{T}_j),\Delta(\theta_c^t;\mathcal{T}_j)\right] = \nabla_{\theta^t}\tfrac{1}{|\mathcal{T}_j|}L\left(\mathcal{T}_j;\theta^{t'}\right)\left[\mathbf{I} - \eta\tfrac{1}{|\mathcal{T}_i|}\left(\tfrac{\partial^2 L\left(\mathcal{T}_i;\theta^t\right)}{\partial\left(\theta^t\right)^2}\right)\right]$$
8:     Parameter update by:
$$\theta_b \leftarrow \theta_b - \alpha\left[\Delta(\theta_b;\mathcal{S}_i) + \Delta(\theta_b;\mathcal{T}_j)\right]$$
$$\theta_c^t \leftarrow \theta_c^t - \alpha\Delta(\theta_c^t;\mathcal{T}_j)$$
$$\theta_c^s \leftarrow \theta_c^s - \alpha\Delta(\theta_c^s;\mathcal{S}_i)$$
9: **end while**

Modified from Adapted from Springer, ECCV, Fine-Grained Visual Categorization using Meta-Learning Optimization with Sample Selection of Auxiliary, Yabin Zhang, Hui Tang, Kui Jia (2018).

5.5.3 One-shot fine-grained visual recognition

Fine-grained visual tasks face severe difficulties with large-scale datasets. One typical solution is to employ an off-the-shelf generator, such as GANs, to generate extensive numbers of synthesis images to alleviate the problem of data scarcity. However, classifiers learning from such images often perform more poorly than those trained on real images. This is due to existing distribution bias in the synthesis images caused by the original image distribution. This negative impact becomes more prominent in one-shot regimes. An off-the-shelf generator designed explicitly for one-shot learning is unable to effectively tackle these issues.

Tsutsui et al. (2019) proposed an end-to-end approach to one-shot fine-grained visual recognition through an off-the-shelf GAN (Goodfellow et al., 2014) and an image classifier called the Meta Image Reinforcing Network (MetaIRNet). The modified GAN is a pretrained generator based on ImageNet-2012.

This framework aims to classify based on few examples and productively enhances the generated images. It is trained on a hybrid dataset consisting of generated images, where the mixed dataset efficiently improves generalization ability rather than naively expanding the training set with generated images. See the comprehensive workflow and high-level architecture in Fig. 5.9. The official code is available at https://github.com/apple2373/MetaIRNet.

The generator G in the off-the-shelf GAN is introduced to produce more images in the targeted data-scarce domain. The loss function with $\mathcal{L}_1$ distance is expressed in Eq. (5.64), where I_z denotes a generated image from input signal z, $\mathcal{L}_{EM}$ represents the earth mover distance of z and random noise r, perceptual loss $\mathcal{L}_{perc}$ with coefficient λ_p.

$$\mathcal{L}_G(G, I_z, z) = \mathcal{L}_1(G(z), I_z) + \lambda_p \mathcal{L}_{perc}(G(z), I_z) + \lambda_z \mathcal{L}_{EM}(z, r) \tag{5.64}$$

The MetaIRNet consists of a classification network C for one-shot learning and an image fusion network F (Tsutsui et al., 2019). The image fusion network splits images into a 3×3 grid, then linearly integrates the cells associated with weights w generated by a CNN based on two

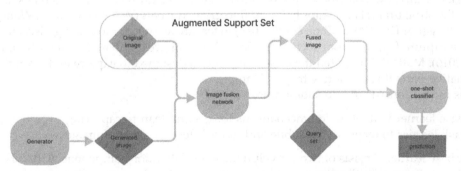

FIG. 5.9 General workflow of meta-image reinforcing network with two modules: an Image Fusion Network and a One-Shot Classifier.
Modified from Tsutsui, S., Fu, Y., & Crandall, D. (2019). Meta-reinforced synthetic data for one-shot fine-grained visual recognition. In: NeurIPS.

images, as expressed in Eq. (5.65). I_{syn} means a synthesized image, I_g is a corresponding generated image to a real image I, and $\odot$ denotes element-wise multiplication.

$$I_{syn} = w \odot I + (1 - w) \odot I_g \tag{5.65}$$

The one-shot classification network C produces the average feature vector by processing prototype vectors p_c for each class c, which is expressed in Eq. (5.66), with each class probability formulation in Eq. (5.67). $\widetilde{S}_c$ means augmented support set for class c, I_i is query set, and $\|\cdot\|$ presents Euclidean distance.

$$p_c = \frac{1}{\left|\widetilde{S}_c\right|} \sum_{(I_i, y_i) \in \widetilde{S}_c} C(I_i) \tag{5.66}$$

$$P(y_i = c | I_i) = \frac{exp\left(-\|C(I_i) - p_c\|\right)}{\sum_{k=1}^{n} exp\left(-\|C(I_i) - p_k\|\right)} \tag{5.67}$$

This approach is assessed with Caltech UCSD Birds (CUB; Wah et al., 2011) and North American Birds (NAB; Horn et al., 2015).

5.5.4 Few-shot fine-grained image recognition

Subordinate object labeling requires a much higher degree of expertise than labelling for generic object categories, a necessity that brings with it considerable expense. Furthermore, it is impossible to collect large-scale data for certain categories, such as endangered animals or rare diseases. Few-shot fine-grained recognition approaches have been implemented in this field, yet they are significantly lacking in comprehensive, in-depth investigation.

To solve these issues, Zhu, Liu, and Jiang (2020) presented an end-to-end approach for few-shot fine-grained image recognition (FSFGIR; Chai, Lempitsky, & Zisserman, 2013; Xie, Tian, Hong, Yan, & Zhang, 2013) named Multi-Attention Meta-Learning (MattML). The traditional strategies of unknown part-based annotations (Xiao et al., 2015) occur in two types: investigating the structural relationships between fine-grained labels (Wang et al., 2015; Wang, Wu, Shen, Hengel, & Dick, 2015; Zhou & Lin, 2016) in feature learning or localizing discriminative parts to capture features from such parts (Xiao, Xu, et al., 2015; Zhang, Xiong, Zhou, Lin, & Tian, 2016). MattML integrated these elements and is designed to explore and learn the discriminative parts through a few training samples.

This model consists of two submodules:

- A base learner with attention mechanisms for general feature capturing
- A task learner to focus on the subtle and local-difference parts of images

The base learner consists of two convolutional block attention components (CBAMs; Woo, Park, Lee, & Kweon, 2018) without residual operations, a feature-embedding component, and one classifier.

The task learner contains an encoder-decoder to learn and process task representations. A weight generator conducts task representations to support the classifier's weight initialization of the base learner. The reconstructed loss $\mathcal{L}_r$ of the task-embedding network is expressed in Eq. (5.68), for each task $\mathcal{T}_i$, where $\forall j$, $g_{i,\,j} = RNN_{enc}(E(x_{i,\,j}), g_{i,\,j-1})$, RNN_{dec} and RNN_{enc} mean recurrent decoder and encoder, respectively, and $E(\cdot)$ is the embedding network:

$$\mathcal{L}_r(D_{\mathcal{T}_i,\,S}) = \frac{1}{n_s}\sum_{j}^{n_s}\left\|RNN_{dec}\left(g_{i,j}\right) - E\left(x_{i,j}\right)\right\|_2^2 \tag{5.68}$$

The objective function of meta-training is expressed in Eq. (5.69), where $D_{\mathcal{T}_i,S}$ denotes the support set, Θ^i represents the task-specific learnable parameters across all sampled tasks, $D_{\mathcal{T}_i,T}$ is the target set, and ξ is a fixed balancing factor:

$$\min_{\Phi}\sum_{\mathcal{T}_i}\mathcal{L}\left(D_{\mathcal{T}_i,T};\Theta^i\right) + \xi\mathcal{L}_r(D_{\mathcal{T}_i,S}) \tag{5.69}$$

Its performance is evaluated in four fine-grained public benchmarks: CUB Bird (Wah et al., 2011), Stanford Dogs (Khosla et al., 2011), Stanford Cars (Krause et al., 2013), and FGVC Aircraft (Maji, Kannala, et al., 2013; Maji, Rahtu, et al., 2013). It conducts a comparison of multiple meta-learning methods—including MAML, Prototypical Networks (Snell et al., 2017), Matching Networks (Vinyals et al., 2016), and Relation Networks (Sung et al., 2018).

5.6 Image segmentation

5.6.1 Introduction

Image segmentation is a fundamental technique of various deep learning applications (Forsyth & Ponce, 2002), including medical image analysis, self-driven vehicles (e.g., pedestrian detection and navigable surface), video surveillance, virtual reality and augmented reality, scene understanding, robotic perception, and image compression, among others.

Modern development

In contrast to classic computer vision-based image segmentation through grayscale value (pixel value), neural network-based image segmentation can be categorized into three main types: semantic segmentation, instance segmentation, and panoptic segmentation. Image segmentation involves classifying each pixel in an image with the correct label so that pixels sharing the same label have certain characteristics. Semantic segmentation is a pixel-level classification problem with semantic labels (i.e., a set of objects). Instance segmentation performs pixel classification for the partitioning of individual objects. In effect, instance segmentation improves the scope and capability of semantic segmentation by adopting detection and portraying every single object of interest from the image.

Long, Shelhamer, and Darrell (2015) proposed the first neural network-based model for semantic image segmentation through a fully convolutional network (FCN). One limitation of FCN family segmentation is a failure in analyzing potentially useful scene-level semantic context. This problem is addressed by methods equipped with probabilistic graphical models (e.g., Chen, Chen, & Hsu, 2014; Lin et al., 2016; Liu et al., 2015).

Encoder-decoder backbone segmentation has attracted much research interest. Noh, Hong, and Han (2015) introduced a deconvolution-based model with a few parameters. The HR-Net by Yuan, Chen, and Wang (2019) tackled the encoder-decoder model issue regarding the loss function of fine-grained knowledge on an image.

The **regional convolutional network** (R-CNN) serves as the most popular backbone for instance segmentation. It is usually combined with a region proposal network (RPN) for locating the bounding box. Some modifications include the Mask R-CNN (He, Gkioxari, et al., 2017; He, Zhang, & Sun, 2017), Path Aggregation Network (PANet) based on Mask R-CNN and FPN, multitask network (Dai, He, & Sun, 2016), Mask-Lab (Chen et al., 2018) through Faster R-CNN, DeepMask (Pinheiro, Collobert, & Dollar, 2015), and TensorMask (Chen et al., 2019). The meta-learning framework by Yan et al. (2020) is also motivated by this idea, as detailed later.

Dilated convolution is primarily used in real-time segmentation, such as DeepLabv1 (Chen, Chen, & Hsu, 2014), DeepLabv2 (Chen, Papandreou, Kokkinos, Murphy, & Yuille, 2017), DeepLabv3 (Chen et al., 2017), and DeepLabv3+ (Chen et al., 2018) through pointwise convolution and atrous separable convolution. Besides these elements mentioned, structure backbones, the recurrent neural network (RNN), attention mechanisms, GANs, and CNN incorporated with active contour models (ACMs) have all became popular in image segmentation.

Recent meta-learning methods are mainly trained on a 2D dataset, such as PASCAL Visual Object Classes (VOC), PASCAL Context (Xia & Kulis, 2017), Microsoft Common Objects in Context (MS COCO; Lin et al., 2014), Cityscapes (Cordts et al., 2016), and others. However, many 3D datasets and 2.5D datasets (color RGB and depth) are available, such as NYU-D Y2 (Silberman, Hoiem, Kohli, & Fergus, 2012), SUN-3D (Xiao, Owens, & Torralba, 2013), SUN RGB-D (Song, Lichtenberg, & Xiao, 2015), Stanford 2D-3D (Armeni, Sax, Zamir, & Savarese, 2017), ShapeNet Core (Chang et al., 2015), and Sydney Urban Objects Dataset (Deuge, Quadros, Hung, & Douillard, 2013).

Although current studies are achieving remarkable success in image segmentation, researchers are still facing multiple difficulties. The distributions over the massive datasets of the pretrained models differ from the data distributions of low-data inference samples. This may cause biases and weak generalization, even under a long-lasting training process. Instance-level segmentation is also under-explored in few-shot regimes. Complex backgrounds may confuse the model by blending objects with novel classes to objects with other classes when multiple objectives are displayed together.

Meta-features connect task-specific and task-agnostic knowledge to tackle these difficulties. First, meta-learners are trained to extract meta-features across shared tasks that are beneficial for classifying each pixel and project task-specific domains to a shared feature space. Moreover, meta-learning concentrates on region-of-interest features, which are leveraged to output class labels, bounding boxes, and segmentation tasks through meta-learner predictor heads.

The following two sections explore two types of meta-learning strategies as stated above. Section 5.6.2 presents a paradigm of semantic segmentation, and Section 5.6.3 provides an illustration of instance segmentation. They offer a brief conceptual outline, the components of main modules, unique design or techniques, overall architecture and workflow, and the corresponding benchmarks.

5.6.2 Multiobject few-shot semantic segmentation

Existing few-shot approaches leverage extra information to obtain sufficient prior knowledge, limiting their applications and generalization ability. Some negative impacts of this include the following: (1) pretraining on ImageNet is usually required, yet the distribution of ImageNet may be significantly different from that of the dataset used in few-shot segmentation; (2) regular few-shot learning methods for image segmentation only focus on a single object in one image, as there is currently no promising strategy for multiple objects; and (3) a high degree of computational complexity leads to difficulties during the training process.

Tian et al. (2020) focused on practical semantic segmentation through learning from meta-knowledge for K-way N-shot (K: the number of classes, K > 1; N: the number of training samples for each class) few-shot learning. They presented a framework named MetaSegNet to view the problem from a pixel classification perspective.

MetaSegNet consists of two modules:

- A linear classifier as a base learner for classification
- A novel embedding module that extracts both global and local features by two submodels (a feature extractor and a feature fusion module) and uses meta-knowledge for better classifying each pixel

The learning process of a base learner Λ is formulated in Eq. (5.70), where X denotes the pixel feature matrix generated from the embedding network, with the label Y over task $\mathcal{T}_i = \left(D_i^{train}, D_i^{test}\right)$.

$$\Lambda\left(\mathbf{X}\right) = \underset{w}{\mathrm{argmin}}||\mathbf{X}w - \mathbf{y}||^2 + \lambda||\mathbf{w}||^2 \tag{5.70}$$

The meta-learning objective function is expressed in Eq. (5.71), where the scale and bias are denoted as α and β, respectively, ϕ is the meta-learner for mapping task-specific domain to a shared feature space, λ signifies learnable parameters, and $\mathcal{I}$ represents a set of pixels of an image. An unseen new class is equipped during meta-testing.

$$L^{meta}\left(T; w, \alpha, \beta, \lambda, \phi\right) = -\frac{1}{|T| \cdot |D_i^{test}||\mathcal{I}|} \sum_{i \in T} \sum_{(x,y) \in D_i^{test}} \sum_{p \in \mathcal{I}} \log\left(S_{py_p}\right) \tag{5.71}$$

where the $S_{pc} = \exp(s_{pc})/\sum_{k=1}^{N} \exp(s_{pk})$.

This model utilizes an end-to-end structure with episode-based training on PASCAL VOC 2012 (Hariharan, Arbelaez, Gir-Shick, & Malik, 2015) and COCO 2014 (Lin et al., 2014) and is evaluated in terms of intersection-over-union (IoU) metrics.

5.6.3 Few-shot static object instance-level detection

Compared to image-level tasks, which require extensive hand-crafted annotation, instance-level tasks necessitate an even greater amount of detail-oriented annotation, including bounding box, segmentation mask, and other structure labels. The requirement of significant resources, both in terms of time and money, is just one of the several dilemmas faced by instance-level tasks. This is a field in which few-shot strategies remain significantly underexplored. The model is also easily misled by objects with novel classes being blended with those with other classes when multiple objectives are displayed together.

Yan et al. (2020) proposed a meta-learning model for few-shot instance-level object detection and segmentation, named Meta R-CNN. It consists of Faster/Mask R-CNN (He, Gkioxari, et al., 2017; He, Zhang, & Sun, 2017; Ren et al., 2015) as a backbone and is equipped with a predictor-head remodeling network (PRN). This model performs well on an image with complex background and multiple objects through bounding boxes or masks, channel-wise soft-attention, and meta-learning on region-of-interest (RoI) features. PRN provides information on the category, position, and structure knowledge of the objects. See the official open-source code at https://yanxp.github.io/metarcnn.html.

Fig. 5.10 shows the architecture and workflow of this framework.

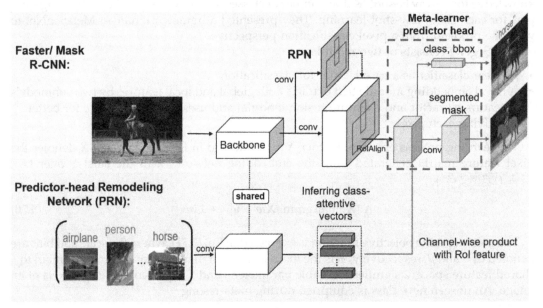

FIG. 5.10   General pipeline of Meta R-CNN, which consists of Faster/ Mask R-CNN and Predictor-Head Remodeling Network (PRN). An image is fed into the Faster/Mask R-CNN to generate RoI features through Region Proposal Network (RPN) equipped with RoIAlign. A set of K-shot M-class resized images with annotated labels (segmentation masks and bounding boxes) are sent to the predictor-head remodeling network (PRN) to produce m class-attentive vectors. Then, a channel-wise soft-attention processes each RoI feature. Hence, the meta-learner predictor head performs object detection or segmentation.

© 2022 IEEE. Reprinted, with permission, from Yan, X., Chen, Z., Xu, A., Wang, X., Liang, X., & Lin, L. (2020). Meta R-CNN: Towards general solver for instance-level low-shot learning. In ICCV 2019.

The objective function is expressed in Eq. (5.72) as follows:

$$\min_{\theta, \phi} L(\theta, \phi)_{cls} + L(\theta, \phi)_{reg} + \lambda L(\theta, \phi)_{mask} + L(\phi)_{meta} \tag{5.72}$$

In an illustration of meta-learning over RoI in Meta R-CNN, the training image contains a person and a horse, so $C_{meta} = ("person", "horse")$ and K-shot of "person" and "horse" samples with their labels in D_{meta}. Both C_{meta} and D_{meta} keep changing adaptively the training image changes during iterations.

This framework produces several advantages, as it:

- is generic (universal backbones in Faster/Mask R-CNN);
- is practical and concise;
- is productive (few-shot detection and segmentation leading to state-of-the-art outcomes); and
- supports rapid inference (preprocessed class-attentive vectors created before testing).

Meta R-CNN is valid in the object-detection tracks of PASCAL VOC and MS-COCO (Lin et al., 2014) in terms of metrics IoU and mAP.

Meta R-CNN implemented ResNet-50 as a backbone and accessed the performance of few-shot (K = 5, 10, 20) instance-level object segmentation in 60 categories from MS COCO and 20 from PASCAL VOC.

5.7 Object tracking

5.7.1 Introduction

Object tracking has a variety of implements in computer vision, some of which apply to tasks related to motion-based recognition, visual navigation, traffic monitoring, automated video surveillance, video indexing, and retrieval. Object tracking can be a time-consuming process. The difficulty of this task is due to multiple reasons: background noise, loss of information via projection from 3D real-world to 2D images, complex object movements, object nature, complex object shape, partial or complete object occlusions, scene illumination, and real-time processing criteria.

To represent the appearance feature of objects, common approaches usually involve the probability density of object appearance (e.g., Gaussian [Paragios & Deriche, 2002] or Parzen windows [Elgammal, Duraiswami, Harwood, & Davis, 2002]), templates with simple silhouettes or geometric shapes (Fieguth & Terzopoulos, 1997), active-appearance models with landmarks to enhance object shape (Edwards, Taylor, & Cootes, 1998), and multiview active models to produce subspace through Principal Component Analysis (PCA) or Independent Component Analysis (ICA).

In multiple-object tracking (MOT), regular strategies include four stages: detection, feature extraction and motion prediction, affinity (computing similarity between pairs of detections based on feature and motion prediction), and association (assigning an ID based on similarity ranking and identifying target).

In the **detection** stage, with the development of deep learning, Simple Online and Realtime Tracking (SORT; Bewley, Ge, Ott, Ramos, & Upcroft, 2016) became the first MOT pipeline through CNNs. Yu et al. (2016) proposed a Fast R-CNN-based approach equipped with skip-pooling (Bell, Zitnick, Bala, & Girshick, 2016) and multiregion features (Gidaris & Komodakis, 2015). Zhang et al. (2019) introduced an SSD detector supported by Discriminative Correlation Filters (DCF) online tracking methods. Bullinger, Bodensteiner, and Arens (2017) presented a Multi-Task Network Cascade (Dai et al., 2016) to replace the traditional bounding boxes.

During **feature extraction** and **motion prediction**, autoencoder-based methods were first provided by Wang et al. (2014). Kim, Li, Ciptadi, and Rehg (2015) discussed the implementation of CNN backbone visual feature extraction in the novel Multiple Hypothesis Tracking strategy. Kim, Nam, and Ko (2018) developed a YOLOv2 CNN object detector to extract features. Wang et al. (2017) proposed a correlation filter (Ma, Huang, Yang, & Yang, 2015) to generate a response map of the tracked target.

LSTM and CNN backbones can directly produce an output in the **affinity** period. Milan, Rezatofighi, Dick, Reid, and Schindler (2017) proposed the first RNN based on an end-to-end online learner to mock Bayesian filter methods. Motivated by the Markov Decision Process, Sadeghian, Alahi, and Savarese (2017) introduced three LSTM to generate affinity scores. Wan, Wang, and Zhou (2018) processed a Siamese LSTM with a Hungarian algorithm, compared detection, and predicted target position through IOU. Zhu et al. (2018) developed a bidirectional LSTM on a feature extracted by a Spatial Attention Network. Lee and Kim (2019) presented a CNN-Based Feature Pyramid Siamese Network to capture appearance features.

Deep reinforcement learning (DRL) is one of the promising strategies for decision-making during the association stage. Rosello and Kochenderfer (2018) implemented a DRL agent with a Kalman filter to handle multiple tracked objects, indicating when to start and stop tracking. Ren et al. (2018) trained a DRL in a collaborative environment, consisting of a CNN backbone prediction network and a decision network, equipped with a modified MDNet (Nam & Han, 2016) for feature extraction on MOT15 (Leal-Taixe, Milan, Reid, Roth, & Schindler, 2015) and MOT16 (Milan, Leal-Taixe, Reid, Roth, & Schindler, 2016).

Even though multiple paradigms have accomplished impressive results, some drawbacks limited object tracking applications. Current online object tracking studies require a time-consuming training period and an extensive dataset for a pretrained model. On the other hand, while offline object trackers save time, the generalization capacity remains inefficient compared to online models. Furthermore, offline learners rely heavily on the ground truth of the target object's appearances at the first frame. In addition, the target classification module needs to diligently update the target object's appearance even with limited samples, which leads to overfitting, and commonly happens as the pipeline is decoupled to multiple components instead of an end-to-end architecture.

Meta-learning provides various solutions to these scenarios. One way is to concentrate on the future frames' error indications by determining the optimal gradient descent direction, instead of directly minimizing the loss of current frames in standard methods. In reverse, the first frame ground truth of the target object's appearances can still be utilized, employing a rapid meta-learning-based adaptive module. Moreover, in the real-time object tracking model, meta-learning presents a task-specific feature space for more details of the appearance features of the target object. Additionally, object tracking can be viewed as special instance detection, equipped with meta-learning to construct an optimal initialization of the detector, which enables quick adaptation to new instances when only the initial frame is available.

The following three sections will examine further research on meta-learning object tracking chronologically: Section 5.7.2 introduces an offline object tracker and Section 5.7.3 presents online real-time object tracking. Section 5.7.4 focuses on real-time object tracking but is equipped with channel pruning; whereas Section 5.7.5 explores instance detection on object tracking. Each section offers an introduction, the motivation behind the design, primary paradigm and components, creative techniques, and the corresponding datasets.

5.7.2 Offline object tracking

As a fundamental task in computer vision, object tracking attempts to differentiate the object of interest from a complicated background, as well as from similar distractors belonging to the same categories. Traditional approaches are based on online adaptation equipped with deep neural networks. The model is initialized during the first frame and updating is maintained during the succeeding frames. While it may have achieved promising results, however, a few important drawbacks are worthy of attention here: (1) it requires a large-scale dataset for pretraining and long-lasting initial training and (2) although an offline solution enables high speed, its performance remains below that of online adaptive trackers.

Meta-Tracker, an influential model-agnostic offline tracking method that seeks to improve online adaptation-based tracking, was proposed by Park and Berg (2018). Meta-Tracker focuses on error signals from future frames by finding the optimal direction of gradient descent and generic initialization, rather than minimizing the loss function on the current frames like traditional strategies. Meta-Tracker primarily reduces overfitting to the background clutter or distractors in the current frame. The official code is released at https://github.com/silverbottlep/meta_trackers. It applies to any learning-based tracking approach with slight modifications and offers time-saving and robustness benefits, based on a small amount of training data within few interactions through meta-learning. See Fig. 5.11 for details.

The step-by-step pseudocode is summarized in Table 5.17.

The original paper illustrated this strategy by incorporating it with two SOTA (state-of-the-art) tracking frameworks:

- MDNet with tracking-by-detection paradigm (Nam & Han, 2016)
- CREST with a correlation paradigm (Song et al., 2017) by adding a 1x1 convolutional layer behind feature capture and sharing its weight with the meta-learner alongside a correlation filter

The framework performed state-of-the-art benchmarks in OTB2015 (Wu, Lim, & Yang, 2015) and VOT2016 (Kristan, Leonardis, Matas, & Felsberg, 2016).

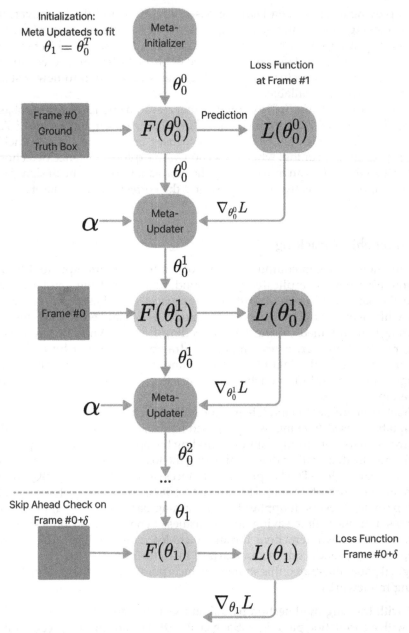

FIG. 5.11 General pipeline of meta-tracker.
Adapted from Springer, ECCV, Meta- Tracker: Fast and Robust Online Adaptation for Visual Object Trackers, Park, E., & Berg, A. C. (2018).

TABLE 5.17 General methods of meta-tracker.

```
Input: θ₀ and α under randomly initialization
       D, training dataset
Output: θ₀* and α*
```

```
1: while not converged do
   # Initialize using zero vector
2:    grad_θ₀, grad_α = 0
3:    for all k∈{0,...,N_mini-1} do
         # Sample a training instance
4:          S,j,δ~p(D)
5:          θ₀⁰=θ₀
6:          for all t ∈ {0,...,T - 1) do
7:             ŷⱼ = F(xⱼ,θ₀ᵗ)
8:             θ₀ᵗ⁺¹ = θ₀ᵗ - α⊙∇_θ₀ᵗ L(yⱼ,ŷⱼ;θ₀ᵗ)
9:          end for
10:         θ₁=θ₀ᵀ
11:         ŷⱼ₊δ = F(xⱼ₊δ,θ₁)
12:         grad_θ₀ = grad_θ₀ + ∇_θ₀ L(yⱼ₊δ,ŷⱼ₊δ)
            # Compute the gradients
13:         grad_α = grad_α + ∇_α L(yⱼ₊δ,ŷⱼ₊δ)
14:    end for
   # update model parameters by
15:    θ₀= Optimizer (θ₀,grad_θ₀)
16:    α=Optimizer(α,grad_α)
17: end while
```

Modified from Park, E., & Berg, A. C. (2018). Meta-tracker: Fast and robust online adaptation for visual object trackers. In: ECCV.

5.7.3 Real-time online object tracking

While deep neural network technology has already had a powerful influence on object tracking tasks, several problems result from the fact that these approaches are usually decoupled into two different components, including deep feature modules and targe classifier modules; the target classifier module requires constant, active updating of the target object's appearance, even though positive samples remain limited. As a result, overfitting occurs frequently due to training sample scarcity, while the generalization capability is also reduced.

In contrast to the strategy of traditional discriminative feature visual tracking through CNN—which tackles complex optimization for adapting an unseen target object's appearance—Choi et al. (2019) generated the target-specific feature space (TSFS) to provide more appearance features of the target object.

This approach aims to contrive a feature space to discriminate the target object's appearance from a complicated background to avoid overfitting. Choi's work presented a real-time online object-tracking framework consisting of two submodules:

1. A Siamese matching network (Bertinetto, Valmadre, Henriques, Vedaldi, & Torr, 2016) for task seeking.

This Siamese matching network generates the final response map $f_W(x,z)$ through cross-correlation computation $\divideontimes$ between the feature maps, as expressed in Eq. (5.73), where w is the trained kernel weights, ϕ_w represents the CNN-based N-layer feature extractor, x denotes the target image patch, and z is the image patch concerning the massive context region contained the target:

$$f_{\boldsymbol{w}}(x,z) = \phi_{\boldsymbol{w}}(x) \divideontimes \phi_{\boldsymbol{w}}(z) \tag{5.73}$$

The averaged negative gradient δ is utilized as the last layer's loss function in the Siamese network, as expressed in Eq. (5.74), where $\widetilde{y}_i$ represents the generated binary response map with the assumption that the target is located in the correct region within the context patch z_i (Choi et al., 2019):

$$\delta = \sum_{i=1}^{M} -\frac{1}{M} \frac{\partial \ell \left(f_{\boldsymbol{w}}(x, z_i), \widetilde{y}_i \right)}{\partial w_N} \tag{5.74}$$

2. A meta-learner network for presenting target-specific parameterization and updating target-specific adaptive feature space. The TSFS parameters are provided immediately through a forward-pass without further iteration for optimization or overfitting.

The overall meta-learning visual tracking appears in Table 5.18.

TABLE 5.18 General methods of the proposed methods.

Input: L, length of tracking sequence
      s_1, initial target state
      x, initial target template
Output: tracked target states s_t

\# *For each frame in the tracking scenes*
1. for t = 2, ..., L do
2.   Get a context image of candidate z' through s_{t-1}
3.   Get a response map y through the matching network
4.   Implement cosine window h to y, figure out the position and scale, and the
   new state s_t;
          \# *If confident, save context image*
5.   if $y\,[s_t] > \tau$ then
6.   Get a new context image z through s_t and save in the memory z_{mem}
7.   end if

          \# *Weights updating for each T frames*
8.   if (t mod T) = 0 then
9.   Select M samples z_δ from memory z_{mem} based on minimum entropy metric
10.   Evaluate loss gradient δ
11.   Compute target-specific adaptive weights w^{target}
12.   Update w^{adapt} for the matching network
13.   end if

14. end for

Modified from Choi, J., Kwon, J., & Lee, K. M. (2019). Deep meta learning for real-time target-aware visual tracking. In: ICCV.

The matching network is trained on datasets ILSVRC 2015 (Russakovsky et al., 2015) and ILSVRC 2017, and the minimum extropy metric is expressed in Eq. (5.75):

$$\underset{\widehat{y_i} \in \widehat{y_{mem}}}{\text{argmin}} - \sum_{p \in P} \rho(\widehat{y}_i[p]) \, log \, (\rho(\widehat{y}_i[p])) \tag{5.75}$$

The performance is assessed in five different public benchmarks: OTB2015/2013 (Wu et al., 2015, p. 51), LaSOT (Fan et al., 2019), TC-128 (Liang, Blasch, & Ling, 2015), UAV20L (Mueller, Smith, & Ghanem, 2016), and VOT-2016 (Cehovin, Leonardis, & Kristan, 2016).

5.7.4 Real-time object tracking with channel pruning

Meta-Tracker, an offline object tracker, relies heavily on the ground truth target object annotation during the first frame. Motivated by the Meta-Tracker (Park & Berg, 2018; explored in Section 5.7.2)—which employed an estimation from ground-truth of future frames—Jung et al. (2020) presented a MAML-based real-time object-tracking framework. This real-time model explores the target ground-truth label annotation at the first frame, with the advantages of fast model adaptation.

This model investigates two model-adaptation scenarios:

- During initial adaptation, the model optimizes parameters through the one-shot object ground-truth at the first frame.
- In online adaptation, the parameters are enhanced through the tracking object's estimated label annotation based on the previous frames, where the Meta-Tracker solely centralizes on this scenario.

The loss function of model adaptation is expressed in Eq. (5.76), where x is the input patch, and the output is $f(x;\theta)$:

$$\mathcal{L}(D;\boldsymbol{\theta}) = -\mathbb{E}_{p_D(x,y)} \left[y^{\top} log \left[Soft \, max \, (f(\boldsymbol{x};\boldsymbol{\theta})) \right] \right] \tag{5.76}$$

In contrast to the regular tracking algorithm, which seeks to estimate targets during every frame, the tracking simulation episode conduces only an initial adaptation and one online adaptation from datasets simulated from $\mathcal{V}$.

The parameters of initial adaptation and online adaptation are presented in Eqs. (5.77), (5.78), respectively, where k = 1, ..., K_{init}, α presents the learning rate, D_{init} denotes the ground-truth dataset, and D_{on} is the online dataset with a sample from the estimated targets:

$$\boldsymbol{\theta}_{init}^k = \boldsymbol{\theta}_{init}^{k-1} - \boldsymbol{\alpha}_{init}^k \odot \nabla_{\theta_{init}^{k-1}} \mathcal{L}\left(\boldsymbol{D}_{init}; \boldsymbol{\theta}_{init}^{k-1}\right) \tag{5.77}$$

$$\boldsymbol{\theta}_{on}^k = \boldsymbol{\theta}_{on}^{k-1} - \boldsymbol{\alpha}_{on}^k \odot \nabla_{\theta_{on}^{k-1}} \mathcal{L}\left(\boldsymbol{D}_{on}; \boldsymbol{\theta}_{on}^{k-1}\right) \tag{5.78}$$

The loss function in testing is a combination of cross-entropy and a triplet loss, as expressed in Eqs. (5.79), (5.80), where D_{test} is the test dataset, D_{test}^{std} is a dataset with annotated video, ξ presents a margin, and x^+ and x^- indicate positive and hard samples, respectively:

$$\mathcal{L}_{test}(D_{test};\boldsymbol{\theta}) = \mathcal{L}\left(D_{test}^{std};\boldsymbol{\theta}\right) + \gamma\mathcal{L}_{tri}(D_{test};\boldsymbol{\theta}) \tag{5.79}$$

$$\mathcal{L}_{tri}(D_{test};\boldsymbol{\theta}) = \mathbb{E}_{p_{D_{test}}(x,x^+,x^-)}\left[(\xi + \triangle(x,x^+;\boldsymbol{\theta}) - \triangle(x,x^-;\boldsymbol{\theta}))_+\right] \tag{5.80}$$

The Euclidean distance between L_2 normalization $\Delta(\mathbf{x}_1,\mathbf{x}_2;\boldsymbol{\theta})$ is indicated in Eq. (5.81):

$$\Delta(\mathbf{x}_1,\mathbf{x}_2;\boldsymbol{\theta}) := \left\| \frac{\mathbf{f}(\mathbf{x}_1;\boldsymbol{\theta})}{\|\mathbf{f}(\mathbf{x}_1;\boldsymbol{\theta})\|^2} - \frac{\mathbf{f}(\mathbf{x}_2;\boldsymbol{\theta})}{\|\mathbf{f}(\mathbf{x}_2;\boldsymbol{\theta})\|^2} \right\|^2 \tag{5.81}$$

The loss function of the meta-optimization is provided in Eq. (5.82), whereas the gradient descent to update the meta-parameters is presented in Eq. (5.83):

$$\mathcal{L}_{\text{meta}}(\mathcal{M}) = \mathbb{E}_{p(\tau)}\left[\mathcal{L}_{test}\left(\mathcal{D}_{test};\boldsymbol{\theta}_{init}^{K_{init}}\right) + \mathcal{L}_{test}\left(\mathcal{D}_{test};\boldsymbol{\theta}_{on}^{K_{on}}\right)\right] \tag{5.82}$$

$$\nabla_{\mathcal{M}}\mathcal{L}_{\text{meta}} = \mathbb{E}_{p(\tau)}\left[\frac{\partial\mathcal{L}_{test}\left(\mathcal{D}_{test};\boldsymbol{\theta}_{init}^{K_{init}}\right)}{\partial\boldsymbol{\theta}_{init}^{K_{init}}}\frac{\partial\boldsymbol{\theta}_{init}^{K_{init}}}{\partial\mathcal{M}} + \frac{\partial\mathcal{L}_{test}\left(\mathcal{D}_{test};\boldsymbol{\theta}_{on}^{K_{on}}\right)}{\partial\boldsymbol{\theta}_{on}^{K_{on}}}\left\{\frac{\partial\boldsymbol{\theta}_{on}^{K_{on}}}{\partial\mathcal{M}} + \frac{\partial\boldsymbol{\theta}_{on}^{K_{on}}}{\partial\boldsymbol{\theta}_{init}^{K_{init}}}\frac{\partial\boldsymbol{\theta}_{init}^{K_{init}}}{\partial\mathcal{M}}\right\}\right] \tag{5.83}$$

The comprehensive methods of the proposed simulated tracking episodes are described in Table 5.19.

TABLE 5.19   General training methods of the proposed methods.

```
Input: Γ, training video set
       M = {θ⁰init, Ainit, Aon}, meta-parameters
Output: updated meta-parameters M*
```

```
1: while not meeting stopping criteria do
2:      Select a labeled video mini-batch from Γ
3:      for each video V in the mini-batch do

4:          Gather Dinit with V
5:          for all k in 1, ..., Kinit do
6:              θᵏinit = θᵏ⁻¹init − αᵏinit ⊙ ∇θᵏ⁻¹init L(Dinit; θᵏ⁻¹init)
            end for

7:          Gather Don with V and θKinitinit
8:          for all k ∈ 1, ..., Kon do
9:              θᵏon = θᵏ⁻¹on − αᵏon ⊙ ∇θᵏ⁻¹on L(Don; θᵏ⁻¹on)
            end for #where θᵏon=θKinitinit
10:         Gather Dtest with V and Γ − V
11:         Set τ = (Dinit, Don, Dtest, {θᵏinit}Kinitk=1, {θᵏon}Konk=1)
        end for

12:     Evaluate Lmeta on a mini-batch of τ
13:     M ← optimize(M, ∇M Lmeta)
14: end while
```

Modified from Jung, I., You, K., Noh, H., Cho, M., & Han, B. (2020). Real-time object tracking via meta-learning: Efficient model adaptation and one-shot channel pruning. In: AAAI.

One-shot channel pruning

Additionally, Jung's research proposed a channel pruning technique in one-shot scenarios through lasso pruning (He, Gkioxari, et al., 2017; He, Zhang, & Sun, 2017), allowing for a meta-learning network to drive efficient target-specific model compression (Choi et al., 2018; Han, Pool, Tran, & Dally, 2015; Han, Mao, & Dally, 2016; He, Gkioxari, et al., 2017; He, Zhang, & Sun, 2017; Wen, Wu, Wang, Chen, & Li, 2016) by the first frame's ground-truth annotation.

The objective function of the simulated tracking episode in terms of lasso pruning is expressed in Eq. (5.84), which aims to determine a single $\mathcal{B}$ to minimize $\mathcal{L}_{Lasso}$ based on multi-pairs of parameters and datasets during an episode. τ is the episode trajectory.

$$\mathcal{L}_{ep}(\tau, \mathcal{B}) = \mathcal{L}_{lasso}\left(\mathcal{D}_{init}, \mathcal{B}; \theta_{init}^{K_{int}}\right) + \sum_{k=1}^{K_{on}} \mathcal{L}_{lasso}\left(\mathcal{D}_{on}, \mathcal{B}; \theta_{on}^{k}\right) + \mathcal{L}_{lasso}\left(\mathcal{D}_{test}, \mathcal{B}; \theta_{on}^{K_{on}}\right) \tag{5.84}$$

This method is implemented with RT-MDNet (Jung, Son, Baek, & Han, 2018), and employs the datasets OTB2015 (Wu et al., 2015) and TempleColor (Liang et al., 2015).

5.7.5 Object tracking via instance detection

Object tracking can be thought of as a unique situation of object detection, referred to as instance detection. However, while the object detector can be converted to a robust tracker, reaching the optimal initiation with a high degree of efficiency and without overfitting remains a highly challenging issue.

Wang, Luo, Sun, Xiong, and Zeng (2020) suggested viewing object tracking as an instance-detection problem by applying MAML as a weight initialization on top of two different object trackers—one combined with RetinNet (Lin et al., 2017), named Retina-MAML, and another with FCOS (Tian et al., 2020), named FCOS-MAML. The critical part of converting object tracking to instance detection is the optimal initialization of the detector, allowing quick adaptation to new instances when only the initial frame is available.

The following three-staged guidance describes how to construct and train this tracker:

1. Learning an instance detector through MAML

   The k-step gradient descent in the support set, namely inner-level optimization, is expressed in Eq. (5.85). The loss function in the target dataset is described in Eq. (5.86), where $\mathcal{D}_i^s$ is the training set, $h(x; \theta_{k-1})$ represents the detector model with the input image x, and the detector's parameter is θ.

$$\theta_k \mathscr{E} \equiv \mathrm{GD}_k\left(\theta_0, \mathcal{D}_i^s\right) \tag{5.85}$$

and

$$\theta_k = \theta_{k-1} - \alpha \frac{1}{\left|\mathcal{D}_i^s\right|} \sum_{(xy) \in \mathcal{D}_i^s} \nabla_{\theta_{k-1}} \mathcal{L}(h(x; \theta_{k-1})y) \tag{5.86}$$

The overall training objective function in Eqs. (5.87), (5.88) is called outer-level optimization. N denotes the number of videos, $\mathcal{D}_i^t$ is the target set, and $\mathcal{D}_i$ is the mixture of target and training set.

$$F(\theta_0, \mathcal{D}_i) = \frac{1}{\left|\mathcal{D}_i^t\right|} \sum_{(x,y) \in \mathcal{D}_i^t} \mathcal{L}(h(x; \theta_k), y) \tag{5.87}$$

$$\boldsymbol{\theta}^* = \arg\min_{\boldsymbol{\theta}_0} \frac{1}{N} \sum_i^N F(\boldsymbol{\theta}_0, \mathcal{D}_i) \tag{5.88}$$

The multistep loss optimization function in Eq. (5.89), motivated by MAML++ (Antoniou, Edwards, & Storkey, 2018), selects parameters after each step of inner-level optimization, rather than parameters after the final steps, which is essential to maintain gradient stability:

$$F(\boldsymbol{\theta}_0, \mathcal{D}_i) = \frac{1}{|\mathcal{D}_i^t|} \sum_{(x,y)\in\mathcal{D}_i^t} \sum_{k=0}^{K} \gamma_k \mathcal{L}(h(x;\boldsymbol{\theta}_k), y) \tag{5.89}$$

2. Initializing the detector by offline training on many tracking sequences by feature capture through ResNet-18.
3. Domain adaptation through an initial frame within only a few steps of gradient descent given the initial frame of test series, as summarized in Table 5.20.

TABLE 5.20 General methods of the proposed methods.

```
Input: {I_i}_{i=1}^N, frame sequence
  h(·;θ), detector
  B_1, initial bounding box
  u, update interval
Output: tracking consequence {B_i}_{i=1}^N
```

```
# Produce search region image
1: S_1←SR(I_1,B_1)
# Initialize the support set
2: D^s ← {DataAug(S_1)}
3: Update θ ← GD_5(θ,D^s) with Eq. (5.53)

4: for i=2, ..., N do
  # Detect the displayed objects using the bounding box and score
5:    {B_det^j, c_j}_{j=1}^M←h(SR(I_i,B_{i-1});θ)

6:    if all c_j<0.1 then
7:            B_i←B_{i-1}
8:            continue
9:    end if

10:   Insert punishment and window before {B_det^j c_j}_{j=1}^M
11:   # Choose the box with the highest score c*
      B_i ← B_det^*
      # Linear interpolate shape
12:   B_i←Inter(B_i,B_{i-1})
13:   Update D^s

14:   if i mod u=0 or distractor detected then
15:           Update with Eq. (5.53) θ ← GD_1(θ,D^s)
16:   end if
17:end for
```

Modified from Wang, Z., Hu, G., & Hu, Q. (2020). Training noise-robust deep neural networks via meta-learning. In: Proceedings of the IEEE/CVF conference on computer vision and pattern recognition (pp. 4524–4533).

These methods are assessed on four public benchmarks: OTB-100 (Wu et al., 2015), TrackingNet (Muller, Bibi, Giancola, Subaihil, & Ghanem, 2018), VOT-2018 (Kristan et al., 2018), and LaSOT (Fan et al., 2019).

5.8 Label noise

5.8.1 Introduction

The success of deep neural networks in a variety of machine learning tasks has heavily relied on large-scale datasets. However, the ratio of unreliable labels in public datasets is estimated at 8.0%–38.5% (Lee et al., 2018; Li, Wang, Li, Agustsson, & Gool, 2017; Song et al., 2019; Xiao, Xu, et al., 2015). Such unreliable labels are named noisy labels—corruption from ground-truth. This label noise significantly limits the generalization capability of a training model.

Angluin and Laird (1988) suggested that label noise occurs when the true class is given but the preprocessing method contains noise. This chapter refers to the definition from Frenay's research (Frenay and Verleysen, 2014) where the method may pollute labels is label noise, which does not include correctly labeled outliers or feature noise which may influence features' value. The process of learning a dataset with label noise is named *imperfectly supervised*, creating a learning scenario "between supervised and unsupervised" (Frenay & Verleysen, 2014).

Label noise can occur in two types:

- Instance-independent label noise assumes the label corruption is conditionally irrelevant to data features given the ground-truth.
- Instance-dependent label noise assumes the probability of corruption is conditioned on the two of data features and class annotation.

Approaches

Deep learning methods tackle this through five different paradigms:

1. DNN architecture modification: inserting a noise adaptation layer into a network or proposing an architecture for supporting various types of label noise, such as Webly learning (Chen & Gupta, 2015) and NLNN (Bekker & Goldberger, 2016), probabilistic noise modeling (Xiao, Xu, et al., 2015), and contrastive-additive noise network (Yao et al., 2018)
2. Regularization: annotator confusion (Tanno, Saeedi, Sankaranarayanan, Alexander, & Silberman, 2019), PHuber (Menon, Rawat, Reddi, & Kumar, 2020), and label smoothing (Pereyra, Tucker, Chorowski, Kaiser, & Hinton, 2017)
3. Loss function, such as generalized cross-entropy (GCE; Zhang & Sabuncu, 2018) and active-passive loss (APL; Ma, Huang, et al., 2020; Ma, Meng, et al., 2020)
4. Loss adjustment: suggesting a confidence factor of the given loss function via correction, reweighting, etc. (e.g., approaches based on meta-learning, as explored below) (Song, Kim, Park, Shin, & Lee, 2022).

5. Sample selection: implementing multinetwork or multiround learning to recognize and identify the true-labeled samples, such as the co-teaching series (Han et al., 2018; Yu et al., 2019), ITLM (Shen & Sanghavi, 2019), and SELF (Nguyen et al., 2020)

Benchmarks

Four public benchmarks of noisy labels are commonly accessed: ANIMAL-10N, Food-101N (Kaster, Menze, Weber, & Hamprecht, 2010), Clothing 1M (Ganapathiraju & Picone, 2000), and WebVision (Biggio, Nelson, & Laskov, 2011). Multiple typical evaluation metrics assess the prediction accuracy of unbiasedness and unused true-labeled samples, including text accuracy, validation accuracy, label precision, label recall, and correction error.

As merging of large-scale datasets, feature representation achieves promising outcomes through deep neural networks. However, noisy labels are inevitable. There are two standard research lines for noisy labels: (a) weighting and (b) label noise correction. The confidence score may not cover comprehensive core elements for noise-label confusion in weighting approaches. Current studies of reweighting methods require hand-crafted, predefined weighting functions and pressure researchers with an in-depth understanding of the complicated data properties, specifically low-quality datasets. The confusion matrix is impractical from the massive dataset in label noise correction methods. Additionally, carefully removing mislabeled train-test paired data is trivial.

In addition to the two regular research lines for processing noisy labels, meta-learning helps leverage datasets with a mixture of noisy and clean labels. A meta-learning reweighting strategy arranges validation right after each training iteration to monitor the current weights automatically. The hyperparameters and weighting function can be automatically obtained from a meta-learner. A meta-weighting framework introduces data coefficients in dense label noise regimes. Moreover, a teacher-student approach addresses the noisy label problem without clean labels. Another strategy explores the relationship between images within the same categories. In a nondifferentiable sampling process where gradient-based optimization is invalid, a meta-learner equipped with reinforcement learning handles noisy labels.

The rest of this section summarizes multiple meta-learning approaches that either clean the representation of noisy labels or build a novel loss to manage the label noise. There are two standard techniques to manage noisy labels: the reweighting model and label correlation. Unlike classic examples of reweighting solutions with the assumption of noisy and skewed training samples, a novel automatic online meta-learning reweighting strategy through online approximation on a much more generic and practical assumption is reviewed in Section 5.8.2. Section 5.8.3 introduces MetaCleaner to integrate a noise weight and a clean hallucinating generator. In Section 5.8.4, a reinforcement learning-based solution is discussed, which consists of a data value estimator and a target task predictor. In contrast to the mix of labeled and unlabeled dataset regimes in previous sections, Section 5.8.5 introduces Meta-Learning-based Noise-Tolerant, a strategy using a teacher-student structure to avoid human interaction and overfitting with a wide variety of synthetic noisy labels. Meta-Weight-Net attempts to create a reweighting model that is easier to implement in a real-world situation. Different training samples and problem sets lead to various weighting schemes; see Section 5.8.6 for a detailed explanation. Section 5.8.7 investigates a loss correction adjustment to approach a noise transition matrix through a three-stage framework. Section 5.8.8 describes how to leverage low-quality labels by suggesting the concept and theory of Data Coefficients. Meta-label correction (MLC), discussed in Section 5.8.9, presents bi-level processing as one model to correct mislabeled data and make predictions based on the initially accurate labels.

5.8.2 Reweighting examples through online approximation

In contrast to the contemporary example of reweighting approaches, Ren, Zeng, et al. (2018) offer a different view to estimate the weights for each training sample by relying on gradient direction. The traditional paradigm usually follows a tricky model assumption in noisy and imbalanced training samples. This proposed approach was developed under a generic assumption: the optimal example weighting aims to reduce the loss across many clean validation examples that are unbiased and consistent with the evaluation methods. Instead of evaluating a validation set after finalizing the comprehensive training on the entire data, the proposed method processes validation right after each training iteration to monitor the current weights closely. This is an automatic online meta-learning reweighting strategy based on MAML without an offline training procedure, which can be applied to all kinds of deep neural networks without tuning extra hyperparameters. The official code is available at https://github.com/uber-research/learning-to-reweight-examples.

It attempts to minimize the weighted loss rather than the average loss to enhance the meta-objectives and leverage reweighting of inputs; see Eq. (5.90), where $f_i(\theta)$ represents loss function of data x_i:

$$\theta^*(w) = \arg\min_\theta \sum_{i=1}^{N} w_i f_i(\theta) \tag{5.90}$$

The selection of optimal w is expressed in Eq. (5.91), which relies on the validation performance:

$$w^* = \arg\min_{w, w \geq 0} \frac{1}{M} \sum_{i=1}^{M} f_i^v(\theta^*(w)) \tag{5.91}$$

To avoid complicated and expensive nested loops, the proposed method processes an online approximation by monitoring the gradient descent direction of training samples from the training loss surface and reweighting them based on the similarity to the gradient descent direction of the validation loss surface. The parameters are updated according to Eq. (5.92), where α denotes the step size:

$$\theta_{t+1} = \theta_t - \alpha \nabla \left(\frac{1}{n} \sum_{i=1}^{n} f_i(\theta_t) \right) \tag{5.92}$$

The overall algorithm with automatic differentiation is summarized in Table 5.21. This method is evaluated on MNIST and CIFAR datasets.

TABLE 5.21 General methods of the reweight examples via automatic differentiation.

Input: θ_0, the initial parameters
Output: θ_T, the updated parameters

1: for $t=0\ldots T-1$ do
2:      Obtain $\{X_f, y_f\} \leftarrow \text{MiniBatch}(\mathcal{D}_f, n)$ through randomly sample
3:      Obtain $\{X_g, y_g\} \leftarrow \text{MiniBatch}(\mathcal{D}_g, m)$ through randomly sample
4:      **Obtain** $\hat{y}_f$ $using$ Forward computation (X_f, y_f, θ_t)
5:      Obtain ϵ $using$ $0; l_f \leftarrow \sum_{i=1}^{n} \epsilon_i C\left(y_{f,i}, \hat{y}_{f,i}\right)$
6:      Obtain $\nabla \theta_t using$ BackwardAD computation (l_f, θ_t)
7:      Obtain $\hat{\theta}_t \leftarrow \theta_t - \alpha \nabla \theta_t$
8:      Obtain $\hat{y}_g u\,sing$ Forward computation$\left(X_g, y_g, \hat{\theta}_t\right)$
9:      Obtain $l_g \leftarrow \frac{1}{m}\sum_{i=1}^{m} C\left(y_{g,i}, \hat{y}_{g,i}\right)$
10:     Obtain $\nabla \epsilon \leftarrow$ BackwardAD computation(l_g, ϵ)
11:     Obtain $\tilde{w} \leftarrow \max(-\nabla \epsilon, 0)$ and $w \leftarrow \sum_j \tilde{w} + \delta\left(\sum_j \tilde{w}\right)$
12:     Obtain $\hat{l}_f \leftarrow \sum_{i=1}^{n} w_i C\left(y_i, \hat{y}_{f,i}\right)$
13:     Obtain $\nabla \theta_t u\,sing$ BackwardAD computation $\left(\hat{l}_f, \theta_t\right)$
14:     Obtain $\theta_{t+1} using$ OptimizerStep computation $(\theta_t, \nabla \theta_t)$
15: end for

Modified from Ren, M., Zeng, W., Yang, B., & Urtasun, R. (2018). Learning to reweight examples for robust deep learning. International conference on machine learning (pp. 4334–4343). PMLR.

5.8.3 Hallucinated clean representation for noisy-labeled visual recognition

To reduce the adverse effects caused by noisy labels, such as overfitting, two standard approaches include label noise correction and weighting. However, despite their benefits, they both suffer from certain limitations. Label noise correction demands a confusion matrix to bridge clean and dirty data, which is usually highly impractical to obtain in large-scale datasets. In the weighting strategies, the confidence score may neglect a core component for noise-label confusion. Additionally, splitting noisy labeled data and hard clean data is a demanding task requiring complicated paradigm design.

Zhang, Wang, and Qiao (2019) proposed a prototypical network-suited (Snell et al., 2017) noisy labeled visual recognition softmax classifier, named MetaCleaner, to address the overfitting problem in noisy labels. In contrast to the existing noisy labeled recognition methods (e.g., Jiang, Zhou, Leung, Li, & Fei-Fei, 2018; Lee, He, Zhang, & Yang, 2018a, 2018b; Ren, Zeng, et al., 2018) and metric distance classifier under low-shot leaning (Snell et al., 2017), MetaCleaner emphasizes the importance of the relationships between multiple images in the subsets of a category and suggests to hallucinate clean representation for shot-free denoise.

This label noise correction framework consists of two primary modules:

1. Noisy weighting compared the semantic representations of a category's image subset to measure the confidence scores of all images in the noisy subset
2. Clean hallucinating produces a clean representation of the given noisy subset considering different weights to different image representations

Given a noisy set with one noisy sample and four clean samples, Noisy Weighting measures the importance of each individual sample through the comparisons of all representations within the set (visualized as weighted representation). Hence, Clean Hallucinating estimates the clean representation v_c using $v_c = \dfrac{\sum_i \alpha_i v_i}{\sum_i \alpha_i}$. The three representations are displayed as noisy representation, weighted representation, and clean representation.

The detailed structure of MetaCleaner is explored along with the prototypical network in Chapter 3. See theoretical perspective introduction and analysis of the network architecture and its two submodules (noisy weighting and clean hallucination) in Extended Algorithm 3 in Section 3.4.

MetaCleaner is reported to improve the robustness on noisy labels and is assessed in datasets Food-101N (Lee et al., 2018a, 2018b), Clothing1M (Xiao, Xia, Yang, Huang, & Wang, 2015), CIFAR-10 (He et al., 2016), and ImageNet (Deng et al., 2009).

5.8.4 Data valuation using reinforcement learning

A large-scale dataset is urgently needed in deep learning as a data-hungry technology; however, not all data are equally helpful and beneficial in training a deep neural network for promising generalization capability, as reported in research by Toneva et al. (2018). To improve performance, removing mislabeled or low-quality data is an ideal choice, suggested by multiple publications (Frenay & Verleysen, 2014). But given a tricky situation where the train-test mismatch cannot be easily removed or is inevitable, carefully culling the noisy data and selecting the most useful data are essential to avoid training inefficiency and to keep the mismatch manageable.

For data valuation, Yoon et al. (2019) suggested a meta-learning framework to value data jointly with the corresponding target task, entitled Data Valuation using Reinforcement Learning (DVRL). This approach aims to train the deep neural network through a meta-reinforcement learning approach. It consists of two processors: a data value estimator based on a deep neural network and a target task predictor. The data value estimator holds a nondifferentiable sampling process; thus, gradient-based optimization is no longer appropriate. Instead, the REINFORCE paradigm is conducted as a policy gradient optimization to stimulate the exploration of the optimal policy. More specifically, a reward is produced as an evaluation of the performance on a microscale validation set; this reward is a reinforcement signal for learning the likelihood of each datum during the training of the target task predictor. The official DVRL code is available at https://github.com/google-research/google-research/tree/master/dvrl.

This framework can be generalized in different scenarios to maintain impressive data selection, including the following:

- Mislabeled data
- Heterogeneous data distribution due to varying collection methods

- Low-quality data
- irrelevant data to target tasks

DVRL employs two learnable functions:

- One for target task predictor as $f_\theta : \mathcal{X} \rightarrow \mathcal{Y}$, which aims to minimize a certain weighted loss $\mathcal{L}_f$, as expressed in Eq. (5.93), where h_ϕ is the data value estimator:

$$f_\theta = \arg \min_{\hat{f} \in \mathcal{F}} \frac{1}{N} \sum_{i=1}^{N} h_\phi(x_i, y_i) \cdot \mathcal{L}_f\left(\hat{f}(x_i), y_i\right) \qquad (5.93)$$

- Another for data value estimator $h_\phi : \mathcal{X} \cdot \mathcal{Y} \rightarrow [0,1]$. The data value estimator adjusts the output weights to find out the selection likelihood distribution of the selected samples in the training of the predictor model f_θ. The optimization method is summarized in Eq. (5.94) based on samples of validation dataset x^v and y^v:

$$\min_{h_\phi} \mathbb{E}_{(x^v, y^v) \sim P^t}\left[\mathcal{L}_h\left(f_\theta(x^v), y^v\right)\right]$$

$$s.t. f_\theta = \arg \min_{\hat{f} \in \mathcal{F}} \mathbb{E}_{(xy) \sim P}\left[h_\phi(xy) \cdot \mathcal{L}_f\left(\hat{f}(x)y\right)\right] \qquad (5.94)$$

The overall training method of DVRL is summarized in Table 5.22.

TABLE 5.22   General training methods of data valuation using reinforcement learning.

```
Input: α and β, the hyperparameters of learning rate
Bₚ and Bₛ, the size of mini-batch
Nᵢ, number of inner iteration count
T, moving average window
D, training dataset
Dᵛ={(xₖᵛ,yₖᵛ)}ₖ₌₁ᴸ, the validation dataset
```

1: $\theta, \phi \rightarrow$ initialization and moving average $\delta=0$
2: **while** not convergence **do**
3:    randomly sample a mini-batch from the training dataset $D_B = (x_j, y_j)_{j=1}^{B_S} \sim D$

4:    **for** $j=1, \ldots, B_S$ **do**
5:       compute selection probabilities using $w_j = h_\phi(x_j, y_j)$
6:       randomly sample selection vector using $s_j \sim Ber(w_j)$

7:    **for** $t = 1, \ldots, N_I$ **do**
8:       randomly sample a mini-batch as $(\tilde{x}_m, \tilde{y}_m, \tilde{s}_m)_{m=1}^{B_P} \sim (x_j, y_j, s_j)_{j=1}^{B_S}$

9:       update the predictor model network using $\theta \leftarrow \theta - \alpha \frac{1}{B_P} \sum_{m=1}^{B_P} \tilde{s}_m \cdot \nabla_\theta \mathcal{L}_f(f_\theta(\tilde{x}_m), \tilde{y}_m)$

10:    update the data value estimator using

$$\phi \leftarrow \phi - \beta \left[\frac{1}{L} \sum_{k=1}^{L} [\mathcal{L}_h(f_\theta(x_k^v), y_k^v) - \delta] \nabla_\phi \log \pi_\phi(D_B, (s_1, \ldots, s_{B_s})) \right]$$

11:    update the moving average base line using

$$\delta \leftarrow \frac{T-1}{T} \delta + \frac{1}{LT} \sum_{k=1}^{L} [\mathcal{L}_h(f_\theta(x_k^v), y_k^v)]$$

Modified from Yoon et al. (2019).

This framework is assessed in 12 public benchmarks and datasets, including:

- two language datasets—Enron Email Dataset and SMS Spam;
- three public tabular datasets—UCI BlogFeedback, UCI Adult, and Kaggle Rossmann Store Sales Dataset; and
- seven image datasets—HAM10000, MNIST, USPS, Kaggle Flower Recognition Dataset, Fashion-MNIST, CIFAR-10, and CIFAR-100.

5.8.5 Teacher-student networks for image classification on noisy labels

Unlike the previous strategy that relied on a mixture of clean labels and noise labels, as discussed previously, Li et al. (2019) presented the Meta-Learning-based Noise-Tolerant (MLNT) paradigm to leverage noisy annotated data and avoid overfitting without human supervision or any support from clean labels. MLNT consists of a teacher network (through a self-ensembling algorithm developed by Tarvainen & Valpola, 2017) and a student network (which is guided by the teacher network during meta-testing) to obtain parameters that are more tolerant of low-quality data. Diverse synthetic noisy labels are produced for the same images on each mini-batch of training samples to enhance the consistency of predictions and to model immune to synthetic noise. This strategy executes meta-objectives before regular gradient updates. It is model-agnostic and easy to apply in gradient-based learning algorithms. In contrast to classification loss used in the meta-test from MAML, MLNT employs consistency loss in the teacher model with the self-ensembling method. The official code is available at https://github.com/LiJunnan1992/MLNT.

There are two procedures: meta-training and meta-testing.

- During meta-training, the updating rule occurs by one-step gradient descent with synthetic mini-batch $(X, \widehat{Y}_m)$, as expressed in Eq. (5.95), where $\mathcal{L}_c$ is cross-entropy loss and α represents step size:

$$\theta'_m = \theta - \alpha \nabla_\theta \mathcal{L}_c \left(X, \widehat{Y}_m, \theta \right) \tag{5.95}$$

- In meta-testing, MLNT sets consistency loss $\mathcal{J}\left(\theta'_m\right)$ as KL divergence D_{KL} between the predictions by the updated model $f(X, \theta_m')$ and the teacher network $f\left(X, \widetilde{\theta}\right)$, as expressed in Eq. (5.96):

$$
\begin{aligned}
\mathcal{J}\left(\theta'_m\right) &= \frac{1}{k} \sum_{i=1}^{k} D_{KL}\left(f\left(x_i, \widetilde{\theta}\right) \middle\| f\left(x_i, \theta'_m\right)\right) \\
&= \frac{1}{k} \sum_{i=1}^{k} \mathbb{E}\left(\log\left(f\left(x_i, \widetilde{\theta}\right)\right) - \log\left(f\left(x_i, \theta'_m\right)\right)\right)
\end{aligned}
\tag{5.96}
$$

The meta-loss—averaging all consistency losses—is expressed in Eq. (5.97), which describes the updating parameter, where η denotes the meta-learning rate:

TABLE 5.23   General training methods of meta-learning based noise-tolerant.

1: $\boldsymbol{\theta}\to$ random initialization
2: $\tilde{\boldsymbol{\theta}}=\boldsymbol{\theta}\to$ teacher model initialization

3: while not done do
4:      Randomly sample a mini-batch denoted as $(\boldsymbol{X},\boldsymbol{Y})$ from $\mathcal{D}$ in k size.

5:      for m=1, 2, ..., M do
6:          Produce synthetic noisy labels $\hat{Y}_m$ using random neighbour label transferring
7:          Compute the updated model parameters under gradient descent:
$$\boldsymbol{\theta}'_m = \boldsymbol{\theta} - \alpha\nabla_{\boldsymbol{\theta}}\mathcal{L}_c\left(\boldsymbol{X},\hat{Y}_m,\boldsymbol{\theta}\right)$$
8:          Evaluate consistency loss using teacher module:
$$\mathcal{J}\left(\boldsymbol{\theta}'_m\right)=\tfrac{1}{k}\textstyle\sum_{i=1}^{k}D_{\mathrm{KL}}\left(f\left(x_i,\tilde{\boldsymbol{\theta}}\right)\,\|\,f\left(x_i,\boldsymbol{\theta}'_m\right)\right)$$
9:      end for

10:      Compute meta-loss $\mathcal{L}_{\mathrm{meta}}(\boldsymbol{\theta})=\tfrac{1}{M}\sum_{m=1}^{M}\mathcal{J}\left(\boldsymbol{\theta}'_m\right)$
11:      Meta-learning update using $\boldsymbol{\theta}\leftarrow\boldsymbol{\theta}-\eta\nabla\mathcal{L}_{\mathrm{meta}}(\boldsymbol{\theta})$
12:      Compute classification loss $\mathcal{L}_c(\boldsymbol{X},\boldsymbol{Y},\boldsymbol{\theta})$
13:      Update $\boldsymbol{\theta}\leftarrow\boldsymbol{\theta}-\beta\nabla\mathcal{L}_c(\boldsymbol{X},\boldsymbol{Y},\boldsymbol{\theta})$
14:      Obtain teacher model using $\tilde{\boldsymbol{\theta}}=\gamma\tilde{\boldsymbol{\theta}}+(1-\gamma)\boldsymbol{\theta}$
15: end while

Modified from Li, J., Wong, Y., Zhao, Q., & Kankanhalli, M. S. (2019). Learning to learn from noisy labeled data. In: Proceedings of the IEEE/CVF conference on computer vision and pattern recognition (pp. 5051–5059).

$$\mathcal{L}_{\mathrm{meta}}(\boldsymbol{\theta}) = \frac{1}{M}\sum_{m=1}^{M}\mathcal{J}\left(\boldsymbol{\theta}'_m\right)$$

$$= \frac{1}{M}\sum_{m=1}^{M}\mathcal{J}\left(\boldsymbol{\theta}-\alpha\nabla_{\boldsymbol{\theta}}\mathcal{L}_c\left(\boldsymbol{X},\hat{Y}_m,\boldsymbol{\theta}\right)\right).$$

$$\boldsymbol{\theta}\leftarrow\boldsymbol{\theta}-\eta\nabla\mathcal{L}_{\mathrm{meta}}(\boldsymbol{\theta}) \tag{5.97}$$

The summarized training method is outlined in Table 5.23. This method is assessed on two general benchmarks: CIFAR-10 and Clothing1M.

5.8.6 Sample reweighting function construction

Sample reweighting is an effective strategy to reduce the issues caused by a skewed distribution, such as bias, overfitting, and poor generalization capabilities. Current sample reweighting approaches require a hand-crafted, predefined weighting function and its related hyperparameters. This impedes some real-world applications, however, by requiring the researcher to carry out an in-depth examination of the often complicated training sample or data properties, particularly low-quality datasets.

Shu et al. (2019) suggested a strategy named Meta-Weight-Net (MW-Net) to overcome the problem with the traditional reweighting model in biased training samples (i.e., imbalanced and low-quality data with corrupted labels), which proved difficult to implement in real-world scenarios due to various weighting schemes led by different training samples and problem sets. MW-Net aims to learn the hyper-parameter Θ automatically through meta-learning and adaptively leverage an explicit m directly from data. This weighting function consists of a multiple-layer perceptron with one hidden layer as a general approximator for most continuous functions. The small unbiased validation set is fulfilled with accurate labels and balanced data distribution $\{x_i^{(meta)}, y_i^{(meta)}\}_{i=1}^M$ instructs the training for all parameters. The official code is available at https://github.com/xjtushujun/meta-weight-net.

The optimal classifier parameter $\mathbf{w}^*$ is obtained by minimizing the weighted loss as expressed in Eq. (5.98), where $\mathcal{V}(\ell; \Theta)$ presents the weight net.

$$\mathbf{w}^*(\Theta) = \arg\min_{\mathbf{w}} \mathcal{L}^{\text{train}}(\mathbf{w}; \Theta) \triangleq \frac{1}{N}\sum_{i=1}^{N} \mathcal{V}\big(L_i^{\text{train}}(\mathbf{w}); \Theta\big) L_i^{\text{train}}(\mathbf{w}) \tag{5.98}$$

The optimal parameter Θ^* is learned by minimizing the meta-loss, as expressed in Eqs. (5.99), (5.100):

$$\Theta^* = \arg\min_{\Theta} \mathcal{L}^{\text{meta}}(\mathbf{w}^*(\Theta)) \triangleq \frac{1}{M}\sum_{i=1}^{M} L_i^{\text{meta}}(\mathbf{w}^*(\Theta)) \tag{5.99}$$

where

$$L_i^{\text{meta}}(w) = \ell\left(y_i^{(meta)}, f\left(x_i^{(meta)}, w\right)\right) \tag{5.100}$$

Analogous to the online approximation to save single optimization in Section 5.8.2, the summarized training method of MW-Net is demonstrated in Table 5.24. This strategy is evaluated on multiple public benchmarks, including long-tailed CIFAR-10 and long-tailed CIFAR-100.

TABLE 5.24 General training methods of meta-weight-net.

Input: $\mathcal{D}$, training samples
      $\widehat{\mathcal{D}}$, the metadata set
      n and m, batch size
      T, maximum iterations
Output: $\mathbf{w}^{(T)}$, parameters of the classifier network

1: $\mathbf{w}^{(0)} \rightarrow$ parameters of the classifier network initialization
2: $\Theta^{(0)} \rightarrow$ parameter of Meta-Weight-Net initialization
3: for $t=0, 1, \ldots, T-1$ do
4:       $\{x, y\} \leftarrow$ Mini-Batch $(\mathcal{D}, n)$ through randomly sample
5:       $\{x^{(meta)}, y^{(meta)}\} \leftarrow$ Mini-Batch $\left(\widehat{\mathcal{D}}, m\right)$ through randomly sample
6:       Obtain the classifier learning function $\hat{\mathbf{w}}^{(t)}(\Theta)$ using
      $\hat{\mathbf{w}}^{(t)}(\Theta) = \mathbf{w}^{(t)} - \alpha \frac{1}{n}\sum_{i=1}^{n} \mathcal{V}\left(L_i^{\text{train}}(\mathbf{w}^{(t)}); \Theta\right) \nabla_{\mathbf{w}} L_i^{\text{train}}(\mathbf{w})\Big|_{\mathbf{w}^{(t)}}$.
7:       Evaluate $\Theta^{(t+1)}$ using $\Theta^{(t+1)} = \Theta^{(t)} - \beta \frac{1}{m}\sum_{i=1}^{m} \nabla_{\Theta} L_i^{\text{meta}}\left(\hat{\mathbf{w}}^{(t)}(\Theta)\right)\Big|_{\Theta^{(t)}}$.
8:       Evaluate $\mathbf{w}^{(t+1)}$ using
      $\mathbf{w}^{(t+1)} = \mathbf{w}^{(t)} - \alpha \frac{1}{n}\sum_{i=1}^{n} \mathcal{V}\left(L_i^{\text{train}}(\mathbf{w}^{(t)}); \Theta^{(t+1)}\right) \nabla_{\mathbf{w}} L_i^{\text{train}}(\mathbf{w})\Big|_{\mathbf{w}^{(t)}}$.
9: end for

Modified from Shu, J., Xie, Q., Yi, L., Zhao, Q., Zhou, S., Xu, Z., & Meng, D. (2019). Meta-weight-net: Learning an explicit mapping for sample weighting. In: Advances in Neural information processing systems (pp. 1917–1928).

5.8.7 Loss correction approach

Wang, Hu, and Hu (2020) presented a model-agnostic loss correction (LC) meta-learner, applicable in computer vision and natural language processing, named meta-loss correction (MLC). Loss correction approaches assume an unknown noise transition matrix T, which causes the corruption of noisy labels from ground-truth. This framework is aim to learn and approach this matrix accurately. The official code is released at https://github.com/ZhenWang-PhD/Training-Noise-Robust-Deep-Neural-Networks-via-Meta-Learning in a PyTorch version.

In the traditional LC strategy, the unknown noise transition matrix T is introduced to correct the ground-truth label. T is learned from prior knowledge to accurately estimate maximum predictions (Patrini, Rozza, Menon, Nock, & Qu, 2017) and mean predictions (Hendrycks, Mazeika, Wilson, & Gimpel, 2018). It relies on the "perfect example" assumption (Patrini et al., 2017). In contrast, this approach learns directly from data through meta-learning and viewing it as a meta-parameter (Ren, Zeng, et al., 2018).

MLC can be divided into three components: (1) virtual-train, (2) meta-train, and (3) actual-train.

Virtual-train is used to optimize the backbone network's weights θ^t relied on a corrected loss function, expressed in Eq. (5.101), where n is the batch size, T^t represents noise transition matrix, and $\widetilde{y}_i$ denotes noisy label for classes C:

$$l_{\text{virtual-trn}} = -\frac{1}{n} \sum_{i=1}^{n} \widetilde{y}_i \log \left(T^t f \left(x_i; \theta^t \right) \right) \tag{5.101}$$

The weights $\widehat{\theta}^{t+1}$ of the one-step-forward "virtual" model are updated according to the gradient descent rule in Eq. (5.102), where α denotes the learning rate:

$$\widehat{\theta}^{t+1} \left(T^t \right) = \theta^t - \alpha \nabla_{\theta^t} l_{\text{virtual-trn}} \tag{5.102}$$

Given the backbone from virtual-train, meta-train optimizes the optimal T^{t+1} on its validation set, as expressed in Eq. (5.103):

$$l_{\text{meta-trn}} = -\frac{1}{M} \sum_{i=1}^{M} y_i \log \left(f \left(x_i; \widehat{\theta}^{t+1} \right) \right) \tag{5.103}$$

An approximation on a mini-batch of the validation set to save time and memory is indicated in Eq. (5.104), where m is mini-batch size:

$$l_{\text{meta-trn}} = -\frac{1}{m} \sum_{i=1}^{m} y_i \log \left(f \left(x_i; \widehat{\theta}^{t+1} \right) \right) \tag{5.104}$$

The transition matrix T performs gradient descent through Eq. (5.105), where u^{t+1} is the raw one-step-forward noise transition matrix that is neither always nonnegative nor normalized; the β denotes the learning rate:

$$u^{t+1} = T^t - \beta \nabla_{T^t} l_{\text{meta-trn}} \tag{5.105}$$

It can fix to nonnegative and normalization by Eqs. (5.106), (5.107), respectively:

TABLE 5.25 General training methods of meta-loss correction.

```
Input:  {θᵗ, Tᵗ}, Randomly initialized
        Dₙ, noisy training set
        Dᵥ, clean validation set
        I, number of iterations
Output: Updated parameter θᴵ⁺¹
```

1. for iteration =1, ..., I do
   # Virtual-Training
2.   Updated the virtual network weights $\hat{\theta}^{t+1}$ with D_η using $\hat{\theta}^{t+1}(T^t) = \theta^t - \alpha\nabla_{\theta^t}l_{\text{virtual-trn}}$,

   where

$$l_{\text{virtual-trn}} = -\frac{1}{n}\sum_{i=1}^{n}\tilde{y}_i \log\left(T^t f(x_i;\theta^t)\right)$$

   # Meta-train
3.   Updated the transition matrix T^{t+1} with D_v under Eqs. (5.103)–(5.107)
   # Actual-Training
4.   Updated the actual network weights θ^{t+1} with D_η using

$$\theta^{t+1} = \theta^t - \gamma\nabla_{\theta^t}\left(-\frac{1}{n}\sum_{i=1}^{n}\tilde{y}_i \log\left(T^{t+1}f(x_i;\theta^t)\right)\right)$$

5. End for

Modified from Wang, Z., Hu, G., & Hu, Q. (2020). Training noise-robust deep neural networks via meta-learning. In: CVPR.

$$\tilde{T}^{t+1} = \max\left(u^{t+1}, 0\right) \tag{5.106}$$

$$T_j^{t+1} = \frac{\tilde{T}_j^{t+1}}{\sum \tilde{T}_j^{t+1} + \delta\left(\sum \tilde{T}_j^{t+1}\right)}, \delta(a) = \begin{cases} 1, & \text{if } a = 0 \\ 0, & \text{if } a \neq 0 \end{cases} \tag{5.107}$$

The actual-train optimizes the "actual" network via gradient descent, as expressed in Eq. (5.108), where γ denotes the learning rate:

$$\theta^{t+1} = \theta^t - \gamma\nabla_{\theta^t}\left(-\frac{1}{n}\sum_{i=1}^{n}\tilde{y}_i \log\left(T^{t+1}f(x_i;\theta^t)\right)\right) \tag{5.108}$$

See the comprehensive methods of MLC in Table 5.25.

MLC is evaluated in multiple datasets: MNIST (Deng, 2012), CIFAT-10 (He et al., 2016), CIFAR-100 , and Clothing1M (Xiao, Xia, et al., 2015) for visual loss correction tasks, and Twitter (Gimpel et al., 2010) for natural language processing and computer vision LC benchmarks.

5.8.8 Meta-relabeling through data coefficients

Cleaning data with the annotated label is usually expensive due to costly manual crafting by domain experts, while noise samples with mislabeled annotations are much cheaper. How to leverage noise labels is a practical problem that has provoked much research. Zhang et al.

(2020) suggested a meta-reweighting framework based on a highly noise-robust strategy. It aims to produce exemplar weights using the minimal trusted set while generating pseudo-labels to noise data by measuring data coefficients in a dense label noise regime, consisting of a few trusted clean labels combined with many noise or mislabeled samples. Data coefficients refer to the process of valuing exemplar weights based on noise labels and predicting the correct labels. This framework is grounded in the L2R model (Ren, Zeng, et al., 2018), a meta-learning reweighting algorithm that minimizes the loss of an unbiased trusted set. The official code of this method is available at https://github.com/google-research/google-research/tree/master/ieg.

This framework can be divided into four steps:

1. Soft pseudo-label initialization is a standard method used to leverage unannotated training samples in semisupervision. Instead of applying neural networks as unstable approaches to augmentation, this step employs soft pseudo with K random augmentation (as shown by Berthelot et al., 2019), which is expressed in Eqs. (5.109), (5.110). $\hat{x}_k$ denotes the kth random augmentation from input x, $g(x)_i$ represents the probability of pseudo-label x over ith class. τ indicates the softmax temperature scaling factors for sharpening the distribution of pseudo-labels, where the suggested value is $\tau = 0.5$, and Φ represents the targeting neural network.

$$g(x, \Phi)_i = \Pr_i^{\frac{1}{\tau}} / \sum_j \Pr_j^{\frac{1}{\tau}} \qquad (5.109)$$

where

$$\Pr = \frac{1}{K} \left(\Phi(x) + \sum_{k=1}^{K-1} \Phi(\hat{x}_k) \right) \qquad (5.110)$$

2. Enhance the initialization. For effectiveness in the final supervised learning, the sharpness and consistency of augmented inputs are crucial. To minimize the inconsistency of augmentation prediction, an enhanced pseudo-label initialization with Kullback-Leibler (KL) divergence loss is equipped. It punishes the inconsistent augmentations $\hat{x}_i$ of input x_i, as expressed in Eq. (5.111):

$$\min_\Theta L_{KL} = \frac{1}{N} \sum_i^N KL(\Phi(x_i; \Theta) \| \Phi(\hat{x}_i; \Theta)) \qquad (5.111)$$

3. Meta-relabeling aims to produce the optimal combination λ_i of the original ground truth label y_i and pseudo-label $g(x, \Phi)$ through the meta-learning approach by Ren, Zeng, et al. (2018). See Eqs. (5.112), (5.113) for details on the differentiable function $\mathcal{P}$ of parameter λ_i, which clarifies backpropagation:

$$\Theta^*(\omega, \lambda) = \arg\min_\Theta \sum_{i=1}^N \omega_i L(\mathcal{P}(\lambda_i), \Phi(x_i; \Theta)) \qquad (5.112)$$

$$\mathcal{P}(\lambda_i) = \lambda_i y_i + (1 - \lambda_i) g(x_i \Phi) \text{ s.t. } 0 \leq \lambda_i \leq 1 \qquad (5.113)$$

The pseudo-label is eventually expressed as Eqs. (5.114), (5.115), where λ_i^* denotes the sign of gradient as the following:

$$y_i^* = \begin{cases} y_i, & \text{if } \lambda_i^* > 0 \\ g(x_i, \Phi), & \text{otherwise} \end{cases} \tag{5.114}$$

$$\lambda_i^* = \left[\text{sign}\left(-\frac{\partial}{\partial \lambda_i} \mathbb{E}\left[L^p |_{\lambda=\lambda_0, \omega=\omega_0} \right] \right) \right]_+ \tag{5.115}$$

To obtain y_i^* and ω_i^*, two cross-entropy loss functions are expressed in Eqs. (5.116), (5.117):

$$L_{\omega^*} = \sum_i^N \omega_i^* L(\mathcal{P}(\lambda_0), \Phi(x_i; \Theta)) \tag{5.116}$$

$$L_{\lambda^*} = \sum_i^N \omega_0 L\left(y_i^*, \Phi(x_i; \Theta)\right) \tag{5.117}$$

4. Supervision learning. The pairwise mixed collection of input batch and its arbitrary permutation is expressed in Eq. (5.118) for sample x_a from the concatenated pool $D_p \cup \hat{D}_u \cup D_u$:

$$x_\beta = \text{Mix}_\beta(x_a, x_b), y_\beta = \text{Mix}_\beta(y_a, y_b), \text{where } \left\{ (x_a, y_a), (x_b, y_b) \in D_p \cup \hat{D}_u \cup D_u \right\} \tag{5.118}$$

The overall training method is summarized in Table 5.26.

TABLE 5.26 General training methods of the proposed method.

Input: Θ^t, the model parameters at the current step
       A batch of training data X_u from D_u
       $X_p \sim D_p$, a batch of probe data
       k and p, the loss weight
       T, the threshold
Output: Θ^{t+1}, the updated model parameters after training

1: Produce augmentation $\hat{X}_u$ based on X_u
2: Evaluate the pseudo labels through $g(x_u, \Phi), x_u \sim X_u \cup \hat{X}_u$
3: Evaluate optimal data coefficients λ^* and ω^*
4: Separate the training batch X_u and corresponding $\hat{X}_u$ if applicable, to (1) potential correctly labelled batch X_u^c and (2) potential mislabeled batch X_u^u via the binary criterion $\mathbb{I}(\omega* < T)$.
5: Obtain the joint batch set $X_p \cup X_u^u \cup X_u^c \cup \hat{X}_u^u \cup \hat{X}_u^c$, where $\hat{X}_u^u \cup X_u^u$ employs pseudo labels evaluated using $g(\cdot, \Phi)$.
6: Evaluate the overall loss for parameters updating using $L_{\omega^*} + L_{\lambda^*} + L_\beta^p + p L_\beta^u + k L_{KL}$.
7: Obtain Θ^{t+1} by performing one step stochastic gradient descent

Modified from Zhang, Z., Zhang, H., Arik, S. O., Lee, H., & Pfister, T. (2020). Distilling effective supervision from severe label noise. In: Proceedings of the IEEE/CVF conference on computer vision and pattern recognition (pp. 9294–9303).

This framework is evaluated in dataset CIFAR-10, a subset of WebVision (Jiang, Zhou, et al., 2018), Clothing1M, and Food101 (Lee et al., 2018a, 2018b) for scaling to a real-world examination. CIFAR-100 is used to assess generalization in a semisupervised setting.

5.8.9 Meta-label correction

There are two research lines on handling low-quality data with mislabeled annotations: (1) reweighting methods (see related approach in Section 5.8.6) and (2) label correction through a label corruption matrix. Motivated by the idea of "learning to correct," Zheng et al. (2021) provided MLC, a framework with two models trained jointly as a bi-level optimization to deal with noisy labels. The meta-learning-based label correction network generates correct labels for mislabeled data (i.e., noisy labels, $D = \{x, y\}^m$). At the same time, the main model predicts from both the initially accurate labeled data (i.e., clean labels, $D' = \{x, y'\}^M$) and corrected noisy data produced by the meta-model, where $M \gg m$. This can be viewed as a weak supervision solution for image recognition and text classification problems. The official code is available at https://github.com/microsoft/MLC.

The bi-level optimization through the main model and the label correction network is formulated as Eqs. (5.119), (5.120), where w is the main parameter from main model and α denotes meta-parameters from the label correction network. f is the main model, g represents the meta-model, $h(x)$ mean the feature representation from the main classifier, and y' denotes the weak label.

$$\min_{\alpha} \mathbb{E}_{(x,y) \in D} \ell \left(y, f_{w_{\alpha}^*}(x) \right) \tag{5.119}$$

$$\text{s.t. } w_{\alpha}^* = \arg\min_{w} \mathbb{E}_{(xy') \in D'} \ell \left(g_{\alpha}(h(x)y') f_{w}(x) \right) \tag{5.120}$$

To reduce computing complexity on solving optimal w^*, the one-step stochastic gradient descent adjusts w to approximate the favorable main model. This is shown in Eq. (5.121), where η is the learning rate and $\mathcal{L}_{D'}$ represents the loss of noisy dataset:

$$w_{\alpha}^* \approx w'(\alpha) = w - \eta \nabla_w \mathcal{L}_{D'}(\alpha, w) \tag{5.121}$$

Hence, the proxy optimization is formulated in Eq. (5.122), where $\mathcal{L}_{D'}(\alpha, w)$ and $\mathcal{L}_D(w)$ denote the lower-level and upper-level objective function, respectively:

$$\min_{\alpha} \mathcal{L}_D(w'(\alpha)) = \mathcal{L}_D(w - \eta \nabla_w \mathcal{L}_{D'}(\alpha, w)) \tag{5.122}$$

Table 5.27 briefly outlines the summarized methods of meta-label correction. This framework is evaluated on three public benchmarks (CIFAR-10, CIFAR-100, and Clothing1M) with uniform label noise, flipped label noise, and real-world noisy labels.

TABLE 5.27 General training methods of MLC—meta-label correction.

```
1. while not converged do
2.         Update meta-parameters α
3.         Update model parameters w through ∇_w L_D'(α, w)
4. end
```

Modified from Zheng, G., Awadallah, A. H., & Dumais, S.(2021). Meta label correction for noisy label learning. In: Proceedings of the AAAI conference on artificial intelligence, Vol. 35, No. 12 (pp. 11053–11061).

5.9 Superresolution

5.9.1 Introduction

Superresolution technology is a class of techniques that reestablishes an image or a sequence of observations from low-resolution to higher-resolution. Superresolution (SR) imaging has become an active research area in many practical applications, such as medical imaging. As deep learning emerged, researchers implemented various CNN-based frameworks, such as SRCNN (Dong, Loy, He, & Tang, 2014, 2016) and GANs-based (Goodfellow et al., 2014) models (e.g., SRGAN (Ledig et al., 2017). These deep-learning SR techniques can be divided into three groups: unsupervised superresolution, supervised superresolution, and domain-specific superresolution.

Approaches

For supervised SR, there are four primary frameworks. Dong and colleagues (Dong et al., 2014, 2016) proposed the first preupsampling superresolution, SRCNN. However, preupsampling SR is time-consuming with noise amplification and blurring. To address these issues, postupsampling superresolution consists of end-to-end upsampling layers and anterior CNN. Although postupsampling SR essentially decreases the computational complexity, the upsampling is only processed under a single step, making the learning difficult for significant scaling factors. To tackle the limitation for multiscale SR, progressive upsampling superresolution is built on Laplacian pyramid SR (LabSRN; Lai, Huang, Ahuja, & Yang, 2017) with several variations, such as MS-LabSRN (Lai, Huang, Ahuja, & Yang, 2018) and progressive SR (ProSR). Iterative up-and-down sampling superresolution is designed for the shared dependency of LR-HR pairwise images: SRFBN (Li, Wong, et al., 2019) captures better representations through an iterative up-and-down sampling feedback module, whereas RBPN (Haris, Shakhnarovich, & Ukita, 2019) focuses on continuous video scenes.

A variety of popular neural networks pair with these four fundamental frameworks. ResNet (He et al., 2016) is considered an essential scheme for SR tasks, with many implements through either local residual learning or global residual learning. Others have incorporated recursive learning (e.g., DRCN; Kim, Lee, & Lee, 2016a, 2016b), DRRN (Tai et al., 2017), CARN (Ahn, Kang, & Sohn, 2018), multipath learning (MPL, such as global MPL) LapSRN, local MPL MSRN, scale-specific MPL MDSR (Lim, Son, Kim, Nah, & Lee, 2017), DenseNet (Huang, Liu, Maaten, & Weinberger, 2017), channel attention mechanism (Hu, Dollar, et al., 2018; Hu, Shen, & Sun, 2018), nonlocal attention models (Zhang et al., 2019), and dilated convolution.

Early research typically employs pixel-wise L2 loss function. However, it fails to accurately evaluate the reconstruction quality. L1 loss boosts the convergence and performance more than L2 loss, whereas L2 loss punishes major errors more, but is more open to minor errors, which could lead to outcomes that are too smooth. For later discovery, content loss, adversarial loss, texture loss, cycle consistency loss, total variation loss, and prior-based loss have attracted increasing attention.

Gathering many images with the same scene but multiple resolutions is not always practical. Thus, unsupervised superresolution has drawn greater expectations. Unsupervised SR mainly focuses on three parts: zero-shot SR, weakly supervised SR, and deep image prior. One common approach of zero-shot super-resolution (ZSSR) proposed by Shocher, Cohen, and Irani (2018) is to incorporate an unsupervised SR through an image-specific SR network during testing instead of producing a generic model based on an external dataset. However, the existing ZSSR methods are still challenging due to time-consuming inference from distinct models for training and testing.

Datasets and benchmarks

SR public datasets have been summarized by Wang, Chen, and Hoi (2020). Some image datasets for other computer vision tasks are also appropriate for SR benchmarks, including ImageNet (Deng et al., 2009), MS-COCO (Lin et al., 2014), VOC2012 (Everingham et al., 2015), CelebA (Liu et al., 2015), T91 jointly with BSD300 (Kim et al., 2016a, 2016b; Lai et al., 2017; Tai, Yang, & Liu, 2017; Tai, Yang, Liu, & Xu, 2017), or DIV2K jointly with Flickr2K (Haris, Shakhnarovich, & Ukita, 2018; Lim et al., 2017).

For SR evaluation criteria, the general image quality assessment (IQA) contains two parts: human perception and the objective computational scheme. Human perception can be subjective depending on the individual visual perception system; more research to evaluate performances has relied on objective IQA. The three types of objective IQA (Wang, Bovik, Sheikh, & Simoncelli, 2004; Wang, Chen, & Hoi, 2020) are: "full-reference" IQA (FR-IQA), based on reference images, "reduced-reference" IQA (RR-IQA), equipped with extracted features comparison, and "no-reference" IQA (also named blind IQA or NR-IQA), without reference images.

Among various existing superresolution strategies, several deficiencies need to be highlighted. Current studies commonly neglect to leverage the nonlocal self-similarity (NSS)—an essential prior of natural images. Additionally, most existing attempts have failed to investigate superresolution in few-shot regimes with expensive massive datasets. The internal properties of the testing image remain under-explored in supervised methods, self-supervised solutions fail to maintain a precise but efficient computation complexity, and the sizeable models aggravate practical experiences. Furthermore, zero-shot strategies need long-lasting inference periods because of inefficient self-training and the failure to leverage prior knowledge from pretrained models, which is inconvenient in real-world situations.

On the other hand, meta-learning has shed light on some new solutions to these issues. Meta-learning is conducted to rapidly adapt any unseen low-resolution test image based on a small number of samples. It meta-learns the shared prior across multiple tasks and then fine-tunes the prior model for unknown distortion. Moreover, a zero-shot kernel-based approach achieves a time-shrink inference and exploits the internal structure and patterns by integrating meta-learning and transfer learning.

The following three sections will delve into: multiple illustrations of zero-shot SR in Section 5.9.2; nonreference SR in Section 5.9.3; and low-resolution/high-resolution image pair SR in Section 5.9.4. Each section will start with a short conceptual introduction and explore related motivations, the central paradigm, novel techniques, a comprehensive pipeline, and the training/testing datasets.

5.9.2 Meta-transfer learning for zero-shot superresolution

As a line of research in the area of superresolution, single image superresolution demonstrates the implementation of deep neural network technology in image reconstruction. However, there are several issues with this approach: (1) current attempts rely on supervised methods requiring extensive training data, which is expensive to label and collect; (2) the need to iterate through thousands of gradient descents increases the inference time; (3) due to the previous two factors, the number of parameters increases dramatically, resulting in a very large model that is impractical when it comes to fitting real-world applications; and (4) the internal or structural information of an image remains underexplored, particularly its NSS, a powerful natural image prior.

To solve these problems, Soh and colleagues (Soh et al., 2020) introduced kernel-agnostic meta-transfer learning for zero-shot superresolution (MZSR; Shocher et al., 2018). This framework was built on a modified MAML training by only one gradient update, seeking to tackle the MZSR issues of long inference time and solely exploit the internal structure and patterns that cannot employ external datasets. This research argued that simple transfer learning and fine-tuning do not yield a promising result; instead, the framework couples transfer learning and meta-learning with a novel training method to handle internal and external samples. The official code is available at https://github.com/JWSoh/MZSR.

During large-scale training, this model is training on a paired dataset (I_{HR}, I_{LR}^{bic}) and processed under bicubic degradation from a large-scale high-resolution dataset D_{HR} to learn super-resolution by minimizing the loss function, as expressed in Eq. (5.123). This is a pixel-wise L1 loss between estimation and ground truth. The pretrained approach is also helpful in stabilizing MAML.

$$L^D(\theta) = \mathbb{E}_{D \sim (I_{HR}, \ I_{LR}^{bic})} \left[\left\| I_{HR} - f_\theta(I_{LR}^{bic}) \right\|_1 \right] \tag{5.123}$$

This framework employs an external dataset in meta-training and an internal dataset for meta-testing. The meta-objective function is expressed in Eq. (5.124), where α denotes the task-level learning rate:

$$\underset{\theta}{\mathrm{argmin}} \sum_{T_i \sim p(T)} L_{T_i}^{te}(\theta_i) = \underset{\theta}{\mathrm{argmin}} \sum_{T_i \sim p(T)} L_{T_i}^{te} \left(\theta - \alpha \nabla_\theta L_{T_i}^{tr}(\theta) \right) \tag{5.124}$$

The update rule is formulated in Eq. (5.125), where β denotes the meta-learning rate:

$$\theta \leftarrow \theta - \beta \nabla_\theta \sum_{T_i \sim p(T)} L_{T_i}^{te}(\theta_i) \tag{5.125}$$

This method is summarized in Table 5.28. The large-scale training is outlined in lines 3–7. Meta-transfer learning is shown in lines 11–14, and the meta-learner optimization appears in lines 15–16.

In meta-testing, the information of a single low-resolution image is learned in internal learning to model its superresolved target image, as demonstrated in Table 5.29.

Similar to work from Hu et al. (2019), this rapid and efficient self-supervised method is valid on the following datasets under "bicubic" downsampling (a technique using a weighted average is better than average downsampling but time-consuming):

TABLE 5.28　General training methods of the proposed model.

```
Input: 𝒟_HR, high-resolution dataset
       p(k), blur kernel distribution
       α, β: learning rates
Output: Updated parameter θ_M
```

```
1  Randomly initialize θ
2  Generate paired dataset 𝒟 by bicubically downsampling 𝒟_HR
3  while not done do
4        Sample LR-HR batch from 𝒟
5        Estimate ℒ^D with L^D(θ) = 𝔼_{D∼(I_HR, I^{bic}_{LR})}[‖I_HR − f_θ(I^{bic}_{LR})‖_1]
6        Update θ by ℒ^D
7  end while

8  Produce task distribution p(𝒯) with 𝒟_HR and p(k)
9  while not done do
10       Sample task batch 𝒯_i ∼ p(𝒯)

11   for all 𝒯_i do
12          Compute training loss (𝒟_tr): ℒ^{tr}_{𝒯_i}(θ)
13          Compute adapted parameters θ_i: θ_i = θ − α∇_θℒ^r_{𝒯_i}(θ)
14   end for

15   Update θ by average test loss (𝒟_te):
16     θ ← θ − β∇_θ∑_{𝒯_i∼p(𝒯)}ℒ^{te}_{𝒯_i}(θ_i)
17 end while
```

Modified from Soh, J. W., Cho, S., & Cho, N. I. (2020). Meta-Transfer Learning for Zero-Shot Super-Resolution. In: CVPR.

TABLE 5.29　General testing methods of the proposed model.

```
Input: I_LR, LR test image
       θ_M, model parameter trained by meta-transfer
       n, number of gradient updates
       α, learning rate
Output: Super-resolution image I_SR
```

```
1  Initialize θ with θ_M
2  Produce LR son I_son by downsampling I_LR through corresponding blur kernel

3  for n steps do
4        Compute loss ℒ(θ) = ‖I_LR − f_θ(I_son)‖_1
5        Update model parameters by θ ← θ − α∇_θℒ(θ)
6  end for

7  return I_SR = f_θ(I_LR)
```

Modified from Soh, J. W., Cho, S., & Cho, N. I. (2020). Meta-Transfer Learning for Zero-Shot Super-Resolution. In: CVPR.

- Set5 (Bevilacqua, Roumy, Guillemot, & Alberi-Morel, 2012)
- BSD100 (Martin, Fowlkes, Tal, & Malik, 2001)
- Urban100 (Huang, Singh, & Ahuja, 2015)
- SSIM (Wang et al., 2004)
- DIV2K (Agustsson & Timofte, 2017)

5.9.3 LR-HR image pair superresolution

With an increasing number of super-resolution techniques available, multiple paradigms are now being applied in this area. Supervised learning, involving extensive training datasets, constitutes one of the most basic, intuitive approaches in this regard. Yet it is deficient when it comes to examining the internal properties of test images. While self-supervised methods can be employed to address this issue, they fail to maintain a computation complexity that is both precise and efficient. Additionally, this popular approach already appears to have reached its limit based on the peak signal-to-noise ratio. Furthermore, regular zero-shot learners are time-consuming during inference due to the fact that they are inefficient at self-training and struggle to leverage the prior knowledge from pretrained models trained on large-scale datasets.

Park et al. (2020) proposed a model-agnostic kernel-agnostic MAML backbone learner for single-image super-resolution, named meta-learning for super-resolution (MLSR). Similar to the approach of Soh et al. (2020), this model initializes the conventional SR networks—SRCNN (Dong et al., 2014, 2016), ENET (Sajjadi, Scholkopf, & Hirsch, 2017), IDN (Hui, Wang, & Gao, 2018), and RCAN (Zhang et al., 2018)—with a large external training dataset from DIV2K (Agustsson & Timofte, 2017). It modified MAML as a backbone for rapidly fine-tuning the pretrained parameters to adapt any new low-resolution (LR) test image quickly. Patch recurrence property successfully handles the nonbicubic SR kernel issue (Michaeli & Irani, 2013; Shocher et al., 2018) and essentially improves the performance of the SR pretrained network. The overall scheme of this framework is displayed in Fig. 5.12 with three different stages:

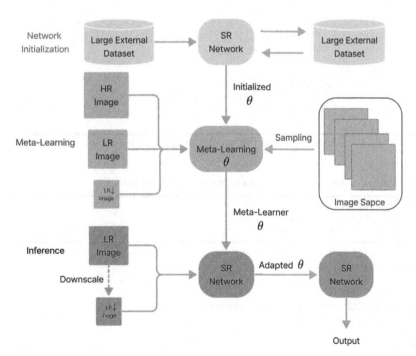

FIG. 5.12 High-level workflow of (A) network initialization, (B) meta-learning, and (C) inference.
Adapted from Springer, CVPR, Fast Adaptation to Super-Resolution Networks via Meta-Learning, Park, S., Yoo, J., Cho, D., Kim, J., & Kim, T. H. (2020).

initialization, meta-training, and meta-testing. The official code is available at https://github. com/parkseobin/MLSR.

The loss function and the gradient updating rule are expressed in Eqs. (5.126), (5.127), respectively.

$$L\big(f_\theta(LR), HR\big) = \big\|f_\theta(LR) - HR\big\|_2^2 \tag{5.126}$$

$$\theta \leftarrow \theta - \beta\nabla_\theta L\Big(f_{\theta_i}(LR_i), HR_i\Big) \tag{5.127}$$

The inner loop updating is expressed in Eq. (5.128), where α is the learning rate:

$$\theta_i \leftarrow \theta - \alpha\nabla_\theta L\Big(f_{\theta_i}(LR_i\downarrow), LR_i\Big) \tag{5.128}$$

Meta-training and meta-testing methods are summarized in Tables 5.30 and 5.31, where $(LR\downarrow)$ denotes down-sized low-resolution images.

This performance is compared with the ZSSR (Shocher et al., 2018) method and meta-trained IDN with nonbicubic SR kernel.

TABLE 5.30   General training methods of meta-learning for super-resolution.

```
Input: p(I): Distribution of images
    α, β: Hyperparameters of step-size
```

```
1 Initialize θ

2 while not converged do
3       Sample a batch from {Iᵢ}~p(I)
4       Produce {HRᵢ}, {LRᵢ}, {LRᵢ↓} based on {Iᵢ}

5       for each t do
6           Evaluate ∇θℒ(fθ(LRᵢ↓),LRᵢ) with ℒ
7         # Employ SGD for adapted parameters computation
              θᵢ ← θ - α∇θℒ(fθ(LRᵢ↓),LRᵢ)
8     θ ← θ - β∇θ∑ᵢℒ(fθᵢ(LRᵢ),HRᵢ)
```

Modified from Park, S., Yoo, J., Cho, D., Kim, J., & Kim, T. H. (2020). Fast adaptation to super-resolution networks via meta-learning. In: CVPR.

TABLE 5.31   General testing methods of meta-learning for super-resolution.

```
Input: I: the given image
       α: Hyperparameter of step-size
       n: number of gradient updates
```

```
1 Initialize θ with meta-trained parameter
2 Produce LR, LR↓ with I
3 i←0
4 while i<n do
5         # employ SGD for adapted parameters
6         θ ← θ - α∇θℒ(fθ(LR↓),LR)
7         i←i+1
8 end while
9 Compute fθ(LR)
```

Modified from Park, S., Yoo, J., Cho, D., Kim, J., & Kim, T. H. (2020). Fast adaptation to super-resolution networks via meta-learning. In: CVPR.

5.9.4 No-reference image quality assessment

Since the distortion types remain unknown in real-world scenarios, the CNN-based approach of general-purpose no-reference IQA seems to be a potential one-size-fits-all solution. Yet in spite of many remarkable efforts in this direction, several challenges still constitute significant barriers. The existing large-scale annotated datasets for IQA are in short supply due to the expensive nature of assembling a large number of high-quality samples. Hence, overfitting is inevitable when using DCNNs as they are trained on small-scale datasets. One typical solution is to pretrain the model on a large-scale dataset, such as ImageNet, but this often performs poorly because the distortion types are unknown.

Zhu et al. (2020) suggested a deep meta-learning solution for no-reference image quality metrics (NR-IQA; Ye, Kumar, Kang, Doermann, & Jun., 2012), named MetaIQA. This model aims to improve generalization abilities on various distortions in the real-world no-reference IQA scenario when full-reference IQA and reduce-reference IQA are not practical. The official code is available at https://github.com/zhuhancheng/MetaIQA.

The MetaIQA approach consists of two stages:

- Meta-learning for a shared quality prior model based on numerous NR-IQA tasks
- Fine-tuning the prior model on undetermined distortions NR-IQA

The loss function is built on squared Euclidean distance, as expressed in Eq. (5.129), where the ground truth quality score of the image x is denoted as y:

$$L = \left\| f_\theta(x;\theta) - y \right\|_2^2 \tag{5.129}$$

Unlike ordinary optimization, MetaIQA implements a bi-level gradient optimization (i.e., two-level stochastic gradient descent methods from the support set to the query set) based on various distortion-specific NR-IQA.

The two-level Adam optimization of the support set is expressed in Eqs. (5.130), (5.131). $Adam(L_{T_i}, \theta)$ is the first level, and $Adam(L_{T_i}, \theta_i')$ the second level, where $m_{\theta(s)}$ denotes the first moment of gradients, $v_{\theta(s)}$ is the second moment, α is the inner loop learning rate, and ϵ is a constant.

$$\text{Adam}(\mathcal{L}_{\tau_i}, \theta) : \theta_i' \leftarrow \theta - \alpha \sum_{s=1}^{S} \frac{m_{\theta(s)}}{\sqrt{v_{\theta(s)}} + \epsilon} \tag{5.130}$$

$$\text{Adam}\left(\mathcal{L}_{\tau_i}, \theta_i'\right) : \theta_i \leftarrow \theta_i' - \alpha \sum_{s=1}^{S} \frac{m_{\theta'(s)}}{\sqrt{v_{\theta'(s)}} + \epsilon} \tag{5.131}$$

The step-by-step methods of MetaIQA are summarized in Table 5.32.

This model is evaluated in synthetically and authentically distorted IQA databases with assessment metrics of Spearman's rank-order correlation coefficient (SROCC) and Pearson's linear correlation coefficient (PLCC). Synthetically distorted databases include TID2013 (Ponomarenko et al., 2015) and KADID-10K (Lin, Hosu, Saupe, & Jun., 2019). However,

TABLE 5.32 General training methods of MetaIQA and fine-tuning for NR-IQA task.

Input: meta-train $\mathcal{D}_{meta}^{p(\tau)} = \left\{ \mathcal{D}_{s}^{\tau_i}, \mathcal{D}_{q}^{\tau_i} \right\}_{i=1}^{N}$ where $\mathcal{D}_{tr_s}^{\tau_i}$ denotes the task-support set and $\mathcal{D}_{tr_q}^{\tau_i}$ is the task-query set

      N: the total quantity of tasks
      M: training images of a target NR-IQA task
      x: query image
      β: hyperparameter of learning rate
Output: estimated quality score y corresponding to x

1: θ initialization
2: # meta-train

3: for = 1, 2, ... do
4:     Select a mini-batch containing k tasks from $\mathcal{D}_{meta}^{p(\tau)}$

5:   for i=1, 2, ..., k do
6:       # first level computation
7:       $\theta_i' = \text{Adam}(\mathcal{L}_{\tau_i}, \theta)$ on $\mathcal{D}_{s}^{\tau_i}$
8:       # second level computation
9:       $\theta_i = \text{Adam}(\mathcal{L}_{\tau_i}, \theta_i')$ on $\mathcal{D}_{q}^{\tau_i}$
10:   end for

11:   $\theta \leftarrow \theta - \beta \frac{1}{k} \sum_{i=1}^{k} (\theta - \theta_i)$
12:end for

13:# fine-tuning concerning NR-IQA task
14:$\theta_{te} = \text{Adam}(\mathcal{L}, \theta)$ over the NR-IQA task
15:Take x as input of the quality model $f_{\theta_{te}}$

16:return $\hat{y}$

Modified from Zhu, Y., Liu, C., & Jiang, S. (2020). Multi-attention meta learning for few-shot fine-grained image recognition.

authentically distorted IQA databases include CID2013 (Virtanen, Nuutinen, Vaahteranoksa, Oittinen, & Hakkinen, 2015), LIVE challenge (Ghadiyaram & Bovik, 2016), and KonIQ-10K (Lin, Hosu, & Saupe., D., 2018).

5.10 Multimodal learning

5.10.1 Introduction

In many real-world scenarios, multiple sensors with particular characteristics are equipped to process and analyze global and local patterns in terms of versatile size, dimensions, format, and scope from various data streams. One major difficulty is to extract visual features across multiple modalities through the multimodal fusion of these heterogeneous features and represent them in a shared common space (Bayoudh, Knani, Hamdaoui, & Mtibaa, 2021). These modalities may cover data sources of textual, auditory, visual, and encoding information by specific methods or mechanisms. There are many tasks in multimodal learning worth exploration, such as embodied question answering and image retrieval; however, this introduction will concentrate more on the corresponding background related to the following meta-learning implementations in Section 5.10.2—image captioning and visual question answering (VQA).

Image captioning—the process of automatic generation of a textual description of an image—has developed a range of real-life applications, such as social media recommendations, image annotation, image indexing, and others. It incorporates a machine vision for looking and reading the image and natural language processing for language expression. The typical evaluation metrics include the BLEU metric, Meteor metric, ROUGE metric, and CIDEr metric.

Deep learning approaches

There are three main types of image captioning through deep neural networks (Liu et al., 2018):

- Retrieval-based method, which relies on an image search engine to procure visual words based on features from images.
- Template-based method, which is a two-staged strategy through object detection and classification, as well as sentence generation based on an object's attribute and the relationship between objects and environments.
- End-to-end learning-based method, which integrates DCNN with RNN as a joint model directly trained by maximizing the likelihood probability $p(S|I)$ for the generated language expression $S = (S_1, S_2, \ldots)$ with input image I. Classic models include neural image caption (NIC; Farhadi et al., 2010), spatial attention mechanism (e.g., show-and-tell framework; Vinyals, Toshev, Bengio, & Erhan, 2015), semantic attention (You, Jin, Wang, Fang, & Luo, 2016), self-adaptive attention mechanism (Lu, Xiong, Parikh, & Socher, 2016), context-based captioning (Krause, Johnson, et al., 2016), and image paragraph (Krause, Sapp, et al., 2016).

VQA is one of the most developed research lines in understanding and reasoning the correct answer given a query question. The standard approaches can be categorized into four types:

- Joint-embedding methods, motivated by image captioning, with image representations extracted through pretraining CNN on object recognition and text representations captured by pretraining word embedding, such as Neural-Image-QA (Malinowski, Rohrbach, & Fritz, 2015)
- Attention mechanisms, assigning different weights of various features from separate locations to show the model "where to look" (Wu et al., 2016), such as SMem (Xu & Saenko, 2015)
- Compositional models, which stimulate transfer learning and the optimal use of supervision, such as Neural Module Networks (Andreas, Rohrbach, Darrell, & Klein, 2016)
- Knowledge base-enhanced approaches, requiring prior nonvisual information ranging from common sense to domain-specific knowledge, such as FVQA

Benchmarks

The taxonomy of public benchmarks is summarized in DAQUAR (Malinowski & Fritz, 2014), COCO-QA (Ren et al., 2015), FM-IQA (Gao et al., 2015), VQA-real (Antol et al.,

2015), Visual Genome (Krishna et al., 2016), VQA-abstract (Antol et al., 2015), FVQA, and KB-VQA (Wang, Shen, et al., 2015; Wang, Wu, et al., 2015). Typical evaluation metrics involve accuracy and Wu-Palmer similarity (WUPS; Wu & Palmer, 1994).

The remaining sections discuss different multimodal applications, offering an in-depth exploration of specific techniques. Section 5.10.2 demonstrates an effective prototypical meta-learner that employs a nonlinear transformation function for a VQA system.

5.10.2 Visual question answering system

Typical VQA approaches are closely aligned with the mapping between predefined images and questions with fixed terms and vocabularies. During the conversation, open domains are forcefully concentrated into finite parameters, leading to inherent scalability issues. The scope of these approaches is also rather narrow, since answers can only be given when the question is highly similar to one used during the training process. Additionally, the extensibility of such a model is relatively limited, as the only way to modify or expand the domain is to begin training again from the start.

To tackle this issue, Teney and van den Hengel (2018) brought a meta-learner into a VQA system (Jabri, Joulin, & van der Maaten, 2016; Kazemi & Elqursh, 2017; Wu et al., 2017; Yang, He, Gao, Deng, & Smola, 2016) to enhance the recall of rare answers and generate appropriate novel answers corresponding to an unseen query (i.e., the optimal answer to a question related to a visual image). This framework converges a multimodal problem between joint computer vision, natural language processing, incremental learning (Fernando et al., 2017; Rebuffi, Kolesnikov, & Lampert, 2016), and continuum learning (Aljundi, Chakravarty, & Tuytelaars, 2016; Lopez-Paz & Ranzato, 2017; Yoon, Yang, Lee, & Ju Hwang, 2017).

This meta-framework was motivated by prototypical networks (Snell et al., 2017) and the Meta-Network (Munkhdalai & Yu, 2017); its architecture can be divided into two parts (see Fig. 5.13):

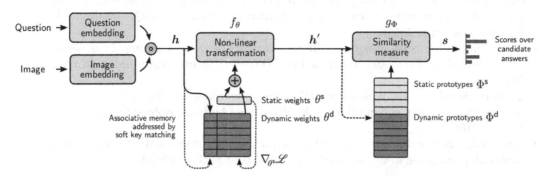

FIG. 5.13   The gneral structure of the proposed meta-learner.
Teney, D., & van den Hengel, A. (2017). Visual question answering as a meta learning task. In Proceedings of the European conference on computer vision (ECCV) (pp. 219–235).

1. A nonlinear transformation $f_\theta(\cdot)$ acts as an embedding part to encode the input questions and images h through a gated hyperbolic tangent layer (Dauphin, Fan, Auli, & Grangier, 2016); the element-wise Hadamard product ∘ is employed in Eq. (5.132), where σ present logistic activation function, and b and b' are the bias:

$$f_\theta(h) = \sigma(Wh + b) \circ \tanh\left(W'h + b'\right) \tag{5.132}$$

2. A similarity measure $g_\Phi(\cdot)$ addresses reasoning and real question answering. The mapping $g_\Phi(h)$ of the output of nonlinear transformation to a numerical vector score $s \in [0,1]^A$ over the set of candidates' answers is defined in Eq. (5.133), where the b'' denotes the learned bias, $d(\cdot, \cdot)$ represents the similarity estimation, and i index the N^a support samples contains a as correct answer:

$$g_\phi^a(h') = \sigma\left(\frac{1}{N^a}\sum_{i=1}^{N^a} d\left(h', \phi_i^a\right) + b''\right) \tag{5.133}$$

This framework has built prototypes $\Phi = \{\phi_i^a\}_{i,\,a}$ for potential answers. See the methods from Eqs. (5.134), (5.135), where w''' denotes the learned weights where d_{dot} presents a dot-product similarity. Step-by-step methods are demonstrated in Table 5.33.

$$d_{\text{dot}}(h, \theta) = h^\top \theta \tag{5.134}$$

$$d_{\text{L1}}(h, \theta) = w'''|h - \theta| \tag{5.135}$$

TABLE 5.33 General training and testing methods of the proposed model.

```
Input: S = {(Qᵢ,Iᵢ,ŝᵢ)}ᵢ, support set
    Instances for evaluating (Q,I,ŝ) with training set or testing set
Output: s, prediction scores over candidate answers
Φᵈ←∅, for initializing dynamic prototypes
M←∅, for initializing memory of dynamic weights
```

```
1. for each element i in S do
2.     if training with probability p then
3.         Drop random support elements end
4.         continue
5.     end if
6.         Forward- and back-propagation of (Qᵢ,Iᵢ,ŝᵢ) with static weights θˢ and
           prototypes Φˢ
7.         Gather hᵢ
```

$$h_i' = f_\theta(h_i)$$

$$s_i = g_\Phi\left(h_i'\right)$$

$$\nabla_{\theta^s}\mathcal{L}(L_i, \hat{s}_i)$$

Continued

TABLE 5.33   General training and testing methods of the proposed model—cont'd

```
# Store in memory of dynamic weights in terms of (key, value)
```

$$\mathcal{M} \leftarrow \mathcal{M} \cup (\boldsymbol{h}, \nabla_{\theta^s}\mathcal{L}(s_i, \hat{s}_i))$$

```
8. end for
```

```
# One average value each answer
```

$$\phi^a = \frac{1}{N^a}\sum_{i:\hat{s}_i^a=1}^{N^a} \boldsymbol{h}_i' \quad \forall a$$

```
# Dynamic prototypes storage
```

$$\Phi^d = \cup_a \phi^a$$

```
9. Forward-propagation of (Q, I) using static and dynamic parameters
```

```
# testing/inference period
10. if testing then
11.         Return prediction scores  s=g_Φ(f_θ(h))
# training period
12. else if training then
13.      Employ back-propagation and gradient descent
14.      Update static parameters θˢ, φˢ, b″, w′, w‴, as well as that of the question
         and image embeddings
15. end if
```

Modified from Zhu, Y., Liu, C., & Jiang, S. (2020). Multi-attention meta learning for few-shot fine-grained image recognition.

$$d_{L2}(\boldsymbol{h}, \boldsymbol{\theta}) = \boldsymbol{w}'''(\boldsymbol{h} - \boldsymbol{\theta})^2$$

This approach reaches state-of-the-art performance on the VQA v2 benchmark (Goyal, Khot, Summers-Stay, Batra, & Parikh, 2016) under the scenario of a constantly increasing support set without continual retraining.

5.11 Other emerging topics

5.11.1 Domain generalization

Domain generalization and domain adaptation are different types of domain shift solutions in transfer learning. Domain generalization (DG) is to generalize a model for unseen domains that cannot be accessed in training methods (i.e., explicit knowledge of target distributions is not allowed). In domain adaptation (DA), both the labeled source data distribution and the unlabeled (or sparsely labeled) target data distribution can be learned during training (Li, Wong, et al., 2019). Some researchers view DG as a special case of DA.

Balaji et al. (2018) introduced MetaReg, a meta-learning framework to produce an novel regularization function for optimal performance in domain generalization problem. MetaReg also addresses the limitations caused by MAML and meta-learning domain generalization

(MLDG) on DG—weak scalability to develop MLDA into deep structures of neural networks and ineffective MAML-like objective functions. MAML is SOTA for fast task adaptation, but limited to domain generalization.

MetaReg proposes structures to tackles these problems in two stages:

1. Developing a novel regularization function from task specific to task general representations in each training episode to enhance the meta-training effectiveness
2. Processing meta-learning solely on the task network while freezing the feature network to support its scalability

This framework aims to minimize the cross entropy loss function expressed in Eq. (5.136), where M_Θ represents a deep neural network and $\Theta = \{\psi, \theta\}$, F denotes the feature network with weights ψ, and T denotes the task network with weights θ. $y_j^{(i)}$ demonstrates a one-shot vector on label $\boldsymbol{y}_j^{(i)}$ and " . " represents dot product.

$$L(\psi, \theta) = \mathbb{E}_{(x,y) \sim D}\left[-y \cdot \log\left(M_\Theta(x)\right)\right] = \sum_{i=1}^{p}\sum_{j=1}^{N_i} -y_j^{(i)} \cdot \log\left(M_\Theta\left(x_j^{(i)}\right)\right) \tag{5.136}$$

The regularizer update procedure is expanded in Eqs. (5.137), (5.138) and describes samples of domain a utilized in task network a, which also leverages well on domain b:

$$\widehat{\theta}_a^{(k)} = \beta^\ell \tag{5.137}$$

$$\phi^{(k+1)} = \phi^{(k)} - \alpha\nabla_\phi L^{(b)}\left(\psi^{(t)}, \widehat{\theta}_a^{(k)}\right)\bigg|_{\phi=\phi^{(k)}} \tag{5.138}$$

The comprehensive meta-training algorithm is summarized in Table 5.34. It shows how MetaReg, the pipeline with feature network and task networks, works, and the optimization update of MetaReg.

TABLE 5.34 General training and testing methods of MetaReg.

Input: N_{iter}, number of iterations in training Output: α_1 and α_2, hyperparameters of learning rate
1: for $t = 1, \ldots, N_{iter}$ do
2:    for $i = 1, \ldots, p$ do 3:   randomly sample n_b labelled image $\{(x_j^{(i)}, y_j^{(i)})\}$ from D_i 4:   update supervised classification using $$\psi^{(t)} \leftarrow \psi^{(t-1)} - \alpha_1 \nabla_\psi L^{(i)}\left(\psi^{(t-1)}, \theta^{(t-1)}\right)$$ $$\theta_i^{(t)} \leftarrow \theta_i^{(t-1)} - \alpha_1 \nabla_{\theta_i} L^{(i)}\left(\psi^{(t-1)}, \theta^{(t-1)}\right)$$
5: end for
6: randomly select $a, b \in \{1, 2, \ldots, p\}$ as $a \neq b$

Continued

TABLE 5.34   General training and testing methods of MetaReg—cont'd

```
7:   β¹ ← θₐ⁽ᵗ⁾
8:   for i = 2, 3, ... ℓ do
9:      randomly sample meta-train set {(xⱼ⁽ᵃ⁾, yⱼ⁽ᵃ⁾)} from Dₐ
```

$$\beta^i = \beta^{i-1} - \alpha_2 \nabla_{\beta^{i-1}} \left[L^{(a)}\left(\psi^{(t)}, \beta^{i-1}\right) + R_\phi\left(\beta^{i-1}\right) \right]$$

```
10:  end for
11:  θ̂ₐ⁽ᵗ⁾ = βₗ
12:  randomly sample meta-test set {(xⱼ⁽ᵇ⁾, yⱼ⁽ᵇ⁾)} from Dᵦ
13:  meta-update the regularizer using
```

$$\phi^{(t)} \leftarrow \phi^{(t-1)} - \alpha_2 \nabla_\phi L^{(b)}\left(\phi^{(t)}, \widehat{\theta}_a^{(t)}\right)\Big|_{\phi = \phi^{(t)}}$$

```
14:  end for
```

Modified from Balaji, Y., et al. (2018). Metareg: Towards domain generalization using meta-regularization. In: NIPS.

This model is evaluated in four public datasets: the Photo, Art painting, Cartoon, and Sketch (PACS) datasets (Li, Yang, Song, & Hospedales, 2018). In four separate experiments, one of the four domains is hidden as the target domain while the other three are trained as source domains. With the advantages of scalability and efficiency, MetaReg outperforms MAML-based MLDG and creates a state-of-the-art benchmark in all four categories (art painting, cartoon, photo, sketch, and average) in the PACS dataset.

5.11.2 High-accuracy 3D appearance-based gaze estimation in few-shot regimes

Gaze estimation is a task regarding eye fixations, seeking to locate where a person is looking at and what is being stared at. It is primarily implemented in human-machine interaction and virtual reality. It remains one of the challenging research areas in computer vision due to the uniqueness and diversity of eye appearance, head position, image quality, occlusion, and illumination conditions. Highly accurate 3D gaze estimation is rarely achieved due to the requirement of explicit or implicit fitting of eyeball movement in the context of various face appearances and measurements of visual and optical axes. Additionally, over-parameterization caused by training on low-data personalization regimes and image variations beyond regulated settings pose significant difficulties in gaze estimation.

Park et al. (2019) proposed a MAML-based meta-learning framework for tackling person-independent human gaze estimation that relied on only a few calibration instances (no more than nine), few-shot adaptive gaze estimation (FAZE). FAZE concentrates on the condensed person-specific latent representation based on various gazes, appearances, and head poses through the Disentangling Transforming Encoder-Decoder (DT-ED), a disentangling encoder-decoder network. The official code is available at https://github.com/NVlabs/few_shot_gaze.

This framework consists of two main modules: (1) the DT-ED that processes a rotation-aware implicit gaze embedding and (2) a meta-learning-oriented adaptable gaze estimator.

During gaze-equivariance feature processing, the multiobjective loss function in DT-ED is expressed in Eq. (5.139), where the empirically suggested values are $\lambda_{recon}=1$, $\lambda_{EC}=2$, $\lambda_{gaze}=0.1$.

$$\mathcal{L}_{full} = \lambda_{recon}\mathcal{L}_{recon} + \lambda_{EC}\mathcal{L}_{EC} + \lambda_{gaze}\mathcal{L}_{gaze} \tag{5.139}$$

Each component of this multiobjective loss function is described below:

- The reconstruction loss function $\mathcal{L}_{recon}$ controls the encoding-decoding part, which is expressed in Eq. (5.140), where x_b denotes input image with pixels u, and $\hat{x}_b$ means a reconstructed image with pixels $\hat{u}$ obtained through decoding the image x_a's rotated embeddings $\hat{z}_b$:

$$\mathcal{L}_{recon}(\mathbf{x}_b, \hat{\mathbf{x}}_b) = \frac{1}{|\mathbf{x}_b|} \sum_{u \in x_b, \hat{u} \in \hat{x}_b} |\hat{u} - u| \tag{5.140}$$

- The embedding consistency component allows the encoder to focus on face images with various appearances and the same eye fixation directions and encode them to analogous features. The embedding consistency loss function is expressed in Eq. (5.141), where the frontalized implicit gaze features $f(z^g)=(R^g)^{-1}z^g$ with rotation matrix R^g and ground-truth eye fixation direction g for mini-batch B:

$$\mathcal{L}_{EC} = \frac{1}{B} \sum_{i=1}^{B} \max_{\substack{j=1\dots B \\ id(i)=id(j)}} d\left(f\left(\mathbf{z}_i^g\right), f\left(\mathbf{z}_j^g\right)\right) \tag{5.141}$$

- The gaze direction loss function through a multiple-layer perceptron is expressed in Eq. (5.142):

$$\mathcal{L}_{gaze}(\hat{\mathbf{g}}, \mathbf{g}) = \arccos\left(\frac{\hat{\mathbf{g}} \cdot \mathbf{g}}{\|\hat{\mathbf{g}}\| \|\mathbf{g}\|}\right) \tag{5.142}$$

In Adaptable Gaze Estimator (AdaGEN) learning, MAML is employed to handle few-shot regimes. The updating rules during meta-training and meta-testing are expressed in Eqs. (5.143), (5.144), respectively, where α and η represent the learning rates:

$$\theta'_n = f(\theta_n) = \theta_n - \alpha\nabla\mathcal{L}_{p^{train}}^c(\theta_n) \tag{5.143}$$

$$\theta_{n+1} = \theta_n - \eta\nabla\mathcal{L}_{p^{train}}^v(f(\theta_n)) \tag{5.144}$$

The overall person-specific learner P^{test} is obtained by fine-tuning the few-shot person-specific learner M_{θ^*} on k calibration samples, as shown in Eq. (5.145):

$$\theta_{p^{test}} = \theta^* - \alpha\nabla\mathcal{L}_{p^{test}}^c(\theta^*) \tag{5.145}$$

This framework is assessed on two public benchmarks: GazeCapture (Krafka et al., 2016) and MPIIGaze (Zhang, Sugano, Fritz, & Bulling, 2015).

5.11.3 Benchmark of cross-domain few-shot learning in vision tasks

Cross-domain few-shot learning, differing from traditional few-shot learning, explores how to deal with the significant divergence between novel class domains and base class domains. It can be formulated through source domains $(\mathcal{X}_s, \mathcal{Y}_s)$ over distribution P_s and target domains $(\mathcal{X}_t, \mathcal{Y}_t)$ over distribution P_t, $P_{\mathcal{X}_t} \neq P_{\mathcal{X}_s}$ and $\mathcal{Y}_s \cap \mathcal{Y}_t = \varnothing$. The expected error is expressed in Eq. (5.146), with model f_θ and parameter θ:

$$\epsilon(f_\theta) = E_{(x,\ y)\sim P}\left[\ell(f_\theta(x), y)\right] \tag{5.146}$$

In this way, standard natural images may not be the best choices due to their high visual similarity across primary images, which limits the development of benchmarks in this area and related model performances. However, real-world images under different imaging procedures using various forms of energy—such as high-energy radiation (e.g., X-ray) and high-energy sound (e.g., ultrasound)—shed light on this problem. Guo et al. (2020) designed and constructed a public benchmark for cross-domain visual tasks under few-shot regimes, namely the Broader Study of Cross-Domain Few-Shot Learning (BSCD-FSL). It gathers countless images with distinct perspectives: semantic content, color depth, and perspective distortion. The official code for the experiments is available at https://github.com/IBM/cdfsl-benchmark.

There are two procedures during few-shot methods: meta-training and meta-testing. During the meta-training procedure, many base category classes will be learned under low-data regimes concentrated on a specific domain. In meta-testing methods, unseen classes with few examples per class are adapted based on the learned model. In BSDC-FSL, the natural images from ImageNet are fed as the source domain, while the diverse target domains gather versatile images from the following collections:

- Skin lesion images from ISIC2018
- Satellite images with large perspective distortions from EuroSAT (Helber, Bischke, Dengel, & Borth, 2019)
- Radiological images with various perspective distortions but no natural scenes and two lost color channels from ChestX (Wang et al., 2017)
- Natural images specializing in plant disease from CropDisease (Mohanty, Hughes, & Salathé, 2016)

  Several meta-learning backbones are assessed in proposed benchmarks:

- Matching Network (see Section 3.3)
- MAML (see Section 4.3)
- Prototypical Network (see Section 3.4)
- Relation Network (see Section 3.5)
- MetaOpt (Lee et al., 2019)
- FWT (Tseng, Lee, Huang, & Yang, 2020)

5.11.4 Latent embedding optimization in low-dimensional space

The gradient-based meta-learning method highlights a variety of application and research problems, attempting to obtain a single set of particular parameters to adapt individual tasks rapidly within a few steps of gradient descent. Many widely used algorithms like MAML and

Reptile deliver impressive benefits—fast adaptation and optimal initialization—on multiple practice areas and offer backbone models to countless modifications for specific scenarios. See a detailed introduction of critical optimization-based meta-learning approaches in Chapter 4.

However, gradient-based meta-learners face difficulties regarding their generalization capability in high-dimensional parameter spaces under a shared initialization for task-specific adaptation with an exceptionally small number of training samples. Rusu et al. (2018) provided the LEO strategy to tackle this issue through an encoder, decoder, and Relation Net. LEO decouples the gradient-based adaptation mechanism from the high-dimensional parameter space Θ, then applies it into low-dimensional latent space $\mathcal{Z}$. Instead of conducting one optimal parameter $\theta^* \in \Theta$, LEO provides a more expressive way through a data-dependent conditional probability distribution over Θ. It concentrates on a generative distribution of parameters that aim for the same goal. The official code is available at https://github.com/deepmind/leo.

This approach provides two benefits:

- The initialization of a new task can leverage a joint relationship with all input data by equipping a relation network with the encoder; this allows a task-specific initialization for adaptation
- A more effective adaptation is performed when this approach optimizes low-dimensional space; the ambiguities in low-data regimes are also expressed as in a stochastic process

During the encoding procedure, a sample from the given problem instance $T_i = (D^{tr}, D^{val}) \sim p(T)$ is projected from the input space to a code from a hidden-layer space $\mathcal{H}$ via an encoder model as $g_{\phi_e}: R^{n_x} \to R^{n_h}$. The relation network g_{ϕ_r} aggregates codes from $\mathcal{H}$ related to various training samples as pair-wise concatenation, and it obtains $(NK)^2$ pairs for K-shot N-way classification. The probability distribution in low-dimensional latent space $\mathcal{Z} = R^{n_z}$ with the number of 2N parameters is obtained by averaging within each group of $(NK)^2$ outputs, which is divided by n classes as $D_n^{tr} = \{(x_n^k, y_n^k) | k = 1 \dots K\}$. The encoding procedure can be summarized into Eq. (5.147), where $diag$ denotes a diagonal covariance:

$$\mu_n^e, \sigma_n^e = \frac{1}{NK^2} \sum_{k_n=1}^{K} \sum_{m=1}^{N} \sum_{k_m=1}^{K} g_{\phi_r}\left(g_{\phi_e}\left(x_n^{k_n}\right) g_{\phi_e}\left(x_m^{k_m}\right) \right)$$

$$z_n \sim q\left(z_n | \mathcal{D}_n^{tr}\right) = \mathcal{N}\left(\mu_n^e \operatorname{diag}\left(\sigma_n^{e2}\right)\right) \tag{5.147}$$

In the decoding procedure, the decoder network $g_{\phi_d}: \mathcal{Z} \to \Theta$ maps the latent codes $z_n \in \mathcal{Z}, n = 1 \dots N$ to a Gaussian distribution under diagonal covariance in the parameter space Θ. This is expressed in Eq. (5.148), where w_n denotes class-dependent parameters:

$$\mu_n^d, \sigma_n^d = g_{\phi_d}(z_n)$$

$$w_n \sim p(w|z_n) = \mathcal{N}\left(\mu_n^d, \operatorname{diag}\left(\sigma_n^{d2}\right)\right) \tag{5.148}$$

The classification loss function in the inner loop based on the decoding parameters is expressed in Eq. (5.149):

$$\mathcal{L}_{T_i}^{tr}\left(f_{\theta_i}\right) = \sum_{(x,y) \in \mathcal{D}^{tr}} \left[-w_y \cdot x + \log\left(\sum_{j=1}^{N} e^{w_j \cdot x} \right) \right] \tag{5.149}$$

TABLE 5.35   General training methods of latent embedding optimization.

Input: $\mathcal{S}^{tr}{\in}\mathcal{T}$, the training meta-set
         α and η, hyperparameters of learning rates

1: ϕ_e, ϕ_r, $\phi_d{\rightarrow}$ randomly initialization
2: Assign $\phi{=}\{\phi_e,\phi_r,\phi_d,\alpha\}$

3: while not converged do
4:     for number of tasks in batch do
5:             Randomly sample task instance $\mathcal{T}_i$ from $\mathcal{S}^{tr}$
6:             Assign $(\mathcal{D}^{tr},\mathcal{D}^{val}) = \mathcal{T}_i$
7:             Encode $\mathcal{D}^{tr}$ to z via g_{ϕ_e} and g_{ϕ_r}
8:             Decode z to initial params θ_i by g_{ϕ_d}
9:             Initialize $z'{=}z$, $\theta_i'{=}\theta_i$

10:            for number of adaptation steps do
11:                    Evaluate training loss $\mathcal{L}_{\mathcal{T}_i}^{tr}\left(f_{\theta_i'}\right)$
12:                    Compute gradient step w.r.t. $z' \leftarrow z' - \alpha\nabla_{z'}\mathcal{L}_{\mathcal{T}_i}^{tr}\left(f_{\theta_i'}\right)$
13:                    Obtain θ_i' by decoding z' by g_{ϕ_d}
14:            end for

15:            Evaluate validation loss $\mathcal{L}_{\mathcal{T}_i}^{val}\left(f_{\theta_i}\right)$
16:    end for

17:    Compute gradient step w.r.t $\phi \leftarrow \phi - \eta\nabla_\phi\sum_{\mathcal{T}_i}\mathcal{L}_{\mathcal{T}_i}^{val}\left(f_{\theta_i}\right)$
18: end while

Modified from Rusu, A.A., Rao, D., Sygnowski, J., Vinyals, O., Pascanu, R., & Osindero, S., et al. (2018). Meta-learning with latent embedding optimization. arXiv preprint, arXiv:1807.05960.

Hence, the objective function in the outer loop is indicated in Eq. (5.150), where βD_{KL} is a weighted KL-divergence term as a regularization:

$$\min_{\phi_e,\phi_r,\phi_d} \sum_{\tau_i \sim p(\mathcal{T})} \left[\mathcal{L}_{\mathcal{T}_i}^{val}\left(f_{\theta_i}\right) + \beta D_{KL}\left(q(\mathbf{z}_n|\mathcal{D}_n^{tr}) \| p(\mathbf{z}_n)\right) + \gamma\| \operatorname{stopgrad}(\mathbf{z}_n') - \mathbf{z}_n \|_2^2\right] + R \quad (5.150)$$

The summarized methods of LEO are outlined in Table 5.35. This method is evaluated in the image classification problem of five-way one-shot and five-way five-shot settings under two public benchmarks—miniImageNet and tieredImageNet.

5.11.5 Image captioning

Reinforcement learning provides the advantage of optimizing nondifferentiable metrics through a reward mechanism. However, this also entails the problem of reward hacking. The reward signal acts as an agent's guide when choosing the optimal policy; the cumulative reward increase indicates a potential corrective action determined by the agent in the name of maximizing the cumulative reward. Reward hacking occurs when the agent invests its effortsolely in maximizing the reward rather than detecting and executing the optimal policy.

Li et al. (2009) introduced a MAML-based meta-learning driver, offering a globally optimal solution to avoid reinforcement learning (RL) reward-hacking obstacles by simultaneously performing distinctive gradient steps for the task with reinforcement learning and task supervision. This model of image captioning referred to Anderson's work (2018) by employing a soft attention long-short term memory (LSTM) and a language LSTM.

These two tasks are defined in this framework as:

1. A supervision task $T1$: maximization of probability of the label annotation caption
2. A reinforcement learning task $T2$: maximization of the generated caption-reward function

Therefore, meta-updating is the MLE + RL combination through $(\nabla L_1, \theta_1)$ for MLE and $(\nabla L_2, \theta_2)$ for RL.

To maximize the probability of the label annotation, the supervision task aims to reduce each batch variance and stimulates the distinctiveness of the generated caption. The gradient $\nabla_{\theta_1'} L_1(\theta_1')$ is demonstrated in Eqs. (5.151), (5.152), where S^+ denotes the paired caption, S^- shows the unpaired caption, and I presents image:

$$\nabla_{\theta_1} L_1\left(\theta_1'\right) = -\frac{1}{\nabla_{\theta_1} G(S^+, I)} - \frac{1}{1 - \nabla_{\theta_1} G(S^-, I)} \tag{5.151}$$

$$\nabla_{\theta_1} G(S, I) = \nabla_{\theta_1} \sigma\left(\log\left(p_{\theta_1}(S|I) \right) \right) \tag{5.152}$$

Inspired by Rennie, Marcheret, Mroueh, Ross, and Goel (2017) regarding using a reinforcement learning task to maximize total reward, this model computes the baseline reward b by greedy sampling. As illustrated in Eq. (5.153), this is accomplished by diminishing the variance of the gradient estimate without changing the expected value. $p(w_t)$ represents the probability of word w_t, and reward function $r(S)$ as CIDEr+SPICE.

$$E[r(S)] = E\left[\sum_{t=1}^{N} (r(w_t) - b) \log p(w_t) \right] \tag{5.153}$$

The gradient $\nabla_{\theta_2'} L_2(\theta_2')$ is summarized through the policy gradient, as expressed in Eq. (5.154), where $r(S)$ denotes the reward function:

$$\nabla_{\theta_2'} L_2\left(\theta_2'\right) = -\nabla_{\theta_2'} E[r(S)]$$

$$= -E\left[\sum_{t=1}^{N} (r(w_t) - b) \nabla_{\theta_2'} \log p_{\theta_2'}(w_t) \right] \tag{5.154}$$

The updating of a task-specific parameter θ_i' is expressed in Eq. (5.155), where α is the learning rate:

$$\theta_i' = \theta - \alpha \nabla_\theta L_i(\theta), i = 1, 2 \tag{5.155}$$

The meta-parameter θ update across all tasks is expressed in Eq. (5.156), where a constant value $\lambda \in [0, 1]$ determines the ratio of the reinforcement learning task and the supervision task in this meta-learner. β is the learning rate.

$$\theta \leftarrow \theta - \beta \nabla_\theta \left(\lambda L_1\left(\theta_1'\right) + L_2\left(\theta_2'\right) \right) \tag{5.156}$$

Its performance is evaluated on the MS COCO dataset (Lin et al., 2014).

5.11.6 Memorization issue

Meta-learning technology has achieved remarkable success in processing a small number of data under diverse scenarios, such as few- and zero-shot learning. However, one requirement sets barriers to the usage of meta-learning—the memorization issue. First, meta-overfitting differs from regular overfitting during supervised learning. Memorization issues can cause meta-overfitting, which happens when a meta-learner impresses on memorizing a function to process all meta-training tasks (i.e., remembering the task information of each meta-training task) but fails in learning for adapting unseen tasks. The formal definition of memorization has been described by Yin et al. (2019) as follows:

Complete memorization in meta-learning is when the learned model ignores the task training data such that $I(\widehat{y}^*; D| x^*, \theta) = 0$ (i.e., $q(\widehat{y}^*|x^*, \theta, D) = q(\widehat{y}^*|x^*, \theta) = \mathbb{E}_{D'|x^*}[q(\widehat{y}^*|x^*, \theta, D')]$.

To avoid this memorization problem, mutually exclusive task distributions are required on a general meta-learning model. The task information that can be solely inferred from testing inputs can be avoided. Currently, standard solutions primarily rely on the elaborate design of meta-training tasks by, for instance, label shuffling or withdrawing task information.

Yin et al. (2019) proposed the meta-regularization (MR) strategy through information theory to free the requirement for mutually exclusive meta-training tasks and execute promising generalization smoothly across a variety of nonmutually exclusive meta-training tasks. The official code is available at https://github.com/google-research/google-research/tree/master/meta_learning_without_memorization.

Meta-regularization aims to increase mutual information $I(\widehat{y}^*; D| x^*, \theta)$ and to diminish memorization by executing meta-regularization on the following two perspectives: activation and weights. The general architecture is demonstrated in Fig. 5.14.

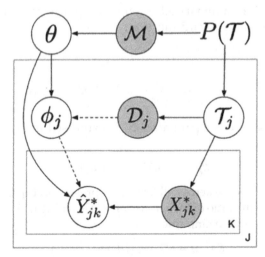

FIG. 5.14 The general pipeline of meta-regularization.
From Yin, M., Tucker, G., Zhou, M., Levine, S., & Finn, C. (2019). Meta-learning without memorization. arXiv preprint, arXiv:1912.03820. In ICLR.

- As meta-regularization concentrates on activations, the goal is to maximize mutual information $I(\hat{y}^*; D | x^*, \theta)$ and minimize the training loss function. The meta-regularized training objective function is expressed in Eq. (5.157), where β adjusts the meta-regularizer, $r(z^*)$ is a set of $N(z^*; 0, I)$, z^* denotes an intermediate stochastic bottleneck variable, ϕ means task-specific parameter, and θ is the meta-parameter. $\mathcal{D}_i$ and $\mathcal{D}_i^*$ represent training and testing set, respectively, which are contained in the meta-training set $\mathcal{M}$.

$$\frac{1}{N}\sum_i \mathbb{E}_{q(\theta|\mathcal{M})q(\phi|\mathcal{D}_i, \theta)}\left[-\frac{1}{K}\sum_{(x^*, y^*)\in\mathcal{D}_i^*}\log q(\hat{y}^* = y^*|x^*, \phi, \theta) + \beta D_{\mathrm{KL}}(q(z^*|x^*, \theta) \,\|\, r(z^*)) \right] \quad (5.157)$$

- As meta-regularization focuses on weights, the meta-regularized objective function is expressed in Eq. (5.158):

$$\frac{1}{N}\sum_i \mathbb{E}_{q(\theta; \theta_\mu, \theta_\sigma)q(\phi|\mathcal{D}_i, \tilde{\theta})}\left[-\frac{1}{K}\sum_{(x^*, y^*)\in\mathcal{D}_i^*}\log q\left(\hat{y}^* = y^*|x^*, \phi, \theta, \tilde{\theta}\right) + \beta D_{\mathrm{KL}}\left(q(\theta; \theta_\mu, \theta_\sigma) \,\|\, r(\theta)\right) \right]$$
$$(5.158)$$

The summarized method of meta-regularization on weights under conditional neural processes (MR-CNP) is outlined in Table 5.36.

TABLE 5.36 General training methods of meta-regularization on weights under conditional neural processes.

```
Input: p(T), task distribution
       q(θ;τ) = N(θ;τ) Encoder weights distribution with Gaussian parameters τ=(θμ,θσ);
       r(θ), prior distribution
       β, Lagrangian multiplier
       hθ̃(·), feature extractor
       Tθ̃(·),decoder
       α, hyper-parameter of step size
Output: τ and θ̃,the updated parameters
```

1	$\tau, \tilde{\theta} \rightarrow$ random initialization
2	**while** not converged **do**
3	Randomly sample a mini-batch of task as $\{\mathcal{T}_i\} \sim p(\mathcal{T})$;
4	Randomly sample $\theta \sim q(\theta; \tau)$ through reparameterization;
5	**for** all $\mathcal{T}_i \in \{\mathcal{T}_i\}$ **do**
6	Randomly sample $\mathcal{D}_i = (x_i, y_i)$ and $\mathcal{D}_i^* = (x_i^*, y_i^*)$ from $\mathcal{T}_i$;
7	Encode observation $z_i = g_\theta(x_i)$ and $z_i^* = g_\theta(x_i^*)$;
8	Evaluate task context $\phi_i = a(h_{-\theta}(z_i, y_i))$ via aggregator $a(\cdot)$;
9	Update $\tilde{\theta} \leftarrow \tilde{\theta} + \alpha\nabla_{\tilde{\theta}}\sum_{\mathcal{T}_i}\log q(y_i^*|T_{-\theta}(z_i^*, \phi_i))$;
10	Update $\tau \leftarrow \tau + \alpha\nabla_\tau\left[\sum_{\mathcal{T}_i}\log q\left(y_i^*|T_{\tilde{\theta}}(z_i^*, \phi_i)\right) - \beta D_{\mathrm{KL}}(q(\theta; \tau) \,\|\, r(\theta))\right]$

Modified from Yin, M., Tucker, G., Zhou, M., Levine, S., & Finn, C. (2019). Meta-learning without memorization. arXiv preprint, arXiv:1912.03820. In ICLR.

TABLE 5.37   General training methods of meta-regularized MAML.

Input: $p(\mathcal{T})$, task distribution
     $q(\theta;\tau)=\mathcal{N}(\theta;\tau)$ Encoder weights distribution with Gaussian parameters $\tau=(\theta_\mu,\theta_\sigma)$;
     $r(\theta)$, prior distribution
     β, Lagrangian multiplier
     $h_{\tilde{\theta}}(\cdot)$, feature extractor
     $T_{\tilde{\theta}}(\cdot)$, decoder
     α and α', hyperparameter of step size
Output: τ and $\tilde{\theta}$, the updated parameters

---

1 $\tau, \tilde{\theta} \to$ random initialization

2 **while** not converged **do**
3   Randomly sample a mini-batch of task as $\{\mathcal{T}_i\} \sim p(\mathcal{T})$;
4   Randomly sample $\theta \sim q(\theta;\tau)$ through reparameterization;

5   **for** all $\mathcal{T}_i \in \{\mathcal{T}_i\}$ **do**
6   Randomly sample $\mathcal{D}_i = (x_i, y_i)$ and $\mathcal{D}_i^* = (x_i^*, y_i^*)$ from $\mathcal{T}_i$;
7   Encode observation $z_i = g_\theta(x_i)$ and $z_i^* = g_\theta(x_i^*)$;
8   Obtain task-specific parameter $\phi_i = \tilde{\theta} + \alpha' \nabla_{\tilde{\theta}} \log q\left(y_i | z_i, \tilde{\theta}\right)$;

9   Update $\tilde{\theta} \leftarrow \tilde{\theta} + \alpha \nabla_{\tilde{\theta}} \sum_{\mathcal{T}_i} \log q\left(y_i^* | z_i^*, \phi_i\right)$;
10   Update $\tau \leftarrow \tau + \alpha \nabla_\tau \left[\sum_{\mathcal{T}_i} \log q\left(y_i^* | z_i^*, \phi_i\right) - \beta D_{\mathrm{KL}}(q(\theta;\tau) \parallel r(\theta)) \right]$

Modified from Yin, M., Tucker, G., Zhou, M., Levine, S., & Finn, C. (2019). Meta-learning without memorization. arXiv preprint, arXiv:1912.03820. In ICLR.

The outlined paradigm of meta-regularized MAML (MR-MAML) is shown in Table 5.37.

Table 5.38 Indicates the meta-regularized methods in meta-testing regarding MR-MAML and MR-CNP.

TABLE 5.38   Summarized meta-testing method of meta-regularized MAML.

Input: $\mathcal{T}$, meta-testing task
     $\mathcal{D} = (x, y)$, training data
     x^*, testing input
     τ and $\tilde{\theta}$, optimized parameters
Output: $\hat{y}^*$, prediction

---

1 **for** $k = 1, \ldots, K$ **do**
2   Randomly sample θ_k from $q(\theta;\tau)$;
3   Encode observation $z_k = g_{\theta_k}(x)$, $z_k^* = g_{\theta_k}(x^*)$;
4   Evaluate task-specific parameter $\phi_k = a\left(h_{\tilde{\theta}}(z_k, y)\right)$ for MR-CNP and

       $\phi_k = \tilde{\theta} + \alpha' \nabla_{\tilde{\theta}} \log q\left(y | z_k, \tilde{\theta}\right)$ for MR-MAML;
5   Make prediction as $\hat{y}_k^* \sim q(\hat{y}^* | z_k^*, \phi_k, \overline{\theta})$

6 Return prediction $\hat{y}^* = \frac{1}{K} \sum_{k=1}^{K} \hat{y}_k^*$

Modified from Yin, M., Tucker, G., Zhou, M., Levine, S., & Finn, C. (2019). Meta-learning without memorization. arXiv preprint, arXiv:1912.03820. In ICLR.

This strategy is algorithm-agnostic in optimization-based and contextual meta-learning algorithms. Meta-regularization is evaluated in several public benchmarks, including Omniglot and *mini*ImageNet, for few-shot classification and regression tasks.

5.11.7 Meta-pseudo label

Teacher-student learning is one of the training approaches in semisupervised learning. The main difference between supervised and semisupervised learning is that a set of numerous unlabeled data is contained in semisupervised learning but not in supervised learning. Thus, instead of directly training a method on the raw data in supervised learning, considering the labeled and unlabeled datasets in semisupervised learning, one common strategy involves using a teacher model T to guide the student model S to mimic the same output as the teacher model. The teacher model is first trained on the labeled dataset. Hence, the teacher model generates soft labels (i.e., class probabilities or likelihood) on the unlabeled samples. For example, in a classification task, soft labels are like "cat 0.4, dog 0.6" instead of hard labels like "cat 0, dog 1." Soft labels offer much more information to the student model, such as this specific dog looks somewhat similar to a cat. Then, the student model is trained on samples with soft labels and perfectly labeled data. The final student model is compressed compared to the larger teacher model, while previous attempts show that student models can outperform teacher models.

Motivated by teacher-student techniques in pseudo-labeling methods and self-training approaches, Pham et al. (2021) proposed an upgraded semisupervised method named meta-pseudo label. It is analogous to pseudo labeling, with a teacher model to produce pseudo labels for unannotated data and lead the student model. However, in contrast with pseudo labeling, where the teacher model remains fixed during the entire training, Meta-pseudo label equips a teacher network that can actively adapt the evaluation of generalization performance on an annotated dataset from the student network. See Fig. 5.15 for the general pipeline of meta-pseudo label and regular pseudo labels. The official code is available at https://github.com/google-research/google-research/tree/master/meta_pseudo_labels.

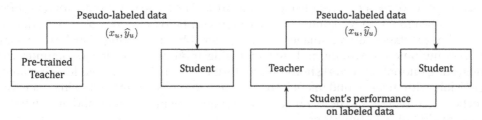

FIG. 5.15 Workflow of meta-pseudo label. The conventional approach, pseudo label, equips a pretrained teacher module to produce pseudo labels; in contrast, the teacher module from meta-pseudo label is learned with the student module jointly. The teacher module is trained by the student module's performance on labeled data, while the student module leverages pseudo-labeled data.

This method performs a bi-level optimization when training the teacher-student cyclic pipeline:

- The student network selects a batch of the unlabeled example x_u, then samples the pseudo-labeled data estimated by the teacher network. The objective function is expressed in Eq. (5.159), where η_S is the learning rate:

$$\theta'_S = \theta_S - \eta_S \nabla_{\theta_S} \mathcal{L}_u(\theta_T, \theta_S) \tag{5.159}$$

- The teacher network updates on a batch of labeled data (x_l, y_l) according to the feedback on performance from the student network. The objective function is expressed in Eq. (5.160), where η_T is the learning rate:

$$\theta'_T = \theta_T - \eta_T \nabla_{\theta_T} \mathcal{L}_l(\underbrace{\theta_S - \nabla_{\theta_S} \mathcal{L}_u(\theta_T, \theta_S)}_{=\theta'_S \text{ reused from student's update}}) \tag{5.160}$$

This method employed EfficientNet-L2 (Tan & Le, 2020) and EfficientNet-B6-Wide with an ImageNet training set as annotated samples and a JFT dataset as unannotated samples. It is assessed on datasets CIFAR-10-4K, Stree View House Number Dataset (SVHN-1K; Netzer et al., 2011), and ImageNet-10%.

5.12 Summary

The development of machine learning, and particularly deep learning, signals an important success in simulating human intelligence processes by machine vision. Despite this achievement, the learning process of current intelligent agents is still challenged by the mechanisms of understanding, analyzing, planning, and reasoning, and by the speed of humans continuously learning based on limited data on versatile scenarios. Meta-learning serves as a bridge from classical AI to artificial general intelligence (AGI)—which allows intelligent agents to analyze any task in the way a human brain does.

This chapter probes 49 pieces of state-of-the-art (SOTA) research from various subfields: image classification, face recognition and face representation attacks, object detection, fine-grained image classification, image segmentation, object tracking, label noise, super-resolution, multimodal learning, and other emerging applications related to computer vision.

Interesting tutorials and workshops present further discussions on meta-learning for computer vision, with diverse fundamental concepts and knowledge referred to in reviews or introduction lecture notes. These range from reinforcement learning and gradient-based learning to algorithm optimization:

- Conference on Computer Vision and Pattern Recognition (CVPR) 2019 workshop at https://metalearning-cvpr2019.github.io
- Association for the Advancement of Artificial Intelligence (AAAI) 2021 first international workshop on meta-learning for computer vision (MeL4CV) workshop at http://iab-rubric.org/mel4cv/

References

Ager, S. (2020). *Omniglot—writing systems and languages of the world*. Retrieved from www.omniglot.com.

Agustsson, E., & Timofte, R. (2017). Ntire 2017 challenge on single image super-resolution: Dataset and study. In *IEEE conference on computer vision and pattern recognition workshops* (pp. 126–135).

Ahmad, M. (2019). *MIT indoor scenes*. Retrieved from Kaggle: https://www.kaggle.com/itsahmad/indoor-scenes-cvpr-2019.

Ahn, N., Kang, B., & Sohn, K.-A. (2018). Fast, accurate, and lightweight super-resolution with cascading residual network. In *The European Conference on Computer Vision (ECCV)* (pp. 252–268).

Ajayi, G. (2018). *Multi-class weather dataset for image classification*. Retrieved from Mendeley Data: https://data.mendeley.com/datasets/4drtyfjtfy/1.

Aljundi, R., Chakravarty, P., & Tuytelaars, T. (2016). *Expert gate: Lifelong learning with a network of experts*. Retrieved from arXiv preprint: arXiv:1611.06194.

Andreas, J., Rohrbach, M., Darrell, T., & Klein, D. (2016). Neural module networks. In *IEEE conference on computer vision and pattern recognition*.

Andrychowicz, M., Denil, M., Gomez, S., Hoffman, M. W., Pfau, D., Schaul, T., ... Freitas, N. D. (2016). Learning to learn by gradient descent by gradient descent. In *NeurIPS*.

Angluin, D., & Laird, P. (1988). Learning from noisy examples. *Machine Learning, 2*(4), 343–370.

Antol, S., Agrawal, A., Lu, J., Mitchell, M., Batra, D., Zitnick, C. L., & Parikh, D. (2015). VQA: Visual question answering. In *IEEE international conference on computer vision*.

Antoniou, A., & Storkey, A. (2019). *Assume, augment and learn: Unsupervised few-shot meta-learning via random labels and data augmentation*. arXiv: 1902.09884.

Antoniou, A., Edwards, H., & Storkey, A. (2018). *How to train your maml*. Retrieved from arXiv preprint.

Arashloo, S. R., Kittler, J., & Christmas, W. (2017). An anomaly detection approach to face spoofing detection: A new formulation and evaluation protocol. In *IEEE Access*.

Armeni, I., Sax, A., Zamir, A. R., & Savarese, S. (2017). *Joint 2D-3D-semantic data for indoor scene understanding*. ArXiv e-prints.

Bachman, P., Hjelm, R. D., & Buchwalter, W. (2019). Learning representations by maximizing mutual information across views. In *Advances in neural information processing systems* (pp. 15509–15519).

Balaji, Y., et al. (2018). Metareg: Towards domain generalization using meta-regularization. In *NIPS*.

Bansal, P. (2019). *Intel image classification*. Retrieved from Kaggle: https://www.kaggle.com/puneet6060/intel-image-classification/version/2.

Bayoudh, K., Knani, R., Hamdaoui, F., & Mtibaa, A. (2021). *A survey on deep multimodal learning for computer vision: Advances, trends, applications, and datasets*. Retrieved from The Visual Computer. https://doi.org/10.1007/s00371-021-02166-7.

Bekker, A. J., & Goldberger, J. (2016). Training deep neural-networks based on unreliable labels. In *ICASSP* (pp. 2682–2686).

Bell, S., Zitnick, C. L., Bala, K., & Girshick, R. (2016). Inside-outside net: Detecting objects in context with skip pooling and recurrent neural networks. In *IEEE conference on computer vision and pattern recognition* (pp. 2874–2883).

Belongie, S., Malik, J., & Puzicha, J. (2002). Shape matching and object recognition using shape contexts. In *IEEE TPAMI* (pp. 509–522).

Bendale, A., & Boult, T. E. (2016). Towards open set deep networks. In *IEEE computer society conference on computer vision and pattern recognition*.

Berg, T., Liu, J., Lee, S. W., Alexander, M. L., Jacobs, D. W., & Belhumeur, P. N. (2014). Birdsnap: Large-scale fine-grained visual categorization of birds. In *CVPR* (pp. 2019–2026).

Berthelot, D., Carlini, N., Goodfellow, I., Papernot, N., Oliver, A., & Raffel, C. A. (2019). Mixmatch: A holistic approach to semi-supervised learning. In *Advances in neural information processing systems* (pp. 5050–5060).

Berthelot, D., Carlini, N., Cubuk, E. D., Kurakin, A., Sohn, K., Zhang, H., & Raffel, C. (2020). ReMixMatch: Semi-supervised learning with distribution alignment and augmentation anchoring. In *International conference on learning representation*.

Berthelot, D., Raffel, C., Roy, A., & Goodfellow, I. (2018). *Understanding and improving interpolation in autoencoders via an adversarial regularizer*. Retrieved from arXiv preprint arXiv:1807.07543.

Bertinetto, L., Henriques, J. F., Torr, P. H., & Vedaldi, A. (2018). *Meta-learning with differentiable closed-form solvers*. Retrieved from arXiv preprint : arXiv:1805.08136.

Bertinetto, L., Valmadre, J., Henriques, J., Vedaldi, A. D., & Torr, P. H. (2016). *Fully-convolutional siamese networks for object tracking*. Retrieved from arXiv:1606.09549.

Bevilacqua, M., Roumy, A., Guillemot, C., & Alberi-Morel, M. L. (2012). Low-complexity single-image super-resolution based on nonnegative neighbor embedding. In *BMVC*.

Bewley, A., Ge, Z., Ott, L., Ramos, F., & Upcroft, B. (2016). Simple online and realtime tracking. In *IEEE international conference on image processing (ICIP)* (pp. 3464–3468).

Biederman, I. (1987). Recognition by components: A theory of human image understanding. *Psychological Review, 94*(2), 115.

Biggio, B., Nelson, B., & Laskov, P. (2011). Support vector machines under adversarial label noise. In *ACML* (pp. 97–112).

Boccolini, A., Fedrizzi, A., & Faccio, D. (2019). Ghost imaging with the human eye. *Optics Express, 27*(6), 9258–9265.

Boulkenafet, Z. A. (2017). Oulu-npu: A mobile face presentation attack database with real-world variations. In *FG*. Retrieved from FG.

Bullinger, S., Bodensteiner, C., & Arens, M. (2017). Instance flow based online multiple object tracking. In *IEEE international conference on image processing (ICIP)* (pp. 785–789).

Caron, M., Bojanowski, P., Joulin, A., & Douze, M. (2018). Deep clustering for unsupervised learning of visual features. In *The European conference on computer vision (ECCV)* (pp. 132–149).

Cehovin, L., Leonardis, A., & Kristan, M. (2016). Visual object tracking performance measures revisited. *IEEE Transactions on Image Processing, 25*(3), 1261–1274.

Chai, Y., Lempitsky, V., & Zisserman, A. (2013). Symbiotic segmentation and part localization for fine-grained categorization. In *ICCV* (pp. 321–328).

Chang, A. X., Funkhouser, T., Guibas, L., Hanrahan, P., Huang, Q., Li, Z., ... Su, H. (2015). *Shapenet: An information-rich 3d model repository*. arXiv preprint arXiv:1512.03012.

Chang, J., Wang, L., Meng, G., Xiang, S., & Pan, C. (2017). Deep adaptive image clustering. In *IEEE 29 international conference on computer vision (ICCV)* (pp. 5880–5888).

Charikar, M., Chen, K., & Farach-Colton, M. (2002). *ICALP. Finding frequent items in data streams* (pp. 693–703).

Chen, Y., Liu, Z., Xu, H., Darrell, T., & Wang, X. (2021). Meta-baseline: Exploring simple meta-learning for few-shot learning. In: *Proceedings of the IEEE/CVF international conference on computer vision* (pp. 9062–9071).

Chen, L.-C., Papandreou, G., Kokkinos, I., Murphy, K., & Yuille, A. L. (2017). Deeplab: Semantic image segmentation with deep convolutional nets, atrous convolution, and fully connected crfs. In: *IEEE transactions on pattern analysis and machine intelligence*.

Chen, X., & Gupta, A. (2015). Webly supervised learning of convolutional networks. In *ICCV* (pp. 1431–1439).

Chen, Z., Fu, Y., Wang, Y. X., Ma, L., Liu, W., & Hebert, M. (2019). Image deformation meta-networks for one-shot learning. In: *Proceedings of the IEEE/CVF conference on computer vision and pattern recognition* (pp. 8680–8689).

Chen, B.-C., Chen, C.-S., & Hsu, W. H. (2014). Cross-age reference coding for age-invariant face recognition and retrieval. In *European conference on computer vision* (pp. 768–783). Springer.

Chen, W.-Y., Liu, Y.-C., Kira, Z., Wang, Y.-C. F., & Huang, J.-B. (2019). A closer look at few-shot classification. In *ICLR*.

Chen, H., Wang, Y., Wang, G., & Qiao, Y. (2018). LSTD: A low-shot transfer detector for object detection. In *AAAI*.

Chingovska, I., Anjos, A., & Marcel, S. (2012). On the effectiveness of local binary patterns in face anti-spoofing. In *BIOSIG*.

Choi, J., Chang, H. J., Fischer, T., Yun, S., Lee, K., Jeong, J., ... Choi, J. Y. (2018). Context-aware deep feature compression for high-speed visual tracking. In *CVPR*.

Choi, J., Kwon, J., & Lee, K. M. (2019). Deep meta learning for real-time target-aware visual tracking. In *ICCV*.

Chollet, F. (2016). *Xception: Deep learning with depthwise separable convolutions*. Retrieved from ArXiv: https://arxiv.org/abs/1610.02357.

Cordts, M., Omran, M., Ramos, S., Rehfeld, T., Enzweiler, M., Nenson, R. B., ... Schiele, B. (2016). The cityscapes dataset for semantic urban scene understanding. In *IEEE conference on computer vision and pattern recognition* (pp. 3213–3223).

CrowdFlower. (2016). *Image classification: People and food*. Retrieved from data.world: https://data.world/crowdflower/image-classification-people-an.

Cubuk, E. D., Zoph, B., Mane, D., Vasudevan, V., & Le, Q. V. (2019). Autoaugment: Learning augmentation strategies from data. In *The IEEE conference on computer vision and pattern recognition*.

Cui, Y., Zhou, F., Wang, J., Liu, X., Lin, Y., & Belongie, S. (2017). Kernel pooling for convolutional neural network. In *CVPR* (pp. 2921–2930).

Dai, B. L. (2017). Contrastive learning for image captionin. In *NIPS*.

Dai, J., He, K., & Sun, J. (2016). Instance-aware semantic segmentation via multi-task network cascades. In *IEEE conference on computer vision and pattern recognition* (pp. 3150–3158).

Dalal, N., & Triggs, B. (2005). Histograms of oriented gradients for human detection. In *CVPR* (pp. 886–893).

Dauphin, Y., Fan, A., Auli, M., & Grangier, D. (2016). *Language modeling with gated convolutional networks*. Retrieved from arXiv preprint: arXiv:1612.08083.

Deng, L. (2012). The mnist database of hand written digit images for machine learning research. *IEEE Signal Processing Magazine*, *29*(6), 141–142.

Deng, J., Dong, W., Socher, R., Li, L.-J., Li, K., & Fei-Fei, L. (2009). Imagenet: A large-scale hierarchical image database. In *CVPR*.

Deng, J., Guo, J., Xue, N., & Zafeiriou, S. (2019). Arcface: Additive angular margin loss for deep face recognition. In *IEEE conference on computer vision and pattern recognition* (pp. 4690–4699).

Deuge, M. D., Quadros, A., Hung, C., & Douillard, B. (2013). Unsupervised feature learning for classification of outdoor 3d scans. In *Australasian conference on robitics and automation*.

Dhillon, G. S., Chaudhari, P., Ravichandran, A., & Soatto, S. (2020). *A baseline for few-shot image classification*. Retrieved from https://arxiv.org/abs/1909.02729.

Dinh, C., Tran, N., & Nguyen, J. (2020). Personalized federated learning with moreau envelopes. *Advances in Neural Information Processing Systems*, *33*, 21394–21405.

Doersch, C., Gupta, A., & Efros, A. A. (2015). Unsupervised visual representation learning by context prediction. In *IEEE international conference on computer vision (ICCV)* (pp. 1422–1430).

Dong, C., Loy, C. C., He, K., & Tang, X. (2014). Learning a deep convolutional network for image super-resolution. In *ECCV*.

Dong, C., Loy, C. C., He, K., & Tang, X. (2016). Image super-resolution using deep convolutional networks. In *TPAMI*.

Dosovitskiy, A., Fischer, P., Springenberg, J. T.-B., Riedmiller, M., & Brox, T. (2018). Discriminative unsupervised feature learning with exemplar convolutional neural networks. In *IEEE transactions on pattern analysis and machine intelligence*.

Dubey, A., Gupta, O., Raskar, R., & Naik, N. (2018). Maximum entropy fine-grained classification. In *NeurIPS* (pp. 637–647).

Edwards, H., & Storkey, A. (2017). Towards a neural statistician. In *5th International conference on learning representations (ICLR 2017)*.

Edwards, G., Taylor, C., & Cootes, T. (1998). Interpreting face images using active appearance models. In *International conference on face and gesture recognition* (pp. 300–305).

Elgammal, A., Duraiswami, R., Harwood, D., & Davis, L. (2002). Background and foreground modeling using nonparametric kernel density estimation for visual surveillance. *Proceedings of IEEE*, *90*(7), 1151–1163.

Everingham, M., Eslami, S. A., Gool, L. V., Williams, C. K., Winn, J., & Zisserman, A. (2015). The pascal visual object classes challenge: A retrospective. In *IJCV*.

Fan, H., Lin, L., Yang, F., Ch, P., Deng, G., Yu, S., … Ling, H. (2019). Lasot: A high-quality benchmark for large-scale single object tracking. In *CVPR* (pp. 5374–5383).

Farhadi, A., Hejrati, M., Sadeghi, M. A., Young, P., Rashtchian, C., Hockenmaier, J., & Forsyth, D. (2010). Every picture tells a story: Generating sentences from images. In *European conference on computer vision* (pp. 15–29). Berlin, Heidelberg: Springer.

Fernando, C., Banarse, D., Blundell, C., Zwols, Y., Ha, D., Rusu, A., … Wierstra, D. (2017). *Pathnet: Evolution channels gradient descent in super neural networks*. Retrieved from arXiv preprint : arXiv:1701.08734.

Fieguth, P., & Terzopoulos, D. (1997). Color-based tracking of heads and other mobile objects at video frame rates. In *IEEE conference on computer vision and pattern recognition (CVPR)* (pp. 21–27).

Forsyth, D., & Ponce, J. (2002). *Computer vision: a modern approach*. Retrieved from Prentice Hall Professional Technical Reference.

Frenay, B., & Verleysen, M. (2014). Classification in the presence of label noise: A survey. In *Vol. 25(5). IEEE transactions on neural networks and learning systems*.

Ganapathiraju, A., & Picone, J. (2000). Support vector machines for auto-matic data cleanup. In *ICSLP*.

Gansbeke, W. V., Vandenhende, S., Georgoulis, S., Proesmans, M., & Gool, L. V. (2020). *SCAN: Learning to classify images without labels*. Retrieved from https://arxiv.org/abs/2005.12320.

Gao, H., Mao, J., Zhou, J., Huang, Z., Wang, L., & Xu, W. (2015). Are you talking to a machine? Dataset and methods for multilingual image question answering. In *Advances in neural inf. process. syst.*

Gao, Y., Beijbom, O., Zhang, N., & Darrell, T. (2016). Compact bilinear poolin. In *CVPR* (pp. 317–326).

Ge, Z., Demyanov, S., & Garnavi, R. (2019). *Generative OpenMax for multi-class open set classification*.

Ghadiyaram, D., & Bovik, A. C. (2016). Massive online crowd-sourced study of subjective and objective picture quality. *IEEE Transactions on Image Processing, 25*(1), 372–387.

Gidaris, S., & Komodakis, N. (2015). Object detection via a multi-region and semantic segmentation-aware cnn model. In *IEEE international conference on computer vision* (pp. 1134–1142).

Gidaris, S., Singh, P., & Komodakis, N. (2018). Unsupervised representation learning by predicting image rotations. In *International conference on learning representations* (pp. 1–16).

Gimpel, K., Schneider, N., O'Connor, B., Das, D. P., Mills, D., Eisenstein, J., … Smith, N. A. (2010). *Part-of-speech tagging for twitter: Annotation, features, and experiments. Technical report.* Carnegie-Mellon Univ Pittsburgh Pa School of Computer Science.

Girshick, R. (2015). *Fast R-CNN.* Retrieved from arXiv https://arxiv.org/abs/1504.08083.

Girshick, R., Donahue, J., Darrell, T., & Malik, J. (2013). *Rich feature hierarchies for accurate object detection and semantic segmentation.* Retrieved from arXiv https://arxiv.org/abs/1311.2524.

Goodfellow, I., Pouget-Abadie, J., Mirza, M., Xu, B., Warde-Farley, D., Ozair, S., … Bengio, Y. (2014). Generative adversarial nets. In *Neural Information Processing Systems (NIPS).*

Goyal, Y., Khot, T., Summers-Stay, D., Batra, D., & Parikh, D. (2016). *Making the V in VQA matter: Elevating the role of image understanding in visual question answering.* Retrieved from arXiv preprint: arXiv:1612.00837.

Grill, J.-B., et al. (2020). Bootstrap your own latent: A new approach to self-supervised Learning. In *Advances in Neural Information Processing Systems 33 pre-proceedings (NeurIPS 2020).*

Gross, R., Matthews, I., Cohn, J., Kanade, T., & Baker, S. (2010). Multi-pie. *Image and Vision Computing, 28*(5), 807–813.

Guo, J., Zhu, X., Zhao, C., Cao, D., Lei, Z., & Li, S. Z. (2020). Learning meta face recognition in unseen domains. In *CVPR.*

Guo, Y., Codella, N. C., Karlinsky, L., Codella, J. V., Smith, J. R., Saenko, K., et al. (2020). A broader study of cross-domain few-shot learning. In *European conference on computer vision* (pp. 124–141). Cham: Springer.

Guo, J., Zhu, X., Lei, Z., & Li, S. Z. (2018). Face synthesis for eyeglass-robust face recognition. In *Chinese conference on biometric recognition* (pp. 275–284). Springer.

Gupta, A., Dollar, P., & Girshick, R. (2019). LVIS: Adataset for large vocabulary instance segmentation. In *IEEE conference on computer vision and pattern recognition.*

Han, B., Yao, Q., Yu, X., Niu, G., Xu, M., Hu, W., … Sugiyama, M. (2018). *Co-teaching: Robust training of deep neural networks with extremely noisy labels* (pp. 8527–8537). NeurIPS.

Han, S., Mao, H., & Dally, W. J. (2016). Deep compression: compressed deep neural networks with pruning, trained quantization, and huffman coding. In *ICLR.*

Han, S., Pool, J., Tran, J., & Dally, W. (2015). Learning both weights and connections for efficient neural network. In *NeurIPS.*

Hariharan, B., & Girshick, R. (2017). Low-shot visual recognition by shrinking and hallucinating features. In *ICCV.*

Hariharan, B., Arbelaez, P. A., Gir-Shick, R. B., & Malik, J. (2015). Hypercolumns for object segmentation and fine-grained localization. In *CVPR.*

Haris, M., Shakhnarovich, G., & Ukita, N. (2018). Deep backp-rojection networks for super-resolution. In *CVPR.*

Haris, M., Shakhnarovich, G., & Ukita, N. (2019). Recurrent back-projection network for video super-resolution. In *CVPR.*

He, K., Fan, H., Wu, Y., Xie, S., & Girshick, R. (2020). Momentum contrast for unsupervised visual representation learning. In *The IEEE/CVF conference on computer vision and pattern recognition* (pp. 9729–9738).

He, K., Gkioxari, G., Dollár, P., & Girshick, R. (2017). *Mask R-CNN.* Retrieved from arXiv https://arxiv.org/abs/1703.06870.

He, Y., Zhang, X., & Sun, J. (2017). Channel pruning for accelerating very deep neural networks. In *ICCV.*

He, K., Zhang, X., Ren, S., & Sun, J. (2016). Deep residual learning for image recognition. In *Proceedings of the IEEE conference on computer vision and pattern recognition* (pp. 770–778). IEEE.

Helber, P., Bischke, B., Dengel, A., & Borth, D. (2019). Eurosat: A novel dataset and deep learning benchmark for land use and land cover classification. *IEEE Journal of Selected Topics in Applied Earth Observations and Remote Sensing, 12*(7), 2217–2226.

Henaff, O. J., Srinivas, A., Fauw, J. D., Razavi, A., Doersch, C., Eslami, S. M., & Oord, A. V. (2020). Data-efficient image recognition with contrastive predictive coding. In *The 37th international conference on machine-learning.*

Hendrycks, D., Mazeika, M., Wilson, D., & Gimpel, K. (2018). Using trusted data to train deep networks on labels corrupted by severe noise. In *NIPS.*

Hjelm, R. D., Fedorov, A., Marchildon, S. L., Grewal, K., Bachman, P., Trischler, A., & Bengio, Y. (2019). Learning deep representations by mutual information estimation and maximization. In *International conference on learning representation*.

Horn, G. V., Branson, S., Farrell, R., Haber, S., Barry, J., Ipeirotis, P., ... Belongie, S. (2015). Building a bird recognition app and large scale dataset with citizen scientists: The fine print in fine-grained dataset collection. In *IEEE conference on computer vision and pattern recognition (CVPR)*.

Horn, G. V., Aodha, O. M., Song, Y., Cui, Y., Sun, C., Shepard, A., ... Belongie, S. (2017). The iNaturalist species classification and detection dataset. In *CVPR* (pp. 8769–8778).

Hou, S., Feng, Y., & Wang, Z. (2017). VegFru: A domain-specific dataset for fine-grained visual categorization. In *ICCV* (pp. 541–549).

Howard, A. G., Zhu, M., Chen, B., Kalenichenko, D., Wang, W., Weyand, T., ... Adam, H. (2017). *MobileNets: Efficient convolutional neural networks for mobile vision applications*. Retrieved from arXiv https://arxiv.org/abs/1704.04861.

Hsu, K., Levine, S., & Finn, C. (2018). *Unsupervised learning via meta-learning*. Retrieved from arXiv preprint arXiv:1810.02334.

Hu, X., Mu, H., Zhang, X., Wang, Z., Tan, T., & Sun, J. (2019). Meta-SR: A magnification-arbitrary network for super-resolution. In *CVPR*.

Hu, R., Dollar, P., He, K., Darrell, T., & Girshick, R. (2018). Learning to segment every thing. In *CVPR*.

Hu, W., Miyato, T., Tokui, S., Matsumoto, E., & Sugiyama, M. (2017). Learning discrete representations via information maximizing self-augmented training. In *The 34th international conference on machine learning*.

Hu, J., Shen, L., & Sun, G. (2018). Squeeze-and-excitation networks. In *CVPR*.

Huang, G., Liu, Z., Maaten, L. V., & Weinberger, K. Q. (2017). Densely connected convolutional networks. In *CVPR*.

Huang, J.-B., Singh, A., & Ahuja, N. (2015). Single image super-resolution from transformed self-exemplars. In *IEEE conference on computer vision and pattern recognition*.

Hui, Z., Wang, X., & Gao, X. (2018). Fast and accurate single image super-resolution via information distillation network. In *IEEE conference on computer vision and pattern recognition (CVPR)*.

Izmailov, P., Podoprikhin, D., Garipov, T., Vetrov, D., & Wilson, A. G. (2018). Averaging weights leads to wider optima and better generalization. In *Conference on uncertainty in artificial intelligence*.

Jabri, A., Joulin, A., & van der Maaten, L. (2016). *Revisiting visual question answering baselines*.

Jamal, M. A., Brown, M., Yang, M.-H., Wang, L., & Gong, B. (2020). *Rethinking class-balanced methods for long-tailed visual recognition from a domain adaptation perspective*. Retrieved from ArXiv, abs/2003.10780.

Jiang, L., Zhou, Z., Leung, T., Li, L.-J., & Fei-Fei, L. (2018). Mentornet: Learning data-driven curriculum for very deep neural networks on corrupted labels. In *ICML*.

Jung, I., Son, J., Baek, M., & Han, B. (2018). Real-Time MDNet. In *ECCV*.

Jung, I., You, K., Noh, H., Cho, M., & Han, B. (2020). Real-time object tracking via meta-learning: efficient model adaptation and one-shot channel pruning. In *AAAI*.

Kang, B., Liu, Z., Wang, X., Yu, F., Feng, J., & Darrell, T. (2019). Few-shot object detection via feature reweighting. In *ICCV*.

Kang, B., Xie, S., Rohrbach, M., Yan, Z., Gordo, A., Feng, J., & Kalantidis, Y. (2020). Decoupling representation and classifier for long-tailed recognition. In *International conference on learning representations*. p. abs/1910.09217.

Kaster, F. O., Menze, B. H., Weber, M.-A., & Hamprecht, F. A. (2010). Comparative validation of graphical models for learning tumor segmentations from noisy manual annotations. In *MICCAI* (pp. 74–85).

Kazemi, V., & Elqursh, A. (2017). *Show, ask, attend, and answer: A strong baseline for visual question answering*. Retrieved from arXiv preprint: arXiv:1704.03162.

Khodadadeh, S., Bölöni, L., & Shah, M. (2019). Unsupervised meta-learning for few-shot image classification. In *CVPR*.

Khosla, A., Jayadevaprakash, N., Yao, B., & Li, F. (2011). Novel dataset for fine-grained image categorization: Stanford dogs. In *Vol. 2. CVPR workshop on fine-grained visual categorization (FGVC)*.

Kim, J., Lee, J. K., & Lee, K. M. (2016a). Accurate image super-resolution using very deep convolutional networks. In *CVPR*.

Kim, J., Lee, J. K., & Lee, K. M. (2016b). Deeply-recursive convolutional network for image super-resolution. In *CVPR*.

Kim, C., Li, F., Ciptadi, A., & Rehg, J. M. (2015). Multiple hypothesis tracking revisited. In *IEEE international conference on computer vision* (pp. 4696–4704).

Kim, S. J., Nam, J.-Y., & Ko, B. C. (2018). Online tracker optimization for multi-pedestrian tracking using a moving vehicle camera. In *IEEE Access.*

Kong, S., & Fowlkes, C. (2017). Low-rank bilinear pooling for fine-grained classification. In *CVPR* (pp. 365–374).

Krafka, K., Khosla, A., Kellnhofer, P., Kannan, H., Bhandarkar, S., Matusik, W., et al. (2016). Eye tracking for everyone. In: *Proceedings of the IEEE conference on computer vision and pattern recognition* (pp. 2176–2184).

Krause, J., Sapp, B., Howard, A., Zhou, H., Toshev, A., Duerig, T., … Fei-Fei, L. (2016). The unreasonable effectiveness of noisy data for fine-grained recognition. In *European conference on computer vision* (pp. 301–320). Springer.

Krause, J., Johnson, J., Krishna, R., & Li, F. (2016). *A hierarchical approach for generating descriptive image paragraphs.* arXiv. preprint arXiv:1611.06607.

Krause, J., Stark, M., Deng, J., & Fei-Fei, L. (2013). 3D object representations for fine-grained categorization. In *ICCV workshop on 3D representation and recognition.*

Krishna, R., Zhu, Y., Groth, O., Johnson, J., Hata, K., Kravitz, J., … Fei-Fei, L. (2016). *Visual genome: Connecting language and vision using crowdsourced dense image annotations.* arXiv preprint arXiv:1602.07332.

Kristan, M., Leonardis, A., Matas, J., Berg, M. F., Pflugfelder, R., Zajc, L. C., … Abdelrahman Eldesokey, E. A. (2018). The sixth visual object tracking vot2018 challenge results. In *ECCV.*

Kristan, M., Leonardis, A., Matas, J., & Felsberg, M. (2016). The visual object tracking vot2016 challenge results. In *ECCV Workshop.*

Krizhevsky, A. (2009). *Learning multiple layers of features from tiny images.* Technical report.

Kuznetsova, A., Rom, H., Alldrin, N., Uijlings, J., Krasin, I., & PontTuset, J.e. (2018). *The open images dataset v4: Unified image classification, object detection, and visual relationship detection at scale.* Retrieved from arXiv: arXiv:1811.00982.

Lai, W.-S., Huang, J.-B., Ahuja, N., & Yang, M.-H. (2017). Deep laplacian pyramid networks for fast and accurate superresolution. In *CVPR.*

Lai, W.-S., Huang, J.-B., Ahuja, N., & Yang, M.-H. (2018). Fast and accurate image super-resolution with deep laplacian pyramid networks. In *TPAMI.*

Laine, S., & Aila, T. (2017). Temporal ensembling for semi-supervised learning. In *International conference on learning representations.*

Leal-Taixe, L., Milan, A., Reid, I., Roth, S., & Schindler, K. (2015). *Motchallenge 2015: Towards a benchmark for multi-target tracking.* arXiv preprint arXiv:1504.01942.

Ledig, C., Theis, L., Huszar, F., Caballero, J., Cunningham, A., Acosta, A., … Wang, Z. (2017). Photo-realistic single image super-resolution using a generative adversarial network. In *CVPR.*

Lee, D.-H. (2013). Pseudo-label: The simple and efficient semi-supervised learning method for deep neural networks. In *ICML.*

Lee, H., Hwang, S. J., & Shin, J. (2020). Self-supervised label augmentation via input transformations. In *International conference on machine learning* (pp. 5714–5724). PMLR.

Lee, S., & Kim, E. (2019). Multiple object tracking via feature pyramid siamese networks. In *IEEE Access.*

Lee, K.-H., He, X., Zhang, L., & Yang, L. (2018a). CleanNet:Transfer learning for scalable image classifier training with label noise. In *CVPR* (pp. 5447–5456).

Lee, K.-H., He, X., Zhang, L., & Yang, L. (2018b). Cleannet: Transfer learning for scalable image classifier training with label noise. In *CVPR.*

Lee, K., Maji, S., Ravichandran, A., & Soatto, S. (2019). Meta-learning with differentiable convex optimization. In *IEEE conference on computer vision and pattern recognition* (pp. 10657–10665).

Li, N., Chen, Z., & Liu, S. (2019). *Meta learning for image captioning, 33(01),* 8626–8633.

Li, J., Wong, Y., Zhao, Q., & Kankanhalli, M. S. (2019). Learning to learn from noisy labeled data. In: *Proceedings of the IEEE/CVF conference on computer vision and pattern recognition* (pp. 5051–5059).

Li, Z., & Hoiem, D. (2018). Learning without forgetting. In *IEEE transactions on pattern analysis and machine intelligence.*

Li, K., & Malik, J. (2017). Learning to optimize. In *ICLR.*

Li, W., Wang, L., Li, W., Agustsson, E., & Gool, L. V. (2017). *Webvision database: Visual learning and understanding from web data.* arXiv preprint arXiv:1708.02862.

Li, D., Yang, Y., Song, Y.-Z., & Hospedales, T. M. (2018). Learning to generalize: Meta-learning for domain generalization. In *Thirty-second AAAI conference on artificial intelligence.*

Li, S., Yi, D., Lei, Z., & Liao, S. (2013). The casia nir-vis 2.0 face database. In *IEEE conference on computer vision and pattern recognition workshops* (pp. 348–353).

Liang, P., Blasch, E., & Ling, H. (2015). Encoding color information for visual tracking: Algorithms and benchmark. *IEEE Transactions on Image Processing, 24*(12), 5630–5644.

Lim, B., Son, S., Kim, H., Nah, S., & Lee, K. M. (2017). Enhanced deep residual networks for single image super-resolution. In *CVPRW*.

Lin, T.-Y., Maire, M., Belongie, S., Hays, J., Perona, P., Ramanan, D., … Zitnick, C. L. (2014). Microsoft COCO: Common objects in context. In *ECCV*.

Lin, T.-Y., Goyal, P., Girshick, R., He, K., & Dollar, P. (2017). Focal loss for dense object detection. In *ICCV* (pp. 2980–2988).

Lin, H., Hosu, V., & Saupe., D. (2018). Koniq-10k: Towards an ecologically valid and large-scale iqa database. In *CoRR*.

Lin, H., Hosu, V., Saupe, D., & Jun. (2019). Kadid-10k: A large-scale artificially distorted iqa database. In *IEEE international conference on quality of multimedia experience (QoMEX)* (pp. 1–3).

Lin, T.-Y., RoyChowdhury, A., & Maji, S. (2015). Bilinear CNN models for fine-grained visual recognition. In *ICCV* (pp. 1449–1457).

Lin, G., Shen, C., Hengel, A. V., & Reid, I. (2016). Efficient piecewise training of deep structured models for semantic segmentation. In *The IEEE conference on computer vision and pattern recognition* (pp. 3194–3203).

Liu, W., Anguelov, D., Erhan, D., Szegedy, C., Reed, S., Fu, C. Y., et al. (2016). SSD: Single shot multibox detector. In *European conference on computer vision* (pp. 21–37). Cham: Springer.

Liu, Y., Lee, J., Park, M., Kim, S., Yang, E., Hwang, S. J., & Yang, Y. (2018). Learning to propagate labels: Transductive propagation network for few-shot learning. *arXiv preprint*, arXiv:1805.10002.

Liu, B., Kang, H., Li, H., Hua, G., & Vasconcelos, N. (2020). Few-shot open-set recognition using meta-learning. In: *Proceedings of the IEEE/CVF conference on computer vision and pattern recognition* (pp. 8798–8807).

Llamas, J. (2021). *Architectural heritage elements image dataset*. Retrieved from datahub: https://old.datahub.io/dataset/architectural-heritage-elements-image-dataset.

Long, J., Shelhamer, E., & Darrell, T. (2015). Fully convolutional networks for semantic segmentation. In *The IEEE conference on computer vision and pattern recognition* (pp. 3431–3440).

Lopez-Paz, D., & Ranzato, M. (2017). *Gradient episodic memory for continuum learning*. Retrieved from arXiv preprint: arXiv:1706.08840.

Lu, D., & Weng, Q. (2007). A survey of image classification methods and techniques for improving classification performance. *International Journal of Remote Sensing, 28*(5), 823–870.

Lu, J., Xiong, C., Parikh, D., & Socher, R. (2016). *Knowing when to look: Adaptive attention via a visual sentinel for image captioning*. arXiv preprint arXiv:1612.01887.

Ma, X., Huang, H., Wang, Y., Romano, S., Erfani, S., & Bailey, J. (2020). Normalized loss functions for deep learning with noisy labels. In *ICML* (pp. 6543–6553).

Ma, C., Huang, J.-B., Yang, X., & Yang, M.-H. (2015). Hierarchical convolutional features for visual tracking. In *IEEE international conference on computer vision* (pp. 3074–3082).

Ma, F., Meng, D., Dong, X., & Yang, Y. (2020). Self-paced multi-view co-training. *Journal of Machine Learning Research, 21*(57), 1–38.

Maji, S., Kannala, J., Rahtu, E., Blaschko, M., & Vedaldi, A. (2013). *Fine-grained visual classification of aircraft*. arXiv preprint arXiv:1306.5151.

Maji, S., Rahtu, E., Kannala, J., Blaschko, M., & Vedaldi, A. (2013). *Fine-grained visual classification of aircraft*. Technical report.

Malinowski, M., & Fritz, M. (2014). A multi-world approach to question answering about real-world scenes based on uncertain input. In *Advances in neural inf. process. syst* (pp. 1682–1690).

Malinowski, M., Rohrbach, M., & Fritz, M. (2015). Ask your neurons: A neural-based approachto answering questions about mages. In *IEEE international conference on computer vision*.

Martin, D., Fowlkes, C., Tal, D., & Malik, J. (2001). A database of human segmented natural images and its application to evaluating segmentation algorithms and measuring ecological statistics. In *ICCV*.

Menon, A. K., Rawat, A. S., Reddi, S. J., & Kumar, S. (2020). Can gradient clipping mitigate label noise? In *ICLR*.

Michaeli, T., & Irani, M. (2013). Nonparametric blind super-resolution. In *IEEE international conference on computer vision (ICCV)*.

Milan, A., Leal-Taixe, L., Reid, I., Roth, S., & Schindler, K. (2016). *Mot16: A benchmark for multi-object tracking*. arXiv preprint arXiv:1603.00831.

Milan, A., Rezatofighi, S. H., Dick, A., Reid, I., & Schindler, K. (2017). Online multi-target tracking using recurrent neural networks. In *AAAI conference on artificial intelligence*.

Ming, Z., Visani, M., Luoman, M. M., & Burie, J.-C. (2020). *A survey on anti-spoofing methods for face recognition with rgb cameras of generic consumer devices*. Retrieved from https://arxiv.org/abs/2010.04145.

Mishra, N., Rohaninejad, M., Chen, X., & Abbeel, P. (2018). *A simple neural attentive meta-learner*. Retrieved from arXiv:1707.03141.

Miyato, T., Maeda, S.-I., Koyama, M., Ishii, S., & Koyama, M. (2018). Virtual adversarial training: a regularization method for supervised and semi-supervised learning. In *IEEE transactions on pattern analysis and machine intelligence*.

Mohanty, S. P., Hughes, D. P., & Salathé, M. (2016). Using deep learning for image-based plant disease detection. *Frontiers in Plant Science, 7*, 1419.

Mooney, P. (2018). *Blood cell images*. Retrieved from Kaggle: https://www.kaggle.com/paultimothymooney/blood-cells.

Mueller, M., Smith, N., & Ghanem, B. (2016). A benchmark and simulator for uav tracking. In *ECCV*.

Muller, M., Bibi, A., Giancola, S., Subaihil, S. A., & Ghanem, B. (2018). Trackingnet: A large-scale dataset and benchmark for object tracking in the wild. In *ECCV* (pp. 300–317).

Munkhdalai, T., Yuan, X., Mehri, S., Wang, T., & Trischler, A. (2017). Learning rapid-temporal adaptations.

Munkhdalai, T., & Yu, H. (2017). Meta networks. In *International conference on machine learning (ICML)* (pp. 2554–2563).

Murase, H., & Nayar, S. (1995). Visual learning and recognition of 3d objects from appearance. *International Journal of Computer Vision, 14*(1), 5–24.

Nam, H., & Han, B. (2016). Learning multi-domain convolutional neural networks for visual tracking. In *CVPR*.

Neal, L., Olson, M., Fern, X., Wong, W. K., & Li, F. (2018). Open set learning with counterfactual images. In *Lecture notes in computer science (including subseries lecture notes in artificial intelligence and lecture notes in bioinformatics)*. pp. 11210 LNCS(1):620–635.

Netzer, Y., Wang, T., Coates, A., Bissacco, A., Wu, B., & Ng, A. Y. (2011). Reading digits in natural images with unsupervised feature learning. In *NIPS workshop on deep learning and unsupervised feature learning*. Retrieved from http://ufldl.stanford.edu/housenumbers/.

Nguyen, D. T., Mummadi, C. K., Ngo, T. P., Nguyen, T. H., Beggel, L., & Brox, T. (2020). SELF: Learning to filter noisy labels with self-ensembling. In *ICLR*.

Nichol, A., & Schulman, J. (2018). *Reptile: a scalable metalearning algorithm*. arXiv preprint arXiv: 1803.02999.

Nichol, A., Achiam, J., & Schulman, J. (2018). *On first-order meta-learning algorithms*. Retrieved from arXiv preprint: arXiv:1803.02999.

Nikisins, O., Mohammadi, A., Anjos, A., & Marcel, S. (2018). On effectiveness of anomaly detection approaches against unseen presentation attacks in face anti-spoofing. In *International conference on biometrics (ICB)* (pp. 75–81).

Nilsback, M.-E., & Zisserman, A. (2008). Automated flower classification over a large number of classes. In *Indian conf. on comput. vision, graph. and image process* (pp. 722–729).

Noh, H., Hong, S., & Han, B. (2015). Learning deconvolution network for semantic segmentation. In *the IEEE international conference on computer vision* (pp. 1520–1528).

Noroozi, M., & Favaro, P. (2016). Unsupervised learning of visual representations by solving jigsaw puzzles. In *European conference on computer vision* (pp. 69–84).

Oltean, M. (2021). *Fruits 360*. Retrieved from Kaggle: https://www.kaggle.com/moltean/fruits.

Oord, A. V., Li, Y., & Vinyals, O. (2018). *Representation learning with contrastive predictive coding*. arXiv preprint arXiv:1807.03748.

Oreshkin, B. N., López, P. R., & Lacoste, A. (2018). TADAM: Task dependent adaptive metric for improved few-shot learning. In: *Proc. NIPS*.

Özgenel, Ç. F. (2019). *Concrete crack images for classification*. Retrieved from Mendeley Data: https://data.mendeley.com/datasets/5y9wdsg2zt/2.

Paragios, N., & Deriche, R. (2002). Geodesic active regions and level set methods for supervised texture segmentation. *International Journal of Computer Vision, 46*(3), 223–247.

Park, E., & Berg, A. C. (2018). Meta-tracker: Fast and robust online adaptation for visual object trackers. In *ECCV*.

Park, S., De Mello, S., Molchanov, P., Iqbal, U., Hilliges, O., & Kautz, J. (2019, October 14). *Few-shot adaptive gaze estimation*. arXiv.org. Retrieved June 4, 2022, from: https://arxiv.org/abs/1905.01941.

Park, S., Yoo, J., Cho, D., Kim, J., & Kim, T. H. (2020). Fast adaptation to super-resolution networks via meta-learning. In *CVPR*.

Parkhi, O. M., Vedaldi, A., & Zisserman, A. (2015). Deep face recognition. In *Vol. 1. BMVC* (p. 6).

Patacchiola, M., Turner, J., Crowley, E. J., O'Boyle, M., & Storkey, A. J. (2020). Bayesian meta-learning for the few-shot setting via deep kernels. *Advances in Neural Information Processing Systems, 33*, 16108–16118.

Patrini, G., Rozza, A., Menon, A. K., Nock, R., & Qu, L. (2017). Making deep neural networks robust to label noise: A loss correction approach. In *CVPR* (pp. 2233–2241).

Pereira, T. D., Anjos, A., Martino, J. M., & Marcel, S. (2013). Can face anti-spoofing countermeasures work in a real world scenario? In *International conference on biometrics (ICB)* (pp. 1–8).

Pereyra, G., Tucker, G., Chorowski, J., Kaiser, Ł., & Hinton, G. (2017). Regularizing neural networks by penalizing confident output distributions. In *ICLRW*.

Pfulb, B., & Gepperth, A. (2019). *A comprehensive, application-oriented study of catastrophic forgetting in dnns.*

Pham, N., & Pagh, R. (2013). Fast and scalable polynomial kernels via explicit feature maps. In *KDD* (pp. 239–247).

Pham, H., Dai, Z., Xie, Q., Luong, M.-T., & Le, Q. V. (2021, March 1). *Meta pseudo labels.* arXiv.org. Retrieved June 4, 2022, from: https://arxiv.org/abs/2003.10580.

Pinheiro, P. O., Collobert, R., & Dollar, P. (2015). Learning to segment object candidates. In *Advances in neural information processing systems* (pp. 1990–1998).

Ponomarenko, N., Jin, L., Ieremeiev, O., Lukin, V., Egiazarian, K., Astola, J., … Battisti, F. (2015). Image database TID2013: Peculiarities, results and perspectives. *Signal Processing: Image Communication, 30*, 57–77.

Qiao, S., Liu, C., Shen, W., & Yuille, A. L. (2018). Few-shot image recognition by predicting parameters from activations. In: *Proceedings of the IEEE conference on computer vision and pattern recognition*(pp. 7229–7238).

Qin, Y., Zhao, C., Zhu, X., Wang, Z., Yu, Z., Fu, T., … Lei, Z. (2020). Learning meta model for zero- and few-shot face anti-spoofing. In *AAAI*.

Rajasegaran, J., Khan, S., Hayat, M., Khan, F. S., & Shah, M. (2020). iTAML: An incremental task-agnostic meta-learning approach. In *CVPR*.

Ravi, S., & Larochelle, H. (2017). Optimization as a model for few-shot learning. In *ICLR*.

Rebuffi, S., Kolesnikov, A., & Lampert, C. (2016). *icarl: Incremental classifier and repre- sentation learning.* Retrieved from arXiv preprint: arXiv:1611.07725.

Redmon, J., Divvala, S., Girshick, R., & Farhadi, A. (2016). You only look once: Unified, real-time object detection. In: *Proceedings of the IEEE conference on computer vision and pattern recognition* (pp. 779–788).

Ren, M., Triantafillou, E., Ravi, S., Snell, J., Swersky, K., Tenenbaum, J. B., et al. (2018). Meta-learning for semi-supervised few-shot classification. *arXiv preprint.* arXiv:1803.00676.

Ren, J., Yu, C., Sheng, S., Ma, X., Zhao, H., Yi, S., & Li, H. (2020). Balanced meta-softmax for long-tailed visual recognition. In *NeurIPS*.

Ren, S., He, K., Girshick, R., & Sun, J. (2015). Faster R-CNN: Towards real-time object detection with region proposal networks. In *NeurIPS*.

Ren, M., Zeng, W., Yang, B., & Urtasun, R. (2018). Learning to reweight examples for robust deep learning. In *International conference on machine learning* (pp. 4334–4343). PMLR.

Rennie, S. J., Marcheret, E., Mroueh, Y., Ross, J., & Goel, V. (2017). Self-critical sequence training for image captioning. In *CVPR*.

Requeima, J., Gordon, J., Bronskill, J., Nowozin, S., & Turner, R. E. (2020). *Fast and flexible multi-task classification using conditional neural adaptive processes.* arXiv.org. Retrieved June 4, 2022, from: https://arxiv.org/abs/1906.07697.

Riemer, M., Cases, I., Ajemian, R., Liu, M., Rish, I., Tu, Y., & Tesauro, G. (2019). Learning to learn without forgetting by maximizing transfer and minimizing interference. In *The international conference on learning representation*.

Rosello, P., & Kochenderfer, M. J. (2018). Multi-agent reinforcement learning for multi-object tracking. In *The 17th international conference on autonomous agents and multiagent systems* (pp. 1397–1404).

Russakovsky, O., Deng, J., Su, H., Krause, J., Satheesh, S. J., Ma, S., …. (2015). Imagenet large scale visual recognition challenge. *International Journal of Computer Vision, 115*(3), 211–252.

Rusu, A. A., Rao, D., Sygnowski, J., Vinyals, O., Pascanu, R., Osindero, S., et al. (2018). Meta-learning with latent embedding optimization. *arXiv preprint*, arXiv:1807.05960.

Sadeghian, A., Alahi, A., & Savarese, S. (2017). Tracking the untrackable: Learning to track multiple cues with long-term dependencies. In *IEEE international conference on computer vision* (pp. 300–311).

Sajjadi, M., Scholkopf, B., & Hirsch, M. (2017). Enhancenet: Single image super-resolution through automated texture synthesis. In *IEEE international conference on computer vision (ICCV)*.

Salimans, T., Goodfellow, I., Zaremba, W., Cheung, V., Radford, A., Chen, X., & Chen, X. (2016). Improved techniques for training gans. In *29. Advances in neural information processing systems* (pp. 2234–2242).

Schlachter, P., Liao, Y., & Yang, B. (2019). *Open-set recognition using intra-class splitting*.

Schmarje, L., Brunger, J., Santarossa, M., Schroder, S.-M., Kiko, R., & Koch, R. (2020). *Beyond cats and dogs: Semi-supervised classification of fuzzy labels with overclustering*. arXiv. preprint arXiv: 2012.01768.

Schmarje, L., Santarossa, M., Schroder, S.-M., & Koch, R. (2021). *A survey on semi-, self- and unsupervised learning in image classification*. Retrieved from arXiv: https://arxiv.org/pdf/2002.08721.pdf.

Schroff, F., Kalenichenko, D., & Philbin, J. (2015). Facenet: A unified embedding for face recognition and clustering. In *CVPR* (pp. 815–823).

Schwartz, E., Karlinsky, L., Shtok, J., Harary, S., Marder, M., Pankanti, S., ... Bronstein, A. M. (2019). Rep-Met: Representative-based metric learning for classification and one-shot object detection. In *CVPR*.

Shao, R., Lan, X., & Yuen, P. C. (2020). Regularized fine-grained meta face anti-spoofing. In *AAAI*.

Shao, R., Lan, X., Li, J., & Yuen, P. C. (2019). Multi-adversarial discriminative deep domain generalization for face presentation attack detection. In *CVPR*.

Shen, Y., & Sanghavi, S. (2019). Learning with bad training data via iterative trimmed loss minimization. In *ICML*.

Shocher, A., Cohen, N., & Irani, M. (2018). *"zero-shot" super-resolution using deep internal learning*. CVPR.

Shu, J., Xie, Q., Yi, L., Zhao, Q., Zhou, S., Xu, Z., & Meng, D. (2019). Meta-weight-net: Learning an explicit mapping for sample weighting. In *Advances in neural information processing systems* (pp. 1917–1928).

Silberman, N., Hoiem, D., Kohli, P., & Fergus, R. (2012). Indoor segmentation and support inference from rgbd images. In *European conference on computer vision* (pp. 746–760). Springer.

Simonyan, K., & Zisserman, A. (2014). *Very deep convolutional networks for large-scale image recognition*. Retrieved from arXiv preprint: arXiv:1409.1556.

Sinha, A., Sarkar, M., Mukherjee, A., & Krishnamurthy, B. (2017). Introspection: Accelerating neural network training by learning weight evolution. In *ICLR*.

Snell, J., Swersky, K., & Zemel, R. S. (2017). Prototypical networks for few-shot learning. In *NIPs*.

Soh, J. W., Cho, S., & Cho, N. I. (2020). Meta-transfer learning for zero-shot super-resolution. In *CVPR*.

Sohn, K., Berthelot, D., Li, C.-L., Zhang, Z., Carlini, N., Cubuk, E. D., ... Raffel, C. (2020). FixMatch: simplifying semi-supervised learning with consistency and confidence. In *Advances in neural information proces*.

Song, Y., Ma, C., Gong, L., Zhang, J., Lau, R., & Yang, M. (2017). CREST:Convolutional residual learning for visual tracking. In *ICCV*.

Song, H., Kim, M., & Lee, J.-G. (2019). SELFIE: Refurbishing unclean samples for robust deep learning. In *ICML* (pp. 5907–5915).

Song, H., Kim, M., Park, D., Shin, Y., & Lee, J.-G. (2022). Learning from noisy labels with deep neural networks: A survey. *IEEE Transactions on Neural Networks and Learning Systems*.

Song, S., Lichtenberg, S. P., & Xiao, J. (2015). Sun rgb-d: A rgb-d scene understanding benchmark suite. In *IEEE conference on computer vision and pattern recognition* (pp. 567–576).

Sun, Q., Liu, Y., Chua, T. S., & Schiele, B. (2019). Meta-transfer learning for few-shot learning. In: *Proceedings of the IEEE/CVF conference on computer vision and pattern recognition* (pp. 403–412).

Sun, Y., Wang, X., & Tang, X. (2015). Deeply learned face representations are sparse, selective, and robust. In *CVPR* (pp. 2892–2900).

Sung, F., Yang, Y., Zhang, L., Xiang, T., Torr, P. H., & Hospedales, T. M. (2018). Learning to compare: Relation network for few-shot. In *CVPR*.

Swain, M., & Ballard, D. (1991). Color indexing. *International Journal of Computer Vision*, 7(1), 11–32.

Szegedy, C., Liu, W., Jia, Y., Sermanet, P., Reed, S., Anguelov, D., ... Rabinovich, A. (2014). *Going deeper with convolutions*. Retrieved from arXiv: https://arxiv.org/abs/1409.4842.

Szegedy, C., Vanhoucke, V., Ioffe, S., Shlens, J., & Wojna, Z. (2015). *Rethinking the inception architecture for computer vision*. Retrieved from arXiv: https://arxiv.org/abs/1512.00567.

Tai, Y., Yang, J., & Liu, X. (2017). Image super-resolution via deep recursive residual network. In *CVPR*.

Tai, Y., Yang, J., Liu, X., & Xu, C. (2017). Memnet: A persistent memory network for image restoration. In *ICCV*.

Taigman, Y., & Yang, M. (2014). Deepface: Closing the gap to human-level performance in face verification. In *CVPR* (pp. 1701–1708).

Tan, M., & Le, Q. V. (2020). *EfficientNet: Rethinking model scaling for convolutional neural networks*. Retrieved from arXiv: https://arxiv.org/pdf/1905.11946.pdf.

Tanno, R., Saeedi, A., Sankaranarayanan, S., Alexander, D. C., & Silberman, N. (2019). Learning from noisy labels by regularized estimation of annotator confusion. In *CVPR* (pp. 11244–11253).

Tarvainen, A., & Valpola, H. (2017). Mean teachers are better role models: Weight-averaged consistency targets improve semi-supervised deep learning results. In *International conference on learning representations*.

Teney, D., & van den Hengel, A. (2017). Visual question answering as a meta learning task. In *Proceedings of the European conference on computer vision (ECCV)* (pp. 219–235).

Teney, D., Anderson, P., He, X., & van den Hengel, A. (2017). *Tips and tricks for visual question answering: Learnings from the 2017 challenge*. Retrieved from arXiv preprint: arXiv:1708.02711.

TensorFlow. (2021a). *patch_camelyon*. Retrieved from TensorFlow: https://www.tensorflow.org/datasets/catalog/patch_camelyon.

Tensorflow. (2021b). *Tensorflow*. Retrieved from sun397: https://www.tensorflow.org/datasets/catalog/sun397.

Tian, P., Wu, Z., Qi, L., Wang, L., Shi, Y., & Gao, Y. (2020). Differentiable meta-learning model for few-shot semantic segmentation. In: *Proceedings of the AAAI conference on artificial intelligence, Vol. 34, No. 07* (pp. 12087–12094).

Toneva, M., Sordoni, A., Combes, R. T. D., Trischler, A., Bengio, Y., & Gordon, G. J. (2018). An empirical study of example forgetting during deep neural network learning. *arXiv preprint*, arXiv:1812.05159.

Tseng, H. Y., Lee, H. Y., Huang, J. B., & Yang, M. H. (2020). Cross-domain few-shot classification via learned feature-wise transformation. *arXiv preprint*, arXiv:2001.08735.

Tsutsui, S., Fu, Y., & Crandall, D. (2019). Meta-reinforced synthetic data for one-shot fine-grained visual recognition. In *NeurIPS*.

Turk, M. A., & Pentland, A. (1991). Face recognition using eigenfaces. In *CVPR* (pp. 586–591).

Vedaldi, A., Ji, X., Henriques, J. F., & Vedaldi, A. (2019). Invariant information clus- tering for unsupervised image classification and segmentation. In *The IEEE international conference on computer vision (Iic)* (pp. 9865–9874).

Verma, V., Lamb, A., Kannala, J., Bengio, Y., Lopez-Paz, D., Kawaguchi, K., … Lopez-Paz, D. (2019). Interpolation consistency training for semi-supervised learning. In *The twenty-eighth international joint conference on artificial intelligence*.

Vermaak, J., Maskell, S., & Briers, M. (2005). Online sensor registration. In *IEEE aerospace conference*.

Vinyals, O., Blundell, C., Lillicrap, T. P., Kavukcuoglu, K., & Wierstra, D. (2016). Matching networks for one shot learning. In *NeurIPS*.

Vinyals, O., Toshev, A., Bengio, S., & Erhan, D. (2015). Show and tell: a neural image caption generator. In *Computer vision and pattern recognition* (pp. 3156–3164).

Viola, P., & Jones, M. (2001). Rapid object detection using a boosted cascade of simple features. In *CVPR* (pp. 1–8).

Virtanen, T., Nuutinen, M., Vaahteranoksa, M., Oittinen, P., & Hakkinen, J. (2015). CID2013: a database for evaluating noreference image quality assessment algorithms. *IEEE Trans. Image Process, 24*(1), 390–402.

Vos, K. (2019). *CoastSat image classification training data*. Retrieved from Zenodo Dataset. https://doi.org/10.5281/zenodo.3334147.

Wah, C., Branson, S., Welinder, P., Perona, P., & Belongie, S. (2011). *The Caltech-UCSD birds-200-2011 dataset*. Tech. Report CNS-TR-2011-001.

Wan, X., Wang, J., & Zhou, S. (2018). An online and flexible multi-object tracking framework using long short-term memory. In *Conference on computer vision and pattern recognition workshops* (pp. 1230–1238).

Wang, Z., Hu, G., & Hu, Q. (2020). Training noise-robust deep neural networks via meta-learning. In: *Proceedings of the IEEE/CVF conference on computer vision and pattern recognition* (pp. 4524–4533).

Wang, M., & Deng, W. (2020). *Deep face recognition: A survey*. Retrieved from arXiv. https://arxiv.org/abs/1804.06655.

Wang, Y., & Hebert, M. (2016a). Learning to learn: Model regression networks for easy small sample learning. In *IEuropean conference on computer vision (ECCV), October, Amsterdam, The Netherlands* (pp. 616–634).

Wang, Y.-X., & Hebert, M. (2016b). Learning to learn: Model regression networks for easy small sample learning. In *ECCV*.

Wang, L., Pham, N. T., Ng, T.-T., Wang, G., Chan, K. L., & Leman, K. (2014). Learning deep features for multiple object tracking by using a multi-task learning strategy. In *IEEE international conference on image processing (ICIP)* (pp. 838–842).

Wang, D., Shen, Z., Shao, J., Zhang, W., Xue, X., & Zhang, Z. (2015). Multiple granularity descriptors for fine-grained categorization. In *ICCV* (pp. 2399–2406).

II. Applications

Wang, X., Peng, Y., Lu, L., Lu, Z., Bagheri, M., & Summers, R. M. (2017). Chestx-ray8: Hospital-scale chest x-ray database and benchmarks on weakly-supervised classification and localization of common thorax diseases. In: *Proceedings of the IEEE conference on computer vision and pattern recognition* (pp. 2097–2106).

Wang, Z., Bovik, A. C., Sheikh, H. R., & Simoncelli, E. P. (2004). Image quality assessment: From error visibility to structural similarity. In *IEEE transactions on image processing*.

Wang, Z., Chen, J., & Hoi, S. C. (2020). *Deep learning for image super-resolution: A survey*. Retrieved from arxiv: https://arxiv.org/abs/1902.06068.

Wang, Y.-X., Girshick, R., Hebert, M., & Ran, B. H. (2018). Low-shot learning from imaginary data. In *CVPR*.

Wang, Y. X., Ramanan, D., & Hebert, M. (2019). Meta-learning to detect rare objects. In: *Proceedings of the IEEE/CVF international conference on computer vision* (pp. 9925–9934).

Wang, Z., Hu, G., & Hu, Q. (2020). Training noise-robust deep neural networks via meta-learning. In *CVPR*.

Wang, G., Luo, C., Sun, X., Xiong, Z., & Zeng, W. (2020). Tracking by instance detection: A meta-learning approach. In *Proceedings of the IEEE/CVF conference on computer vision and pattern recognition* (pp. 6288–6297).

Wang, P., Wu, Q., Shen, C., Hengel, A. V., & Dick, A. (2015). *Explicit knowledge-based reasoning for visual question answering*. arXiv preprint arXiv:1511.02570.

Wei, X.-S., Cui, Q., Yang, L., Wang, P., & Liu, L. (2019). *RPC: A large- scale retail product checkout dataset*. arXiv preprint arXiv:1901.07249.

Wei, X.-S., Wu, J., & Cui, Q. (2019). *Deep learning for fine-grained image analysis: A survey*. Retrieved from arXiv: https://arxiv.org/abs/1907.03069.

Wen, D., Han, H., & Jain, A. K. (2015). Face spoof detection with image distortion analysis. *IEEE Transactions on Information Forensics and Security, 10*(4), 746–761.

Wen, W., Wu, C., Wang, Y., Chen, Y., & Li, H. (2016). Learning structured sparsity in deep neural networks. In *NeurIPS*.

Wiles, O., Koepke, A., & Zisserman, A. (2018). X2face: A network for controlling face generation using images, audio, and pose codes. In: *Proceedings of the European conference on computer vision (ECCV)* (pp. 670–686).

Woo, S., Park, J., Lee, J.-Y., & Kweon, I. S. (2018). Cbam: Convolutional block attention module. In *ECCV* (pp. 3–19).

Wu, Z., & Palmer, M. (1994). Verbs semantics and lexicalselection. In *Conference association for computational linguistics*.

Wu, Q., Teney, D., Wang, P., Shen, C., Dick, A., & Hengel, A.v. (2016). *Visual question answering: A survey of methods and datasets*. Retrieved from arXiv: https://arxiv.org/abs/1607.05910.

Wu, Y., Chen, Y., Wang, L., Ye, Y., Liu, Z., Guo, Y., & Fu, Y. (2019). Large scale incremental learning. In *IEEE conference on computer vision and pattern recognition*.

Wu, Y., Lim, J., & Yang, M.-H. (2015). Object tracking benchmark. In *IEEE transactions on pattern analysis and machine intelligence*.

xhlulu. (2019). *Recursion cellular image classification: 224 JPG*. Retrieved from Kaggle: https://www.kaggle.com/xhlulu/recursion-cellular-image-classification-224-jpg.

Xia, X., & Kulis, B. (2017). *W-net: A deep model for fully unsupervised image segmentation*. Retrieved from arXiv: arXiv:1711.08506.

Xiao, Y., & Marlet, R. (2020, July 23). *Few-shot object detection and viewpoint estimation for objects in the wild*. arXiv.org. Retrieved June 4, 2022, from: https://arxiv.org/abs/2007.12107.

Xiao, T., Xu, Y., Yang, K., Zhang, J., Peng, Y., & Zhang, Z. (2015). The application of two-level attention models in deep convolutional neural network for fine-grained image classification. In *CVPR* (pp. 842–850).

Xiao, J., Owens, A., & Torralba, A. (2013). Sun3d: A database of big spaces reconstructed using sfm and object labels. In *IEEE international conference on computer vision* (pp. 1625–1632).

Xiao, T., Xia, T., Yang, Y., Huang, C., & Wang, X. (2015). Learning from massive noisy labeled data for image classification. In *CVPR*.

Xie, J., Girshick, R. B., Farhadi, A., Cs, A. L., & Edu, W. (2016). Unsupervised deep embedding for clustering analysis. In *Vol. 1. 33rd international conference on machine learning* (pp. 740–749).

Xie, L., Tian, Q., Hong, R., Yan, S., & Zhang, B. (2013). Hierarchical part matching for fine-grained visual categorization. In *ICCV* (pp. 1641–1648).

Xu, W., Xu, Y., Wang, H., & Tu, Z. (2021). Attentional constellation nets for few-shot learning. In: *International conference on learning representations*.

Xu, H., & Saenko, K. (2015). *Ask, attend and answer: Exploring question-guided spatial attention for visual question answering*. arXiv preprint arXiv:1511.05234.

Yan, X., Chen, Z., Xu, A., Wang, X., Liang, X., & Lin, L. (2020). Meta R-CNN: Towards general solver for instance-level low-shot learning. In *ICCV 2019*.

Yang, Z., He, X., Gao, J., Deng, L., & Smola, A. (2016). *Stacked attention networks for image question answering*. Retrieved from IEEE Conf. Comp. Vis. Patt. Recogn.

Yao, J., Wang, J., Tsang, I. W., Zhang, Y., Sun, J., Zhang, C., & Zhang, R. (2018). Deep learning from noisy image labels with quality embedding. In *IEEE transactions on image processing* (pp. 1909–1922).

Ye, P., Kumar, J., Kang, L., Doermann, D., & Jun. (2012). Unsupervised feature learning framework for no-reference image quality assessment. In *IEEE conference on computer vision and pattern recognition (CVPR)* (pp. 1098–1105).

Yin, M., Tucker, G., Zhou, M., Levine, S., & Finn, C. (2019). Meta-learning without memorization. *arXiv preprint*, arXiv:1912.03820. In *ICLR*.

Yoon, J., Arik, S., & Pfister, T. (2020). Data valuation using reinforcement learning. In *International conference on machine learning* (pp. 10842–10851). PMLR.

Yoon, J., Yang, E., Lee, J., & Ju Hwang, S. (2017). *Lifelong learning with dynamically expandable networks*. Retrieved from arXiv preprint: arXiv:1708.01547.

You, Q., Jin, H., Wang, Z., Fang, C., & Luo, J. (2016). Image captioning with semantic attention. In *IEEE conference on computer vision and pattern recognition* (pp. 4651–4659).

Yu, F., Li, W., Li, Q., Liu, Y., Shi, X., & Yan, J. (2016). Poi: Multiple object tracking with high performance detection and appearance feature. In *European conference on computer vision* (pp. 36–42). Springer.

Yu, X., Han, B., Yao, J., Niu, G., Tsang, I. W., & Sugiyama, M. (2019). How does disagreement help generalization against label corruption? In *ICML*.

Yuan, Y., Chen, X., & Wang, J. (2019). *Object-contextual representations for semantic segmentation*. Retrieved from arXiv: arXiv:1909.11065.

Yue, Z., Zhang, H., Sun, Q., & Hua, X. S. (2020). Interventional few-shot learning. *Advances in Neural Information Processing*, 33, 2734–2746.

Zakharov, E., Shysheya, A., Burkov, E., & Lempitsky, V. (2019, September 25). *Few-shot adversarial learning of realistic neural talking head models*. arXiv.org. Retrieved June 4, 2022, from: https://arxiv.org/abs/1905.08233.

Zhai, X., Oliver, A., Kolesnikov, A., & Beyer, L. (2019). S4L: Self-supervised semi-supervised learning. In *The IEEE international conference on computer vision* (pp. 1476–1485).

Zhang, R., Che, T., Ghahramani, Z., Bengio, Y., & Song, Y. (2018). Metagan: An adversarial approach to few-shot learning. *Advances in Neural Information Processing Systems*, 31.

Zhang, X., Sugano, Y., Fritz, M., & Bulling, A. (2015). *Appearance-based gaze estimation in the wild*. Chicago: MPIIGaze.

Zhang, Z., Zhang, H., Arik, S. O., Lee, H., & Pfister, T. (2020). Distilling effective supervision from severe label noise. In: *Proceedings of the IEEE/CVF conference on computer vision and pattern recognition* (pp. 9294–9303).

Zhang, Z., & Sabuncu, M. (2018). Generalized cross entropy loss for training deep neural networks with noisy labels. In *NeurIPS* (pp. 8778–8788).

Zhang, Z., Yan, J., Liu, S., Lei, Z., Yi, D., & Li, S. Z. (2012). A face antispoofing database with diverse attacks. In *5th IAPR international conference on biometrics (ICB)*.

Zhang, W., Wang, Y., & Qiao, Y. (2019). Metacleaner: Learning to hallucinate clean representations for noisy-labeled visual recognition. In: *Proceedings of the IEEE/CVF conference on computer vision and pattern recognition* (pp. 7373–7382).

Zhang, X., Xiong, H., Zhou, W., Lin, W., & Tian, Q. (2016). Picking deep filter responses for fine-grained image recognition. In *CVPR* (pp. 1134–1142).

Zheng, G., Awadallah, A. H., & Dumais, S. (2021). *Meta label correction for noisy label learning*, 35(12), 11053–11061.

Zhou, F., & Lin, Y. (2016). Fine-grained image classification by exploring bipartite-graph labels. In *CVPR* (pp. 1124–1133).

Zhou, B., Cui, Q., Wei, X.-S., & Chen, Z. (2019). *Bbn: Bilateral-branch network with cumulative learning for long-tailed visual recognition*. Retrieved from ArXiv, abs/1912.02413.

Zhou, B., Lapedriza, A., Khosla, A., Oliva, A., & Torralba, A. (2017). Places: A 10 million image database for scene recognition. In *IEEE transactions on pattern analysis and machine intelligence* (pp. 1452–1464).

Zhu, J., Yang, H., Liu, N., Kim, M., Zhang, W., & Yang, M.-H. (2018). Online multi-object tracking with dual matching attention networks. In *European conference on computer vision (ECCV)* (pp. 366–382).

Zhu, X., Liu, H., Lei, Z., Shi, H., Yang, F., Yi, D., … Li, S. Z. (2019). Large-scale bisample learning on id versus spot face recognition. *International Journal of Computer Vision, 127*(6–7), 684–700.

Zhu, Y., Liu, C., & Jiang, S. (2020). Multi-attention meta learning for few-shot fine-grained image recognition. In: *IJCAI* (pp. 1090–1096).

Zoph, B., Vasudevan, V., Shlens, J., & Le, Q. V. (2018). *Learning transferable architectures for scalable image recognition.* Retrieved from arXiv https://arxiv.org/pdf/1707.07012.pdf.

6

Meta-learning for natural language processing

6.1 Introduction

In the 1950s, Alan Turing proposed the renowned "Turing test" in his paper "Computing Machinery and Intelligence" regarding natural language interpretation and generation. Natural language processing (NLP) is an interaction of machine-readable programs and human languages, aiming to guide the machine to understand, process, and analyze infinite natural language data, such as natural language understanding and generation. A significant amount of early success concentrated on machine translation, primarily relying on the existing multilingual corpora translated from government official documentation by the European Union and Parliament of Canada. However, the shortage of corpora in a range of other tasks promotes researchers' focus on more efficient solutions based on limited samples. After the rule-based and statistical-based milestones, representation learning through neural networks became mainstream in NLP problems. Supervised learning generates highly accurate performance at the cost of extensive datasets. On the other hand, semisupervised and unsupervised learning bridge the gap of sample scarcity by leveraging the nonlabelled data—but with a trade-off of inferior generalization.

6.1.1 Limitations

Although deep learning technology has dominated NLP for decades with impressively extensive success across diverse fields, some challenging issues limit its applications:

- In contrast to massive datasets that rely on hand-crafted labeling for supervised learning, sample scarcity, and imbalanced and long-tailed datasets have become the mainstream in practical situations. This has severely limited the supervised learning applications and generalization capabilities of current solutions.
- Furthermore, large-scale human engineering datasets frequently experience monotonic and straightforward utterances with minimal linguistic variations. This challenge could

209

increase overfitting and limit the technology's generalization capability. However, current studies aim to produce synthesis samples, which are highly noisy, for training. Even though a set of samples with commonly shared features are assembled as "tasks," such tasks are not available in the standard datasets. Consequently, a model that can perform powerful generalizations based primarily on prior knowledge within low-data regimes is required.

- Although generic models offer promising results across typical scenarios, personalized approaches have successfully handled various customized situations—conditioned on various persona, context, etc. The effectiveness of using a single model to handle diverse situations remains lacking.
- Large-scale parallel corpora within particular domains are challenging to obtain; this leads to difficulties in multilingual tasks, such as machine translation.
- Although domain adaptation is widely applied, gaps among multiple domains inhibit its performance. Considerable differences between various domains reduce generalization in the regular adaptation by leveraging knowledge extracted from high-resource to low-resource domains.
- Few-shot or missing knowledge graph relations commonly exist, for instance, long-tailed knowledge graph relations or knowledge graph incompleteness. These few-shot relations severely reduce the efficiency of knowledge graphs.

This chapter investigates 20 advanced pieces of research, all of which can be divided into seven taxonomies according to their tasks to solve, as outlined in Table 6.1: semantic parsing, sentiment analysis, machine translation, dialogue system, knowledge graph (including named entity recognition and question answering), relation extraction, and emerging topics (e.g., domain-specific word embedding, multilabel classification, compositional generalization, query suggestion). Numerous attempts are discussed across various research areas, including domain adaption, few-shot/zero-shot learning, and a lifelong learning setting.

TABLE 6.1 Summary of meta-learning techniques for natural language processing.

References	Task	Method	Conferences
6.2 Semantic parsing			
Huang, Wang, Singh, Yih, and He (2018)	Natural language to structured query generation in few-shot learning	Pseudo-Task MAML (PT-MAML)	ACL
Sun et al. (2019)	Semantic parsing in low-resource scenarios	Back-Translation, MAML-based	AAAI
Guo, Tang, Duan, Zhou, and Yin (2019)	Context-dependent semantic parser with few-shot learning	Retrieval-MAML	ACL
6.3 Machine translation			
Gu, Wang, Chen, Cho, and Li (2018)	Multidomain neural machine translation in low-resource scenarios	MetaNMT	ACL
Li, Feng, et al. (2020)	Multilingual neural machine translation in few-shot scenarios	MetaMT	AAAI

TABLE 6.1 Summary of meta-learning techniques for natural language processing—cont'd

References	Task	Method	Conferences
6.4 Dialogue system			
Lin, Madotto, Wu, and Fung (2019)	Few-shot personalizing dialogue generation	Persona-agnostic meta-learning (PAML)	ACL
Qian and Yu (2019)	Domain adaptation in a dialogue system	DAML	ACL
Mi, Huang, Zhang, and Faltings (2019)	Natural language generation by few-shot learning concerning task-oriented dialogue systems	Meta-NLG	IJCAI
6.5 Knowledge graph			
Lv et al. (2019)	Multihop knowledge graph reasoning in few-shot scenarios	Meta-KGR	ACL
Chen, Zhang, Zhang, Chen, and Chen (2019)	Knowledge graphs link prediction in few-shot scenarios	Meta Relationship Learning (MetaR)	ACL
Hua, Li, Haffari, Qi, and Wu (2020)	Knowledge base complex question answering	Meta Retrieval Learning (MARL)	IJCAI
Wu et al. (2020)	Named-entity recognition in cross-lingual scenarios	mBERT, MAML-based	AAAI
6.6 Relation extraction			
Obamuyide and Vlachos (2019)	Few-shot supervised relation classification	Meta-Learning Relation Classification (MLRC)	ACL
Qu, Gao, Xhonneux, and Tang (2020)	Relation extraction with few-shot and zero-shot learning	Bayesian Meta-Learning-Based	ICML
6.7 Sentiment analysis			
Zhao and Ma (2019)	Text emotion distribution learning with small samples	EDL-Meta	ACL
6.8 Other emerging topics			
Xu, Liu, Shu, and Yu (2018)	Domain-specific word embedding under lifelong learning setting	Lifelong Domain Embedding via Meta-Learning (L-DEM)	IJCAI
Wu, Xiong, and Wang (2019)	Multi-label classification	GRU-based	ACL
Dou, Yu, and Anastasopoulos (2019)	Representation under a low-resource setting	MAML, First-Order MAML, Reptile	ACL
Lake (2019)	Compositional generalization	Meta Sequence-to-Sequence (Meta seq2seq)	NeurIPS
Han et al. (2020)	Zero-shot transfer learning for query suggestion	Reptile-Based	KDD

Each section outlines the definition of relevant terminology, early attempts, current status, multiple research lines, milestones of model architecture, distribution and general purposes, remarkable techniques, objective function and pseudocode of critical methods, regular datasets, and benchmarks.

The state-of-the-art meta-learning approaches covered in the following sections were selected due to their fundamental influence on current methods or theories, with a particular focus on: (a) their significant and broadly practical contributions in diverse applications; (b) their remarkable influence in academia according to their advanced performance and significant potential for further investigation; (c) the impressive solutions they present as integral components, which are rarely discussed but important to meta-learning in natural language processing. These pieces of research recursively track related bibliographies in papers accepted at premier academic conferences: AAAI, ACL, ICML, IJCAI, KDD, and NeurIPS.

6.2 Semantic parsing

6.2.1 Introduction

Semantic parsing is a fundamental component of natural language processing tasks. It is widely executed in versatile applications ranging from robotic navigation (Artzi & Zettlemoyer, 2013; Tellex et al., 2011), object recognition (Krishnamurthy & Kollar, 2013; Matuszek, FitzGerald, Zettlemoyer, Bo, & Fox, 2012), machine translation, code generation, question answering, and conversational agents like Apple's Siri and the Google Assistant.

As logician Richard Montague stated, there is no significant conceptual difference between natural languages and the logicians' artificial languages (Montague, 1973). Semantic parsing analyzes the variance between natural language and logic (Liang, 2016). It is a task that focuses on mapping a natural language (NL) utterance to a machine-understandable logical form for disclosing fundamental meanings to execute the desired behavior (Berant, Chou, Frostig, & Liang, 2013; Jia & Liang, 2016; Kamath & Das, 2019). If the goal is to understand the natural language accurately and comprehensively, semantic parsing is highly recommended. It converts the natural language to a formal meaning representation that can be understood by a machine. On the other hand, due to the broad applications of semantic parsing in NLP and extensive datasets with various formats, the definition of semantic parsing can be extended by specifying the type of tasks, overall goal, and corresponding domains.

Development

Early efforts heavily relied on handcrafted rule-based systems (Johnson, 1984; Woods, 1973; Woods, Kaplan, & Webber, 1972) with limitations due to narrow domains and complexity of general language. Then, statistical semantic parsing approaches (Thompson & Mooney, 2003; Zelle & Mooney, 1996) illuminated a more in-depth understanding but essentially counted on labeled data of annotated utterance-logical form pairs. As the parameters-learning method and the semistructured table (Pasupat & Liang, 2015) drove developments, it became possible for semantic parsing to be trained on wide-ranging knowledge bases with multiple major approaches: maximum marginal likelihood (MML) with full supervision and weakly supervision (Clarke, Goldwasser, Chang, & Roth, 2010; Liang, Jordan, & Klein, 2011) in online search (Liang et al., 2011; Pasupat & Liang, 2015) and offline search (Krishnamurthy, Dasigi, & Gardner, 2017), reinforcement learning methods (Guu, Pasupat, Liu, & Liang, 2017; Liang, Berant, Le, Forbus, & Lao, 2016; Liang, Norouzi, Berant, Le, & Lao, 2018), and maximum margin reward (MMR; Iyyer, Yih, & Chang, 2017; Misra, Chang, He, & Yih, 2018). As the technology of machine learning and deep learning emerged, remarkable models largely relied on recurrent neural network-based models, encoder-decoder-based structures, transformer-based architectures, etc., as popular frameworks such as Cornell Semantic Parsing Framework.

Benchmarks

Some standard benchmarks are outlined below, with their goals or attributes:

- AMR Bank (Banarescu et al., 2013), a graph-based abstract meaning representation
- ATIS (Hemphill, Godfrey, & Doddington, 1990), a corpus with audio record of requesting airline information
- ComplexWebQuestions (Talmor & Berant, 2018), a dataset fulfilled with complex questions
- FrameNet (Baker, Fillmore, & Lowe, 1998), a lexical database with frames, lexical units, frame relations, etc.
- Geo880 (Zelle & Mooney, 1996), a dataset with questions and answers of geographical facts
- SparC (Yu et al., 2019), a dataset for cross-domain context-dependent tasks
- SQA (Iyyer et al., 2017), a dataset for questions answering
- SCAN (Lake & Baroni, 2018), a dataset with navigation command and action sequences
- SPIDER (Yu et al., 2018), a dataset for cross-domain tasks
- WikiSQL (Zhong, Xiong, & Socher, 2017), a dataset for code generation
- WebQuestions (Berant et al., 2013), a dataset utilizing Freebase as its knowledge base
- WebQuestionsSP (Yih, Richardson, Meek, Chang, & Suh, 2016), a dataset for knowledge-based question answering
- WikiTableQuestions (Pasupat & Liang, 2015), a dataset for question answering

Semantic parsing is a fundamental task for high-level natural language processing implementations; despite various existing approaches that are broadly applied, some drawbacks remain. Deep learning in semantic parsing achieved impressive performance but relied heavily on extensive training data in supervised learning. Moreover, existing generic strategies with context-independent retrievers frequently fail on context-dependent semantic parsing tasks. Personalized semantic parsers can tackle this problem by mapping the natural language utterances to structural logic forms conditioned to different scenarios. However, conventional personalized approaches are still deficient and pose the following dilemmas: (a) the generalization capability is harmfully diminished by sample scarcity in supervised learning; and (b) a predefined "task" for assembling a set of samples with a shared common feature does not exist in the standard datasets.

In contrast, meta-learning provides novel directions for solving these issues. By leveraging prior knowledge from minimal mapping rules, meta-learners efficiently perform semantic parsing based on low-data regimes. Furthermore, a personalized semantic parser is implemented by retrieving similar samples via a context-aware retriever in mate-learning approaches. It can also be accomplished by treating each text sample as the individual pseudo-task in a meta-learner, with support from domain-dependent relevant functions.

This section introduces multiple semantic parsers employed with meta-learning in practical scenarios. Section 6.2.2 discusses a MAML (see detailed exploration in Section 4.3) backbone method for structured query generation. A model-agnostic semantic parsing system with a few annotated samples for few-shot learning is presented in Section 6.2.3 to handle SQL queries, conversational follow-up questions and answers, and knowledge-based large-scale datasets. Section 6.2.4 focuses on a context-dependent semantic parser through a classical encoder-decoder pipeline.

6.2.2 Natural language to structured query generation in few-shot learning

Compared with the generic one-size-fits-all solution, a personalized approach seems more reasonable in complex situations with various inputs. However, two contradicting scenarios regarding a personalized approach have attracted attention. First, as the number of tasks increases, the sample for each task decreases dramatically, which negatively impacts the model's generalization in the case of supervised learning. Second, a set of samples with certain common features are denoted as a "task"; however, such a task does not directly present in a standard dataset.

To tackle these issues, Huang and colleagues (Huang et al., 2018) proposed a solution to re-discuss the supervised training into a few-shot problem named Pseudo-Task MAML (PT-MAML), which views each test example as an individual pseudo-task supported by a MAML backbone meta-learner and a domain-dependent relevance function. This framework is based on semantic parsing tasks. The official code is available at https://github.com/Microsoft/PointerSQL.

Problem-dependent relevance function produces higher scores when the examples belong to the same type of SQL query (i.e., overall five different types from WikiSQL dataset). This relevance function maintains two factors: the length of the question and the predicted SQL type.

The high-level workflow is displayed in Fig. 6.1.

FIG. 6.1   General pipeline of pseudo-task MAML. The support set is selected from all training datapoints conditioned on the relevance function. Datapoint $\mathcal{D}'_j$ is given for setting up the pseudo-task $\mathcal{T}_j$.
Modified from Huang, P.-S., Wang, C., Singh, R., Yih, W.-t., & He, X. (2018). Natural language to structured query generation via meta-learning. In ACL.

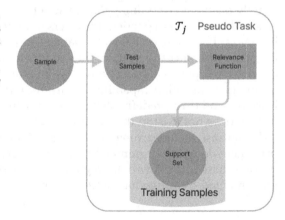

Implementation

The workflow with the MAML backbone is summarized in Table 6.2.

TABLE 6.2 Summarized methods of pseudo-task MAML.

Input: $\mathcal{D} = \{x^{(j)}, y^{(j)}\}$, training samples
$\quad$ α, β: hyperparameters of step size
$\quad$ K: hyperparameter of support set size

1: Apply a support set $\mathcal{S}_K^{(j)}$ and a test example $\mathcal{D}'_j = (x^{(j)}, y^{(j)})$ to construct a task $\mathcal{T}_j$
2: Set the distribution over tasks as $p(\mathcal{T})$
3: Randomly initialize θ

4: **while** not done **do**
5: $\quad$ Construct batch of tasks $\mathcal{T}_i \sim p(\mathcal{T})$

6: $\quad$ **for all** $\mathcal{T}_i$ **do**
7: $\quad\quad$ Apply $\mathcal{S}_K^{(j)}$ to obtain $\nabla_\theta \mathcal{L}_{\mathcal{T}_i}(f_\theta)$
8: $\quad\quad$ Evaluate adapted parameters as $\theta'_i = \theta - \alpha \nabla_\theta \mathcal{L}_{\mathcal{T}_i}(f_\theta)$
9: $\quad$ **end for**

$\quad$ # **Meta-update**
10: $\quad$ Evaluate $\theta \leftarrow \theta - \beta \nabla_\theta \sum_{\mathcal{T}_i \sim p(\mathcal{T})} \mathcal{L}_{\mathcal{T}_i}(f_{\theta'_i})$

11: **end while**

Modified from Huang, P.-S., Wang, C., Singh, R., Yih, W.-t., & He, X. (2018). Natural language to structured query generation via meta-learning. In ACL.

This model is assessed in dataset WikiSQL (Zhong et al., 2017) with question-query pairs processed under Stanford Stanza (Manning et al., 2014), and achieves 1.1%–5.4% improvement in absolute accuracy compared to nonmeta-learning methods.

6.2.3 Semantic parsing in low-resource scenarios

Extensive training data are necessary for supervising learning strategies. Current deep learning methods can achieve impressive semantic parsing but are heavily reliant on these massive datasets. In reality, a model may be only supported by the prior knowledge with a few simple rules without annotated programs or execution results.

Sun et al. (2019) introduced a MAML backbone semantic parsing system in a low-resource scenario. Unlike regular approaches, this framework does not rely on annotated logical forms or execution results during training. Instead, it focusses on prior knowledge of a few simple mapping rules and domain-independent word-level matching tables.

This framework first gathers a small number of query-program pairs based on the given rules and then boosts the generality and accuracy through artificially generated samples.

This method is implemented through three submodules:

- A data generator, which has two components motivated by the back-translation paradigm (Lample, Ott, Conneau, De-Noyer, & Ranzato, 2018; Sennrich, Haddow, & Birch, 2016a): a semantic parser (to map a natural language utterance q to a logic form lf) and a question-generation model (to map the logic form lf to a natural language question a).
- A quality controller qc that removes noise from the artificially generated samples (Ren, Zhang, Liu, Zhou, & Ma, 2019) by maintaining high-frequency mapping patterns while obliterating low-frequencies as noise.

TABLE 6.3   Summarized training methods of the proposed strategy.

Input: Q, a set of UL questions
$\quad\quad$ LF, a gather of sampled logical patterns
$\quad\quad$ r, a rule: projects q to lf if satisfied
$\quad\quad$ α, β, hyperparameters of step size

1: Acquire training data D_0 through implement r to Q
2: Initialization of $\theta_{q \to lf}$ and $\theta_{lf \to q}$ through D_0

3: **while** not done **do**
4:$\quad\quad$ Conduct $f_{q \to lf}$ to Q whereas $f_{lf \to q}$ to LF
5:$\quad\quad$ Evaluate the phrase table from qc (the quality controller) through $f_{q \to lf}(Q)$ and
$\quad\quad$ $f_{lf \to q}(LF)$
6:$\quad\quad$ Evaluate $\theta_{lf \to q}$ via D_0 and $qc(f_{q \to lf}(Q))$

7:$\quad\quad$ **for** Task $\mathcal{T}_i \in \{r = T, r = F\}$ **do**
$\quad\quad\quad$ # base learner update
8:$\quad\quad\quad$ Randomly sample $\mathcal{D}_i$ from $\{D_0, qc(f_{q \to lf}(Q)), qc(f_{lf \to q}(LF))\}$ for task $\mathcal{T}_i$
9:$\quad\quad\quad$ Apply $\mathcal{D}_i$ and $\mathcal{L}$ to obtain gradients, then evaluate $\theta_i = \theta - \alpha \nabla_\theta \mathcal{L}(f_\theta)$
$\quad\quad\quad$ # meta learner meta-update
10:$\quad\quad\quad$ Randomly sample $\mathcal{D}'_i$ from $\{D_0, qc(f_{q \to lf}(Q)), qc(f_{lf \to q}(LF))\}$
11:$\quad\quad\quad$ Apply $\mathcal{D}'_i$ and $\mathcal{L}$ to obtain gradients, then evaluate $\theta = \theta - \beta \nabla_\theta \mathcal{L}(f_{\theta_i})$
12:$\quad\quad$ **end for**

13:$\quad\quad$ Repeatedly evaluate $\theta^{r=T}_{q \to lf}$ and $\theta^{r=F}_{q \to lf}$ through θ
14: **end while**

Modified from Sun, Y., Tang, D., Duan, N., Gong, Y., Feng, X., Qin, B., & Jiang, D. (2019). Neural semantic parsing in low-resource settings with back-translation and meta-learning. In AAAI.

- A model-agnostic meta-learner via MAML (see the detailed pseudocode in Table 6.3) handles samples covered and not covered by rules with good performances on and balances of model stability (by learning the task-specific model θ' for examples covered by rules) and versatility (by considering θ' as updating the cross-task parameter θ in the inner-loop and inputting the output from qc as input for inner-loop and outer-loop, as shown by lines 8–11 in Table 6.3).

This model applies to three different scenarios as follows:

- a single-turn table-based semantic parsing trained on a web table with SQL query from dataset WikiSQL (Zhong et al., 2017)
- a multiturn conversational table-based semantic parsing trained on follow-up questions conducted in dataset SequentialQA (Iyyer et al., 2017)
- a single-turn knowledge-based semantic parsing trained on the large-scale dataset SimpleQuestions (Bordes, Usunier, Chopra, & Weston, 2015)

6.2.4 Context-dependent semantic parser with few-shot learning

A context-dependent semantic parser projects a natural language into a structural logical form based on the conditioned context. Compared to conventional or generic approaches, a personalized solution is required. Most current retrieve-and-edit solutions employ a context-independent retriever (where even context-aware retrievers can act as core components in these tasks); however, they may fail to handle a scenario when the pattern of a structural logical form is related to various retrieved examples.

Analogous to the concept of semantic parsing in Section 6.2.1, context-dependent semantic parsing (CDSP) aims to map NL utterance to a logical form with respect to the underlying context environment (e.g., a database or knowledge base; Krishnamurthy & Mitchell, 2012; Liang, 2016). Guo et al. (2019) suggested a system to retrieve similar data points as compelling evidence in context-dependent semantic parsing tasks, named Retrieval-MAML. This system couples two components:

- A context-aware retriever based on a variational auto-encoder (VAE) structure encodes a natural language utterance that is conditioned on the given context environments into latent variables (the two latent variables include a current utterance and a context environment) that are prepared to generate structural logic patterns. It equips bidirectional RNNs with LSTM as the encoder and LSTM as decoder without an attention mechanism or a copying process.
- A meta-learner through MAML generates such logic patterns based on a sample number of retrieved samples (treated as the support set in meta-training), as presented in Fig. 6.2.

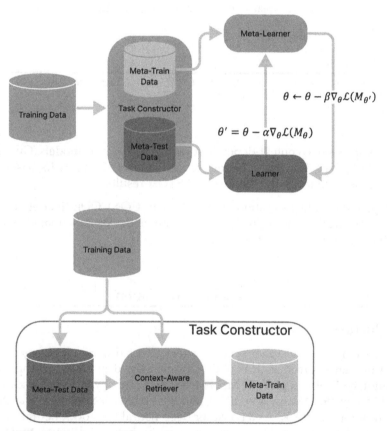

FIG. 6.2 General pipeline of retrieval-MAML.
Modified from Guo, D., Tang, D., Duan, N., Zhou, M., & Yin, J. (2019). Coupling retrieval and meta-learning for context-dependent semantic parsing. In ACL.

Table 6.4 Summarizes the comprehensive training methods.

TABLE 6.4   Summarized methods of retrieval-MAML.

Input: D, training dataset s.t. $D = (x^{(j)}, c^{(j)}, y^{(j)})$
    α, β, hyperparameters of step size
Output: M, updated meta-learner

1: Apply D to obtain a context-aware retriever R

2: **for** each example d **do**
3:    Acquire a support set S^d through R
4: **end for**

meta-learner M initialization
5: Randomly initialize θ
6: **while** not done **do**
7:    Sample test examples as a batch of examples D' in D
8:    Set $S' = \bigcup_{d \in D'} S^d$ as training examples
9:        Apply S' to compute $\nabla_\theta \mathcal{L}(M_\theta)$, then evaluate adapted parameters as $\theta' = \theta - \alpha \nabla_\theta \mathcal{L}(M_\theta)$
        # meta-update
10:        Evaluate $\theta \leftarrow \theta - \beta \nabla_\theta \mathcal{L}(M_{\theta'})$ with D'
11: **end while**

Modified from Guo, D., Tang, D., Duan, N., Zhou, M., & Yin, J. (2019). Coupling retrieval and meta-learning for context-dependent semantic parsing. In ACL.

This model employs two context-dependent sequence-to-action models (Guo, Tang, Duan, Zhou, & Yin, 2018; Iyer, Konstas, Cheung, & Zettlemoyer, 2018) as its baseline semantic parsers. It examines two tasks and has reached STOA results:

- Context-dependent code generation on benchmarks CONCODE (Iyer et al., 2018)
- Conversational question answering based on a knowledge base evaluated on CSQA (Saha, Pahuja, Khapra, Sankaranarayanan, & Chandar, 2018)

6.3 Machine translation

6.3.1 Introduction

Machine translation can decipher speech or text across different languages through software without human interaction. It is widely implemented in daily life applications, such as Google Language Tool, GoogleTalk, MSN Messenger, and Skype. René Descartes proposed an equivalent idea in 1629 (Knowlson, 1975), and the first MT intervention was developed by Georges Artsrouni in the 1930s. As a boost for deep neural networks, neural machine translation (NMT) achieves competitive performance in both traditional topics and open questions.

The development of machine translation proceeded through three milestones (Yang, Wang, & Chu, 2020):

- Rule-based machine translation (Forcada et al., 2011)
- Statistical machine translation (SMT; Koehn, Och, & Marcu, 2003; Koehn et al., 2007)
- Neural machine translation (Cho, Van Merrinboer, Bahdanau, & Bengio, 2014)

Even with the support of many early MT attempts, researchers still face several significant pitfalls: (a) a word that carries more than one meaning, (b) casual speech with nonstandard language, and (c) named entities required to be distinguished from common nouns. Rule-based MT requires an extensive amount of hand-crafted annotation for extracting linguistic information, and the adaptation to different domains remains weak. Furthermore, SMT shares limited flexibility on cross-lingual samples; thus, the benefits of leveraging from the Western languages rarely aid other language pairs. On the other hand, NMT offers advantages in simple architecture, processing on long dependency within a sentence, and avoiding flawed representation due to hand-crafted features (Song & Croft, 1999; Wallach, 2006). NMT utilized embedding representation of words and internal states through deep learning, and replaced the language model, reordering model, and translation model. The widely implemented NMT strategy follows the embed-encode-attend-decode protocol (Dabre, Chu, & Kunchukuttan, 2020). The primary five categories of this paradigm are as follows (Yang et al., 2020):

- Shallow layer NLM (Allen, 1987; Chrisman, 1991; Pollack, 1990)
- Statistical machine translation supported by NLM (Cho et al., 2014)
- NMT through a deep neural network (e.g., ComS2S (Gehring, Auli, Grangier, Yarats, & Dauphin, 2017), RNMT+ (Chen et al., 2018); Kalchbrenner & Blunsom, 2013; Sutskever, Vinyals, & Le, 2014; Wu et al., 2016)
- NMT through an attention mechanism (Bahdanau, Cho, & Bengio, 2014; Luong, Pham, & Manning, 2015; You, Sun, & Iyyer, 2020)
- Self-attention-based NMT (Schlag, Irie, & Schmidhuber, 2021; Vaswani et al., 2017)

Multilingual NMT (MNMT) aims to handle "translation between as many languages as possible by effective use of available linguistic resources" (Dabre et al., 2020). MNMT aims to obtain a single model for translating among diverse languages. Leveraging multiple languages can improve the generalization of a single model on a low-resource translation. Thus, few-shot translation has received increasing interest in cases of limited or no parallel corpora for language pairs. Two common approaches are (a) transferrable knowledge learned from a high-resources language pair applied to a low-resources language pair, or (b) a common parallel corpus shared with one or more pivot language(s). Standard datasets for MNMT include the Asian Scientific Paper Excerpt Corpus (ASPEC; Nakazawa et al., 2016) and the Tatoeba Translation Challenge (Tiedemann, 2020). Section 6.3.3 presents a different solution to learn parameters and address the mismatch between various language pairs.

Due to the limited size of domain-specific corpora and the quantity and quality of accessible domains, SMT and NMT remain unsatisfactory in their performance in domain-specific translation under sample scarcity (Duh, Neubig, Sudoh, & Tsukada., H., 2013; Sennrich, Schwenk, & Aransa, 2013; Zoph, Yuret, May, & Knight, 2016). **Domain adaptation for NMT** offers multiple solutions in two groups (Chu & Wang, 2018):

1. Data-oriented approaches through monolingual corpora (Gulcehre et al., 2015), generation of synthetic parallel corpora (Sennrich, Haddow, & Birch, 2016b), out-of-domain parallel corpora (Chu, Dabre, & Kurohashi, 2017; Khandelwal, Fan, Jurafsky, Zettlemoyer, & Lewis, 2021), or data selection (Wang, Finch, Utiyama, & Sumita, 2017)
2. Model-oriented approaches with various techniques, including fine-tuning (Luong & Manning, 2015), instance weighting (Wang, Utiyama, Liu, Chen, & Sumita, 2017), multidomain with fine-tuning (Chu et al., 2017; Liang, Zhao, Wang, Qiu, & Li, 2021), regularization (Barone, Haddow, Germann, & Sennrich, 2017), domain discriminator (Britz, Le, & Pryzant, 2017), domain control (Chen, Bogoychev, & Germann, 2020; Kobus, Crego, & Senellart, 2016), shallow fusion (Gulcehre et al., 2015), ensembling (Freitag & Al-Onaizan, 2016), and natural lattice search (Khayrallah, Kumar, Duh, Post, & Koehn, 2017)

Although current algorithms have achieved promising levels of generalization, some difficulties continue to constrain neural machine translation applications in real-world scenarios. Latency issues, specifically with low-data language pairs, frequently cause unsatisfactory experiences during human interaction with the translation system. In addition, massive parallel corpora for multidomain neural machine translation training are expensive and difficult to obtain in particular domains. Training based on limited data becomes challenging. Due to sample scarcity, vocabulary problems (a different word for the same meaning) and polysemy problems (an identical word with a different meaning) confuse the model, dramatically reducing generalization.

However, meta-learning provides these few-shot regimes with practical solutions and solid generalization. A generic framework for low-resource, multilingual neural machine translation can be implemented with meta-learning and versal lexical representation to improve the mismatch among various languages. Meta-learning also encourages the representational space across different domains and domain-invariant word representation based on limited training samples without language-specific features. These can effectively block vocabulary and polysemy problems.

This section outlines two approaches to neural machine translation under different use cases. Section 6.3.2 offers a contrast solution to conventional domain adaptation NMT, which is based on domain-invariant word representation through a meta-learner for a multidomain problem. Section 6.3.3 discusses a state-of-the-art framework for multilingual NMT with 18 European languages as source tasks and five languages as target tasks.

6.3.2 Multidomain neural machine translation in low-resource scenarios

Large-scale parallel corpora are powerful and can avoid overfitting, ideally during multidomain neural machine translation training. Nevertheless, it is difficult and expensive to construct extensive parallel corpora within specific domains. The shortage of domain-specific parallel corpora seriously reduces the generalization performance of neural machine translation systems in a particular domain. Fortunately, domain adaptation NMT can help to further investigate these issues.

Li and colleagues (Li, Wang, & Yu, 2020) presented MetaMT to tackle two neural machine translation issues in multiple domains with limited resource corpora via meta-training: the vocabulary problem (a different word for the same meaning) and the polysemy problem (an identical word with a different meaning). Unlike MetaNMT (discussed in Section 6.3.2), this framework only focuses on translating English to Spanish and needs no language-specific features. The regular NMT model employs an encoder-decoder with an attention model relying on a large scale of parallel corpora. In MetaMT, meta-learning supports the representational space across different domains through a few training samples. This framework takes Transformer as a baseline equipped with multihead self-attention.

MetaMT proposed domain-invariant word representation. It maps all words from different domains into the same semantic space (i.e., domain-invariant semantic space) shared by multiple domains. Meta-parameters are fine-tuned to decrease domain divergence, analogous to prior work (Gu et al., 2018). Eqs. (6.1) and (6.2) express the design of words represented in domain-invariant space through an additional transmission layer, where E^G denotes the word embedding formated as $n * d$ matrix based on general domain corpora without optimization for any domain-specific data, and $\vec{w}_k^i$ is the representation of word w_k in domain i. A^i presents a learnable $d \times d$ matrix during training.

$$a_j^i = \vec{w}_k^i * A^i * E^G[j] \tag{6.1}$$

$$\vec{w}_k = \sum_{j=1}^{n} a_j^i * E^G[j] \tag{6.2}$$

Table 6.5 contains comprehensive methods for both model training (line 2) and meta-parameter training (line 3).

This method is evaluated on 7 Greek for Spanish (En-Es) parallel datasets from OPUS-covered (Tiedemann, 2012) diverse domains:

- IRCAcquis (Steinberger et al., 2006), a legal document collection
- Global Voices (Prokopidis, Papavassiliou, & Piperidis, 2016), a gather of blogs on different social networks of Global Voices news
- OpenSub (Lison & Tiedemann, 2016), a collection of Movie and TV subtitles
- Europarll (Koehn, 2005), collected from the European Parliament

TABLE 6.5 Summarized training methods of MetaMT.

Input: $D = \{D^0, D^1, ..., D^{n-1}\}$, a collect of datasets
$M(\theta)$, translation model

1. for $D^i, D^j \in D$ do
   # optimize the translation model during model train
2. $\theta_i \leftarrow$ arg min Loss($D_{tr}^i, D_{dev}^i; M(\theta)$)
   # optimize the transmission layers and the encoder during meta-train
3. $\theta_i' \leftarrow$ arg min Loss($D_{dev}^j; M(\theta_i)$)
4. end for

5. $\theta \leftarrow$ arg min $\sum_{i=0}^{n-1}$ Loss($D_{tr}^i; M(\theta_i')$)
   # fine-tune on D_d from domain d
6. $\theta \leftarrow$ arg min Loss($D_{tr}^d, D_{dev}^d; M(\theta)$)
7. return $M(\theta)$

Modified from Li, R., Wang, X., & Yu, H. (2020). MetaMT, a meta learning method leveraging multiple domain data for low resource machine translation.

- UN Para (Rafalovitch, Dale, et al., 2009), a collection of text in the six official language used in United Nations
- Medline (Liu & Cai, 2015), a collection of biomedical articles on the NIH's MedlinePlus
- EU Bookshops dataset (Skadins, Tiedemann, Rozis, & Deksne, 2014), a collection of EU publications

6.3.3 Multilingual neural machine translation in few-shot scenarios

Standard neural machine translation systems have been reported to experience latency issues compared to traditional machine translation, particularly in cases that included a small number of language pairs.

To overcome this difficulty, Gu et al. (2018) suggested MetaNMT as a generic framework for low-resource multilingual neural machine translation. In contrast to traditional neural machine translation (NMT) research (Bojar et al., 2016), MetaNMT modifies MAML as a backbone and implements versal lexical representation (Gu et al., 2018) to improve the mismatch between different languages in input-output pairs. A meta-learning implementation aims to find an optimal initialization for fast adaptation within a few steps, differing from the function of meta-learning in MetaNT (introduced in Section 6.3.3). See Fig. 6.3 for the overall pipeline of MetaNMT.

This framework exploits five languages as target tasks (Romanian, Latvian, Finnish, Turkish, and Korean) and 18 European languages as source tasks from six language families:

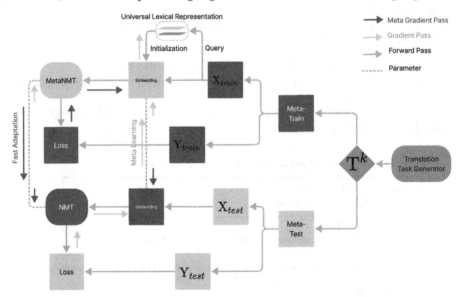

FIG. 6.3 General training pipeline of MetaNMT. This process consists of two procedures: meta-learning (denoted by *yellow boxes* (*light gray* in print version) and *arrows*) and language-specific learning (displayed by *red boxes* (*dark gray* in print version) and *arrows*).
Modified from Gu, J., Wang, Y., Chen, Y., Cho, K., & Li, V. O. (2018). Meta-learning for low-resource neural machine translation. In ACL.

- Bulgarian (a South Slavic language), Czech (a Balto-Slavic language), Lithuanian (a Balto-Slavic language), Slovene (a Balto-Slavic language), Slovak (as a language of the Czech-Slovak group), Polish (a West Slavic language), and Russian (an East Slavic language)
- Danish (a Germanic family language), German (a West Germanic language), Dutch (part of the Germanic family), Swedish (a North Germanic language)
- Greek (an independent family of Indo-European languages)
- Spanish (a Romance language), French (a Romance language), Italian (a Romance language), Portuguese (a West Romance language)
- Estonian (a Finnic language)
- Hungarian (a Uralic language)

The language-specific learning method $Learn(D_T; \theta^0)$ is expressed in Eq. (6.3) based on data D_T. $1/\beta$ represents the variance from the prior distribution $\theta_i \sim N(\theta_i^0, 1/\beta)$, and $p(Y|\theta)$ is a uniform distribution.

$$\text{Learn}(D_{\mathcal{T}}; \theta^0) = \arg\max_\theta \mathcal{L}^{D_{\mathcal{T}}}(\theta)$$
$$= \arg\max_\theta \sum_{(X,Y)\in D_{\mathcal{T}}} \log p(Y|X,\theta) - \beta\|\theta - \theta^0\|^2 \qquad (6.3)$$

The objective function of meta-training with stochastic approximation (Robbins & Monro, 1951) is expressed in Eq. (6.4), where k denotes each meta-training episode. $D_{\mathcal{T}^k}$ and $D'_{\mathcal{T}^k}$ are two independent sets of training data.

$$\mathcal{L}(\theta) = \mathbb{E}_k \mathbb{E}_{D_{\mathcal{T}^k}, D'_{\mathcal{T}'}} \left[\sum_{(X,Y)\in D'_{\mathcal{T}^k}} \log p\big(Y|X; \text{Learn}(D_{\mathcal{T}^k}; \theta)\big) \right] \qquad (6.4)$$

Language-specific learning is simulated in Eq. (6.5), where η denotes the learning rate:

$$\theta'_k = \text{Learn}(D_{\mathcal{T}^k}; \theta) = \theta - \eta\nabla_\theta\mathcal{L}^{D_{\mathcal{T}^k}}(\theta) \qquad (6.5)$$

Then, the updated parameters θ_k' are evaluated on $D'_{\mathcal{T}^k}$ through a meta-gradient, as expressed in Eq. (6.6), where the second-order derivatives are neglected due to computational complexity:

$$\nabla_\theta\mathcal{L}^{D'}(\theta') \approx \nabla_{\theta'}\mathcal{L}^{D'}(\theta') \qquad (6.6)$$

The universal lexical representation is utilized to address the input-output discrepancy between multilingual pairs. A language-specific embedding vector is expressed in Eqs. (6.7) and (6.8) as token x in language k. $\epsilon^0[x]$ is the universal lexical representation as a constant, α_i is a fixed factor during meta-training, and ϵ_u denotes a universal embedding matrix.

$$\epsilon^k[x] = \epsilon^0[x] + \Delta\epsilon^k[x] \qquad (6.7)$$

where:

$$\epsilon^0[x] = \sum_{i=1}^{M} \alpha_i\epsilon_u[i] \qquad (6.8)$$

MetaNMT has been compared with standard transfer learning methods (Zoph et al., 2016) and reaches state-of-the-art performance.

6.4 Dialogue system

6.4.1 Introduction

A dialogue system is a machine-based system that aims to communicate with humans through conversation via text, speech, images, and other communication modes as input or output. Dialogues systems are broadly implemented in banking, client services, human resources management, education, governments, etc. Dialogue systems can be categorized into task-oriented approaches and nontask-oriented approaches (Chen, Liu, Yin, & Tang, 2018). Task-oriented approaches aim to complete specific tasks for end-users, such as booking hotels or recommending products (e.g., see Qin, Xu, Che, Zhang, & Liu, 2020; Xie et al., 2022). Nontask-oriented ones, such as a personal companion chatbot, usually concentrate on continuing a diverse, vivid, and relevant conversation with end-users on an open domain (e.g., Gritta, Lampouras, & Iacobacci, 2021).

A task-oriented dialogue system consists of four components:

- Natural language understanding (NLU), which converts the end user's utterance to a specific semantic pattern depending on the actual scenario
- A dialogue state tracker, which determines the current dialogue state based on the historical conversation
- Dialogue policy learning, which produces the following system action (e.g., as the dialogue state tracker returns the "alarm," the "set the alarm" action is triggered)
- Natural language generation (NLG), which generates the corresponding reply to end-users

Intent detection as an essential element of a task-oriented dialogue system for mining the user's goal or motivation during **natural language understanding** has been the subject of many discussions. Intent detection aims to categorize an utterance according to predefined intents through a convolutional neural network (CNN) backbone for query classification (Hashemi, Asiaee, & Kraft, 2016; Huang et al., 2013; Shen, He, Gao, Deng, & Mesnil, 2014).

The traditional statistical dialogue system provides different methods for **dialogue state tracking**, such as the hand-crafted rule (Wang & Lemon, 2013) and conditional random fields (Lee & Eskenazi, 2013). The development of deep learning has also led to many contributions, such as a multidomain recurrent neural network (RNN) dialogue state tracking framework (Mrksic et al., 2015) and a neural belief tracker (Mrksic, Seaghdha, Wen, Thomson, & Young, 2017).

As Stent, Marge, and Singhai (2005) have stated, the quality of **natural language generation** is measured via adequacy, fluency, readability, and variation. Deep learning-based dialogue systems enhance the variability of natural language, robustness, and learning capability. Various neural network approaches represent numerous attempts, such as LSTM-based (Wen, Gasic, Kim, et al., 2015; Wen, Gasic, Mrksic, et al., 2015) and equipping extra cells for a dialogue act (Tran & Nguyen, 2017). A few-shot NLG solution is offered in Section 6.4.4.

Nontask-oriented dialogue systems involve generative methods and retrieval-based methods. Generative methods aim to keep the conversation smooth and diverse. One way to improve diversity is through the learning of inherent attributes, particularly personality. Many studies have focused on the person who associates with the conversation (Choudhary, Srivastava, Ungar, & Sedoc, 2017; Xing et al., 2017) through emotion embedding (Zhou, Huang, Zhang, Zhu, & Liu, 2017) and user profile (Qian, Huang, Zhao, Xu, & Zhu,

2017). The approach investigated in Section 6.4.2 provides a different way to construct personalized dialogue generation without a profile description.

Public benchmarks and datasets for task-oriented dialogue systems include:

- Schema-Guided Dialogue (SGD; Rastogi, Zang, Sunkara, Gupta, & Khaitan, 2019)
- KVRET (Eric & Manning, 2017)
- MuTual (Cui, Wu, Liu, Zhang, & Zhou, 2020)
- CrossWOZ (Zhu, Huang, Zhang, Zhu, & Huang, 2020)
- Open-Domain Spoken Question Answering (ODSQA; Lee, Wang, Chang, & Lee, 2018)
- BiToD (Lin et al., 2021)
- Incremental Dialogue Dataset (Wang et al., 2019)
- MultiWOZ-coref (Han et al., 2020)
- Action-Based Conversations Dataset (ABCD; Chen, Chen, Yang, Lin, & Yu, 2021)
- KILT, which is the benchmark related to the open-domain dialogue systems (Petroni et al., 2021)

Dialogue systems have been extensively implemented in various communication systems. However, the persona extraction from a few sentences of real-person conversation remains deficient. Accordingly, an adaptation from a high-resource domain to a low-resource domain is widely implemented in dialogue systems. However, the differences among various domains still limit the generalization capabilities.

Current studies of meta-learning illuminate these issues. Meta-training supports a persona-independent framework for fast adaptation on minimal historical dialogues without persona descriptions. In addition, the meta-learner leverages knowledge from high-resource source domains then enables the adaptation of low-data target domains within a few steps of gradient updating. For task-oriented dialogue systems, meta-learning also achieves a rapid adaptation of novel insinuations.

This section discusses how to implement a modified meta-learner into various applications of dialogue systems. Section 6.4.2 focuses on personalizing dialogue generation with only a few historical dialogues and without a persona description. Section 6.4.3 explores a two-stage end-to-end dialogue-generation strategy through transferrable knowledge from a high-resources source domain to a low-resources target domain. Section 6.4.4 presents an approach to a task-oriented dialogue system by viewing utterances from different domains and dialogue act types as various tasks.

6.4.2 Few-shot personalizing dialogue generation

Personalizing dialogue has become more popular in today's world. However, accurately capturing a persona remains challenging, primarily because learning from a few sentences and extracting personal descriptions according to real-person conversations is insufficient for constructing a persona.

To tackle this issue by solely leveraging a collection of conversations with the same persona, Lin and colleagues (Lin et al., 2019) proposed a personalized dialogue system with a MAML backbone trained on a few historical dialogues without persona descriptions. This persona-independent framework is named Persona-Agnostic Meta-Learning (PAML). The official code is available at https://github.com/HLTCHKUST/PAML. It treats different personas as diverse tasks under meta-training and learns initialization for fast adaptation based on limited dialogue data.

In contrast, regular persona-conditioned dialogue systems are expressed in Eq. (6.9), where $Y = u_t$ denotes the output response given all previous utterances $X = \{u_1, \ldots, u_{t-1}\}$, $P = \{p_1, \ldots, p_m\}$ denotes a collection of sentences for persona description, and f_θ represents a personalized dialogue model:

$$f_\theta(Y|X, P; \theta) = p\big(u_t|u_{1:t-1}, p_{1:m}; \theta\big) \tag{6.9}$$

PAML is only conditioned on the dialogue history formatted in Eq. (6.10), without a persona representation ($P = \{p_1, p_2, \ldots, p_m\}$):

$$f_\theta(Y|X; \theta) = p(u_t|u_{1:t-1}; \theta) \tag{6.10}$$

Referring to the work of Finn's team (2017), the meta-objective function is expressed in Eq. (6.11), where $f_{\theta'_{p_i}}$ denotes an adaptative model for novel dialogues in a validation set as a batch of personas $\mathcal{D}_{p_i}^{\text{valid}}$, and α is the learning rate of inner optimization:

$$\min_\theta \sum_{\mathcal{D}_{p_i} \sim \mathcal{D}_{\text{train}}} \mathcal{L}_{\mathcal{D}_{p_i}^{\text{valid}}}\left(f_{\theta'_{p_i}}\right) = \sum_{\mathcal{D}_{p_i} \sim \mathcal{D}_{\text{train}}} \mathcal{L}_{\mathcal{D}_{p_i}^{\text{valid}}}\left(f_{\theta - \alpha \nabla_\theta \mathcal{L}_{\mathcal{D}_{pi}^{\text{train}}}(f_\theta)}\right) \tag{6.11}$$

The meta-updating rule is expressed in Eq. (6.12) with second-order optimization partial derivatives. β denotes the learning rate in the outer optimization.

$$\theta \leftarrow \theta - \beta \sum_{\mathcal{D}_{p_i} \sim \mathcal{D}_{\text{train}}} \nabla_\theta \mathcal{L}_{\mathcal{D}_{p_i}^{\text{valid}}}\left(f_{\theta'_{p_i}}\right) \tag{6.12}$$

This baseline is conducted by a standard Transformer architecture (Vaswani et al., 2017) and pretrained Glove embedding (Pennington, Socher, & Manning, 2014). The step-by-step PAML algorithm is outlined in Table 6.6.

This model is assessed on the Persona-Chat dataset (Zhang et al., 2018) in automatic measures and human-evaluated fluency and consistency. Quantitative evaluation metrics include perplexity (PPL), the Bilingual Evaluation Understudy score (BLEU; Papineni, Roukos, Ward, & Zhu, 2002), and a customized consistency score.

TABLE 6.6 Summarized methods of persona-agnostic meta-learning.

Input: $\mathcal{D}_{\text{train}}$, training dataset
$\quad\quad\quad \alpha, \beta$: hyperparameters of step size
1: Randomly initialize θ
2: **while** not done **do**
3: $\quad$ Sample a batch of persona $\mathcal{D}_{p_i} \sim \mathcal{D}_{\text{train}}$
4: $\quad$ **for all** $\mathcal{D}_{p_i}$ **do**
5: $\quad\quad$ Construct $\left(\mathcal{D}_{p_i}^{\text{train}}, \mathcal{D}_{p_i}^{\text{valid}}\right) \sim \mathcal{D}_{p_i}$
6: $\quad\quad$ Apply $\mathcal{D}_{p_i}^{\text{train}}$ to obtain $\nabla_\theta \mathcal{L}_{\mathcal{D}_{p_i}^{\text{train}}}(f_\theta)$
7: $\quad\quad$ Evaluate adapted parameters as $\theta'_{p_i} = \theta - \alpha \nabla_\theta \mathcal{L}_{\mathcal{D}_{p_i}^{\text{train}}}(f_\theta)$
8: $\quad$ **end for**
9: $\quad$ Update $\theta \leftarrow \theta - \beta \sum_{\mathcal{D}_{p_i} \sim \mathcal{D}_{\text{train}}} \nabla_\theta \mathcal{L}_{\mathcal{D}_{p_i}^{\text{valid}}}\left(f_{\theta'_{p_i}}\right)$
10: **end while**

Modified from Lin, Z., Madotto, A., Wu, C.-S., & Fung, P. (2019). Personalizing dialogue agents via meta-learning. In ACL.

6.4.3 Domain adaptation in a dialogue system

Due to the scarcity of training data, an adaptation from the existing sample-sufficient domain to the new sample-insufficient domain has become a standard approach in dialogue system tasks. Nevertheless, differences between each domain can be large. This divergence leads to difficulty when leveraging knowledge from the sample-sufficient to the sample-insufficient domain.

Qian and Yu (2019) proposed a robust end-to-end domain-adaptive dialogue generation method built on MAML, named DAML. It conducts a two-step gradient update to learn from different source domains that are sample-sufficient, and then adapts target domains with sample-insufficient training samples. The official code is available at https://github.com/qbetterk/DAML.git. The architecture comparison between DAML and the regular dialogue system is indicated in Fig. 6.4.

DAML consists of a two-stage CopyNet (Gu, Lu, Li, & Li, 2016) and an extended Sequicity model (Lei et al., 2018) under a single seq2seq encoder-decoder structure. This framework equips MAML for the initialization of an efficient adaptation. Table 6.7 summarizes its step-by-step methods, r represents the system responses, c denotes the context, such as $c = \{B_{t-1}, R_{t-1}, U_t\}$ at time t where B_{t-1} means the belief span at a previous time step $t-1$, R_{t-1} denotes the previous system responses, and U_t is the user utterance at the current time step t.

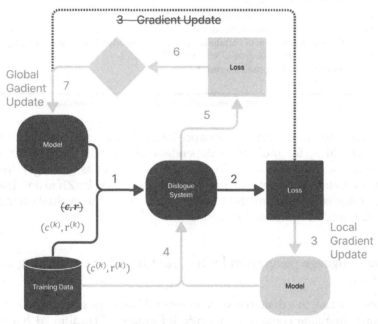

FIG. 6.4 General pipeline of DAML. The regular gradient update procedure is denoted by *red boxes* (*dark gray* in print version), step numbers, and *arrows*. The DAML procedure is built on the regular procedures with modifications displayed by *yellow boxes* (*light gray* in print version), *arrows*, and step numbers. The *dashed line* and step 3 gradient update in *red* (*dark gray* in print version) is replaced by the updated steps 3–7 in *yellow* (*light gray* in print version). *Modified from Qian, K., & Yu, Z. (2019). Domain adaptive dialog generation via meta learning. In ACL.*

TABLE 6.7 Summarized methods of DAML.

Input: dataset on source domain D_{train}^S
    $\alpha; \beta$, hyperparameters
    c, context
Output: a updated meta-learner $\mathcal{M}$

---

1. *Randomly initialize model $\mathcal{M}$*

2. **while** *not done* **do**

3.   **for** $S_k \in$ *Source Domain* **do**

4.   Sample data $c^{(k)}$ from D_{train}^S

5.   Evaluate $\mathcal{M}'_k = \mathcal{M} - \alpha \nabla_{\mathcal{M}} \mathcal{L}_{S_k}\left(\mathcal{M}, c^{(k)}\right)$

6.   Compute $\mathcal{L}_{S_k}\left(\mathcal{M}'_k, c^{(k)}\right)$

7.   **end for**

8. $\mathcal{M} \leftarrow \mathcal{M} - \beta \nabla_{\mathcal{M}} \sum_{S_k} \mathcal{L}_{S_k}\left(\mathcal{M}'_k, c^{(k)}\right)$

9. **end while**

10. Compute loss function $\mathcal{L}(\mathcal{M}, c)$

11.   **return** *cross-entropy* $(\mathcal{M}(c))$

 # Dialogue system

12. Compute $\mathcal{M}\left(c^{(k)} = \left\{B_{t-1}^{(k)}, R_{t-1}^{(k)}, U_t^{(k)}\right\}\right)$

       # Obtain $E_{B_{t-1}}, E_{R_{t-1}}, E_{U_t}$

13.   Obtain $h = \text{Encoder}(B_{t-1}^{(k)}, R_{t-1}^{(k)}, U_t^{(k)})$

14.   Obtain $B_t = \text{BspanDecoder}(h)$

       # Input the outputs of Database $m_t^{(k)}$, Bspan Decoder B_t, Encoder $E_{B_{t-1}}, E_{R_{t-1}}, E_{U_t}$

15.   Obtain $R_t = \text{ResponseDecoder}(h, B_t^{(k)}, m_t^{(k)})$

       # Output of Response Decoder

16.   **return** R_t

Modified from Qian, K., & Yu, Z. (2019). Domain adaptive dialog generation via meta learning. In ACL.

DAML achieved state-of-the-art performance based on the simulated dataset by SimDial (Zhao & Eskenazi, 2018) for multiple independent domains. It utilizes three domains—restaurant, weather, and bus—as source data and takes movies as the target domain. DAML outperforms the selected zero-shot dialogue generation method by Zhao and Eskenazi (2018) and the chosen transfer learning method by Caruana (1997). The evaluation metrics refer to the BLEU score, Entity F1 score, and adapting time.

6.4.4 Natural language generation by few-shot learning concerning task-oriented dialogue systems

As a fundamental task in a dialogue system, natural language generation aims to generate natural-sounding language containing specific information. Traditional hand-crafted and rule-based strategies rely heavily on large-scale human engineering, resulting in monotonic and straightforward utterances with minimal linguistic variations. Due to dataset limitations, considerable overfitting remains inevitable concerning domain adaptation.

Mi and colleagues (Mi et al., 2019) focused on natural language generation (NLG) under a few resources setting and proposed a model-agnostic optimization-based task-oriented dialogue system, namely Meta-NLG. This framework aims to train a good initialization for fast adaptation through MAML. It treats utterances in different domains and dialog-act types as various tasks.

NLG problems conditioned on semantic representation (i.e., dialogue act; DA) can be formulated into Eq. (6.13). The output sentence in length T is generated based on all words before the current term and DA of the sentence. $\mathbf{d}$ denotes the representations of dialogue act of sentences $\mathbf{Y} = (y_0, ..., y_T)$.

$$f_\theta = P(\mathbf{Y}|\mathbf{d}; \theta) = \prod_{t=1}^{T} P(y_t|y_0, ..., y_{t-1}, \mathbf{d}; \theta) \qquad (6.13)$$

The general idea of Meta-NLG is to train a base model f_θ with high-resource source tasks, followed by fine-tuning on low-resource target tasks during meta-training, as expressed in Eq. (6.14), where θ^S denotes a pretrained initialization parameter θ^s with DA-utterance pairs $D_S = \{(d_j, Y_j)\}_{j \in S}$ from high-resource NLG source tasks. It implements LSTM as its base model f_θ. $\mathcal{D}_t = (\mathbf{d}_t, \mathbf{Y}_t)$ is DA-utterance pairs from a set of low-resource target tasks.

$$\begin{aligned} \theta^* &= \text{Adapt}(\mathcal{D}_t, \theta = \theta^s) = \arg\max_\theta \mathcal{L}_{\mathcal{D}_t}(f_\theta) \\ &= \arg\max_\theta \sum_{(\mathbf{d}_t, \mathbf{Y}_t) \in \mathcal{D}_t} \log p(\mathbf{Y}_t|\mathbf{d}_t; \theta) \end{aligned} \qquad (6.14)$$

The meta-learning objective function is explored in Eqs. (6.15) and (6.16), where $\mathcal{D}_{\mathcal{T}_i}$ denotes meta-training sets and $\mathcal{D}'_{\mathcal{T}_i}$ is meta-test sets under standard meta-learning episode training. θ'_i denotes the updated parameters and α is the learning rate.

$$\theta^{Meta} = \text{MetaLearn}(\boldsymbol{\mathcal{T}}_1, ..., \boldsymbol{\mathcal{T}}_K) = \arg\max_\theta \mathbb{E}_i \mathbb{E}_{\mathcal{D}_{\mathcal{T}_i}, \mathcal{D}'_{\mathcal{T}_i}} \mathcal{L}_{\mathcal{D}'_{\mathcal{T}_i}}\left(f_{\theta'_i}\right) \qquad (6.15)$$

$$\theta'_i = \text{Adapt}(\mathcal{D}_{\mathcal{T}_i}, \theta) = \theta - \alpha \nabla_\theta \mathcal{L}_{\mathcal{D}_{\mathcal{T}_i}}(f_\theta) \qquad (6.16)$$

Referring to MAML, Meta-NLG utilized the Hessian matrix H_θ for the second-order gradient, expressed in Eq. (6.17), where β denotes the hyperparameter of the learning rate with recommended value of 0.001:

$$\begin{aligned} \theta^* &= \theta - \beta \sum_{i=1}^{K} \nabla_\theta \mathcal{L}_{\mathcal{D}'_{\mathcal{T}_i}}\left(f_{\theta'_i}\right) \\ &= \theta - \beta \sum_{i=1}^{K} \nabla_\theta \mathcal{L}_{\mathcal{D}'_{\mathcal{T}_i}}\left(f_{\theta'_i}\right) \cdot \nabla_\theta(\theta'_i) \\ &= \theta - \beta \sum_{i=1}^{K} \nabla_\theta \mathcal{L}_{\mathcal{D}'_{\mathcal{T}_i}}\left(f_{\theta'_i}\right) \cdot \nabla_\theta\left(\theta - \alpha \nabla_\theta \mathcal{L}_{\mathcal{D}_{\mathcal{T}_i}}(f_\theta)\right) \\ &= \theta - \beta \sum_{i=1}^{K} \nabla_\theta \mathcal{L}_{\mathcal{D}'_{\mathcal{T}_i}}\left(f_{\theta'_i}\right) - \alpha \nabla_{\theta'_i} \mathcal{L}_{\mathcal{D}'_{\mathcal{T}_i}}\left(f_{\theta'_i}\right) \cdot H_\theta\left(\mathcal{L}_{\mathcal{D}_{\mathcal{T}_i}}(f_\theta)\right) \end{aligned} \qquad (6.17)$$

The detailed Meta-NLG methods are demonstrated in Table 6.8.

TABLE 6.8   Summarized training methods of meta-NLG.

Input: $f_\theta, \theta_0, \mathcal{D}_s, \alpha, \beta$
Output: θ^{Meta}

1: Initialize θ
2: **while** θ not converge **do**
3:      Imitate a batch of *Meta NLG* tasks $\left\{ \mathcal{T}_i = \left(\mathcal{D}_{\mathcal{T}_i}, \mathcal{D}'_{\mathcal{T}_i} \right) \right\}_{i=1}^{K}$

4:      **for** $i = 1 \ldots K$, **do**
5:          Update $\theta'_i = \theta - \alpha \nabla_\theta \mathcal{L}_{\mathcal{D}_{\mathcal{T}_i}} \left(f_\theta \right)$
6:      **end for**

     # **meta-update**
7:      Update $\theta = \theta - \beta \sum_{i=1}^{K} \nabla_\theta \mathcal{L}_{\mathcal{D}'_{\mathcal{T}_i}} \left(f_{\theta'_i} \right)$
8: **end while**

9: Return θ^{Meta}

Modified from Mi, F., Huang, M., Zhang, J., & Faltings, B. (2019). Meta-learning for low-resource natural language generation in task-oriented dialogue systems. In IJCAI.

This system is evaluated on a multidomain dialogue dataset MultiWOZ (Budzianowski et al., 2018), which contains versatile linguistic variations. The evaluation metrics include:

- The BLEU (Papineni et al., 2002)
- The slot error rate (ERR; Chinchor, 1995) for domain-adaptation performance
- The informativeness (i.e., whether the result captures comprehensive information)
- The naturalness (i.e., whether the result is reasonably similar to an expression generated by a human)
- The Fleiss kappa value (Fleiss, 1971) for interrater consistency

Meta-NLG also achieved good performance in near-domain adaptations with a small adaptation size. However, the performance is reduced as the target and source domains become more different or the adaption size increases.

6.5 Knowledge graph

6.5.1 Introduction

In 1956 the equivalent concept of graphical knowledge representation was first proposed by Richens as an idea of semantic net (Richens, 1956). Knowledge-based reasoning grew in use among various systems that expected high-degree expertise in particular domains, such as protein structure analysis and construction-site layout (Ji, Pan, Cambria, Marttinen, & Yu, 2021). As Google's search engine dominated internet search tools through the knowledge fusion approach named Knowledge Vault (Dong et al., 2014) in 2012, large-scaled knowledge graphs attracted more attention. While no single formal definition is widely accepted, many researchers have provided multiple definitions of knowledge graphs from various views (Ehrlinger & Woß, 2016; Hogan et al., 2021; Paulheim, 2017; Wang, Mao, Wang, & Guo, 2017).

A knowledge graph is a multirelational graph of entities, relations, and facts. There are four taxonomies of tasks in a knowledge graph (Ji et al., 2021):

- Knowledge representation learning primarily focused on representation space, encoding model, scoring function, and auxiliary information
- Knowledge acquisition, where subtasks include knowledge graph completion (KGC), named entity recognition (NER), and relation extraction (RE; see explorations in Section 6.7)
- Temporal knowledge graphs that conduct temporal knowledge for representation learning
- Knowledge-aware applications, such as dialog system

Knowledge graph completion concentrates on learning embeddings in low dimensions for triple prediction. Reinforcement (RL) learning-based pathfinding—one of the major approaches—uses multihop reasoning with deep RL methods, particularly the Markov decision process (MDP). The policy-based agent aims to extend the reasoning paths based on the knowledge graph environment through policy gradient methods. Various attempts include DeepPath (Xiong, Hoang, & Wang, 2017), MINERVA (Das et al., 2018), Hop (Lin, Socher, & Xiong, 2018), M-Walk (Shen, Chen, Huang, Guo, & Gao, 2018), and CPL (Fu, Chen, Qu, Jin, & Ren, 2019). Section 6.5.2 discusses a meta-learning approach based on MAML under a few-shot setting.

Named entity recognition aims to provide tags to entities. Named-entity recognition (NER; also named entity extraction, entity identification, or entity chunking) is a subfield of information extraction and retrieval, which detects and categories named entities from an unstructured text into predetermined categories (e.g., person, location, organization). For example, the natural language as

Gina went to Google in 2010.

is detected and classified as:

$$[\text{Gina}]_{\text{person}} \text{ went to } [\text{Google}]_{\text{organization}} \text{ in } [2010]_{\text{time}}.$$

Early research heavily relied on hand-crafted features, whereas current attempts implement neural architectures, such as MGNER (Xia et al., 2019) and work by Hu, Dou, Nie, and Wen (2020), Lample, Ballesteros, Subramanian, Kawakami, and Dyer (2016), Chiu and Nichols (2016), and Li and colleagues (2020). Section 6.5.5 presents a cross-lingual NER framework that operates via transferrable knowledge from sample-sufficient source languages to sample-insufficient target languages.

Deep learning-based methods for **knowledge graph question answering** (KG-QA) aim to project answers and natural language questions into a semantic space or to employ symbolic knowledge injection for common-sense reasoning (Ji et al., 2021). Variety discussions can be divided into two types: single-fact QA (see (Chen et al., 2019); Dai, Li, & Xu, 2016) and complex multihop reasoning (see Bauer, Wang, & Bansal, 2018; Zhang et al., 2018).

The common datasets and benchmarks for the general knowledge graph include Cord-19 (Wang et al., 2020), Atomic (Sap et al., 2019), semantic scholar (Ammar et al., 2018), ReDial (Li et al., 2018), MetaQA (Zhang, Dai, Kozareva, Smola, & Song, 2018), and ComplexWeb-Question (Talmor & Berant, 2018). For task-specific datasets, see Table 6.9.

Even though knowledge graphs aid natural language processing tasks in multiple fields, researchers still face some challenges. It is impractical to assume that all relations within knowledge graphs are sufficiently trained. The long-tailed knowledge graph only contains several triples as few-shot relations. Additionally, the process of answering complex

TABLE 6.9　Details of datasets and benchmarks regarding knowledge graph tasks.

Task	Dataset	References
Knowledge representation learning	WN18-IMG	Xie, Liu, Luan, and Sun (2017)
Relation extraction	SemEval 2010	Hendrickx et al. (2009)
	NYT	Riedel, Yao, and McCallum (2010)
Sentiment analysis	IsaCore	Cambria, Song, Wang, and Howard (2012)
Few-shot relation classification	FewRel	Han et al. (2018)
Entity alignment	DBP15K	Sun, Hu, and Li (2017)
Multiview knowledge graphs	DB111K-174	Hao, Chen, Yu, Sun, and Wang (2019)
	YAGO26K-906	Hao et al. (2019)
Multilanguage	ConceptNet	Speer et al. (2017)

Modified from Ji, S., Pan, S., Cambria, E., Marttinen, P., & Yu, P. S. (2021). A survey on knowledge graphs: Representation, acquisition and applications. IEEE Transactions on Neural Networks and Learning Systems.

questions over the knowledge base maintains unique discrete aggregation behaviors. Furthermore, transfer learning becomes inapplicable for named-entity recognition when the target languages have no annotated samples.

Meta-learning approaches offer more possibilities to solve these issues. Multihop reasoning can be conducted on knowledge graphs, and reasonable and efficient methods through meta-learning can address few-shot relations. Moreover, knowledge graph incompleteness can be solved via link prediction, particularly with training sample scarcity.

The rest of this section will review multiple subfields under the knowledge graph and provide different ways to solve the problems or format the tasks. Section 6.5.2 explores multihop reasoning through a relation-specific multihop reasoning agent based on the policy method and meta-learning. Section 6.5.3 discusses a subtask of knowledge graph completion—link prediction—through relation-specific meta information. Section 6.5.4 examines a single-round question answering system based on a complex knowledge base. In contrast, Section 6.5.5 presents an approach for cross-lingual named entity recognition from sample-sufficient languages to sample-insufficient target languages.

6.5.2　Multihop knowledge graph reasoning in few-shot scenarios

Knowledge graphs play a vital role in natural language processing tasks. Most of standard knowledge graph-based approaches assume that all relations have sufficient training triples. Conversely, few-shot relations commonly exist, such as long-tailed knowledge graph relations, which only maintain a few triples. The current zero-shot and one-shot solutions either lack interpretability or are impractical in real-world situations.

To solve this issue, Lv et al. (2019) proposed few-shot relations for multihop reasoning over a knowledge graph named Meta-KGR. This approach equipped multihop reasoning over knowledge graphs and constructed reasonable and efficient methods through meta-learning. The multihop reasoning is usually conducted on query answering systems over incomplete knowledge graphs with a reinforcement learning setup (Lin et al., 2018). It focuses on the symbolic inference rules learned from relational paths and is viewed as a sequence of decision problems. This framework applies knowledge graph embedding (Bordes, Usunier, Duran, Weston, & Yakhnenko, 2013) methods. It projects entities and relations from high-dimensional spaces into low-dimensional ones; a score function $f(e_s, r, e_o)$ estimates the probability of whether a triple is true. A meta-learner (i.e., a modified MAML) is involved in rapid task adaption through an optimal initiation over few-shot relations through shared and common features among different tasks. It treats the triple queries that share the same relation r over KGs as one task. The official code is available at https://github.com/ THU-KEG/MetaKGR.

This approach consists of two modules:

- A relation-specific multihop reasoning agent is based on an on-policy method to determine the target entities and effective reasoning paths for a given relation r. The searching approach can be viewed as a customized Markov decision process (MDP). In a parametrized policy network defined as Eq. (6.18), the search path can be encoded through an LSTM, as expressed in Eq. (6.19). $\pi_\theta(a_t | s_t)$ indicates the probability distribution of all potential actions, $\mathbf{A}_t$ denotes an action space, $\widehat{\mathbf{e}}_t$ is the current entity over knowledge graph, $\mathbf{r}_q$ means query relation, and $\mathbf{h}_t$ represents the encoded search path through LSTM on the pervious action $\mathbf{a}_{t-1}$.

$$\pi_\theta(a_t | s_t) = \text{softmax}\left(\mathbf{A}_t\left(\mathbf{W}_2 \text{ReLU}\left(\mathbf{W}_1\left[\widehat{\mathbf{e}}_t; \mathbf{h}_t; \mathbf{r}_q\right]\right)\right)\right) \qquad (6.18)$$

where

$$\mathbf{h}_t = \text{LSTM}(\mathbf{h}_{t-1}, \mathbf{a}_{t-1}) \qquad (6.19)$$

The overall loss function of this module is expressed in Eq. (6.20), where e_s and e_o denote the source and target entity, respectively, s_T represents the state space, and r is the relation:

$$\mathcal{L}_r^{\mathcal{D}}(\theta) = -\mathbb{E}_{(e_s, r, e_o) \in \mathcal{D}} \mathbb{E}_{a_1, \dots, a_{T-1} \in \pi_\theta}[R(s_T | e_s, r)] \qquad (6.20)$$

- A MAML-based meta-learner is trained according to methods summarized in Table 6.10.

TABLE 6.10   Summarized methods of meta-KGR.

Input: $p(\mathcal{R})$: distribution over relations α, β: learning rate hyperparameters
1: Randomly initialize θ 2: **while** *not converged* **do** 3:   Construct a batch of relations $r \sim p(\mathcal{R})$ 4:   **for** all relation r **do** 5:   Construct support set $\mathcal{D}_S$, query set $\mathcal{D}_Q$ respect to task $\mathcal{T}_r$ 6:   Compute $\nabla_\theta L_r^{\mathcal{D}_S}(\theta)$ with Eq. (6.20) 7:   Evaluate adapted parameters as $\theta_r' = \theta - \alpha \nabla_\theta L_r^{\mathcal{D}_S}(\theta)$ 8:   **end for** 9:   Update $\theta \leftarrow \theta - \beta \nabla_\theta \sum_{\mathcal{T}_r} L_r^{\mathcal{D}_Q}(\theta_r')$ 10: **end while**

Modified from Lv, X., Gu, Y., Han, X., Hou, L., Li, J., & Liu, Z. (2019). Adapting meta knowledge graph information for multi-hop reasoning over few-shot Relations. In ACL.

This approach is trained and evaluated on two public datasets: Freebase (FB15K-237l; Toutanova et al., 2015) and NELL (NELL-995; Xiong et al., 2017).

6.5.3 Knowledge graphs link prediction in few-shot scenarios

Knowledge graph (KG) incompleteness is a problem that considerably reduces the efficiency of KGs. One issue in this regard is few-shot relations, which occur when KG relations only have minimal triples.

To tackle this problem, (Chen et al. (2019) proposed a meta-learning-based few-shot learner for knowledge graphs link prediction, namely Meta Relationship Learning (MetaR). Link prediction is a fundamental task of KGC. In contrast to the solution discussed in Section 6.5.2 through knowledge graph embedding, link prediction maintains good performance even when the training samples are limited. Xiong, Yu, Chang, Guo, and Wang (2018) proposed the first attempt at few-shot link prediction for knowledge graphs, whereas MetaR serves as the second trial. MetaR concentrates on the shared and common knowledge within one task (named relation-specific meta-information), which can rapidly adopt new tasks based on a few training samples and pass on shared relation knowledge from existing triples to incomplete ones. The official code is released at https://github.com/AnselCmy/MetaR.

This model aims to estimate new triples relations based on only a few associative triples by transferring the mutual relation-specific meta-knowledge learned from the support set to the query set. The overall pipeline of this model is shown in Fig. 6.5. MetaR is independent of

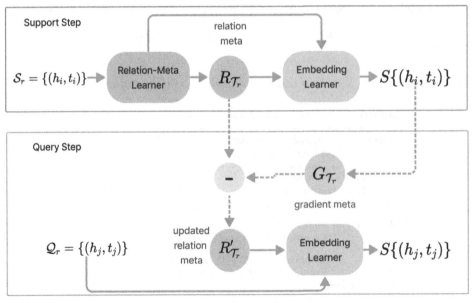

FIG. 6.5 General architecture of MetaR.
Modified from Chen, M., Zhang, W., Zhang, W., Chen, Q., & Chen, H. (2019). Meta relational learning for few-shot link prediction in knowledge graphs. arXiv preprint arXiv:1909.01515.

background knowledge graphs but heavily relies on the number of tasks and sparsity of entities. The model consists of two essential types of meta-information:

- Relation meta-information, in terms of a vector to represent the relation between head entities and tail ones, is extracted in each task via a relation meta-learner. It is passed from the support set to the query set.
- Gradient meta-information, which is the loss gradient of relation meta in a support set, demonstrates the path of relation meta to reach the loss minimal and performs fast learning.

The overall training method of the MetaR algorithm based on these two modules is described in Table 6.11.

The updating policy in relation to meta is expressed in Eqs. (6.21) and (6.22), where R_{T_r}' denotes the updated relation meta from original relation meta R_{T_r}, and β is the step size in gradient meta G_{T_r}. $R_{(h_i,ti)}$ presents a relation meta from the head entity h_i and tail entity t_i, K is the number of samples in support set S_r, γ denotes the hyperparameter for margin, and $s_{(h_i,ti)}$ and $s_{(h_i,ti')}$ represent the score of the positive sample (h_i, t_i) and negative sample (h_i, t_i'), respectively.

$$R_{T_r}' = R_{T_r} - \beta G_{T_r},\tag{6.21}$$

where:

$$R_{T_r} = \frac{\sum_{i=1}^{K} R_{(h_i,t_i)}}{K}, G_{T_r} = \nabla_{R_{T_r}} L(S_r), L(S_r) = \sum_{(h_i,t_i)\in S_r} \left[\gamma + s_{(h_i,t_i)} - s_{(h_i,t_i')}\right]_+\tag{6.22}$$

TABLE 6.11 Summarized training methods of MetaR.

Input: T_{train}, training tasks
   emb, embedding layer
   ϕ, parameter of relation-meta learner

1: **while** not done **do**
2: Construct $T_r = \{S_r, Q_r\}$ from T_{train}
3: Obtain R_{T_r} from S_r, using $x^0 \& = h_i \oplus t_i$, $x^l \& = \sigma(W^l x^{l-1} + b^l)$, $R_{(h_i,ti)} \& = W^L x^{L-1} + b^L$ and $R_{T_r} = \frac{\sum_{i=1}^{K} R_{(h_i,t_i)}}{K}$
4: Evaluate loss function $L(S_r)$ in S_r using $L(S_r) = \sum_{(h_i,t_i)\in S_r}\left[\gamma + s_{(h_i,t_i)} - s_{(h_i,t_i')}\right]+$
5: Obtain G_{T_r} by gradient of R_{T_r} using $G_{T_r} = \nabla_{R_{T_r}} L(S_r)$
6: Evaluate R_{T_r} by G_{T_r} using $R_{T_r}' = R_{T_r} - \beta G_{T_r}$
7: Compute objective function $L(Q_r)$ in Q_r using $L(Q_r) = \sum_{(h_j,t_j)\in Q_r}\left[\gamma + s_{(h_j,t_j)} - s_{(h_j,t_j')}\right]+$
8: Evaluate ϕ and *emb* by loss in Q_r
9: **end while**

Modified from Chen, M., Zhang, W., Zhang, W., Chen, Q., & Chen, H. (2019). Meta relational learning for few-shot link prediction in knowledge graphs. arXiv preprint arXiv:1909.01515.

The training objective is shown in Eq. (6.23), where $Q_r = \{(h_j, t_j)\}$ denotes the query set:

$$L(Q_r) = \sum_{(h_j, t_j) \in Q_r} \left[\gamma + s_{(h_j, t_j)} - s_{(h_j, t_j')} \right]_+ \tag{6.23}$$

This strategy is evaluated using NELL-One (Carlson et al., 2010) and Wiki-One (Vrandecic & Krotzsch, 2014) datasets.

6.5.4 Knowledge base complex question answering

Knowledge base (KB) complex question answering (CQA) is a task-focused on mapping a natural language query to a logical form to execute the desired answers over the knowledge base (Berant et al., 2013; Shen et al., 2019). CQA maintains unique discrete aggregation actions (e.g., intersection, union, count) to produce answers (Hua et al., 2020).

Hua et al. (2020) introduced a meta-learning neural programmer-interpreter system for CQA over a knowledge base, named Meta Retrieval Learning (MARL). It aims to adapt and convert the unseen question quickly to a series of actions to produce correct answers over the knowledge base. Unlike the previous meta-learner, Seq2Action model (S2A; Guo et al., 2019) trains retrievers and programmers independently on a multiround conversation to tackle context-dependent questions. MARL focuses on a single-round question training retriever and programmer jointly and alternately. The official code is available at https://github.com/DevinJake/MARL.

MARL addresses broadly diverse questions across less common knowledge bases through two-stage weak supervision with two networks (see Fig. 6.6 for its workflow):

- A programmer network $\pi(\tau \,|\, q_i; \theta)$ under an encoder-decoder structure supported by Reptile (see detailed exploration in Section 4.4) to transform primary questions into programs that can be executed over KB
- A retriever network $\pi(q_{c_i} \,|\, q_{pri}; \phi)$ to capture the top-N similar questions (i.e., the secondary questions) to the primary question through REINFORCE (Sutton, McAllester, Singh, & Mansour, 1999)

In the first stage (lines 4–13 in Table 6.12), the programmer is optimized by a meta-reinforcement learning method (meta-RL), fixing the parameters in a retriever. At the second stage (lines 16–30), this framework applies a reinforcement learning method to refer to the reward as a signal to improve the retriever policy.

FIG. 6.6 High-level architecture of two-staged MARL consists of a programmer parameterized by θ and a retriever parameterized by ϕ.
Modified from Hua, Y., Li, Y.-F., Haffari, G., Qi, G., & Wu, W. (2020). Retrieve, program, repeat: Complex knowledge base question answering via alternate meta-learning. In IJCAI.

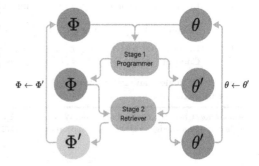

TABLE 6.12 Summarized training methods of MARL.

Input: D_{train}, training set
$\quad\quad$ η_1, η_2, η_3, hyperparameters of step size
Output: The learned parameters θ^* and ϕ^*

---

1 Initialize groups vector ψ, randomly initialize θ and ϕ

2 while *not converged* **do**

3 $\quad$ # **1st stage: the programmer is optimized by the meta-RL while fixing parameters in a retriever**

4 $\quad\quad$ **for** *iteration* **do**

5 $\quad\quad\quad$ Construct a batch of primary questions $D_{\text{pri}} \sim D_{\text{train}}$

6 $\quad\quad\quad$ **for each** $q_{pri} \in D_{pri}$ **do**

7 $\quad\quad\quad\quad$ Retrieve $s^{q_{pri}}$ using ϕ and ψ

8 $\quad\quad\quad\quad$ Evaluate $\mathcal{L} = \sum_{q_i \in s^{q_{pri}}} \mathbb{E}_{\tau \sim \pi(\tau | q_i; \theta)}[R(\tau)]$

9 $\quad\quad\quad\quad$ Obtain adapted parameters as $\theta' \leftarrow \theta + \eta_1 \nabla_\theta \mathcal{L}$

10 $\quad\quad\quad\quad$ Compute $J_{q_{pri}}(\theta') \overset{\text{def}}{=} \mathbb{E}_{\tau' \sim \pi(\tau' | q_{pri}; \theta')}[R(\tau')]$

11 $\quad\quad\quad$ **end for**

12 $\quad\quad\quad$ Evaluate $\theta \leftarrow \theta + \eta_2 \nabla_\theta \sum_{q_{pri} \in D_{pri}} J_{q_{pri}}(\theta')$

13 $\quad\quad$ **end for**

14 $\quad$ $\theta^* \leftarrow \theta$

15 $\quad$ # **2nd stage: apply a reinforcement learning method to refer to the reward as a signal to improve the reliever policy**

16 $\quad\quad$ **for** *iteration* **do**

17 $\quad\quad\quad$ Construct a batch of primary questions $D_{\text{pri}} \sim D_{\text{train}}$

18 $\quad\quad\quad$ **for each** $q_{pri} \in D_{pri}$ **do**

19 $\quad\quad\quad\quad$ Obtain $\tau^* \leftarrow \text{decode}(\pi(\tau | q_{pri}; \theta^*))$

20 $\quad\quad\quad\quad$ Evaluate reward function $R(\tau^*)$

21 $\quad\quad\quad\quad$ Construct support sets $\mathcal{M}$ using ϕ and ψ

22 $\quad\quad\quad\quad$ **for each** $s_m^{q_{pri}} \in \mathcal{M}$ **do**

23 $\quad\quad\quad\quad\quad$ Obtain $\theta_m^{*'} \leftarrow \theta^* + \eta_1 \nabla_{\theta^*} \sum_{q_i \in s_m^{q_{pri}}} \mathbb{E}_{\tau \sim \pi(\tau | q_i; \theta^*)} R(\tau)$

24 $\quad\quad\quad\quad\quad$ Obtain $\tau_m^{*'} \leftarrow \text{decode}(\pi(\tau | q_{pri}; \theta_m^{*'}))$

25 $\quad\quad\quad\quad\quad$ Evaluate reward function $R(\tau_m^{*'})$

26 $\quad\quad\quad\quad$ **end for**

27 $\quad\quad\quad\quad$ Compute $J_{q_{pri}}(\phi) \overset{\text{def}}{=}$

28 $\quad\quad\quad$ **end for**

29 $\quad\quad\quad$ Evaluate $\mathbb{E}_{s_m^{q_{pri}} \sim P(s^{q_{pri}})}[R(\tau_m^{*'}) - R(\tau^*)]$

30 $\quad\quad$ **end for**

31 $\quad$ $\phi^* \leftarrow \phi$
32 end while

33 Return the learned θ^* and ϕ^*

Modified from Hua, Y., Li, Y.-F., Haffari, G., Qi, G., & Wu, W. (2020). Retrieve, program, repeat: Complex knowledge base question answering via alternate meta-learning. In IJCAI.

6.5.5 Named-entity recognition in cross-lingual scenarios

Named-entity recognition is a foundation of a variety of downstream tasks. A common strategy, based on transfer learning, is to leverage knowledge from a high-resources source language, which will have sufficient annotated training samples, to a low-resource target language with a typically small amount of annotated data. One extreme situation in this regard is where only a high-resources source language is available, while other target languages include no annotated samples.

To solve this problem, Wu et al. (2020) proposed a MAML backbone cross-lingual strategy for named-entity recognition in low-resource annotated languages. Motivated by Wu and Dredze (2019) and Lample and Conneau (2019), this framework transfers knowledge from a well-studied high-resource source language (e.g., English, which maintained the 93.39% of F-measure on MUC-7, whereas human experts scored 97.60% and 96.95%; Chinchor, 2005; Marsh & Perzanowski, 1998) to low-resource target languages (e.g., Spanish, Dutch, German, French, and Chinese) with limited labeled data.

To enhance the capability of transferring knowledge among different languages, the strategy proposed a masking scheme on named entities and inserted a maximum term into the loss function during meta-training. It utilizes sentence cosine similarities to perform multiple pseudo-NER tasks during meta-training. The official code is released at https://github.com/microsoft/vert-papers/tree/master/papers/Meta-Cross.

This framework employs multilingual BERT (mBERT; Devlin, Chang, Lee, & Toutanova, 2018) as the base model for word representations with WordPiece embeddings (Wu et al., 2016) for tokenization. A SoftMax linear classification layer is added to the pretrained mBERT, as expressed in Eqs. (6.24) and (6.25). A sequence $x = \{x_l\}_{l=1}^{L}$ with L tokens is fed into the pretrained mBERT model to produce , which represents the probability distribution with respect to x_l. is the intermediate output with input x_l from mBERT. W and are learnable parameters.

$$h = \text{mBERT}(x) \tag{6.24}$$

$$\hat{y}_l = \text{softmax}(Wh_l + b) \tag{6.25}$$

The step-by-step meta-training methods are outlined in Table 6.13, where the model is tested on the unlabeled data.

Notice that g_i is the meta-gradient on each task with first-order approximation instead of the Jacobian matrix $\nabla_\theta(\theta_i')$, as expanded in Eq. (6.26). $D_{test}^{\mathcal{T}_i}$ presents testing set for meta-task $\mathcal{T}_i$ and θ_i' denotes the updated parameter:

$$g_i = \nabla_{\theta_i'} \mathcal{L}_{D_{test}^{\mathcal{T}_i}} (\theta_i') \tag{6.26}$$

A masking scheme (Devlin et al., 2018), [MASK], conducts token-level mask entities in each training sample so that "each token inside an entity can be randomly masked under a given probability" (Wu et al., 2020). This leads to lower dependence of target entity representations and stimulates the framework to predict based on context information.

A max loss function drives the framework to pay more attention to the token with higher losses than others, as expressed in Eq. (6.27), where λ denotes the weighting coefficient, and y_i and $\hat{y}$ represent the ground truth label and estimated label, respectively:

TABLE 6.13 Summarized meta-training and adaptation methods of cross-lingual named-entity recognition.

Input: D_{train}^{S}
       D_{test}^{T}

1: # META-TRAIN (D_{train}^{S}, α, β)
2:     Set $\mathcal{T} = \{\mathcal{T}_i\}$ from D_{train}^{S}
3:     Apply the pre-trained base model $\mathcal{M}_\theta$ for initialization
4:     **while** not done **do**
5:         Sample a batch of $\mathcal{T}_i$ from $\mathcal{T}$, $\mathcal{T}_i$ are source tasks
6:         **for all** $\mathcal{T}_i$ **do**
7:             Evaluate $\theta_i' = U^n(\theta; \alpha)$.
8:             Evaluate $g_i = \nabla_{\theta_i'} \mathcal{L}_{D_{\text{test}}^{T_i}(\theta_i)}$.
9:         **end for**
10:     Evaluate $\theta \leftarrow \theta - \beta \sum_i g_i$
11:     **end while**
12: # θ^* **denotes the overall updated** θ
13:     **return** $\mathcal{M}_{\theta^*}$

14:   # ADAPTATION $\left(\mathcal{M}_{\theta^*}, D_{\text{train}}^{S}, D_{\text{test}}^{T}, \gamma\right)$
15:     **for all** $x^{(j)} \in D_{\text{test}}^{T}$ **do**
16:         $D_{\text{test}}^{T_j} = x^{(j)}$, built $D_{\text{train}}^{T_j}$ from D_{train}^{S}
17:         Evaluate $\hat{\theta}_j = \theta^* - \gamma \nabla_{\theta^*} \mathcal{L}_{D_{\text{train}}^{T_j}}$
18:         Apply $\mathcal{M}_{\hat{\theta}_j}$ to assign label $x^{(j)}$ to $D_{\text{test}}^{T_j}$
19:     **end for**

Modified from Wu, Q., Lin, Z., Wang, G., Chen, H., Karlsson, B. F., Huang, B., & Lin, C.-Y. (2020). Enhanced meta-learning for cross-lingual named entity recognition with minimal resources. In AAAI.

$$\mathcal{L}(\theta) = -\frac{1}{L} \sum_{i=1}^{L} CrossEntropy(y_i, \hat{y}_i) - \lambda \max_{i \in 1,2,\ldots,L} CrossEntropy(y_i, \hat{y}_i) \tag{6.27}$$

The masking scheme and max loss-function structures lead to an 8.76% improvement in F1-score as the state-of-the-art performance.

The experiments are evaluated on four benchmark datasets:

- CoNLL-2002 (Tjong Kim Sang, 2002) for Spanish and Dutch NER
- CoNLL-2003 (Tjong Kim Sang and De Meulder, 2003) for English and German NER
- Europeana Newspapers (Neudecker, 2016) for French NER
- MSRA (Cao, Chen, Liu, Zhao and Liu, 2018) for Chinese NER

6.6 Relation extraction

6.6.1 Introduction

Relation extraction (RE) is a task seeking to extract structured information from unstructured artifacts. It has many applications, such as bio-text mining and named entity recognition. The relation is defined as a tuple $t = (e_1, e_2, ..., e_n)$, and the e_i denotes the entities of a predetermined relation r within document D.

Early attempts at supervised relation extraction heavily leaned on feature-based approaches (Kambhatla, 2004; Zhao & Grishman, 2005) and kernel algorithms, such as tree kernel methods (Zelenko, Aone, & Richardella, 2003). Then, semisupervised methods and bootstrapping strategies drew increasing interest, including DIPRE (Brin, 1998) and Snowball (Agichtein & Gravano, 2000).

Recent approaches equipped with deep neural networks can be divided into the following categories (Aydar, Bozal, & Ozbay, 2020; Gao, 2019):

- Sentence-level relation extraction aims to classify the relations of new entity pairs in a sentence based on a set of predefined relations. Huge consumption of labeled training data is the major limitation of this most classically supervised RE task
- Bag-level relation extraction is usually under distant or weak supervision: the dataset is still large-scale but noisy, imbalanced, or long-tailed. Knowledge graphs (KG) with existing relation triples essentially sort the weakly annotated training data as a reference. The entities in the artifacts are automatically referred to those in the KG. The sentences have the same entity pair, named "bag"
- In document-level relation extraction, multiple entities share complex intersentence structures that the relations can only be understood across numerous sentences. Regular intrasentence relation extraction typically focuses on single entity pairs
- Few-shot relation extraction combines few-shot learning with relation extraction to improve the learning ability based on a few training samples. Han's team contributed to dataset FewRel (Gao, Han, Zhu et al., 2019), whereas persuasive research efforts include those by Soares, FitzGerald, Ling, and Kwiatkowski (2019), Ye and Ling (2019), and Gao, Han, Liu, and Sun (2019)

The widespread benchmarks and datasets include:

- SemEval 2010 Task-8 (Hendrickx et al., 2009)
- NYT10 (Riedel et al., 2010)
- FewRel (Gao, Han, Zhu, et al., 2019)
- TAC Relation Extraction Dataset (TACRED)
- 2005 Automatic Content Extraction (ACE-2005; Walker, Strassel, Medero, & Maeda, 2005)
- WebNLG (Gardent, Shimorina, Narayan, & Perez-Beltrachini, 2017)
- DocRED (Yao et al., 2019)
- Wiki80 (a dataset modified from FewRel)
- MUC and MEDLINE (PubMed, 2007) for protein-protein interaction and gene building

The regular metrics for evaluation are precision, recall, and F-measure.

Relation classification, a subtask of RE, is prevalent in natural language processing for determining the relationship between two entities. It is primarily applied in question-answering systems, knowledge-based populations, and web searches. Typical relation classifiers are based on recursive networks (Hashimoto, Miwa, Tsuruoka, & Chikayama, 2013; Socher, Huval, Manning, & Ng, 2012), convolutional neural networks (Nguyen & Grishman, 2015; Zeng, Liu, Lai, Zhou, & Zhao, 2014), or recurrent neural networks (Xu et al., 2015; Zhang & Wang, 2015) structures.

Relation extraction is a primary task for a variety of downstream tasks; however, some deficiencies limit their applications and scope. Extensive training datasets are usually unavailable, owing to the cost of expert labeling and sample assembles, as annotated sentences remain in shortage. Distance supervision could produce many synthesis samples, but these are highly noisy. Existing meta-learning approaches provide some improvements, but their generalization performance remains unsatisfactory.

Nevertheless, current studies of meta-learning addresses these dilemmas. Few-shot relation classification is accomplished with a meta-learning framework using gradient-optimized base models for relation classification. In addition, Bayesian meta-learning generates novel relations and tasks under a few-shot or zero-shot setting to tackle sample scarcity in few-shot regimes.

This section investigates relation extraction through three different sides. Section 6.6.2 mainly inspects the relation reclassification in a few-shot setting. Section 6.6.3 concentrates on Bayesian meta-learning to optimize the posterior distribution via stochastic gradient, Langevin dynamic methods.

6.6.2 Few-shot supervised relation classification

Due to the need for human labeling and sample collection, large labeled datasets are expensive to obtain. Thus, practical solutions based on a small number of examples, are required.

Obamuyide and Vlachos (2019) provided a meta-learning strategy tackling relation classification problems under limited supervision and few training data elements within few-step updates, which is named the Meta-Learning Relation Classification (MLRC). This framework is generally model-agnostic to any gradient-optimized base models for relation classification. It treats each relation R_i over distribution $p(R)$ as a task and offers an optimal joint initialization for all relations.

The comprehensive MLRC methods are described in Table 6.14.

TABLE 6.14 Summarized methods of meta-learning relation classification.

Input: $p(\mathcal{R})$, distribution over relations
f_θ, function of relation classification
ϵ, hyperparameter of step size
α : hyperparameter of learning rate

1: Random initialization of θ
2: **while** not done **do**
3:      Sample a batch $\mathcal{B}$ from relations $\mathcal{R}_i \sim p(\mathcal{R})$
4:      **for** all $\mathcal{R}_i$ **do**
5:          Set $\mathcal{D} = \{x^{(j)}, y^{(j)}\}$ from $\mathcal{R}_i$ as training data
6:          Apply $\mathcal{D}$ to obtain $\nabla_\theta \mathcal{L}_{\mathcal{R}_i}(f_\theta)$
7:          Evaluate adapted parameters as $\theta'_i = SGD(\theta_i, \nabla_\theta \mathcal{L}_{\mathcal{R}_i}(f_\theta), \alpha)$
8:      **end for**
meta-update
9:      Evaluate meta-parameters as $\theta = \theta - \epsilon \frac{1}{\mathcal{B}} \sum_{i=1}^{i=\mathcal{B}} (\theta'_i - \theta)$
10: **end while**
11: Regular supervised learning for fine-tuning f_θ

Modified from Obamuyide, A., & Vlachos, A. (2019). Model-agnostic meta-learning for relation classification with limited supervision. In ACL.

This model was applied on top of two supervised multiclass relation classification learners: the position-aware model (TACRED-PA) and the contextual graph convolution network (C-GCN; Zhang et al. (2018)). This strategy is evaluated using two relation classification datasets: SemEval-2010 (SemEval) task 8 (Iris Hendrickx et al., 2009) and TACRED.

6.6.3 Relation extraction with few-shot and zero-shot learning

Relationship extraction, a key element of many natural language processing tasks, is typically examined through supervised learning methods with numerous labeled training sentences. Annotated sentences regarding these tasks are still lacking. One standard approach is distant supervision, which aims to generate additional training samples; however, these generated examples are highly noisy. Another common strategy is meta-learning, which provides some improvements but its generalization performance is weak.

To tackle this issue, Qu and colleagues (Qu et al., 2020) proposed an end-to-end Bayesian meta-learning strategy for relation extraction to estimate the relation for paired entities from a sentence. It aims to address the limitation posed by the lack of labeled training data and expensive computing costs for supervised and semisupervised approaches. Essentially, this strategy seeks to generate novel relations and tasks as supporting training data under a few-shot or zero-shot setting and then extract the global relationship between different relations through a global relation graph, which represents all potential relations. The strategy simulates the uncertainty of prototypical vectors by adding random noises to each gradient descent step like a stochastic modification of MAML. This framework focuses on the prototype vectors' posterior distribution from different relations and optimizes the posterior distribution via a stochastic gradient Langevin dynamics method (Welling & Teh, 2011) over various distributions. The official code is available at https://github.com/DeepGraphLearning/FewShotRE.

The steps are summarized in Table 6.15.

This framework employs Monte Carlo sampling to simulate the log-probability $\log p\left(y_Q|x_Q, x_S, y_S, \mathcal{G}\right)$, as expressed in Eq. (6.28), where $\mathcal{G}$ represents the global relation

TABLE 6.15 Summarized training methods of the proposed strategy.

Input: $\mathcal{R}$, a relation set
$\mathcal{G}$, a global relation graph

1. **while** not converged **do**
2. Construct the targets as a subset of relations $\mathcal{T} \subseteq \mathcal{R}$
3. Construct a support set (x_S, y_S) and a query set (x_Q, y_Q)
4. Conduct GNN $\mathcal{F}$ on the global relation graph $\mathcal{G}$ to evaluate relations' summary vectors $h_\mathcal{T}$
5. Apply equations 6.30 and 6.31 for prototype vectors $\left\{v_\mathcal{T}^{(\ell)}\right\}_{\ell=1}^{L}$ initialization
6. Apply equation 6.29 to evaluate $\widehat{v_\mathcal{T}}$ for M steps
7. Apply equation 6.28 to maximize the log-likelihood function
8. **end while**

Modified from Qu, M., Gao, T., Xhonneux, L.-P. A., & Tang, J. (2020). Few-shot relation extraction via Bayesian meta-learning on relation graphs. In ICML.

graph, y_Q denotes the estimated label for query text x_Q with support sentences (x_S, y_S), and $v_{\mathcal{T}}^{(l)} \sim p(v_{\mathcal{T}}|x_S, y_S, \mathcal{G})$ represents samples selected from the posterior distribution:

$$\log p\left(\mathbf{y}_Q|\mathbf{x}_Q, \mathbf{x}_S, \mathbf{y}_S, \mathcal{G}\right) = \log \mathbb{E}_{p(\mathbf{v}_{\mathcal{T}}|\mathbf{x}_S, \mathbf{y}_S, \mathcal{G})}\left[p\left(\mathbf{y}_Q|\mathbf{x}_Q, \mathbf{v}_{\mathcal{T}}\right)\right] \approx \log \frac{1}{L}\sum_{l=1}^{L} p\left(\mathbf{y}_Q|\mathbf{x}_Q, \mathbf{v}_{\mathcal{T}}^{(l)}\right) \quad (6.28)$$

The updating rule is expressed in Eq. (6.29), where $\hat{v}_T$ denotes the sampled prototypical vector and $\hat{z} \sim \mathcal{N}(0, I)$ is a sample dropped from a standard normal distribution. The component $\nabla_{\hat{v}_T} \log p(\mathbf{y}_S|\mathbf{x}_S, \hat{v}_T)p(\hat{v}_T|h_T)$, as with MAML, strives to maximize the likelihood based on a support set and adjust to the target relations in T. ϵ denotes the step size.

$$\hat{\mathbf{v}}_{\mathcal{T}} \leftarrow \hat{\mathbf{v}}_{\mathcal{T}} + \frac{\epsilon}{2}\nabla_{\hat{\mathbf{v}}_{\mathcal{T}}} \log p(\mathbf{y}_S|\mathbf{x}_S, \hat{\mathbf{v}}_{\mathcal{T}})p(\hat{\mathbf{v}}_{\mathcal{T}}|\mathcal{G}) + \sqrt{\epsilon}\hat{\mathbf{z}} \quad (6.29)$$

Due to the burn-in period—a time-consuming situation in Langevin dynamics—the time-saving initialization is expressed in Eqs. (6.30) and (6.31), where h_r denotes the latent embedding for relation r, m_r represents the mean encoding for all sentences of the support set under relation r, and m means the mean encoding for all sentences of the support set:

$$\hat{\mathbf{v}}_{\mathcal{T}} \leftarrow \{\hat{\mathbf{v}}_r\}_{r\in\mathcal{T}} \quad (6.30)$$

with each:

$$\hat{\mathbf{v}}_r \leftarrow \mathbf{m}_r + \mathbf{h}_r - \mathbf{m} \quad (6.31)$$

This framework is assessed on two benchmarks: the FewRel dataset (Gao, Han, Zhu, et al., 2019; Han et al., 2018) and NYT-25, a modified subset of FewRel.

6.7 Sentiment analysis

6.7.1 Introduction

Sentiment analysis, a subfield of natural language processing, aims to find out multiple opinion elements, including sentiments, emotions, attitudes toward entities, and opinions based on someone's writing, facial expressions, speech, music, actions, etc. (Zhang, Wang, & Liu, 2018). Sentiment analysis is widely implemented in real-world applications, including the feedback of consumers in material like social media and product reviews. This section refers to the definition from Liu (2012) regarding the objective of sentiment analysis as follows: "given an opinion document d, the goal of sentiment analysis is to discover all opinion quintuples $(e_i, a_{ij}, s_{ijkl}, h_k, t_l)$ in d," where e_i denotes the name of the entity, a_{ij} represents the aspect of e_i, s_{ijkl} means the sentiment of aspect a_{ij} of an entity e_i, h_k denotes the opinion holder, and t_l reflects the time of opinion executed by h_k.

Among a significant number of varied problems and tasks, sentiment analysis can be divided into two groups: opinion mining and emotion mining. Opinion mining aims to process expressions of opinions in terms of positive/negative/neutral. On the other hand, emotion mining attempts to handle the statement of emotion in times of frustration, sadness, happiness, etc. (Yadollahi, Shahraki, & Zaiane, 2018). It focused on detecting, analyzing, and evaluating the given emotion regarding various events, issues, activities, services, etc. Among them, the typical tasks of emotion-mining can be categorized into four groups:

- **Emotion detection** determines whether a given text contains any type of emotion (e.g., DialogueRNN Majumder et al., 2019)
- **Emotion polarity classification** concentrates on the polarity of the detected emotion
- **Emotion classification** offers a fine-grained classification of an existing motion into multiple predefined emotions (e.g., SpanEmo (Alhuzali & Ananiadou, 2021)).
- **Emotion cause detection** seeks to discover the cause of multiple types of emotions

With the emergence of machine learning and deep learning technology, emotion polarity classification has attracted a surge in interest. There are three types of emotion polarity classification according to scale:

- Document level targets the entire document as a primary information unit with an expression of polarity toward a single entity
- Sentence level deals with the polarity of a given sentence
- Aspect level, also named feature-based opinion mining, focuses on sentences with various opinions on different aspects; for example, "the restaurant is in a good location but extremely overpriced"

Early attempts in textual emotion mining emerged from social information processing (SIP; Walther (1992)), followed by social emotion detection (Lei, Rao, Li, Quan, & Wenyin, 2014). The lexical-based classification was popular since 2009. Meanwhile, rule-based approaches grew (e.g., Affect Analysis Model, UPAR7 (Chaumartin, 2007)). An unsupervised method has been offered by Strapparava and Mihalcea (2008) based on news headlines, while deep neural networks are involved in emotion mining from classification (e.g., Socher et al., 2013) to representation. Meantime, emotion recognition in conversation (Poria, Majumder, Mihalcea, & Hovy, 2019) is widely applied in healthcare analysis and education. Textual conversation emotion detection with a knowledge-enriched transformer has also been launched (Zhong, Wang, & Miao, 2019). Regarding the ongoing pandemic, in 2020, a multilingual emotion prediction about COVID-19 was proposed based on tweets and emoji (Stoikos & Izbicki, 2020).

Benchmark and dataset

Public datasets and benchmarks of emotion mining include:

- Amazon (Blitzer, Dredze, & Pereira, 2007)
- Movies ((Pang & Lee, 2005)
- Blogs (Melville, Gryc, & Lawrence, 2009)

Other emotion-related datasets are offered in:

- ISEAR (Scherer & Wallbott, 1994)
- Fairytales (Alm & Sproat, 2005)
- SemEval 2007, TEC (Mohammad, 2012)
- CBET (Shahraki & Zaiane, 2017)

6.7.2 Text emotion distribution learning with small samples

Emotion distribution learning (EDL) is one type of emotion mining (Zhou, Zhang, Zhou, Zhao, & Geng, 2016). EDL seeks to "decode fine-grained composition and magnitude of emotions in text, the human perception of which can be highly subtle and personal" (Volkova, Mohler, Meurers, Gerdemann, & Lthoff, 2010). It aims to predict an emotion description degree to find the emotion distribution of a text (i.e., to project a sentence from semantic space $\mathcal{S}$ to the corresponding emotion distribution space $\mathcal{Y}$).

Zhao and Ma (2019) suggested a meta-learning strategy, EDL-Meta, to tackle the text emotion distribution from a small number of training samples. This work was motivated by earlier work (Vilalta & Drissi, 2002). The official code is released at https://github.com/zhaozj89/EDL-Meta.

The key ideas are described and summarized as follows:

- To classify each training data point through K-Nearest Neighbors (k-NN) methods with K-nearest semantically similar neighbors
- To learn the low-rank embeddings of a sentence through tensor decomposition to figure out the contextual semantic similarity

  ○ The CANDECOMP/PARAFAC method (Sidiropoulos et al., 2017) is equipped for tensor decomposition, as expressed in Eq. (6.32). $\widehat{\mathcal{V}}$ is an estimated 3D tensor through the outer product $\otimes$ as $w_r \otimes w_r \otimes s_r(i,j,k) = w_r(i) \cdot w_r(j) \cdot s_r(k)$. $w_r \in \mathbb{R}^V$ and $s_r \in \mathbb{R}^D$, where V denotes the number of words, and D represents the sum of numbers of training and testing tasks. R means the rank.

$$\widehat{\mathcal{V}} = \sum_{r=1}^{R} \mathbf{w}_r \otimes \mathbf{w}_r \otimes \mathbf{s}_r \tag{6.32}$$

This strategy applies a convolutional neural network as a backbone equipped with Kullback-Leibler (K-L) divergence as the objective function to estimate the distance between the predicted distribution and the ground truth distribution. These methods are outlined in Table 6.16.

TABLE 6.16 Summarized meta-training and adaptation methods of EDL-meta.

Data: $\mathcal{D}_{\text{train}}$, training set
$\mathcal{D}_{\text{test}}$, testing set
$\alpha, \beta, \gamma, H, R, K, niter, L$, hyperparameters
Result: learner f_{θ_s} for each sentence in s

 # Task Generation
1 obtain sentence embeddings C of each datapoint in $\mathcal{D}_{\text{train}}$
2 construct $\mathcal{T}_{\text{train}}$ with the corresponding KNNs

#Meta-Learner Training
3 initialize θ
4 for *iteration* in 1, 2, ..., niter **do**

Continued

TABLE 6.16 Summarized meta-training and adaptation methods of EDL-meta—cont'd

5	randomly sample L tasks from $\mathcal{T}_{\text{train}}$
6	**for** l in 1, 2, ..., L **do**
7	Update $\theta'_l \leftarrow \theta - \alpha \nabla_\theta \mathcal{L}_{T_i(S)}\left(f_\theta\right)$
8	**end**
9	Updated $\theta \leftarrow \theta - \beta \nabla_\theta \sum_l \mathcal{L}_{T_i(Q)}\left(f_{\theta'_l}\right)$
10 **end**	

#Meta-Learner Adaptation
11 **for** *each sentence s* in $\mathcal{D}_{\text{test}}$ **do**
12   Obtain KNNs $\mathcal{K}_s$ of s in $\mathcal{D}_{\text{train}}$;
13   Update $\theta_s \leftarrow \theta - \nabla_\theta \mathcal{L}_{\mathcal{K}_s}\left(f_\theta\right)$
14 **end**

Modified from Zhao, Z., & Ma, X. (2019). Text emotion distribution learning from small sample: A meta-learning approach. In ACL.

This method is evaluated with six metrics (Euclidean, SØrensen, Squared χ^2, K-L, Fidelity, and Intersection; Geng & Ji, 2013) in SemEval 2007 Task 14 (Strapparava & Mihalcea, 2007), concentrating on English language emotion distribution.

6.8 Emerging topics

6.8.1 Domain-specific word embedding under lifelong learning setting

Background knowledge

Word embeddings (e.g., word2Vec (Mikolov, Chen, Corrado, & Dean, 2013)) have achieved widely promising results in general domains and semantic relations among frequent and common terms; domain-specific word embeddings are still in their emergent stage. Many previous studies (Bollegala, Maehara, Yoshida, & Kawarabayashi, 2015; Hamilton, Clark, Leskovec, & Jurafsky, 2016) have shown that embeddings from one domain to another are distinctive due to various keywords and semantic variations.

Compared to two major models (Skip-gram and CBOW), several attempts (Leeuwenberg, Vela, Dehdari, & van Genabith, 2016; Van der Plas & Tiedemann, 2006) have reported that CBOW outperforms Skip-gram in "all semantic relation tasks" (Nooralahzadeh, Øvrelid, & Lønning, 2018). Despite this finding, regular approaches remain weak in domain-specific synonymy detection, with 6.5% precision and 29% recall (Nooralahzadeh et al., 2018). A small amount of statistical support from the underlying corpora also makes it challenging (Bollegala et al., 2015; Pilehvar & Collier, 2016).

Methodology

Xu and colleagues (Xu et al., 2018) proposed a meta-solver that tackled domain-specific word embedding problems (Mnih & Hinton, 2007) based on a lifelong learning setup: the $(n+1)-th$ task, which heavily relied on the information obtained from the previous n tasks. This framework—Lifelong Domain Embedding via Meta-Learning (L-DEM)—provides a novel approach to expand the in-domain corpus.

There are two implicit dilemmas regarding the productiveness of the embedding method to down-stream tasks:

- The sample size of the training embedding should be much larger than that of the training downstream tasks. This model focuses on addressing this limitation since the training data for embedding methods can be limited in reality. L-DEM illustrates classification as its downstream tasks for experiments and evaluation
- The domains of embedding should be closely related to those of the downstream tasks, such as where GloVe embedding (Pennington et al., 2014) is involved in this dilemma

Regarding the lifelong learning setting mentioned earlier, L-DEM can be divided into two stages under the support of a meta-learner (see overall pipeline in Fig. 6.7.):

1. Automatic detection and recognition of the relevant knowledge A from the previous n task without user interactions. Inspired by early attempts (Ganin et al., 2016; Thrun & Pratt, 2012), a multidomain meta-learner M identifies such knowledge through the similarities among domain contexts (i.e., the surrounding words around an item in a domain corpora) of the same word in many domain corpora. It takes a pair of word features as the input and outputs the similarity score of such word features. See lines 6–15 in Table 6.17 for details.
2. Merging the obtained relevant knowledge into the $(n+1)-th$ domain corpus. The framework applied the Skip-gram model (Mikolov, Sutskever, Chen, Corrado, & Dean, 2013), where its objective functions are expressed in Eqs. (6.33)–(6.35). $\mathcal{L}'_{D_{n+1}}$ is the overall

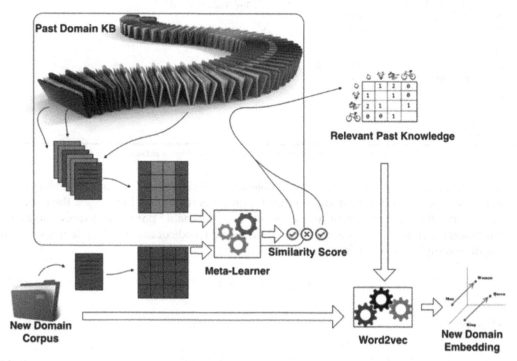

FIG. 6.7 General architecture of L-DEM.
From Xu, H., Liu, B., Shu, L., & Yu, P. S. (2018). Lifelong domain word embedding via meta-learning. In IJCAI.

TABLE 6.17 Summarized training methods of lifelong domain embedding via meta-learning.

Input: $\mathcal{K}.V_{wf}$, a knowledge base $\mathcal{K}$ containing a vocabulary

$\mathcal{K}.M$, a base meta-learner, which produces a similarity score of two feature.

$\mathcal{K}_{m+1:n}$, domain knowledge

D_{n+1}, a new domain corpus

Output: $\mathcal{A}$, relevant past knowledge (each element with a key-value pair $(w_t, \mathcal{C}_{w_t})$, where $\mathcal{C}_{w_t}$ denotes a set of context words from all similar domain for w_t)

---

1 $(V_{m+1:n}, C_{m+1:n}, E_{m+1:n}) \leftarrow \mathcal{K}_{m+1:n}$

\# **Input a new domain corpus D_{n+1} into the BuildVocab**
2 Evaluate $V_{n+1} \leftarrow \text{BuildVocab}(D_{n+1})$

\# **Input a new domain corpus D_{n+1} and the output of BuildVocab V_{n+1}**
3 Evaluate $C_{n+1} \leftarrow \text{ScanContextWord}(D_{n+1}, V_{n+1})$

\# **Input a new domain corpus D_{n+1} and knowledge base $\mathcal{K}.V_{wf}$**
4 Evaluate $E_{n+1} \leftarrow \text{BuildFeatureVector}(D_{n+1}, \mathcal{K}.V_{wf})$

\# **Feed the output of BuildFeatureVector $E_{n+1}, E_{m+1:n}$ and base meta-learner $\mathcal{K} \cdot M$ to generate similarity score**
5 Evaluate $M_{n+1} \leftarrow \text{AdaptMeta-learner}(\mathcal{K} \cdot M, E_{m+1:n}, E_{n+1})$

\# **clean the past knowledge to empty**
6 $\mathcal{A} \leftarrow \varnothing$

7 **for** $(V_j, C_j, E_j) \in (V_{m+1:n}, C_{m+1:n}, E_{m+1:n})$ **do**
8   Set O as $V_j \cap V_{n+1}$
9   Evaluate $F \leftarrow \{(\mathbf{x}_{o,j,1}, \mathbf{x}_{o,n+1,1}) \mid o \in O \text{ and } \mathbf{x}_{o,j,1} \in E_j \text{ and } \mathbf{x}_{o,n+1,1} \in E_{n+1}\}$
10   Evaluate $S \leftarrow M_{n+1}. \text{ inference } (F)$
11   Evaluate $O \leftarrow \{o \mid o \in O \text{ and } S[o] \geq \delta\}$

12   **for** $o \in O$ **do**
13   Perform $\mathcal{A}[o]. \text{ append } (C_j[o])$
14   **end for**

15 **end for**

16 Evaluate $\mathcal{K}_{n+1} \leftarrow (V_{n+1}, C_{n+1}, E_{n+1})$
17 **return** $\mathcal{A}$

Modified from Xu, H., Liu, B., Shu, L., & Yu, P. S. (2018). Lifelong domain word embedding via meta-learning. In IJCAI.

objectives, which consists of the original objective of Skip-gram $\mathcal{L}_{D_{n+1}}$ and the objectives of skip-gram model for the past knowledge $\mathcal{L}_{\mathcal{A}}$ on pairs $(w_t, \mathcal{C}_{w_t})$, where $\mathcal{C}_{w_t}$ is the context words from the similar domain for w_t. $\boldsymbol{u}$ and $\boldsymbol{v}$ are learnable parameters under sigmoid activation function σ. $\mathcal{W}_{w_t}$ presents the surrounding words of w_t, and $\mathcal{N}_{w_t}$ denotes a set of negative samples selected from vocabulary for w_t.

$$\mathcal{L}'_{D_{n+1}} = \mathcal{L}_{D_{n+1}} + \mathcal{L}_{\mathcal{A}} \tag{6.33}$$

where:

$$\mathcal{L}_{\mathcal{A}} = \sum_{(w_t, \mathcal{C}_{w_t}) \in \mathcal{A}} \left(\sum_{w_c \in \mathcal{C}_{w_t}} \left(\log \sigma \left(\boldsymbol{u}_{w_t}^{\mathrm{T}} \cdot v_{w_c} \right) + \sum_{w_{c'} \in \mathcal{N}_{w_t}} \log \sigma \left(-\boldsymbol{u}_{w_t}^{\mathrm{T}} \cdot v_{w_{c'}} \right) \right) \right) \tag{6.34}$$

$$\mathcal{L}_{D_{n+1}} = \sum_{t=1}^{T} \left(\sum_{w_c \in \mathcal{W}_{w_t}} \left(\log \sigma \left(u_{w_t}^T \cdot v_{w_c} \right) + \sum_{w_{c'} \in \mathcal{N}_{w_t}} \log \sigma \left(-u_{w_t}^T \cdot v_{w_{c'}} \right) \right) \right) \quad (6.35)$$

The base meta-learner M is a four-layer pairwise model, which produces a similarity score between two feature vectors.

This model uses multidomain corpora Amazon Review datasets (He & McAuley, 2016) to evaluate its performance.

6.8.2 Multilabel classification

Background knowledge

Multilabel classification is a task that aims to learn from an instance that belongs to one or more disjointed class labels, with various applications in text categorization, semantic image labeling, etc. According to Sorower (2010), conventional methods exist in five groups:

- Elementary problem transformation approaches (e.g., calibrated label ranking)
- Elementary algorithm adaptation approaches (e.g., boosting tree algorithms)
- Ensemble approaches
- Generative modeling
- Dimensionality reduction and subspace-based approaches (e.g., subspace sharing)

The Canonical Correlated AutoEncoder (C2AE) served as the first deep-learning-based embedding solution (Yeh, Wu, Ko, & Wang, 2017). Then, many attempts built on deep neural networks (e.g., Liu, Chang, Wu, & Yang, 2017; Nam, Kim, Mencia, Gurevych, & Furnkranz, 2014; Zhang & Zhou, 2006; Zhou & Feng, 2017).

Methodology

Traditional approaches to multilabel classification have limitations in handling various complexities and dependencies of different labels: they set a one-for-all prediction policy among various labels and neglect the explicit and implicit label dependencies. Wu and colleagues (Wu et al., 2019) proposed a model-agnostic meta-learner equipped with a gated recurrent unit (GRU; Chung, Gulcehre, Cho, & Bengio, 2014) backbone to tackle this problem, which can automatically pattern the implicit and explicit label dependencies. See the overall pipieline in Fig. 6.8. This framework meta-learns a training policy w_t and a prediction policy p_t as meta-policies to adjust model parameters simultaneously and jointly (see lines 9 and 10 in Table 6.18). It treats these policies as a series of hyperparameters determined by the meta-learner.

This framework contains a classifier and a GRU-based meta-learner. The weighted cross-entropy objective function for the classifier is expressed below in Eq. (6.36). B_t denotes a batch of samples from the training set at time t, $y_i^{*(j)}$ present the ground truth prediction with respect to the ith sample from B_t, $y_i^{(j)}$ means the jth entry of output y_i, and N denotes the classes of classifier C.

$$L\left(\theta_t^C \right) = -\sum_{i}^{B_t} \sum_{j}^{N} w_t^{(j)} N \left\{ y_i^{*(j)} \log y_i^{(j)} + \left(1 - y_i^{*(j)} \right) \log \left(1 - y_i^{(j)} \right) \right\} \quad (6.36)$$

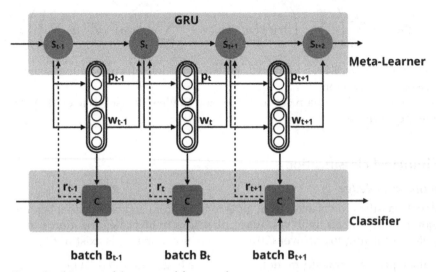

FIG. 6.8   General architecture of the proposed framework.
From Wu, J., Xiong, W., & Wang, W. Y. (2019). Learning to learn and predict: A meta-learning approach for multi-label classification. In ACL.

TABLE 6.18   Summarized training methods of the proposed strategy.

Input: a training dataset
1 **for** episode in $l, ..., M$ **do**
w_0 **and** p_0 **initialization**
2       $w_0 \leftarrow \left(\frac{1}{N}, \frac{1}{N}, \cdots, \frac{1}{N}\right) \in \mathbb{R}^N$
3       $p_0 \leftarrow (0.5, 0.5, \cdots, 0.5) \in \mathbb{R}^N$
4   **for** t in $l, ..., T$ **do**
5   Compute $s_t \leftarrow \text{GRU}\left(s_{t-1}, \begin{bmatrix} p_{t-1} \\ w_{t-1} \end{bmatrix}\right)$
6   Compute $w_t \leftarrow \text{softmax}(W_w s_t + b_w)$
7   Compute $p_t \leftarrow \text{sigmoid}(W_p s_t + b_p)$
8   Construct a batch B_t from U
9   Apply B_t under w_t-based objective function in Eq. (6.36) to obtain C
10   Apply p_t in Eq. (6.37) to obtain reward r_t
11   Evaluate θ_{meta} with $g \propto \nabla_\theta J(\theta_{\text{meta}})$

Modified from Wu, J., Xiong, W., & Wang, W. Y. (2019). Learning to learn and predict: A meta-learning approach for multi-label classification. In ACL.

For training a joint function of training policy w_t and prediction policy p_t, a reward function r_t is introduced in Eq. (6.37), where the goal of the meta-learner is to select w_t and p_t at time t to maximize the future reward.

$$r_t = \sum_{i}^{B_t} \sum_{j=1}^{N} (-1)^{y_i^*(j)} \frac{p_t^{(j)} - y_i^{(j)}}{p_t^{(j)}} \tag{6.37}$$

Table 6.18 indicates the comprehensive training methods of this meta-learning framework. The framework evaluates state-of-the-art performance on two tasks:

- The task of fine-grained entity typing, where the entities are associated with knowledge graphs (i.e., the labels obtain explicit hierarchical dependencies) on datasets FIGER (Ling & Weld, 2012), OntoNotes (Weischedel et al., 2013), and BBN (Weischedel & Brunstein, 2005).
- The task of text classification without explicit correlation, which needs to figure out the implicit label dependencies on the Reuters-21578 (Nam et al., 2014; Yang, 2001) and RCV1-V2 (Lewis, Yang, Rose, & Li, 2004) datasets.

6.8.3 Representation under a low-resource setting

Background knowledge

General language representation ranges from a minimal unit to a large volume, spanning characters, subwords, words, phrases, sentences, and documents. This procedure of "representing text elements as continuous and dense vectors" is called embedding (Babić, Martinčić-Ipšić, & Meštrović, 2020).

In long decades, numerous research efforts has emphasized character-level embedding (e.g., CharCNN (Kim, Jernite, Sontag, & Rush, 2016), FastText (Bojanowski, Grave, Joulin, & Mikolov, 2017) through n-grams), word embedding (e.g., term frequency-inverse document frequency (TFIDF; Manning, Raghavan, & Schütze, H., 2008)), and sentence representation (e.g., Le & Mikolov, 2014). Recent research interests include contextualized word embedding (i.e., representing a word conditioned on its surrounding context) with permission performance (e.g., BERT; Devlin et al., 2018). Despite some impressive results achieved by contemporary (e.g., GTP-based) frameworks, the rational cognitive processes behind the black box remain unknown.

Methodology

Dou and colleagues (Dou et al., 2019) investigated a text representation task under a low-resource setting and proposed an approach by implementing three optimization-based meta-learner backbones on top of the pretrained BERT: MAML, First-Order MAML (FOMAML), and Reptile (Nichol, Achia, & Schulman, 2018). This framework aims to generate good initialization for fast adaptation on diverse tasks through meta-learning. The comprehensive training framework is based on MAML and its variants (i.e., FOMAML and Reptile), while these three meta-learners can substitute for each other. See the generic methods in Table 6.19.

Eq. (6.38) indicates a gradient descent of k steps during parameter updating, where $k \geq 1$. α denotes the hyperparameter of the learning rate:

$$\theta_i^{(k)} = \theta_i^{(k-1)} - \alpha \nabla_{\theta_i^{(k-1)}} L_i \left(f_{\theta_i^{(k-1)}} \right) \tag{6.38}$$

The *metaUpdate( )* methods are demonstrated in Eq. (6.39) and noted in Table 6.19. MAML, FOMAML, and Reptile provide three different ways to implement a meta-learner.

$$\theta = \text{MetaUpdate} \left(\theta; \left\{ \theta_i^{(k)} \right\} \right) \tag{6.39}$$

These three methods are described in Eqs. (6.40)–(6.42). Different datasets are fed in the gradient descent update method (i.e., Eq. 6.38) and meta-update method (i.e., Eq. 6.39). Applying MAML, the *metaUpdate( )* method is implemented in Eq. (6.40). β denotes the hyperparameter of the learning rate.

TABLE 6.19 Summarized training methods of the proposed strategy.

Input: θ parameters of a pre-train model

1. **while** not converged **do**
2.   Construct a batch of tasks $\{T_i\} \sim p(T)$

3.   **for all** T_i **do**
            # **Gradient descent of k steps during parameter updating as k ≥1**
4.   Evaluate $\theta_i^{(k)}$ using Eq. (6.38).
5.   **end for**

            # **Fed with three different meta approaches: MAML,**
              FOMAML, Reptile
6.   Evaluate θ using either equation of Eqs. (6.40)–(6.42).

7. **end while**
8. Fine-tune θ on the target task.

Modified from Dou, Z.-Y., Yu, K., & Anastasopoulos, A. (2019). Investigating meta-learning algorithms for low-resource natural language understanding tasks. In ACL.

$$\theta = \theta - \beta \sum_{T_i \sim p(T)} \nabla_\theta L_i\left(f_{\theta_i^{(k)}}\right) \tag{6.40}$$

For First-Order MAML, the *metaUpdate( )* is implemented as presented in Eq. (6.41).

$$\theta = \theta - \beta \sum_{T_i \sim p(T)} \nabla_{\theta_i^{(k)}} L_i\left(\theta_i^{(k)}\right) \tag{6.41}$$

For Reptile, the *metaUpdate( )* method is implemented in Eq. (6.42) as follows:

$$\theta = \theta + \beta \frac{1}{|\{T_i\}|} \sum_{T_i \sim p(T)} \left(\theta_i^{(k)} - \theta\right) \tag{6.42}$$

This model is accessed on the GLUE benchmark (Wang et al., 2019). The four rich-resource source tasks include the Stanford Sentiment Treebank (SST-2; Socher et al., 2013), Quora Question Pairs (QQP; Iyer, Dandekar and Csernai, 2017), Multi-Genre Natural Language Inference (MNLI; Williams, Nangia and Bowman, 2018), and Question-answering NLI (QNLI; Rajpurkar, Zhang, Lopyrev and Liang, 2016). Then, this framework is fine-tuned on target tasks: Corpus of Linguistic Acceptability (CoLa; Warstadt, Singh and Bowman, 2018), Microsoft Research Paraphrase Corpus (MRPC; Dolan and Brockett, 2005), Semantic Textual Similarity (STS-B; Cera et al., 2017), and Recognising Textual Entailment (RTE; Dagan, Glickman and Magnini, 2005). The performance generalization ability is evaluated on the SciTail dataset (Khot, Sabharwal and Clark, 2018).

6.8.4 Compositional generalization

Background knowledge

Systematic compositionality is a critical ability for understanding and generating infinite combinations with finite components. For instance, as long as a person understands the terms "Google," "Facebook," or how to "click," they will easily understand new phrases such as "click twice," "Google a picture," and "Facebook immediately" (Bastings, Baroni, Weston, Cho, & Kiela, 2018; Lake & Baroni, 2018; Loula, Baroni, & Lake, 2018).

Neural networks had a known lack of compositionality for decades, until recent attempts, as similar data exist between the training set and testing set through RNN and the attention mechanism (Chang, Gupta, Levine, & Griffiths, 2018; Kliegl & Xu, 2018). Compositionality remains a challenging task regarding image captioning, visual question answering, and embodied question answering (Li, Zhao, Wang, & Hestness, 2019).

Methodology

Lake (2019) proposed a meta-based memory-augmented neural network framework named Meta Sequence-to-Sequence (Meta seq2seq). It focused on compositionality, particularly for combinations of existing concepts and novel concepts. This framework learns from training a variety of seq2seq tasks to establish the ability to understand and handle compositionality through three main modules. The official code is released at https://github.com/facebookresearch/meta_seq2seq.

The high-level workflow is indicated in Fig. 6.9, in which:

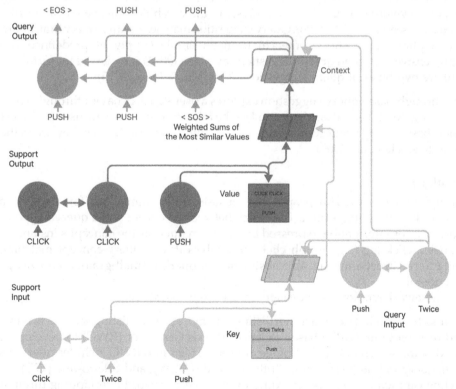

FIG. 6.9 General workflow of meta sequence-to-sequence.
Modified from Lake, B. M. (2019). Compositional generalization through meta sequence-to-sequence learning. In NIPS.

1. An input encoder *(red)* *(gray* in print version) employs a bidirectional long short-term memory encoder (biLSTM; Hochreiter & Schmidhuber, 1997). It encodes the compositional query (e.g., "click twice") via the symbols first (e.g., "click").
2. An output encoder *(blue)* *(light gray* in print version) also equips a biLSTM encoder and encodes the symbols first.
3. An output decoder *(green)* *(dark gray* in print version) is supported by an RNN or LSTM equipped with a Luong-style attention mechanism (Luong et al., 2015).

In the meta-learning episode-training stage, each episode contains a novel seq2seq question with support samples and query samples under a negative log-likelihood loss function. This model is evaluated on a compositional query from the SCAN (Lake & Baroni, 2018) dataset.

6.8.5 Zero-shot transfer learning for query suggestion

Background knowledge

The internet serves as an extensive information-retrieval system based on a giant collection of information. The effectiveness of each keyword search depends on multiple factors related to the accuracy of a keyword in a query, such as polysemy and vocabulary mismatch (briefly discussed in Section 6.2.1; see Xu & Croft, 1996). Query suggestion matches a search query to an appropriate concept (a phrase or a short sentence) from an ample supply of predefined concepts. A comprehensive survey on query suggestions by Meng (2014) is reviewed for further interest.

There are two types of query suggestions (Ooi, Ma, & Liew, 2015):

- Click-through-based query suggestion explores a user's click behavior through a search log (e.g., Leung, Ng, & Lee, 2008; Meng, 2014)—the following approach focuses on this category
- Session-based query suggestion assumes every query is related, since they are in the same session (e.g., He et al., 2009)

Methodology

Han and colleagues (2020) proposed a meta-learning framework for a query-concept matching task—query suggestion. The match between a concept and a query happens when the knowledge or information expressed by the given query is the concept's instance. It puts an unlabeled click log (e.g., graph click) and solves it as a query-concept matching task, expecting to construct a manageable abstraction of queries' small-grained knowledge from an open domain.

This framework employs a two-stage, coarse-to-fine strategy:

1. It shrinks the search space via a shortlisting scheme. The shortlisting scheme was built by a gated recurrent unit (GRU)-based Relevant Words Generator (RWG) to develop a broad context of the search query. The range of tasks to feed into RWG includes query-to-query (Q2Q), query-to-title (Q2T), query/title-to-word (QT2W), and title-to-title (T2T).
2. Selecting candidate concepts according to their score of word overlapping through two submodals:

   ○ A BERT (Devlin et al., 2018) pretrained pair-wise classifier under meta-fine-tuning

○ A Reptile backbone for meta-learning with the objective function expressed in Eq. (6.43), where $\mathfrak{D}^{meta}$ is denoted as $\left\{ \mathfrak{D}_1^{train}, \mathfrak{D}_2^{train}, \dots \right\}$

$$\max_{\phi} \ \log p\left(\phi | \mathcal{D}^{meta}\right) \tag{6.43}$$

The click graph is formatted into two collections regarding relevant words (RW), queries, and labels during the training phase. Hence, meta-fine-tuning is performed for a classification. After postprocessing the relevant word, relevant word generation is conducted.

6.9 Summary

While deep learning dominates countless research projects on natural language processing, deep learning techniques are unfavorable for data-consuming and complex computation. Many real-world scenarios cannot afford such a high cost of training samples and computing resources, limiting deep learning methods from dealing with practical problems. Meta-learning fills this gap with its "learning to learn" benefits of fast task adaptation, optimal initialization, meta-knowledge across all tasks, inner-/outer-loop architecture, and beyond. Although meta-learning-based natural language processing is still in its early growth stage, several attempts have been made to discover novel directions for conventional and contemporary tasks and other open questions.

This chapter investigates 20 advanced pieces of research, all of which can be divided into seven taxonomies according to their tasks to solve: semantic parsing, sentiment analysis, machine translation, dialogue system, knowledge graph (including named entity recognition and question answering), relation extraction, and emerging topics (e.g., domain-specific word embedding, multilabel classification, compositional generalization, query suggestion).

Multiple lectures highlight the global online discussion about meta-learning for natural language processing. These are organized by key academic conferences:

- Association for Computational Linguistics (ACL) 2021 workshop at https://meta-nlp-2021.github.io/#reading
- Seminar by Hung-Yi Lee at https://www.youtube.com/watch?v=wurPYalweeo
- Stanford University lectures *CS 330: Deep Multi-Task and Meta-Learning* by Chelsea Finn at http://cs330.stanford.edu

References

Agichtein, E., & Gravano, L. (2000). Snowball: Extracting relations from large plain-text collections. In *The fifth ACM international conference on digital libraries*.

Alhuzali, H., & Ananiadou, S. (2021). SpanEmo: Casting multi-label emotion classification as span-prediction. In *EACL*.

Allen, R. (1987). Several studies on natural language and back-propagation. In *Vol. 2. IEEE first international conference on neural networks* (p. 341). IEEE Piscataway. No. S 335.

Alm, C. O., & Sproat, R. (2005). Emotional sequencing and development in fairy tales. In *International conference on affective computing and intelligent interaction* (pp. 668–674). Berlin, Heidelberg: Springer.

Ammar, W., Groeneveld, D., Bhagavatula, C., Beltagy, I., Crawford, M., Downey, D., et al. (2018). *Construction of the literature graph in semantic scholar. arXiv preprint arXiv:1805.02262.*

Artzi, Y., & Zettlemoyer, L. (2013). Weakly supervised learning of semantic parsers for mapping instructions to actions. *Transactions of the Association for Computational Linguistics (TACL)*, 1, 49–62.

Aydar, M., Bozal, O., & Ozbay, F. (2020). *Neural relation extraction: A survey*. Retrieved from arXiv http://arxiv.org/abs/2007.04247v1.

Babić, K., Martinčić-Ipšić, S., & Meštrović, A. (2020). Survey of neural text representation models. *Information*, 11(11), 511.

Bahdanau, D., Cho, K., & Bengio, Y. (2014). *Neural machine translation by jointly learning to align and translate. arXiv preprint arXiv:1409.0473*.

Baker, C. F., Fillmore, C. J., & Lowe, J. B. (1998). The berkeley FrameNet project. In *ACL*.

Banarescu, L., Bonial, C., Cai, S., Georgescu, M., Griffitt, K., Hermjakob, U., ... Schneider, N. (2013). Abstract meaning representation for sembanking. In *WS*.

Barone, A. V., Haddow, B., Germann, U., & Sennrich, R. (2017). Regularization techniques for fine-tuning in neural machine translation. In *The 2017 conference on empirical methods in natural language processing*.

Bastings, J., Baroni, M., Weston, J., Cho, K., & Kiela, D. (2018). Jump to better conclusions: SCAN both left and right. In *The EMNLP BlackboxNLP Workshop*.

Bauer, L., Wang, Y., & Bansal, M. (2018). Commonsense for generative multi-hop question answering tasks. In *EMNLP* (pp. 4220–4230).

Berant, J., Chou, A., Frostig, R., & Liang, P. (2013). Semantic parsing on Freebase from question-answer pairs. In *EMNLP*.

Blitzer, J., Dredze, M., & Pereira, F. (2007). Biographies, bollywood, boom-boxes and blenders: Domain adaptation for sentiment classification. In *Proceedings of the 45th annual meeting of the association of computational linguistics* (pp. 440–447).

Bojanowski, P., Grave, E., Joulin, A., & Mikolov, T. (2017). Enriching word vectors with subword information. In *Trans. Assoc. Comput. Linguist*.

Bojar, O., Chatterjee, R., Federmann, C., Graham, Y., Haddow, B., Huck, M., ... (2016). Findings of the 2016 conference on machine translation. In *ACL—First conference on machine translation (WMT16)*.

Bollegala, D., Maehara, T., Yoshida, Y., & Kawarabayashi, K. I. (2015). Learning word representations from relational graphs. In *Twenty-Ninth AAAI conference on artificial intelligence*.

Bordes, A., Usunier, N., Chopra, S., & Weston, J. (2015). Large-scale simple question answering with memory networks. *CoRR*. abs/1506.02075.

Bordes, A., Usunier, N., Duran, A. G., Weston, J., & Yakhnenko, O. (2013). Translating embeddings for modeling multi-relational data. In *NIPS*.

Brin, S. (1998). Extracting patterns and relations from the world wide web. In *6th international conference on extending database technology, EDBT '98*.

Britz, D., Le, Q., & Pryzant, R. (2017). Effective domain mixing for neural machine translation. In *The second conference on machine translation* (pp. 118–126).

Budzianowski, P., Wen, T.-H., Tseng, B.-H., Casanueva, I., Ultes, S., Ramadan, O., & Gasic, M. (2018). Multiwoza large-scale multi-domain wizard-of-oz dataset for task-oriented dialogue modelling. In *The 2018 conference on empirical methods in natural language processing* (pp. 5016–5026).

Cambria, E., Song, Y., Wang, H., & Howard, N. (2012). Semantic multidimensional scaling for open-domain sentiment analysis. *IEEE Intelligent Systems*, 29(2), 44–51.

Cao, P., Chen, Y., Liu, K., Zhao, J., & Liu, S. (2018). Adversarial transfer learning for Chinese named entity recognition with self-attention mechanism. In *EMNLP* (pp. 182–192).

Carlson, A., Betteridge, J., Kisiel, B., Settles, B., Hruschka, E. R., & Mitchell, T. M. (2010). Toward an architecture for never-ending language learning. In *Twenty-fourth AAAI conference on artificial intelligence*.

Caruana, R. (1997). Multitask learning. *Machine Learning*, 28(1), 41–75.

Cera, D., Diabb, M., Agirrec, E., Lopez-Gazpioc, I., Speciad, L., & Donostia, B. C. (2017). Semeval-2017 task 1: Semantic textual similarity multilingual and cross-lingual focused evaluation. In *11th international workshop on semant*.

Chang, M. B., Gupta, A., Levine, S., & Griffiths, T. L. (2018). *Automatically composing representation transformations as a means for generalization. arXiv preprint arXiv:1807.04640*.

Chaumartin, F. R. (2007). UPAR7: A knowledge-based system for headline sentiment tagging. In *SemEval* (p. 422). ACL Workshop.

Chen, H., Liu, X., Yin, D., & Tang, J. (2018). *A survey on dialogue systems: Recent advances and new frontiers*. Retrieved from https://arxiv.org/abs/1711.01731.

Chen, M., Zhang, W., Zhang, W., Chen, Q., & Chen, H. (2019). Meta relational learning for few-shot link prediction in knowledge graphs. *arXiv preprint*, arXiv:1909.01515.

Chen, M. X., Firat, O., Bapna, A., Johnson, M., Macherey, W., Foster, G., et al. (2018). The best of both worlds: Combining recent advances in neural machine translation. *arXiv preprint*, arXiv:1804.09849.

Chen, P.-Z., Bogoychev, N., & Germann, U. (2020). Character mapping and Ad-hoc adaptation: Edinburgh's IWSLT 2020 open domain translation system. In *WS*.

Chen, D., Chen, H., Yang, Y., Lin, A., & Yu, Z. (2021). Action-based conversations dataset: A corpus for building more in-depth task-oriented dialogue systems. In *NAACL*.

Chinchor, N. (1995). Four scorers and seven years ago: the scoring method for MUC-6. In *The 6th conference on message understanding* (pp. 33–38). https://doi.org/10.3115/1072399.1072403.

Chinchor, N. (2005). *MUC-07 proceedings (named entity tasks)*. Retrieved from https://www-nlpir.nist.gov/related_ projects/muc/proceedings/muc_7_toc.html#named.

Chiu, J. P., & Nichols, E. (2016). Named entity recognition with bidirectional LSTM-CNNs. *Transactions of ACL, 4*, 357–370.

Cho, K., Van Merrinboer, B., Bahdanau, D., & Bengio, Y. (2014). On the properties of neural machine translation: Encoder-decoder approaches. *arXiv preprint*, arXiv:1409.1259.

Choudhary, S., Srivastava, P., Ungar, L., & Sedoc, J. (2017). *Domain aware neural dialog system*. Retrieved from arXiv preprint arXiv:1708.00897.

Chrisman, L. (1991). Learning recursive distributed representations for holistic computation. *Connection Science, 3*(4), 345–366.

Chu, C., & Wang, R. (2018). A Survey of domain adaptation for neural machine translation. In *ACL*. https:// aclanthology.org/C18-1111/.

Chu, C., Dabre, R., & Kurohashi, S. (2017). An empirical comparison of domain adaptation methods for neural machine translation. In *The 55th annual meeting of the association for computational linguistics*.

Chung, J., Gulcehre, C., Cho, K., & Bengio, Y. (2014). *Empirical evaluation of gated recurrent neural networks on sequence modeling. arXiv preprint arXiv:1412.3555*.

Clarke, J., Goldwasser, D., Chang, M., & Roth, D. (2010). Driving semantic parsing from the world's response. In *Computational natural language learning (CoNLL)* (pp. 18–27).

Cui, L., Wu, Y., Liu, S., Zhang, Y., & Zhou, M. (2020). MuTual: A dataset for multi-turn dialogue reasoning. In *ACL*.

Dabre, R., Chu, C., & Kunchukuttan, A. (2020). A survey of multilingual neural machine translation. *ACM Computing Surveys, 53*(5), 1–38. https://doi.org/10.1145/3406095.

Dagan, I., Glickman, O., & Magnini, B. (2005). The pascal recognising textual entailment challenge. In *Machine learning challenges work-shop* (pp. 177–190). Springer.

Dai, Z., Li, L., & Xu, W. (2016). *CFO: Conditional focused neural question answering with large-scale knowledge bases*. arXiv preprint, arXiv:1606.01994.

Das, R., Dhuliawala, S., Zaheer, M., Vilnis, L., Durugkar, I., Krishnamurthy, A., … McCallum, A. (2018). Go for a walk and arrive at the answer: Reasoning over paths in knowledge bases using reinforcement learning. In *ICLR* (pp. 1–18).

Devlin, J., Chang, M., Lee, K., & Toutanova, K. (2018). *Bert: Pre-training of deep bidirectional transformers for language understanding*. arXiv:1810.04805.

Dolan, W. B., & Brockett, C. (2005). Automatically constructing a corpus of sentential paraphrases. In *The third international workshop on paraphrasing (IWP2005)*.

Dong, X., Gabrilovich, E., Heitz, G., Horn, W., Lao, N., Murphy, K., … Zhang, W. (2014). Knowledge vault: A web-scale approach to probabilistic knowledge fusion. In *SIGKDD* (pp. 601–610).

Dou, Z.-Y., Yu, K., & Anastasopoulos, A. (2019). Investigating meta-learning algorithms for low-resource natural language understanding tasks. In *ACL*.

Duh, K., Neubig, G., Sudoh, K., & Tsukada, H. (2013). Adaptation data selection using neural language models: Experiments in machine translation. In *The 51st annual meeting of the association for computational linguistics*.

Ehrlinger, L., & Woß, W. (2016). Towards a definition of knowledge graphs. In *Vol. 48. SEMANTiCS (Posters, Demos, SuCCESS)* (pp. 1–4).

Eric, M., & Manning, C. D. (2017). *Key-value retrieval networks for task-oriented dialogue*. Retrieved from https://arxiv.org/pdf/1705.05414v2.pdf.

Fleiss, J. L. (1971). Measuring nominal scale agreement among many raters. *Psychological Bulletin, 76*(5), 378.

Forcada, M. L., Ginest-Rosell, M., Nordfalk, J., ORegan, J., Ortiz-Rojas, S., Prez-Ortiz, J. A., … Tyers, F. M. (2011). Apertium: A free/open-source platform for rule-based machine translation. *Machine Translation, 25*(2), 127–144.

Freitag, M., & Al-Onaizan, Y. (2016). *Fast domain adaptation for neural machine translation. arXiv preprint arXiv:1612.06897.*

Fu, C., Chen, T., Qu, M., Jin, W., & Ren, X. (2019). Collaborative policy learning for open knowledge graph reasoning. In *EMNLP* (pp. 2672–2681).

Ganin, Y., Ustinova, E., Ajakan, H., Germain, P., Larochelle, H., Laviolette, F., et al. (2016). Domain-adversarial training of neural networks. *The Journal of Machine Learning Research, 17*(1). 2096–2030.

Gao, T. (2019). *Settings and benchmark.* Retrieved from OpenNRE: https://opennre-docs.readthedocs.io/en/latest/get_started/benchmark.html.

Gao, T., Han, X., Zhu, H., Liu, Z., Li, P., Sun, M., & Zhou, J. (2019). *Fewrel 2.0: Towards more challenging few-shot relation classification. arXiv preprint arXiv:1910.07124.*

Gao, T., Han, X., Liu, Z., & Sun, M. (2019). Hybrid attention-based prototypical networks for noisy few-shot relation classification. In *Proceedings of the AAAI conference on artificial intelligence Vol. 33, No. 01* (pp. 6407–6414). No. 01.

Gardent, C., Shimorina, A., Narayan, S., & Perez-Beltrachini, L. (2017). The WebNLG challenge: Generating text from RDF data. In *The 10th international conference on natural language generation* (pp. 124–133).

Gehring, J., Auli, M., Grangier, D., Yarats, D., & Dauphin, Y. N. (2017). Convolutional sequence to sequence learning. In *Vol. 70. The 34th international conference on machine learning* (pp. 1243–1252).

Geng, X., & Ji, R. (2013). Label distribution learning. In *The 13th IEEE inter-national conference on data mining workshops* (pp. 377–383).

Gritta, M., Lampouras, G., & Iacobacci, I. (2021). Conversation graph: Data augmentation, training, and evaluation for non-deterministic dialogue management. *Transactions of the Association for Computational Linguistics, 9,* 36–52.

Gu, J., Lu, Z., Li, H., & Li, V. O. (2016). Incorporating copying mechanism in sequence-to-sequence learning. *CoRR.* abs/1603.06393.

Gu, J., Wang, Y., Chen, Y., Cho, K., & Li, V. O. (2018). Meta-learning for low-resource neural machine translation. In *ACL.*

Gulcehre, C., Firat, O., Xu, K., Cho, K., Barrault, L., Lin, H.-C., … Bengio, Y. (2015). On using monolingual corpora in neural machine translation. *CoRR.* abs/1503.03535.

Guo, D., Tang, D., Duan, N., Zhou, M., & Yin, J. (2018). Dialog-to-action: Conversational question answering over a large-scale knowledge base. *Advances in Neural Information Processing Systems, 31.*

Guo, D., Tang, D., Duan, N., Zhou, M., & Yin, J. (2019). Coupling retrieval and meta-learning for context-dependent semantic parsing. In *ACL.*

Guu, K., Pasupat, P., Liu, E. Z., & Liang, P. (2017). *From language to programs: Bridging reinforcement learning and maximum marginal likelihood. arXiv preprint arXiv:1704.07926.*

Hamilton, W. L., Clark, K., Leskovec, J., & Jurafsky, D. (2016). Inducing domain-specific sentiment lexicons from unlabeled corpora. In *Retrieved from the 2016 conference on empirical methods in natural language processing.*

Han, X., Zhu, H., Yu, P., Wang, Z., Yao, Y., Liu, Z., & Sun, M. (2018). Fewrel: A large-scale supervised few-shot relation classification dataset with state-of-the-art evaluation. In *EMNLP.*

Han, F.X., Niu, D., Chen, H., Guo, W., Yan, S., & Long, B. (2020). Meta-learning for query conceptualization at web scale.

Hao, J., Chen, M., Yu, W., Sun, Y., & Wang, W. (2019). Universal representation learning of knowledge bases by jointly embedding instances and ontological concepts. In *KDD.* https://github.com/JunhengH/joie-kdd19.

Hashemi, H. B., Asiaee, A., & Kraft, R. (2016). Query intent detection using convolutional neural networks. In *International conference on web search and data mining, workshop on query understanding.*

Hashimoto, K., Miwa, M., Tsuruoka, Y., & Chikayama, T. (2013). Simple customization of recursive neural networks for semantic relation classification. In *Conference on empirical methods in natural language processing.*

He, R., & McAuley, J. (2016). Ups and downs: Modeling the visual evolution of fashion trends with one-class collaborative filtering. In *WWW* (pp. 507–517).

He, Q., Jiang, D., Liao, Z., Hoi, S. C., Chang, K., Lim, E.-P., & Li, H. (2009). Web query recommendation via sequential query prediction. In *IEEE international conference on data engineering.*

Hemphill, C. T., Godfrey, J. J., & Doddington, G. R. (1990). The ATIS spoken language systems pilot corpus. In *The workshop on speech and natural language* (pp. 96–101). Retrieved from https://www.kaggle.com/siddhadev/ms-cntk-atis.

Hendrickx, I., Kim, S. N., Kozareva, Z., Nakov, P., OSeaghdha, D., Pado, S., ... Szpakowicz, S. (2009). Semeval-2010 task 8: Multi-way classification of semantic relations between pairs of nominals. In *The workshop on semantic evaluations: Recent achievements and future directions* (pp. 94–99).

Hochreiter, S., & Schmidhuber, J. (1997). Long short-term memory. *Neural Computation, 9*(8), 1735–1780.

Hogan, A., Blomqvist, E., Cochez, M., d'Amato, C., de Melo, G., Gutierrez, C., ... Rula, A. (2021). Knowledge graphs. *ACM Computing Surveys, 54*(4), 1–37. arXiv:2003.02320 https://doi.org/10.1145/3447772.

Hu, A., Dou, Z., Nie, J.-Y., & Wen, J.-R. (2020). Leveraging multi-token entities in document-level named entity recognition. In *AAAI* (pp. 7961–7968).

Hua, Y., Li, Y.-F., Haffari, G., Qi, G., & Wu, W. (2020). Retrieve, program, repeat: Complex knowledge base question answering via alternate meta-learning. In *IJCAI*.

Huang, P.-S., He, X., Gao, J., Deng, L., Acero, A., & Heck, L. (2013). Learning deep structured semantic models for web search using clickthrough data. In *The 22nd ACM international conference on conference on information & knowledge management*.

Huang, P.-S., Wang, C., Singh, R., Yih, W.-t., & He, X. (2018). Natural language to structured query generation via meta-learning. In *ACL*.

Iris Hendrickx, S. N., Nakov, P., OSeaghdha, D., Pado, S., Pennacchiotti, M., Romano, L., & Szpakowicz, S. (2009). Semeval-2010 task 8: Multi-way classification of semantic relations between pairs of nominals. In *The workshop on semantic evaluations: Recent achievements and future directions*.

Iyer, S., Dandekar, N., & Csernai, K. (2017). *First quora dataset release: Question Pairs*. Retrieved from Quora https://quoradata.quora.com/First-Quora-Dataset-Release-Question-Pairs.

Iyer, S., Konstas, I., Cheung, A., & Zettlemoyer, L. (2018). Mapping language to code in programmatic context. In *The 2018 conference on empirical methods in natural language processing* (pp. 1643–1652).

Iyyer, M., Yih, W.-T., & Chang, M.-W. (2017). Search-based neural structured learning for sequential question answering. In *The 55th annual meeting of the association for computational linguistics (Volume 1: Long papers)*.

Ji, S., Pan, S., Cambria, E., Marttinen, P., & Yu, P. S. (2021). A survey on knowledge graphs: Representation, acquisition and applications. In *IEEE transactions on neural networks and learning systems*.

Jia, R., & Liang, P. (2016). *Data recombination for neural semantic parsing*. Retrieved from arXiv: arXiv:1606.03622.

Johnson, T. (1984). Natural language computing: The commercial applications. *The Knowledge Engineering Review, 1*(3), 11–23.

Kalchbrenner, N., & Blunsom, P. (2013). Recurrent continuous translation models. In *The 2013 conference on empirical methods in natural language processing* (pp. 1700–1709).

Kamath, A., & Das, R. (2019). A survey on semantic parsing. In *Automated knowledge base construction*.

Kambhatla, N. (2004). Combining lexical, syntactic, and semantic features with maximum entropy models for extracting relations. In *Proceedings of the ACL 2004*.

Khandelwal, U., Fan, A., Jurafsky, D., Zettlemoyer, L., & Lewis, M. (2021). Nearest neighbor machine translation. In *ICLR*.

Khayrallah, H., Kumar, G., Duh, K., Post, M., & Koehn, P. (2017). Neural lattice search for domain adaptation in machine translation. In *The eighth international joint conference on natural language processing*.

Khot, T., Sabharwal, A., & Clark, P. (2018). Scitail: A textual entailment dataset from science question answering. In *AAAI*.

Kim, Y., Jernite, Y., Sontag, D., & Rush, A. (2016). Character-aware neural language models. In *The thirtieth AAAI conference on artificial intelligence*.

Kliegl, M., & Xu, W. (2018). *More systematic than claimed: Insights on the scan tasks*.

Knowlson, J. (1975). *Universal language schemes in England and France 1600–1800*. University of Toronto Press. ISBN 978-0-8020-5296-4.

Kobus, C., Crego, J., & Senellart, J. (2016). *Domain control for neural machine translation. arXiv preprint arXiv:1612.06140*.

Koehn, P. (2005). Europarl: A parallel corpus for statistical machine translation. In *Vol. 5. MT summit* (pp. 79–86).

Koehn, P., Hoang, H., Birch, A., Callison-Burch, C., Federico, M., Bertoldi, N., ... Dyer, C. (2007). Moses: Open source toolkit for statistical machine translation. In *The 45th annual meeting of the association for computational linguistics*.

Koehn, P., Och, F. J., & Marcu, D. (2003). Statistical phrase-based translation. In *Vol. 1. The 2003 conference of the north american chapter of the association for computational linguistics on human language technology* (pp. 48–54).

Krishnamurthy, J., & Kollar, T. (2013). Jointly learning to parse and perceive: Connecting natural language to the physical world. *Transactions of the Association for Computational Linguistics (TACL), 1*, 193–206.

Krishnamurthy, J., & Mitchell, T. M. (2012). Weakly supervised training of semantic parsers. In *The 2012 joint conference on empirical methods in natural language processing and computational natural language learning* (pp. 754–765).

Krishnamurthy, J., Dasigi, P., & Gardner, M. (2017). Neural semantic parsing with type constraints for semi-structured tables. In *Empirical methods in natural language processing* (pp. 1516–1526).

Lake, B. M. (2019). Compositional generalization through meta sequence-to-sequence learning. In *NIPS*.

Lake, B. M., & Baroni, M. (2018). Generalization without systematicity: On the compositional skills of sequence-to-sequence recurrent networks. In *ICML*.

Lample, G., & Conneau, A. (2019). Cross-lingual language model pretraining. *CoRR*. abs/1901.07291.

Lample, G., Ballesteros, M., Subramanian, S., Kawakami, K., & Dyer, C. (2016). Neural architectures for named entity recognition. In *NAACL* (pp. 260–270).

Lample, G., Ott, M., Conneau, A., De-Noyer, L., & Ranzato, M. (2018). Phrase-based & neural unsupervised machine translation. In *EMNLP*.

Le, Q., & Mikolov, T. (2014). Distributed representations of sentences and documents. In *The international conference on machine learning* (pp. 1188–1196).

Lee, S., & Eskenazi, M. (2013). Recipe for building robust spoken dialog state trackers: Dialog state tracking challenge system description. In *SIGDIAL* (pp. 414–422).

Lee, C.-H., Wang, S.-M., Chang, H.-C., & Lee, H.-Y. (2018). *ODSQA: Open-domain spoken question answering dataset.* Retrieved from https://arxiv.org/pdf/1808.02280v1.pdf.

Leeuwenberg, A., Vela, M., Dehdari, J., & van Genabith, J. (2016). A minimally supervised approach for synonym extraction with word embeddings. *The Prague Bulletin of Mathematical Linguistics, 105*, 111–142. Retrieved from.

Lei, J., Rao, Y., Li, Q., Quan, X., & Wenyin, L. (2014). Towards building a social emotion detection system for online news. *Future Generation Computer Systems, 37*, 438–448.

Lei, W., Jin, X., Kan, M.-Y., Ren, Z., He, X., & Yin, D. (2018). Sequicity: Simplifying task-oriented dialogue systems with single sequence-to-sequence architectures. In *The 56th annual meeting of the association*.

Leung, K. W.-T., Ng, W., & Lee, D. L. (2008). Personalized concept-based clustering of search engine queries. In *IEEE transactions on knowledge and data engineering*.

Lewis, D. D., Yang, Y., Rose, T. G., & Li, F. (2004). Rcv1: A new benchmark collection for text categorization research. *Journal of Machine Learning Research, 5*, 361–397.

Li, R., Ebrahimi Kahou, S., Schulz, H., Michalski, V., Charlin, L., & Pal, C. (2018). Towards deep conversational recommendations. *Advances in Neural Information Processing Systems, 31*.

Li, X., Feng, J., Meng, Y., Han, Q., Wu, F., & Li, J. (2020). A unified MRC framework for named entity recognition. In *ACL* (pp. 5849–5859).

Li, R., Wang, X., & Yu, H. (2020). MetaMT, a meta learning method leveraging multiple domain data for low resource machine translation. In *AAAI*.

Li, Y., Zhao, L., Wang, J., & Hestness, J. (2019). *Compositional generalization for primitive substitutions.* arXiv preprint, arXiv:1910.02612.

Liang, P. (2016). Learning executable semantic parsers for natural language understanding. *Communications of the ACM, 59*(9), 68–76.

Liang, J., Zhao, C., Wang, M., Qiu, X., & Li, L. (2021). Finding sparse structures for domain specific neural machine translation. In *Proceedings of the AAAI conference on artificial intelligence, Vol. 35, No. 15* (pp. 13333–13342).

Liang, C., Berant, J., Le, Q., Forbus, K. D., & Lao, N. (2016). *Neural symbolic machines: Learning semantic parsers on freebase with weak supervision. arXiv preprint arXiv:1611.00020.*

Liang, P., Jordan, M. I., & Klein, D. (2011). Learning dependency-based compositional semantics. *Computational Linguistics, 39*(2), 389–446.

Liang, C., Norouzi, M., Berant, J., Le, Q. V., & Lao, N. (2018). Memory augmented policy optimization for program synthesis and semantic parsing. In *Advances in neural information processing systems* (pp. 10015–10027).

Lin, Z., Madotto, A., Winata, G. I., Xu, P., Jiang, F., Hu, Y., … Fung, P. (2021). *BiToD: A bilingual multi-domain dataset for task-oriented dialogue modeling.* Retrieved from https://arxiv.org/pdf/2106.02787v1.pdf.

Lin, Z., Madotto, A., Wu, C.-S., & Fung, P. (2019). Personalizing dialogue agents via meta-learning. In *ACL*.

Lin, X. V., Socher, R., & Xiong, C. (2018). Multi-hop knowledge graph reasoning with reward shaping. In *EMNLP*.

Ling, X., & Weld, D. S. (2012). Fine-grained entity recognition. In *The 26th AAAI conference on artificial intelligence (AAAI)*.

Lison, P., & Tiedemann, J. (2016). *Opensubtitles2016: Extracting large parallel corpora from movie and tv subtitles.*

Liu, B. (2012). *Sentiment analysis and opinion mining.* Retrieved from https://www.cs.uic.edu/~liub/FBS/SentimentAnalysis-and-OpinionMining.pdf.

Liu, W., & Cai, S. (2015). Translating electronic health record notes from english to spanish: A preliminary study. *BioNLP*, *15*, 134–140.

Liu, J., Chang, W., Wu, Y., & Yang, Y. (2017). Deep learning for extreme multi-label text classification. In *SIGIR* (pp. 115–124).

Loula, J., Baroni, M., & Lake, B. M. (2018). *Rearranging the familiar: Testing compositional generalization in recurrent networks. arXiv preprint.*

Luong, M.-T., & Manning, C. D. (2015). Stanford neural machine translation systems for spoken language domains. In *The 12th international workshop on spoken language translation* (pp. 76–79).

Luong, M. T., Pham, H., & Manning, C. D. (2015). *Effective approaches to attention-based neural machine translation. arXiv preprint arXiv:1508.04025.*

Lv, X., Gu, Y., Han, X., Hou, L., Li, J., & Liu, Z. (2019). Adapting meta knowledge graph information for multi-hop reasoning over few-shot relations. In *ACL*.

Majumder, N., Poria, S., Hazarika, D., Mihalcea, R., Gelbukh, A., & Cambria, E. (2019). DialogueRNN: An attentive RNN for emotion detection in conversations. *In Proceedings of the AAAI conference on artificial intelligence, Vol. 33, No.01, 6818–6825.*

Manning, C. D., Surdeanu, M., Bauer, J., Finkel, J. R., Bethard, S., & McClosky, D. (2014). The Stanford CoreNLP natural language processing toolkit. In *Association for computational linguistics (ACL) system demonstrations.*

Manning, C., Raghavan, P., & Schütze, H. (2008). *Introduction to information retrieval.* Cambridge, UK: Cambridge University Press.

Marsh, E., & Perzanowski, D. (1998). *MUC-7 evaluation of IE technology: Overview of results.* Retrieved from https://www-nlpir.nist.gov/related_projects/muc/proceedings/muc_7_proceedings/marsh_slides.pdf.

Matuszek, C., FitzGerald, N., Zettlemoyer, L., Bo, L., & Fox, D. (2012). A joint model of language and perception for grounded attribute learning. In *International conference on machine learning (ICML)* (pp. 1671–1678).

Melville, P., Gryc, W., & Lawrence, R. D. (2009). Sentiment analysis of blogs by combining lexical knowledge with text classification. In *Proceedings of the 15th SIGKDD international conference on knowledge discovery and data mining* (pp. 1275–1284).

Meng, L. (2014). A survey on query suggestion. *International Journal of Hybrid Information Technology*, *7*(6), 43–56.

Mi, F., Huang, M., Zhang, J., & Faltings, B. (2019). Meta-learnaing for low-resource natural language generation in task-oriented dialogue systems. In *IJCAI*.

Mikolov, T., Sutskever, I., Chen, K., Corrado, G. S., & Dean, J. (2013). Distributed representations of words and phrases and their compositionality. *Advances in Neural Information Processing Systems*, *26*.

Mikolov, T., Chen, K., Corrado, G., & Dean, J. (2013). *Efficient estimation of word representations in vector space.* Retrieved from Computing Research Repository, abs/1301.3781.

Misra, D., Chang, M.-W., He, X., & Yih, W.-T. (2018). *Policy shaping and generalized update equations for semantic parsing from denotations. arXiv preprint arXiv:1809.01299.*

Mnih, A., & Hinton, G. (2007). Three new graphical models for statistical language modelling. In *ICML* (pp. 641–648).

Mohammad, S. (2012). #Emotional tweets. In **SEM 2012: The first joint conference on lexical and computational semantics—Volume 1: Proceedings of the main conference and the shared task, and Volume 2: Proceedings of the sixth international workshop on semantic evaluation (SemEval 2012)* (pp. 246–255).

Montague, R. (1973). The proper treatment of quantification in ordinary English. In *Approaches to natural language* (pp. 221–242). Dordrecht/Chicago: Springer.

Mrksic, N., Seaghdha, D. O., Thomson, B., Gasic, M., Su, P. H., Vandyke, D., … Young, S. (2015). Multi-domain dialog state tracking using recurrent neural networks. In *The 7th international joint conference on natural language processing.*

Mrksic, N., Seaghdha, D. O., Wen, T.-H., Thomson, B., & Young, S. (2017). Neural belief tracker: Data-driven dialogue state tracking. In *The 55th annual meeting of the association for computational linguistics.*

Nakazawa, T., Yaguchi, M., Uchimoto, K., Utiyama, M., Sumita, E., Kurohashi, S., & Isahara, H. (2016). ASPEC: Asian scientific paper excerpt corpus. In *LREC*.

Nam, J., Kim, J., Mencia, E. L., Gurevych, I., & Furnkranz, J. (2014). Large-scale multi-label text classification—Revisiting neural networks. In *ECML-PKDD* (pp. 437–452).

Neudecker, C. (2016). An open corpus for named entity recognition in historic newspapers. In *LREC*.

Nguyen, T. H., & Grishman, R. (2015). Relation extraction: Perspective from convolutional neural networks. In *The 1st workshop on vector space modeling for natural language processing.*

Nichol, A., Achia, J., & Schulman, J. (2018). *On first-order meta-learning algorithms.* Retrieved from arXiv preprintarXiv:1803.02999.

Nooralahzadeh, F., Øvrelid, L., & Lønning, J. T. (2018). Evaluation of domain-specific word embeddings using knowledge resources. In *Proceedings of the eleventh international conference on language resources and evaluation (LREC 2018)*.

Obamuyide, A., & Vlachos, A. (2019). Model-agnostic meta-learning for relation classification with limited supervision. In *ACL*.

Ooi, J., Ma, X., & Liew, S.-C. (2015). *A survey of query expansion, query suggestion and query refinement techniques*. Retrieved from https://www.researchgate.net/publication/282610255.

Pang, B., & Lee, L. (2005). Seeing stars: Exploiting class relationships for sentiment categorization with respect to rating scales. *arXiv preprint*, cs/0506075.

Papineni, K., Roukos, S., Ward, T., & Zhu, W. J. (2002). Bleu: A method for automatic evaluation of machine translation. In *Proceedings of the 40th annual meeting of the association for computational linguistics* (pp. 311–318).

Pasupat, P., & Liang, P. (2015). Compositional semantic parsing on semi-structured tables. In *Association for Computational Linguistics (ACL)*.

Paulheim, H. (2017). Knowledge graph refinement: A survey of approaches and evaluation methods. *Semantic Web*, *8*(3), 489–508.

Pennington, J., Socher, R., & Manning, C. (2014). Glove: Global vectors for word representation. In *The 2014 conference on empirical methods in natural language processing (EMNLP)* (pp. 1532–1543).

Petroni, F., Piktus, A., Fan, A., Lewis, P., Yazdani, M., Cao, N. D., … Riedel, S. (2021). KILT: A benchmark for knowledge intensive language tasks. In *NAACL*.

Pilehvar, M. T., & Collier, N. (2016). Improved semantic representation for domain-specific entities. In *Retrieved from the 15th workshop on biomedical natural language processing*.

Pollack, J. B. (1990). Recursive distributed representations. *Artificial Intelligence*, *46*(1–2), 77–105.

Poria, S., Majumder, N., Mihalcea, R., & Hovy, E. (2019). Emotion recognition in conversation: Research challenges, datasets, and recent advances. *IEEE Access*, *7*, 100943–100953.

Prokopidis, P., Papavassiliou, V., & Piperidis, S. (2016). Parallel global voices: A collection of multilingual corpora with citizen media stories. In *The tenth international conference on language resources and evaluation (LREC 2016)*.

PubMed. (2007). *PubMed home*. Medline. http://www.ncbi.nlm.nih.gov/sites/entrez.

Qian, K., & Yu, Z. (2019). Domain adaptive dialog generation via meta learning. In *ACL*.

Qian, Q., Huang, M., Zhao, H., Xu, J., & Zhu, X. (2017). *Assigning personality/identity to a chatting machine for coherent conversation generation*. Retrieved from arXiv preprint arXiv:1706.02861.

Qin, L., Xu, X., Che, W., Zhang, Y., & Liu, T. (2020). Dynamic fusion network for multi-domain end-to-end task-oriented dialog. In *ACL*.

Qu, M., Gao, T., Xhonneux, L.-P. A., & Tang, J. (2020). Few-shot relation extraction via Bayesian meta-learning on relation graphs. In *ICML*.

Rafalovitch, A., Dale, R., et al. (2009). United nations general assembly resolutions: A six-language parallel corpus. In *Vol. 12. The MT Summit* (pp. 292–299).

Rajpurkar, P., Zhang, J., Lopyrev, K., & Liang, P. (2016). Squad: 100,000+ questions for machine comprehension of text. In *The 2016 conference on empirical methods in natural language processing* (pp. 2383–2392).

Rastogi, A., Zang, X., Sunkara, S., Gupta, R., & Khaitan, P. (2019). *Towards scalable multi-domain conversational agents: The schema-guided dialogue dataset*. Retrieved from https://arxiv.org/abs/1909.05855.

Ren, S., Zhang, Z., Liu, S., Zhou, M., & Ma, S. (2019). Unsupervised neural machine translation with smt as posterior regularization. In *AAAI*.

Richens, R. H. (1956). Preprogramming for mechanical translation. *Mechanical Translation*, *3*(1), 20–25.

Riedel, S., Yao, L., & McCallum, A. (2010). Modeling relations and their mentions without labeled text. In *European conference on machine learning and knowledge discovery in databases* (pp. 148–163). Springer.

Robbins, H., & Monro, S. (1951). A stochastic approximation method. *The Annals of Mathematical Statistics*, 400–407.

Saha, A., Pahuja, V., Khapra, M. M., Sankaranarayanan, K., & Chandar, S. (2018). Complex sequential question answering: Towards learning to converse over linked question answer pairs with a knowledge graph. In *Thirty-second AAAI conference on artificial intelligence*.

Sap, M., Le Bras, R., Allaway, E., Bhagavatula, C., Lourie, N., Rashkin, H., et al. (2019). Atomic: An atlas of machine commonsense for if-then reasoning. In *Proceedings of the AAAI conference on artificial intelligence, Vol. 33, No. 01* (pp. 3027–3035).

Scherer, K. R., & Wallbott, H. G. (1994). Evidence for universality and cultural variation of differential emotion response patterning. *Journal of Personality and Social Psychology*, *66*(2), 310.

Schlag, I., Irie, K., & Schmidhuber, J. (2021). Linear transformers are secretly fast weight programmers. *International Conference on Machine Learning* (pp. 9355–9366). PMLR.

Sennrich, R., Haddow, B., & Birch, A. (2016a). *Edinburgh neural machine translation systems for wmt 16*. Retrieved from arXiv preprint arXiv:1606.02891.

Sennrich, R., Haddow, B., & Birch, A. (2016b). Improving neural machine translation models with monolingual data. In *The 54th annual meeting of the association for computational linguistics (Volume 1: Long papers)* (pp. 86–96).

Sennrich, R., Schwenk, H., & Aransa, W. (2013). A multi-domain translation model framework for statistical machine translation. In *The 51st annual meeting of the association for computational linguistics (Volume 1: Long papers)*.

Shahraki, A. G., & Zaiane, O. R. (2017). Lexical and learning-based emotion mining from text. In *Proceedings of the international conference on computational linguistics and intelligent text processing Vol. 9* (pp. 24–55).

Shen, T., Geng, X., Qin, T., Guo, D., Tang, D., Duan, N., ... Jiang, D. (2019). Multi-task learning for conversational question answering over a large-scale knowledge base. In *Conference on empirical methods in natural language processing and the 9th international joint conference on natural language processing (EMNLP-IJCNLP)* (pp. 2442–2451).

Shen, Y., Chen, J., Huang, P.-S., Guo, Y., & Gao, J. (2018). M-Walk: Learning to walk over graphs using monte carlo tree search. In *NeurIPS* (pp. 6786–6797).

Shen, Y., He, X., Gao, J., Deng, L., & Mesnil, G. (2014). Learning semantic representations using convolutional neural networks for web search. In *The 23rd international conference on World Wide Web* (pp. 373–374).

Sidiropoulos, N. D., Lathauwer, L. D., Fu, X., Huang, K., Papalexakis, E. E., & Faloutsos, C. (2017). Tensor decomposition for signal processing and machine learning. *IEEE Transactions on Signal Processing, 65*(13), 3551–3582.

Skadins, R., Tiedemann, J., Rozis, R., & Deksne, D. (2014). Billions of parallel words for free: Building and using the eu bookshop corpus. In *LREC*.

Soares, L. B., FitzGerald, N., Ling, J., & Kwiatkowski, T. (2019). *Matching the blanks: Distributional similarity for relation learning. arXiv preprint arXiv:1906.03158*.

Socher, R., Perelygin, A., Wu, J., Chuang, J., Manning, C. D., Ng, A., & Potts, C. (2013). Recursive deep models for semantic compositionality over a sentiment tree-bank. In *The 2013 conference on empirical methods in natural language processing*.

Socher, R., Huval, B., Manning, C. D., & Ng, A. Y. (2012). Semantic composition-ality through recursive matrix-vector spaces. In *The 2012 joint conference on empirical methods in natural language processing and computational natural language learning*.

Song, F., & Croft, W. B. (1999). A general language model for information retrieval. In *The eighth international conference on Information and knowledge management*.

Sorower, M. S. (2010). *A literature survey on algorithms for multi-label learning. Vol. 18* (pp. 1–25). Corvallis: Oregon State University.

Speer, R., Chin, J., & Havasi, C. (2017). Conceptnet 5.5: An open multilingual graph of general knowledge. In *Thirty-first AAAI conference on artificial intelligence*.

Steinberger, R., Pouliquen, B., Widiger, A., Ignat, C., Erjavec, T., Tufis, D., & Varga, D. (2006). *The jrc-acquis: A multilingual aligned parallel corpus with 20+ languages. arXiv preprint cs/0609058*.

Stent, A., Marge, M., & Singhai, M. (2005). Evaluating evaluation methods for generation in the presence of variation. In *International conference on computational linguistics and intelligent text processing* (pp. 341–351).

Stoikos, S., & Izbicki, M. (2020). Multilingual emoticon prediction of tweets about COVID-19. In *COLING (PEOPLES)*.

Strapparava, C., & Mihalcea, R. (2008). Learning to identify emotions in text. In *Proceedings of the 2008 symposium on Applied computing* (pp. 1556–1560).

Strapparava, C., & Mihalcea, R. (2007). Semeval-2007 task 14: Affective text. In *The 4th international workshop on semantic evaluations, SemEval '07* (pp. 70–74).

Sun, Y., Tang, D., Duan, N., Gong, Y., Feng, X., Qin, B., & Jiang, D. (2019). Neural semantic parsing in low-resource settings with back-translation and meta-learning. In *AAAI*.

Sun, Z., Hu, W., & Li, C. (2017). Cross-lingual entity alignment via joint attribute-preserving embedding. In *ISWC* (pp. 628–644).

Sutskever, I., Vinyals, O., & Le, Q. V. (2014). Sequence to sequence learning with neural networks. In *Advances in neural information processing systems* (pp. 3104–3112).

Sutton, R. S., McAllester, D., Singh, S., & Mansour, Y. (1999). *Policy gradient methods for reinforcement learning with function approximation*. Retrieved from NIPS https://papers.nips.cc/paper/1999/file/464d828b85b0bed98e80ade0a5c43b0f-Paper.pdf.

Talmor, A., & Berant, J. (2018). *The web as a knowledge-base for answering complex questions. arXiv preprint arXiv:1803.06643*.

Tellex, S., Kollar, T., Dickerson, S., Walter, M. R., Banerjee, A. G., Teller, S. J., & Roy, N. (2011). Understanding natural language commands for robotic navigation and mobile manipulation. In *The advancement of artificial intelligence (AAAI)*.

Thompson, C. A., & Mooney, R. J. (2003). Acquiring word-meaning mappings for natural language interfaces. *Journal of Artificial Intelligence Research, 18*(1), 1–44.

Thrun, S., & Pratt, L. (2012). *Learning to learn.* Springer.

Tiedemann, J. (2012). Parallel data, tools and interfaces in opus. In *Vol. 2012. Lrec* (pp. 2214–2218).

Tiedemann, J. (2020). *MT, The tatoeba translation challenge—Realistic data sets for low resource and multilingual.* https://arxiv.org/pdf/2010.06354v1.pdf.

Tjong Kim Sang, E. F. (2002). ntroduction to the CoNLL-2002 shared task: Language-independent named entity recognition. In *CoNLL*.

Tjong Kim Sang, E. F., & De Meulder, F. (2003). Introduction to the CoNLL-2003 shared task: Language-independent named entity recognition. In *CoNLL* (pp. 142–147).

Toutanova, K., Chen, D., Pantel, P., Poon, H. F., Choudhury, P., & Gamon, M. (2015). Representing text for joint embedding of text and knowledge bases. In *EMNLP*.

Tran, V. K., & Nguyen, L. M. (2017). Semantic refinement gru-based neural language generation for spoken dia- logue systems. In *PACLING*.

Van der Plas, L., & Tiedemann, J. (2006). Finding synonyms using automatic word alignment and measures of distributional similarity. In *Retrieved from 21st international conference on computational linguistics*.

Vaswani, A., Shazeer, N., Parmar, N., Uszkoreit, J., Jones, L., Gomez, A. N., … Polosukhin, I. (2017). Attention is all you need. *Advances in Neural Information Processing Systems, 30,* 5998–6008.

Vilalta, R., & Drissi, Y. (2002). A perspective view and survey of meta-learning. *Artificial Intelligence Review, 18*(2), 77–95.

Volkova, E. P., Mohler, B. J., Meurers, D., Gerdemann, D., & Lthoff, H. H. (2010). Emotional perception of fairy tales: Achieving agreement in emotion annotation of text. In *The NAACL HLT 2010 workshop on computational approaches to analysis and generation of emotion in text, CAAGET '10*.

Vrandecic, D., & Krotzsch, M. (2014). Wikidata: A free collaborative knowledge base. *Communications of the ACM, 57*(10), 78–85.

Walker, C., Strassel, S., Medero, J., & Maeda, K. (2005). *Ace 2005 multilingual training corpus-linguistic data consortium..* https://catalog.ldc.upenn.edu/LDC2006T06.

Wallach, H. M. (2006). Topic modeling: beyond bag-of-words. In *The 23rd international conference on Machine learning* (pp. 977–984).

Walther, J. B. (1992). Interpersonal effects in computer-mediated interaction: A relational perspective. *Communication Research, 19*(1), 52–90.

Wang, Z., & Lemon, O. (2013). A simple and generic belief tracking mechanism for the dialog state tracking challenge: On the believability of observed information. In *SIGDIAL* (pp. 423–432).

Wang, W., Zhang, J., Li, Q., Hwang, M.-Y., Zong, C.-q., & Li, Z. (2019). Incremental learning from scratch for task-oriented dialogue systems.

Wang, L. L., Lo, K., Chandrasekhar, Y., Reas, R., Yang, J., Eide, D., et al. (2020). *Cord-19: The covid-19 open research dataset. ArXiv.*

Wang, R., Finch, A., Utiyama, M., & Sumita, E. (2017). Sentence embedding for neural machine translation domain adaptation. In *The 55th annual meeting of the association for computational linguistics (Volume 2: Short papers)*.

Wang, Q., Mao, Z., Wang, B., & Guo, L. (2017). Knowledge graph embedding: A survey of approaches and applications. In *Vol. 29. IEEE TKDE* (pp. 2724–2743). no. 12.

Wang, R., Utiyama, M., Liu, L., Chen, K., & Sumita, E. (2017). Instance weighting for neural machine translation domain adaptation. In *The 2017 conference on empirical methods in natural language processing* (pp. 1482–1488).

Warstadt, A., Singh, A., & Bowman, S. R. (2018). *Neural network acceptability judgments. arXiv preprint arXiv:1805.12471.*

Weischedel, R., & Brunstein, A. (2005). *Bbn pronoun coreference and entity type corpus.* Linguistic Data Consortium (LDC).

Weischedel, R., Palmer, M., Mitchell Marcus, E. H., Ramshaw, L., Xue, N., Taylor, A., et al. (2013). *Ontonotes release 5.0 ldc2013t19.* Linguistic Data Consortium (LDC).

Welling, M., & Teh, Y. W. (2011). Bayesian learning via stochastic gradient langevin dynamics. In *ICML*.

Wen, T.-H., Gasic, M., Mrksic, N., Su, P.-H., Vandyke, D., & Young, S. (2015). Semantically conditioned lstm-based natural language generation for spoken dialogue systems. In *EMNLP*.

Wen, T.-H., Gasic, M., Kim, D., Mrksic, N., Su, P.-H., Vandyke, D., & Young, S. (2015). Stochastic language generation in dialogue using recurrent neural networks with convolutional sentence reranking. In *Proceedings of the 16th annual meeting of the special interest group on discourse and dialogue*.

Williams, A., Nangia, N., & Bowman, S. (2018). A broad-coverage challenge corpus for sentence understanding through inference. In *NAACL*.

Woods, W. A. (1973). Progress in natural language understanding: an application to lunar geology. In *ACM-national computer conference and exposition* (pp. 441–450).

Woods, W. A., Kaplan, R. M., & Webber, B. N. (1972). *The lunar sciences natural language information system: Final report.* Technical report, BBN Report 2378, Bolt Beranek and Newman Inc.

Wu, S., & Dredze, M. (2019). Beto, bentz, becas: The surprising cross-lingual effectiveness of BERT. *CoRR*. abs/1904.09077.

Wu, Y., Schuster, M., Chen, Z., Le, Q. V., Norouzi, M., Macherey, W., … Klingner, J. (2016). *Google's neural machine translation system: Bridging the gap between human and machine translation. arXiv preprint arXiv:1609.08144.*

Wu, Q., Lin, Z., Wang, G., Chen, H., Karlsson, B. F., Huang, B., & Lin, C.-Y. (2020). Enhanced meta-learning for cross-lingual named entity recognition with minimal resources. In *AAAI*.

Wu, J., Xiong, W., & Wang, W. Y. (2019). Learning to learn and predict: A meta-learning approach for multi-label classification. In *ACL*.

Xia, C., Zhang, C., Yang, T., Li, Y., Du, N., Wu, X., … Yu, P. (2019). Multi-grained named entity recognition. In *ACL* (pp. 1430–1440).

Xie, T., Wu, C. H., Shi, P., Zhong, R., Scholak, T., Yasunaga, M., … Xiong, C. (2022). *UnifiedSKG: Unifying and multi-tasking structured knowledge grounding with text-to-text language models. arXiv preprint, arXiv:2201.05966.*

Xie, R., Liu, Z., Luan, H., & Sun, M. (2017). Image-embodied knowledge representation learning. In *IJCAI* (pp. 3140–3146).

Xing, C., Wu, W., Wu, Y., Liu, J., Huang, Y., Zhou, M., & Ma, W.-Y. (2017). Topic aware neural response generation. In *AAAI*.

Xiong, W., Hoang, T., & Wang, W. Y. (2017). Deeppath: A reinforcement learning method for knowledge graph reasoning. In *EMNLP*.

Xiong, W., Yu, M., Chang, S., Guo, X., & Wang, W. Y. (2018). One-shot relational learning for knowledge graphs. In *The 2018 conference on empirical methods in natural language processing* (pp. 1980–1990).

Xu, J., & Croft, W. B. (1996). Query expansion using local and global document analysis. In *SIGIR '96 proceedings of the 19th annual international ACM SIGIR conference on research and development in information retrieval*.

Xu, Y., Mou, L., Li, G., Chen, Y., Peng, H., & Jin, Z. (2015). Classifying relations via long short term memory networks along shortest dependency paths. In *Conference on empirical methods in natural language processing*.

Xu, H., Liu, B., Shu, L., & Yu, P. S. (2018). Lifelong domain word embedding via meta-learning. In *IJCAI*.

Yadollahi, A., Shahraki, A., & Zaiane, O. (2018). *Current state of text sentiment analysis from opinion to emotion mining.* Retrieved from ACM Computing Surveys.

Yang, Y. (2001). A study of thresholding strategies for text categorization. In *The 24th annual international ACM SIGIR conference on research and development in information retrieval (SIGIR)* (pp. 137–145).

Yang, S., Wang, Y., & Chu, X. (2020). *A survey of deep learning techniques for neural machine translation.* Retrieved from https://arxiv.org/abs/2002.07526.

Yao, Y., Ye, D., Li, P., Han, X., Lin, Y., Liu, Z., … Sun, M. (2019). *Docred: A large-scale document-level relation extraction dataset. arXiv preprint arXiv:1906.06127.*

Ye, Z.-X., & Ling, Z.-H. (2019). *Multi-level matching and aggregation network for few-shot relation classification. arXiv preprint arXiv:1906.06678.*

Yeh, C., Wu, W., Ko, W., & Wang, Y. F. (2017). Learning deep latent space for multi-label classification. In *AAAI* (pp. 2838–2844).

Yih, W.-T., Richardson, M., Meek, C., Chang, M.-W., & Suh, J. (2016). The value of semantic parse labeling for knowledge base question answering. In *ACL*.

You, W., Sun, S., & Iyyer, M. (2020). Hard-coded gaussian attention for neural machine translation. In *ACL*.

Yu, T., Zhang, R., Yang, K., Yasunaga, M., Wang, D., Li, Z., … Radev, D. (2018). Spider: A large-scale human-labeled dataset for complex and cross-domain semantic parsing and text-to-SQL task. In *EMNLP*.

Yu, T., Zhang, R., Yasunaga, M., Tan, Y. C., Lin, X. V., Li, S., … Radev, D. (2019). SParC: Cross-domain semantic parsing in context. In *ACL*.

Zelenko, D., Aone, C., & Richardella, A. (2003). Kernel methods for relation extraction. *Journal of Machine Learning Research, 3*(Feb), 1083–1106.

Zelle, M., & Mooney, R. J. (1996). Learning to parse database queries using inductive logic programming. In *AAAI* (pp. 1050–1055).

Zeng, D., Liu, K., Lai, S., Zhou, G., & Zhao, J. (2014). Relation classification via convolutional deep neural network. In *The 25th international conference on computational linguistics: Technical papers*.

Zhang, D., & Wang, D. (2015). *Relation classification via recurrent neural network. arXiv preprint arXiv:1508.01006*.

Zhang, M.-L., & Zhou, Z.-H. (2006). Multilabel neural networks with applications to functional genomics and text categorization. *IEEE Transactions on Knowledge and Data Engineering, 18*(10), 1338–1351.

Zhang, Y., Dai, H., Kozareva, Z., Smola, A. J., & Song, L. (2018). Variational reasoning for question answering with knowledge graph. In *Thirty-second AAAI conference on artificial intelligence*.

Zhang, S., Dinan, E., Urbanek, J., Szlam, A., Kiela, D., & Weston, J. (2018). Personalizing dialogue agents: I have a dog, do you have pets too? *arXiv preprint*, arXiv:1801.07243.

Zhang, L., Wang, S., & Liu, B. (2018). *Deep learning for sentiment analysis: A survey*. Retrieved from https://arxiv.org/abs/1801.07883.

Zhao, T., & Eskenazi, M. (2018). Zero-shot dialog generation with cross-domain latent actions. *CoRR*. abs/1805.04803.

Zhao, S., & Grishman, R. (2005). Extracting relations with integrated information using kernel methods. In *The 43rd annual meeting on association for computational linguistics* (pp. 419–426).

Zhao, Z., & Ma, X. (2019). Text emotion distribution learning from small sample: A meta-learning approach. In *ACL*.

Zhong, P., Wang, D., & Miao, C. (2019). Knowledge-enriched transformer for emotion detection in textual conversations. In *IJCNLP*.

Zhong, V., Xiong, C., & Socher, R. (2017). Seq2SQL: Generating structured queries from natural language using reinforcement learning. In *CoRR*.

Zhou, Z., & Feng, J. (2017). Deepforest: Towards an alternativet o deep neural networks. In *IJCAI* (pp. 3553–3559).

Zhou, H., Huang, M., Zhang, T., Zhu, X., & Liu, B. (2017). *Emotional chatting machine: Emotional conversation generation with internal and external memory*. Retrieved from arXiv preprint arXiv:1704.01074.

Zhou, D., Zhang, X., Zhou, Y., Zhao, Q., & Geng, X. (2016). Emotion distribution learning from texts. In *The 2016 conference on empirical methods in natural language processing* (pp. 638–647). Austin, Texas.

Zhu, Q., Huang, K., Zhang, Z., Zhu, X., & Huang, M. (2020). CrossWOZ: A large-scale chinese cross-domain task-oriented dialogue dataset. In *TACL*.

Zoph, B., Yuret, D., May, J., & Knight, K. (2016). Transfer learning for low-resource neural machine translation. In *EMNLP*.

CHAPTER

7

Meta-reinforcement learning

7.1 Background knowledge

Reinforcement learning is one of the three machine learning paradigms, differing from supervised learning (relying on input-output labeled data) and unsupervised learning (training without annotation). It concentrates on forming a policy of action behavior to maximize the overall reward and balancing the trade-off between exploration (in the unknown situation) and exploitation (in currently known information).

Deep reinforcement learning (DRL) is concerned with how an artificial agent solves a range of complex decision-making tasks based on given environments, previous experience, and a sequence of actions to maximize the cumulative reward. DRL is a type of reinforcement learning, combined with the deep learning technology (Goodfellow, Bengio, & Courville, 2016; LeCun, Bengio, & Hinton, 2015; Schmidhuber, 2015) for function approximation (like policy and value function estimation), which can be estimated through linear models as well. DRL is widely helpful in raw, high-dimensional states and action spaces for decision-making that rely on reward signals (François-Lavet, Henderson, Islam, Bellemare, & Pineau, 2018).

Reinforcement learning problems are formulated in a mathematical model, the Markov decision process (MDP). The MDP, a classical stochastic control method, is popular in solving optimization problems via dynamic programming. The MDP is a fundamental principle of reinforcement learning that assumes finite states with probabilistic transactions, and the Markov property indicates that the next state is solely dependent on current states. Per these assumptions, if the current state is unsure, it may be considered a hidden Markov process.

7.1.1 Basic components of a deep reinforcement learning system

DRL implements a deep neural network on state representation and function approximation for the four main components in the DRL system: a policy, a value function, a reward signal, and a model of the environment.

- A *policy* is a behavior an agent pursues during a given period. It can be a straightforward function, a lookup table, or a complicated computation.

Meta-Learning
https://doi.org/10.1016/B978-0-323-89931-4.00011-0

- A *value function* indicates what is good for the long term. In contrast, the reward presents the immediate and intrinsic benefits of environmental states, and value functions demonstrate the long-term benefits of states that are likely to task as follows.
- A *reward signal* defines the goal; the agent aims to maximize the cumulative sum of rewards during learning/reward-driven behavior, such that $R_T = \sum_{i=0}^{T} r_{t+1}$, where R_T is the total rewards and r_{t+1} is the immediate reward of taking action at time t on the environment regarding state s_{t+1}.
- A *model of the environment* enables the inference of the environment's behavior. An environment of reinforcement learning is regularly described as MDP.

The value function $v_\pi(s)$ of state s with discount γ of reward r under policy π is defined in Eq. (7.1) (Sutton & Barto, 2018):

$$v_\pi(s) = \mathbb{E}[R_t|s_t = s] = \mathbb{E}\left[\sum_{k=0}^{\infty} \gamma^k r_{t+k}|s_t = s\right] \tag{7.1}$$

It can be broken into the Bellman equation (Dixit & Sherrerd, 1990) based on action a taken at time t in Eq. (7.2), where s' denotes the state at time $t+1$ after the action (i.e., next state):

$$v_\pi(s) = \sum_a \pi(a|s) \sum_{s',r} p(s',r|s,a)[r + \gamma v_\pi(s')] \tag{7.2}$$

The action-value function $q_\pi(s,a) = \mathbb{E}[R_t|s_t = s, a_t = a]$ transitions into the Bellman equation, as expressed in Eq. (7.3):

$$q_\pi(s,a) = \sum_{s',r} p(s',r|s,a)\left[r + \gamma \sum_{a'} \pi(a'|s')q_\pi(s',a')\right] \tag{7.3}$$

7.1.2 Model-based and model-free approaches

Model-based reinforcement learning refers to obtaining the prime behavior obliquely through training a model concerning the surrounding environment through actions response and estimating the outcomes that may occur in the coming state and the instant reward (Ray & Tadepalli, 2011). The "model" means a transition probability distribution related to MDP and the reward function. In the model-based approach, the agent can predict the next state and reward before actually taking each action. Nevertheless, the model-based approach consumes more computing power due to its higher complexity than model-free approaches; furthermore, the effectiveness of the model-based approach can be limited by the ability to estimate the model. In contrast, *model-free* reinforcement learning means an "explicit trial-and-error" algorithm that cannot make such predictions (Sutton & Barto, 2018). There are two categories of model-free reinforcement learning paradigms: on-policy [e.g., State-Action-Reward-State-Action (SARSA), Actor-Critic and Proximal Policy ptimization (PPO)] and off-policy [e.g., Q-learning and Deep Q Network (DQN)].

7.1.3 Simulated environments

As stated above in Section 7.1.1, reinforcement learning heavily relied on given simulated environments. Existed reinforcement learning environments include:

- Arcade Learning Environment (Bellemare, Naddaf, Veness, & Bowling, 2013), for Atari 2600 games
- VizDoom (Kempka, Wydmuch, Runc, Toczek, & Jaśkowski, 2016), with semirealistic 3D environment
- TorchCraft (Synnaeve et al., 2016), supported by Facebook AI for real-time strategy games
- StarCraft II (Vinyals et al., 2017), developed by Blizzard based on StarCraft 2 game
- Quake III Arena first-person shooter engine byid Software in 2012, a classical simulator
- Project Malmo (Johnson, Hofmann, Hutton, & Bignell, 2016), supported by Microsoft for Minecraft game
- MuJoCo Physics Engine (Todorov, Erez, & Tassa, 2012) for general-purpose physics simulated environments
- OpenAI Gym (Brockman et al., 2016) with multiple games for algorithm comparison
- MuJoCo Control (Finn, Abbeel, & Levine, 2017) with two main environments: Forward/ Backward Ant and HalfCheetch, and Random Ant and HalfCheetch from MuJoCo Control (Finn et al., 2017), which are considered as baseline tasks in meta-reinforcement learning
- Robotic Manipulation (Gupta, Mendonca, Liu, Abbeel, & Levine, 2018) consists of tasks to move one or more blocks into a target region with sparse rewards
- MuJoCo 2D Locomotion (Gupta et al., 2018) conducts sparse rewards
- Maze2D and Maze3D (Kamienny et al., 2020) split exploration and exploitation
- Krazy-World (Stadie et al., 2018), officially released at https://github.com/bstadie/ krazyworld. This high-dimensional grid world game forces the agent to recognize and adapt multiple factors: various tile types, color palettes, and dynamics, leveraging high-level structures
- Meta-World, a novel set of benchmarks for meta-reinforcement learning tasks, see Section 7.6.1 for an explanation

7.1.4 Limitations of deep reinforcement learning

DRL fills the gap of various computing scenarios with diverse beneftis, such as tackling complex decision making in dynamic enviroments. However, challenges faced by DRL are still obvious, including:

- *Extensive training data* are consumed during computation, which is time-consuming, expensive, difficult to gather, and even more data-hungry than deep learning
- *High computational complexity* is associated with long-range time dependencies
- The *curse of dimension* remains, as even DRL allows agents to be trained in a high-dimensional state and action spaces; this issue still blocks DRL applications in certain situations
- *Time-consuming training* due to weak inductive bias: DRL require a long time for training until convergence; as reported by Botvinick et al. (2019), this is caused by weak inductive bias (discussed in Chapter 1, Section 1.2) and, Although weak inductive bias enables DRL to handle large variance, the trade-off is *low sample efficiency*

- For *credit assignment*, the impact of reward from the action solely should be split among the effects of reward from other factors and subsequent actions (Sutton & Barto, 2018)
- The trade-off between *exploration and exploitation*. DRL concerns the balance between exploration and exploitation: under what condition should the agent explore the environment via nonoptimal actions to improve the policy? and under what condition should the agent obey the optimal action as exploitation? Efficient exploration is one of the challenging issues in the DRL system. Early attempts to address this have offered many solutions (see Fu, Luo, & Levine, 2017; Houthooft et al., 2016; Kocsis & Szepesvári, 2006; Osband, Blundell, Pritzel, & Van Roy, 2016; Tang et al., 2017)
- *Standardized assessment and evaluation* for new techniques are lacking. Although DRL attracts much attention from academia and industries, such as the computer gaming community, the standard benchmarks to measure the performance across various existing and emerging techniques are still lacking

7.2 Meta-reinforcement learning introduction

Meta-reinforcement learning (Meta-RL) is an ambitious technology step toward general AI (also named Artificial general intelligence; AGI) , where AGI aims to learn as automatically and efficiently as, or even exceeding, human beings (Clune, 2019). In contrast to relying on hand-crafted learning strategies, the robust solution with Meta-RL depends on (a) the design of meta-learning, (b) the capability of meta-learning on the learning algorithms, and (c) the effectiveness of produced environments (Clune, 2019). Meta-RL aims to implement meta-learning approaches in the area of reinforcement learning, where the training and testing tasks are disjointed from each other, such as $\{T_{tra}\} \cap \{T_{test}\} = \emptyset$, but can be sampled from the same type of problems. It offers novel directions to tackle the limitations of the DRL approach.

7.2.1 Early development

The first Meta-RL approach can be traced back to 2001, which was proposed by Hochreiter and colleagues (Hochreiter, Younger, & Conwell, 2001), even before the formulation of Meta-RL was formalized. This is a supervised leaning approach rather than standard reinforcement learning method, but it shed light on early Meta-RL methods and developed the fundamental intuition behind many affinities shared with current Meta-RL algorithms. Hochreiter and colleagues proposed a recurrent neural network architecture with long short-term memory (LSTM) as a meta-learner to set up approximation of any quadratic function (e.g., $ax_1^2 + bx_2^2 + cx_1x_2 + dx_1 + ex_2 + f$, where a-f are constants and x is variable) via as few as 35 training samples. This approach consists of a subordinate and the supervisory system. The training data is a set of sequences $\{s_k\}$, $k = 1, \ldots, K$, and each sequences contain N samples, such that:

$$input : (x_k(j), y_k(j-1)) \to label : y_k(j)$$

$$where\ y_k(j) = f_k(x_k(j))$$

$$for\ j = 1, \ldots, N$$

Due to the volume conserving requirement, LSTM—its hidden states acting as the memory of trajectories for knowledge extraction—is selected as the optimal architecture for internalizing the pervious inputs and productively computing the weights through Back-Propagation Through Time (BPTT) and Real Time Recurrent Learning (RTRL).

7.2.2 Formalism

Although many researchers in the reinforcement learning community attempt to discuss the general intuition behind Meta-RL, Wang's team (2016) and Duan (2016) proposed the formal description of Meta-RL in the same year. Given a distribution D of tasks, each task of which is formularized to a MDP or slight modification of D, such as $D_i \in D$, each MDP is expressed with the four components as $D_i = \langle S, A, R_i, P_i \rangle$. On the other hand, some current researchers attempted to add or remove some component of them. For example, RL^2 (Duan et al., 2017) inserted an extra parameter T as horizon and NoRML (Yang, Caluwaerts, Iscen, Tan, & Finn, 2019) removed the reward term R. S and A denote a set of states and a set of actions, respectively, R_i represents the reward function, and P_i means the transition probability function.

Meta-RL makes it possible to leverage from prior knowledge through a recurrent model and interactions with a sequence of MDP environments in each episode to maximize the cumulative rewards. In contrast with reinforcement learning, the Meta-RL policy $\pi_\theta(a_{t-1}, r_{t-1}, s_t)$, which is estimated by the neural network parameters θ, leverages the last reward r_{t-1} and the last action a_{t-1} besides the current state s_t. Specifically, the set of states $\{x_s\}_{0 \leq s \leq t}$, the set of rewards $\{r_s\}_{0 \leq s \leq t}$, and the set of actions $\{a_s\}_{0 \leq s \leq t}$ are under measured from the start of the episode. The action $a_t \in A$ is processed as a function based on the comprehensive history $\mathcal{H}_t = \{x_0, a_0, r_0, ..., x_{t-1}, a_{t-1}, r_{t-1}, x_t\}$ for step t, of interaction with the MDP in the current episode.

During the bi-level optimization of Meta-RL, the inner loop implements the DRL method to guide the agent with surrounding environment to generate the maximum cumulative rewards. The outer loop conducts a novel environment for each iteration and adjusts parameters regarding the agent's behavior (Majid et al., 2021).

As training is finished, the parameters of the optimal policy will be frozen and assessed on a set of MDP from D or slight modification of D as testing tasks.

The overall setting of DRL and Meta-RL is generally similar, the main difference is that the last action a_{t-1} and the last reward r_{t-1} are involved as two additional parameters in the policy π_θ processing, such as $\pi_\theta(a_{t-1}, r_{t-1}, s_t)$ in Meta-RL, rather than $\pi_\theta(s_t)$ in the regular DRL which only involved s_t, where s_t denotes current state.

In general, the regular Meta-RL training steps can be summarized as follows:

1. Randomly sampling a MDP D_i
2. Initializing the hidden states
3. Performing and gathering a variety of trajectories while updating parameters
4. Repeating these above methods until convergence

7.2.3 Fundamental components

The three fundamental components for the basic policy computation are summarized below (Weng, 2019):

- A memory: a reasoning capacity based on the knowledge learning from interaction with the current environment at the current tasks. The recurrent models equipped hidden states for memorization by updating them during learning. Without memory, Meta-RL cannot be achieved.
- A Meta-RL paradigm is the key for rapid adaptation to unseen tasks during testing time by leveraging knowledge through training across a set of tasks.
- A MDPs distribution: the distribution for training and testing tasks under the assumption of MDPs

These three parts will be explored in detail in the following sections. Section 7.3 discusses different approaches regarding memory. Even as Meta-RL is just emerging, the passion from the researcher is dramatically increasing while a variety of Meta-RL methods has been proposed for multiple scenarios. These are investigated in Section 7.4. Section 7.5 examines the reward function and environments for the Meta-RL setup. Besides the above essential components during Meta-RL training periods, a standardized benchmark for broad Meta-RL assessments and evolution is reviewed in Section 7.6.

Meta-RL has obtained a surge of interest from many researchers and developed various novel directions and research lines since 2006. The rest of this chapter covers 25 state-of-the-art pieces of research, among which nine approaches are explored in detail, as summarized in Table 7.1. Although these 25 approaches certainly are milestones of various perspectives of Meta-RL, the selection is based on the relevance to the flow of this chapter.

TABLE 7.1 This table covers the mentioned nine pieces of research from Sections 7.3 to 7.7 from premier academic conferences. All this research either achieved state-of-the-art performance or contributed an influential impact on academia or industries.

Reference	Task	Method	Conference
7.3 Memory			
Hill et al. (2020)	External read-write memory for agents with multiple modalities	Dual-coding episodic memory	ICLR
7.4 Meta-reinforcement learning methods			
Al-Shedivat et al. (2018)	Continuous adaptation in nonstationary environment	MAML-based	ICLR
Gupta et al. (2018)	Exploration with structured noise	Model-agnostic exploration with structured noise (MAESN)	NeurIPS
Rothfuss, Lee, Clavera, Asfour, and Abbeel (2019)	Credit assignment	Proximal metapolicy search (ProMP)	ICLR
Song et al. (2020)	Second-order computation in MAML	Evolution strategies-MAML (ES-MAML)	ICLR

TABLE 7.1 This table covers the mentioned nine pieces of research from Sections 7.3 to 7.7 from premier academic conferences. All this research either achieved state-of-the-art performance or contributed an influential impact on academia or industries—cont'd

Reference	Task	Method	Conference
7.5 Reward & environment			
Campero, Raileanu, Küttler, and Grefenstette (2021)	Sparse extrinsic reward in procedurally generated environments	Adversarial motivated intrinsic goals (AMIGo)	ICLR
7.6 Benchmark			
Yu et al. (2021)	Meta-World	Meta-World	CoRL
7.7 Visual navigation			
Wortsman, Ehsani, Rastegari, Farhadi, and Mottaghi (2019)	Visual navigation to unseen scenes	Self-adaptive visual navigation	CVPR
Li et al. (2020)	Visual navigation	Unsupervised reinforcement learning of transferable meta-skills	CVPR

All the selected technologies deliver essential and fundamental influences as a solid foundation of the widely spread methods or theories either (i) with significantly and broadly practical contributions in diverse applications, (ii) shedding light on an important mainstream in academia with huge potential space for further exploration and investigation, (iii) or with promising solutions for the fundamental components that are hardly discussed but important to Meta-RL. This research recursively tracked to the related bibliographies in papers accepted at leading academic conferences: ICLR, CoRL, CVPR, and NeurIPS.

7.3 Memory

7.3.1 External read-write memory for agents with multiple modalities

One-shot and few-shot language models have attracted a surge of interest in machine learning communities. Fast mapping is a quick language-learning ability demonstrated by child development in which a new word can be rapidly learned by contrasting it with a familiar word. Hill et al. (2020) proposed a method to achieve fast mapping based on one-shot language processing in a 3D physical environment through a memory architecture named dual-coding episodic memory (DCEM).

This method aimed to produce an embodied learning system that supports processing of fast mapping and slow word learning in a 3D game-based simulated environment. The intelligent agent can learn the names of novel objects based on a single episode. Hence, the agent utilizes this knowledge to offer instructions on these objects right away. For instance, the agent can assess "move back an empyrean" with "move back" through slow learning and "empyrean" with fast mapping. The agent is trained with new external memory through conventional reinforcement and semisupervised predictive learning.

This 3D room environment is constructed by Unity (game engine), which contains N daily objects (e.g., teddy bear, pots) from a collection G. Each episode has a discovery phase and an instruction phase. A nonsense term is randomly assigned to each object as a preepisode setup. The agent needs to memorize the connection of words and objects during the discovery phase and then utilize the learner episode-specification knowledge to execute actions in the instruction phase.

Motivated by dual-coding theory (Paivio, 1969) in human memory, DCEM provides an external memory architecture for multiple modalities to find the keys (i.e., queries) and values needed to determine the keys and values among different modalities. In this 3D room task, the keys are associated with language, and the values are associated with vision. The overall pipeline of DCEM is displayed in Fig. 7.1. The agent writes the linguistic observation embeddings at the current timestep to the keys and the visual observation embeddings at the current timestep at the values of the memory for each timestep. For reading from memory, an estimated query is compared with the keys through cosine similarity, then the value with the most similar keys is returned. The similarities are utilized to weight the memories. These weighted memories are sent via a self-attention layer to generate a vector concatenated with new input and a state as a latent vector to pass to the LSTM core memory. Thus, the next state and the latent vector are generated.

DCEM is also compared to the architecture of Gated Transformer (Vaswani et al., 2017) as core memory by equipping a four-layer transformer with eight parallel heads for querying and a key-value size of 32 for each layer. In experiments of 100 timesteps, the Gated Transformer employs XL window-recurrence to send information to context windows, and DCEM uses an LSTM controller for obtaining information beyond 100 timesteps. As a result, DCEM appears much more memory-efficient than Gated Transformer.

The general architecture of the intelligent agent with memory is displayed in Fig. 7.2.

7.4 Meta-reinforcement learning methods

7.4.1 Continuous adaptation in nonstationary environments

Traditional reinforcement learning approaches concentrate on a stationary environment, which is too simplistic compared to real-world situations. These nonstationary environments are dynamic and may dramatically change all the time. Nonstationary environments force intelligent agents to adapt rapidly and continuously during training and execution. Regular solutions for nonstationary environments usually employ context detection (Silva, Basso, Bazzan, & Engel, 2006) and tracking (Sutton, Koop, & Silver, 2007) by repeatedly fine-tuning the policy in response to changes that happen in the environments. Due to the scarce interactions before the environment changes, sample inefficiency is another challenge. This continuous adaptation problem, an important aspect of continual learning (Ring, 1994) and never-ending learning (Mitchell et al., 2015), aims to learn a single and nonstationary task or environment. A basic fine-tuning strategy is not practical, as agents need to adapt to the dynamic changes in nonstationary environments during execution time with the hardship of scarce data. Thus, meta-learning is demanded.

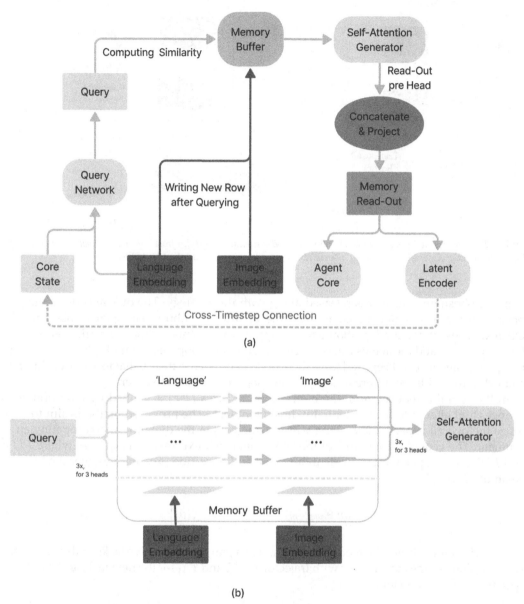

FIG. 7.1 Workflow of dual-coding episodic memory. *Modified from Hill, F., Tieleman, O., Glehn, T.V., Wong, N., Merzic, H., & Clark, S. (2020). Grounded language learning fast and slow. In: ICLR.*

Al-Shedivat et al. (2018) proposed a Meta-RL approach for multiagents for continuous adaptation. The agent is trained with an opponent based on low-data regimes under a nonstationary and adversarial environment. The proposed methods treat a nonstationary environment as multiple stationary tasks in chronological order to convert continuous adaptation into multiple tasks in a modified MAML. This learning is built on a 3D simulated environment

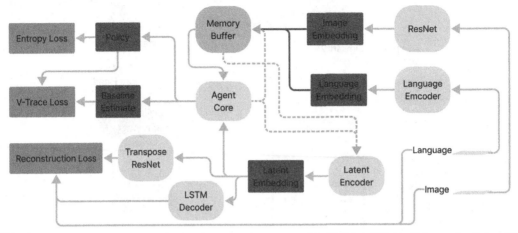

FIG. 7.2 General Architecture of dual-coding episodic memory. *Modified from Hill, F., Tieleman, O., Glehn, T.V., Wong, N., Merzic, H., & Clark, S. (2020). Grounded language learning fast and slow. In: ICLR.*

named Robosumo, which was released along with this strategy. The official code of the proposed approach and Robosumo is available at https://github.com/openai/robosumo by OpenAI. These iterated adaptation games support two agents competing against each other (i.e., opponent), and the agents can compete with the same opponent in multiple rounds. Thus, this pair of agents can keep updating their policy and adjust their behaviors under different competitions and three different design of agents—ant, bug, and spider.

In these multiagent regimes, the distribution of tasks $D(T)$ is shaped by environmental changes and altered to the sequentially dependent task. The proposed methods aim to minimize the overall expected loss along with interactions in the dynamic and competing environment. The goal of the length L of the task sequence is expressed in Eq. (7.4), where $\mathcal{P}(T_0)$ and $\mathcal{P}(T_{i+1}|T_i)$, respectively, represent the initial and transition probabilities over the Markov chain of tasks:

$$\min_\theta \mathbb{E}_{\mathcal{P}(T_0),\mathcal{P}(T_{i+1}|T_i)}\left[\sum_{i=1}^{L}\mathcal{L}_{T_i,T_{i+1}}(\theta)\right] \tag{7.4}$$

Eq. (7.5) demonstrates the meta-loss function of a pair of consecutive tasks as the following, where T_i denotes the current task with trajectories $\tau_{i,\theta}^{1:K}$ and T_{i+1} for the next task, and ϕ as task-specific policy parameters.

$$\mathcal{L}_{T_i,T_{i+1}}(\theta):=\mathbb{E}_{\tau_{i,\theta}^{1:K}\sim P_{T_i}(\tau|\theta)}\left[\mathbb{E}_{\tau_{i+1,\phi}\sim P_{T_{i+1}}(\tau|\phi)}\left[L_{T_{i+1}}\left(\tau_{i+1,\phi}\right)|\tau_{i,\theta}^{1:K},\theta\right]\right] \tag{7.5}$$

The core methods of the M-step meta-gradient can be summarized in Eqs. (7.6)–(7.8), denoting the set of step sizes in meta-gradient simultaneously optimized with θ. $\{\alpha_m\}_{m=1}^{M}$ denotes the learnable meta-gradient step size optimized jointly with parameter θ.

$$\phi_i^0:=\theta,\tau_\theta^{1:K}\sim P_{T_i}(\tau|\theta) \tag{7.6}$$

$$\phi_i^m := \phi_i^{m-1} - \alpha_m \nabla_{\phi_i^{m-1}} L_{T_i}\left(\tau_{i,\phi_i^{m-1}}^{1:K}\right), m = 1,\ldots,M-1 \qquad (7.7)$$

$$\phi_{i+1} := \phi_i^{M-1} - \alpha_M \nabla_{\phi_i^{M-1}} L_{T_i}\left(\tau_{i,\phi^{M-1}}^{1:K}\right) \qquad (7.8)$$

The policy gradient for T_i and T_{i+1} is expressed in Eq. (7.9), where π_θ and π_ϕ denote the initial policy and meta-updated policy, respectively:

$$\nabla_{\theta,\alpha}\mathcal{L}_{T_i,T_{i+1}}(\theta,\alpha) = \mathop{\mathbb{E}}_{\substack{\tau_{i,\phi} \\ \tau_{i,\theta,\phi}\sim P_{T_{i+1}}^{1:K}\sim P_{T_i}(\tau|\theta)}}\left[L_{T_{i+1}}\left(\tau_{i+1,\phi}\right)\left[\nabla_{\theta,\alpha}\log\pi_\phi\left(\tau_{i+1,\phi}\right) + \nabla_\theta \sum_{k=1}^K \log\pi_\theta\left(\tau_{i,\theta}^k\right)\right]\right]$$

$$(7.9)$$

The importance-corrected single-step meta-update for adaption during execution is expressed in Eq. (7.10), where K is the number of trajectories, and $\pi_{\phi_{i-1}}$ and π_θ are outputted from T_{i-1} and T_i, separately:

$$\phi_i := \theta - \alpha \frac{1}{K} \sum_{k=1}^K \left(\frac{\pi_\theta\left(\tau^k\right)}{\pi_{\phi_{i-1}}\left(\tau^k\right)}\right)\nabla_\theta L_{T_{i-1}}\left(\tau^k\right), \tau^{1:K} \sim P_{T_{i-1}}(\tau|\phi_{i-1}) \qquad (7.10)$$

This approach enables process adaptation in both meta-training and execution time. Table 7.2 indicates meta-training methods, whereas Table 7.3 outlines the adaptation during execution.

TABLE 7.2   General meta-learning process.

Input: $P(T_i, T_{i+1})$, distribution over pairs-wise tasks
  β, hyperparameter of learning rate
Output: $\theta*$ and $\alpha*$, optimal parameters

1: θ and $\alpha \rightarrow$ random initialization

2: **repeat**
3:   Randomly sample a batch pair-wise tasks, $\{(T_i, T_{i+1})\}_{i=1}^n$

4:   **for all** pair-wise task (T_i, T_{i+1}) in the batch **do**
5:     Randomly sample trajectory $\tau_\theta^{1:K}\sim T_i$ through π_θ
6:     Evaluate $\phi = \phi(\tau_\theta^{1:K}, \theta, \alpha)$
7:     Randomly sample trajectory $\tau_\phi \sim T_{i+1}$ through π_ϕ
8:   **end for**

9:   Evaluate $\nabla_\theta L_{T_i,T_{i+1}}$ and $\nabla_\alpha L_{T_i,T_{i+1}}$ through $\tau_\theta^{1:K}$ and τ_ϕ
10:   Update $\theta \leftarrow \theta + \beta \nabla_\theta L_T(\theta,\alpha)$
11:   Update $\alpha \leftarrow \alpha + \beta \nabla_\alpha L_T(\theta,\alpha)$

12: **until** Convergence

Modified from Al-Shedivat, M., Bansal, T., Burda, Y., Sutskever, I., Mordatch, I., & Abbeel, P. (2018). Continuous adaptation via meta-learning in nonstationary and competitive environments. In ICLR.

TABLE 7.3   General adaption process.

Input: A sequence of tasks $T_1, T_2, T_3, \dots$

1: $\phi = \theta$

2: **while** novel incoming tasks **do**
3:      Obtain a new task T_i from the sequence
4:      Process T_i through π_ϕ policy
5:      Gather trajectories $\tau_{i,\,\phi}^{1:K}$ as processing T_i
6:      Update $\phi \leftarrow \phi(\tau_{i,\,\phi}^{1:K}, \theta^*, \alpha^*)$ through importance-corrected meta-update
7: **end while**

Modified from Al-Shedivat, M., Bansal, T., Burda, Y., Sutskever, I., Mordatch, I., & Abbeel, P. (2018). Continuous adaptation via meta-learning in nonstationary and competitive environments. In ICLR.

Related Meta-RL algorithms for sample efficiency

Regarding the sample efficiency task, other Meta-RL methods also achieve state-of-the-art performance. Rakelly and colleagues (Rakelly, Zhou, Quillen, Finn, & Levine, 2019) developed an off-policy Meta-RL to improve sample efficiency. Frans and colleagues (Frans, Ho, Chen, Abbeel, & Schulman, 2018) leveraged hierarchically structured policies with a higher sample efficiency when adapting to novel situations. Nagabandi and colleagues (Nagabandi, Finn, & Levine, 2019) developed a continued adaptation method incorporating model-based reinforcement learning algorithms through meta-learning for online learning (MOLe).

7.4.2 Exploration with structured noise

Exploration is one of the critical topics that reinforcement learning attempts to solve, particularly for productive exploring in novel scenarios. However, traditional Meta-RL approaches face several difficulties:

- Optimal policies are qualitatively distinct from powerful exploration strategies. Optimal policies have deterministic behavior under completed known environments. In contrast, efficient exploration in new scenarios heavily relies on stochasticity. Early approaches, such as MAML, failed to explore efficiency because of the deficient structured stochasticity. The balance of optimal policies and exploratory strategies is not effective with standard time-invariant representation for action distributions.
- Many attempts of existing Meta-RLs develop the behavior of learning the entire learning method. In this way, the asymptotic performance is constrained because the learned algorithm is irrelated to the convergent iterative optimization procedure.

To tackle these problems, Gupta et al. (2018) proposed a Meta-RL approach named Model-Agnostic Exploration with Structured Noise (MAESN) based on MAML. This method implements prior experience to initialize a policy and obtain a latent exploration space. The latent exploration space can sample temporally coherent structured behaviors, producing stochastic exploration strategies that allow leveraging prior knowledge more robustly than simple random noise. The official code is available at https://github.com/russellmendonca/maesn_suite.

The general meta-training problem can be described in several steps from Eqs. (7.11) to (7.14) and contains two objectives—one for the postupdate expected reward of each task expressed in Eq. (7.11) and another with KL divergence between the variational parameters of each task and the prior knowledge, as expressed in Eq. (7.12). α denotes the per-parameter step sizes, and $\circ$ represents the elementwise product. μ_i, and σ_i denote preupdate variational parameters, μ_i', and σ_i' represent the latent distribution parameters, and z_i is fixed latent variable. R_i represents the reward function, α_μ, α_σ, and α_θ are the hyperparameters of step size.

$$\max_{\theta,\mu_i,\sigma_i} \sum_{i \in \text{tasks}} E_{a_t \sim \pi(a_t|s_t;\theta_i',z_i')} \left[\sum_{z_i' \sim \mathcal{N}(\mu_i',\sigma_i')} R_i(s_t) \right] - \sum_{i \in \text{tasks}} D_{KL}(\mathcal{N}(\mu_i,\sigma_i) \| \mathcal{N}(0,I)) \qquad (7.11)$$

$$\mu_i' = \mu_i + \alpha_\mu \circ \nabla_{\mu_i} E_{a_t \sim \pi(a_t|s_t;\theta,z_i)} \left[\sum_t \sim R_i(s_t) \right] \qquad (7.12)$$

$$\sigma_i' = \sigma_i + \alpha_\sigma \circ \nabla_{\sigma_i} E_{a_t \sim \pi(a_t|s_t;\theta,z_i)} \left[\sum_{z_i \sim \mathcal{N}(\mu_i,\sigma_i)} R_i(s_t) \right] \qquad (7.13)$$

$$\theta_i' = \theta + \alpha_\theta \circ \nabla_\theta E_{a_t \sim \pi(a_t|s_t;\theta,z_i)} \left[\sum_z R_i \sim \mathcal{N}(\mu_i,\sigma_i) \right] \qquad (7.14)$$

The summarized methods of MAESN are outlined in Table 7.4.

TABLE 7.4   General training methods of MAESN meta-RL.

1: Initialize variational parameters μ_i, σ_i for each training task τ_i

2: **for** $k \in \{1,\ldots,K\}$ **do**
3:     Randomly sample a batch of training tasks over $p(\tau)$

4:     **for** $\tau_i \in \{1,\ldots,K\}$ **do**
5:         Collect data by latent conditioned policy θ, (μ_i,σ_i)
6:         Evaluate gradient of inner policy with variational parameters by
$\mu_i' = \mu_i + \alpha_\mu \circ \nabla_{\mu_i} E a_t \sim \pi(a_t|s_t;\theta,z_i) \left[\sum_t R_i(s_t)\right]$ and $\sigma_i' = \sigma_i + \alpha_\sigma \circ \nabla_{\sigma_i} E a_t \sim \pi(a_t|s_t;\theta,z_i) \left[\sum_t R_i(s_t)\right]$
$\qquad z_i \sim \mathcal{N}(\mu_i,\sigma_i) \qquad\qquad\qquad\qquad\qquad\qquad\qquad z_i \sim \mathcal{N}(\mu_i,\sigma_i)$

7:     **end for**

8:     Perform meta-updating based on latent and policy parameters, using

$\max_{\theta,\mu_i,\sigma_i} \sum_{i \in \text{tasks}} E_{a_t \sim \pi(a_t|s_t;\theta_i',z_i')} \left[\sum_t R_i(s_t)\right] - \sum_{i \in \text{tasks}} D_{KL}(\mathcal{N}(\mu_i,\sigma_i)\|\mathcal{N}(0,I))$ with TRPO
$\qquad z_i' \sim \mathcal{N}(\mu_i',\sigma_i')$
9: **end for**

Modified from Gupta, A., Mendonca, R., Liu, Y., Abbeel, P., & Levine, S. (2018). Meta-reinforcement learning of structured exploration strategies. https://arxiv.org/abs/1802.07245.

Related Meta-RL approaches for exploration

Motivated by MAESN, Xu et al. (2020) proposed exploration with structured noise in parameter space (ESNPS) to extract prior knowledge for efficient exploration. Garcia and Thomas (2019) solved the exploration issue by treating exploration itself as a reinforcement learning task in a MDP and introducing the Meta-MDP framework. In contrast to typical noise adding, Xu and colleagues (Xu, Liu, Zhao, & Peng, 2018) presented a meta-policy gradient method based on Deep Q-learning (DQN) and Deep Deterministic Policy Gradient (DDPG). Moreover, Zintgraf et al. (2020) conducted meta-learning into Bayesian reinforcement learning and approximate variational inference to tackle exploration through the learner variational Bayes-Adaptive Deep RL (variBAD). Stadie et al. (2018) offer two Meta-RLs—Extension of MAML (E-MAML) and Extension of RL^2 (E-RL^2)—for more efficient exploration.

7.4.3 Credit assignment

Credit assignment, which stems from Richard Sutton's research in 1984 of temporal credit assignment in reinforcement learning, is an issue related to measuring the future reward caused by an action. Credit assignment is discussed and evaluated in various learning approaches—not only in reinforcement learning but also in supervised learning. It seeks to segregate the influence on reward caused by the action solely and the impact of consecutive actions and other factors. For a long time, credit assignment has been neglected in preupdate distribution (Finn et al., 2017) or naively implemented (Al-Shedivat et al., 2018).

Previous attempts employed vanilla policy gradient (VPG) and trust region policy optimization (TRPO; Schulman, Levine, Abbeel, Jordan, & Moritz, 2015) for optimization. The regular solution uses finite difference methods, but the approximation errors are considerable. Rothfuss et al. (2019) focused on the credit assignment in gradient-based Meta-RL approaches. This essential but insufficiently investigated issue may lead to ineffective task distribution and low sample efficiency. Rothfuss et al. (2019) proposed a Meta-RL method called Proximal Meta-Policy Search (ProMP). The implementation of ProMP allows careful execution of multiple meta-gradients from the same sampled data with a current policy π_{θ_o}. ProMp equips the likelihood ratio $\frac{\pi_\theta(a_t|s_t)}{\pi_{\theta_o}(a_t|s_t)}$, and the objective J_T^{LR} is expressed in Eq. (7.15), where $\pi_\theta(a_t|s_t)$ is the preupdated action distribution,

$$J_T^{LR}(\theta) = \mathbb{E}_{\tau \sim P_T(\tau,\theta_o)}\left[\sum_{t=0}^{H-1} \frac{\pi_\theta(a_t|s_t)}{\pi_{\theta_o}(a_t|s_t)} A^{\pi_{\theta_o}}(s_t,a_t)\right] \tag{7.15}$$

The overall objective J_T^{ProMP} over task T under distribution $\rho(T)$ is expressed in Eq. (7.16), by modifying the clipped meta-objective $J_T^{CLIP}(\theta)$ with a KL-penalty operation, where η denotes the KL-penalty coefficient, α represents the step size, and θ' is the adapted policy parameter:

$$J_T^{ProMP}(\theta) = J_T^{CLIP}(\theta') - \eta\overline{D}_{KL}(\pi_{\theta_o},\pi_\theta) \text{ s.t. } \theta' = \theta + \alpha\nabla_\theta J_T^{LR}(\theta), T \sim \rho(T) \tag{7.16}$$

where $J_T^{CLIP}(\theta)$ is the meta-objective of a surrogate clipping, as expressed in Eq. (7.17), and $H-1$ denotes the time horizon at the previous step:

$$J_T^{\mathrm{CLIP}}(\theta) = \mathbb{E}_{\tau \sim P_T(\tau,\theta_o)} \left[\sum_{t=0}^{H-1} \min \left(\frac{\pi_\theta(a_t|s_t)}{\pi_{\theta_o}(a_t|s_t)} A^{\pi_{\theta_o}}(s_t,a_t), \mathrm{clip}_{1-\epsilon}^{1+\epsilon} \left(\frac{\pi_\theta(a_t|s_t)}{\pi_{\theta_o}(a_t|s_t)} \right) A^{\pi_{\theta_o}}(s_t,a_t) \right) \right] \quad (7.17)$$

Table 7.5 outlines the steps of ProMP.

TABLE 7.5 General training methods of Proximal Meta-Policy Search.

Input: Task distribution ρ, step sizes α, β, KL-penalty coefficient η, clipping range ϵ
1: $\theta \rightarrow$ random initialization
2: **while** θ not converged **do**
3: $\qquad$ Randomly sample batch of tasks $T_i \sim \rho(T)$
4: $\qquad$ **for** $n=0, \ldots, N-1$ **do**
5: $\qquad\qquad$ **if** $n=0$ **then**
6: $\qquad\qquad\qquad$ Let $\theta_o \leftarrow \theta$
7: $\qquad\qquad\qquad$ **for all** $T_i \sim \rho(T)$ **do**
8: $\qquad\qquad\qquad\qquad$ Randomly sample preupdate trajectories $D_i = \{\tau_i\} \sim T_i$ via π_θ
9: $\qquad\qquad\qquad\qquad$ Evaluate adapted parameters $\theta'_{o,\,i} \leftarrow \theta + \alpha \nabla_\theta J_{T_i}^{LR}(\theta)$ via $D_i = \{\tau_i\}$
10: $\qquad\qquad\qquad\qquad$ Randomly sample postupdate trajectories $D_i' = \{\tau_i'\} \sim T_i$ via $\pi_{\theta'_{o,\,i}}$
11: $\qquad\qquad$ Update $\theta \leftarrow \theta + \beta \sum_{T_i} \nabla_\theta J_{T_i}^{ProMP}(\theta)$ using each $D_i' = \{\tau_i'\}$

Modified from Song, X., Yang, Y., Choromanski, K., Pacchiano, A., Gao, W., & Tang, Y. (2020). ES-MAML: Simple Hessian-free meta learning. In ICLR.

This method is evaluated in simulated environments through OpenAI Gym and the Mujoco simulator (Brockman et al., 2016). ProMP reaches the state-of-the-art performance of other Meta-RL approaches with better sample efficiency and asymptotic performance.

7.4.4 Second-order computation in MAML

Model-agnostic meta-learning (MAML) is the most successful gradient-based meta-learning strategy but faces difficulties estimating second-order derivatives through backpropagation based on stochastic policies (Song et al., 2020). For MAML implemented in reinforcement learning, each task $T_i \in \mathcal{T}$ appears under the MDP with transition distribution $q_i(s_{t+1}|s_t,a_t)$, total reward function $R(\tau)$, and trajectory $\tau = (s_0, a_1, \ldots, a_{H-1}, s_H)$. A policy is a function of a stochastic policy or a deterministic policy. Stochastic policy projects the state S to probability distributions of the action space $P(A)$ as $\pi: S \rightarrow P(A)$. Deterministic policy is

$\pi : S \rightarrow A$. The gradient of the adaptation operator $\nabla_\theta U(\theta, T)$ is a second-order derivative, as expressed in Eq. (7.18), where α is the step size:

$$\nabla_\theta U = 1 + \alpha \int \mathcal{P}_T(\tau|\theta)\nabla_\theta^2 \log \pi_\theta(\tau)R_T(\tau)d\tau + \alpha \int \mathcal{P}_T(\tau|\theta)\nabla_\theta \log \pi_\theta(\tau)\nabla_\theta \log \pi_\theta(\tau)^T R_T(\tau)d\tau$$

(7.18)

Due to the trivial implementation of MAML, researchers proposed the Development of Unbiased Higher-Order Estimators (DiCE) (Foerster et al., 2018) and credit assignment analysis (see Section 7.4.3 for exploration). Additionally, the high variance inherence in policy gradient causes trouble.

Song et al. (2020) introduced an extended framework of MAML aggregating with evolution strategies (ES; Wierstra, Schaul, Peters, & Schmidhube, 2008) named ES-MAML to prevent multiple concerns: specifically, high variance on policy gradients, trivial Hessian estimation, and unstable stochastic policies. ES-MAML tackled these issues by processing nonsmooth adaptation for better generalization on sparse-reward environments with a simple and easily applied algorithm. ES-MAML can be equipped with ES improvement and generates more feasibility for handling various adaptation operators. The benefits of ES-MAML are summarized as follows:

- Preventing second-order computation: ES-MAML does not require second-order derivatives estimating, avoiding the potential issue of valuing second-order derivatives with backpropagation on stochastic policies
- Preventing backpropagation: since the algorithm can be run solely in CPUs, ES remains much more accessible to implement than policy gradients, and no backpropagation is needed
- Offering flexibility with various adaptation operators
- Using deterministic policies and other compact policies

In zero-order ES-MAML, the Gaussian smoothing $\tilde{J}_\sigma$ of MAML reward is employed, and $\tilde{J}_\sigma$ is optimized through the ES paradigm with the joint sampling mechanism and evaluation of $f^T(U(\theta + \sigma g, T))$. The gradient $\nabla \tilde{J}_\sigma$ is expressed in Eq. (7.19), where U denotes the adaptation operator and σ represents the precision parameter:

$$\nabla \tilde{J}_\sigma(\theta) = \mathbb{E}_{\substack{T \sim \mathcal{P}(T) \\ g \sim \mathcal{N}(0,I)}} \left[\frac{1}{\sigma} f^T(U(\theta + \sigma \mathbf{g}, T))\mathbf{g} \right]$$

(7.19)

The Zero-Order ES-MAML with ES gradient adaptation is indicated in Table 7.6, which is based on the Monte Carlo ES Gradient (ESGrad) method, as described in Table 7.7.

The Zero-Order ES-MAML with ES-Gradient Adaptation is summarized in Table 7.8.

The First-Order ES-MAML is summarized in Table 7.9, and Monte Carlo ES Hessian (ESHess) is outlined in Table 7.10.

This framework is executed in a sparse-reward environment to test its exploratory ability. The Four Corners benchmark, introduced by Rothfuss (Rothfuss et al., 2019), has two tasks: a single goal exploration game and a six circles game. The agent needs to reach six target points in the six circles game. Otherwise, it will continue receiving negative rewards. ES-MAML is

TABLE 7.6   General training methods of Zero-Order ES-MAML.

Input: θ_0, the initial policy
β, the hyperparameter of meta-step size
$U\,(\cdot,\,T))$, the general adaption operator

 # Procedure of Zero-Order ES-MAML

1 **for** $t = 0, 1, \ldots$ **do**
2   *Sample n tasks $T_1, \ldots, T_n$ and iid vectors $g_1, \ldots, g_n$ from $N(0,I)$*

3   **foreach** (T_i, g_i) **do**
4         $v_i \leftarrow f^{T_i}(U(\theta_t + \sigma g_i, T_i))$
5   **end**

6   Update $\theta_{t+1} \leftarrow \theta_t + \frac{\beta}{\sigma n} \sum_{i=1}^{n} v_i g_i$
7 **end**

Modified from Song, X., Yang, Y., Choromanski, K., Pacchiano, A., Gao, W., & Tang, Y. (2020). ES-MAML: Simple Hessian-free meta learning. In ICLR.

TABLE 7.7   General methods of Monte Carlo ES Gradient.

---

inputs: f, function
θ, policy
n, number of perturbations
σ, precision

 # Procedure of Monte Carlo ES Gradient

1 **ESGrad** (f, θ, n, σ)
2   Randomly sample n i.i.d from $N(0,I)$ vectors $g_1, \ldots, g_n$
3   **return** $\frac{1}{n\sigma} \sum_{i=1}^{n} f(\theta + \sigma g_i) g_i;$

Modified from Song, X., Yang, Y., Choromanski, K., Pacchiano, A., Gao, W., & Tang, Y. (2020). ES-MAML: Simple Hessian-free meta learning. In ICLR.

TABLE 7.8   General training methods of Zero-Order ES-MAML with ES-Gradient Adaptation.

Input: θ_0, initial policy
α, hyperparameter of adaptation step size
β, hyperparameter of meta-step size
K, number of queries

 # Procedure of Zero-Order ES-MAML with ES-Gradient Adaptation

1 **for** $t = 0, 1, \ldots$ **do**
2   Randomly sample n tasks $T_1, \ldots, T_n$ and iid vectors $g_1, \ldots, g_n$ from $N(0,I)$

3   **for each** (T_i, g_i) **do**
4   Obtain $d^{(i)} \leftarrow ESGRAD(f^{T_i}, \theta_t + \sigma g_i, K, \sigma)$;
5   Obtain $\theta_i^{(i)} \leftarrow \theta_t + \sigma g_i + \alpha d^{(i)}$
6   Obtain $v_i \leftarrow f^{T_i}(\theta_i^{(i)})$

7   **end**

8   Update $\theta_{t+1} \leftarrow \theta_t + \frac{\beta}{\sigma n} \sum_{i=1}^{n} v_i g_i$
9 **end**

Modified from Song, X., Yang, Y., Choromanski, K., Pacchiano, A., Gao, W., & Tang, Y. (2020). ES-MAML: Simple Hessian-free meta learning. In ICLR.

TABLE 7.9 General training methods of First-Order ES-MAML.

Input: θ_0, initial policy
　　　　α, hyperparameter of adaptation step size
　　　　β, hyperparameter of meta-step size
　　　　K, number of queries

 # Procedure of First Order ES-MAML

1 **for** $t = 0, 1, \ldots,$ **do**
2 　　Randomly sample n tasks $T_1, \ldots, T_n$

3 　　**for each** T_i **do**
4 　　　　　Obtain $d_1^{(i)} \leftarrow ESGRAD(f^{T_i}, \theta_t, K, \sigma)$
5 　　　　　Obtain $H^{(i)} \leftarrow ESHESS(f^{T_i}, \theta_t, K, \sigma)$
6 　　　　　Obtain $\theta_t^{(i)} \leftarrow \theta_t + \alpha \cdot d_i$;
7 　　　　　Obtain $d_2^{(i)} \leftarrow ESGRAD(f^{T_i}, \theta_t^{(i)}, K, \sigma)$
8 　　**end**

9 　　Update $\theta_{t+1} \leftarrow \theta_t + \frac{\beta}{n} \sum_{i=1}^{n} \left(I + \alpha H^{(i)} \right) d_2^{(i)}$
10 **end**

Modified from Song, X., Yang, Y., Choromanski, K., Pacchiano, A., Gao, W., & Tang, Y. (2020). ES-MAML: Simple Hessian-free meta learning. In ICLR.

TABLE 7.10 General training methods of Monte Carlo ES Hessian.

Inputs: f, function
　　　　θ, policy
　　　　n, number of perturbations
　　　　σ, precision

 # Procedure of Monte Carlo ES Hessian

1 **ESHess** (f, θ, n, σ)
2 　　Randomly sample i.i.d. from $N(0, I)$ vectors $g_1, \ldots, g_n$
3 　　Obtain $v \leftarrow \frac{1}{n} \sum_{i=1}^{n} f(\theta + \sigma g_i)$
4 　　Obtain $H^0 \leftarrow \frac{1}{n} \sum_{i=1}^{n} f(\theta + \sigma g_i) g_i g_i^T$;
5 　　**return** $\frac{1}{\sigma^2} (H^0 - v \cdot I)$

Modified from Song, X., Yang, Y., Choromanski, K., Pacchiano, A., Gao, W., & Tang, Y. (2020). ES-MAML: Simple Hessian-free meta learning. In ICLR.

also evaluated in four MuJoCo environments: (1) HalfCheetah, (2) Swimmer, (3) Walker2d, and (4) Ant, to perform two tasks of forward-backward and goal-velocity.

Related Meta-RL algorithms based on MAML modifications

Similar to ES-MAML, various extensions of MAML have been built for diverse purposes. Liu and colleagues (Liu, Socher, & Xiong, 2019) suggested a surrogate objective function called Taming MAML, which removes bias terms in gradient estimation to accelerate the training time. Nagabandi et al. (2019) proposed a meta-learner to train the prior knowledge for rapid adaptation to novel scenarios.

7.5 Reward signals and environments

7.5.1 Sparse extrinsic reward in procedurally generated environments

The dense reward or flawless environment is commonly employed in conventional reinforcement learning settings to encourage learning and offer smooth searching. This led to impressive performance, such as the ability to play Go. However, its reasonably dense reward is quite impractical and leads to a significant gap in real-world scenarios, as real-world environments provide extremely sparse rewards rather than dense ones. Thus, regular random exploration experiences difficulty with addressing adequate reward signals and holds low sample efficiency.

Campero et al. (2021) proposed a meta-learning framework to help agent learning in environments with sparse extrinsic rewards by implementing a teacher-student structure—a goal-depended student policy trained by a goal-created teacher policy through the Adversarially Motivated Intrinsic Goals framework, or AMIGo. The official code is available at https://github.com/facebookresearch/adversarially-motivated-intrinsic-goals.

This framework consists of two modules: the teacher policy module guides the training, and the student policy module is the original policy network in policy-gradient approaches. The idea behind this approach is to provide progressively more challenging goals to the agent constantly and promote learning actively in dynamic environments. The teacher policy behaves as a constructive adversary against the student policy by offering more and more complex (but achievable) goals with different objectives. The student module is rewarded for achieving the given goal with discounts among specific steps. Both the teacher and student modules get a reward as the agent tackles the completed task. r^T is the teacher's reward function, where α and β denote the hyperparameters determining the weight of positive or negative teacher rewards, respectively. t^* represents a threshold of the number of steps to achieve the goal, and t^+ is the number of steps to achieve the goal by the student module. r_t^g presents the undiscounted intrinsic reward function, s_t is the state at time t and g denotes the intrinsic goal offered by the teacher module.

$$r^T = \begin{cases} +\alpha & \text{if } t^+ \geq t^* \\ -\beta & \text{if } t^+ < t^* \end{cases}$$

$$r_t^g = v(s_t, g) = \begin{cases} +1 & \text{if the state } s_t \text{ satisfies the goal } g \\ 0 & \text{otherwise} \end{cases}$$

This framework can be viewed as an augmentation for policy gradient-based approaches; see Fig. 7.3 for the general architecture.

Rather than solving a particular task, this framework is evaluated in several procedurally generated environments on MiniGrid (Chevalier-Boisvert, Willems, & Pal, 2018). Such environments force the agent to handle a set of tasks under more sizeable observation spaces and

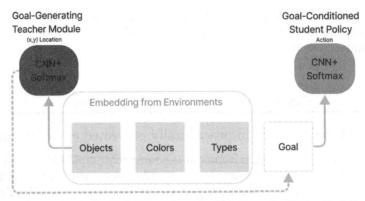

FIG. 7.3   General pipeline of AMIGo. *Modifed from Campero, A., Raileanu, R., Küttler, H., & Grefenstette, E. (2021). Learning with Amigo: Adversarially motivated intrinsic goals.. ICLR.*

generalize among varying environment layouts and transition dynamics. These procedurally generated environments include:

- KeyCorrS3R3 (KCmedium)
- ObstrMaze1D1 (OMmedium)
- ObstrMaze2D1hb (OMmedhard)
- KeyCorrS4R3 (KChard)
- KeyCorrS5R3 (KCharder)
- ObstrMaze1Q (OMhard)

Related Meta-RL algorithms for reward signal

Besides, many other Meta-RL algorithms also discuss the reward signal from versatile perspectives. Yang et al. (2019) suggested a MAML-based self-adaptation approach without reward signal through no-reward meta-learning (NoRML). Yu and colleagues (Yu, Yu, Finn, & Ermon, 2019) employed meta-inverse reinforcement learning for reward function in real-world applications by proposing a deep latent variable model to leverage rewards from unstructured data in novel structured situations. Xu, Ratner, Dragan, Levine, and Finn (2019) also demonstrated an inverse reinforcement learning-based approach to recover reward function for unseen situations.

7.6 Benchmark

7.6.1 Meta-World

Meta-RL aims to meta-learn reinforcement learning tasks through an agent that can productively solve novel tasks. Meta-RL task distribution needs to be extensive enough to incorporate novel tasks so that the agent can solve the novel tasks much more rapidly than the traditional reinforcement learning approach, which must solve from scratch. Current Meta-RL only concentrates on restricted task distributions; thus, the policy cannot generalize extensively enough for rapidly adapting to novel tasks and quickly obtaining new behavior. For example, multitask reinforcement learning approaches in Atari games achieved hardly any efficiency in learning across diverse games (Parisotto, Ba, & Salakhutdinov, 2015).

To solve this problem, Yu et al. (2021) offered a simulated standardized benchmark and evaluation protocol for Meta-RL and multitask reinforcement learning through 50 different Sawyer robotic manipulation tasks to speed the accession in novel tasks, calling the benchmark Meta-World. This completely open-sourced benchmark aims to provide a practical and systematic design and evaluation protocol for various paradigms and to support the fast generalization and adaptation to relevantly shared distinct tasks. Nonparametric and parametric variations are presented in the goal positions and objects. The efficiency gains of adaptation of novel tasks heavily rely on commonly shared structures across tasks. In this way, the meta-training and meta-testing tasks necessitate two assumptions:

- The task distribution $P(T)$ of meta-training and meta-testing is the same
- Commonly, shared structures are presented in the task distribution $P(T)$ for improvement in efficient adaptation

Among these 50 Sawyer robotic manipulation tasks, 45 are meta-training tasks, and five are meta-testing tasks. The agent needs either to move one object to a 3D position of the flexible goal or to move two objects to a 3D position of the fixed goal. The observation space is laid out as a sextuplet of the following:

- 3D Cartesian locations of the end-effector
- The open condition of the gripper under normalized measurement
- The 3D position and quaternion of the first object
- The 3D position and quaternion of the second object
- Comprehensive previous measures in the environment
- The 3D location of the goal

The names of these 45 meta-training robotic tasks in Meta-World are illustrated as the following (Yu et al., 2021):

- Ball-related tasks: basketball, soccer
- Wall-related tasks: button press top-down wall, button press wall, reach wall, push wall, pick place wall
- Open and close tasks: drawer close, door open, drawer open, faucet open, faucet close, window open, window close
- Pull and push tasks: coffee pull, handle pull side, handle pull, lever pull, stick pull, stick push, push, push back, coffee push
- Press tasks: button press top-down, button press, handle press side, handle press
- Other actions: assembly, disassemble, coffee button, dial turn, door unlock, hammer, peg insert side, peg unplug side, pick out of hole, pick place, plate slide, plate slide side, plate slide back, plate slide back side, reach, shelf place, sweep into, sweep

Similarly, the names of the five meta-testing tasks in Meta-World are listed as the following: bin picking, box close, door lock, door unlock, and hand insert.

The official code regarding this benchmark is available at https://github.com/rlworkgroup/metaworld, and the video illustration of all 50 robotic tasks is featured at https://meta-world.github.io.

Per reward function, there are two requirements: (a) the reward function needs to have a shared structure among different tasks and (b) the task should be within the scope of current single-task reinforcement learning methods.

Per evaluation protocol, the evaluation can be divided into the following groups:

- Meta-learning 1 (ML1): few-shot adaptation of an unseen object or goal via sole task
- Multitask 1 (MT1): obtaining sole multitask policy generalized to 50 tasks under the same environment
- Multitask 10, Multitask 50 (MT10, MT50): obtaining sole multitask policy generalized to 50 tasks under 10 different training environments with overall 500 training tasks, or under 50 training environments with overall 2500 training tasks
- Meta-learning 10, Meta-learning 45 (ML10, ML45): few-shot adjustment of verifying generalization for novel tasks based on 10 or 45 meta-training tasks
- The success metrics are the distance between the final goal g and the task-relevant object o

7.7 Visual navigation

7.7.1 Introduction

Visual navigation is the task of navigating a mobile AI robot in a given environment through visual information of the system. It is a process of determining the shortest safe and appropriate path from the starting position to the goal position.

Five approaches to the taxonomy of visual navigation are incorporated with DRL paradigms (Zeng, Wang, & Ge, 2020).

(1) Direct DRL visual navigation

As the most straightforward strategy, a DRL algorithm is directly embedded in the visual navigation system to guide and analyze the movements of the mobile agents in a given environment to reach the goal and maximize cumulative rewards. In these methods, the agents instruct the movement through sparse rewards and utilize auxiliary tasks in training, where the goal is demonstrated through the state, or the corresponding map would be offered. Furthermore, DRL can be conducted for a single task in visual navigation, such as mapping, localization, or path planning. Previous attempts include optimal path routing (Pan, You, Wang, & Lu, 2017), mapping (Bhatti et al., 2016; Brunner, Richter, Wang, & Wattenhofer, 2018; Gupta, Davidson, Levine, Sukthankar, & Malik, 2017), active neural localization (ANL; Chaplot, Parisotto, & Salakhutdinov, 2018) for localization, and value iteration networks (VIN; Tamar, Wu, Thomas, Levine, & Abbeel, 2016) for path planning.

(2) Hierarchical DRL visual navigation

Hierarchical reinforcement learning tackles long-horizon decision-making tasks by splitting such tasks into multiple simpler subtasks. This type of approach benefits the high-dimension state by reducing dimensional disaster in visual navigation processing. There are two subgroups of hierarchical DRL visual navigation:

- Hierarchical abstract machines (HAM) for DRL visual navigation: Due to highly sparse extrinsic rewards, the agents cannot explore the given environment sufficiently and thoroughly. Thus, it is challenging for the agent to determine the optimal policy or nearly optimal policy. HAM for DRL solves this issue by representing hierarchical temporal abstraction to encourage exploration by intrinsic rewards. Intrinsic rewards or motivations mean the agent is rewarded for performing specific behaviors rather than related to achieving any tasks (i.e., extrinsic reward). Additionally, the environments with sparse rewards are converted to ones with dense rewards. Moreover, a subgoal is indicated before the agent makes decisions. Once the agent accomplishes a subgoal, another subgoal is proposed to step closer toward the final goal.

- Option DRL visual navigation, which treats the navigation tasks as a couple of options: the option is a sequence of actions on a state subspace. The option DRL approach aims to execute a navigation subgoal through a specific policy via the given pseudo rewards and subgoals; e.g., hierarchical deep deterministic policy gradient (h-DDPG; Yang, Merrick, Jin, & Abbass, 2018).

(3) Multitask DRL visual navigation

Multitask DRL tackles this problem through mutual parameters across similar or relevant tasks and parameters with mutual knowledge of navigation to benefit data efficiency and navigation transferability. This can be achieved via two categories of strategies:

- Distillation DRL visual navigation, which extracts commonly shared knowledge among multiple tasks, can be implemented in complicated environments. However, the drawback is decreasing sample efficiency and weak assumption that is hard to maintain.
- Progressive DRL visual navigation, which can cover the disadvantages noted earlier, casts previously learned features by leveraging prior knowledge (see Mirowski et al., 2018; Rusu et al., 2016; Schaul, Horgan, Gregor, & Silver, 2015).

(4) Memory-inference DRL visual navigation

Memory acts as an essential function in DRL to supply the reasoning capacity, usually through deep learning models like LSTM and RNN. However, regular internal memory units integrate computation and memorization in parameters, yielding an increasing amount of parameters as more memory is occupied during navigation. In this way, the researcher recommends lots of external memory, including replay buffer, memory networks (e.g., memory Q-network and recurrent memory Q-network), episodic memory, and differentiable neural computer (e.g., Graves et al., 2016; Graves, Wayne, & Danihelka, 2014; Pritzel et al., 2017; Weston, Chopra, & Bordes, 2014).

(5) Vision-language DRL visual navigation

Navigation relies on multimodel inputs of vision, and natural language demands a robust analyzing capability of associating natural language guidance with vision knowledge about the environment to plan and move toward a goal position. Early research has yielded multiple approaches, such as reinforced cross-modal matching (RCM; Wang et al., 2019).

Despite the rapid developments of AI technology and many DRL methods supported for visual navigation tasks, several fundamental difficulties remain, including:

- Poor data efficiency due to many interactions of environments and sparse rewards

- Weak generalization among various simulated environments because of different data distribution; once the target changes, retraining is ultimately required despite the same scenes
- Deficient generalization from simulated environments to real-world environments

On the other hand, meta-learning sheds light on the above issues. Meta-learning enables self-adaptive visual navigation for a rapid adaptation in unseen environments within a few steps of gradient descent. In addition, unsupervised Meta-RL obtains transferable meta-features from unannotated environments during meta-training. This tackles the annotated environment scarcity.

Section 7.7.2 introduces SAVN via two objectives. Section 7.7.3 investigates the transferrable meta-knowledge obtained for an unsupervised approach.

7.7.2 Visual navigation to unseen scenes

Learning to navigate during training is a prevalent and standard approach. However, navigating is challenging in unseen environment scenes where the object's appearance and the scene's structure are unfamiliar to the agent during training. In other words, the agent is required to perform learning and rapid adaptation in training and testing, which can be solved through meta-learning.

Inspired by previous meta-learning researches (Clavera et al., 2018; Yu et al., 2018), Wortsman et al. (2019) proposed a Meta-RL approach, namely the SAVN method. SAVN focuses on learning a self-supervised interaction loss to lead to efficient visual navigation in unseen environments. This method utilized MAML (Finn et al., 2017) as a backbone supported by the AI2-THOR environment (Kolve et al., 2017) and applied meta-learning in training and testing periods. The official code and benchmarks are released at https://github.com/allenai/savn.

In this end-to-end architecture, SAVN contains two objective functions:

1. A novel self-supervised interaction loss $\mathcal{L}_{\text{int}}^{\phi}$ that continually updates the policy as it corresponds to an environment
2. A navigation loss $\mathcal{L}_{\text{nav}}$, which is a supervised actor-critic (A3C) navigation loss (Mirowski et al., 2017; Zhu et al., 2017)

In the training objective for the navigation method, the training objection function is expressed in Eq. (7.20), and a Taylor expansion approximation version in Eq. (7.21), where the $\langle \bullet, \bullet \rangle$ represents the inner product, α denotes the step size hyper-parameter. $\mathcal{D}_{\tau}^{\text{int}}$ represents the actions, observations, and internal state for the first k steps, whereas $\mathcal{D}_{\tau}^{\text{nav}}$ is the similar representation for the rest of trajectory τ.

$$\min_{\theta} \sum_{\tau \in \mathcal{T}_{\text{train}}} \mathcal{L}_{\text{nav}}\left(\theta - \alpha \nabla_{\theta} \mathcal{L}_{\text{int}}\left(\theta, \mathcal{D}_{\tau}^{\text{int}}\right), \mathcal{D}_{\tau}^{\text{nav}}\right) \tag{7.20}$$

$$\min_{\theta} \sum_{\tau \in \mathcal{T}_{\text{train}}} \mathcal{L}_{\text{nav}}\left(\theta, \mathcal{D}_{\tau}^{\text{nav}}\right) - \alpha \left\langle \nabla_{\theta} \mathcal{L}_{\text{int}}\left(\theta, \mathcal{D}_{\tau}^{\text{int}}\right), \nabla_{\theta} \mathcal{L}_{\text{nav}}\left(\theta, \mathcal{D}_{\tau}^{\text{nav}}\right) \right\rangle \tag{7.21}$$

Two types of hand crafted interaction objective functions are suggested in learning to learn how to learn the method:

1. A diversity loss $\mathcal{L}_{\text{int}}^{\text{div}}$ to increase the variety of agent's actions (move ahead, rotate left/right, look down/up, done), expressed in Eq. (7.22), where $g(s_i, s_j)$ is an indicator that equals 1 as the pixel differences between s_i and s_j below a predefined threshold, and equals 0 otherwise:

$$\mathcal{L}_{\text{int}}^{\text{div}}\left(\theta, \mathcal{D}_\tau^{\text{int}}\right) = \sum_{i<j\leq k} g\left(s_i, s_j\right) \log\left(\pi_\theta^{(a_i)}\left(s_j\right)\right) \tag{7.22}$$

2. A prediction loss $\mathcal{L}_{\text{int}}^{\text{pred}}$ to estimate the success possibility from each action, expressed in Eq. (7.23), where $\mathcal{H}$ means the standard binary cross-entropy, $q_\theta^{(a_i)}$ denotes the success prediction, and g present a reliable function:

$$\mathcal{L}_{\text{int}}^{\text{pred}}\left(\theta, \mathcal{D}_\tau^{\text{int}}\right) = \sum_{t=0}^{k-1} \mathcal{H}\left(q_\theta^{(a_t)}(s_t), 1 - g(s_t, s_{t+1})\right) \tag{7.23}$$

The comprehensive training and testing methods are outlined in Tables 7.11 and 7.12, respectively.

The quantitative and qualitative state-of-the-art performances are achieved in the results, as implemented in AI2-THOR 3D synthetic indoor scenes of kitchen, living, bedroom, and bathroom.

TABLE 7.11 General training methods of SAVN.

Procedure of SAVN-Training
1: θ and $\phi \rightarrow$ random initialization
2: **while** not meeting stopping criteria **do**
3:     **for** each mini-batch over tasks $\tau_i \in T_{train}$ **do**
4:         $\theta_i \leftarrow \theta$
5:         $t \leftarrow 0$
6:         **while** not meeting stopping criteria **do**
7:             Execute action $a \sim \pi_{\theta_i}(s_t)$
8:             $t \leftarrow t+1$
9:             **if** t can be divisible by k **then**
10:                 Update $\theta_i \leftarrow \theta_i - \alpha \nabla_\theta L_{\text{int}}^\phi(\theta_i, D_\tau^{(t,k)})$
11:     Update $\theta \leftarrow \theta - \beta_1 \sum_i \nabla_\theta L_{\text{nav}}(\theta_i, D_\tau)$
12:     Update $\phi \leftarrow \phi - \beta_2 \sum_i \nabla_\phi L_{\text{nav}}(\theta_i, D_\tau)$
13: **return** θ, ϕ

Modified from Wortsman, M., Ehsani, K., Rastegari, M., Farhadi, A., & Mottaghi, R. (2019). Learning to learn how to learn: Self-adaptive visual navigation using meta-learning. In CVPR.

TABLE 7.12   General testing methods of SAVN.

Procedure of SAVN-Testing
1: **for** mini-batch over tasks $\tau_i \in T_{\text{test}}$ **do**
2:       $\theta_i \leftarrow \theta$
3:       $t \leftarrow 0$
4:       **while** not meeting stopping criteria **do**
5:             Execute action $a \sim \pi_{\theta_i}(s_t)$
6:             $t \leftarrow t+1$
7:             **if** t can be divisible by k **then**
8:                   Update $\theta_i \leftarrow \theta_i - \alpha \nabla_{\theta_i} L_{int}^{\phi}(\theta_i, D_{\tau}^{(t,k)})$

Modified from Wortsman, M., Ehsani, K., Rastegari, M., Farhadi, A., & Mottaghi, R. (2019). Learning to learn how to learn: Self-adaptive visual navigation using meta-learning. In CVPR.

7.7.3 Transferable meta-knowledge in unsupervised visual navigation

Conventional DRL requests a large amount of annotated training data, particularly in visual navigation tasks; a significant number of 3D simulated environments and elaborately annotated object information are demanded. However, this costly data labeling takes a long time and cannot guarantee a practical mimic in real-world scenarios.

Li et al. (2020) introduced a Reptile-based (Nichol, Achiam, & Schulman, 2018) reinforcement learning approach to learn transferable meta-knowledge by actively interacting with unannotated environments. Unlike meta-training based on unannotated environments, some annotated environments with the corresponding reward are presented during meta-testing. This framework is named Unsupervised Reinforcement Learning of Transferable Meta-skills (ULTRA).

The curriculum-based adversarial training process is highlighted in this framework, evolved as a task generator (one agent) and a meta-learner (another agent): the task generator produces a sequence of tasks according to the increasing difficulty level. The meta-learner learns the meta-skills by conducting these tasks. During this process, the meta-learner learns multiple transferable subpolicies related to particular meta-skills or motor primitives (e.g., move straight, go around obstacles). After learning the subpolicies, the agent needs to know a task-specific master policy and combine both policies to accomplish fast adaption of visual navigation, where the subpolicies are parameters shared by all tasks.

ULTRA adds a task diversity component D into the reward function to help achieve a better understanding in visual and physical on the corresponding environments through a more extensive state space, as expressed in Eq. (7.24), where π is the current policy, π' indicates the previous policy, and $\prod$ denotes the prior polices. s_t denotes the state at time t from trajectory τ.

$$D = \sum_{s_t \in \tau} \sum_{\pi' \in \Pi} D_{KL}(\pi'(\cdot \ |s_t) \ \| \ \pi(\cdot \ \| \ s_t)) \tag{7.24}$$

The overall task generator total reward function R_G is expressed in Eq. (7.25), where λ and η denote weight hyper-parameters, n represents the number of actions produced from the task generator. k denotes the scaling factor and r means the success rate.

TABLE 7.13 General training methods of the proposed solution.

1: $\theta, \phi, \mu \rightarrow$ random initialization
2: $\Pi \leftarrow \Pi$ while not converged do

4: **while** not converged **do**
5:       gather rollout $\tau_i^G(s_0, s_1, \ldots, s_T)$ via π_μ^G
6:       $s^* \leftarrow s_T$
7:       $o^* \leftarrow O_T$
8:       Let task $\tau_i = SetTask(s_0, s^*, o^*)$
        # warm-up
9:       **for** $w = 0, 1, \ldots W$ **do**
10:            gather rollout τ_i^w via $\pi_{\phi_i, \theta}^M$
11:            update $\phi_i \leftarrow \phi_i + \alpha \nabla_\phi J(\tau_i^w, \pi_{\phi_i, \theta}^M)$
12:      **end for**
13:      $\tilde{\theta} = \theta$
        # joint updating
14:      **for** $j = 0, 1, \ldots J$ **do**
15:            gather rollout τ_i^j via $\pi_{\phi_i, \tilde{\theta}}^M$

16:            update $\phi_i \leftarrow \phi_i + \alpha \nabla_\phi J\left(\tau_i^j, \pi_{\phi_i, \tilde{\theta}}^M\right)$

17:            update $\tilde{\theta} \leftarrow \tilde{\theta} + \alpha \nabla_\theta J\left(\tau_i^j, \pi_{\phi_i, \tilde{\theta}}^M\right)$
18:      **end for**

19:      update $\theta \leftarrow \theta + \beta\left(\tilde{\theta} - \theta\right)$
20:      Compute R_G and update π_μ^G

21:      **if** $len(\Pi) == 4$ **then**
22:            $\Pi.\text{pop}(0)$
23:      **end if**

24:      $\Pi.\text{append}(\mu)$
25: **end while**

Modified from Li, J., Wang, X., Tang, S., Shi, H., Wu, F., Zhuang, Y., & Wang, W. Y. (2020). Unsupervised reinforcement learning of transferable meta-skills for embodied navigation. In CVPR.

$$R_G = k * (1 - r) - \lambda * n + \eta * \sum_{s_t \in \tau} \sum_{\pi' \in \Pi} D_{KL}(\pi'(\cdot \mid s_t) \parallel \pi(\cdot \parallel s_t)) \qquad (7.25)$$

The step-by-step pseudocode of ULTRA is summarized in Table 7.13. Note that, unlike the original Reptile methods to update the entire parameters, ULTRA solely keeps the subpolicies parameters updating and freezes them during testing. Similar to SAVN (Wortsman et al., 2019), ULTRA is also implemented in AI2-THOR 3D synthetic environment (Kolve et al., 2017) with six actions (go ahead, rotate right/left, look down/up, done).

7.8 Summary

Meta-RL delivers remarkable achievements in a variety of challenging situations and offers potential solutions. However, the current Meta-RL is at an early emerging stage, with plenty of room for further exploration and investigation, and it has some deficiencies that need to be addressed. Existing studies of Meta-RL primarily rely on simulated environments rather than smoothly implementing complicated real-world scenarios. Moreover, intensive model complexity may lead to time-consuming training phases. In addition, the high consumption of computational power also limits its scope and applications.

On the other hand, and more importantly, Meta-RL offers a novel direction and practical research path to achieve the primary goal of Artificial General Intelligence (also named general AI or AGI): learning any intellectual task as a human being does. Meta-RL technology enables many AI researchers to move one more step from narrow AI toward general AI—tackling diverse known and unknown problems by learning automatically, efficiently, and continuously.

References

Al-Shedivat, M., Bansal, T., Burda, Y., Sutskever, I., Mordatch, I., & Abbeel, P. (2018). Continuous adaptation via meta-learning in nonstationary and competitive environments. In *ICLR*.

Bellemare, M. G., Naddaf, Y., Veness, J., & Bowling, M. (2013). The arcade learning environment: An evaluation platform for general agents. *Journal of Artificial Intelligence Research, 47*, 253–279.

Bhatti, S., Desmaison, A., Miksik, O., Nardelli, N., Siddharth, N., & Torr, P. H. (2016). *Playing doom with SLAM-augmented deep reinforcement learning*. http://arxiv.org/abs/1612.00380.

Botvinick, M., Ritter, S., Wang, J. X., Kurth-Nelson, Z., Blundell, C., & Hassabis, D. (2019). Reinforcement learning, fast and slow. *Trends in Cognitive Sciences, 23*(5), 408–422.

Brockman, G., Cheung, V., Pettersson, L., Schneide, J., Schulman, J., Tang, J., & Zaremba, W. (2016). *OpenAI gym*. Technical report http://arxiv.org/abs/1606.01540.

Brunner, G., Richter, O., Wang, Y., & Wattenhofer, R. (2018). Teaching a machine to read maps with deep reinforcement learning. In *AAAI* (pp. 1–8).

Campero, A., Raileanu, R., Küttler, H., & Grefenstette, E. (2021). Learning with Amigo: Adversarially motivated intrinsic goals. In *ICLR*.

Chaplot, D. S., Parisotto, E., & Salakhutdinov, R. (2018). Active neural localization. In *Proceedings of interenational conference on learning representations* (pp. 1–15).

Chevalier-Boisvert, M., Willems, L., & Pal, S. (2018). *Minimalistic gridworld environment for OpenAI gym*. https://github.com/maximecb/gym-minigrid.

Clavera, I., Nagabandi, A., Fearing, R. S., Abbeel, P., Levine, S., & Finn, C. (2018). *Learning to adapt: Meta-learning for model-based control*. Retrieved from arXiv.

Clune, J. (2019). *AI-GAs: AI-generating algorithms, an alternate paradigm for producing general artificial intelligence*.

Dixit, A. K., & Sherrerd, J. J. (1990). *Optimization in economic theory*. Oxford University Press on Demand.

Duan, Y. (2016). *RL2: Fast reinforcement learning via slow reinforcement learning*. arXiv preprint arXiv:1611.02779.

Duan, Y., Schulman, J., Chen, X., Bartlett, P. L., Sutskever, I., & Abbeel, P. (2017). RL2: Fast reinforcement learning via slow reinforcement learning. In *ICLR*.

Finn, C., Abbeel, P., & Levine, S. (2017). Model-agnostic meta-learning for fast adaptation of deep networks. In *Vol. 70. The 34th international conference on machine learning* (pp. 1126–1135).

Foerster, J., Farquhar, G., Al-Shedivat, M., Rocktäschel, T., Xing, E., & Whiteson, S. (2018). DiCE: The infinitely differentiable Monte Carlo estimator. In *Proceedings of the 35th international conference on machine learning. Vol. 80* (pp. 1529–1538).

François-Lavet, V., Henderson, P., Islam, R., Bellemare, M. G., & Pineau, J. (2018). An introduction to deep reinforcement learning. *Foundations and Trends in Machine Learning, 11*(3–4), 219–354.

Frans, K., Ho, J., Chen, X., Abbeel, P., & Schulman, J. (2018). Meta learning shared hierarchies. In *ICLR*.

Fu, J., Luo, K., & Levine, S. (2017). Learning robust rewards with adversarial inverse reinforcement learning. *arXiv preprint*, arXiv:1710.11248.

Garcia, F. M., & Thomas, P. S. (2019). *A meta-MDP approach to exploration for lifelong reinforcement learning*. Retrieved from NeurIPS.

Goodfellow, I., Bengio, Y., & Courville, A. (2016). *Deep learning*. MIT Press.

Graves, A., Wayne, G., & Danihelka, I. (2014). *Neural turing machines*. http://arxiv.org/abs/1410.5401.

Graves, A., Wayne, G., Reynolds, M., Harley, T., Danihelka, I., Grabska-Barwinska, A., ... Blunsom, P. (2016). Hybrid computing using a neural network with dynamic external memory. *Nature, 538*(7626), 471.

Gupta, A., Mendonca, R., Liu, Y., Abbeel, P., & Levine, S. (2018). *Meta-reinforcement learning of structured exploration strategies*. https://arxiv.org/abs/1802.07245.

Gupta, S., Davidson, J., Levine, S., Sukthankar, R., & Malik, J. (2017). Cognitive mapping and planning for visual navigation. In *CVPR* (pp. 2616–2625).

Hill, F., Tieleman, O., Glehn, T. V., Wong, N., Merzic, H., & Clark, S. (2020). Grounded language learning fast and slow. In *ICLR*.

Hochreiter, S., Younger, A. S., & Conwell, P. R. (2001). Learning to learn using gradient descent. In *ICANN*.

Houthooft, R., Chen, X., Duan, Y., Schulman, J., De Turck, F., & Abbeel, P. (2016). Vime: Variational information maximizing exploration. *Advances in Neural Information Processing Systems, 29*.

Johnson, M., Hofmann, K., Hutton, T., & Bignell, D. (2016). The malmo platform for artificial intelligence experimentation. In *IJCAI* (pp. 4246–4247). AAAI Press.

Kamienny, P. A., Pirotta, M., Lazaric, A., Lavril, T., Usunier, N., & Denoyer, L. (2020). Learning adaptive exploration strategies in dynamic environments through informed policy regularization. *arXiv preprint*, arXiv: 2005.02934.

Kempka, M., Wydmuch, M., Runc, G., Toczek, J., & Jaśkowski, W. (2016). Vizdoom: A doom-based ai research platform for visual reinforcement learning. In *2016 IEEE conference on computational intelligence and games (CIG)* (pp. 1–8). IEEE.

Kocsis, L., & Szepesvári, C. (2006). Bandit based monte-carlo planning. In *European conference on machine learning* (pp. 282–293). Berlin, Heidelberg: Springer.

Kolve, E., Mottaghi, R., Gordon, D., Zhu, Y., Gupta, A., & Farhadi, A. (2017). *AI2-THOR: An interactive 3D environment for visual AI*. Retrieved from arXiv.

LeCun, Y., Bengio, Y., & Hinton, G. (2015). Deep learning. *Nature, 521*(7553), 436–444.

Li, J., Wang, X., Tang, S., Shi, H., Wu, F., Zhuang, Y., & Wang, W. Y. (2020). Unsupervised reinforcement learning of transferable meta-skills for embodied navigation. In *CVPR*.

Liu, H., Socher, R., & Xiong, C. (2019). Taming MAML: Efficient unbiased meta-reinforcement learning. In *ICML*.

Majid, A. Y., Saaybi, S., van Rietbergen, T., Francois-Lavet, V., Prasad, R. V., & Verhoeven, C. (2021). *Deep reinforcement learning versus evolution strategies: A comparative survey. TechRxiv*. Preprint. https://doi.org/10.36227/techrxiv. 14679504.v2.

Mirowski, P., Grimes, M., Malinowski, M., Hermann, K. M., Anderson, K., Teplyashin, D., ... Hadsell, R. (2018). *Learning to navigate in cities without a map* (pp. 2419–2430).

Mirowski, P., Pascanu, R., Viola, F., Soyer, H., Ballard, A. J., Banino, A., ... Hadsell, R. (2017). Learning to navigate in complex environments. In *ICLR*.

Mitchell, T. M., Cohen, W. W., Jr., Hruschka, E., Talukdar, P., Betteridge, J., Carlson, A., ... Krishnamurthy, J. (2015). Never ending learning. In *AAAI* (pp. 2302–2310).

Nagabandi, A., Clavera, I., Liu, S., Fearing, R. S., Abbeel, P., Levine, S., & Finn, C. (2019). Learning to adapt in dynamic, real-world environments through meta-reinforcement learning. In *ICLR*.

Nagabandi, A., Finn, C., & Levine, S. (2019). Deep online learning via meta-learning: Continual adaptation for model-based RL. In *ICLR*.

Nichol, A., Achiam, J., & Schulman, J. (2018). *On first-order meta-learning algorithms*. Retrieved from arXiv preprint: arXiv:1803.02999.

Osband, I., Blundell, C., Pritzel, A., & Van Roy, B. (2016). Deep exploration via bootstrapped DQN. *Advances in Neural Information Processing Systems, 29*.

Paivio, A. (1969). Mental imagery in associative learning and memory. *Psychological Review, 76*(3), 241.

Pan, X., You, Y., Wang, Z., & Lu, C. (2017). *Virtual to real reinforcement learning for autonomous driving*.

Parisotto, E., Ba, J. L., & Salakhutdinov, R. (2015). *Actor-mimic: Deep multitask and transfer reinforcement learning*. arXiv:1511.06342.

Pritzel, A., Uria, B., Srinivasan, S., Badia, A. P., Vinyals, O., Hassabis, D., ... Blundell, C. (2017). Neural episodic control. In *PMLR* (pp. 2827–2836).

Rakelly, K., Zhou, A., Quillen, D., Finn, C., & Levine, S. (2019). Efficient off-policy meta-reinforcement learning via probabilistic context variables. In *ICML*.

Ray, S., & Tadepalli, P. (2011). Model-based reinforcement learning. In C. Sammut, & G. I. Webb (Eds.), *Encyclopedia of machine learning*. Boston, MA: Springer. https://doi.org/10.1007/978-0-387-30164-8_556.

Ring, M. B. (1994). *Continual learning in reinforcement environments*. Ph.D. thesis Austin, TX: University of Texas at Austin Austin.

Rothfuss, J., Lee, D., Clavera, I., Asfour, T., & Abbeel, P. (2019). Promp: Proximal meta-policy search. In *7th international conference on learning representations*.

Rusu, A. A., Rabinowitz, N. C., Desjardins, G., Soyer, H., Kirkpatrick, J., Kavukcuoglu, K., ... Hadsell, R. (2016). *Progressive neural networks*. http://arxiv.org/abs/1606.04671.

Schaul, T., Horgan, D., Gregor, K., & Silver, D. (2015). Universal value function approximators. In *PMLR* (pp. 1312–1320).

Schmidhuber, J. (2015). Deep learning in neural networks: An overview. *Neural Networks, 61*, 85–117.

Schulman, J., Levine, S., Abbeel, P., Jordan, M., & Moritz, P. (2015). Trust region policy optimization. In *International conference on machine learning* (pp. 1889–1897). PMLR.

Silva, B. C., Basso, E. W., Bazzan, A. L., & Engel, P. M. (2006). Dealing with non-stationary environments using context detection. In *The 23rd international conference on machine learning. ACM* (pp. 217–224).

Song, X., Yang, Y., Choromanski, K., Pacchiano, A., Gao, W., & Tang, Y. (2020). ES-MAML: Simple Hessian-free meta learning. In *ICLR*.

Stadie, B. C., Yang, G., Houthooft, R., Chen, X., Duan, Y., Wu, Y., et al. (2018). Some considerations on learning to explore via meta-reinforcement learning. *arXiv preprint*, arXiv:1803.01118.

Sutton, R. S., & Barto, A. G. (2018). *Reinforcement learning: An introduction*. MIT Press.

Sutton, R. S., Koop, A., & Silver, D. (2007). On the role of tracking in stationary environments. In *The 24th international conference on machine learning. ACM* (pp. 871–878).

Synnaeve, G., Nardelli, N., Auvolat, A., Chintala, S., Lacroix, T., Lin, Z., et al. (2016). Torchcraft: A library for machine learning research on real-time strategy games. *arXiv preprint*, arXiv:1611.00625.

Tamar, A., Wu, Y., Thomas, G., Levine, S., & Abbeel, P. (2016). Value iteration networks. *Advances in Neural Information Processing Systems, 29*.

Tang, H., Houthooft, R., Foote, D., Stooke, A., Xi Chen, O., Duan, Y., et al. (2017). #Exploration: A study of count-based exploration for deep reinforcement learning. *Advances in Neural Information Processing Systems, 30*.

Todorov, E., Erez, T., & Tassa, Y. (2012). MuJoCo: A physics engine for model-based control. In *2012 IEEE/RSJ international conference on intelligent robots and systems* (pp. 5026–5033). IEEE.

Vaswani, A., Shazeer, N., Parmar, N., Uszkoreit, J., Jones, L., Gomez, A. N., ... Polosukhin, I. (2017). Attention is all you need. In *Advances in neural information processing systems* (pp. 5998–6008).

Vinyals, O., Ewalds, T., Bartunov, S., Georgiev, P., Vezhnevets, A. S., Yeo, M., et al. (2017). Starcraft ii: A new challenge for reinforcement learning. *arXiv preprint*, arXiv:1708.04782.

Wang, J. X., Kurth-Nelson, Z., Tirumala, D., Soyer, H., Leibo, J. Z., Munos, R., ... Botvinick, M. (2016). *Learning to reinforcement learn*. https://arxiv.org/abs/1611.05763v1.

Wang, X., Huang, Q., Celikyilmaz, A., Gao, J., Shen, D., Wang, Y.-F., ... Zhang, A. L. (2019). Reinforced cross-modal matching and self-supervised imitation learning for vision-language navigation. In *CVPR*.

Weng, L. (2019). *Meta reinforcement learning*. Retrieved from lilianweng.github.io/lil-log http://lilianweng.github.io/lil-log/2019/06/23/meta-reinforcement-learning.html.

Weston, J., Chopra, S., & Bordes, A. (2014). *Memory networks*. http://arxiv.org/abs/1410.3916.

Wierstra, D., Schaul, T., Peters, J., & Schmidhube, J. (2008). Natural evolution strategies. In *2008 IEEE congress on evolutionary computation* (pp. 3381–3387).

Wortsman, M., Ehsani, K., Rastegari, M., Farhadi, A., & Mottaghi, R. (2019). Learning to learn how to learn: Self-adaptive visual navigation using meta-learning. In *CVPR*.

Xu, H., Zhang, C., Wang, J., Ouyang, D., Zheng, Y., & Shao, J. (2020). *Exploring parameter space with structured noise for meta-reinforcement learning*. Retrieved from IJCAI.

Xu, K., Ratner, E., Dragan, A., Levine, S., & Finn, C. (2019). Learning a prior over intent via meta-inverse reinforcement learning. In *ICML*.

Xu, T., Liu, Q., Zhao, L., & Peng, J. (2018). *Learning to explore via meta-policy gradient*. Retrieved from ICML.

Yang, Y., Caluwaerts, K., Iscen, A., Tan, J., & Finn, C. (2019). NoRML: No-reward meta learning. In *AAMAS*. https://arxiv.org/abs/1903.01063; (2019).

Yang, Z., Merrick, K., Jin, L., & Abbass, H. A. (2018). *Hierarchical deep reinforcement learning for continuous action control*.

Yu, L., Yu, T., Finn, C., & Ermon, S. (2019). Meta-inverse reinforcement learning with probabilistic context variables. In *NeurIPS*.

Yu, T., Finn, C., Xie, A., Dasari, S., Zhang, T. H., Abbeel, P., & Levine, S. (2018). One-shot imitation from observing humans via domain-adaptive meta-learning. In *RSS*.

Yu, T., Quillen, D., He, Z., Julian, R., Narayan, A., Shively, H., ... Levine, S. (2021). *Meta-world: A benchmark and evaluation for multi-task and meta reinforcement learning*. https://github.com/rlworkgroup/metaworld.

Zeng, F., Wang, C., & Ge, S. S. (2020). A survey on visual navigation for artificial agents with deep reinforcement learning. In *IEEE*. https://doi.org/10.1109/ACCESS.2020.3011438.

Zhu, Y., Mottaghi, R., Kolve, E., Lim, J. J., Gupta, A., Fei-Fei, L., & Farhadi, A. (2017). Target-driven visual navigation in indoor scenes using deep reinforcement learning. In *ICRA*.

Zintgraf, L., Shiarlis, K., Igl, M., Schulze, S., Gal, Y., Hofmann, K., & Whiteson, S. (2020). VariBAD: A very good method for Bayes-adaptive deep RL via meta-learning. In *ICLR*.

8

Meta-learning for healthcare

8.1 Introduction

Healthcare is one of the most stimulating domains of rapid AI development with transformative power in applications ranging from medical imaging computing to electronic health record (EHR) analysis and other highly specialized scenarios. Meta-learning has quickly become one of the most efficient quantitative methodologies in clinical research and clinic management. It assists clinical risk prediction in hospitals and predicts disease through EHRs, reconstructs low-dose computed tomography (CT) imaging, assists in magnetic resonance imaging (MRI) analysis, and personalizes medical treatments. It also can be used to perform disease prognoses for patients and offers novel treatment options for children and adults with specific health conditions.

This chapter starts from primary machine learning concepts and deals with cutting-edge meta-learning models in the context of diverse modalities of healthcare data, including medical imaging, electrocardiography, time-series data with nonuniform time intervals, multimodal data, facial imaging captured from a video camera, and others. This chapter investigates 15 interesting contributions to the field, all of which can be divided into three taxonomies according to their tasks to solve, as outlined in Table 8.1: medical imaging analysis (image classification, lesion classification, image segmentation, and image reconstruction), computing based on EHRs, and applications in specialized areas (cardiac and disease diagnosis). In-depth overviews are offered of studies per practice area: breast, chest, cardiac, tongue, abdominal, pulmonary, and dermatologic.

The selected techniques have developed essential and fundamental influences as a solid foundation of the widely spread methods or theories either (i) with significantly and broadly practical contributions in diverse applications with state-of-the-art results, (ii) shedding light on an important mainstream in academia with huge potential space for further exploration and investigation, (iii) or with promising solutions for the fundamental components that are hardly discussed but important to the corresponding fields in healthcare. Some pieces of research recursively track related bibliographies in papers accepted at premier academic conferences and journals: ICML, ISBI, ECCV, CVPR, KDD, MICCAI, NeurIPS, NSS/MIC, and PubMed Central.

TABLE 8.1 Summarized paradigms of meta-learning for healthcare.

References	Topic	Tasks	Method	Conferences
Part I Medical imaging computing				
8.2 Image classification				
Maicas, Nguyen, Motlagh, Nascimento, and Carneiro (2020)	Breast dynamic contrast-enhanced magnetic resonance imaging		Deep Clustering	ISBI
Qiu (2020)	Tongue identification		Prototypical Networks-Based	
8.3 Dermatology				
Prabhu et al. (2019)	Fine-grained skin disease classification		Prototypical Cluster Network (PCN)	
Li et al. (2020)	Difficulty-aware rare disease classification		Difficulty-Aware Meta Learner (DAML)	MICCAI
Mahajan, Sharma, and Vig (2020)	Rare disease diagnostics: skin lesion		Meta-Derm Diagnosis	CVPR
8.4 Image segmentation				
Wu, Xie, Qu, Dai, and Chen (2020)	Medical ultra-resolution image segmentation		Meta Segmentation Network (MSN)	
8.5 Image reconstruction				
Zhu et al. (2019)	Chest and abdomen computed tomography image reconstruction	Low-dose computed tomography imaging reconstruction	MetaCT	NSS/MIC
Part II/8.6 Electronic health records analysis				
Zhang, Tang, Dodge, Zhou, and Wang (2019)	Disease prediction in a low-resource setting	Outcome prediction	MetaPred	KDD
Gheissari and Huang (2020)	Disease classification in a few-shot setting	Outcome prediction	Latent-ODE, ODE-RNN	
Part III Application area				
8.7 Cardiology				
Lee, Chen, and Lee (2020)	Remote heart rate measurement in a few-shot setting		Meta-rPPG	ECCV
Kan et al. (2018)	Customized pulmonary valve conduit reconstruction		General Regression Neural Network (GRNN), Practice Swarm Optimization (PSO)	

TABLE 8.1 Summarized paradigms of meta-learning for healthcare—cont'd

References	Topic	Tasks	Method	Conferences
Lin, Kan, Wang, Chen, and Chen (2018)	Cardiac arrhythmia auto-screening	Pattern recognition	Discrete Fractional-Order Integration (DFIO), GRNN, PSO	
8.8 Disease diagnostics				
Suo, Chou, Zhong, and Zhang (2020)	Fine-grained disease classification under task heterogeneity	Image classification	TAdaNet	KDD
Alaa and Schaar (2018)	Clinical prognosis with Bayesian optimization	Disease prognosis	AutoPrognosis	ICML
8.9 Data modality				
Rahman and Bhattacharya (2016)	Modality detection of biomedical images	Image classification	Multiclass SVM, MLR	

Part I: Medical imaging computing

Medical imaging computing is an interdisciplinary field involving machine learning, computer vision, image science (radiology, biomedical), and image processing. Widely used medical imaging techniques include X-ray radiation, computed tomography (CT), and magnetic resonance imaging (MRI). According to Litjens's work (2017), dominant modalities in medical imaging analysis are ranked as follows: magnetic resonance imaging, microscopy imaging, computed tomography, ultrasound imaging, X-ray imaging, mammography, other medical imaging, multiple medical imaging, and color fundus photography; application areas are "pathology, brain, lung, abdomen (belly), cardiac, breast, bone, retina, and multiple" (Litjens et al., 2017).

Medical imaging seeks to represent the interior body for clinical diagnosis and medical intervention by the visual representation of tissues and organs. About 30 years ago, as supervised methods bloomed, the interest in medical image analysis steadily increased through remarkable techniques, such as active shape models (ASMs), atlas methods, feature extraction, and statistical classifiers. As the achievements of handcrafted features grew, the idea of using a machine to learn features automatically for representation data brought the first success of a practical deep learning technique, known as LeNet (LeCun, Bottou, Bengio, & Haffner, 1998). Hence, the convolutional neural network (CNN) remains the most effective model for image analysis.

Besides, a computer-aided diagnosis (CAD) system—an intelligent agent to assist radiologists in analyzing images—was developed over many years. However, it has proved to be limited due to both the lack of annotated training samples and label noise. Insufficient labeled training data have also led to the weak performance of some baseline models. This negatively influenced the development of advanced frameworks until meta-learning showed impressive results in multiple real-world scenarios.

In Part I of this chapter (Sections 8.2–8.5), multiple medical imaging tasks under meta-learning tools are discussed. Section 8.2 explores the image classification of breast MRI and tongue diagnostics. Skin lesion classifications are detailed in Section 8.3. Ultra-Resolution Image semantic segmentation of breast cancer is presented in Section 8.4, whereas Section 8.5 offers an investigation of low-/high-dose computed tomography image reconstruction.

8.2 Image classification

Medical image classification, usually inputs one image or multiple images and outputs one diagnostic variable. Transfer learning plays a crucial role in conventional medical image classification, considering the limited amounts of clinical training data compared to the numerous training sets of typical computer vision tasks. Early attempts ranged from neuroimaging analysis (Brosch & Tam, 2013; Suk & Shen, 2016) to brain MRI analysis (Kawahara et al., 2016). In this way, pretrained CNN became a medical standard architecture.

Extensive datasets with perfectly annotated samples are expensive and difficult to obtain, mainly due to the low population of patients with rare diseases but also because of the requirement of a high-level expert to label such data. Some examples are image datasets of different types of breast cancer and image datasets of the tongue regarding its color, "fur," shape, etc. Even existing solutions of deep learning achieve promising generalizations in certain medical imaging tasks, they rely heavily on the costly, hand-crafted design process for classification task operations.

On the other hand, current studies of meta-learning shed light on these issues. Unsupervised meta-learning frameworks enable numerous classification tasks from medical breast screening under sample scarcity situation, through a Bayesian hierarchical model in meta-training. Moreover, meta-learning enables a prototypical network-based classification with attention dedicated to tongue diagnosis.

Section 8.2.2 discusses a model-agnostic meta-solver for dynamically contrast-enhanced magnetic resonance imaging of breast malignancies. Section 8.2.3 outlines tongue diagnostics relying on the ordinal images of the organ's shape, "fur," shape, texture, etc.

8.2.1 Breast magnetic resonance imaging

Large-scale training datasets of breast imaging could be high-priced to obtain; hence, it is inappropriate to apply conventional supervised learning in such a situation. Although the existing meta-learning approach (Maicas, Bradley, Nascimento, Reid, & Carneiro, 2018) produces superior outcomes when compared to regular pretraining strategies, the meta-training still relies extensively on high-cost, handcrafted processes to generate classification tasks.

To solve this issue, Maicas et al. (2020) suggested an unsupervised framework based on numerous classification tasks from medical breast screening via dynamic contrast-enhanced magnetic resonance imaging (DCE-MRI). To address the severe lack of annotated training data in medical images, this framework aims to apply annotated training data during meta-training, and fine-tuning for unseen classification tasks. It implemented MAML (Grant, Finn, Levine, Darrell, & Griffiths, 2018) with a Bayesian hierarchical model in meta-training.

This approach uses deep clustering (Caron et al., 2018) as a base model to generate a set of clusters for the unsupervised methods of the classification tasks stated as following. The overall goal is expressed in Eq. (8.1). The classifier g_ω parameterized by ω, and unsupervised leaner f_θ parameterized by θ. $\ell(\cdot)$ denotes the cross-entropy loss, and $\widetilde{y}_i$ represents the pseudo-label for the input from a dataset $\mathcal{D} = \left\{ (v_i, t_i, b_i, y_i) \right\}_{i=1}^{|\mathcal{D}|}$. v and t represent the first DCE-MRI subtraction volume and the T1-weighted MRI to split the breast regions within the volume. b indicates the right or left breast, and y denotes the binary classification label of whether or not malignancy is found.

$$\underset{\theta, \omega}{\operatorname{argmin}} \frac{1}{|\mathcal{D}|} \sum_{i=1}^{|\mathcal{D}|} \ell\left(g_\omega(f_\theta(v_i)), \widetilde{y}_i\right) \tag{8.1}$$

Then, the K centroids C are found through the objective function, as expressed in Eq. (8.2). They relied on the L binary classification with the pseudo-labels $\widetilde{y}_i$, where $\widetilde{y}_i$ is a K-dim one-shot representation, and θ^* denotes the optimal parameters.

$$\underset{C}{\min} \frac{1}{|\mathcal{D}|} \sum_{i=1}^{|\mathcal{D}|} \underset{\widetilde{y}_i}{\min} \left\| f_{\theta*}(v_i) - C\widetilde{y}_i \right\|_2^2 \tag{8.2}$$

The objective function of meta-training is shown in Eq. (8.3), which can be approximated with a lower bound maximization through Jensen's inequality (Bishop, 2006), as shown in Eq. (8.4). ψ and ϕ_l denote meta-parameters and the parameters regarding task $\mathcal{T}_l$, and $Y_l^{(t)} = \left\{ \sim y_i^{(lt)} \right\}_{i=1}^M$, $Y_l^{(v)} = \left\{ \sim y_i^{(lv)} \right\}_{i=1}^N$, $V_l^{(v)} = \left\{ v_i^{(lv)} \right\}_{i=1}^N$, and $V_l^{(t)} = \left\{ v_i^{(l,t)} \right\}_{i=1}^M$ from training set $\left\{ v_i^{(l,t)}, \widetilde{y}_i^{(l,t)} \right\}_{i=1}^M$ and testing set $\left\{ v_i^{(l,v)}, \widetilde{y}_i^{(l,v)} \right\}_{i=1}^N$. $p(\phi_l | Y_l^{(t)}, V_l^{(t)}, \psi)$ represents the posterior.

$$\underset{\psi}{\max} \; \log p\left(Y_{l=1\ldots T}^{(v)} \middle| Y_{l=1\ldots T}^{(t)}, V_{l=1\ldots T}^{(v)}, V_{l=1\ldots T}^{(t)}, \psi \right) \tag{8.3}$$

$$\log p\left(Y_{l=1\ldots T}^{(v)} \middle| Y_{l=1\ldots T}^{(t)}, V_{l=1\ldots T}^{(v)}, V_{l=1\ldots T}^{(t)}, \psi \right) \geq \sum_{l=1}^{T} \mathbb{E}_{p\left(\phi_l | Y_l^{(t)}, V_l^{(t)}, \psi\right)} \left[\log p\left(Y_l^{(v)} \middle| V_l^{(v)}, \phi_l \right) \right] \tag{8.4}$$

The meta-update with truncated gradient descent is expressed in Eq. (8.5):

$$\phi_l^* = \psi - a\nabla_{\phi_l} \left[-\log p\left(Y_l^{(t)} \middle|, V_l^{(t)}, \phi_l \right) \right] \tag{8.5}$$

This framework is evaluated in the DCE-MRI dataset (McClymont, Mehnert, Trakic, Kennedy, & Crozier, 2014), an imaging modality of breast screening processes for patients who are likely to be at high risk. The dataset provides a region of the breast {left, right} and a binary label of malignant or not {1, 0}.

8.2.2 Tongue identification

A tongue diagnosis is essential in traditional Chinese medicine (TCM) to evaluate personal health conditions. Typical characteristics observed include shape, color, texture, body features, coating of fur, and fur features. Qiu (2020) introduced a prototypical network-based classification for tongue diagnosis (Zhu, 2018), and the prototypical network worked as a classifier.

There are three main modules in this framework: (1) feature representation, (2) prototype generation, and (3) distance estimation.

The feature representation module is built as a four-layer convolution, consisting of the following:

- Residual convolutional block (He, Zhang, Ren, & Sun, 2016)
- Spatial attention network
- Feature selection layer with attention mechanism (Vaswani et al., 2017) to improve accuracy
- Domain knowledge of TCM tongue diagnosis (e.g., the color of the tongue coating, tongue body, tongue tip, and allocation of the tongue coating)

The prototype is estimated in Eq. (8.6), where $EMBED_{j,i}$ denotes the ith feature embedding for j-type prototype among overall n types:

$$P_j = \sum_i EMBED_{j,i}/n \qquad (8.6)$$

The overall cross-entropy loss function $CE(\cdot)$ aims to reduce intra-class distance while expanding interclass distance, as represented in Eq. (8.7), where y_t and y_1 represent the ground truth and estimated label, $EMBED_1$ denotes the feature embedding of the query image, a_1, a_2, and a_3 are the predefined coefficient for weighting, and P_t denotes the prototype of ground truth label:

$$loss = a_1{}^*CE\left(y_t, y_1\right) + a_2{}^*L1(EMBED_1, P_t) + a_3/\sum_{i,j}L2\left(P_i, P_j\right) + 1 \qquad (8.7)$$

This research assessed datasets from miniImageNet and self-collected tongue images; however, other tongue image sample sets may provide more diverse data: Hou Jun's (Hou et al., 2017), Zheng's (Huo et al., 2017), Sun's (Fu et al., 2017), and Li's (Li, Wen, & Zeng, 2019).

8.3 Lesion classification

Although more than half of the population in the world suffers from skin diseases—which are a potential indicator of severe conditions, such as cancer—they often go mistreated or untreated. Unfortunately, primary doctors are usually more familiar with typical skin lesions than with rare skin lesions. Lesion classification focuses on the small parts of an image. The local features of lesion appearance and global contextual information are two key components; the integration of these components stimulated the popularity of multistream networks. A skin lesion classification with multistream CNN was proposed by Kawahara and

Hamarneh (2016), whereas Setio et al. (2016) provided a multistream CNN on chest CT. As the end-to-end application blossomed, attempts with various structures presented versatile solutions, such as restricted Boltzmann machines, stacked auto-encoders, and convolutional sparse auto-encoders (CSAE; Litjens et al., 2017). However, performance of the supplementary machine learning analyzer may be inferior because of the long-tailed data distribution and the various intra-class variations. In addition, transfer learning based on imbalanced data leads to a high possibility of overfitting.

Meta-learning has demonstrated a fair amount of novel research possibilities to solve these challenges. Fine-grained classification—through the extension of the prototypical network—allows a primary doctor to obtain a comprehensive list of potential skin lesion diagnoses based on minimal training samples.

Section 8.3 focuses on skin lesions, which are experienced by significant portion of the population. A fine-grained dermatological disease classification based on a Prototypical Clustering Network is presented in Section 8.3.2. Section 8.3.3 offers a difficulty-aware meta-learner for rare skin diagnostics by first learning from common skin alignments and then adapting to rare dermatological diseases. Building on this, Section 8.3.4 evaluates the performance of the Reptile and Prototypical Network on the same skin lesion diagnostic problem, in which Reptile achieved better results.

8.3.1 Fine-grained skin disease classification

Skin disease affects 30%–70% of people worldwide (Johnson & Roberts, 1978). Mistreated or untreated skin issues can increase the risk of potential disability and even death (Basra & Shahrukh, 2009). However, accurate and fast dermatological disease diagnostics suffer from two significant limitations in clinical and quantitative analysis:

- Primary care doctors are usually trained to recognize the most common skin conditions, while, according to the International Classification for human Diseases (ICD), there are thousands of skin or skin-relevant diseases (Wilmer et al., 2014)
- Most real-patient skin lesion datasets are long-tailed samples, and the intra-class variations are huge

As clinical image classification has achieved massive success in assisting disease diagnostics for general physicians, Prabhu et al. (2019) presented a fine-grained classifier named Prototypical Clustering Network (PCN). It applies a nonlinear extension of a prototypical network (see a detailed discussion in Section 3.4) and aims to assist primary care doctors by offering a list of possible skin disease diagnoses.

Differing from a standard prototypical network of a single prototype for each class, PCN expanded to a collection $\{\mu_{z,k}\}_{z=1}^{M_k}$ of prototypes M_k for every class k.

To avoid the imbalance of sampling between hand and tail, this framework involved K-means in the cluster prototype for each class. From Eqs. (8.8) to (8.10), the terms $2W_{k,x}^T f_\phi(x)$ and $b_{k,x}$ capture the nonlinearity of samples, as demonstrated in Eq. (8.8). $w_{k,x}$ is the example-specific prototypical representation through the posterior probability of intra-class cluster assignments. $q(z|k,x)$ is the critical determinator of prototype methods, processing standard prototype methods if the posterior is confident; otherwise, PCN involves $q(z|k,x)$ to adjust prototypes.

$$-\sum_z q(z|k,x)\|f_\phi(x)-\mu_{z,k}\|^2 = \text{const. for k} + 2\sum_z q(z|k,x)f_\phi(x)^T\mu_{z,k}$$

$$-\sum_z q(z|k,x)\mu_{z,k}^T\mu_{z,k} \qquad (8.8)$$

$$= \text{const. for k} + 2w_{k,x}^T f_\phi(x) - b_{k,x}$$

where:

$$w_{k,x} = \sum_z q(z|k,x)\mu_{z,k}$$

$$b_{k,x} = \sum_z q(z|k,x)\mu_{z,k}^T\mu_{z,k} \qquad (8.9)$$

Resembling most meta-learners in needing to train on an episode strategy (see a detailed discussion of episode-based training in Section 3.3), the overall training method of PCN is summarized in Table 8.2. This framework is evaluated on a customized image dataset from Dermnet: Skin Disease Atlas (Dermnet, 1998).

TABLE 8.2   General training methods of prototypical clustering network.

Input: Training set $\mathcal{D} = \{(x_1,y_1), \cdots, (x_N,y_N)\}$, and $y_i \in \{1,\cdots,K\}$.

     $\mathcal{D}_k$ denotes the subset of $\mathcal{D}$ with all class prototypes, i.e., $(x_i,y_i) = \{\mu_{z,k}\}_{z=1}^{M_k} \forall k \in \{1,\cdots,K\}$

Output: The loss L_ϕ with respect to a randomly generated training episode

---

1: $V \leftarrow$ randomly sample $(\{1,\cdots,K\}, N_C)$

2: **for** $k \in \{1,\cdots,N_C\}$ **do**

     # Construct support set and query set

3:      $S_k \leftarrow$ randomly sample $(\mathcal{D}_{v_k}, N_S)$

4:      $Q_k \leftarrow$ randomly sample $(\mathcal{D}_{v_k \setminus S_k}, N_Q)$

     # Evaluate probabilistic assignment of x to clusters of y

5:      **for** $z \in \{1,\cdots,M_k\}$ **do**

6:          **for** $(x,y) \in S_k$ **do**

7:              $q(z|k,x) = \dfrac{\exp\left(-d(f_\phi(x),\mu_{z,k})/\tau\right)}{\sum_{z'} \exp\left(-d(f_\phi(x),\mu_{z',k})/\tau\right)}$

8:          **end for**

9:          $\mu_{z,k}^{\text{new}} \leftarrow \alpha\mu_{z,k}^{\text{old}} + (1-\alpha)\dfrac{\sum_{(x,y)\in S_k} q(z|k,x)f_\phi(x)}{\sum_{(x,y)\in S_k} q(z|k,x)}$

10:     **end for**

11: **end for**

12: $L_\phi \leftarrow 0$

13: **for** $k \in \{1,\cdots,N_C\}$ **do**

14:     **for** $(x,y) \in Q_k$ **do**

15:         $r_{x,y} \leftarrow \sum_z q(z|k,x)d(f_\phi(x),\mu_{z,k}) + \log \sum_{k'} \exp(-\sum_{z'} q(z'|k',x)d(f_\phi(x),\mu_{z',k'}))$

16:         $L_\phi \leftarrow L_\phi + \frac{r_{x,y}}{N_C N_Q}$

17:     **end for**

18: **end for**

Modified from Prabhu, V., Kannan, A., Ravuri, M., Chablani, M., Sontag, D., & Amatriain, X. (2019). Few-shot learning for dermatological disease diagnosis. Retrieved from http://proceedings.mlr.press/v106/prabhu19a/prabhu19a.pdf.

8.3.2 Difficulty-aware rare disease classification

Meta-learning approaches have become valuable in rare disease diagnostics, as the training data are extremely limited due to the population of corresponding patients. In contrast, transfer learning through fine-tuning the minimal amount of data causes serious overfitting, which a meta-learner can avoid.

To address the lack of training data samples of rare disease diagnosis, Li et al. (2020) provided a Difficulty-Aware Meta-Learning (DAML) framework and illustrated dermatological imaging classification as examples. The general strategy of this framework is first to train the meta-learner based on a set of tasks on common diseases classification, hence adapting the meta-knowledge to the tasks of rare disease classification based on a few samples. Fig. 8.1 demonstrates the overall pipeline of DAML.

Analogous to the attention mechanism, the difficulty-aware module interactively reduces the importance of easy tasks while emphasizing the tough ones. In meta-optimization, the cross-entropy loss in the adaptation steps is expressed in Eq. (8.10).

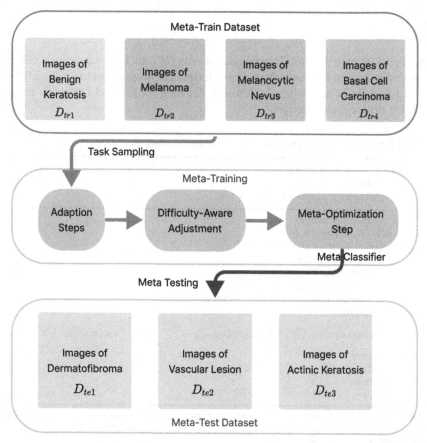

FIG. 8.1 General pipeline of difficulty-aware meta-learning in meta-training and meta-testing. *Adapted from Springer, MICCAI, Difficulty-Aware Meta-learning for Rare Disease Diagnosis, Xiaomeng Li, Lequan Yu, Yueming Jin, Chi-Wing Fu, Lei Xing, Pheng-Ann Heng, (2020).*

η denotes the scaling factor, $\in$ represents the smallest positive such that $(\epsilon, 1 - \mathcal{L}_{T_i}) > 0$, ϕ is the parameters of base model, α means the meta-learning rate, and $\mathcal{L}_{T_i}$ is the original cross-entropy loss for task T_i.

$$\mathcal{L}_{DA\_meta} = \sum_{T_i \sim p(T)} - \mathcal{L}_{T_i}{}^{\eta} \log \left(\max \left(\epsilon, 1 - \mathcal{L}_{T_i} \right) \right)$$

$$\phi \leftarrow \phi - \alpha \nabla_\phi \sum_{T_i \sim p(T)} - \mathcal{L}_{T_{DA\_meta}}$$

(8.10)

Table 8.3 summarizes the general method of DAML.
The seven common skin conditions D_{tr} covers are:

- Melanocytic nevus
- Melanoma
- Benign keratosis
- Dermatofibroma
- Basal cell carcinoma
- Actinic keratosis
- Vascular lesion

The three types of rare dermatological alignments (D_{te}) include squamous cell carcinoma, pyogenic granuloma, and hemangioma. This model is evaluated on the ISIC 2018 skin alignment dataset (Codella et al., 2018b; Li, Yu, Fu, & Heng, 2018) and Dermofit Image Library (Jia et al., 2018) under AUC metrics.

TABLE 8.3   General training methods of difficulty-aware meta-learner.

Input: D_{tr}, Meta-train dataset
  α, Meta learning rate
  γ, inner-loop adaptation learning rate

1. $\phi \leftarrow$ randomly initialize
2. **while** not converged **do**
3.   Sample batch of tasks from D_{tr}
4.   **for** each task T_i **do**
5.   **for** number of adaptation steps **do**
6.   evaluate $\mathcal{L}_{T_i}\left(f_{\phi_i}\right)$ by cross entropy loss for T_i
7.   obtain gradient descent through $\phi'_i \leftarrow \phi_i - \gamma \nabla_\phi \mathcal{L}_{T_i}\left(f_{\phi_i}\right)$
8.   **end for**

9.   evaluate $\mathcal{L}_{D\,A_{meta}}\left(f_{\phi_i}\right)$ through $\mathcal{L}_{D\,A\_meta} = \sum_{T_i \sim p(T)} - \mathcal{L}_{T_i}{}^{\eta} \log \left(\max \left(\epsilon, 1 - \mathcal{L}_{T_i} \right) \right)$

10.   **end for**
11.   update $\phi \leftarrow \phi - \alpha \nabla_\phi \sum_{T_i \sim p(T)} - \mathcal{L}_{T_{D\,A\_meta}}$
12. **end while**
13. **return** ϕ

Modified from Li, X., Yu, L., Jin, Y., Fu, C. W., Xing, L., & Heng, P. A. (2020). Difficulty-aware meta-learning for rare disease diagnosis. International conference on medical image computing and computer-assisted intervention (pp. 357–366). Cham: Springer.

8.3.3 Rare disease diagnostics: Skin lesion

Due to the low population of people who have suffered from rare diseases, the amount of annotated training data could be minimal. This sample scarcity leads deep learning-based diagnostics to be much more challenging. In addition, many existing datasets experience imbalanced or long-tailed data distributions, which may cause deficient generalizations. Novel classes in the inference phase, which have never been seen during training, increase the difficulties of classification tasks.

Continuing the interest in rare disease and heavy-tailed data from Section 8.3.2, Mahajan et al. (2020) introduced a classifier—Meta-DermDiagnosis—that tackled rare or novel disease classification and long-tailed data.

Like the previous sections, this framework also addresses the scarcity of labeled data, the long-tailed class distributions, and significant fine-grained variations. However, Meta-DermDiagnosis works with both gradient-based (e.g., Reptile, see Section 4.4) and metric-based (e.g., Prototypical Net, see Section 3.4) meta-learning methods.

Table 8.4 summarizes the overall methods when implementing Reptile.

TABLE 8.4 General training methods of Meta-DermDiagnosis.

Algorithm 1 implementing Reptile
1: θ initialization
2: **for** $i = 1, 2, \ldots$ **do**
3:    sample task T with loss L_T for weight vectors θ
4:    obtain $\sim \theta = U_T^k(\theta)$ under k steps of SGD or Adam
5:    evaluate $\theta \leftarrow \theta + \epsilon(\sim \theta - \theta)$, where ϵ denotes the parameter of step size
6: end **for**

Modified from Mahajan, K., Sharma, M., & Vig, L. (2020). Meta-DermDiagnosis: Few-shot skin disease identification using meta-learning. Retrieved from https://openaccess.thecvf.com/content_CVPRW_2020/ papers/w42/Mahajan_Meta-DermDiagnosis_Few-Shot_Skin_Disease_Identification_Using_Meta-Learning_CVPRW_2020_paper.pdf.

It applies Euclidean distance $d(\cdot)$ for the prototypical network, where the distribution of the predicted label y as class c for input x is expressed in Eqs. (8.11) and (8.12). g denotes the embedding function such that $\mathbf{z} = g(x, \theta)$, and m_c is the prototype vector computed from the support set S_c of class c.

$$p(y = c|x, m_c) = \frac{\exp\left(-d(\mathbf{z}, m_c)\right)}{\sum_{c'} \exp\left(-d(\mathbf{z}, m_{c'})\right)} \tag{8.11}$$

where

$$m_c = \frac{1}{|S_c|} \sum_{(x_j, y_j) \in S_c} g(x_j, \theta) \tag{8.12}$$

This project was trained on skin lesion datasets ISIC 2018 (Codella et al., 2019), Derm7pt (Kawahara, Daneshvar, Argenziano, & Hamarneh, 2019), and SD-198 (Sun, Yang, Sun, & Wang, 2016).

8.4 Image segmentation

Medical imaging segmentation represents the organs and their substructure in terms of volume and shape, encouraging a variety of analyses focused on relevant clinical parameters. Chapter 5, Section 5.5.5 delivers a fundamental of general image segmentation; this section specifically focuses on medical imaging segmentation and its various approaches. Influential U-net-based (Ronneberger, Fischer, & Brox, 2015) techniques—an hourglass structured neural network specific to biomedical image segmentation—have captured a surge of interest. Cicek, Lienkamp, Brox, and Ronneberger (2016) proposed a 3D U-net to achieve volumetric segmentation through scantly labeled volumetric images. Milletari and colleagues (Milletari, Navab, & Ahmadi, 2016) introduced V-net, a U-net-modified 3D deep net structure for volumetric medical image segmentation. Other variants include the Kaggle-winning structure TernausNet (Iglovikov & Shvets, 2018), a U-net backbone with an ImageNet pretrained VGG-11 encoder. In contrast, there are significant impacts from distributions based on a recurrent neural network (RNN; Stollenga, Byeon, Liwicki, & Schmidhuber, 2015; Xie, Zhang, Sapkota, & Yang, 2016), a fully convolutional neural network (FCNN; Shakeri et al., 2016; Song et al., 2015), and a patch-trained neural network (Ciresan, Giusti, Gambardella, & Schmidhuber, 2012).

Section 8.4.1 presents a meta-learning approach that aims to reduce the model complexity and redundancy caused by the conventional fusion structure. This represents a novel direction to solve this challenging problem and avoid the loss of detailed features and global information caused by traditional solutions.

8.4.1 Medical ultra-resolution image segmentation

There are current studies of image segmentation that employ multibranch architecture to aggregate context information. However, two deficiencies need to be addressed: elaborate fusion mechanisms may lead to model redundancy, and all branches are independently trained from scratch, which results in a considerable difference in parameters.

Wu and colleagues (Wu et al., 2020) introduced Meta Segmentation Network (MSN) to solve model complexity and redundancy caused by conventional fusion structure. Two typical approaches are used to deal with ultra-resolution images (URIs). Although both of them reduce computational burdens to some degree, serious drawbacks are worth noting:

- Image down-sampling (i.e., resizing an image into an appropriate size), which may lose detailed information
- Sliding patches (i.e., splitting the image into different small patches) that lack global features

MSN aims to maintain a good balance of computational burdens and segmentation performance by a simple but robust meta-learner. It conducts a unique weight-sharing process that leads to fast knowledge adaptation and parameters reduction.

This framework contains two modules:

1. The multibranch model, named Mainbody, is an all-in-one multibranch (high-resolution, mid-resolution, and low-resolution branches) deep model for URI segmentation. It consists of three parts

   (a) The meta-branch, which has a reference branch and carries critical parameters that are necessarily shared with other branches.

   (b) The memory feature pool (Mem-FP) as storage of meta-features from the meta-branch.

   (c) The memory recall module (Mem-RM) recaps missing features from gap layers in Mem-FP, which is processed as expressed in Eq. (8.13). $\hat{B}$ denotes the output from Mem-RM through nonlinear transformation function f, where $cat(\cdot)$, $up(\cdot)$ and $crop$ $(\cdot)$ represent concatenation, upsampling and cropping operations, respectively.

$$\hat{B} = f(cat(B, up(crop(A)))) \tag{8.13}$$

2. The meta-fusion module (Meta-FM) merges multiple branches.

The cross-entropy loss function of the MSN is expressed in Eq. (8.14), where P and Y denote the estimated segmentation maps and corresponding ground truth labels:

$$L(P, Y) = - \sum_{i}^{N} \sum_{j \in P_i} Y_{i,j} \log P_{i,j} \tag{8.14}$$

This framework implemented BiSeNet (Yu et al., 2018) as the backbone (a CNN-based three-branches network in Mainbody) and was equipped with OpenSlide (Goode, Gilbert, Harkes, Jukic, & Satyanarayanan, 2013) to input various resolution pyramids.

The model is validated on medical datasets BACH (breast cancer; Aresta et al., 2019) and ISIC (Codella et al., 2018a; Tschandl, Rosendahl, & Kittler, 2018) with ultra-resolution medical images.

8.5 Image reconstruction

Following conventional hand-craft modeling, and combined hand-craft and data-driven modeling, there have been significant distributions by deep learning techniques since 2012 through two general strategies: postprocessing and raw-to-image. Postprocessing approaches (Chang, Meng, Haber, Tung, & Begert, 2018; He et al., 2016; Jin, Mccann, Froustey, & Unser, 2017) aim to reconstruct the image through pairs of low-quality images and their high-quality counterparts. However, due to limited measurements, related noise, and missing information, which remains difficult to remove with deep neural networks, postprocessing is appropriate for initial reconstructed images that are fairly high quality. In contrast, versatile deep neural network architectures effectively support raw-to-image approaches, such as ADMM-Net (Sun, Li, & Xu, 2016), PD-Net (Adler & Oktem, 2018), and JSR-Net (Dong, Li, & Shen, 2013), relying on the "mapping between the raw data and the reconstruction image" (Zhang & Dong, 2020). The significant differences between the distribution from the raw data domain and the construction image domain make this approach challenging.

Section 8.5.1 offers a low-dose CT image reconstruction method through a teacher-student model based on high-dose counterparts. This exciting strategy combines with transfer learning to produce pseudo-labeled data.

8.5.1 Chest and abdomen computed tomography image reconstruction

High-dose computed tomography (CT) images (200 mAs) are commonly helpful as labels, but considering the cancer risk of high-dose scanning, high-dose images are not widely available. Although unannotated low-dose images (20 or 50 mAs) are easy to gather, a neural network usually fails on learning latent information. Some attempts rely on precollection of high-dose/low-dose paired images, but these results are time-intensive and hard to get.

Zhu et al. (2019) presented a teacher-student model called metaCT, which aims to apply unlabeled low-dose CT images to generate high-dose ones. MetaCT can reconstruct many low-dose CT images with only a few labeled samples.

This strategy refers to a meta-learning-like concept but is implemented based on transfer learning. The teacher network aims to learn the image reconstruction based on a few high-dose/low-dose paired images. Then, this pretrained teacher network processes numerous unlabelled data points and generates pseudo-labels. Finally, the student network is trained by both ground-truth labeled data and pseudo-labeled data. The teacher and student models utilize recursive ResNet (Ren, Zuo, Hu, Zhu, & Meng, 2019).

This strategy is evaluated on chest and abdomen images from a Mayo Clinic dataset (Chen et al., 2016; He et al., 2018).

Part II: Electronic health records analysis
8.6 Electronic health records

Electronic health record (EHR) systems have developed rapidly in the last decade, partially due to the 2009 Health Information Technology for Economic and Clinical Health (HITECH) ACT, which invested $30 billion to help hospitals install and process EHR systems (Shickel, Tighe, Bihorac, & Rashidi, 2017). EHRs are an informatic digital means of storing data associated with each patient's medical and treatment history, including demographical information, nurse notes, medication records, physician notes, lab testing reports and results, current and past diagnoses, classification schema (e.g., ICD-10, CPT, LOINC, and RxNorm) and radiological images.

Multiparameter Intelligent Monitoring in Intensive Care (MIMIC-III; Johnson et al., 2016) is a remarkable open-source real-world EHR dataset with 38,597 adult patients and 49,785 hospital admissions after deidentification from 2001 to 2012 (Pishgar, Theis, Del Rios, et al., 2022); others refer to MIMIC-CXR (Johnson, Pollard, Mark, Berkowitz, & Horng, 2019) or MIMIC-CXR-JPG (Johnson, Pollard, Greenbaum, et al., 2019). The standard evaluation consists of regular classification metrics, including AUC, accuracy, precision, recall, and F1-score.

The heterogeneous characteristics of this abundance of information create challenges of diverse data types, including:

- Numerical quantities (e.g., resting heart rate)
- Datetime objects (e.g., date of vaccine)
- Categorical values (e.g., codes of ICD-10)
- Natural language text (e.g., physicians' notes)
- Derived time series (e.g., time records created by ICU instruments)

Typical EHR-related machine learning tasks appear in the following groupings (Shickel, Tighe, Bihorac, & Rashidi, 2017):

- EHR information extracting
- EHR representation
- Clinical outcome predicting or treatment outcome predicting
- Computational phenotyping
- Deidentification of patient data

For outcome prediction, there are two subcategories: static outcome prediction (e.g., eyelid cancer prediction based on information from a single encounter) and temporal outcome prediction (e.g., staging prediction for pancreatic cancer). Commonly used deep neural network architectures are CNN (Cheng, Wang, Zhang, Xu, & Hu, 2015; Liang, Zhang, Huang, & Hu, 2014), RBM (Jacobson & Dalianis, 2016), LSTM (Nickerson, Tighe, Shickel, & Rashidi, 2016; Pham, Tran, Phung, & Venkatesh, 2016), autoencoder (Miotto, Li, Kidd, & Dudley, 2016), DBM (Tran, Nguyen, Phung, & Venkatesh, 2015), and GRU (Choi, Bahadori, Schuetz, Stewart, & Sun, 2016).

Although conventional machine learning approaches have achieved remarkable success, some deficiencies remain. Clinical risks, such as in-hospital mortality, inherently influence hospital management and the rehabilitation conditions of patients. The high cost of EHR data limits the number of training samples. Moreover, regular recurrent neural networks face several dilemmas in disease classification due to data scarcity and nonuniform time intervals.

Conversely, meta-learning can perform diverse quantitative analyses and predictions based on EHRs. Disease prediction through irregularly timed data from EHRs is permitted with meta-learning based on limited training samples. Meta-learning equipped with deep neural networks (e.g., LSTM or CNN) is helpful for predicting clinical risks from longitudinal patient EHRs.

Section 8.6.2 demonstrates a prediction framework of multiple clinical risks, such as chronic disease onset, to avoid and forecast potential catastrophes. Section 8.6.3 presents a solution through latent-ordinary differential equations to understand the hidden state of time-series data with nonuniform time intervals in EHRs.

8.6.1 Disease prediction in a low-resource setting

Predictive modeling of clinical risk has attracted keen interest as an emerging application of electronic health records with machine learning. It provides suggestions for in-hospital mortality, 30-day readmission, emergency medical readmission, chronic disease, condition of readmission and death, etc. This analysis is vital for identifying early stage hidden risks at the clinical level and understanding and processing EHRs characteristics such as sparsity, irregularity, and temporality.

Besides expensive costs as the main reason for scarce training data, real-world EHRs data are minimal for the following reasons:

- Patients of rare diseases are few and spread across various locations, limiting new data collection
- The biological mechanisms and effective treatments behind the majority of fatal diseases remain unknown, which leads to complicated clinical risk assessments

To analyze the existing limited EHRs more intensely, Zhang and colleagues (Zhang et al., 2019) suggest a meta-learner named MetaPred to estimate clinical risks based on EHRs and patient data (Jensen, Jensen, & Brunak, 2012). This strategy applied MAML as backbone based on a few samples from a set of relevant disease risk-prediction tasks, implementing a convolutional neural network-based (CNN) or long short-term memory-based (LSTM) network as base predictors for fully supervised sequence representation.

The base learner conducts a cross-entropy loss function, as expressed in Eq. (8.15), where estimated probability for matrix X_i as $\widehat{y}_i = f(X_i; \Theta)$, y_i denotes the target disease label, and N represents the size of training set:

$$\mathcal{L}(\Theta) = -\frac{1}{N} \sum_{i=1}^{N} \left((y_i)^T \log (\widehat{y}_i) + (1 - y_i)^T \log (1 - \widehat{y}_i) \right) \tag{8.15}$$

The main procedure of MetaPred can be divided into four steps:

1. Sampling source domains D_S and simulated target domain D_{T^s} to generate episodes
2. Training the model through base learning and meta-learning (see general training methods in Table 8.5)

3. Apple the target domain D_{T^v} to fine-tune the pretrained model parameter
4. Making predictions on the target clinical risks (see the overall methods of adaptation and prediction in Table 8.6)

Several diseases are discussed during experiments, including:

- Mild cognitive impairment (MCI)
- Alzheimer's disease (AD)
- Parkinson's disease (PD)
- Dementia (DM)
- Amnesia (AM)

Its performance is measured in AUC metrics and F1 scores on the longitudinal real-patient EHRs from Research Data Warehouse (RDW) by the Oregon Health & Science University Hospital and the Oregon Clinical and Translational Research Center (OCTRI).

TABLE 8.5 General training methods of MetaPred.

Input: $\mathcal{S}^i$, source domains
$\qquad \mathcal{T}^0$, target domain
$\qquad \alpha, \beta, \mu$, hyperparameters

1: Randomly initialize Θ

 # Outer-loop
2: **while** not meeting stopping criteria **do**
3: $\qquad$ Sample $\{\mathcal{D}_{epi}\}$ batch of episodes from $\mathcal{D}_{\mathcal{S}^i}$ and $\mathcal{D}_{\mathcal{T}^s}$

$\qquad$ **# Inner-loop**
4: $\qquad$ **while** not meeting stopping criteria **do**
5: $\qquad\qquad \left\{(\mathbf{X}_{\mathcal{S}^i}, \mathbf{y}_{\mathcal{S}^i})\right\}_{i=1}^{K-1}, \left\{(\mathbf{X}_{\mathcal{T}^s}, \mathbf{y}_{\mathcal{T}^s})\right\} = \{\mathcal{D}_{epi}\}$
6: $\qquad\qquad$ Obtain $\mathcal{L}_{\mathcal{S}^i} = \mathcal{L}\left(\mathbf{y}_{\mathcal{S}^i}, f(\mathbf{X}_{\mathcal{S}^i}, \Theta)\right)$, where $i = 1, \cdots, K-1$
7: $\qquad\qquad$ Execute fast adaption by $\Theta' = \Theta - \alpha \nabla_\Theta \sum_i^{K-1} \mathcal{L}_{\mathcal{S}^i}$
8: $\qquad$ **end while**

9: $\qquad$ Obtain $\mathcal{L}_{\mathcal{T}^s} = \mathcal{L}\left(\mathbf{y}_{\mathcal{T}^s}, f(\mathbf{X}_{\mathcal{T}^s}, \Theta')\right)$
10: $\qquad$ Evaluate $\Theta = \Theta - \beta \nabla_\Theta \left(\mathcal{L}_{\mathcal{T}^s} + \mu \sum_i^{K-1} \mathcal{L}_{\mathcal{S}^i}\right)$ through Adam
11: **end while**

Modified from Zhang, X. S., Tang, F., Dodge, H., Zhou, J., & Wang, F. (2019). MetaPred: Meta-learning for clinical risk prediction with limited patient electronic health records. Retrieved from https://arxiv.org/abs/1905.03218.

TABLE 8.6 General methods of adaptation and prediction through MetaPred.

Input: $\mathcal{S}^i$, source domains
$\qquad \mathcal{T}^0$, target domain
$\qquad \Theta$, learned parameter

1: construct testing episodes $\{\mathcal{D}_{epi}\}$ by randomly sampling from $\mathcal{D}_{\mathcal{S}^i}$
2: $\left\{(\mathbf{X}_{\mathcal{S}^i}, \mathbf{y}_{\mathcal{S}^i})\right\}_{i=1}^{K-1}, \left\{(\mathbf{X}_{\mathcal{T}^0}, \mathbf{y}_{\mathcal{T}^0})\right\} = \{\mathcal{D}_{epi}\}$
3: Obtain $\mathcal{L}_{\mathcal{S}^i} = \mathcal{L}\left(\mathbf{y}_{\mathcal{S}^i}, f(\mathbf{X}_{\mathcal{S}^i}, \Theta)\right)$, where $i = 1, \cdots, K-1$
4: Execute fast adaption by $\Theta' = \Theta - \alpha \nabla_\Theta \sum_i^{K-1} \mathcal{L}_{\mathcal{S}^i}$
5: Obtain predicted results of learner $\left(\left\{(\mathbf{X}_{\mathcal{T}^0}, \mathbf{y}_{\mathcal{T}^0})\right\}; \Theta'\right)$

Modified from Zhang, X. S., Tang, F., Dodge, H., Zhou, J., & Wang, F. (2019). MetaPred: Meta-learning for clinical risk prediction with limited patient electronic health records. Retrieved from https://arxiv.org/abs/1905.03218.

8.6.2 Disease classification in a few-shot setting

Targeting EHRs in terms of numerical, structured, and textual data, Gheissari and Huang (2020) presented a meta-learner for disease classification based on irregularly timed data from EHRs samples. These cause the standard strategies on dense data to be ineffective, as with recurrent neural networks (RNN).

This framework conducts latent-ordinary differential equations (latent-ODE; Mozer, Kazakov, & Lindsey, 2017) and ODE-RNN (Rubanova, Chen, & Duvenaud, 2019) as a base learner to model the hidden state on time-series data. See Table 8.7 for the ODE-RNN training method and Table 8.8 for the latent-ODE training procedure. Meta-LSTM (see an in-depth discussion in Section 4.1) is equipped as a meta-learner, and this framework is assessed on the MiniImageNet dataset.

TABLE 8.7 General training methods of ODE-RNN.

Input: Data points with time stamps $\{(x_i, t_i)\}_{i=1...N}$
Output: Last hidden state
　　　　　output at each time stamp

procedure ODE-RNN
1: $h_0 \leftarrow 0$ initilization
2: **for** i in 1, 2, ..., N **do**
3: 　$h_i' = $ ODESolve $(f_\theta, h_{i-1}, (t_{i-1}, t_i))$
4: 　$h_i = $ GRUCell (h_i', x_i)
5: **end for**
6: $o_i = $ OutputNN (hi) **for all** i$=1...$N
7: **return** $\{o_i\}_{i=1...}; h_N$

Modified from Gheissari, P., & Huang, Y. (2020). Meta-learning in medicine.

TABLE 8.8 General training methods of latent-ODE.

Input: Data points with time stamps $\{(x_i, t_i)\}_{i=1..N}$

procedure LATENT-ODE
1: 　$z_0' = $ ODE $-$ RNN$(\{x_i\}_{i=1...N})$
2: 　# g_μ **and** g_δ **denote MLPs**
3: 　$\mu_{z_0} = g_\mu(z_0')$
4: 　$\sigma_{z_0} = g_\sigma(z_0')$
5: 　$z_0 \sim \mathcal{N}(\mu_{z_0}, \sigma_{z_0})$
6: 　$\{z_i\} = $ ODE$(f, z_0, (t_0...t_N))$
7: 　$\widetilde{x}_i = $ Output $NN(z_i)$ **for all** $i=1..N$
8: 　**return** $\{\widetilde{x}_i\}_{i=1...N}$

Modified from Gheissari, P., & Huang, Y. (2020). Meta-learning in medicine.

Part III: Application areas

Despite the tremendous developments in medical imaging computing, meta-learning techniques also have many applications in areas such as cardiac, dermatological, and rare disease diagnostics. These real-world situations pose challenges to transfer learning and supervision learning methods due to low-resource datasets, long-tailed class distribution, minimal new data collection, complex task distributions, etc.

The rest of this chapter will perform several discussion of meta-learning. First, remote heartbeat measurement without wearable devices is a fundamental method for monitoring and detecting potential cardiovascular disease. Traditional supervised learning with extensive training data faces difficulties in sample scarcity. In addition, patients with leaky pulmonary valves need implantation of a customizable pulmonary valve conduit based on their blood pressure, heart condition, etc. Due to the significant variations among each individual, conventional transfer learning leads to inferior generalization and potential overfitting.

Second, task heterogeneity happens during meta-training when the distributions of various tasks have significant variations, which can reduce the generalization capability. Although multiple types of patient data could be used for analysis (e.g., bio-information, testing results, and EHRs), the lack of high-expertise annotation limits the sizes of training datasets for traditional deep learning.

Fortunately, pioneering treatments for heart diseases can be accomplished through meta-learning strategies. The pattern of electrocardiogram and photoplethysmogram detection and pattern recognition achieves impressive performance and accuracy based on only a few samples. A customized pulmonary valve conduit for adults and children can obtain the optimal pulmonary tri-leaflet valve parameters after meta-training.

Incorporating an external knowledge graph in meta-learning approaches supports disease classification in the domain-specific knowledge graph of multiple diseases. In addition, there is an automatic clinical prognosis system with common machine learning algorithms, embedded meta-learning, and Bayesian optimization that has demonstrated advanced interpretability.

Part III consists of three categories that investigate in-depth multiple meta-learning approaches in different clinical applications. Section 8.7 introduces how meta-learning is applied in cardiac-related illness. Section 8.7.1 shows a novel approach to remote heart rate measurement through facial image and photoplethysmography signals. For example, when a standard-sized pulmonary valve stent is not appropriate for young children and adults with certain health conditions, a customized pulmonary valve conduit reconstruction can be prepared with personalized pulmonary tri-leaflet valves parameters, as discussed in Section 8.7.2. Section 8.7.3 provides a novel approach to familiar cardiac arrhythmia auto-screening using electrocardiography (ECG).

General disease diagnostics with task heterogeneity and a clinical prognosis system has received a recent surge of interest, and Section 8.8 introduces several attempts. Section 8.8.1 outlines a task-adaptive meta-learner with a domain-knowledge graph. A system of clinical prognosis based on Bayesian optimization is explored in Section 8.8.2.

Section 8.9 discusses the versatile data modality. Section 8.9.1 investigates a meta-learner for the different medical imaging modalities, ranging from microscopic images to graphics. This is rising field of machine learning for healthcare, which offers essential features for accurate and fast results using medical retrieval systems.

8.7 Cardiology

8.7.1 Remote heart rate measurement in a few-shot setting

A remote photoplethysmography signal is applied through a video camera to measure heart rate without the need of a physical connection between devices and patients. However, various face structures, skin tones, and lighting conditions may confound accurate measurement. When training data distribution differs from the testing data distribution, existing supervised learning approaches become inferior, in addition, failing to produce promising generalizations based on minimal training samples.

Lee and colleagues (Lee et al., 2020) proposed a transductive meta-learning framework (Hu et al., 2020; Liu et al., 2019) for remote heart rate (HR) detection and measurement without any wearable equipment or physical contact with the subjects; this framework was named Meta-rPPG. It applies remote photoplethysmography (rPPG) signals (e.g., from an electrocardiogram (ECG) or photoplethysmogram (PPG)) to detect and measure a subject's heart rate and heart rate variation (HRV). Meta-rPPG takes face video as inputs through a video camera. A two-second warm-start time is employed for the adaptation of distributional changes and improving performance. The official code is available at https://github.com/eugenelet/Meta-rPPG.

This framework can be divided into three parts (see Fig. 8.2 for a demonstration of the general pipeline):

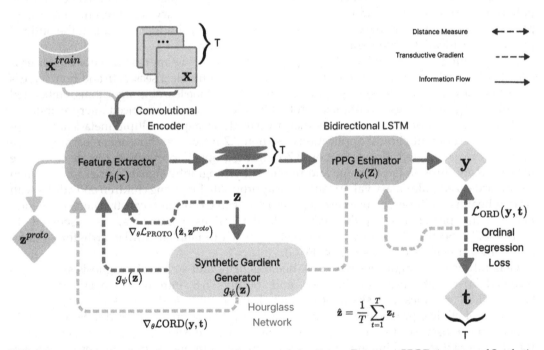

FIG. 8.2 Architecture of transductive system with three modules: Feature Extractor, rPPG Estimator, and Synthetic Gradient Generator. *Adapted from Springer, ECCV, Meta-rPPG: Remote Heart Rate Estimation Using a Transductive Meta-Learner, Lee, E., Chen, E., & Lee, C.-Y. (2020).*

- A ResNet-alike encoder as a feature extractor
- A bidirectional LSTM-based rPPG estimator from visual sequences from a video camera
- A synthetic gradient generator via an hourglass network (Newell, Yang, & Deng, 2016)

Table 8.9 offers a detailed demonstration of Meta-rPPG training methods. The methods are validated on two public heart rate datasets: MAHNOB-HCI (Soleymani, Lichtenauer, Pun, & Pantic, 2011) and UBFC-rPPG (Bobbia, Macwan, Benezeth, Mansouri, & Dubois, 2019).

TABLE 8.9 General training methods of Meta-rPPG training methods.

Input: $p(\mathcal{T})$: distribution of tasks

\# **Pre-train network in R epochs**

2: **for** $i \leftarrow 1, R$ **do**

3:     Sample batch of tasks $\mathcal{T}_i$ from $p(\mathcal{T})$

4:     **for** $(x, t) \sim \mathcal{T}_i$ **do**

5:         Update θ and ϕ through $\mathcal{L}_{\text{ORD}}(y, t) = -\frac{1}{T} \sum\limits_{t=1}^{T} \sum\limits_{s=1}^{S} t_{t,s} lop\left(p_\phi\left(y_{t,s} | z_{t:t+T}\right)\right) + (1 - t_{t,s}) \log\left(1 - p_\phi\left(y_{t,s} | z_{t:t+T}\right)\right)$

6:     **end for**

7: **end for**

\# **transductive meta − learning**

8: **while** not done **do**

9:     Sample batch of tasks $\mathcal{T}_i$ from $p(\mathcal{T})$

10:     **for** $(x, t) \sim \mathcal{T}_i$ **do**

11:       $\{\hat{x}, \hat{t}\}, \{\tilde{x}, \tilde{t}\} \leftarrow x, t$

12:       **for** $i \leftarrow 1, L$ **do**

          \# **Adaptive phase**

13:           Update $\theta \leftarrow \theta - \alpha\left(\nabla_\theta \mathcal{L}_{\text{proto}}\left(\hat{z}, \hat{z}^{\text{proto}}\right) + \nabla_\theta \mathcal{L}_{\text{ORD}}\left(\hat{y}, \hat{t}\right) + f_\psi(\hat{z})\right)$

14:       **end for**

      \# **Learn phase**

15:       $\psi = \psi - \eta \nabla_\psi \mathcal{L}_{\text{SYN}}\left(f_\psi(\tilde{z}), \nabla_{\tilde{z}} \mathcal{L}_{\text{ORD}}\left(\tilde{y}, \tilde{t}\right)\right)$

16:       $\theta = \theta - \eta \nabla_\theta \mathcal{L}_{\text{ORD}}\left(\tilde{y}, \tilde{t}\right)$

17:       $\phi = \phi - \eta \nabla_\phi \mathcal{L}_{\text{ORD}}\left(\tilde{y}, \tilde{t}\right)$

18:       $z^{\text{proto}} = \gamma z^{\text{proto}} + (1 - \gamma) \mathbb{E}_{\tilde{x}(i) \sim \tilde{x}} \frac{1}{T} \sum_{t=1}^{T} f_\theta\left(\tilde{x}_t^{(i)}\right)$

19:     **end for**

20: **end while**

Modified from Lee, E., Chen, E., & Lee, C.-Y. (2020). Meta-rPPG: Remote heart rate estimation using a transductive meta-learner. *Retrieved from https://arxiv.org/abs/2007.06786.*

8.7.2 Customized pulmonary valve conduit reconstruction

Patients with congenital heart disease with narrowed or leaky pulmonary valves will require percutaneous pulmonary valve implantation (PPVI), which can significantly improve the outcomes of surgical operations. Some patients (e.g., infants) with specific health conditions cannot receive valve stents due to the constraints of stent size. The need for a customizable pulmonary valve conduit is evident, as patients with different heart rates, blood pressure, blood flow volumes, etc., need varying sizes of this pulmonary valve.

Kan et al. (2018) proposed a customized pulmonary valve conduit for adults and children by computing the optimal pulmonary tri-leaflet valve parameters. This meta-learning strategy employs a general regression neural network-based (GRNN; Specht, 1991) estimator and particle swarm optimization (PSO; Ratnaweera, Halgamuge, & Watson, 2004; Li et al., 2017) as a meta-learning approach.

This framework can be divided into two stages:

1. Base learning seeks to find the globally optimal solution through a gradient descent-based approach to learning many training patterns
2. Meta-learning seeks to modify part of the parameters through PSO for the optimal smoothing parameters.

   The general searching procedure can be summarized into:

   (1) Constructing initial random population with G particles such that $\delta^p_{cg} = [\sigma^p_{c1}, \sigma^p_{c2}, \sigma^p_{c3}, ..., \sigma^p_{cG}]$

   (2) Obtaining objective function using either one of the below MSEF equations

$$MSEF_1 = \min \left(\sum_{j=1}^{3} \frac{1}{N_1 + N} \sum_{k=1}^{N_1 + N} \left[T_{1j}(k) - y_j(k) \right]^2 \right) \leq \varepsilon$$

$$MSEF_2 = \min \left(\sum_{j=1}^{3} \frac{1}{N_2 + N} \sum_{k=1}^{N_2 + N} \left[T_{2j}(k) - y_j(k) \right]^2 \right) \leq \varepsilon$$

   (3) Obtaining the optimal individual $\sigma best_{cg}$ and the optimal global $\sigma best$ according to each search stage
   (4) Evaluating the velocity of each particle according to each search stage using
   $$\Delta\sigma_{cg}(p + 1) = a_c \left[\Delta\sigma_{cg}(p) + c_1 rand_1 \left(\sigma best_{cg} - \sigma_{cg}(p) \right) + c_2 rand_2 \left(\sigma best - \sigma_{cg}(p) \right) \right]$$
   (5) Hence, evaluating the center position of each practice using $\sigma_{cg}(p+1) = \sigma_{cg}(p) + \Delta\sigma_{cg}(p+1)$
   (6) Terminate this searching procedure if either reaching the maximum number of iterations p_{max}, or MSEF $< \varepsilon$; otherwise, repeat from step (2)

8.7.3 Cardiac arrhythmia auto-screening

The clinical use of 12-lead electrocardiography (ECG) concentrates on detecting heart electrical potentials. Normal and abnormal ECG waveforms are used to recognize multiple patterns of heartbeats.

Lin and colleagues (Lin et al., 2018) introduced a classifying algorithm to detect and process ECG-based real-time screening of cardiac arrhythmias, which aims to process signals, perform feature representation, and recognize patterns of different heartbeats.

Similar to the approach introduced in Section 8.7.2, this framework is equipped with a generalized regression neural network (GRNN) and particle swarm optimization (PSO; Li et al.,

2017; Ratnaweera et al., 2004). It enhances accuracy by fine-tuning each of seven subestimators (N, V, A, R, L, O, and F beats) after learning from the input-output pairs through PSO.

The entire system contains three main modules:

1. A discrete fractional-order integration (DFOI; Wang, Ye, Pan, & Gao, 2015; Wu, Li, Chen, Ho, & Lin, 2017) performs feature extraction of the QRS wave complex (the combined Q wave, R wave, and S wave comprise a cardiac electrical impulse).
2. A general regression neural network (GRNN) is a primary estimator with sufficient training samples to settle the general patterns (Chen, Kan, Lin, & Mai, 2018).
3. A PSO-based meta-learner tunes the parameters of each subestimator (N, V, A, R, L, O, and F beats).

This framework is an evaluated dataset from the Massachusetts Institute of Technology—Beth Israel Hospital (MIT-BIH) dataset (Birkhead, Klompas, & Shah, 2001; Goldberger et al., 2000).

8.8 Disease diagnostics

8.8.1 Fine-grained disease classification under task heterogeneity

Task heterogeneity occurs when the distributions of tasks differ from each other. As meta-learning relies on a set of tasks, task heterogeneity may challenge the generalization of meta-learners (see more details of task heterogeneity in Chapter 1, Section 1.1—Evaluation). There are two main ways to tackle this problem. Some attempts aim to learn task-specific knowledge to adapt shared task-invariant information across all tasks (Lee & Choi, 2018; Li et al., 2020; Yoon, Seo, & Moon, 2019). Other research has concentrated on task relatedness by understanding the relationships among tasks through training samples (Yao et al., 2020; Yao, Wei, Huang, & Li, 2019). Besides these existing research lines, Suo and colleagues (Suo et al., 2020) introduced a task-adaptive metric-based approach based on a graph-based prototypical network and a domain-knowledge graph, namely TAdaNet. It provides a novel direction of task heterogeneity in meta-learning by referring to an external knowledge graph. The official code is released at https://github.com/OpenXAIProject/TAEML.

This paradigm is designed for disease classification among the hierarchical nodes in the domain-specific knowledge graph of multiple diseases. A graph $\mathcal{G}(y, \varepsilon)$ denotes the graph-based associative relationships with two types of nodes: child nodes y^t as the fine-grained disease classes and parent nodes y^c as coarse disease classes to present supplementary knowledge in the few-shot classification. There are two main modules: task context embedding and customized target prediction.

The comprehensive methods of TAdaNET are summarized in Table 8.10.

TABLE 8.10   General training methods TAdaNet.

Input: $p(\mathcal{T})$, task distribution
$\mathcal{G}$, hierarchy graph

1: θ, φ, $\mathcal{M}$ ←Randomly initialization
2: **for** iterations **do**
3:    Sample a batch of tasks from $p(\mathcal{T})$
4:    Sample $\mathcal{D}_i^{tr}$ and $\mathcal{D}_i^{te}$ for task $\mathcal{T}_i$

5:    **for** all task $\mathcal{T}_i$ **do**

6:       # **Obtain the prototype c_i^k of each support class k**
7:

$$c_i^{k,0} = \frac{1}{n_i^{tr,k}} \sum_{(x_{i,j}, y_{i,j}) \in \mathcal{D}_i^{tr,k}} f_\theta(x_{i,j})$$

8:       $$c_i^{k,l+1} = \sum_{p \in N_k \cup k} att\left(c_i^{p,l}, c_i^{k,l}\right) c_i^{p,l}$$

9:       $$c_i^k = (1-\lambda)c_i^{k,\,0} + \lambda c_i^{k,\,L}$$

10:       # **Obtain task representation $\tilde{\tau}_i$**

11:       $$\tau_i = \frac{1}{NK}\sum_{j=1}^{NK} g_\varphi(x_{i,j})$$

12:       $$\alpha_s^k = \frac{exp\left(c_i^k \cdot M(s)\right)}{\sum_{s'=1}^{S} exp\left(c_i^k \cdot M(s')\right)}$$

13:       $$z_i^k = \sum_{s=1}^{S} \alpha_s^k M(s)$$

14:       $$\tilde{\tau}_i = [\tau_i; \tau_i']$$

15:       $$\mathcal{L}_c(\mathcal{T}_i) = \sum_{k=1}^{K} \left\| c_i^k - \frac{1}{n_i^{tr,k}} \sum_{x_{i,j} \in \mathcal{D}_i^{tr,k}} g_\varphi(x_{i,j}) \right\|_F^2$$

16:       $$\eta_i^j = P_c^j(\tilde{\tau}_i), for\, all\, j = 1, \ldots, |\theta|$$

17:       update $\theta_i \leftarrow \eta_i \theta$
18:       # Evaluate the prototype $\tilde{c}_i^k$ and the classification loss $\mathcal{L}_p(\mathcal{T}_i) = -\sum_{k=1}^{K}\sum_{x'_{i,j} \in \mathcal{D}_i^{te,k}} logp\left(y'_{i,j} = k | x'_{i,j}\right)$
19:    **end for**
20:    Update θ, φ, $\mathcal{M}$ through $\mathcal{L}_p + \alpha\mathcal{L}_c$
21: **end for**

Modified from Suo, Q., Chou, J., Zhong, W., & Zhang, A. (2020). TAdaNet: Task-adaptive network for graph-enriched meta-learning.
Retrieved from https://www.kdd.org/kdd2020/accepted-papers/view/tadanet-task-adaptive-network-for-graph-enriched-meta-learning.

These methods are validated on TieredImageNet (Ren et al., 2018) and a public medical analysis dataset named Multiparameter Intelligent Monitoring in Intensive Care (MIMIC-III; Johnson et al., 2016).

8.8.2 Clinical prognosis with Bayesian optimization

Prognosis prediction focuses on the patient's clinical condition, which is based on a multitude of bio-information, lab results, and electronic health records. However, because high-level expertise is required to manually label the data, it is difficult to obtain massive datasets in order to construct a deep learning model that can effectively predict a prognosis.

To prognose diverse health conditions and predict potential risks, Alaa and Schaar (2018) proposed a system for automatic clinical prognosis named AutoPrognosis. Unlike conventional tree-based frameworks, AutoPrognosis is constructed as a principled Gaussian process (GP) based on Bayesian optimization (BO). It aims to process dimension reduction by creating a lower dimensional disintegration from the higher dimensional complex hyperparameter space. In order to improve the interpretability of the system, a rule-based approximation is inserted for assisting clinical decision-makers. The official code is available at https://github.com/ahmedmalaa/AutoPrognosis.

The following list outlines the various computing methods used in the four pipeline stages: data imputation, feature process, prediction, and calibration. Each stage consists of multiple algorithms or mathematical operations, indicated as follows:

- Data imputation: missForest, median, most-frequent, mean, expectation-maximization, matrix completion, multiple imputations by chained equations, or none algorithm applied
- Feature process: feature agglomeration, principal component analysis (PCA), kernel PCA, polynomial, fast independent component analysis, random kitchen sinks, linear support vector machine (SVM), or none algorithm applied
- Prediction: Bernoulli Naive Bayes (NB), AdaBoost, decision tree, gradient boost, Latent Dirichlet Allocation, Gaussian NB, XGBoost, LightGBM, Multinominal NB, random forest, neural networks, log regression, genetic programming, ridge classification, bagging, k-NN
- Calibration: sigmoid, isotonic, or none algorithm applied

Differing from typical meta-learning efforts to create an optimal initialization for fast adaption or a meta-policy for learning among a set of tasks, AutoPrognosis employs meta-learning to transfer a collection of prior knowledge across different datasets. It conducts meta-learning to integrate the optimizer with prior knowledge from previous runs on K supportive datasets $\{D_1, D_2, ..., D_k\}$ with the new dataset D. This aims to obtain an empirical Bayesian estimation of the prior hyperparameters of (M, γ, μ, k), denoted as $(\widehat{M}, \widehat{\gamma}, \widehat{\mu}, \widehat{k})$, which can accelerate the convergence of Bayesian optimization.

The knowledge learned from each supportive dataset includes 55 meta-features $\mathcal{M}(D_k)$: 40 statistical meta-features (e.g., distribution of classes) and 15 clinical meta-features (e.g., physician diagnosis and lab report). This model applies marginal likelihood maximization for hyperparameters $(\widehat{M}, \widehat{\gamma}, \widehat{\mu}, \widehat{k})$ optimization through weights $\{\eta_j\}_j$ such that $\eta_j = \dfrac{\ell_j}{\sum_k \ell_k}$ and $\ell_j = \|\mathcal{M}(D) - \mathcal{M}(D_k)\|_1$.

The output of this pipeline contains two parts: a disease prediction result through the prognostic model and different clinical risk levels (low risk, moderate risk, and high risk;

Richardson, Kriska, Lantz, & Hayward, 2004). This strategy is assessed on nine real-patient datasets covering four aspects of clinical care:

- Preventive care: Meta-Analysis Global Group in Chronic Heart Failure (MAGGIC) database (Wong et al., 2014)
- Heart transplant: the United Network for Organ Sharing database (UNOS; UNOS, 1977)
- Posttransplant healing: UNOS-2
- Cardiovascular comorbidities: surveillance, epidemiology, and end results (SEER) program (Yoo & Coughlin, 2019), including SEER-1 (breast cancer), SEER-2 (colorectal cancer), SEER-3 (leukemia), SEER-4 (respiratory cancers), SEER-5 (cancer of the digestive system), and SEER-6 (cancer of urinary system)

8.9 Data modality

8.9.1 Modality detection of biomedical images

Modality detection among multiple images is essential for a medical retrieval system and its end users. Current search engines, such as Goldminer, can yield inaccurate results due to relying on caption extraction. Rahman and Bhattacharya (2016) provided a multimodal image classifier for a biomedical image retrieval system, integrating various elements from text and visual features to improve performance. This approach employs a multiresponse linear regression (MLR; Zhang & Duin, 2009) as a meta-learner combiner. It merges the class probabilities to the final decision and learning relationship among different variables, plus a multiclass SVM as a base classifier (K classes for K features).

Note that this model differs from regular meta-learners for data-saving or a meta-policy of learning. It attempts to extract meta-knowledge from different features as likely "overall" feature descriptors for classification. While the performance and representation methods may not be robust, the idea of rare multimodal biomedical applications has attracted interest.

These diverse modalities cover eight categories:

- Computerized tomography
- Microscopic imaging
- Magnetic resonance imaging
- Positron emission tomography
- Photography
- Ultrasonography
- X-ray, including angiography
- Graphics

The probability of feature embedding $\mathbf{x}_n$ of nth sample estimated through the K-class SVM backbone classifier is expressed in Eq. (8.16), where $\{\omega_1, \ldots, \omega_m\}$ denotes a set of the labels of m classes:

$$\mathbf{P}_k(\mathbf{X}_n) = \left[P_k\big(\omega_1|\mathbf{X}_n\big), P_k(\omega_2|\mathbf{X}_n), \ldots, P_k(\omega_m|\mathbf{X}_n) \right]^{\mathrm{T}} = \left[P_k^1(x_n), P_k^2(x_n), \ldots, P_k^m(x_n) \right]^{\mathrm{T}}, \quad k = 1, 2, \ldots, K$$

$$(8.16)$$

The MLR selects probabilities $P_k^j(x_n)$ from each class to feed into a linear expression, displayed in Eq. (8.17), where $\{\alpha_k^j\}$ denotes the coefficients:

$$LR_j(x_n) = \sum_{k=1}^{K} \alpha_k^j P_k^j(x_n), \quad j = 1, 2, ..., m \tag{8.17}$$

This framework is evaluated on the dataset ImageCLEFmed (Kalpathy-Cramer et al., 2011; Muller et al., 2010).

8.10 Future work

From chest computed tomography to electrocardiography, research on meta-learning raises challenging clinical questions in highly specialized applications. It supports advanced and complex diagnostics for conditions such as cancer, percutaneous pulmonary valve implantation, and the long-term effects of the COVID-19 pandemic.

This chapter investigates 15 interesting pieces of research, all of which can be divided into three taxonomies according to their tasks to solve: medical imaging analysis (image classification, lesion classification, image segmentation, and image reconstruction), computing based on electronic health records (EHRs), and applications in specialized areas (cardiac and disease diagnosis).

As noted in *Nature* journal and the *British Journal of Cancer*, "meta-learning can facilitate transfer learning and reduce the amount of data that is needed in a target domain by transferring knowledge from abundant genomic data in different source domains, enabling the use of AI in data-scarce scenarios" (Gevaert, 2021).

Generally, from simple to complex, healthcare applications appear in three groupings: patient-oriented, clinician-oriented, and administrative- or operational-oriented (Craft, 2017). More clinically meaningful applications impact patients, caregivers, physicians, clinicians, and the pharmaceutical industry. An illustration of some active research fields and concepts is as follows (Yeung, 2020):

- Multimodal modeling: utilizing useful joint knowledge and reasoning across multiple modalities of data (e.g., text, images, EHRs)
- Capturing useful features for downstream tasks
- Discovering cohorts of similar patients (precision medicine)
- Model interpretability
- Prediction and early warning of fatal medical conditions

Additionally, the global discussion of "how can machine learning be used to help enable healthcare for all?" in NeurIPS 2020 shed light on valuable experiences and remarkable research directions for the future of meta-learning, available at https://nips.cc/Conferences/2020/ScheduleMultitrack?event=16134.

The future of machine learning in medicine could offer a healthcare-oriented combination of meta-learning, natural language processing, machine learning, and improvements in clinical practice over the next decade.

References

Adler, J., & Oktem, O. (2018). Learned primal-dual reconstruction. *IEEE Transactions on Medical Imaging, 37*(6), 1322–1332.

Alaa, A. M., & Schaar, M.v. (2018). AutoPrognosis: Automated clinical prognostic modeling via Bayesian optimization with structured kernel learning. In *ICML*.

Aresta, G., Araujo, T., Kwok, S., Chennamsetty, S. S., Safwan, M., Alex, V., ... Aguiar, P. (2019). Bach: Grand challenge on breast cancer histology images. *Medical Image Analysis, 56*, 122–139.

Basra, M., & Shahrukh, M. (2009). *Burden of skin diseases*. Retrieved from Expert Review Pharmacoeconomics Outcomes Research.

Birkhead, G. S., Klompas, M., & Shah, N. R. (2001). The impact of the MIT-BIH arrhythmia database. In *IEEE engineering in medicine and biology*.

Bishop, C. M. (2006). *Pattern recognition and machine learning*. Springer.

Bobbia, S., Macwan, R., Benezeth, Y., Mansouri, A., & Dubois, J. (2019). Unsupervised skin tissue segmentation for remote photoplethysmography. *Pattern Recognition Letters, 124*, 82–90. Retrieved from https://www.sciencedirect.com/science/article/abs/pii/S0167865517303860.

Brosch, T., & Tam, R. (2013). Manifold learning of brain MRIs by deep learning. In *Med image comput comput assist interv. Vol. 8150 of lect notes comput sci* (pp. 633–640).

Caron, M., et al. (2018). Deep clustering for unsupervised learning of visual features. In *ECCV*.

Chang, B., Meng, L., Haber, E., Tung, F., & Begert, D. (2018). Multi-level residual networks from dynamical systems view. In *ICLR Poster*.

Chen, W.-L., Kan, C.-D., Lin, C.-H., & Mai, Y. C. (2018). Generalized regression estimator improved the accuracy rate of estimated dialysis accesses stenotic condition on in-vitro arteriovenous graft experimental model. *IEEE Access*, 10381–10391.

Chen, B., Leng, S., Yu, L., Holmes, D., III, Fletcher, J., & McCollough, C. (2016). An open library of CT patient projection data. In *Vol. 9783. Medical imaging 2016: Physics of medical imaging* (pp. 330–335). SPIE.

Cheng, Y., Wang, F., Zhang, P., Xu, H., & Hu, J. (2015). Risk prediction with electronic health records: A deep learning approach. In *SIAM international conference on data mining SDM16*.

Choi, E., Bahadori, M. T., Schuetz, A., Stewart, W. F., & Sun, J. (2016). Doctor AI: Predicting clinical events via recurrent neural networks. *Machine learning for healthcare conference* (pp. 301–318). PMLR.

Cicek, A., Lienkamp, S., Brox, T., & Ronneberger, O. (2016). 3D U-Net: Learning dense volumetric segmentation from sparse annotation. In *Med image comput comput assist interv. Vol. 9901 of lect notes comput sci* (pp. 424–432). Springer.

Ciresan, D., Giusti, A., Gambardella, L., & Schmidhuber, J. (2012). Deep neural networks segment neuronal membranes in electron microscopy images. *Advances in Neural Information Processing Systems, 25*.

Codella, N. C., Gutman, D., Celebi, M. E., Helba, B., Marchetti, M. A., Dusza, S. W., ... Halpern, A. (2018a). Skin lesion analysis toward melanoma detection: A challenge at the 2017 international symposium on biomedical imaging (ISBI), hosted by the international skin imaging collaboration (ISIC). In *2018 IEEE 15th international symposium on biomedical imaging (ISBI 2018)* (pp. 168–172). https://doi.org/10.1109/ISBI.2018.8363547.

Codella, N., Gutman, D., Celebi, M., Helba, B., Marchetti, M., Dusza, S., ... Kittler, H. (2018b). Skin lesion analysis toward melanoma detection challenge. In *IEEE international symposium on biomedical imaging* (pp. 168–172).

Codella, N., Rotemberg, V., Tschandl, P., Celebi, M. E., Dusza, S., Gutman, D., ... Halpern, A. (2019). *Skin lesion analysis toward melanoma detection 2018: A challenge hosted by the International Skin Imaging Collaboration (ISIC)*. Retrieved from https://arxiv.org/abs/1902.03368.

Craft, L. (2017). *Emerging applications of Ai for healthcare providers*. GARTNER.

Dermnet. (1998). *Dermnet: Skin disease image atlas*. Retrieved from https://apps.lib.umich.edu/database/link/11961.

Dong, B., Li, J., & Shen, Z. (2013). X-ray CT image reconstruction via wavelet frame based regularization and radon domain inpainting. *Journal of Scientific Computing, 54*(2), 333–349.

Fu, S., Zheng, H., Yang, Z., Yan, B., Su, H., & Liu, Y. (2017). Computerized tongue coating nature diagnosis using convolutional neural network. In *2017 IEEE 2nd international conference* (pp. 730–734).

Gevaert, O. (2021). Meta-learning reduces the amount of data needed to build AI models in oncology. *Br J Cancer, 125*, 309–310. https://doi.org/https://doi.org/10.1038/s41416-021-01358-1.

Gheissari, P., & Huang, Y. (2020). *Meta-learning in medicine*.

Goldberger, A., Amaral, L., Glass, L., Hausdorff, J., Ivanov, P. C., Mark, R., ... Stanley, H. E. (2000). PhysioBank, PhysioToolkit, and PhysioNet: Components of a new research resource for complex physiologic signals. *Circulation*, e215–e220 (Online).

Goode, A., Gilbert, B., Harkes, J., Jukic, D., & Satyanarayanan, M. (2013). Openslide: A vendor-neutral software foundation for digi-tal pathology. *Journal of Pathology Informatics, 4*(1), 27.

Grant, E., Finn, C., Levine, S., Darrell, T., & Griffiths, T. (2018). Recasting gradient-based meta-learning as hierarchical bayes. *arXiv preprint*, arXiv:1801.08930.

He, J., Yang, Y., Wang, Y., Zeng, D., Bian, Z., Zhang, H., ... Ma, J. (2018). Optimizing a parameterized plug-and-play ADMM for iterative low-dose CT reconstruction. *IEEE Transactions on Medical Imaging*, 371–382.

He, K., Zhang, X., Ren, S., & Sun, J. (2016). Deep residual learning for image recognition. In *CVPR* (pp. 770–778).

Hou, J., Su, H.-Y., Yan, B., Zheng, H., Sun, Z.-L., & Cai, X.-C. (2017). Classification of tongue color based on CNN. In *IEEE international conference on big data analysis*.

Hu, S. X., Moreno, P. G., Xiao, Y., Shen, X., Obozinski, G., Lawrence, N. D., & Damianou, A. (2020). Empirical bayes transductive meta-learning with synthetic gradients. In *ICRL*. Retrieved from https://openreview.net/pdf?id=Hkg-xgrYvH.

Huo, C.-M., Zheng, H., Su, H.-Y., Sun, Z.-L., Cai, Y.-J., & Xu, Y.-F. (2017). Tongue shape classification integrating image preprocessing and convolution neural network. In *IEEE intelligent robot systems*.

Iglovikov, V., & Shvets, A. (2018). *TernausNet: U-Net with VGG11 encoder pre-trained on ImageNet for image segmentation*. Retrieved from https://arxiv.org/abs/1801.05746.

Jacobson, O., & Dalianis, H. (2016). Applying deep learning on electronic health records in Swedish to predict healthcare-associated infections. In *ACL 2016*.

Jensen, P. B., Jensen, L. J., & Brunak, S. (2012). *Mining electronic health records: Towards better research applications and clinical care*. Retrieved from Nature https://www.nature.com/articles/nrg3208.

Jia, J., Wang, R., An, Z., Guo, Y., Ni, X., & Shi, T. (2018). Rdad: A machine learning system to support phenotype-based rare disease diagnosis. *Frontiers in Genetics, 9*, 587.

Jin, K. H., Mccann, M. T., Froustey, E., & Unser, M. (2017). Deep convolutional neural network for inverse problems in imaging. *IEEE Transactions on Image Processing, 26*(9), 4509–4522.

Johnson, A., Pollard, T., Mark, R., Berkowitz, S., & Horng, S. (2019). MIMIC-CXR database (version 2.0.0). *PhysioNet*. https://doi.org/https://doi.org/10.13026/C2JT1Q.

Johnson, A. E., Pollard, T. J., Greenbaum, N. R., Lungren, M. P., Deng, C. Y., Peng, Y., et al. (2019). MIMIC-CXR-JPG, a large publicly available database of labeled chest radiographs. *arXiv preprint*, arXiv:1901.07042.

Johnson, A. E., Pollard, T. J., Shen, L., Lehman, L. W. H., Feng, M., Ghassemi, M., et al. (2016). MIMIC-III, a freely accessible critical care database. *Scientific Data, 3*(1), 1–9.

Johnson, M. L. T., & Roberts, J. (1978). *Skin conditions and related need for medical care among persons 1-74 years, United States, 1971-1974 (No. 212)*. Department of Health, Education, and Welfare, Public Health Service, Office of the Assistant Secretary for Health, National Center for Health Statistics.

Kalpathy-Cramer, J., Muller, H., Bedrick, S., Eggel, I., Herrera, A. G., & Tsikrika, T. (2011). Overview of the CLEF 2011 medical image classification and re-trieval tasks. In *CLEF 2011 working notes, Amsterdam, the Netherlands*.

Kan, C.-D., Chen, W.-L., Lin, C.-H., Wang, J.-N., Lu, P.-J., Chan, M.-Y., & Wu, J.-T. (2018). *Customized handmade pulmonary valved conduit reconstruction for children and adult patients using meta-learning based intelligent model*. Retrieved from https://ieeexplore.ieee.org/document/8315005/.

Kawahara, J., Brown, C. J., Miller, S. P., Booth, B. G., Chau, V., Grunau, R. E., ... Hamarneh, G. (2016). Brain-NetCNN: Convolutional neural networks for brain networks. *NeuroImage, 146*, 1038–1049.

Kawahara, J., Daneshvar, S., Argenziano, G., & Hamarneh, G. (2019). *Seven-point checklist and skin lesion classification using multitask multimodal neural nets*. Retrieved from https://ieeexplore.ieee.org/document/8333693.

Kawahara, J., & Hamarneh, G. (2016). Multi-resolution-tract CNN with hybrid pretrained and skin-lesion trained layers. In *Machine learning in medical imaging. Vol. 10019 of lect notes comput sci* (pp. 164–171).

LeCun, Y., Bottou, L., Bengio, Y., & Haffner, P. (1998). Gradient-based learning applied to document recognition. In *IEEE 86* (pp. 2278–2324).

Lee, E., Chen, E., & Lee, C.-Y. (2020). *Meta-rPPG: Remote heart rate estimation using a transductive meta-learner*. Retrieved from https://arxiv.org/abs/2007.06786.

Lee, Y., & Choi, S. (2018). Gradient-based meta-learning with learned layerwise metric and subspace. In *ICML*.

Li, T.-H. S., Liu, C.-Y., Kuo, P.-H., Fang, N.-C., Li, C.-H., Cheng, C.-W., ... Chen, C.-Y. (2017). *A three-dimensional adaptive PSO-based packing algorithm for an IoT-based automated e-fulfillment packaging system*. Retrieved from https://ieeexplore.ieee.org/document/7924336.

Li, H., Wen, G., & Zeng, H. (2019). Natural tongue physique identification using hybrid deep learning methods. *Multimedia Tools and Applications, 78*(6), 6847–6868.

Li, X., Yu, L., Fu, C., & Heng, P. (2018). Deeply supervised rotation equivariant network for lesion segmentation in dermoscopy images. In *OR 2.0 context-aware operating theaters, computer assisted robotic endoscopy, clinical image-based procedures, and skin image analysis* (pp. 235–243). Springer.

Li, X., Yu, L., Jin, Y., Fu, C. W., Xing, L., & Heng, P. A. (2020). Difficulty-aware meta-learning for rare disease diagnosis. In *International conference on medical image computing and computer-assisted intervention* (pp. 357–366). Cham: Springer.

Liang, Z., Zhang, G., Huang, J. X., & Hu, Q. V. (2014). Deep learning for healthcare decision making with EMRs. In *IEEE international conference on bioinformatics and biomedicine* (pp. 556–559).

Lin, C.-H., Kan, C.-D., Wang, J.-N., Chen, W.-L., & Chen, P.-Y. (2018). *Cardiac arrhythmias automated screening using discrete fractional-order integration process and meta learning based intelligent classifier.* Retrieved from https://ieeexplore.ieee.org/document/8466771.

Litjens, G., Kooi, T., Bejnordi, B. E., Setio, A. A. A., Ciompi, F., Ghafoorian, M., et al. (2017). A survey on deep learning in medical image analysis. *Medical Image Analysis, 42,* 60–88.

Liu, Y., Lee, J., Park, M., Kim, S., Yang, E., Hwang, S. J., & Yang, Y. (2019). *Learning to propagate labels: Transductive propagation network for few-shot learning.* Retrieved from https://arxiv.org/abs/1805.10002.

Mahajan, K., Sharma, M., & Vig, L. (2020). *Meta-dermdiagnosis: Few-shot skin disease identification using meta-learning.* Retrieved from https://openaccess.thecvf.com/content_CVPRW_2020/papers/w42/Mahajan_Meta-DermDiagnosis_Few-Shot_Skin_Disease_Identification_Using_Meta-Learning_CVPRW_2020_paper.pdf.

Maicas, G., Bradley, A. P., Nascimento, J. C., Reid, I., & Carneiro, G. (2018). Training medical image analysis systems like radiologists. In *International conference on medical image computing and computer-assisted intervention* (pp. 546–554). Cham: Springer.

Maicas, G., Nguyen, C., Motlagh, F., Nascimento, J. C., & Carneiro, G. (2020). Unsupervised task design to meta-train medical image classifiers. In *2020 IEEE 17th international symposium on biomedical imaging (ISBI)* (pp. 1339–1342). https://doi.org/https://doi.org/10.1109/ISBI45749.2020.9098470.

McClymont, D., Mehnert, A., Trakic, A., Kennedy, D., & Crozier, S. (2014). Fully automatic lesion segmentation in breast MRI using mean-shift and graph-cuts on a region adjacency graph. *Journal of Magnetic Resonance Imaging, 39*(4), 795–804.

Milletari, F., Navab, N., & Ahmadi, S.-A. (2016). *V-Net: Fully convolutional neural networks for volumetric medical image segmentation.* Retrieved from arXiv:1606.04797.

Miotto, R., Li, L., Kidd, B. A., & Dudley, J. T. (2016). Deep patient: An unsupervised representation to predict the future of patients from the electronic health records. *Scientific Reports, 6*(1), 1–10.

Mozer, M. C., Kazakov, D., & Lindsey, R. V. (2017). *Discrete event, continuous time RNNs.* Retrieved from https://arxiv.org/abs/1710.04110.

Muller, H., Kalpathy-Cramer, J., Eggel, I., Bedrick, S., Reisetter, J. C., Jr., & Hersh, W. (2010). Overview of the CLEF 2010 medical image retrieval track. In *Online working notes, September 20–23.* Padua, Italy: CLEF 2012 Evaluation Labs and Workshop.

Newell, A., Yang, K., & Deng, J. (2016). *Stacked hourglass networks for human pose estimation.* Retrieved from https://arxiv.org/abs/1603.06937.

Nickerson, P., Tighe, P., Shickel, B., & Rashidi, P. (2016). Deep neural network architectures for forecasting analgesic response. In *38th annual international conference of the ieee engineering in medicine and biology society (EMBC)* (pp. 2966–2969). IEEE.

Pham, T., Tran, T., Phung, D., & Venkatesh, S. (2016). Deepcare: A deep dynamic memory model for predictive medicine. In *Pacific-Asia conference on knowledge discovery and data mining* (pp. 30–41). Cham: Springer.

Pishgar, M., Theis, J., Del Rios, M., et al. (2022). Prediction of unplanned 30-day readmission for ICU patients with heart failure. *BMC Medical Informatics and Decision Making, 22,* 117. https://doi.org/https://doi.org/10.1186/s12911-022-01857-y.

Prabhu, V., Kannan, A., Ravuri, M., Chablani, M., Sontag, D., & Amatriain, X. (2019). *Few-shot learning for dermatological disease diagnosis.* Retrieved from http://proceedings.mlr.press/v106/prabhu19a/prabhu19a.pdf.

Qiu, T. (2020). Tongue identification for small samples based on meta learning. In *2020 international conference on computer information and big data applications (CIBDA)* (pp. 295–299). Guiyang, China.

Rahman, M. M., & Bhattacharya, P. (2016). Biomedical image classification with multi response linear regression (MLR) as meta-learner combiner and its effectiveness on small to large data sets. In *2016 international conference on computational science and computational intelligence (CSCI)* (pp. 110–115). Las Vegas, NV.

Ratnaweera, A., Halgamuge, S., & Watson, H. (2004). *Self-organizing hierarchical particle swarm optimizer with time-varying acceleration coefficients.* Retrieved from https://ieeexplore.ieee.org/document/1304846.

Ren, M., Triantafillou, E., Ravi, S., Snell, J., Swersky, K., Tenenbaum, J. B., ... Zemel, R. S. (2018). Meta-learning for semi-supervised few-shot classification. In *ICLR*.

Ren, D., Zuo, W., Hu, Q., Zhu, P., & Meng, D. (2019). Progressive image deraining networks: A better and simpler baseline. In *IEEE conference on computer vision and pattern recognition* (pp. 3937–3946).

Ronneberger, O., Fischer, P., & Brox, T. (2015). U-net: Convolutional networks for biomedical image segmentation. In *Med image comput comput assist interv. Vol. 9351 of lect notes comput sci* (pp. 234–241).

Rubanova, Y., Chen, R. T., & Duvenaud, D. (2019). *Latent ODEs for irregularly-sampled time series*. Retrieved from https://arxiv.org/abs/1907.03907.

Setio, A. A. A., Ciompi, F., Litjens, G., Gerke, P., Jacobs, C., Van Riel, S. J., et al. (2016). Pulmonary nodule detection in CT images: false positive reduction using multi-view convolutional networks. *IEEE Transactions on Medical Imaging*, 35(5), 1160–1169.

Shakeri, M., Tsogkas, S., Ferrante, E., Lippe, S., Kadoury, S., Paragios, N., & Kokkinos, I. (2016). Subcortical brain structure segmentation using F-CNNs. In *IEEE int symp biomedical imaging* (pp. 269–272).

Shickel, B., Tighe, P. J., Bihorac, A., & Rashidi, P. (2017). Deep EHR: A survey of recent advances in deep learning techniques for electronic health record (EHR) analysis. *IEEE Journal of Biomedical and Health Informatics*, 22(5), 1589–1604.

Soleymani, M., Lichtenauer, J., Pun, T., & Pantic, M. (2011). *A multimodal database for affect recognition and implicit tagging*. Retrieved from https://ieeexplore.ieee.org/document/5975141.

Song, Y., Zhang, L., Chen, S., Ni, D., Lei, B., & Wang, T. (2015). Accurate segmentation of cervical cytoplasm and nuclei based on multiscale convolutional network and graph partitioning. *IEEE Transactions on Biomedical Engineering*, 62(10), 2421–2433.

Specht, D. F. (1991). A general regression neural network. *IEEE Transactions on Neural Networks*, 2(6), 568–576.

Stollenga, M. F., Byeon, W., Liwicki, M., & Schmidhuber, J. (2015). Parallel multi-dimensional LSTM, with application to fast biomedical volumetric image segmentation. In *Advances in neural information processing systems* (pp. 2998–3006).

Suk, H.-I., & Shen, D. (2016). Deep ensemble sparse regression network for Alzheimer's disease diagnosis. In *Med image comput comput assist interv. vol. 10019 of lect notes comput sci* (pp. 113–121). NeuroImage 129.

Sun, J., Li, H., & Xu, Z. (2016). Deep ADMM-Net for compressive sensing MRI. *Advances in Neural Information Processing Systems*, 29.

Sun, X., Yang, J., Sun, M., & Wang, K. (2016). *A benchmark for automatic visual classification of clinical skin disease images*. Retrieved from https://link.springer.com/chapter/10.1007/978-3-319-46466-4_13.

Suo, Q., Chou, J., Zhong, W., & Zhang, A. (2020). *TAdaNet: Task-adaptive network for graph-enriched meta-learning*. Retrieved from https://www.kdd.org/kdd2020/accepted-papers/view/tadanet-task-adaptive-network-for-graph-enriched-meta-learning.

Tran, T., Nguyen, T. D., Phung, D., & Venkatesh, S. (2015). Learning vector representation of medical objects via EMR-driven nonnegative restricted Boltzmann machines (eNRBM). *Journal of Biomedical Informatics*, 54, 96–105.

Tschandl, P., Rosendahl, C., & Kittler, H. (2018). The ham10000 dataset, a large col- lection of multi-source dermatoscopic images of common pigmented skin lesions. *Scientific Data*, 5(1), 1–9.

UNOS. (1977). *UNOS data and transplant statistics | organ donation data*. Retrieved from https://www.google.com/url?sa=t&rct=j&q=&esrc=s&source=web&cd=&ved=2ahUKEwjI3ba1haT0AhXOrVYBHTzjDdAQFnoECAYQAQ&url=https%3A%2F%2Funos.org%2Fdata%2F&usg=AOvVaw1yIn-LSS7v_KFFwPLL_oW6.

Vaswani, A., Shazeer, N., Parmar, N., Uszkoreit, J., Jones, L., Gomez, A. N., ... Polosukhin, I. (2017). Attention is all you need. In *NIPS*.

Wang, J., Ye, Y., Pan, X., & Gao, X. (2015). Parallel-type fractional zero-phase filtering for ECG signal denoising. *Biomedical Signal Processing and Control*, 18, 36–41.

Wilmer, E., Gustafson, C., Ahn, C., Davis, S., Feldman, S., & Huang, W. (2014). *Most common dermatoogic conditions encountered by dermatologists and nondermatologists*. Retrieved from Cutis, 94(6).

Wong, C. M., Hawkins, N. M., Petrie, M. C., Jhund, P. S., Gardner, R. S., Ariti, C. A., ... Krogsgaard, K. (2014). Heart failure in younger patients: The Meta-Analysis Global Group in Chronic Heart Failure (MAGGIC). *European Heart Journal*, 35(39), 2714–2721.

Wu, J.-X., Li, C.-M., Chen, G.-C., Ho, Y.-R., & Lin, C.-H. (2017). Peripheral arterial disease screening for hemodialysis patients using a fractional-order integrator and transition probability decision-making model. *IET Systems Biology*, 11(2), 69–76.

Wu, T., Xie, Y., Qu, Y., Dai, B., & Chen, S. (2020). *Meta segmentation network for ultra-resolution medical images*. Retrieved from https://arxiv.org/abs/2002.08043.

Xie, Y., Zhang, Z., Sapkota, M., & Yang, L. (2016). Spatial clock-work recurrent neural network for muscle perimysium segmentation. In *International conference on medical image computing and computer-assisted intervention.*

Yao, H., Wei, Y., Huang, J., & Li, Z. (2019). Hierarchically structured meta-learning. In *ICML.*

Yao, H., Wu, X., Li, R., Tao, Z., Li, Y., Ding, B., & Li, Z. (2020). Automated relational meta-learning. In *ICLR.*

Yeung, S. (2020). *Electronic health records: Advanced topics.* Retrieved from https://web.stanford.edu/class/biods220/syllabus.html.

Yoo, W., & Coughlin, S. S. (2019). *Surveillance, epi-demiology, and end results (seer) data for monitoring cancer trends.*

Yoon, S. W., Seo, J., & Moon, J. (2019). TapNet: Neural network augmented with task-adaptive projection for few-shot learning. In *ICML.*

Yu, C., Wang, J., Peng, C., Gao, C., Yu, G., & Sang, N. (2018). Bisenet: Bi-lateral segmentation network for real-time semantic seg- mentation. In *Proceedings of the European conference on computer vision (ECCV)* (pp. 325–341).

Zhang, H. M., & Dong, B. (2020). A review on deep learning in medical image reconstruction. *Journal of the Operations Research Society of China, 8*(2), 311–340.

Zhang, C.-X., & Duin, R. P. (2009). n Empirical study of a linear regression combiner on multi- class data sets. In J. K. J. A. Benediktsson (Ed.), *MCS 2009, LNCS 5519* (p. 478487). Berlin Heidelberg: Springer-Verlag.

Zhang, X. S., Tang, F., Dodge, H., Zhou, J., & Wang, F. (2019). *MetaPred: Meta-learning for clinical risk prediction with limited patient electronic health records.* Retrieved from https://arxiv.org/abs/1905.03218.

Zhu, W. (2018). *Traditional medicine diagnosis* (3rd ed.). Shanghai: Shanghai Science and Technology Press.

Zhu, M., Li, S., Li, D., Gao, Q., Bian, Z., Huang, J., … Ma, J. (2019). Teacher-student network for CT image reconstruction via meta-learning strategy. In *2019 IEEE nuclear science symposium and medical imaging conference (NSS/MIC)* (pp. 1–3). Manchester, United Kingdom.

Meta-learning for emerging applications: Finance, building materials, graph neural networks, program synthesis, transportation, recommendation systems, and climate science

9.1 Introduction

Artificial intelligence has transcended basic techniques to shape our daily lives and social developments, including self-driven vehicles, dialog system, and image recognition. Turning to fields that are hardly touched by conventional techniques, where can meta-learning expand novel interests or open possibilities?

The previous four chapters cover the most well-developed fields; this chapter will examine several emerging areas:

- Finance and economics in Section 9.2
- Building materials in Section 9.3
- Graph neural network in Section 9.4

- Program synthesis in Section 9.5
- Transportation in Section 9.6
- Cold-start problems for a recommendation systems in Section 9.7
- Climate science in Section 9.8

This chapter investigates 17 state-of-the-art contributions to the field, all of which can be divided into several taxonomies according to their tasks to solve, as outlined in Table 9.1: credit card fraud and economic inequality, graph meta-learning, traffic state prediction, climate change, building material defect recognition, program synthesis, etc.

TABLE 9.1 Summary of meta-learning techniques for finance and economics, building materials, graph neural networks, program synthesis, transportation, recommendation systems, and climate science.

Reference	Topic	Task	Method	Conference
9.2 Finance and Economics				
Zheng, Yan, Gou, and Wang (2020)	Detection of Credit Card Transaction Fraud	Fraud Detection	Deep K-tuplet Network	IJCAI
Jamal and Qi (2019)	Task-Agnostic Meta-Learner with Inequality Measurement in Economic		Inequality-Minimization Task-Agnostic Meta-Learning (TAML)	CVPR
9.3 Building Materials				
Mundt, Majumder, Murali, Panetsos, and Ramesh (2019b)	Defect (Crack) Recognition in Concrete in Reinforcement Learning		ENAS-Based, MetaQNN-Based	CVPR
9.4 Graph Neural Network				
Lan et al. (2020)	Node Classification on Graphs with Few-Shot Novel Labels	Node Classification	Meta-Transformed Network Embedding (MetaTNE)	NeurIPS
Huang and Zitnik (2020)	Local Subgraphs for Node Classification and Link Prediction	Node Classification	G-Meta	NeurIPS
Goldblum, Fowl, and Goldstein (2020)	Adversarial Attacks of Node Classification	Node Classification	Adversarial Querying (AQ)	NeurIPS
Yang et al. (2020)	Dual-Graph Structured Approach with Instance- and Distribution-Level Relations		Distribution Propagation Graph Network (DPGN)	CVPR
9.5 Program Synthesis				
Si, Yang, Dai, Naik, and Song (2019)	Syntax-Guided Synthesis		A2C-based	ICRL
9.6 Transportation				
Zang et al. (2020)	Traffic Signal Control		Meta-Light	AAAI

TABLE 9.1 Summary of meta-learning techniques for finance and economics, building materials, graph neural networks, program synthesis, transportation, recommendation systems, and climate science—cont'd

Reference	Topic	Task	Method	Conference
Dong, Chen, and Dolan (2019)	Continuous Trajectory Estimation for Lane Changes under a Few-Shot Setting		Recurrent Induction Network (RMIN)	ICRA
Pan et al. (2019)	Urban Traffic Prediction base nn Spatio-Temporal Correlation		ST-MetaNet	KDD
9.7 Cold-Start Problems in Recommendation Systems				
Vartak, Vartak, Miranda, Bratman, and Larochelle (2017)	Continuously Adding New Items	Item Cold-Start	Nonlinear Bias Adaptation (NLBA)	NeurIPS
Du, Wang, Yang, Zhou, and Tang (2019)	Context-Aware Cross-Domain Recommendation Cold-Start under a Few-Shot Setting	User-Item Cold-Start	Scenario-Specific Sequential Meta-Learner (s^2Meta)	KDD
Lee, Im, Jang, Cho, and Chung (2019)	User Preference Estimator	User Cold-Start, Item Cold-Start	Meta-Learned User Preference Estimator (MeLU)	KDD
Dong, Yuan, Yao, Xu, and Zhu (2020)	Memory-Augmented Recommendation System Meta-optimization	User Cold-Start, Item Cold-Start, User-Item Cold-Start	Memory-Augmented Meta-Optimization (MAMO)	KDD
Lu, Fang, and Shi (2020)	Meta-Learner with Heterogenous Information Networks	User Cold-Start, Item Cold-Start, User-Item Cold-Start	MetaHIN	KDD
9.8 Climate Science				
Kamani, Farhang, Mahdavi, and Wang (2019)	Critical Incident Detection	Few-Shot Object Recognition	Targeted Meta-Learning	ICML

Each section explores the following perspectives:

- Which practice areas are of emerging interest to the meta-learning community?
- What is the current status of the existing research in each of these application areas?
- What and why are meta-learning approaches favorable among different practice areas?
- How do these approaches work theoretically and practically?

The selected state-of-the-art techniques have developed essential and fundamental influences as a solid foundation of the widely spread methods or theories either (i) with significantly and broadly practical contributions in diverse applications, (ii) shedding light on an important mainstream in academia with huge potential space for further exploration and investigation, or (iii) with promising solutions for the fundamental components that are hardly discussed but important to the corresponding fields. Most pieces of research recursively track related bibliographies in papers accepted at premier academic conferences: AAAI, ICML, ICRA, ICRL, IJCAI, CVPR, KDD, and NeurIPS.

9.2 Finance and economics

9.2.1 Introduction

Since the 1980s, financial applications have received a surge of interest from the machine learning community; as the mature option of deep neural networks—a variety of implementation subfields—are investigated (Ozbayoglua, Gudeleka, & Sezera, 2020):

- Algorithmic trading executes orders (i.e., selling or buying decisions) based on preprogrammed and automated trading guidance; typical algorithmic training applications are usually equipped with price-prediction models (e.g., stock prices and index forecasting). While long short-term memory (LSTM) dominates this area (Fischer & Krauss, 2018; Troiano, Villa, & Loia, 2018), successful models based on time-series data with other structures (e.g., GoldAI Sachs [Serrano, 2018; Lu, 2017; Jeong & Kim, 2019; Krauss, Do, & Huck, 2017]) have also achieved good performance.
- Risk assessment (e.g., bankruptcy forecast, credit evaluation, insurance underwriting, corporate credit ratings, and mortgage loan applications) mainly focuses on credit scoring (Chen, Ribeiro, & Chen, 2015; Lahsasna, Ainon, & Teh, 2010) and banking distress classification (Abroyan, 2017; Rawte, Gupta, & Zaki, 2018).
- Fraud detection (e.g., credit card fraud, tax evasion, insurance claim fraud, and money laundering) is one of the most substantially examined areas (Goumagias, Hristu-Varsakelis, & Assael, 2018; Paula, Ladeira, Carvalho, & Marzagao, 2016; Roy et al., 2018; Sohony, Pratap, & Nambiar, 2018; Wang & Xu, 2018).
- Portfolio management maintains and oversees a highly selective collection of investments to meet investors' long-term financial goals with affordable risk-tolerance measures. Impressive attempts include: Chen, Wu, and Tindall (2016); Fu et al. (2018); Jiang, Xu, and Liang (2017); Zhou (2018).
- Asset pricing and derivatives (i.e., financial contracts such as forwards, options, and futures; Iwasaki & Chen, 2018; Culkin & Das, 2017) targets clients from banks, real estate, and corporations, particularly financial modeling, investment strategy development, pricing modeling, and others.
- Cryptocurrency and blockchain are current mainstream digital technologies applied in financial industries, actively impacting the information exchange system. Blockchain is critical for enabling and maintaining the existence of cryptocurrency. Bitcoin, Litecoin, and Dogecoin are common forms of cryptocurrency. Recent attempts have focused on price prediction and automated trading systems (Lopes, 2018; McNally, Roche, & Caton, 2018; Spilak, 2018).
- Behavioral finance studies the emotions, sentiments, psychology, and behaviors of investors and financial markets. It is the most influential factor for leading dramatic changes in investments. With the rising interest in sentiment analysis, several research efforts have shown strong potential (Das, Behera, Kumar, & Rath, 2018; Iwasaki & Chen, 2018; Wang, Xu, & Zheng, 2018).

- Text mining in financial services is the most intensively studied area of social media (e.g., Dang, Sadeghi-Niaraki, Huynh, Min, & Moon, 2018; Huynh, Dang, & Duong, 2017; Lee & Soo, 2017; Li, Cao, & Pan, 2018; Minami, 2018). Systems in text mining have been broadly applied by global financial institutions, such as Deloitte (Moosbrucker, Flisgen, Bauer, & Pachl, 2019).

Approaches

The typical architectures as backbones used in financial applications are as follows:

- Long short-term memory (LSTM)
- Deep multilayer perceptron (DMLP)
- Restricted Boltzmann machine (RBM)
- Convolutional neural network (CNN)
- Recurrent neural network (RNN)
- Deep belief network (DBM)
- Autoencoder (AE)
- Capsule network (CapsNet)
- Deep Gaussian processes (DGP)
- Generative adversarial network (GAN)

According to the report from Ozbayoglua et al. (2020), the most studied application fields are text-mining in financial services, algorithmic training, and risk assessment. Minor emerging areas are asset pricing and derivatives trading cryptocurrency and blockchain trading.

Machine learning has been applied to fraud detection over decades; however, credit card fraud detection and analysis still faces several difficulties. These include long-tailed transaction history data with few illegal activities, barriers to obtaining shared transaction datasets among different banks, data security, and privacy policies.

Currently, federate learning is frequently involved in the current studies of banking system analysis. Meta-learners aid fraud detection based on a bank's local database through federate learning to avoid sensitive data communication among different banks or datasets. A secure analysis can be accomplished based on few-shot samples. Additionally, economic concepts, like income inequality metrics, can be an essential component in the parameter updating rule to minimize the performance variations for tackling task heterogeneity.

Section 9.2.2 presents a federated learning-based meta-classifier, which protects privacy as implemented by local bank databases. Section 9.2.3 presents a paradigm using five economic inequality indexes related to income, wealth, and other metrics (e.g., Gini coefficient) to minimize the overall inequality.

9.2.2 Detection of credit card transaction fraud

Credit card fraud plagues online shopping, e-finance, and mobile transactions, leading to billions of dollars in losses. With the rapid expansion of e-payment methods, the number of credit card transactions has significantly grown in this current decade. However, credit card fraud detection remains a challenging task due to multiple factors, including skewed transaction history data with few overtly illegal activities, limited public datasets, scarcely shared transaction datasets among different banks, data security and privacy, and neglected relationships between training samples. Recently, federated learning has shed light on data exchange and information security.

Zheng et al. (2020) proposed a meta-learning classifier based on federated learning (Yang et al., 2020) to solve issues related to credit card transaction fraud. This framework can learn fraud detection based on a bank's local database rather than a conventional cloud-based dataset.

This relational backbone matching network consists of two submodules:

- A meta-learning-based transferable feature-extraction model by applying a deep K-tuplet network with ResNet 34 (expressed in Eq. 9.1). $f_{\text{network}}(x_a^c)$, $f_{\text{network}}(x_p^c)$, and $f_{\text{network}}(x_{n_i}^c)$ denote the feature maps of an anchor sample x_a^c, a positive sample x_p^c, and a negative sample $x_{n_i}^c$, $[\cdot]_+$ presents the hinge loss, and α_{train} means the hyperparameter margin:

$$L_{extraction}^{feature}\left(x_a^c; x_p^c; x_{n_i}^c\right) = \frac{1}{K}\sum_{i=1}^{K}\left[\left\|f_{network}\left(x_a^c\right)\right\|^2 - \left\|f_{network}\left(x_a^c\right) - f_{network}\left(x_{n_i}^c\right)\right\|^2 + \alpha_{train}\right]_+ \quad (9.1)$$

- A meta-learning-based relation model for sample feature comparison in classification through a mean squared error loss function (expressed in Eq. 9.2). $Judge_{i,j}$ represents the relation score, equal to 1 if similar pair, and equal to 0 if mismatched pair.

$$L_{relation}^c = arg\ min \sum_{i=1}^{n_c^{train}}\sum_{j=1}^{n_c^{support}}\left(Judge_{i,j} - \left(y_i^c == y_j^c\right)\right) \quad (9.2)$$

The overall objective loss function of this federated learning framework is expressed in Eq. (9.3). x_i^c and y_i^c present the credit card transaction sample and its label, n_c denotes the size of the dataset from bank c.

$$\min l(x_i; y_i; w),$$

where

$$l(x_i; y_i; w) = \frac{1}{n_c}\sum_{i \in D_i} L_{relation}^c\left(x_i^c; y_i^c; w\right) \quad (9.3)$$

A summary is displayed in Table 9.2, which can be outlined into five steps:

1. An individual bank accesses the globally shared model by downloading the meta-learning classifier located in the server.
2. The framework learns local data from each bank as a classifier improvement.
3. It collects these small updates and sends them to the server with encrypted communication.
4. The server integrates these updates from all banks to enhance each classifier.
5. These steps are repeated until convergence.

TABLE 9.2 General methods of federated meta-learning approach.

Input: The private dataset from different banks
Output: The trained credit card fraud detection model

1: **Procedure** Server-Update
2:    Detection classifier and its parameters w_0 initialization

3:    **for** each round t:1, 2, 3, ..., T **do**
        # seed: the fraction of banks for computation on each round
4:       Randomly select max (seed $\times C$, 1) banks as N_t

5:       **for** all bank $c \in N_t$ in parallel **do**
            # where $\|L_{\text{relation}_{t+1}}{}^c\|$: the value of L_{relation}^c at $t+1$
6:          Obtain w_{t+1}^c, $\|L_{\text{relation}_{t+1}}{}^c\| \leftarrow$ Bank $-$ Update (n_{whole}, w_t, c);

7:          Evaluate $w_{t+1} \leftarrow \sum_{t=1}^{T} \frac{n_c}{n_{whole}} \times \| L_{\text{relation}_{t+1}}^c \| \times w_{t+1}^c$

8: **Procedure** Bank-Update (n_{whole}, w, c)
9:    Construct $\mathcal{D}_{\text{support}}^c$ and $\mathcal{D}_{\text{meta-train}}^c$;
10:   Meta-Learning-Based Classifier Training
11:   Evaluate $w_{t+1}^c \leftarrow w_t^c - \eta \times \nabla L_{\text{relation}}^c (x_i^c; y_i^c; w)$;
12:   Meta-Learning-Based Classifier Testing
13:   **return** w_{t+1}^c and $\| L_{\text{relation}_{t+1}}^c \|$ to server

Modified from Zheng, W., Yan, L., Gou, C., & Wang, F.-Y. (2020). Federated meta-learning for fraudulent credit card detection. IJCAI.

This strategy is assessed on four public datasets:

- European Credit Card (ECC; Pozzolo, 2015)
- Revolution Analytics (RA; Mohammed, Wong, Shiratuddin, & Wang, 2018)
- A synthetic dataset (SD) from Kaggle at https://www.kaggle.com/ntnu-testimon/paysim
- Vesta at https://www.kaggle.com/c/ieee-fraud-detection/overview

9.2.3 Task-agnostic meta-learner with inequality measurement in economics

Economic inequality measure

Measures of income inequality or expenditure inequality are essential for a social scientist to demonstrate the economic inequality in a given country, as well as worldwide. They act as indicators in a particular stage of an economic cycle, of povery level, and of economic activities in a specific region.

Economic-related inequality measures applied in inequality-minimization-based task-agnostic meta-learning (TAML) (described below) include:

- Theil Index (Theil, 1967)
- Generalized Entropy Index (Cowell, 1980)
- Atkinson Index (Atkinson, 1970)
- Gini-Coefficient (Allison, 1978)
- Variance of Logarithms (Ok & Foster, 1997)

Table 9.3 illustrates five inequality measures used in inequality-minimization-based TAML with definitions of and equations (Eqs. 9.4–9.8) for each kind of measure.

TABLE 9.3 Details of income inequality metrics: (1) Theil Index, (2) Generalized Entropy Index, (3) Atkinson Index, (4) Gini-Coefficient, and (5) Variance of Logarithms.

Metrics	Definition/Function	Equation	Eq. no.
Theil Index	A measure of entropic distance in which everyone shares the same income, which is also used to measure racial segregation	$T_T = \frac{1}{M}\sum_{i=1}^{M}\frac{\ell_i}{\bar\ell}\ln\frac{\ell_i}{\bar\ell}$ with M losses $\{\ell_i \mid i=1,...,M\}$	(9.4)
Generalized Entropy Index	A group of measurements of income inequality	$GE(\alpha) = \begin{cases} \frac{1}{M\alpha(\alpha-1)}\sum_{i=1}^{M}\left[\left(\frac{\ell_i}{\bar\ell}\right)^\alpha - 1\right], & \alpha \neq 0,1, \\ \frac{1}{M}\sum_{i=1}^{M}\frac{\ell_i}{\bar\ell}\ln\frac{\ell_i}{\bar\ell}, & \alpha = 1, \\ -\frac{1}{M}\sum_{i=1}^{M}\ln\frac{\ell_i}{\bar\ell}, & \alpha = 0, \end{cases}$	(9.5)
Atkinson Index	An income inequality measurement to determine the cause of observed inequality	$A_\epsilon = \begin{cases} 1 - \frac{1}{\mu}\left(\frac{1}{M}\sum_{i=1}^{M}\ell_i^{1-\epsilon}\right)^{\frac{1}{1-\epsilon}}, & \text{for } 0 \leq \epsilon \neq 1 \\ 1 - \frac{1}{\bar\ell}\left(\frac{1}{M}\prod_{i=1}^{M}\ell_i\right)^{\frac{1}{M}}, & \text{for } \epsilon = 1, \end{cases}$ where ϵ represents the inequality aversion parameter	(9.6)
Gini-Coefficient	A measure of wealth inequality of a given social group (the variations in the middle of the distribution have more influence than the two sides)	$G = \frac{\sum_{i=1}^{M}\sum_{j=1}^{M}|\ell_i-\ell_j|}{2n\sum_{i=1}^{M}\ell_i}$ where M denotes the number tasks from a batch	(9.7)
Variance of Logarithms	A measure of dispersion	$V_L(\ell) = \frac{1}{M}\sum_{i=1}^{M}[\ln \ell_i - \ln g(\ell)]^2$ where $g(\ell)$ denotes the geometric mean of ℓ	(9.8)

Modified from Jamal, M. A., & Qi, G.-J. (2019). Task agnostic meta-learning for few-shot learning. CVPR.

Jamal and Qi (2019) introduced a meta-learning paradigm named inequality-minimization task-agnostic meta-learning (TAML), which aims to minimize the performance variations among various tasks and generate an unbiased initial model to improve the generalization ability of unseen tasks. This inequality-minimization TAML employs several economic inequality measurements (e.g., of wealth, income, or relevant components among certain racial or social groups).

The objective function is expressed in Eq. (9.9), where $\mathcal{L}_{T_i}(f_{\theta_i})$ is the expected loss with updating, I_ϵ denotes the inequality measurement, and λ denotes the positive balancing coefficient.

$$\mathbb{E}_{T_i \sim p(T)}\left[\mathcal{L}_{T_i}(f_{\theta_i})\right] + \lambda I_\epsilon\left(\left\{\mathcal{L}_{T_i}(f_{\theta_i})\right\}\right) \tag{9.9}$$

This algorithm, as demonstrated in Table 9.4, is evaluated using few-shot classification tasks under public benchmarks Omniglot and MiniImageNet.

TABLE 9.4   Optimization Procedure of TAML.

Input: $p(T)$, distribution over task
       α, β, hyperparameters

1   Random initialization of θ
2   **while** no done **do**
3   Select batch of tasks $T_i \sim p(T)$

4   **for** all T_i **do**
5   Select K sample from T_i
6   Evaluate $\nabla_\theta \mathcal{L}_{T_i}(f_\theta)$ and $\mathcal{L}_{T_i}(f_\theta)$ with K samples
7   Evaluate adapted parameters using gradient descent
8        $\theta_i \leftarrow \theta - \alpha \nabla_\theta \mathcal{L}_{T_i}$
9   Select D_{val} from T_i for meta update
10   **end for**

11   Compute $\theta \leftarrow \theta - \beta \nabla_\theta \left[\mathbb{E}_{T_i \sim p(T)} \mathcal{L}_{T_i}(f_\theta) + \lambda I_\varepsilon \left(\{ \mathcal{L}_{T_i}(f_\theta) \} \right) \right]$ with $D_{val, i}$, $\mathcal{L}_{T_i}$, and I_ε
12   **end while**

Modified from Jamal, M. A., & Qi, G.-J. (2019). Task agnostic meta-learning for few-shot learning. CVPR.

9.3 Building materials

9.3.1 Defect (crack) recognition in concrete in reinforcement learning

Concrete—the most widely used composite material globally—is made in different types with varying surface reflectance, color, and roughness. For the structural safety of concrete bridges, it is essential to distinguish all types of defects (i.e., crack, concrete spalling, exposed rebars, concrete efflorescence, staining concrete, and nondefective background) from surface alterations that do not pose a safety risk. Early research was driven by several attempts: Koch, Georgieva, Kasireddy, Akinci, and Fieguth (2015), Cai, Chen, Zhang, Yu, and Wang (2018), and Kim, Ahn, Shin, and Sim (2018).

Mundt et al. (2019b) proposed two task-specific meta-reinforcement learning strategies to determine automatically the optimal neural network structure for multiclass multitarget defect-recognition of concrete defects, based on MetaQNN (Baker, Gupta, Naik, & Raskar, 2016) and Efficient Neural Architecture Search (ENAS; Pham, Guan, Zoph, Le, & Dean, 2018). Defect images are fed into the feature extractor with spatial pyramidal pooling to output the estimated classification label. The official code is released at https://github.com/MrtnMndt/meta-learning-CODEBRIM, with MetaQNN implemented in PyTorch and ENAS in TensorFlow. The dataset is available at https://zenodo.org/record/2620293#.YZ4G3i0RqQI.

MetaQNN is a Q-learning-based reinforcement algorithm that automatically constructs neural network architecture. Spatial-pyramidal pooling (He, Zhang, Ren, & Sun, 2014) in convolutional layers allows inputs of varying image sizes. The number of convolutional layers is flexible from three to 10 layers.

In contrast, ENAS is a fast and effective learning strategy for neural network design, generating a big computational graph. It aims to learn an autoregressive recurrent neural network through policy gradients (Sutton, McAllester, Singh, & Mansour, 1999) with RNN. Unlike MetaQNN, the nodes' number in the directed acyclic graph (DAG) fixes the ENAS depth. Each node reflects a collection of feature operations.

These methods are evaluated on a high-resolution dataset—the Concrete Defect Bridge Image dataset (CODEBRIM; Mundt, Majumder, Murali, Panetsos, & Ramesh, 2019a)—with annotated bounding boxes and six classes for multitarget defect classification: crack, spallation, exposed bars, efflorescence (calcium leaching), corrosion (stains), and nondefective background.

9.4 Graph neural network

9.4.1 Introduction

Graph neural network (GNN) processes data based on the graph data structure (Scarselli, Gori, Tsoi, Hagenbuchner, & Monfardini, 2009). It contributes many essential variations in neural architectures, such as graph attention networks, graph autoencoders, and graph convolutional networks. GNN has also been broadly applied in diverse practical domains to tackle real-world problems related to daily life and social development (e.g., recommendation systems, traffic prediction, and medicine analysis). However, the availability of only a few training samples limits its applications (Mandal, Medya, Uzzi, & Aggarwal, 2021).

Recent research on meta-learning has shed light on GNN and offered more possibilities. The major tasks of GNN can be categorized into three groups:

- Node classification, a current trend, is a task to classify an unlabeled node based on a partially annotated graph. This aids in protein classification and document categorization (Borgwardt et al., 2005; Tang et al., 2008). It is often challenging due to limited labeled nodes; Section 9.4.2 transforms task-agnostic representations to address task-specific ones for few-shot novel label problems, and Section 9.4.4 outlines adversarial learning methods.
- Link prediction examines relationships between paired nodes. Meta-learning can aid in multirelational graphs, as their dynamic nature poses challenges. Unlike traditional edge/ node-level and graph-level representation, Section 9.4.3 presents a local subgraph-based approach with centroid node embedding for both link prediction and node classification tasks.
- Node embedding aims to project nodes to a low-dimensional space so that similar nodes in the original graph share embeddings that are proximal in the embedding space. Then, the downstream tasks can utilize this embedding without the original network.

As indicated above, there are multiple tasks related to graph neural networks. Regarding node classification tasks, which attempt to assign labels to a nonexisting node property by leveraging the properties of its neighbor nodes, some deficiencies exist in current approaches. In reality, few-shot novel labels occur in many graph neural networks, where a novel label only exists in minimal representative nodes without sufficient knowledge for leveraging. Learning based on such scenarios with limited nodes or edges extensively reduces the generalization capabilities. Furthermore, due to the dependencies of different nodes, such network effects enable indirect adversarial attacks by replacing the prediction of a single node with no need for changes of its attributes or edges.

Meta-learning tackles these issues and solves them from different perspectives. Multiple meta-learning frameworks allow information extraction and learning based on few-shot novel labels for node classification and link prediction. They describe each node with a local subgraph and make predictions by relying on the information from the subgraph surrounding the target node or edge through graph neural networks. Furthermore, meta-learning approaches concentrate on both instance-level and distribution-level relations for solving node classification tasks through a semisupervised strategy or dual-graph structure approach.

Typical benchmarks regarding node classification and link prediction are Cora (Motl & Schulte, 2015), Citesser (Giles, Bollacker, & Lawrence, 1998), PPI (Hamilton, Ying, & Leskovec, 2017), Flickr30k (Young, Lai, Hodosh, & Hockenmaier, 2014), Reddit (Hamilton et al., 2017), IMDb Movie Review (Maas et al., 2011), MovieLens (Harper & Konstan, 2016), Freebase 15K (Bordes, Usunier, Garcia-Duran, Weston, & Yakhnenko, 2013), WorldNet 18 (Bordes et al., 2013), and PubMed (Namata, London, Getoor, & Huang, 2012).

9.4.2 Node classification on graphs with few-shot novel labels

Node classification is a classic task in graph machine learning, aiming to assign labels to a nonexisting node property (i.e., target property) based on the properties of its neighbor nodes. Few-shot novel labels occur when a novel label appears in only a small number of representative nodes including the positive (with the novel label) or the negative (without the novel label) (Lan et al., 2020). The corresponding real-world applications consist of recommendation systems and biological protein-protein networks.

Lan et al. (2020) proposed a Meta-Transformed Network Embedding framework (MetaTNE) for tackling graphs node classification when few-shot novel labels show up. The official code is available at https://github.com/llan-ml/MetaTNE. See Fig. 9.1 for the general pipeline.

This framework consists of two modules:

- A structural module learns representations of each node $v_i \in V$ in latent space while maintaining the graph structure and connections among nodes. Employs conducts a skip-gram architecture (Mikolov, Sutskever, Chen, Corrado, & Dean, 2013).
- A metric-based meta-learning module for few-shot learning involves a transformation function, which is equipped to convert task-agnostic embedding to task-specific ones to improve performance when each node is assigned multiple labels. The loss function of the classification f_{T_i} of each task $T_i = (S_i, Q_i, y_i)$ for each $\left(v_q, \ell_{v_q, y_i}\right) \in Q_i$ is expressed in Eqs. (9.10), (9.11). $\hat{\ell}_{v_q, y_i}$ denotes the estimated probability of query note v_q carries label y_i, and $c_+^{(i)}$ and $c_-^{(i)}$ represent the positive and negative prototype. u_q is the embedding representation of v_q, and dist $(\cdot)$ means the squared Euclidean distance.

$$\mathcal{L}\left(\hat{\ell}_{v_q, y_i}, \ell_{v_q, y_i}\right) = -\ell_{v_q, y_i} \log \hat{\ell}_{v_q, y_i} - \left(1 - \ell_{v_q, y_i}\right) \log \left(1 - \hat{\ell}_{v_q, y_i}\right) \tag{9.10}$$

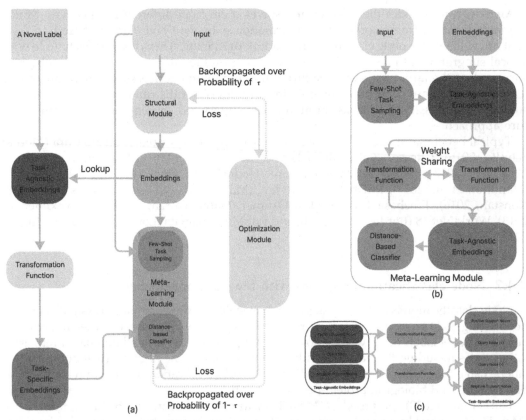

FIG. 9.1 General pipeline of MetaTNE. (A) High-level workflow of the proposed methods. Input is fed into the meta-learning module and structural module; on the other hand, a novel label is sent to the meta-learning module through task-specific embeddings. (B) and (C) Exploration of the meta-learning module. *Modified from Lan, L., Wang, P., Du, X., Song, K., Tao, J., & Guan, X. (2020). Node classification on graphs with few-shot novel labels via meta transformed network embedding. NeurIPS.*

where:

$$\hat{\ell}_{v_q, y_i} = f_{\mathcal{T}_i}\left(v_q | \mathbf{c}_+^{(i)}, \mathbf{c}_-^{(i)}\right) = \frac{\exp\left(-\text{dist}\left(\mathbf{u}_q, \mathbf{c}_+^{(i)}\right)\right)}{\sum_{m \in \{+,-\}} \exp\left(-\text{dist}\left(\mathbf{u}_q, \mathbf{c}_m^{(i)}\right)\right)} \tag{9.11}$$

The projection of the concatenated output vectors of all attentional heads to the original space through the matrix $W_O \in \mathbb{R}^{d \times d'}$ is processed as shown in Eqs. (9.12), (9.13). $\widetilde{u}_{q,m}^{i,h}$ and $\widetilde{u}_{k,q'}^{i,1}$, respectively, denote the query node's output vector and the output vector of the support node designed for the query node.

$$\widetilde{u}_{q,m}^{(i)} = W_O\left(\widetilde{u}_{q,m}^{i,1} \oplus \ldots \oplus \widetilde{u}_{q,m}^{i,H}\right) \tag{9.12}$$

and:

$$\tilde{u}_{k,q}^{(i)} = W_O \left(\tilde{u}_{k,q}^{i,1} \oplus \ldots \oplus \tilde{u}_{k,q}^{i,H} \right) \tag{9.13}$$

where: all $v_k \in V_{S_i^m}$

The overall meta-learning objective function is presented in Eq. (9.14). λ denotes the balancing factor, and $\mathcal{Q}_i$ presents the query set.

$$\min_{U,\Theta} \sum_{T_i} \sum_{\left(v_q, l_{v_q,y_i}\right) \in \mathcal{Q}_i} \mathcal{L}\left(\hat{\ell}_{v_q,y_i}, \ell_{v_q,y_i}\right) + \lambda \sum \|\Theta\|_2^2 \tag{9.14}$$

Hence, optimization concentrates on the structural module first and gradually moves to the meta-learning module. Table 9.5 outlines the general optimizing methods.

Table 9.6 Presents summarizes methods to implement MetaTNE on few-shot novel labels. This framework is evaluated on four public datasets: BlogCatalog (Tang & Liu, 2009), Flickr (Tang & Liu, 2009), PPI (Grover & Leskovec, 2016), and Mashup (Yue et al., 2019).

TABLE 9.5 Optimization methods of MetaTNE.

Input: G, a graph
  N, the total number of steps
  γ, hyperparameter of the decay rate
  N_{decay}, decay period
Output: $U \in \mathbb{R}^{|V| \times M}$, an embedding matrix
  $Tr(\cdot)$, a function

1: Random initialization of U and Θ of $Tr(\cdot)$
2: **for** step $= 0, \ldots, N$ **do**
3:    Evaluate $\tau = \dfrac{1}{\left(1 + \gamma \left\lfloor \frac{\text{step}}{N_{\text{deay}}} \right\rfloor\right)}$
4:    Randomly select a number r from Uniform $(0,1)$
5:    **if** $r < \tau$ **then**
        # enhance the structural procedure
6:        Randomly select a batch of pairs $\{(v_i, v_j) | v_i \in \mathcal{V}, v_j \in \mathcal{N}(v_i)\}$
7:        Update U for $\min \sum_{v_i \in \mathcal{V}} \sum_{v_j \in \mathcal{N}(v_i)} \log \mathbb{P}(v_j | v_i)$
8:    **else**
        # enhance the meta-learning procedure
9:        Select a batch $\mathcal{T}_i$ from $\mathcal{Y}_{\text{known}}$
10:       **for** all $\mathcal{T}_i = (\mathcal{S}_i, \mathcal{Q}_i, y_i)$ **do**
11:          **for** all $v_q \in \mathcal{Q}_i$ **do**
12:             Evaluate the adapted embeddings $\{\tilde{\mathbf{u}}_{k,q}^{(i)} | v_k \in \mathcal{V}_{S_i^m}\}$ and $\tilde{\mathbf{u}}_{q,m}^{(i)}$, where $m \in \{+, -\}$, via Eqs. (9.12) and (9.13)
13:             Evaluate the prototypes $\tilde{\mathbf{c}}_{+,q}^{(i)}$ and $\tilde{\mathbf{c}}_{-,q}^{(i)}$:

$$\tilde{\mathbf{c}}_{m,q}^{(i)} = \frac{1}{|\mathcal{S}_i^m|} \sum_{v_k \in \mathcal{V}_{S_i^m}} \tilde{\mathbf{u}}_{k,q}^{(i)}, m \in \{+, -\}$$

Continued

TABLE 9.5 Optimization methods of MetaTNE—cont'd

14:	Evaluate the predicted probability where v_q holds y_i :

$$\hat{\ell}_{v_q,y_i} = \frac{\exp\left(-\text{dist}\left(\tilde{\mathbf{u}}_{q,+}^{(i)}, \tilde{\mathbf{c}}_{+,q}^{(i)}\right)\right)}{\sum_{m\in\{+,-\}} \exp\left(-\text{dist}\left(\tilde{\mathbf{u}}_{q,m}^{(i)}, \tilde{\mathbf{c}}_{m,q}^{(i)}\right)\right)}$$

15:	**end for**
16:	**end for**
17:	Update U and Θ for $\min_{\mathbf{U},\Theta} \sum_{\mathcal{T}_i} \sum_{(v_q,\ell_{v_q,y_i})\in Q_i} \mathcal{L}\left(\hat{\ell}_{v_q,y_i}, \ell_{v_q,y_i}\right) + \lambda \sum \|\Theta\|_2^2$
18:	**end if**
19:	**end for**

Modified from Lan, L., Wang, P., Du, X., Song, K., Tao, J., & Guan, X. (2020). Node classification on graphs with few-shot novel labels via meta transformed network embedding. NeurIPS.

TABLE 9.6 General methods of MetaTNE with few-shot novel labels.

Input: U, an embedding matrix
$\quad$ Tr$(\cdot)$, the function
$\quad y\in\mathcal{Y}_{novel}$, a novel label
Output: estimated probability $\hat{\ell}_{v_q,y}$ over every query node v_q
1: Obtain the support and query embeddings $\mathbf{u}_k, \mathbf{u}_q$ from **U**
2: **for** v_q in query nodes $\mathcal{V}_Q$ **do**
3: $\quad$ Adapt v_q with positive support nodes $\mathcal{V}_{S^+}$ and evaluate adapted embeddings $\{\tilde{\mathbf{u}}_{q,+}\}\cup\{\tilde{\mathbf{u}}_{k,q}|v_k\in\mathcal{V}_{S^+}\}$
4: $\quad$ Adapt v_q with negative support nodes $\mathcal{V}_{S^-}$ and evaluate adapted embeddings $\{\tilde{\mathbf{u}}_{q,-}\}\cup\{\tilde{\mathbf{u}}_{k,q}|v_k\in\mathcal{V}_{S^-}\}$
5: $\quad$ Get the positive and negative prototypes $\tilde{\mathbf{c}}_{m,q}, m\in\{+,-\}$ for classification
6: $\quad$ Get the predicted probability with $\tilde{\mathbf{c}}_{m,q}$ and $\tilde{\mathbf{u}}_{q,m}$
7: **end for**

Modified from Lan, L., Wang, P., Du, X., Song, K., Tao, J., & Guan, X. (2020). Node classification on graphs with few-shot novel labels via meta transformed network embedding. NeurIPS.

9.4.3 Local subgraphs for node classification and link prediction

Sample scarcity commonly exists in practical situations, where extensive datasets are challenging to obtain. Learning based on a knowledge graph with limited nodes and edges increases the difficulty of generalizing robust performance. Furthermore, fast adaptation performed on novel tasks is accomplished by leveraging prior knowledge via meta-learning.

Huang and Zitnik (2020) proposed a meta-learner strategy for node classification and link prediction, termed G-Meta. Unlike the typical graph meta-learning approach seeking to train the entire graph, G-Meta describes each node with a local subgraph and predicts by relying on the information from the subgraph surrounding the target node or edge through graph neural networks (GNNs). Thus, the task is to train a GNN $f_\theta : S \rightarrow \{1, ..., |Y|\}$ to project the local subgraph S_u of node u to labels from label sets Y based on a few labeled nodes under three scenarios:

- Single graph with disjointed labels: adapt a novel label set $Y_* \sim p(Y|G)$ based on knowledge from disjoint label sets $Y_i \sim p(Y|G)$ and $Y_* \cap Y_i = \varnothing$

- Multiple graphs with shared labels: given a distribution over graphs $p(G)$, adapt a novel graph $G_* \sim p(G)$ based on knowledge from disjointed graph $G_j \sim p(G)$
- Multiple graphs with disjoint labels: given a distribution over label sets $p(Y|\mathcal{G})$ on multiple graphs $\mathcal{G}$ in which each task retains its own label set to Y_i, adapt a novel label set $Y_* \sim p(Y|\mathcal{G})$ based on knowledge from disjointed label sets $Y_i \sim p(Y|\mathcal{G})$ and $Y_* \cap Y_i = \varnothing$

This approach first sets local subgraphs for each node. The h-layer GNN embeds each node of subgraph S_u through centroid node embedding (Chauhan, Nathani, & Kaul, 2020; Xu, Hu, Leskovec, & Jegelka, 2019), where h denotes the subgraph neighborhood size. It applies a prototypical loss for inductive bias and MAML as a meta-optimizer to transfer knowledge across graphs and labels.

Table 9.7 provides the summarized methods of G-Meta.

TABLE 9.7 General training methods of G-Meta.

Input: Graphs $\mathcal{G} = \{G_1, ..., G_N\}$;

1	Random initialization $\theta : [\theta_{\text{GNN}}]$
	# Building local subgraph
2	$S_1, S_2, ..., S_n = \text{Subgraph}(\mathcal{G})$
	# Metatask setup
3	$\{\mathcal{T}\} = \{\mathcal{T}_1, \mathcal{T}_2, ..., \mathcal{T}_m\} \sim p(\mathcal{T})$
4	**while** not done **do**
	# Select a batch of tasks
5	$\{\mathcal{T}_s\} \leftarrow \text{sample}(\{\mathcal{T}\})$
6	**for** $\mathcal{T}_i \in \{\mathcal{T}_s\}$ **do**
	# Mini-batching support subgraphs
7	$\left(\{S\}_{\text{support}}, \mathbf{y}_{\text{support}}\right) \leftarrow \mathcal{T}_i^{\text{support}}$
	# Mini-batching query subgraphs
8	$\left(\{S\}_{\text{query}}, \mathbf{y}_{\text{query}}\right) \leftarrow \mathcal{T}_i^{\text{query}}$
9	$\theta_0 = \theta$
10	**for** j: $1, ..., \eta$ **do**
11	$\mathbf{H}_{\text{support}} \leftarrow \text{GNN}_{\theta_{j-1}}\left(\{S\}_{\text{support}}\right)_{\text{centroid}}$
12	$\mathbf{C} = \frac{1}{N_{k_{\text{support}}}} \sum \left(\mathbf{H}_{\text{support}}\right)$
13	$\mathbf{p} = \frac{\exp\left(-\|\mathbf{H}_{\text{supper}} - \mathbf{C}\|\right)}{\sum_{Y_i} \exp\left(-\|\mathbf{H}_{\text{support}} - \mathbf{C}\|\right)}$
14	$\mathcal{L}_{\text{support}} = \text{L}\left(\mathbf{p}, \mathbf{y}_{\text{support}}\right)$
15	**# Inner Loop Update**
16	$\theta_j = \theta_{j-1} - \alpha \nabla \mathcal{L}_{\text{support}}$
17	$\mathbf{H}_{\text{query}} \leftarrow \text{GNN}_{\theta_j}\left(\{S\}_{\text{query}}\right)_{\text{centroid}}$
18	$\mathbf{p} = \frac{\exp\left(-\|\mathbf{H}_{\text{query}} - \mathbf{C}\|\right)}{\sum_{Y_i} \exp\left(-\|\mathbf{H}_{\text{query}} - \mathbf{C}\|\right)}$
19	$\mathcal{L}_{\text{query}}^{ij} \leftarrow \text{L}\left(\mathbf{p}, \mathbf{y}_{\text{query}}\right)$
20	**end**
21	**end**
	# Outer Loop Update
22	$\theta = \theta - \beta \nabla \sum_i \mathcal{L}_{\text{query}}^{iu}$
23	**end**

Modified from Huang, K., & Zitnik, M. (2020). Graph meta learning via local subgraphs. NeurIPS.

This model is evaluated on seven public datasets, including two synthetic and five real-world datasets:

- Synthetic Cycle
- Synthetic Barabasi-Albert
- ogbn-arxiv (Wang et al., 2020)
- Tissue-PPI (Leskvec, 2017)
- firstMM-DB (Rossi & Ahmed, 2015)
- Fold-PPI (Andreeva, Kulesha, Gough, & Murzin, 2020; Shen et al., 2007; Zitnik & Leskovec, 2017)
- Tree-of-Life (Zitnik, Feldman, & Leskovec, 2019)

9.4.4 Adversarial attacks of node classification

The regular graph convolutional strategies leverage the knowledge from the neighboring nodes to improve the generalization. Unlike standard fundamental assumptions, samples in node classification are no longer independent of each other. This network effect could benefit the classification performance. However, it also allows indirect adversarial attacks: changing the prediction of a single node without changes of its attributes or edges. Although many graph convolutional approaches provide solid solutions per node classification, the vulnerability remains. The following provides a graph neural network-based solution for semisupervised learning by leveraging both instance-level and distribution-level relations through two aggregation modules in a few-shot classification task.

Goldblum and colleagues (Goldblum et al., 2020) proposed a meta-learner named Adversarial Querying (AQ), targeting the adversarial examples with few-shot learning. This algorithm-agnostic method simultaneously improves the few-shot classification's generalization ability and the robustness to adversarial examples. Instead of conducting adversarial training during fine-tuning, AQ generates a robust feature extractor by solving the minimax problem, as expressed in Eq. (9.15), where A denotes the fine-tuning methods for parameters θ, and ϵ presents a p-norm bound of the attacker. δ denotes the adversarial perturbation, x and y present the input image and its label.

$$\min_{\theta} \mathbb{E}_{S,(x,y)} \left[\max_{\|\delta\|_p < \epsilon} \mathcal{L}\left(F_{A(\theta,S)}, x + \delta, y\right) \right] \tag{9.15}$$

Four meta-learning frameworks can operate with AQ: MAML (see Chapter 4, Section 4.3 for details), R2-D2 (see Chapter 5, Section 5.2.8 for details), MetaOptNet (Lee et al., 2019), and Prototypical Network (see Chapter 3, Section 3.4 for details). The official implementation in PyTorch of this model is available at https://github.com/goldblum/AdversarialQuerying.

Comparion and contrast of AQ and prototypical meta-learning

A standard prototypical meta-learning is summarized in Table 9.8, which illustrates the outer and inner loop training under regular prototypical meta-training.

AQ assumes that regular training of a meta-learner is not robust as expected: it is vulnerable to attacks due to the lack of adversarial defenses techniques in few-shot learning. Thus, AQ improves adversarial robustness through the modified meta-training as summarized in

TABLE 9.8 Summarized training methods of standard prototypical meta-learning.

Require: F_θ, Base model

A, fine-tuning algorithm

γ, learning rate

$p(\mathcal{T})$, distribution over tasks

1: Initialize θ, the weights of F;
2: **while** not done **do**
3:    Sample batch of tasks, $\{\mathcal{T}_i\}_{i=1}^n$ such that $\mathcal{T}_i \sim p(\mathcal{T})$ and $\mathcal{T}_i = (\mathcal{T}_i^s, \mathcal{T}_i^q)$

4:    **for** $i=1, ..., n$ **do**
5:       # **Fine-tuning model on $\mathcal{T}_i$ as its inner loop**
6:       $\theta_i = A(\theta, \mathcal{T}_i^s)$
7:       $g_i = \nabla_\theta \mathcal{L}(F_{\theta_i}, \mathcal{T}_i^q)$
8:    **end for**

9:    # **outer loop updating**
10:   $\theta \leftarrow \theta - \frac{\gamma}{n}\sum_i g_i$

11: **end while**

Modified from Goldblum, M., Fowl, L., & Goldstein, T. (2020). Adversarially robust few-shot learning: A Meta-Learning Approach. NeurIPS.

TABLE 9.9 Summarized training methods of adversarial querying.

Require: F_θ, Base model

A, fine-tuning algorithm

γ, learning rate

$p(\mathcal{T})$, distribution over tasks

1: Initialize θ, the weights of F;
2: **while** not done **do**
3:    Sample batch of tasks, $\{\mathcal{T}_i\}_{i=1}^n$ such that $\mathcal{T}_i \sim p(\mathcal{T})$ and $\mathcal{T}_i = (\mathcal{T}_i^s, \mathcal{T}_i^q)$

4:    **for** $i=1, ..., n$ **do**
5:       # **Fine-tuning model on $\mathcal{T}_i$ as its inner-loop**
6:       $\theta_i = A(\theta, \mathcal{T}_i^s)$
7:       Maximize $\mathcal{L}\left(F_{\theta_i}, \widehat{\mathcal{T}}_i^q\right)$ subject to $\left\|\widehat{x}_j^q - x_j^q\right\|_p < \epsilon$ where x_j^q denotes query examples and $\widehat{x}_j^q$ is the associated adversaries
8:       **Evaluate** $g_i = \nabla_\theta \mathcal{L}\left(F_{\theta_i}, \widehat{\mathcal{T}}_i^q\right)$
9:    **end for**

10:   # **outer-loop updating**
11:   $\theta \leftarrow \theta - \frac{\gamma}{n}\sum_i g_i$

12: **end while**

Modified from Goldblum, M., Fowl, L., & Goldstein, T. (2020). Adversarially robust few-shot learning: A Meta-Learning Approach. NeurIPS.

Table 9.9. During its inner loop and outer loop processes, the framework performs backpropagation via the fine-tuning algorithm and minimizes query loss.

This framework achieved a state-of-the-art result after testing against ATM black-box transfer attacks, gradient masking attacks, DeepFool (DF) attacks (Moosavi-Dezfooli,

Fawzi, & Frossard, 2016), Projected Gradient Descent attacks (PGD; Madry, Makelov, Schmidt, Tsipras, & Vladu, 2017), and Momentum Iterative Fast Gradient Sign Method attacks (MI-FGSM; Dong et al., 2018), based on public benchmarks of Mini-ImageNet, CIFAR-FS, and the Omniglot dataset.

9.4.5 Dual-graph structured approach with instance- and distribution-level relations

Traditional few-shot graph neural network approaches primarily concentrate on pair-wise relations (e.g., edge labeling) without much exploration of distribution relations. To investigate both instance-level and distribution-level relations explicitly, Yang et al. (2020) proposed the Distribution Propagation Graph Network (DPGN) with two complete graph networks. This dual-graph structure consists of a point graph (PG) and a distribution graph (DG). The PG produces a DG by collecting one-to-others relations of each sample; meanwhile, the distribution graph adjusts the point graph, which relies on distribution relations among pair-wise examples. DPGN can be extended as a semisupervised method by involving annotated and unannotated data in the support set, where similarity distribution associates between labeled and unlabeled examples. The official code is available at https://github.com/megvii-research/DPGN.

The transformation has two submodules connected to the distribution-level and instance-level representation: point-to-distribution (P2D) aggregation and distribution-to-point (D2P) aggregation.

Within P2D aggregating, each edge of the point graph presents the point similarity (i.e., instance similarity). The initial edge $e_{0,i,j}^p \in \mathbb{R}$ in the first generation (i.e., generation $\ell=0$) is expressed in Eq. (9.16), where $v_{0,i}^p \in \mathbb{R}^m$ and $v_{0,i}^p = f_{emb}(x_i)$ as initialized by the feature extractor f_{emb} of each sample x_i, and m is the feature embedding dimension. $f_{e_\ell^p}: \mathbb{R}^m \to \mathbb{R}$ denotes an encoder to convert point similarity to a specific scale through two Conv-BN-ReLU (Glorot, Bordes, & Bengio, 2011).

$$e_{0,ij}^p = f_{e_0^p}\left(\left(v_{0,i}^p - v_{0,j}^p\right)^2\right) \tag{9.16}$$

The updating rule is expressed in Eq. (9.17) as generation $\ell>0$:

$$e_{l,ij}^p = f_{e_l^p}\left(\left(v_{l-1,i}^p - v_{l-1,j}^p\right)^2\right) \cdot e_{l-1,ij}^p \tag{9.17}$$

The P2D aggregation, the distribution node $v_{0,i}^d \in \mathbb{R}^{NK}$, is initialized as Eq. (9.18), where NK is the number of support samples of each task, $\|\cdot$ denotes concatenation, and $\delta(\cdot)$ computes as Kronecker delta and obtains one if two labels are identical (i.e., $y_i=y_j$) and zero otherwise.

$$v_{0,i}^d = \begin{cases} \|_{j=1}^{NK}\delta\left(y_i, y_j\right) & \text{if } x_i \text{ is labeled,} \\ \left[\dfrac{1}{NK}, \cdots, \dfrac{1}{NK}\right] & \text{otherwise,} \end{cases} \tag{9.18}$$

The updating rule is expressed in Eq. (9.19) as generation $\ell > 0$, where $P2D : (\mathbb{R}^{2NK} \to \mathbb{R}^{NK})$:

$$v_{l,i}^d = \text{P2D}\left(\|_{j=1}^{NK} e_{l,ij}^p, v_{l-1,i}^d \right) \tag{9.19}$$

Within D2P Aggregation, the distribution similarity $e_{0,\, i,\, j}^d \in \mathbb{R}$ is initialized as $\ell = 0$ by an encoder $f_{e_0^d} : \mathbb{R}^{NK} \to \mathbb{R}$ with two Conv-BN-ReLU, as expressed in Eq. (9.20):

$$e_{0,ij}^d = f_{e_0^d}\left(\left(v_{0,i}^d - v_{0,j}^d \right)^2 \right) \tag{9.20}$$

The updating rule is expressed in Eq. (9.21) as generation $\ell > 0$:

$$e_{l,ij}^d = f_{e_l^d}\left(\left(v_{l,i}^d - v_{l,j}^d \right)^2 \right) \cdot e_{l-1,ij}^d \tag{9.21}$$

In D2P aggregation, the node features $v_{l,\, i}^p \in \mathbb{R}^m$ gather the comprehensive node features in the point graph, as expressed in Eq. (9.22), where D2P is an aggregation method such that $D2P : (\mathbb{R}^m, \mathbb{R}^m) \to \mathbb{R}^m$:

$$v_{l,i}^p = \text{D2P}\left(\sum_{j=1}^{T} \left(e_{l,ij}^d \cdot v_{l-1,j}^p \right), v_{l-1,i}^p \right) \tag{9.22}$$

Eqs. (9.23), (9.24) indicate the point loss function and distribution loss function, respectively, where $\mathcal{L}_{CE}$ is cross-entropy loss:

$$\mathcal{L}_l^p = \mathcal{L}_{CE}\left(P(\hat{y}_i | x_i), y_i \right) \tag{9.23}$$

$$\mathcal{L}_l^d = \mathcal{L}_{CE}\left(\text{Softmax}\left(\sum_{j=1}^{NK} e_{l,ij}^d \cdot one - hot\left(y_j \right) \right), y_i \right) \tag{9.24}$$

The overall objective function is provided as Eq. (9.25), where $\hat{\ell}$ denotes the overall DPGN generation and λ_p and λ_d are the weights of the related loss:

$$\mathcal{L} = \sum_{l=1}^{l} \left(\lambda_p \mathcal{L}_l^p + \lambda_d \mathcal{L}_l^d \right) \tag{9.25}$$

This method is evaluated in miniImageNet, Caltech-UCSD Birds (CUB-200-2011), tieredImageNet, and CIFAR-FS.

9.5 Program synthesis

9.5.1 Syntax-guided synthesis

The syntax-guided synthesis (SyGuS) task (Alur et al., 2013) is a general formulation of program synthesis under several syntactic and semantic constraints: context-free grammar G (CFG), background theory T, and correctness specification ϕ. Si and colleagues (2019) introduced an Advantage Actor-Critic (A2C; Mnih et al., 2016) backbone meta-learning framework for syntax-guided synthesis by learning a transferable representation through weak supervision. It aims to provide a bundle of distinctive programs and generation procedures for a variety of constraints. The dataset and official code are available at https://github.com/PL-ML/metal.

This framework consists of three modules for generation procedures:

- A graph neural network-based (GNN) encoder simultaneously embeds the complex grammar and logical specification. Its updating rule is expressed in Eq. (9.26) through a gated graph neural network F (GGNN; Li, Tarlow, Brockschmidt, & Zemel, 2015), where h_v^T denotes a set of node embeddings, $\mathcal{N}(v)$ presents a set of node v's neighbor nodes, and $e_{u,v}$ is the type of edge between node u and v:

$$h_v^{t+1} = Aggregate\left(\left\{F\left(h_u^t, e_{u,v}\right)\right\}_{u \in \mathcal{N}(v)}\right) \tag{9.26}$$

- A grammar-adaptive policy network conducts transfer learning, where the policy is parameterized via decision embedding, as expressed in Eq. (9.27), where $h(\mathcal{G})$ denotes the embedding representation of the graph $\mathcal{G}$:

$$\pi(f|\phi, G) = \prod_{t=1}^{|f|} \pi\left(a_t | h(\mathcal{G}), \mathcal{T}^{(t-1)}\right) \tag{9.27}$$

where $\mathcal{T}^{(t-1)} = \alpha_1 \ldots \alpha_{t-1}$ is the partial tree.

- Actor-critic (A2C) learning with a meta-learner employs a customized sparse reward to learn the embedding and adaptive policy jointly, as demonstrated in Eq. (9.28), where B_ϕ denotes the test case buffer with all observed input and $\widehat{B}_b$ presents a set of the interpolated sample around b:

$$r = \frac{\sum_{b \in B_\phi \cup \widehat{B}_b} [f(b) \equiv \phi(b)]}{|B_\phi \cup \widehat{B}_b|} \tag{9.28}$$

The gradient descent of each instance $\langle \phi_i, G_i \rangle$ is expressed in Eq. (9.29), where γ denotes the discounted factor and V presents a state value estimator of state s_t and parameter ω:

$$d\theta \leftarrow \sum_{t=1}^{|f|} \nabla_\theta \log \pi\left(\alpha_t | h(\mathcal{G}), \mathcal{T}^{(t)}\right)\left(\gamma^{|f|-t} r - V(s_t; \omega)\right) \tag{9.29}$$

9.6 Transportation

9.6.1 Introduction

With rapidly expanding modern urbanization and civilization in contemporary society and the intensive reliance on vehicles, traffic congestion continues to plague urban areas by impairing productivity, wasting time and power, and causing environmental pollution. An intelligent transportation system is an essential part of a data-driven smart city.

The machine learning community has recently experienced a surge of interest in intelligent transportation, with popular applications including self-drive car control, routing planning, traffic light control, and traffic prediction. Current studies of meta-reinforcement learning are making remarkable progress. Nevertheless, traffic light control still faces two dilemmas: different signal phases and the fact that the most recent research of meta-reinforcement algorithms, focused on policy-based paradigms—in contrast with value-based deep reinforcement learning strategies—are inappropriate in traffic light control problems. Moreover, complex traffic conditions and geographical conditions stretch the existing solution to its limit.

Traffic flow prediction measures the number of vehicles entering or leaving a particular road over a specific time interval. It is primarily applied to dynamic traffic control, route scheduling, and taxi navigation. Despite a missing public benchmark in this domain, Caltrans Performance Measurement System (PMS; CA.gov, 2014) remains the most widely used dataset for paradigm training and testing. Common architectures of neural networks range from variants of deep multilayer perceptron (DMLP; Guo & Zhu, 2009; Akiyama & Inokuchi, 2014), deep belief network (DBN; Koesdwiady, Soua, & Karray, 2016; Lv, Duan, Kang, Li, & Wang, 2015), stacked autoencoder (SAE; Leelavathi & Sahana Devi, 2016), convolutional neural network (CNN), and long short-term memory (Wu & Tan, 2016; Wu, Tan, Qin, Ran, & Jiang, 2018). Section 9.6.3 discusses a lane-planning approach based on a modified conditional neural process with asynchronous LSTMs.

Traffic speed prediction aims to forecast the future traffic speed in certain time intervals conditioned on previous speed records within a road segment. There have been many early attempts on DMLP (Huang & Ran, 2003), DBN (Jia, Wu, & Du, 2016), CNN (Ma et al., 2017), LSTM (Jia, Wu, Ben-Akiva, Seshadri, & Du, 2017), SAE (Liu & Chen, 2017), and ST-GCNN (Yu, Yin, & Zhu, 2017). Section 9.6.4 describes an approach to spatial and temporal correlations based on geo-graph attributes.

Traffic signal control teaches a model to control traffic lights to minimize the overall waiting time at multiple intersections. Typically, deep reinforcement learning involves a reward function based on traffic-flow conditions. Standard components of this paradigm consider appropriate states, actions, reward function, and an appropriate paradigm to approximate the Q-learning algorithm. Simulation of Urban Mobility is one of the most popular simulation environments for reinforcement learning. Section 9.6.2 develops model-agnostic meta-reinforcement learning coupled with the DQN backbone.

9.6.2 Traffic signal control

Although many early attempts presented traffic signal control problems (Van der Pol, 2016; Wei, Zheng, Yao, & Li, 2018; Zheng et al., 2019), applying meta-reinforcement learning in this context still faces two dilemmas:

- There are varying numbers of signal phases due to complex combinations of lanes, roads, and intersections, which is defined as heterogeneous scenarios

- Considering the characteristics of small and discrete action spaces, most deep reinforcement learning strategies for traffic signal control are value-based and off-policy. However, current meta-reinforcement algorithms are policy-based and on-policy.

Recently, Zang et al. (2020) proposed a value-based framework with meta-reinforcement learning architecture for an appropriate pattern to control the interaction of traffic signal settings, named MetaLight, which can rapidly adapt to new scenarios. MetaLight is built by a modified model-agnostic gradient-based meta-learner (i.e., MAML) and a structure-agnostic DQN-based traffic control backbone model (i.e., FRAP++; Zheng et al., 2019). The CityFlow simulator (Zhang et al., 2019) is employed as a simulation platform. The official code is available at https://github.com/zxsRambo/metalight, using the four public datasets of multiple cities—Jinan (JN), Hangzhou (HZ), Atlanta (AT), and Los Angeles (LA).

The overall loss function for meta-training is expressed in Eq. (9.30), where D_i denotes the transitions of each intersection I_i, $\mathcal{M}$ denotes the meta-learner, and D_i represents the transitions from an intersection:

$$\{\theta_1,...,\theta_{N_t}\} := \min_{\{\theta_1,\ ...,\theta_{N_t}\}} \sum_{i=1}^{N_t} \mathcal{L}\left(\mathcal{M}\left(f_{\theta_i}\right); D_i\right) \tag{9.30}$$

Two types of adaptation mechanisms are processed in MAML:

- Individual-level adaptation processes each task $\mathcal{T}_i$ with task-specific θ_i, as expressed in Eq. (9.31), where α denotes the step size:

$$\theta_i \leftarrow \theta_i - \alpha \nabla_\theta \mathcal{L}\left(f_\theta; D_i\right) \tag{9.31}$$

- Global-level adaptation over a batch of tasks aims to summarize the adaptation of every intersection. It is expressed in Eq. (9.32), where D_i' represents new transitions, θ_0 denotes initialization, and β denotes the step size:

$$\theta_0 \leftarrow \theta_0 - \beta \nabla_\theta \sum_{\mathcal{T}_i} \mathcal{L}\left(f_\theta; D_i'\right) \tag{9.32}$$

The summarized meta-training and testing methods are outlined in Tables 9.10 and 9.11.

9.6.3 Continuous trajectory estimation for lane changes under a few-shot setting

One of the core components in self-driving vehicles is interactive route planning, where the movement of the vehicle is primarily dependent on the surrounding environment and other vehicles. However, because there is insufficient data of complex driving situations, progress in deep learning implementation remains limited.

Dong and colleagues (Dong et al., 2019) proposed the Recurrent Meta Induction Network (RMIN), a meta-learner based on a Conditional Neural Process (CNP) with an asynchronous Long Short-Term Memory (LSTM) for continuous trajectory estimation in the case of lane changing. It abandons the historic structure to mimic human driving behavior through a

TABLE 9.10 Meta-training methods of MetaLight.

Input: $\mathcal{I}_S$, set of source intersections
$\quad\quad$ α, β, hyperparameters of step sizes
$\quad\quad$ t_θ, frequency of updating meta-parameters
Output: θ_0, optimized parameters initialization

1 Random initialization of θ_0
2 **for** round : 1, ..., N **do**
3 $\quad$ Select a batch of intersections from $\mathcal{E}$
4 $\quad$ **for** $t = 1, t_\theta+1, 2t_\theta+1, ..., T$ **do**
5 $\quad\quad$ **for** $t' = t, ..., \min(t+t_\theta, T)$ **do**
6 $\quad\quad\quad$ **for** each intersection $\mathcal{I}_i$ **do**
7 $\quad\quad\quad\quad$ $\theta_i \leftarrow \theta_0$
8 $\quad\quad\quad\quad$ Produce transitions into $\mathcal{D}$ and select transitions as $\mathcal{D}_i$
9 $\quad\quad\quad\quad$ Evaluate $\theta_i \leftarrow \theta_i - \alpha\nabla_\theta\mathcal{L}(f_\theta; \mathcal{D}_i)$
10 $\quad\quad$ Randomly select new transitions from $\mathcal{D}$ as $\mathcal{D}_i'$
11 $\quad\quad$ Evaluate $\theta_0 \leftarrow \theta_0 - \beta\nabla_\theta\sum_{\mathcal{I}_i}\mathcal{L}(f_\theta; \mathcal{D}_i')$

Modified from Zang, X., Yao, H., Zheng, G., Xu, N., Xu, K., & Li, Z. (2020). MetaLight: Value-based meta-reinforcement learning for traffic signal control. AAAI.

TABLE 9.11 Inference phase of MetaLight.

Input: $\mathcal{I}_T$, set of target intersections
$\quad\quad$ α, hyperparameters of step sizes
$\quad\quad$ θ_0, learned initialization
Output: Optimized parameters θ_t w.r.t. each intersection $\mathcal{I}_t$

1 **for** each $\mathcal{I}_t$ in $\mathcal{I}_T$ **do**
2 $\quad$ $\theta_t \leftarrow \theta_0$
3 $\quad$ **for** $t = 1, ..., T$ **do**
4 $\quad\quad$ produce and select transitions as $\mathcal{D}_t$
5 $\quad\quad$ Evaluate $\theta_t \leftarrow \theta_t - \alpha\nabla_\theta\mathcal{L}(f_\theta; \mathcal{D}_t)$

Modified from Zang, X., Yao, H., Zheng, G., Xu, N., Xu, K., & Li, Z. (2020). MetaLight: Value-based meta-reinforcement learning for traffic signal control. AAAI.

certain stochastic process or distribution. This framework can handle three different scenarios in trajectory estimations:

- Mutual interactions with, at most, five surrounding cars simultaneously
- Lane-changing continuous trajectories prediction
- Few-shot setup with limited training data

As a meta-learning induction algorithm, CNP can be divided into three parts:

- A demonstration network h works as an encoder of the input demonstration, such that $r_i = h(X_i, Y_i)$
- The overall condition r is extracted from n historical demonstration, and each r_i is summarized by aggregation operation $\oplus$, such that $r = r_0 \oplus r_1 ... \oplus r_{n-1}$

- A generator network g works as a decoder to produce an estimated trajectory $\widehat{Y}$, such that $\phi_i = g(X_t, r)$. The output is sent via a fully connected neural network to produce the "overall condition tensor" to pass to the generator network (Zang et al., 2020).

Removing the aggregation operation in the standard CNP (Garnelo et al., 2018), RMIN conducts an asynchronous LSTM within the demonstration network.

The dashed line demonstrates the inner variable transform among multiple LSTMs. The LSTM's outputs will only relay to a fully connected network (FCN) if it obtains sufficient demonstrations; otherwise, it remains internal. These modified methods are expressed in Eqs. (9.33), (9.34). (X_i, Y_{i+1}) is input, as one demonstration: $X_i \in \mathcal{X}_n$ is all vehicles' (including the target and all surrounding vehicles) historical trajectories from the time i. $Y_{i+1} \in \mathcal{Y}_n$ is the trajectory of target vehicles from the time $i+1$. g and h represent the generator and demonstration model.

$$\mathbf{r} = h(\mathcal{X}_n, \mathcal{Y}_n) \tag{9.33}$$

$$\widehat{Y} = g\left(\widehat{X}, \mathbf{r}\right) \tag{9.34}$$

The loss function based on both longitudinal and lateral directions is expressed in Eq. (9.35), where C_{lon} denotes losses in longitudinal directions and C_{lat} in lateral directions. λ denotes a constant with recommended value $\lambda = 10$.

$$C = C_{lon} + \lambda C_{lat} \tag{9.35}$$

This method is trained and accessed by dataset NGSIM (Colyar, 2007; US-101 and I-80 subsets).

9.6.4 Urban traffic prediction based on spatio-temporal correlation

Traffic prediction has appeared in early attempts of multitask learning methods (Liu, Zheng, Liang, Liu, & Rosenblum, 2016; Xu, Tan, Luo, & Zhou, 2016; Zhao et al., 2015). However, two problems persist: complicated spatiotemporal (ST) correlations, and diverse scenarios of such correlations due to geographical conditions.

Pan et al. (2019) suggested ST-MetaNet, a meta-learning framework for urban traffic prediction based on complex spatiotemporal correlations. ST-MetaNet can handle spatiotemporal correlations simultaneously:

- Spatial correlations: traffic in some places changes mutually and dynamically
- Temporal correlations: the current traffic at a given place depends on its precedents

Two geo-graph attributes describe the traffic condition of a place and the mutually interactive relationship:

- Node attributes describe the neighboring environments of a place, its neighboring points of interest (POIs), and the density of road networks (RNs)
- Edge attributes indicate the association among multiple locations (nodes)

Edge characteristics input distance and road networks, where node characteristics process neighboring points of interest (POIs) and location. Node and edge characteristics are passed separately to the ST correlations model through weight generation as spatial and temporal correlation.

This framework consists of four modules:

- An RNN to represent the historical traffic
- A meta-knowledge learner consisting of two submodes to produce weights of a graph attention network (GAT):
  - A node-meta-knowledge learner (NMK) for meta-information from node attributes through a fully connected network
  - An edge-meta-knowledge learner (EMK) for meta-information from edge attributes through a fully connected network
- A meta-graph attention network (Meta-GAT) for attention score computation and aggregation of the hidden state
- A meta-recurrent neural network (Meta-RNN) that processes various temporal correlations to produce the weights of RNN for each place

The overall training method is summarized in Table 9.12.
This method is evaluated through two tasks:

- Taxi flow prediction on the TDrive dataset (Yuan et al., 2010)
- Traffic speed estimation on the METR-LA dataset (Jagadish et al., 2014)

The evaluation metrics include mean absolute error (MAE) and rooted mean square error (RMSE).

TABLE 9.12 General training methods of ST-MetaNet.

Input: $X = (X_1, ..., X_{N_t})$, urban traffic
$\quad\quad \mathcal{V} = \left\{ v^{(1)}, ..., v^{(N_l)} \right\}$, node attributes
$\quad\quad \mathcal{E} = \left\{ e^{(ij)} \right\}$, edge attributes

---

1 $\mathcal{D}_{train} \leftarrow \varnothing$

2 for *available* $t \in \{1, ..., N_t\}$ **do**
3 $\quad$ Obtain $X_{input} \leftarrow (X_{t-\tau_{in}+1}, ..., X_t)$
4 $\quad$ Obtain $Y_{label} \leftarrow (X_{t+1}, ..., X_{t+\tau_{out}})$
5 $\quad$ Set $\left\{ X_{input}, \mathcal{V}, \mathcal{E}, Y_{label} \right\}$ into $\mathcal{D}_{train}$
6 all trainable parameters initialization

7 do
8 $\quad$ Select a batch $\mathcal{D}_{batch}$ from $\mathcal{D}_{train}$
9 $\quad$ Evaluate on $\mathcal{L}_{train}$ by $\mathcal{D}_{batch}$
10 $\quad$ $\omega_1 = \omega_1 - \alpha \nabla_{\omega_1} \mathcal{L}_{train}$
11 $\quad$ $\omega_2 = \omega_2 - \alpha \nabla_{\omega_2} \mathcal{L}_{train}$
12 until converge

13 trained ST-MetaNet model

Modified from Pan, Z., Liang, Y., Wang, W., Yu, Y., Zheng, Y., & Zhang, J. (2019). Urban traffic prediction from spatio-temporal data using deep meta learning. KDD.

9.7 Cold-start problems in recommendation systems

9.7.1 Introduction

Cold-start is a long-standing issue in recommendation systems. It occurs when no inferences are provided for users or items due to a lack of related information, such as item characteristics, user profile, and historical behaviors. It may limit the system's learning capability and lead prediction difficulty to generate a personalized recommendation. The three primary cold-start types can be divided as follows (Bobadilla, Ortega, Hernando, & Bernal, 2012):

- **User cold-start** (UC; also named new user): a newly registered user without interaction with the system has an empty or incomplete user profile
- **Item cold-start** (IC; also named new item): an item is added to the system with some content-based characteristics but a lack of interaction. This becomes a major problem in collaborative filtering algorithms: if no interaction is presented, a pure collaborative algorithm cannot make recommendations. Content-based systems suffer less from this problem
- **User-item cold-start** (UIC; also named new community): the start-up recommendation system has some items but lacks existing users and information on the interaction between users and items

An ideal recommendation system should maintain four characteristics (Gope & Jain, 2017):

- Accuracy: the ratio of the number of related recommendations to the number of total recommendations
- Lack of or reduced bias
- Adaptability (Christakopoulou, Radlinski, & Hofmann, 2016)
- Diversity: to capture users' interest among different domains

The corresponding solutions can be divided into explicit solutions and implicit solutions. An explicit solution aims to collect evidence by directly interacting with users through ratings and questionnaires. It has better control over the evidence contained and can gather more related information, but it requires more time and effort. Active learning and interview-based strategies are two standard techniques for explicit solutions. In contrast, implicit solutions aim to know more about user behavior from a few interactions. This solution concentrates on alternative sources like Facebook data to construct user profiles. Once the user profile is set, filtering methods based on extracted preferences and a rating matrix make recommendations. While implicit solutions reduce users' efforts, the filtering processes based on abundant gathered information should be meticulous.

For finding available user information, two filtering methods are commonly implemented:

- Content-based filtering (Ricci, Rokach, & Shapira, 2011) assumes that if a user likes an item, this user is highly likely to like similar items
- Collaborative filtering (Ricci et al., 2011) has two strategies that require prior knowledge—the Latent Factor Model (Desrosiers & Karypis, 2011) and the neighborhood-based approach (Desrosiers & Karypis, 2011). The neighborhood-based approach assumes if users from a group have similar preferences, they should like similar items. The Latent

Factor Model focuses on users' personalities and psychological activities to recommend appropriate items to them

According to several research efforts (Desrosiers & Karypis, 2011; Koren & Bell, 2011; Ricci et al., 2011), collaborative filtering maintains better performance than content-based filtering.

Existing solutions have been achieved and promise performances outcomes for the above three types of cold-start (UC, IC, UIC). However, certain deficiencies remain. Cold-start can be viewed as a meta-learning problem, as only a small amount of data (user history or item history) is available in the system. The model needs to handle sample scarcity situations; thus, meta-learning offers more possibilities for diverse solutions on cold-start issues.

This section investigates multiple meta-learning-based approaches to tackle cold-start problems (user cold-start, item cold-start, user-item cold-start). Section 9.7.2 presents a nonlinear bias-adaption strategy that focuses on the scenario of new times via continuous adding. A scenario-specific sequential meta-learner dealing with fine-grained situations, such as Black Friday Promotions, is discussed in Section 9.7.3. In Section 9.7.4, a MAML-based user preference estimator for both user cold-start and item cold-start is explored. Section 9.7.5 outlines a memory-augmented meta-optimization that is appropriate for all three cold-start scenarios. Finally, an approach using heterogeneous information networks with meta-learning is offered in Section 9.7.6.

9.7.2 Continuously adding new items

Vartak and colleagues (Vartak et al., 2017) presented a hybrid meta-learning approach to tackle the cold-start issue under the matrix factorization algorithm (Linden, Smith, & York, 2003) due to new items being continuously inserted into a recommendation system. This strategy provides a novel direction of item cold-start (ICS) besides context-based filtering (Lops, Gemmis, & Semeraro, 2011) and item-specific information such as context, description, and implicit feedback.

Named Non-Linear Bias Adaptation (NLBA) for item representations $\mathcal{F}(t_i)$, this is a nonlinear deep neural network classifier with bias adaptation. Considering one user as one task, it aims to learn meta-knowledge across multiple tasks and leverage complex interconnection between ratings (i.e., class $c \in \{0,1\}$ denotes rating, where 0 stands for negative rates and 1 stands for positive ones) and the relationship between the rating and the test items.

In episode-based meta-training, each episode contains a collection of historical items exposed to a specific user and their corresponding engagements. This collection is denoted as $V_j = \{(t_m, e_{mj})\} : t_m \in T_j$. This strategy leaves the upper limit on the size of historical items as a hyperparameter set in advance.

The classifier equipped with H hidden layers is expressed in Eq. (9.36), where $v^0 R_j^0 + v^1 R_j^1$ denotes the bias, w presents the output's weights, $\{v_l^0 R_j^0 + v_l^1 R_j^1\}_{l=1}^H$ denotes the bias, and $\{W_l\}_{l=1}^H$ is a set of all hidden layers' weights. The biases of both output and hidden units are changeable during the adaptation of each user, while all weights of output and weights of the hidden unit remain fixed across multiple users.

$$\left[\mathbf{v}^0 R_j^0 + \mathbf{v}^1 R_j^1, \mathbf{w}, \left\{ \mathbf{V}_l^0 R_j^0 + \mathbf{V}_l^1 R_j^1 \right\}_{l=1}^H, \{\mathbf{W}_l\}_{l=1}^H \right] = \mathcal{H}(V_j) \tag{9.36}$$

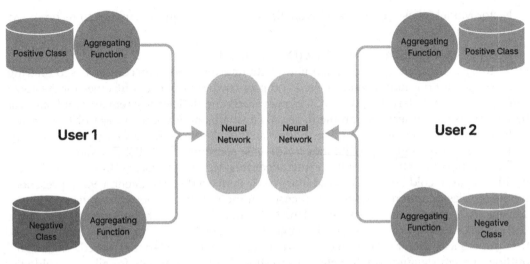

FIG. 9.2 General methods of non-linear bias adaptation. *Modified from Vartak, M., Vartak, M., Miranda, C., Bratman, J., & Larochelle, H. (2017). A meta-learning perspective on cold-start recommendations for items . NIPS.*

The class embedding representation R_j^c is expressed in Eq. (9.37), where $\mathcal{G}$ denotes the aggregating function:

$$R_j^c = \mathcal{G}\big(\{F(t_m)\} : t_m \in T_j \wedge \big(e_{mj} = c\big)\big) \tag{9.37}$$

The overall architecture of NLBA is displayed in Fig. 9.2.

This strategy is designed for Twitter Home Timeline recommendation and has been trained and tested in the Tweet customized dataset.

9.7.3 Context-aware cross-domain recommendation cold-start under a few-shot setting

Du and colleagues (Du et al., 2019) introduced a model-agnostic meta-learner, Scenario-Specific Sequential Meta-Learner (s^2Meta). It discusses the scenario-based cold-start from few-shot interactions between users and items. It aims to recommend user u with top-n item i under scenario c and enhances the likelihood of a user's sequent behaviors. This framework implements meta-learning to instantiate an optimal generalization under a few-shot setting and fast adaptation of unseen tasks. This scenario-specific framework is appropriate when:

- The user behavior significantly changes due to specific events (e.g., Black Friday promotion)
- The long-tailed data lacks user interactions
- It is difficult to set up the combination of hyperparameters in a new scenario
- A minimal collection of user-item interactions is shared across multiple domains

The official code is released at https://github.com/THUDM/ScenarioMeta2, and a video illustration is available at https://youtu.be/TNHLZqWnQwc.

This method applied hinge loss as the loss function, expressed in Eqs. (9.38) and (9.39), where γ denotes margin as a set of 1, θ_c parameters such that $\theta_c = M(D_c^{train}; \omega)$ and i_k^- is the sample of the item set s.t. $(u_k, i_k^-) \notin D_c^{train}$. γ denotes the margin constant.

$$\mathcal{L}_\omega\left(D_c^{test} | D_c^{train}\right) = \sum_{(u_k, i_k, i_k^-) \in D_c^{test}} \frac{\ell\left(u_k, i_k, i_k^-; \theta_c\right)}{|D_c^{test}|} \tag{9.38}$$

$$\ell(u, i, i^-; \theta_c) = max\left(0, \gamma - f(u, i; \theta_c) + f(u, i^-; \theta_c)\right) \tag{9.39}$$

This framework involves the following three steps:

(1) Rather than random initialization, which may cause overfitting in a few-shot setting, parameter $\theta_c^{(0)}$ is initialized from ω_R, which has "global initial values shared across different scenarios" (Du et al., 2019).
(2) Fine-tuning the parameters occurs through updating the controller (Ravi & Larochelle, 2017) equipped with the input gate $\alpha^{(t)}$ and forget gate $\beta^{(t)}$, as expressed in Eq. (9.40):

$$\theta_c^{(t)} = \beta^{(t)} \odot \theta_c^{(t-1)} - \alpha^{(t)} \odot \nabla_{\theta_c^{(t-1)}} \mathcal{L}^{(t)} \tag{9.40}$$

This method conducts LSTM as the encoder of historical information, as expressed in Eqs. (9.41)–(9.43) at time t with the hidden state $h_u^{(t)}$ and cell state $c_u^{(t)}$:

$$h_u^{(t)}, c_u^{(t)} = \text{LSTM}\left(\left[\nabla_{\theta_c^{(t-1)}} \mathcal{L}^{(t)}, \mathcal{L}^{(t)}, \theta_c^{(t-1)}\right], h_u^{(t-1)}, c_u^{(t-1)}\right) \tag{9.41}$$

$$\beta^{(t)} = \sigma\left(W_F h_u^{(t)} + b_F\right) \tag{9.42}$$

$$\alpha^{(t)} = \sigma\left(W_I h_u^{(t)} + b_I\right) \tag{9.43}$$

(3) Preventing overfitting through a learnable stop policy by an LSTM-based stop controller M_s, as demonstrated in Eqs. (9.44), (9.45), where the hidden state of the stop controller $h_s^{(t)}$ at time t:

$$h_s^{(t)}, c_s^{(t)} = \text{LSTM}\left(\left[\mathcal{L}^{(t)}, \left\|\nabla_{\theta_c^{(t-1)}} \mathcal{L}^{(t)}\right\|_2\right], h_s^{(t-1)}, c_s^{(t-1)}\right) \tag{9.44}$$

$$p^{(t)} = \sigma\left(W_s h_s^{(t)} + b_s\right) \tag{9.45}$$

The overall training algorithm is summarized in Table 9.13 with REINFORCE (Williams, 1992).

This method is evaluated in three public datasets: Amazon Review dataset (Brazdil, Giraud-Carrier, Soares, & Vilalta, 2008), Movielens-20M (Harper & Konstan, 2016), and Alibaba Cloud Theme Click Dataset (Tianchi, 2019).

TABLE 9.13   Training methods of scenario-specific sequential meta-learner.

Input: $\mathbb{T}_{\text{metatrain}}$, Meta-training set
$\mathcal{L}$, Loss function

1: Random Initialize ω_u, ω_s, ω_R
#K : thenumberofmeta−trainingsteps
2: **for** $d \leftarrow 1, K$ **do**
3:     Randomly sampling $D_c^{\text{train}}, D_c^{\text{test}}$ from $\mathbb{T}_{\text{metatrain}}$
4:     $\theta_c^{(0)} \leftarrow \omega_R$ and $T \leftarrow 0$

5:     **for** $t:1, \ldots, T_{\max}$ **do**
6:         *Randomly sampling batch $B^{(t)}$ from D_c^{train}*
7:         $\mathcal{L}^{(t)} \leftarrow \mathcal{L}\left(B^{(t)}; \theta_c^{(t-1)}\right)$
8:         $p^{(t)} \leftarrow M_s\left(\mathcal{L}^{(t)}, \parallel \nabla_{\theta_c^{(t-1)}} \mathcal{L}^{(t)} \parallel_2; \omega_s\right)$
          # Randomly stop or not
9:         $s^{(t)} \sim \text{Bernoulli}\left(p^{(t)}\right)$
10:         **if** $s^{(t)} = 1$ **then**
11:             Break;
12:         **end if**
13:         $\theta_c^{(t)} \leftarrow \text{Update } \theta_c^{(t-1)}$
14:         $T \leftarrow T+1$
15:     **end for**

16:     $\mathcal{L}^{\text{test}} \leftarrow \mathcal{L}\left(D_c^{\text{test}}; \theta_c^{(T)}\right)$
17:     Evaluate ω_u, ω_R using $\nabla_{\omega_u} \mathcal{L}^{\text{test}}, \nabla_{\omega_R} \mathcal{L}^{\text{test}}$
18:     $d\omega_s \leftarrow 0$

19:     **for** $j \leftarrow 1, T$ **do**
20:         $d\omega_s \leftarrow d\omega_s + \left(\mathcal{L}^{\text{test}} - \mathcal{L}\left(D_c^{\text{test}}; \theta_c^{(j)}\right)\right) \nabla_{\omega_s} \ln\left(1 - p^{(j)}\right)$
21:     **end for**

22:     Evaluate ω_s using $d\omega_s$
23: **end for**

Modified from Du, Z., Wang, X., Yang, H., Zhou, J., & Tang, J. (2019). Sequential scenario-specific meta learner for online recommendation. KDD.

9.7.4 User preference estimator

Lee and colleagues (Lee et al., 2019) suggested a few-shot MAML-based recommendation system strategy for the cold-start problems of user cold-start and item cold-start, named Meta-Learned User Preference Estimator (MeLU). This approach offers personalized recommendations through the local and global updates for each user based on their personal shopping history of item consumption and interaction preference.

This approach consists of two parts:

- A user preference estimator, in which user profile and item content are inputs for the embedding process. Eq. (9.46) defines the embedding vector for user i profiles U_i and Eq. (9.47) for item j profiles I_j. c_{ip} and c_{jq} present the one-hot embedding of categorical content

$p \in \{1, ..., P\}$ from user i and the one-hot embedding of categorical content $q \in \{1, ..., Q\}$ from item j. e_{ip} and e_{jq} present the embedding matrix of categorical content $p \in \{1, ..., P\}$ from user i and the embedding matrix of categorical content $q \in \{1, ..., Q\}$ from item j.

$$U_i = \left[e_{i1}c_{i1}; \cdots; e_{iP}c_{iP}\right]^\top \tag{9.46}$$

$$I_j = \left[e_{j1}c_{j1}; \cdots; e_{jQ}c_{jQ}\right]^\top \tag{9.47}$$

Hence, it employs an N-layer full-connected neural network as its decision-making layer. The output layer, followed by the decision-making layer, outputs user performance (e.g., rating, feedback). See Eqs. (9.48)–(9.51) for a detailed demonstration, where a means rectified linear unit (ReLU) activation function:

$$x_0 = \left[U_i; I_j\right] \tag{9.48}$$

$$x_1 = a\left(\mathbf{W}_1^\top x_0 + b_1\right)$$
$$\vdots \tag{9.49}$$
$$x_N = a\left(\mathbf{W}_N^\top x_{N-1} + b_N\right) \tag{9.50}$$
$$\hat{y}_{ij} = \sigma\left(\mathbf{W}_o^\top x_N + b_o\right) \tag{9.51}$$

- A meta-learned user preference estimator. This model learns personalized recommendations during the local update through the support set of each user (i.e., item-consumption history and preferences). The loss function of this local update is expressed in Eq. (9.52), where H_i denotes the support set, and y_{ij} and $\hat{y}_{ij}$ denote the ground truth and estimated preference of user i on item j:

$$\mathcal{L}_i = \frac{1}{|H_i|} \sum_{j \in H_i} \left(y_{ij} - \hat{y}_{ij}\right)^2 \tag{9.52}$$

After the local update, this model predicts user preferences for all items that are not rated during global updates over all layers. The comprehensive methods are outlined in Table 9.14.

This strategy is evaluated on MovieLens 1M (Harper & Konstan, 2016) and Book-crossing (Ziegler, McNee, Konstan, & Lausen, 2005) with evaluation metrics of mean absolute error (MAE) and normalized discounted cumulative gain (nDCG).

9.7.5 Memory-augmented recommendation system meta-optimization

Inspired by MeLU (see Section 9.7.3), Dong et al. (2020) presented a Memory-Augmented Meta-Optimization (MAMO) learner. It conducts two memory modules to overcome the local minimum issue caused by the MAML backbone in the cold-start problem; the globally shared initialization parameters may lead the local minimum for various user preference patterns. The official code is released at https://github.com/dongmanqing/Code-for-MAMO.

TABLE 9.14   Training methods of meta-learned user preference estimator.

Input: α, β, hyperparameters of step size

1: randomly initialize θ_1
2: randomly initialize θ_2

3: **while** not converge **do**
4:      sample users batch $B \sim p(\mathcal{B})$

5:      **for** user i in B **do**
6:          let $\theta_2^i = \theta_2$
7:          Compute $\nabla_{\theta_2^i} \mathcal{L}_i\left(f_{\theta_1, \theta_2^i}\right)$
8:          Obtain local update $\theta_2^i \leftarrow \theta_2^i - \alpha \nabla_{\theta_2^i} \mathcal{L}_i'\left(f_{\theta_1, \theta_2^i}\right)$
9:      **end for**

10:      Obtain global update $\theta_1 \leftarrow \theta_1 - \beta \sum_{i \in B} \nabla_{\theta_1} \mathcal{L}_i'\left(f_{\theta_1, \theta_2^i}\right)$

$$\theta_2 \leftarrow \theta_2 - \beta \sum_{i \in B} \nabla_{\theta_2} \mathcal{L}_i'\left(f_{\theta_1, \theta_2^i}\right)$$

11: **end while**

Modified from Lee, H., Im, J., Jang, S., Cho, H., & Chung, S. (2019). MeLU: Meta-learned user preference estimator for cold-start recommendation. SIGKDD.

These two memory modules are explored as follows:

- Feature-specific memory $b_u \leftarrow (p_u, M_U, M_p)$ involves user-embedding memory M_U and profile memory M_p to assist the model through personalized parameter initialization; it aims to produce the retrievable attention value a_u of user-profiles p_u and user embedding memory M_U
- Task-specific memory $M_{U,I} \leftarrow (a_u, M_{u,I})$ with a read head is used to obtain the memory and a write head to re-write the memory $M_{u,I}$ into $M_{U,I}$

The overall model consists of two parts:

- The recommender model $R_\Theta(p_u, p_i)$ estimates user preference; similar to MeLU, it conducts local updating for a single user via personalized recommendations
- The memory-augmented meta-optimizer offers personalized initialization of recommender model parameters Θ, globally updated for all users $u \in D^{train}$; it consists of memory $M = \{M_U, M_P, M_{U,\,I}\}$ and global parameters $\Phi = \{\phi_u, \phi_i, \phi_r\}$

The training and testing methods are displayed in Tables 9.15 and 9.16.

This method is evaluated on the same datasets as MeLU: MovieLens 1M (Harper & Konstan, 2016) and Book-Crossing (Ziegler et al., 2005) with evaluation metrics of MAE and normalized discounted cumulative gain of top N candidates (NDCG@N). It is tested under four scenarios:

- New users with new items (user-item cold-start; UIC)
- Existing users with new items (item cold-start; IC)
- New users with existing items (user cold-start; UC)
- Existing users with existing items (noncold-start)

TABLE 9.15 Training methods of memory-augmented meta-optimization.

Input: U^{train}, training user set
$\{p_u | u \in U^{t\ \text{rain}}\}$, user profile
$\{p_i | i \in (I_u^S, I_u^Q)\}$, Item profile
$\{y_{u,\ i} | u \in U^{train}, i \in (I_u^S, I_u^Q)\}$, user ratings
$\alpha, \beta, \gamma, \tau, \rho, \lambda$, hyper-parameters
Output: ϕ_u, ϕ_i, ϕ_r, meta parameters
$M_P, M_U, M_{U,\ I}$, memories

1 Randomly initialize ϕ_u, ϕ_i, ϕ_r;
2 Randomly initialize $M_P, M_U, M_{U,\ I}$;

3 while n*ot done* **do**

4   **for** $u \in U^{\text{train}}$ **do**
5   Evaluate $b_u \leftarrow (p_u, M_U, M_P)$ as $a_u = \text{attention}(p_u, M_P)$ *and* $b_u = a_u^\top M_U$;
6   Local parameters initializations of $\theta_i, \theta_u, \theta_r$ as $\theta_u \leftarrow \phi_u - \tau b_u, \theta_i \leftarrow \phi_i, \theta_r \leftarrow \phi_r$;
7   Preference memory initializations of $M_{u,\ I} \leftarrow (a_u, M_{U,\ I})$ as $M_{u,\ I} = a_u^\top \cdot M_{U,\ I}$;

8   **for** $i \in I_u^S$ **do**
9   Obtain user and item embedding e_u and e_i as $e_u = f_{\theta_u}(p_u)$, $e_i = f_{\theta_i}(p_i)$;
10   Obtain prediction of $y_{\hat{u}}, i$ as $y_{-u,i} = f_{\theta_r}(e_u, e_i) = FC_{\theta_r}(M_{u,I} \cdot [e_u, e_i])$;
11   Evaluate local update $M_{u,\ I}$;
12   Obtain local update $\theta_u, \theta_i, \theta_r$ as $\theta_* \leftarrow \theta_* - \rho \cdot \nabla_{\theta_0} \mathcal{L}\left(y_{u,i}, y\hat{u}_i\right)$
13   **end for**

14   **end for**

15   Feature-specific memory M_P, M_U update as $M_P = \alpha \cdot (a_u p_u^\top) + (1 - \alpha) M_P$, $M_U =$
$\beta \cdot \left(a_u \nabla_{\theta_u}\left(\mathcal{L}\left(y_{u,i}, y_{u,i}\right)\right)\right) + (1 - \beta) M_U$;
16   Task-specific memory $M_{U,\ I}$ update as $M_{U,\ I} = \gamma \cdot (a_u \otimes M_{u,\ I}) + (1 - \gamma) M_{U,\ I}$;
17   Global parameters ϕ_u, ϕ_i, ϕ_r update as $\phi_* \leftarrow \phi_* - \lambda \Sigma_{u \in U^{\text{train}}} \Sigma_{i \in I_u^Q} \nabla \mathcal{L}\left(\mathcal{R}_{\hat{\theta}_*}\right)$;
18 **end while**

Modified from Dong, M., Yuan, F., Yao, L., Xu, X., & Zhu, L. (2020). MAMO: Memory-augmented meta-optimization for cold-start recommendation. SIGKDD.

TABLE 9.16 Inference with memory-augmented meta-optimization.

Input: U^{test}, testing user set
$\{p_u | u \in U^{\text{test}}\}$, *user profile*
$\{p_i | i \in (I_u^S, I_u^Q)\}$, *item profile*
$\left\{y_{u,i} | u \in U^{\text{test}}, i \in (I_u^S, I_u^Q)\right\}$, *user ratings*
$\alpha, \beta, \gamma, \tau, \rho, \lambda$, *hyperparameters*
ϕ_u, ϕ_i, ϕ_r, meta-parameters
$M_P, M_U, M_{U,\ I}$, memories
Output: $\{y_{u,\ i} | u \in U^{\text{test}}, i \in I_u^Q\}$, predicted user preference

1 **for** $u \in U^{\text{test}}$ **do**
2   Obtain $b_u \leftarrow (p_u, M_U, M_P)$ as $a_u = \text{attention}(p_u, M_P)$, $b_u = a_u^\top M_U$;
3   Local parameters Initialization of $\theta_i, \theta_u, \theta_r$ as $\theta_u \leftarrow \phi_u - \tau b_u, \theta_i \leftarrow \phi_i, \theta_r \leftarrow \phi_r$;

Continued

TABLE 9.16　Inference with memory-augmented meta-optimization—cont'd

4	Preference memory Initialization of $M_{u,\ I}\leftarrow(p_u,M_{U,\ I})$ as $M_{u,\ I}=a_u^\top\cdot M_{U,\ I}$;
5	**for** $i\in I_u^S$ **do**
6	Evaluate user and item embedding e_u and e_i as $e_u=f_{\theta_u}(p_u)$, $e_i=f_{\theta_i}(p_i)$;
7	Evaluate prediction of $y_{\hat{u},i}$ as $y{-}_{u,i}=f_{\theta_r}(e_u,e_i)=FC_{\theta_r}(M_{u,I}\cdot[e_u,e_i])$;
8	Evaluate local update $M_{u,I}$;
9	Obtain local update $\theta_u,\ \theta_i,\ \theta_r$ as $\theta_*\leftarrow\theta_*-\rho\cdot\nabla_{\theta_*}\mathcal{L}\left(y_{u,i},y\hat{u},i\right)$
10	**end for**
11	**for** $i\in I_u^Q$ **do**
12	Evaluate user and item embedding e_u and e_i as $e_u=f_{\theta_u}(p_u)$, $e_i=f_{\theta_i}(p_i)$;
13	Evaluate prediction of $y_{\widehat{u,i}}$ as $y{-}_{u,i}=f_{\theta_r}(e_u,e_i)=FC_{\theta_r}(M_{u,I}\cdot[e_u,e_i])$;
14	**end for**
15	**end for**

Modified from Dong, M., Yuan, F., Yao, L., Xu, X., & Zhu, L. (2020). MAMO: Memory-augmented meta-optimization for cold-start recommendation. SIGKDD.

9.7.6 Meta-learner with heterogeneous information networks

Heterogeneous Information Networks (HIN) explore heterogeneous data and contain various user-item interactions through meta-paths (Sun, Han, Yan, Yu, & Wu, 2011). HIN can be defined as a graph $G=\{V,E,O,R\}$ with nodes V, edges E, a set of objects O, and relation types R if $2<|O|+|R|$. Each node is connected by a type-mapping function $\varphi_O:V\rightarrow O$, and each edge is linked by a type-mapping function $\varphi_R:E\rightarrow R$.

Meta-path is a relation sequence among objects $o_i\in O$ to extract complex semantics. It is defined as $P=o_1\xrightarrow{r_1}o_2\xrightarrow{r_2}\ldots\xrightarrow{r_n}o_{n+1}$, where $r_i\in R$ and n is the length of a meta-path. For example, a meta-path of "User—Book—Author—Book" (i.e., UBAB) encodes the semantic context as "books written by the same author as a book rated by the user."

With the benefit of HIN and meta-paths, Lu et al. (2020) proposed MetaHIN, a coadaptation meta-learning approach to tackle cold-start problems through a meta-learner with semantic-wise adaptation, task-wise adaptation, and a semantic-enhanced task constructor. This strategy performs well under user cold-start, item cold-start, and new users with new items. The official code is released at https://github.com/rootlu/MetaHIN.

MetaHIN consists of two main modules:

1. In semantic-enhanced tasks constructor, assuming the task $T_u=(S_u,Q_u)$ of user u, the semantic-enhanced support set with multifaceted semantic contexts is defined as $S_u=(S_u^R, S_u^P)$ where S_u^R is the set of items rated by user u and S_u^P denotes the semantic contexts along with a set of meta-paths P. For each p-induced semantic context ($p\in P$) such that $S_u^p=\cup_{i\in S_u^R}C_{u,i}^p$, where $C_{u,i}^p=\{j:j\in items\ accessible\ along\ p\ starting\ from\ u-i\}$.

   The semantic-enhanced query set is expressed as $Q_u=(Q_u^R,Q_u^P)$, which disjoints with the support set as $S_u^R\cap Q_u^R=\varnothing$.

2. A coadaptation meta-learner is used for both task- and semantic-wise adaptation:
   - In semantic-wise adaptation, the user-embedding vector represented in semantic space is denoted as $x_u^p=\mathcal{G}_\phi(u,S_u^p)$. The loss function based on the support set is expressed in Eq. (9.53), where r_{ui} denotes the actual rating of item i from user u and $(r_{ui}-h_\omega(x_u^p,\mathbf{e}_i))^2$

represents the preference prediction of item i from user u in the p-induced semantic space:

$$\mathcal{L}_{T_u}\left(\omega, \mathbf{x}_u^p, \mathcal{S}_u^{\mathcal{R}}\right) = \frac{1}{\left|\mathcal{S}_u^{\mathcal{R}}\right|} \sum_{i \in \mathcal{S}_u^{\mathcal{R}}} \left(r_{ui} - h_\omega\left(\mathbf{x}_u^p, \mathbf{e}_i\right)\right)^2 \qquad (9.53)$$

The fine-grained prior knowledge ϕ_u^p of multiple semantic facts is expressed as Eq. (9.54), where α denotes the semantic-wise learning rate:

$$\phi_u^p = \phi - \alpha \frac{\partial \mathcal{L}_{T_u}\left(\omega, \mathbf{x}_u^p, \mathcal{S}_u^{\mathcal{R}}\right)}{\partial \phi} = \phi - \alpha \frac{\partial \mathcal{L}_{T_u}\left(\omega, \mathbf{x}_u^p, \mathcal{S}_u^{\mathcal{R}}\right)}{\partial \mathbf{x}_u^p} \frac{\partial \mathbf{x}_u^p}{\partial \phi} \qquad (9.54)$$

○ In task-wise adaptation, the global prior knowledge ω_u^p of task T_u is presented in Eqs. (9.55), (9.56) with a task-wise learning rate β, an element-wise product $\odot$, and a transformation function by fully connected layer $\kappa(\cdot)$. $\mathbf{x}_u^{p\langle S\rangle}$ represents the embedding representation of user u in the support set's semantic space.

$$\omega_u^p = \omega^p - \beta \frac{\partial \mathcal{L}_{T_u}\left(\omega^p, \mathbf{x}_u^{p\langle S\rangle}, \mathcal{S}_u^{\mathcal{R}}\right)}{\partial \omega^p} \qquad (9.55)$$

where:

$$\omega^p = \omega \odot \kappa\left(\mathbf{x}_u^{p\langle S\rangle}\right) \qquad (9.56)$$

The overall training is outlined in Table 9.17.

TABLE 9.17   Training methods of MetaHIN.

Require: G, a Heterogeneous Information Network
       $\mathcal{P}$, a collection of meta-paths
       $\mathcal{T}^{tr}$, a collection of meta-training tasks
       s, semantic update steps
       t, task-wise update steps
       η, meta-learning rates
       α, semantic-wise
       β, task-wise

1: Randomly initialize $\theta = \{\phi, \omega\}$ and global parameters 2: Setup the meta-training task $\mathcal{T}^{tr}$ support set and query set 3: **while** not done **do** 4:   Sample a batch $\mathcal{T}_u \in \mathcal{T}^{tr}$ 5:   **for** all $\mathcal{T}_u$ regarding to user u **do** 6:   **for** all $p \in \mathcal{P}$ **do** 7:   Obtain $\mathbf{x}_u^p$ using $\mathcal{S}_u^p \subset \mathcal{S}_u^{\mathcal{P}}$ 8:   Compute $\mathcal{L}_{T_u}\left(\omega, \mathbf{x}_u^p, \mathcal{S}_u^{\mathcal{R}}\right)$ 9:   Evaluate semantic-wise adaptation with s updates

Continued

TABLE 9.17 Training methods of MetaHIN—cont'd

10:	Compute $\mathcal{L}_{T_u}\left(\omega^p, \mathbf{x}_u^{p(S)}, \mathcal{S}_u^{\mathcal{R}}\right)$
11:	Evaluate task-wise adaptation with t updates
12:	**end for**
13:	Evaluate ω_u and $\mathbf{x}_u$ under adaptation fusion
14:	**end for**
15:	Update $\Theta \leftarrow \Theta - \eta \nabla_\Theta \sum_{T_{u \sim p(T)}} \mathcal{L}_{T_u}\left(\omega_u, \mathbf{x}_u, Q_u^{\mathcal{R}}\right)$
16:	**end while**

Modified from Lu, Y., Fang, Y., & Shi, C. (2020). Meta-learning on heterogeneous information networks for cold-start recommendation. SIG-KDD.

This method is evaluated on multiple public datasets, including DBook (Shi, Hu, Zhao, & Yu, 2018), MovieLens (Harper & Konstan, 2016), and Yelp (Wang, He, Wang, Feng, & Chua, 2019).

9.8 Climate science

9.8.1 Introduction

As one of the severe issues every nation suffers, contemporary climate change has been challenging people's daily lives, social functioning, and industrial development. Key dangers include global warming led by human activities and the related weather pattern changes—rising sea levels, glaciers melting, and more severe and frequent droughts and wildfires. The emission of greenhouse gases (i.e., carbon dioxide and methane) due to fossil fuels burning primarily cause these emissions. Although artificial intelligence has impacted processes such as clinical diagnosis, traffic analysis, accurate face recognition, and fraud detection, so far, the limitations of computational structure and capability have narrowed their implementations, particularly for applications of climate science (Huntingford et al., 2019).

Early attempts at weather prediction have attracted interest since the 1950s, and a variety of machine learning and deep learning techniques have been applied: artificial neural networks (Gentine, Pritchard, Rasp, Reinaudi, & Yacalis, 2018; Goyal, Bharti, Quilty, Adamowski, & Pandey, 2014), Markov chain Monte Carlo, random forest(Rodriguez-Galiano, Chica-Olmo, Abarca-Hernandez, Atkinson, & Jeganathan, 2012), clustering (Dawson, Palmer, & Corti, 2012), hidden Markov models, generalized regression neural network, principal component analysis, convolutional neural network (Deo & Şahin, 2015; Liu et al., 2016), gradient boosted regression trees , and kernel regression.

Standard datasets regarding climate science include Berkeley Earth Surface Temperature Data (Berkeley, 2016), Global Climate Change Data (World Bank, 2021), International Greenhouse Gas Emissions (Nations, U, 2017), Daily Sea Ice Extent Data (National Snow and Ice Data Center, 2019), Climate Change Adaptation of Coffee Production (Läderach et al., 2016), The Climate Change Knowledge Portal (World Bank, 2021), Climate Change

Projections and Impacts for New York State (New York State Energy Research and Development Authority, 2020), Air Quality in Madrid 2001–2018 (Decide Soluciones, 2018), and Climate Change Tweets Ids (Littman & Wrubel, 2019).

Further discussions on climate science have been aided by machine learning and deep learning techniques ranging from teleconnection identification and Earth system model diagnostics to climatic anomalies detection and prediction. A detection of extreme weather conditions through the warming signal, bow echo, is explored in Section 9.8.2.

9.8.2 Critical incident detection

Long-tailed distribution dominates weather- or climate-related datasets ranging from radar images to real-time temporal and spatial resolution of satellite images. When a large proportion of data concentrates on a few categories while limited data fall into other categories, long-tailed distribution happens, creating imbalanced datasets. Hence, the generalization ability is problematic due to serious bias among datasets. The detection and prediction of critical incidents based on such datasets remains challenging. One important warning of severe weather conditions (e.g., thunderstorms, damaging winds, winter storms, freezing rain, tornadoes) is bow echo. This bow-shaped pattern can be recognized in radar and satellite imagery data (Fujita, 1978; Klimowski, Hjelmfelt, & Bunkers, 2004; Przybylinski, 1995).

Kamani and colleagues (Kamani et al., 2019) proposed a fast and effective meta-learning framework—Targeted Meta-Learning—to deal with imbalanced datasets with a long-tailed distribution and reduce biases in the emerging domains of weather and climate change. The official code is released at https://github.com/mmkamani7/Targeted-Meta-Learning, and an invited talk regarding this framework is available at https://www.climatechange.ai/papers/icml2019/10.html.

This framework conducts a bi-level strategy with two loss functions, as one level supports the main training and another level employs a well-crafted unbiased target dataset V to assist the main training. Fig. 9.3 represents the general pipeline of Targeted Meta-Learning.

The loss function for the main training is expressed in Eq. (9.57), where g_i is the training loss of ith sample point $(x_i, y_i) \in \mathcal{X} \times \mathcal{Y}$ among n training samples in the dataset $\mathcal{T}$ from input space $\mathcal{X}$ to label domain $\mathcal{Y}$, $D \in \{0,1\}^{n \times c}$ represents the assignment of c classes of imbalanced data, and ω denotes the fixed weight, and $g = [g_1, g_2, ..., g_n]^\mathsf{T}$:

$$G(\omega, \theta; \mathcal{T}) = (D\omega)^\mathsf{T} g \qquad (9.57)$$

The loss function of the target dataset is expressed in Eq. (9.58), where $|V|$ is the sample size of V and $\theta^*(\omega)$ comes from the main training:

$$F(\omega, \theta^*(\omega); V) = \frac{1}{|V|} \sum_{(x_i, y_i) \in V} f(\theta^*(\omega); (x_i, y_i)) \qquad (9.58)$$

This framework is assessed on a modified dataset with radar images from the Next Generation Weather Radar (NEXRAD) Level III radar of the National Weather Service (WSR-88D; NOAA, 1988).

FIG. 9.3 General pipeline of targeted meta-learning. *Modified from* Kamani, M. M., Farhang, S., Mahdavi, M., & Wang, J. Z. (2019). Targeted meta-learning for critical incident detection in weather data.

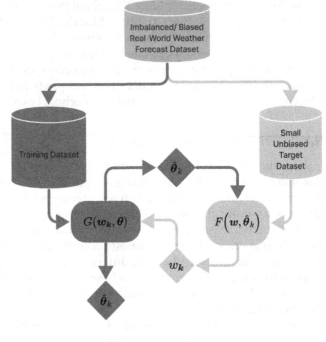

9.9 Summary

From concrete defect identifications to recommendations of new items to new users, the majority of this chapter has focused on meta-learning as a powerful technology for decision-makers in addressing climate change, urban city planning, financial risk analysis, and others. Real-world applications are complex. These solutions provide meaningful opportunities for practical changes and spark academic research discoveries.

This chapter investigates 17 influential contributions to the field, divided into seven taxonomies according to their practice areas to solve: finance and economics, building materials, graph neural network, program synthesis, transportation, cold-start problems in recommendation systems, and climate science.

As some may be interested in taking action on these practice areas or research problems, several recent discussions from the last three years (2019–2021) held by vital academic conferences can shed light on the pathways:

- "Workshop on Computer Assisted Programming" from NeurIPS 2020 at https://nips.cc/Conferences/2020/ScheduleMultitrack?event=16161
- "Tackling Climate Change with Machine Learning" series workshop held by NeurIPS 2019/2020, ICML 2021/2019, ICRL 2020 at https://www.climatechange.ai/events/neurips2021
- "AI for Transportation " from AAAI 2022 at https://aaai.org/Conferences/AAAI-22/ws22workshops/
- "Machine learning in Finance" organized by ACM SIGKDD 2021 at https://sites.google.com/view/kdd-mlf-2021/

References

Abroyan, N. (2017). Neural networks for financial market risk classification. In *Frontiers in signal processing*.

Akiyama, T., & Inokuchi, H. (2014). Long term estimation of traffic demand on urban expressway by neural networks. In *ISIS* (pp. 185–189).

Allison, P. D. (1978). Measures of inequality. *American Sociological Review, 43*, 865–880.

Alur, R., Bodik, R., Juniwal, G., Martin, M. M., Raghothaman, M., Seshia, S. A., et al. (2013). *Syntax-guided synthesis* (pp. 1–8). IEEE.

Andreeva, A., Kulesha, E., Gough, J., & Murzin, A. G. (2020). The scop database in 2020: expanded classification of representative family and superfamily domains of known protein structures. *Nucleic Acids Research, 48*(D1), D376–D382.

Atkinson, A. B. (1970). On the measurement of inequality. *Journal of Economic Theory, 2*, 244–263.

Baker, B., Gupta, O., Naik, N., & Raskar, R. (2016). Designing neural network architectures using reinforcement learning. In *International conference on learning representations (ICLR)*.

Bank, W. (2021). *The climate change knowledge portal*. Retrieved from https://climateknowledgeportal.worldbank.org.

Berkeley. (2016). *Berkeley earth surface temperature data*. Retrieved from https://www.kaggle.com/berkeleyearth/climate-change-earth-surface-temperature-data?ref=hackernoon.com.

Bertinetto, L., Henriques, J. F., Torr, P. H., & Vedaldi, A. (2018). Meta-learning with differentiable closed-form solvers. *arXiv preprint*, arXiv:1805.08136.

Bobadilla, J., Ortega, F., Hernando, A., & Bernal, J. (2012). *A collaborative filtering approach to mitigate the new user cold start problem*. Retrieved from Knowledge-Based Systems:. https://doi.org/10.1016/j.knosys.2011.07.021.

Bordes, A., Usunier, N., Garcia-Duran, A., Weston, J., & Yakhnenko, O. (2013). Translating embeddings for modeling multi-relational data. In *NeurIPS*.

Borgwardt, K. M., Ong, C. S., Schonauer, S., Vishwanathan, S., Smola, A. J., & Kriegel, H.-P. (2005). Protein function prediction via graph kernels. *Bioinformatics, 21*, i47–i56.

Brazdil, P., Giraud-Carrier, C., Soares, C., & Vilalta, R. (2008). *Metalearning: Applications to data mining* (1st ed.). Springer Publishing Company, Incorporated.

CA.gov. (2014). *Performance measurement system (PeMS) data source*. Retrieved from https://dot.ca.gov/programs/traffic-operations/mpr/pems-source.

Cai, H., Chen, T., Zhang, W., Yu, Y., & Wang, J. (2018). Efficient architecture search by network transformation. In *AAAI conference on artificial intelligence*.

Chauhan, J., Nathani, D., & Kaul, M. (2020). Few-shot learning on graphs via super-classes based on graph spectral measures. In *ICLR*.

Chen, J., Wu, W., & Tindall, M. (2016). Hedge fund return prediction and fund selection: A machine-learning approach. In *Occasional papers 16-4* Federal Reserve Bank of Dallas.

Chen, N., Ribeiro, B., & Chen, A. (2015). Financial credit risk assessment: A recent review. *Artificial Intelligence Review, 45*(1), 1–23.

Christakopoulou, K., Radlinski, F., & Hofmann, K. (2016). Towards conversational recommender systems. In *KDD* (pp. 815–824).

Colyar, J. (2007). *NGSIM*. Retrieved from US dep of transportation, NGSIM—Next generation simulation https://data.transportation.gov/Automobiles/Next-Generation-Simulation-NGSIM-Vehicle-Trajector/8ect-6jqj.

Cowell, F. A. (1980). *Generalized entropy and the measurement of distributional change*. European Economic Review.

Culkin, R., & Das, S. R. (2017). *Machine learning in finance: The case of deep learning in option pricing*.

Dang, L. M., Sadeghi-Niaraki, A., Huynh, H. D., Min, K., & Moon, H. (2018). Deep learning approach for short-term stock trends prediction based on two-stream gated recurrent unit network. In *IEEE Access*.

Das, S., Behera, R. K., Kumar, M., & Rath, S. K. (2018). Real-time sentiment analysis of twitter streaming data for stock prediction. *Procedia Computer Science, 132*, 956–964.

Dawson, A., Palmer, T. N., & Corti, S. (2012). Simulating regime structures in weather and climate prediction models. *Geophysical Research Letters, 39*(21).

Deo, R. C., & Şahin, M. (2015). Application of the extreme learning machine algorithm for the prediction of monthly Effective Drought Index in eastern Australia. *Atmospheric Research, 153*, 512–525.

Desrosiers, C., & Karypis, G. (2011). A comprehensive survey of neighborhood-based recommendation methods. In *Recommender systems handbook* (1st ed., pp. 107–144).

Dong, C., Chen, Y., & Dolan, J. M. (2019). Interactive trajectory prediction for autonomous driving via recurrent meta induction neural network. In *ICRA*.

Dong, M., Yuan, F., Yao, L., Xu, X., & Zhu, L. (2020). MAMO: Memory-augmented meta-optimization for cold-start recommendation. In *SIGKDD*.

Dong, Y., Liao, F., Pang, T., Su, H., Zhu, J., Hu, X., et al. (2018). Boosting adversarial attacks with momentum. In *Proceedings of the IEEE conference on computer vision and pattern recognition* (pp. 9185–9193). IEEE.

Du, Z., Wang, X., Yang, H., Zhou, J., & Tang, J. (2019). Sequential scenario-specific meta learner for online recommendation. In *KDD*.

Finn, C., Abbeel, P., & Levine, S. (2017). Model-agnostic meta-learning for fast adaptation of deep networks. In *In International conference on machine learning* (pp. 1126–1135). PMLR.

Fischer, T., & Krauss, C. (2018). Deep learning with long short-term memory networks for financial market predictions. *European Journal of Operational Research, 270*(2), 654–669.

Fu, X., Du, J., Guo, Y., Liu, M., Dong, T., & Duan, X. (2018). *A machine learning framework for stock selection.*

Fujita, T. T. (1978). *Manual of downburst identification for project NIMROD.* Retrieved from Satellite and Mesometeorology Research Project Department of the Geophysical Sciences, University of Chicago.

Garnelo, M., Rosenbaum, D., Maddison, C., Ramalho, T. D., Saxton, M. S., Teh, Y. W., … Eslami, S. M. (2018). Conditional neural processes. In *The 35th international conference on machine learning.*

Gentine, P., Pritchard, M., Rasp, S., Reinaudi, G., & Yacalis, G. (2018). Could machine learning break the convection parameterization deadlock? *Geophysical Research Letters, 45*(11), 5742–5751.

Giles, C. L., Bollacker, K. D., & Lawrence, S. (1998). *CiteSeer: An automatic citation indexing system.*

Glorot, X., Bordes, A., & Bengio, Y. (2011). Deep sparse rectifier neural networks. In *Proceedings of the fourteenth international conference on artificial intelligence and statistics* (pp. 315–323). JMLR Workshop and Conference Proceedings.

Goldblum, M., Fowl, L., & Goldstein, T. (2020). Adversarially robust few-shot learning: A Meta-Learning Approach. In *NeurIPS*.

Gope, J., & Jain, S. K. (2017). *A survey on solving cold start problem in recommender systems.*

Goumagias, N. D., Hristu-Varsakelis, D., & Assael, Y. M. (2018). Using deep q-learning to understand the tax evasion behavior of risk-averse firms. *Expert Systems with Applications, 101*, 258–270.

Goyal, M. K., Bharti, B., Quilty, J., Adamowski, J., & Pandey, A. (2014). Modeling of daily pan evaporation in sub tropical climates using ANN, LS-SVR, Fuzzy Logic, and ANFIS. *Expert Systems With Applications, 41*(11), 5267–5276.

Grover, A., & Leskovec, J. (2016). node2vec: Scalable feature learning for networks. In *SIGKDD*.

Guo, X., & Zhu, Q. (2009). *A traffic flow forecasting model based on bp neural network.* Retrieved from PEITS.

Hamilton, W. L., Ying, R., & Leskovec, J. (2017). GraphSAGE: Inductive representation learning on large graphs. In *NeurIPS*.

Harper, F. M., & Konstan, J. A. (2016). The movielens datasets: History and context. *ACM Transactions on Interactive Intelligent Systems, 5*(4), 19.

He, K., Zhang, X., Ren, S., & Sun, J. (2014). Spatial pyramid pooling in deep convolutional networks for visual recognition. In *European conference on computer vision (ECCV)* (pp. 346–361).

Huang, K., & Zitnik, M. (2020). Graph meta learning via local subgraphs. In *NeurIPS*.

Huang, S.-H., & Ran, B. (2003). *An application of neural network on traffic speed prediction under adverse weather condition* (Ph.D. thesis). University of Wisconsin–Madison.

Huntingford, C., Jeffers, E. S., Bonsall, M. B., Christensen, H. M., Lees, T., & Yang, H. (2019). Machine learning and artificial intelligence to aid climate change research and preparedness. *Environmental Research Letters, 14*, 124007.

Huynh, H. D., Dang, L. M., & Duong, D. (2017). A new model for stock price movements prediction using deep neural network. In *The Eighth International Symposium on Information and Communication Technology—SoICT 2017*ACM Press.

Iwasaki, H., & Chen, Y. (2018). Topic sentiment asset pricing with dnn supervised learning. *SSRN Electronic Journal.* https://doi.org/10.2139/ssrn.3228485.

Jagadish, H., Gehrke, J., Labrinidis, A., Papakonstantinou, Y., Patel, J. M., Ramakrishnan, R., & Shahabi, C. (2014). Big data and its technical challenges. In *ACM*.

Jamal, M. A., & Qi, G.-J. (2019). Task agnostic meta-learning for few-shot learning. In *CVPR*.

Jeong, G., & Kim, H. Y. (2019). Improving financial trading decisions using deep q-learning: Predicting the number of shares, action strategies, and transfer learning. *Expert Systems with Applications, 117*, 125–138.

Jia, Y., Wu, J., Ben-Akiva, M., Seshadri, R., & Du, Y. (2017). Rainfall-integrated traffic speed prediction using deep learning method. In *T-ITS* (pp. 531–536).

Jia, Y., Wu, J., & Du, Y. (2016). Traffic speed prediction using deep learning method. In *ITSC* (pp. 1217–1222).

Jiang, Z., Xu, D., & Liang, J. (2017). *A deep reinforcement learning framework for the financial portfolio management problem.* arXiv preprint arXiv:1706.10059.

Kamani, M. M., Farhang, S., Mahdavi, M., & Wang, J. Z. (2019). Targeted meta-learning for critical incident detection in weather data. In *ICML*.

Kim, H., Ahn, E., Shin, M., & Sim, S. H. (2018). Crack and noncrack classification from concrete surface images using machine learning. *Structural Health Monitoring.*

Klimowski, B. A., Hjelmfelt, M. R., & Bunkers, M. J. (2004). Radar observations of the early evolution of bow echoes. *Weather and Forecasting, 19*(4), 727–734.

Koch, C., Georgieva, K., Kasireddy, V., Akinci, B., & Fieguth, P. (2015). A review on computer vision based defect detection and condition assessment of concrete and asphalt civil infrastructure. *Advanced Engineering Informatics, 29*(2), 196–210.

Koesdwiady, A., Soua, R., & Karray, F. (2016). *Improving traffic flow prediction with weather information in connected cars: A deep learning approach* (pp. 9508–9517).

Koren, Y., & Bell, R. (2011). Advances in collaborative filtering. In *Recommender systems handbook* (1st ed., pp. 145–186).

Krauss, C., Do, X. A., & Huck, N. (2017). Deep neural networks, gradient-boosted trees, random forests: Statistical arbitrage on the s&p 500. *European Journal of Operational Research, 259*(2), 689–702.

Läderach, P., Ramirez-Villegas, J., Navarro-Racines, C., Zelaya, C., Martinez-Valle, A., & Jarvis, A. (2016). *Climate change adaptation of coffee production in space and time.* Retrieved from. https://doi.org/10.1007/s10584-016-1788-9.

Lahsasna, A., Ainon, R. N., & Teh, Y. W. (2010). Credit scoring models using soft computing methods: A survey. *The International Arab Journal of Information Technology, 7*, 115–123.

Lan, L., Wang, P., Du, X., Song, K., Tao, J., & Guan, X. (2020). Node classification on graphs with few-shot novel labels via meta transformed network embedding. In *NeurIPS*.

Lee, C.-Y., & Soo, V.-W. (2017). Predict stock price with financial news based on recurrent convolutional neural networks. In *Conference on technologies and applications of artificial intelligence (TAAI). IEEE.*

Lee, H., Im, J., Jang, S., Cho, H., & Chung, S. (2019). MeLU: Meta-learned user preference estimator for cold-start recommendation. In *SIGKDD*.

Leelavathi, M., & Sahana Devi, K. (2016). *An architecture of deep learning method to predict traffic flow in big data.*

Leskvec, J. (2017). *Tissue-specific protein-protein interaction network.* Retrieved from SNAP: https://snap.stanford.edu/biodata/datasets/10013/10013-PPT-Ohmnet.html.

Li, X., Cao, J., & Pan, Z. (2018). Market impact analysis via deep learned architectures. *Neural Computing and Applications.*

Li, Y., Tarlow, D., Brockschmidt, M., & Zemel, R. (2015). Gated graph sequence neural networks. *arXiv preprint,* arXiv:1511.05493.

Linden, G., Smith, B., & York, J. (2003). Amazon.com recommendations: Item-to-item collaborative filtering. *IEEE Internet Computing, 7*(1), 76–80.

Littman, J., & Wrubel, L. (2019). *Climate change Tweets Ids.* Retrieved from Harvard Dataverse V1. https://doi.org/10.7910/DVN/5QCCUU.

Liu, L., & Chen, R.-C. (2017). A novel passenger flow prediction model using deep learning methods. *Transportation Research Part C: Emerging Technologies, 84*, 74–91.

Liu, Y., Zheng, Y., Liang, Y., Liu, S., & Rosenblum, D. S. (2016). *Urban water quality prediction based on multi-task multi-view learning.*

Lopes, G. D. (2018). *Deep learning for market forecasts.*

Lops, P., Gemmis, M. D., & Semeraro, G. (2011). Content-based recommender systems: State of the art and trends. In *Recommender systems handbook* (pp. 73–105). Springer.

Lu, D. W. (2017). *Agent inspired trading using recurrent reinforcement learning and lstm neural networks.*

Lu, Y., Fang, Y., & Shi, C. (2020). Meta-learning on heterogeneous information networks for cold-start recommendation. In *SIG-KDD*.

Lv, Y., Duan, Y., Kang, W., Li, Z., & Wang, F.-Y. (2015). Traffic flow prediction with big data: A deep learning approach. In *ITS* (pp. 865–873).

Ma, X., Dai, Z., He, Z., Ma, J., Wang, Y., & Wang, Y. (2017). Learning traffic as images: A deep convolutional neural network for large- scale transportation network speed prediction. *Sensors, 17*, 818.

Maas, A. L., Daly, R. E., Pham, P. T., Huang, D., Ng, A. Y., & Potts, C. (2011). Learning word vectors for sentiment analysis. In *ACL*.

Madry, A., Makelov, A., Schmidt, L., Tsipras, D., & Vladu, A. (2017). Towards deep learning models resistant to adversarial attacks. *arXiv preprint*, arXiv:1706.06083.

Mandal, D., Medya, S., Uzzi, B., & Aggarwal, C. (2021). *Meta-learning with graph neural networks: Methods and applications*.

McNally, S., Roche, J., & Caton, S. (2018). Predicting the price of bitcoin using machine learning. In *26th Euromicro international conference on parallel, distributed and network-based processing (PDP)*.

Mikolov, T., Sutskever, I., Chen, K., Corrado, G. S., & Dean, J. (2013). Distributed representations of words and phrases and their compositionality. In *NIPS*.

Minami, S. (2018). Predicting equity price with corporate action events using lstm-rnn. *Journal of Mathematical Finance*, 58–63.

Mnih, V., Badia, A. P., Mirza, M., Graves, A., Lillicrap, T., Harley, T., et al. (2016). Asynchronous methods for deep reinforcement learning. In *International conference on machine learning* (pp. 1928–1937). PMLR.

Mohammed, R. A., Wong, K. W., Shiratuddin, M. F., Wang, X., & Kang, X. G.-H. (2018). Scalable machine learning techniques for highly imbalanced credit card fraud detection: A comparative study. In *PRICAI 2018: Trends in Artificial Intelligence* (pp. 237–246). Springer International Publishing.

Moosavi-Dezfooli, S. M., Fawzi, A., & Frossard, P. (2016). Deepfool: A simple and accurate method to fool deep neural networks. In *Proceedings of the IEEE conference on computer vision and pattern recognition* (pp. 2574–2582). IEEE Computer Society.

Moosbrucker, T., Flisgen, M., Bauer, F., & Pachl, S. (2019). *Text-mining in financial services*. Retrieved from Deloitte https://www2.deloitte.com/content/dam/Deloitte/de/Documents/risk/Flyer-Text-Mining-in-Financial-Services.pdf.

Motl, J., & Schulte, O. (2015). *The CTU prague relational learning repository*.

Mundt, M., Majumder, S., Murali, S., Panetsos, P., & Ramesh, V. (2019a). *CODEBRIM: COncrete DEfect BRidge IMage dataset*. Retrieved from https://zenodo.org/record/2620293#.YI5OVi0RqQI.

Mundt, M., Majumder, S., Murali, S., Panetsos, P., & Ramesh, V. (2019b). *Meta-learning convolutional neural architectures for multi-target concrete defect classification with the COncrete DEfect BRidge IMage Dataset*. arXiv.org. Retrieved June 4, 2022, from https://arxiv.org/abs/1904.08486.

Namata, G., London, B., Getoor, L., & Huang, B. (2012). Query-driven active surveying for collective classification. In *MLG*. Retrieved from https://linqs.soe.ucsc.edu/data.

National Snow and Ice Data Center. (2019). *Daily sea ice extent data*. https://www.kaggle.com/datasets/nsidcorg/daily-sea-ice-extent-data. Retrieved 2022 from.

Nations, U. (2017). *International greenhouse gas emissions*. Retrieved from https://www.kaggle.com/unitednations/international-greenhouse-gas-emissions?ref=hackernoon.com.

New York State Energy Research and Development Authority. (2020). *Climate change projections and impacts for New York State*. https://data.ny.gov/Energy-Environment/Climate-Change-Projections-and-Impacts-for-New-Yor/s7ew-7zev. Retrieved 2022 from.

NOAA. (1988). *Next generation weather radar*. Retrieved from National Centers for Enviromental Information: https://www.ncei.noaa.gov/products/radar/next-generation-weather-radar.

Ok, E. A., & Foster, J. (1997). Lorenz dominance and the variance of logarithms. In *Technical report* C.V. Starr Center for Applied Economics. New York University.

Ozbayoglua, A. M., Gudeleka, M. U., & Sezera, O. B. (2020). *Deep learning for financial applications: A survey*.

Pan, Z., Liang, Y., Wang, W., Yu, Y., Zheng, Y., & Zhang, J. (2019). Urban traffic prediction from spatio-temporal data using deep meta learning. In *KDD*.

Paula, E. L., Ladeira, M., Carvalho, R. N., & Marzagao, T. (2016). Deep learning anomaly detection as support fraud investigation in brazilian exports and anti-money laundering. In *IEEE international conference on machine learning and applications (ICMLA)*.

Pham, H., Guan, M. Y., Zoph, B., Le, Q. V., & Dean, J. (2018). Efficient neural architecture search via parameters sharing. In *ICML*.

Pozzolo, A. D. (2015). *Adaptive machine learning for credit card fraud detection*.

Przybylinski, R. W. (1995). The bow echo: Observations, numerical simulations, and severe weather detection methods. *Weather and Forecasting*, *10*(2), 203–218.

Ravi, S., & Larochelle, H. (2017). Optimization as a model for few-shot learning. In *ICLR*.

Rawte, V., Gupta, A., & Zaki, M. J. (2018). Analysis of year-over-year changes in risk factors disclosure in 10-k filings. In *The fourth international workshop on data science for macro-modeling with financial and economic datasets—DSMM18*.

Ricci, F., Rokach, L., & Shapira, B. (2011). Introduction to recommender systems handbook. In *Recommender systems handbook* (1st ed., pp. 1–35).

Rodriguez-Galiano, V. F., Chica-Olmo, M., Abarca-Hernandez, F., Atkinson, P. M., & Jeganathan, C. (2012). Random forest classification of Mediterranean land cover using multi-seasonal imagery and multi-seasonal texture. *Remote Sensing of Environment, 121*, 93–107.

Rossi, R. A., & Ahmed, N. K. (2015). *The network data repository with interactive graph analytics and visualization*. Retrieved from AAAI http://networkrepository.com.

Roy, A., Sun, J., Mahoney, R., Alonzi, L., Adams, S., & Beling, P. (2018). Deep learning detecting fraud in credit card transactions. In *Systems and information engineering design symposium (SIEDS)*IEEE.

Scarselli, F., Gori, M., Tsoi, A. C., Hagenbuchner, M., & Monfardini, G. (2009). The graph neural network model. *IEEE Transactions on Neural Networks, 20*, 61–80. https://doi.org/10.1109/TNN.2008.2005605. 19068426.

Serrano, W. (2018). Fintech model: The random neural network with genetic algorithm. *Procedia Computer Science, 126*, 537–546.

Shen, J., Zhang, J., Luo, X., Zhu, W., Yu, K., Chen, K., … Jiang, H. (2007). Predicting protein–protein interactions based only on sequences information. *Proceedings of the National Academy of Sciences of the United States of America, 104*(11), 4337–4341.

Shi, C., Hu, B., Zhao, W. X., & Yu, P. S. (2018). Heterogeneous information network embedding for recommendation. In *IEEE TKDE* (pp. 357–370).

Si, X., Yang, Y., Dai, H., Naik, M., & Song, L. (2019). Learning a meta-solver for syntax-guided program synthesis. In *International conference on learning representations* OpenReview.net.

Snell, J., Swersky, K., & Zemel, R. (2017). Prototypical networks for few-shot learning. *Advances in Neural Information Processing Systems, 30*.

Sohony, I., Pratap, R., & Nambiar, U. (2018). Ensemble learning for credit card fraud detection. In *The ACM India joint international conference on data science and Manage- ment of Data—CoDS-COMAD18*ACM Press.

Soluciones, D. (2018). *Air quality in madrid (2001–2018)*. Retrieved from https://www.kaggle.com/decide-soluciones/air-quality-madrid.

Spilak, B. (2018). *Deep neural networks for cryptocurrencies price prediction*.

Sun, Y., Han, J., Yan, X., Yu, P. S., & Wu, T. (2011). Path-sim: Meta path-based top-K similarity search in heterogeneous information networks. In *PVLDB* (pp. 992–1003).

Sutton, S. R., McAllester, D., Singh, S., & Mansour, Y. (1999). Policy gradient methods for reinforcement learning with function approximation. In *NeurIPS* (pp. 1057–1063).

Tang, J., Zhang, J., Yao, L., Li, J., Zhang, L., & Su, Z. (2008). Arnetminer: Extraction and mining of academic social networks. In *KDD*.

Tang, L., & Liu, H. (2009). Relational learning via latent social dimensions. In *KDD*.

Theil, H. (1967). Economics and information theory. In *Studies in mathematical and managerial economics* North-Holland Pub. Co.

Tianchi. (2019). *Cloud theme click dataset*. Retrieved from Tianchi: https://tianchi.aliyun.com/dataset/dataDetail?dataId=9716.

Troiano, L., Villa, E. M., & Loia, V. (2018). Replicating a trading strategy by means of lstm for financial industry applications. *IEEE Transactions on Industrial Informatics, 14*(7), 3226–3234.

Van der Pol, E. A. (2016). Coordinated deep reinforcement learners for traffic light control. In *Learning, inference and control of multi-agent systems*.

Vartak, M., Vartak, M., Miranda, C., Bratman, J., & Larochelle, H. (2017). A meta-learning perspective on cold-start recommendations for items. In *NIPS*.

Wang, K., Shen, Z., Huang, C., Wu, C.-H., Dong, Y., & Kanakia, A. (2020). *Microsoft academic graph: When experts are not enough*. Retrieved from quantitative science studies https://ogb.stanford.edu/docs/nodeprop/.

Wang, Q., Xu, W., & Zheng, H. (2018). Combining the wisdom of crowds and technical analysis for financial market prediction using deep random subspace ensembles. *Neurocomputing, 299*, 51–61.

Wang, X., He, X., Wang, M., Feng, F., & Chua, T.-S. (2019). Neural graph collaborative filtering. In *SIGIR* (pp. 165–174).

Wang, Y., & Xu, W. (2018). Leveraging deep learning with lda-based text analytics to detect automobile insurance fraud. *Decision Support Systems, 105*, 87–95.

Wei, H., Zheng, G., Yao, H., & Li, Z. (2018). Intellilight: A reinforcement learning approach for intelligent traffic light control. In *KDD* (pp. 2496–2505).

II. Applications

Williams, R. J. (1992). Simple statistical gradient-following algorithms for connectionist reinforcement learning. *Machine Learning, 8*, 229–256.

Wu, Y., & Tan, H. (2016). Short-term traffic flow forecasting with spatial-temporal correlation in a hybrid deep learning framework. In *CoRR.* abs/1612.01022.

Wu, Y., Tan, H., Qin, L., Ran, B., & Jiang, Z. (2018). A hybrid deep learning based traffic flow prediction method and its understanding. *Transportation Research Part C: Emerging Technologies, 90*, 166–180.

Xu, J., Tan, P.-N., Luo, L., & Zhou, J. (2016). Gspartan: A geospatio-temporal multi-task learning framework for multi-location prediction. In *SDM. SIAM.*

Xu, K., Hu, W., Leskovec, J., & Jegelka, S. (2019). How powerful are graph neural networks? In *ICLR.*

Yang, L., Li, L., Zhang, Z., Zhou, X., Zhou, E., & Liu, Y. (2020). DPGN: Distribution propagation graph network for few-shot learning. In *CVPR.*

Young, P., Lai, A., Hodosh, M., & Hockenmaier, J. (2014). *From image descriptions to visual denotations: New similarity metrics for semantic inference over event descriptions.* https://shannon.cs.illinois.edu/DenotationGraph/.

Yu, B., Yin, H., & Zhu, Z. (2017). Spatio-temporal graph convolutional neural network: A deep learning framework for traffic forecasting. In *CoRR.* abs/1709.04875.

Yuan, J., Zheng, Y., Zhang, C., Xie, W., Xie, X., Sun, G., & Huang, Y. (2010). T-drive: driving directions based on taxi trajectories. In *SIGSPATIAL. ACM.*

Yue, X., Wang, Z., Huang, J., Parthasarathy, S., Moosavinasab, S., Huang, Y., ... Sun, H. (2019). *Graph embedding on biomedical networks: Methods, applications, and evaluations.* arXiv. preprint arXiv:1906.05017.

Zang, X., Yao, H., Zheng, G., Xu, N., Xu, K., & Li, Z. (2020). MetaLight: Value-based meta-reinforcement learning for traffic signal control. In *AAAI.*

Zhang, H., Feng, S., Liu, C., Ding, Y., Zhu, Y., Zhou, Z., ... Li, Z. (2019). *Cityflow: A multi-agent reinforcement learning environment for large scale city traffic scenario.* p. arXiv preprint arXiv:1905.05217).

Zhao, L., Sun, Q., Ye, J., Chen, F., Lu, C.-T., & Ramakrishnan, N. (2015). Multi-task learning for spatio-temporal event forecasting. In *SIGKDD. ACM.*

Zheng, G., Xiong, Y., Zang, X., Feng, J., Wei, H., Zhang, H., ... Li, Z. (2019). Learning phase competition for traffic signal control. In *CIKM* (pp. 1963–1972).

Zheng, W., Yan, L., Gou, C., & Wang, F.-Y. (2020). Federated meta-learning for fraudulent credit card detection. In *IJCAI.*

Zhou, B. (2018). Deep learning and the cross-section of stock returns: Neural networks combining price and fundamental information. *SSRN Electronic Journal.*

Ziegler, C.-N., McNee, S. M., Konstan, J. A., & Lausen, G. (2005). *Improving recommendation lists through topic diversification.* WWW (pp. 22–32).

Zitnik, M., Feldman, M. W., & Leskovec, J. (2019). Evolution of resilience in protein interactomes across the tree of life. *Proceedings of the National Academy of Sciences of the United States of America, 116*(10), 4426–4433.

Zitnik, M., & Leskovec, J. (2017). Predicting multicellular function through multi-layer tissue. *Bioinformatics, 33*(14), i190–i198. Retrieved from Bioinformatics.

Index

Note: Page numbers followed by *f* indicate figures and *t* indicate tables.

Printed in the United States
by Baker & Taylor Publisher Services